Red Arrow across the Pacific

RED ARROW
ACROSS THE PACIFIC

*The Thirty-Second Infantry Division
during World War II*

MARK D. VAN ELLS

WISCONSIN HISTORICAL SOCIETY PRESS

Published by the Wisconsin Historical Society Press
Publishers since 1855

The Wisconsin Historical Society helps people connect to the past by collecting,
preserving, and sharing stories. Founded in 1846, the Society is one of the nation's
finest historical institutions.
Join the Wisconsin Historical Society: wisconsinhistory.org/membership

Publication of this book was made possible in part by a gift from the estate of Lyle Hougan.

Photographs identified with WHI or WHS are from the Society's collections; address
requests to reproduce these photos to the Visual Materials Archivist at the Wisconsin
Historical Society, 816 State Street, Madison, WI 53706.

Front cover image courtesy of the Wisconsin National Guard, photo by US Army
Signal Corps; back cover image courtesy of the Wisconsin National Guard

Printed in the United States of America
Cover design by TG Design.
Typesetting by Wendy Holdman.

28 27 26 25 24   1 2 3 4 5

Library of Congress Cataloging-in-Publication Data available.

♾ The paper used in this publication meets the minimum requirements of the
American National Standard for Information Sciences—Permanence of Paper for
Printed Library Materials, ANSI Z39.48-1992.

For Jack Robert Mitchell,
may you never know the cruelty and misery of war.

CONTENTS

Note on Language and Terminology

Red Arrow across the Pacific contains extensive quotations from sources that were written many decades ago—wartime press reports, official government records, and the writings of Red Arrow soldiers themselves. Alternative spellings and minor grammatical errors appear in some of these quotations without correction, as they appeared in the original sources. Some quotations use language that today is considered insulting and demeaning. This book, as a history of World War II and the way participants experienced it, also contains graphic descriptions of violence. Place names in the text and in map labels appear as Americans knew them during World War II, and as they appeared in wartime records and press reports. Taiwan is referred to as Formosa, for example, and the present-day nation of Indonesia, then a colony of the Netherlands, is referred to as the Dutch East Indies. Japanese names appear with the family name first, followed by a person's given name, rather than in the Western fashion.

PREFACE

Traveling through the cities and towns of Wisconsin and Michigan, people today often encounter a curious symbol: a red arrow, pointing upward, with a horizontal bar across the shaft. Sightings most commonly occur on historical markers and in parks. On the south side of my own hometown of Manitowoc, Wisconsin, for example, a place called Red Arrow Park sits along the shore of Lake Michigan. My childhood memories of the park are of cool lake breezes, the pungent smell of the vinegar factory across the railroad tracks, and the restaurant across the street with the best fried cheese curds in the world. As a kid, I seldom thought about the park's name, and I was only vaguely aware that it had something to do with war. To the west of Manitowoc, State Highway 32 winds through rolling green countryside, past fields of corn and alfalfa and herds of Holsteins. Here, the red arrow symbol flanks either side of the highway numbers on the road signs. That highway, and the parks and historical markers travelers might happen upon today, are memorials to the Thirty-Second "Red Arrow" Division, a National Guard unit from Wisconsin and Michigan. The Red Arrow Division was created during World War I but saw its most extensive combat and greatest trials in the Pacific during World War II.

Thousands of books have been written about World War II, but historians both popular and academic have paid little attention to the history and significance of the Red Arrow Division. In the eight decades since the war ended, other American fighting units have been lavishly celebrated. The legendary exploits of the US Marine Corps, at places like Guadalcanal and Iwo Jima, have been retold in countless books and films. The US Army's 101st Airborne Division has been featured in popular books like Stephen Ambrose's 1992 bestseller *Band of Brothers* (which in turn inspired the landmark television miniseries of the same name) and Steven Spielberg's 1998 film *Saving Private Ryan*. No such accolades have come to the Red Arrow. Though the division sometimes marches onto the pages of historical works on the Pacific War, it seldom receives more than a supporting role. Even in its home states of Wisconsin and Michigan, the division's

1

World War II record is often not well understood. Walking through a Red Arrow Park—whether in Manitowoc, Marinette, or Milwaukee—people might say to themselves, "My grandpa was in that outfit, but he didn't talk about it much." The details of the division's war experience become increasingly obscure as the World War II generation passes on.[1]

But the Thirty-Second Infantry Division's World War II record deserves more attention. Its history encompassed the entirety of the United States' involvement in the war, from the initial 1940 mobilization of the National Guard to the postwar occupation of Japan. In 1942, while most divisions were still in training in the United States, the Red Arrow was already in action in the South Pacific on the island of New Guinea. It was the first US Army division to fly into a combat zone and the first to go on the offensive against the Japanese. By the time World War II finally ended, the Thirty-Second claimed more hours of combat than any other army division.[2] The Red Arrow played a crucial role at some of the most pivotal moments of the Pacific War, though it did not fight in any of the famous battles like Guadalcanal or Okinawa. Rather, it slogged its way across the Pacific in a long series of lesser known engagements familiar only to the most specialized students of the war: Buna and the Sanananda Track, Saidor, Aitape, Morotai, the Ormoc Valley, the Villa Verde Trail. Such fighting occurred in some of the most forbidding environments on earth—steamy dense jungles, high trackless mountains, fields of razor-sharp kunai grass, and mosquito-infested mangrove swamps that incubated a host of tropical diseases. "Of the many infantry divisions that had the honor and at the same time the misfortune to fight in the Southwest Pacific," wrote historian Robert Young, the Red Arrow Division "stands at the top . . . for it was given one impossible mission after another in the worst possible terrain, understrength, and devoid of support from higher commands."[3]

During its nearly six years of federal service, the Thirty-Second Infantry Division bore witness to the enormous changes the American military experienced during World War II. As a National Guard division, the Red Arrow followed the American military tradition of the militia, dating back to colonial times, in which the ordinary male citizen was expected to drop his plow, pick up his gun, and defend his community in times of emergency. From the moment the first Minutemen met the British at the Battle of Lexington and Concord in 1775, the citizen-soldiers of the militia saw themselves as the backbone of America's national defense. However, when the United States began its preparations for World War II, it became clear that the Red Arrow—like the nation itself—was woefully unprepared for what lay ahead. As the war progressed, the Thirty-Second Division underwent profound changes. Once the division was in federal service, the regular army purged much of the Red Arrow's officer corps (justly or not) and replaced it with professionals and reservists. In the test of battle, some citizen-soldiers turned out to be talented, others lacking, and all too many were killed before they ever got the chance to prove themselves. As the war dragged on, replacements came in to replenish the ranks, but they did so without regard to regional origin; before long the Upper Midwestern character of the division gave way to a nationalized force with members from every corner of the Union. Red Arrowmen came from all walks of life: farmers, factory workers, shopkeepers, pencil-pushing bureaucrats, conservative Christians, communists, and the scions of elite families. The searing experience of combat shattered romantic illusions about war and national defense, but it also forged an effective and battle-hardened fighting force that always prevailed on the battlefield.

What follows is the story of the Thirty-Second Infantry Division during World War II. The goals of the book are twofold. First, it offers a combat chronicle of the Red Arrow Division, tracing the origins of each of the division's battles, the conduct of those operations, and their aftermath. Each engagement is set within the context of the larger strategic situation of the Pacific War and World War II in general. When tracing the movement of regiments, battalions, and companies on the battlefield, we should always bear in mind that soldiers are not chess pieces to be shuffled across a board, but real people with their own stories, feelings, and perspectives. The GIs (as American soldiers during World War II were known) stepped onto the battlefield sure of victory and survival, and innocent to the realities of war. When the first enemy bullets and shells came screeching in, that innocence gave way to the surreal and nightmarish realities of combat. In letters, diaries, memoirs, and postwar interviews, Red Arrow soldiers described their descent into the hellish world of war—the profound fear and sheer horror of battle, the resentment toward incompetent or heartless superiors, the close bonds with fellow soldiers, the struggle to maintain their humanity, their great relief and guilt after surviving a battle, and the emotional agony of having to go back into the fight again and again.

The second goal of this book is to move beyond the traditional "blood

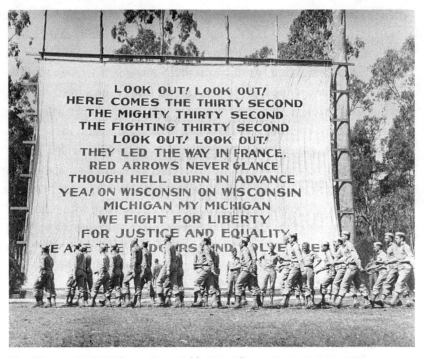

The Thirty-Second Division at Camp Cable, Australia, ca. 1942. WHI IMAGE ID 25162

and guts" approach to military history and examine the Thirty-Second Division's social and cultural world. In virtually any conflict, most of the soldiers' time is spent away from the battlefield. In World War II, GIs endured many hours in training or performing routine tasks—from peeling potatoes to shining their boots—or in transit from one place to another. When not on duty, soldiers received passes and furloughs and sought amusement in nearby communities, enjoying a respite from army life. The National Guard soldiers of the Red Arrow often began the war with strong connections to their families and hometowns. Upon mobilization, division members struggled mightily to maintain those connections, though time, distance, and divergent experiences weakened those links—sometimes to the breaking point. Most Red Arrow soldiers had never before traveled far from home and during the war encountered people and cultures vastly different from their own. Above all else, the Red Arrowmen—like all GIs—struggled to maintain their cherished sense of American individualism and democratic spirit while engulfed in the vast, authoritarian machinery of war.[4]

Each chapter begins with a short summary that introduces the reader to specific phases of the Thirty-Second Division's World War II experience. Chapter 1 places the Red Arrow Division into the historical context of the American citizen-soldier tradition, recounts the division's creation during World War I, and explores how the division evolved between the wars. Chapter 2 outlines the division's entry into federal service in October 1940 and its training in Louisiana. Chapters 3 and 4 cover the period after Pearl Harbor and the United States' entry into the war, during which the Red Arrow Division underwent a major reorganization and was almost constantly on the move, from Louisiana to Massachusetts to California, and then a three-week ocean voyage to Australia—its first foreign land. Chapter 5 brings the Red Arrow to New Guinea, where the jungle itself was an unexpected adversary every bit as unforgiving as the Japanese. Chapter 6 covers the crucible of the division's World War II experience—Buna and the Sanananda Track, where the Red Arrow endured its first combat, learned severe lessons, and took enormous casualties. Chapter 7 describes the rebuilding of the division after Buna, and Chapter 8 recounts the Red Arrow's return to combat along the shores of northern New Guinea in 1944. In Chapters 9 and 10, the Red Arrow moves north to the Philippines for the bloody, back-to-back battles on the islands of Leyte and Luzon that brought the division once again to the brink of collapse. Chapter 11 covers the Red Arrow's final duties in occupied Japan before being demobilized in February 1946.

In essence, this book is a portrait of an American infantry division during World War II, one of ninety-one the US Army mobilized during the conflict. It explores both the combat and noncombat worlds of the Red Arrowmen to help readers better understand the totality of their wartime military experiences in the Pacific. Not only do the stories recounted here depict the war as the ordinary GI saw it, but also the way it smelled, tasted, and felt—what historian Mary Louise Roberts has called the "somatic history of war."[5] In a larger sense, this book also explores how World War II transformed the American military from small, close-knit, and ill-prepared armed services into a gargantuan fighting force of sixteen million men and women—the world's preeminent military power with a vast global reach. The Red Arrow story, in many ways, is a microcosm of the American military experience of World War II.

Red Arrowmen from Wisconsin parade through Milwaukee after their return from France in 1919. WHI IMAGE ID 26240

CHAPTER 1

ROOTS OF THE RED ARROW

The Thirty-Second Division was forged in the fires of World War I. Hastily cobbled together from Wisconsin and Michigan National Guard units in 1917 and then shipped to France, the Red Arrow Division fought in some of the Great War's most crucial battles and earned a reputation as one of the country's most effective fighting units. The division's roots, however, stretched even further back, to the citizen-soldier tradition born at the very founding of the American republic. Historically, Americans preferred to rely on local militias made up of their neighbors for defense, though the professionals of the full-time regular army had long questioned the competence of the part-time citizen-soldier. The Thirty-Second Division proved itself effective during World War I, but afterward it faced significant challenges with recruitment, training, and funding. By the end of the 1930s, a second world war had broken out. Americans ardently hoped to stay out of it, but the dangerous global situation prompted the US to revitalize its defenses. In doing so, the tension between the citizen-soldier and the professional army returned to the forefront of public discussion. In October 1940, the Red Arrow was again mobilized for federal service.

In military parlance, a division is a large, combined arms unit (one that contains multiple combat arms, such as infantry, artillery, and cavalry) capable of independent operations. Designed for tactical effectiveness and bureaucratic efficiency, military divisions first appeared in seventeenth-century Europe. The first American divisions emerged in the early days of the American Revolution in 1775, when General George Washington organized his militia forces around Boston into three divisions of about five thousand soldiers each.[1] During the Revolutionary War, local militia members fought alongside the Continental Army, but Washington found the part-time soldiers unreliable and poorly trained. They sometimes broke and ran under fire, and they went home during harvest time—or pretty much whenever they pleased. Nonetheless, popular lore held that the Minuteman militia had won America's independence.

After the Revolution the United States maintained only a small standing army. The ideology of the early Republic viewed professional soldiers as unnecessary, expensive, and a threat to newly won liberties. Instead, most US leaders at the time believed state-run militias provided the best defense against foreign invasion, domestic disturbance, conflicts with American Indian nations, and rebellions of enslaved people. In the late eighteenth and early nineteenth centuries, Congress passed a series of laws that allowed the president to call up militia forces in times of national emergency, as well as to conscript young white men into service; but in practice, the federal government exercised almost no control over the militias. Early militias operated without standardized training, weapons, or uniforms. During the War of 1812, some governors even refused to allow their militias to serve outside their own state borders.

In the years before the Civil War, volunteer militia organizations proliferated across the United States, including in the new western states like Wisconsin and Michigan. Loosely supervised by state governments, militia units sometimes functioned more like social clubs than military units, akin to the many fraternal organizations popular at the time. Militia units often had colorful names and were sometimes organized along ethnic lines. In Wisconsin, there was the Black Jaeger Rifles, the Milwaukee Dragoons, and Rough and Ready Artillery Company; in Michigan, there was the Detroit Light Guard, the Saginaw City Light Infantry, and the Williams' German Light Artillery.[2]

When the Civil War erupted in 1861, Northern states raised volunteer militias into infantry regiments and artillery batteries, then offered them up for federal service. In Grand Rapids, Michigan, four militia organizations—the Grand Rapids Artillery, the Grand Rapids Light Guard, the Grand Rapids Rifles, and Ringgold's Light Artillery—formed the core of the Third Michigan Volunteer Infantry Regiment, which participated in the war's first major engagement in July 1861, the First Battle of Bull Run in northern Virginia. In Wisconsin, several militia groups, including the Fox Lake Citizens Guard, the Grant County Grays, the La Crosse Light Guards, and the Miners' Guard of Mineral Point, came together to form the Second Wisconsin Volunteer Infantry Regiment. The Second Wisconsin joined with the Sixth and Seventh Wisconsin, the Nineteenth Indiana, and later the Twenty-Fourth Michigan to form what would become known

Members of the Second Wisconsin Infantry Regiment, ca. 1862. The Second Wisconsin was part of the Iron Brigade, which included regiments from Wisconsin, Michigan, and Indiana. WHI IMAGE ID 41960

as the Iron Brigade. The unit earned its nickname in 1862 at the Battle of South Mountain in Maryland, when General George B. McClellan peered through his binoculars to see the brigade advancing under withering Confederate fire and exclaimed that its members "must be made of iron." The Iron Brigade played a critical role in subsequent fights, including the pivotal battles at Antietam and Gettysburg.[3]

In the Union army, two to five regiments made up a brigade, two to four brigades a division, two to three divisions a corps, and two or more corps an army. At the time, the corps was the most important combined arms unit. Each corps was numbered and comprised about fifteen thousand to twenty thousand soldiers. Early in the war, some Union soldiers began to wear distinctive badges to identify the corps to which they were assigned. The practice is attributed to Major General Philip Kearny, who in 1862 had his men wear a diamond insignia on their caps so they could be more easily identified in the field. The practice soon spread and became standardized, and by the Battle of Gettysburg in July 1863, corps badges were nearly universal among Union troops. Each corps adopted a distinctive shape for its badge. For example, I Corps wore a circle, IV Corps a triangle, and XVII Corps a horizontal arrow. Each division within the corps wore its badge in a different color; the first division wore red, the second wore white, and the third wore blue. Thus, the first division of the XVII Corps wore a red arrow. In addition to helping soldiers identify one another, the corps badges became important symbols of pride and connection among the men in each unit. With the end of the war the vast Union army quickly melted away, though for Union veterans the corps badges remained potent symbols of the connection they shared with their wartime comrades, and of their defense of the American Union.

In the years after the Civil War, states reformed their militia forces, providing more money and more supervision, and began to refer to them as the National Guard. Wisconsin adopted the term in 1879 and Michigan in 1891. Governors called on the National Guard to help during emergencies like fires and tornadoes, but most commonly to put down labor strikes. In May 1886, for example, Wisconsin governor Jeremiah M. Rusk sent 250 Wisconsin Guardsmen to contain a demonstration of fifteen hundred workers in Milwaukee who were striking in support of an eight-hour workday. Under Rusk's orders, Guardsmen fired on the workers, who had gathered outside of the Milwaukee Iron Company mill at Bay View, killing seven.[4]

The federal government once again relied on state volunteers during the Spanish-American and Philippine-American Wars, and despite the US victories the regular army raised serious questions about the preparedness of National Guard soldiers. Uniforms and weapons still varied from state to state, as did the capabilities of officers. The United States was a rising world power with grand imperial ambitions and a growing overseas empire, and many in Washington wanted to reform the American military establishment. Secretary of War Elihu Root, who took office in 1899, created a modern general staff and revamped the army's educational system. Root also guided through Congress the Militia Act of 1903, which reorganized and standardized National Guard units across the country. Under the law, the National Guard received the same uniforms, equipment, and weapons as the regular army—and the federal government paid for it. In exchange, Guard units were required to follow minimum training standards, including weekly drills and annual summer encampments, supervised by army regulars. To cultivate qualified leadership, National Guard officers became eligible to attend the regular army's various training schools. The new law also clarified how and when National Guard units could be mobilized

Company K, 127th Infantry Regiment, July 1917. WHI IMAGE ID 87112

for federal service. Further changes came with the National Defense Act of 1916, which, among other provisions, established enlisted and officer reserve forces and created the Reserve Officers Training Corps (ROTC) to train new leaders.

The pace of change accelerated dramatically in 1917 with US entry into World War I. Army reformers had experimented with the creation of permanent, numbered divisions as the principal fighting unit before 1917, but it was the Great War that finally brought these organizations into being. The US Army developed a "square" division consisting of two brigades. Each brigade had two infantry regiments, along with artillery, machine gun, and various support units. As American planners envisioned it, one brigade would attack while the other remained in reserve; when the lead brigade became exhausted, the reserve would then move up, keeping constant pressure on their adversary. The First Division was put together in France, as was the Second, but the rest were born in stateside training camps. Divisions composed of regular army units took the numbers one through twenty. Those composed of National Guard formations were assigned numbers twenty-six through forty-two. The divisions of what was called the National Army, made up of draftees, were numbered seventy-six through ninety-two.

Wisconsin and Michigan National Guard troops came together in the Thirty-Second Division. The division gathered for the first time in September 1917 near Waco, Texas, at Camp MacArthur—named in honor of Milwaukee's Arthur MacArthur, recipient of the Medal of Honor for his heroism at the 1863 Battle of Missionary Ridge. The army reshuffled, broke up, or converted National Guard units as they were integrated into the modernized command structure. Sometimes riflemen became machine gunners, for example, and cavalry troops were reassigned as artillerymen. Existing regiments like the Second Wisconsin and Third Michigan Infantries were renumbered without regard to state identity. "No more did our State Regiments exist with gallant traditions and hopeful futures," wrote Milwaukeean J. Tracy Hale Jr., a reserve lieutenant assigned to the Fifth Wisconsin Infantry Regiment out of Watertown. "All that we had labored so hard to build up in morale for the regiments was to be destroyed."[5]

Regional distinctions did not go away entirely, though. Michigan troops dominated the Sixty-Third Brigade, which included the 125th and 126th Infantry Regiments, while the Sixty-Fourth Brigade, centered on the 127th and 128th Infantry Regiments, was made up of Wisconsin units. A shortage of officers meant that some officers from one state were transferred to units of the other. Hale, for example, took command of Company I of the 125th Infantry Regiment. The Michiganders saw their new lieutenant as an outsider and consequently, as Hale later recounted, "there were many prejudices to contend with."[6] All told, about fifteen thousand Wisconsin troops and eight thousand from Michigan made up the core of the division, with draftees filling out its ranks. Though equipment shortages could sometimes hinder training, at Camp MacArthur the division got down to the business of preparing for war. "A trench system was constructed just outside the camp," noted *The 32nd Division in the World War*, the unit's official World War I history, "infantry and artillery target ranges were prepared early in the training period, and a thorough course of instruction in service firing was given to every man."[7]

In early 1918, the Thirty-Second Division departed for France to join the American Expeditionary Forces under General John J. Pershing.[8] The army sent its untested divisions to "quiet sectors" of the western front to acclimate them to combat conditions. The Thirty-Second went to Alsace, on the southern edge of the front. Stationed in a sector that crossed into the prewar borders of Germany, division members bragged that they were the first American troops on German soil. They first entered the trenches under the tutelage of French trainers, but soon occupied a portion of the front on their own. Here for the first time the division endured enemy machine-gun fire and artillery barrages, staged raids on German positions, and patrolled the no-man's-land between the opposing trench lines. Taking casualties proved sobering. "That brought them down to earth," recalled Sergeant Robert C. McCoy of the 107th Ammunition Train (and son of the 128th Infantry Regiment's commander, Colonel Robert B. McCoy), "and they commenced to be a little more military."[9]

The Thirty-Second Division's first major combat came during the Aisne-Marne Offensive northeast of Paris in July and August. "Although new to the vicious kind of warfare," boasted *The 32nd Division in the World War* of one early engagement, "they rushed the enemy defenses with

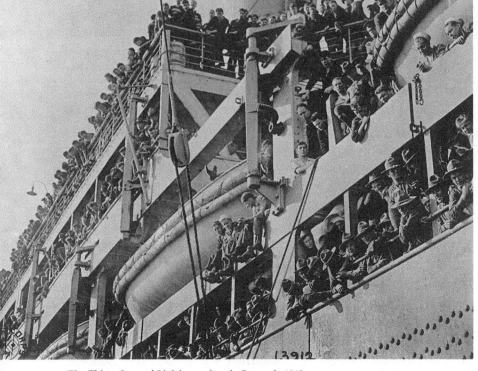

The Thirty-Second Division arrives in France in 1918. WHI IMAGE ID 132644

irresistible determination . . . and completely overwhelmed the strong position which was the day's objective."[10] Tracy Hale, now an intelligence officer, discovered just how vicious the fighting in a major offensive could be. On July 31, battalion headquarters dispatched him into the midst of the battle to locate a missing company. He and another man crawled out onto the field of battle, and when "we rose to take a look," wrote Hale, "an electric shock struck my left arm." A German bullet had ripped into him, causing a "compound fracture just above my left elbow." Machine-gun fire pinned the two men down as Hale lay bleeding, but when it subsided the pair made their way back to headquarters. "Trying to crawl on my right side to keep my left arm off the ground," he recounted, "I felt as conspicuous as a fly on a bald man's head." After reaching headquarters and giving his report, Hale was carted off to an aid station.[11]

Over the next week the Thirty-Second pushed the retreating Germans back ten miles, liberating the villages of Chamery, Coulonges, Cohan, Dravegny, Saint-Gilles, and Mont-Saint-Martin. By August 4, the Thirty-Second Division reached the bluff above Fismes, a small city on the south bank of the Vesle, and moved into its streets that afternoon. The division then spent several days rooting German forces out of the rubble and searching out a spot to cross the Vesle until the Twenty-Eighth Division could relieve it during the night of August 6–7. In little more than a week, the Thirty-Second Division suffered more than seven hundred killed and three thousand wounded but had proven its mettle in combat. One French commander was so impressed with the division's tenacity that he referred to its members as *"les soldats terrible"* (in French the word *terrible* has more of a connotation of ferocity than in English), and the division soon embraced the nickname "Les Terribles."

In late August, the Thirty-Second Division went back into action north of Soissons as part of the Oise-Aisne Offensive. Placed in line west of Juvigny, with French units on either side, the Thirty-Second Division attacked on August 28, with the Michiganders of the Sixty-Third Brigade leading the way. As the brigade's casualties mounted, the Wisconsinites of the Sixty-Fourth Brigade assumed the front during the night of August 29–30. Juvigny fell to the Americans the following day, and the Wisconsin men pressed on until Moroccan troops replaced them during the night of September 1–2.

On September 26, the Allies launched the Grand Offensive to push the Germans back across the Rhine. The American sector of the front lay between the Meuse River and the Argonne Forest in eastern France. At first the Thirty-Second Division remained in reserve, still recovering from the brutal fight at Soissons, but in early October it joined in the Meuse-Argonne Offensive in relief of exhausted comrades. The Thirty-Second pushed forward as usual, wresting fields, woods, and villages away from the Germans. By October 9 the division approached the Germans' main defensive line in the region, the Kreimhilde Stellung, where German soldiers had crammed a wooded ridgeline called the Romagne Heights with trenches, pillboxes, barbed wire, and machine-gun nests. The Thirty-Second reached the outskirts of the small village of Romagne-sous-Montfauçon on the road leading through the Romagne Heights, but then found its advance halted. For several days Les Terribles battled outside Romagne, seizing the best ground it could from which to launch an assault against the Kreimhilde Stellung. That assault came on October 14, part of a massive, coordinated American push across the Meuse-Argonne front. The Thirty-Second Division made the first significant breakthroughs that day. The 128th Infantry Regiment jumped off at 5:30 a.m. and caught the Germans off guard, and the advancing Wisconsinites reached Romagne before noon. The 126th Infantry Regiment also penetrated German lines to the left of the 128th along a spur in the ridgeline called the Côte Dame Marie. The Thirty-Second Division's breakthroughs that morning, as well as the advance of the Fifth Division on its right, forced the Germans to pull back. By the end of the day, elements of the Thirty-Second Division had penetrated half a mile behind the Kreimhilde Stellung.

After breaking through the German line, the Thirty-Second Division continued its slow but relentless drive until the Eighty-Ninth Division relieved it on October 20. The division took another well-deserved rest, but November found it in combat yet again, this time in the heights across the Meuse near the town of Breheville. The division was preparing for an attack on the morning of November 11 when word came that the Germans had agreed to an armistice, effective 11 a.m. The "War to End All Wars" was over.

The announcement sparked wild celebrations among the troops at the front and behind the lines. Tracy Hale was in the French city of Tours, working a desk job while recovering from his wounds. "The streets of Tours were jammed by howling celebrations," Hale recalled, and in the course of the revelries an enthusiastic French soldier "seized me by the wounded left arm and jerked it so hard that I had to report to an American aid station."[12] For the Thirty-Second Division, the Great War's total butcher's bill was 2,915 killed, 10,477 wounded.[13]

After the armistice, the Thirty-Second Division had one final mission: the occupation of Germany. Under the terms of the armistice, Allied soldiers were to occupy German territory west of the Rhine. In addition, they would hold an area east of the Rhine within a thirty-kilometer radius of three key bridges, at Cologne, Koblenz, and Mainz, plus a neutral zone

Corporal George Miner, a member of the Ho-Chunk Nation from Tomah, Wisconsin, served occupation duty in Germany in 1919, as part of the 128th Infantry Regiment.
NATIONAL ARCHIVES

extending another ten kilometers out, giving the Allies a foothold into the German heartland. The Thirty-Second Division was part of the III Corps, along with the First and Second Divisions. *The 32nd Division in the World War* called III Corps "the flower of the American Army" and bragged that "in this brilliant company it is no wonder that our men stepped off toward Germany with their heads held high and the pride of good soldiers in their hearts."[14] The III Corps had the distinction of being the only American troops based east of the Rhine.

Toward the end of the war, American divisions took up the European practice of adopting a distinctive insignia and wearing it on the left shoulder of their uniforms. Like the corps badges during the Civil War, these shoulder patches not only aided unit identification but fostered unit pride. The First Division, for example, adopted an emblem of a prominent red "1" on an olive background, and the division became known as the Big Red One. The members of the Thirty-Second Division, meanwhile, had punctured every German line they encountered. To commemorate this proud achievement, the Thirty-Second Division adopted an emblem of a vertical red arrow, pointing upward, piercing a horizontal red line. The Thirty-Second Division would ever after bear the nickname Red Arrow Division.[15]

In April 1919, the Thirty-Second Division began its withdrawal from Germany. From the Rhine the doughboys made their way to the French port of Brest, and the first elements of the division set sail on May 1. Those

Members of the Wisconsin National Guard at the Wisconsin Military Reservation at Camp Douglas in 1924. WHI IMAGE ID 46186

who arrived at New York aboard the *George Washington* found a delegation of Wisconsin officials there to greet them, including Governor Emanuel Philipp. Transport ships carrying Red Arrow veterans arrived at various ports up and down the East Coast, and from there the doughboys headed to an army post near their home of record for discharge. The Red Arrow Division was no more. Cities and towns across Wisconsin and Michigan held enthusiastic parades and celebrations for their returned soldiers. In Milwaukee, a committee of prominent citizens organized a homecoming parade for Wisconsin's Thirty-Second Division veterans. "It was an impressive occasion," Tracy Hale remembered, though with sadness he also remarked that the old National Guard regiments that "had left Wisconsin at full strength in 1917 marched down Wisconsin Avenue as mere remnants of what they had been when they left."[16]

Shortly after demobilization, the Red Arrow Division gained new life. The National Defense Act of 1920 reorganized the peacetime army, streamlining its command structure and planning for its rapid expansion in case of emergency. The new law created the Army of the United States composed of three segments: the regular army, the National Guard, and the reserves. The law authorized the federal government to maintain permanent divisions in all three segments, reconstituting the divisional system of the Great War. The army divided the continental United States into nine corps

areas of roughly equal populations. Each corps area was to have one regular army division, two National Guard divisions, and three reserve divisions. Under the new arrangement, the Red Arrow was assigned to the VI Corps. Headquartered in Chicago, the VI Corps comprised Illinois, Wisconsin, and Michigan. The Red Arrowmen of the Thirty-Second Division joined the Thirty-Third Division from Illinois to make up the VI Corps National Guard contingent. Washington later superimposed four army areas above the nine corps, and VI Corps became part of the Second Army.[17]

In Wisconsin and Michigan, as across the nation, National Guard units—companies of infantry, batteries of artillery, troops of cavalry— began to reconstitute themselves. The Red Arrow's two wartime brigades and four infantry regiments sprang back to life, as did engineer, medical, quartermaster, and other support units. New organizations emerged as well, reflecting the changing nature of warfare. For example, the Thirty-Second Tank Company was based in Janesville, Wisconsin, and the 107th Aerial Observation Squadron was born in Detroit, with a Milwaukee-based squadron in the works. Guard members once again attended weekly drills at their local armories. Each summer, Michigan troops converged on Camp Grayling in the northern part of the state's Lower Peninsula. Wisconsin soldiers trained at Juneau County's Wisconsin Military Reservation at Camp Douglas—renamed Camp Williams in 1927 in honor of the recently deceased Lieutenant Colonel Charles R. Williams, a longtime Wisconsin National Guard officer and Red Arrow quartermaster during the Great War.

Some World War I veterans resumed their service. In 1919, after being wounded in France, Tracy Hale was discharged from active service and took a reserve commission as a captain. But two years later, he received a telegram asking him to "accept a job in the newly reformed Wisconsin National Guard." Hale needed little convincing and was delighted to be "assigned at once [as] an instructor . . . for training in intelligence and scouting."[18] At various times during the 1920s, Hale served in the cavalry, the artillery, and then the infantry. National Guard units also absorbed new recruits. In Michigan, the *Alma Record* reported that "over one hundred young men from the community" signed up for a new cavalry troop, and "the number who have made application is in excess of the number that the troop will contain."[19]

In Neillsville, Wisconsin, Herbert M. Smith became enamored with the army during World War I. "It should not be surprising that a lad of 16 in 1919 would not have had a profound interest in the military," he later reflected. Smith was too young to join the army, so in 1919 he enlisted in the Wisconsin State Guard, a temporary military organization made up of middle-aged men and teenage boys who took up home defense duties while the National Guard was off to war. With the reconstitution of the Wisconsin National Guard, Smith joined the Neillsville-based service company of the 128th Infantry Regiment.[20] Across the state in Oshkosh, seventeen-year-old Herbert A. Smith "wasn't quite old enough" for the Great War either, though he "always had a hankering for the military."[21] He too enlisted in the State Guard and then joined Company H of the 127th Infantry Regiment. Both of the Herbert Smiths rose quickly through the enlisted ranks and by the end of the 1920s had become officers.

But the military ultimately proved unpopular with most Americans in the 1920s. Concerns that soldiers threatened freedom and liberty remained. Budget hawks complained of the costs of maintaining forces. In the wake of the Great War's bloodshed and destruction, some simply found military affairs revolting. To many, disarmament seemed a better way to keep the peace. At the federal level, the army was constantly starved for funds. At the state level, the National Guard had fallen out of favor as well. In 1923, the Wisconsin Assembly passed a bill to abolish the Wisconsin National Guard altogether by a vote of 64–16—one state representative going so far as to describe Guard members as "legalized hired assassins."[22]

Governor John J. Blaine opposed the measure, as did US senator and Progressive icon Robert M. La Follette, whose opposition to US entry into World War I had made him a pariah in many quarters. La Follette warned of the unintended consequences of such a move. "As everyone knows I have long opposed extravagant expenditures for military purposes in peacetime," La Follette wrote, but "to abolish the national guard at this time . . . would give the militarists of the nation an opportunity to urge an increase in our standing army and to augment our federal expenditures for war purposes."[23] The bill to abolish the Guard died in the state senate, though state lawmakers successfully slashed appropriations for it by more than half.[24]

Support for the Guard was faltering on the other side of Lake Michigan

as well. "Fewer troops will go into camp this year when the Michigan National Guard holds it's [sic] annual field training encampment," reported
the *News-Palladium* of Benton Harbor in 1925, citing "lack of funds."[25]
Tracy Hale recalled "ridicule and abuse" for the citizen-soldier during
those years. "The National Guardsman was not a popular figure," he wrote.
"The term 'boy scout' was applied to him frequently."[26]

Many local armories fell into disrepair. "Our armory had been built
in the 1890's, and had not kept pace with modernization," recalled Herbert M. Smith. "I can recall several drill nights during the winter months
when it was necessary to wear winter overcoats in order to keep warm."[27]
Adjutants general in Wisconsin and Michigan continually asked their state
legislatures for funds for better training facilities. Camp Grayling, encompassing twenty-five thousand acres, offered Michigan soldiers plenty of
room, but in Wisconsin it was a different story.[28] Camp Williams was a
mere one thousand four hundred acres, and by 1930, according to the annual report of the Wisconsin adjutant general, it was "found impractical to
conduct field training."[29] There was little room for artillerymen to train,
for example, and the report noted that "tactical exercises for units larger
than a battalion are not practical." The state leased land from local farmers
to compensate for the lack of space, but by 1930 "it has been found almost
impossible to rent suitable land, since owners have now cleared and have
under cultivation acreage used in the past."[30] To help, the federal government allowed the Wisconsin Guard to use the Sparta Military Reservation
in Monroe County, twenty-five miles west of Camp Williams. In 1926 the
army renamed the facility Camp McCoy in honor of Badger State military
luminary Robert B. McCoy, who had passed away earlier that year.

Despite the challenges of inadequate funding and facilities, Guard
soldiers conducted their weekly drills and summer camps. Herbert M.
Smith respected the "aptitude, personalities, and abilities" of his regular
army trainers. "We had some superior people who were able to inspire,"
he wrote, "if one was willing to follow their suggestions."[31] Not all took
their training so seriously. Armory drills and summer camps often seemed
more of a social occasion, or even an excuse for a party. Smith recalled that
at one summer camp "it was discovered that the keg of moonshine liquor"
that one colonel "had intended for the evening festivities had disappeared

from his tent." Suspicion fell on Smith's service company and the colonel asked Smith to investigate. "I received no leads as to the whereabouts of the keg," Smith wrote, but the "party was held as scheduled; others having the foresight to bring and pool the 'spirits.'"[32] Discipline and military courtesy were often lacking. "I took over a company that was in bad shape," recalled Herbert A. Smith. The previous company commander "laughed at" the idea of military courtesy and set low standards. On the eve of his first federal inspection, Smith found that "the cook's whites hadn't been washed since the camp before," nor had the "sweat and hair" been cleaned from the horse harnesses. Smith worked furiously to get the company into shape, with "practically no help from my supply sergeant." He asked the men to shine their shoes for the inspection, but when Smith went into their lockers the night before he discovered that it had not been done. "I shined thirty-three pairs of shoes," Smith complained, "because I wanted to get a satisfactory rating." The company "barely" passed the inspection, and the supply sergeant lost his job. "The standards hadn't been set for them," Smith lamented.[33]

Poor training and discipline showed in the field. Tracy Hale chronicled several training mishaps at Camp McCoy. "One morning a six inch shell exploded on the Milwaukee Road tracks just south of the reservation," he wrote. "There was a train approaching. The engineer stopped the train and backed up frantically whistling." On another occasion a local farmer appeared at headquarters. "I hope that you will not drop any more of these shells in my backyard," he said. "They make my wife nervous." In yet another incident, Hale recalled a machine-gun crew firing its weapons "over Highway 16, the main highway from Madison to La Crosse." Arriving on the scene, Hale discovered that "the Lieutenant in command was asleep."[34]

Over time, Guard leaders undertook efforts to improve training and readiness. In 1932, for example, the Wisconsin National Guard announced it would no longer promote officers based solely on length of service; instead they were required to complete army extension courses to qualify for promotion.[35] Several Red Arrowmen attended army professional schools. Tracy Hale traveled to the Command and General Staff School at Fort Leavenworth, Kansas. After completing the school, he "rushed to Camp Williams to impart my newfound knowledge to the officers of the

Wisconsin National Guard."[36] Herbert A. Smith attended the Infantry School at Fort Benning, Georgia. "I was number one in my class," he remembered proudly.[37]

Change came slowly, incompletely, and sometimes reluctantly to the Red Arrow Division. "Former WWI officers and non-comms [non-commissioned officers] were dropping out as the requirements were tightened both professionally and physically," observed Herbert M. Smith.[38] Cavalry and transportation formations that had previously used animal power were disbanded or mechanized. Smith recalled that his regiment organized a motor pool in the late 1920s. "All were happy," he thought, "except the stable detail. They were a select group, dedicated to the animals, and woe to anyone making disparaging remarks—even in jest."[39] Indeed, parochialism reigned in many units. In small towns and city neighborhoods, Guardsmen served alongside familiar faces, from neighbors to friends to relatives. "The local banker might be the battalion commander," recounted Madison's Robert Hughes, who joined the Wisconsin National Guard in 1936, "[one] might be the head of the grocery store and be a company commander, maybe the guy pumping gas or running the service station was the platoon leader."[40] Forrest Knox of Janesville's tank company remembered his unit as "a family" in which "everyone had a nickname."[41] Such tight-knit organizations were often wary of outsiders. By the mid-1930s Herbert A. Smith had been promoted to major and was eligible to command a battalion. There were no vacancies for a battalion commander in his 127th Infantry Regiment, so Smith went to the Third Battalion of the 128th based in a different part of the state, but the officers there saw Smith as an intruder and resisted his appointment. "Some even raised a complaint with the adjutant general's office," he remembered. Smith stayed with the Third Battalion for a year and then transferred to the Second Battalion of the 128th when a vacancy opened there. Having been in the regiment for a while, Smith recalled that he got "a much warmer reception."[42]

The entire Thirty-Second Division gathered together only once in the years between the wars, when the Second Army held field maneuvers in southwestern Michigan in the summer of 1936. "For the first time since the World War," noted the Red Arrow Division commander, Major General Guy M. Wilson, "Wisconsin and Michigan Troops will be assembled again as brothers-in-arms." Wisconsin troops boarded car ferries at Milwaukee and sailed to western Michigan ports to participate. After three days of training, the soldiers underwent two days of mock battles. Some found the maneuvers invigorating. "The men seemed to like it," claimed the *Wisconsin National Guard Review*. "They were game, cheerful, and played their part."[43] Tracy Hale thought that "one could feel a different feeling among the officers of the Regiment."[44] Brigadier General Irving A. Fish took command of the division after Wilson's sudden death during the maneuvers. "It was a surprise to me and I think to all of the superior officers," Fish reported, "to find how well the National Guards of the two states comprising the Thirty-Second Division functioned the first time they had been assembled in seventeen years."[45]

During the interwar years, state officials occasionally mobilized Red Arrow troops to respond to natural disasters and other emergencies. In October 1923, for example, Wisconsin's Governor Blaine called up four officers and fifty-five enlisted men from the 120th Field Artillery and the 128th Infantry Regiment to fight forest fires in Douglas County.[46] After a tornado devastated Menomonie, Wisconsin, in 1930, the local Company A of the 128th Infantry Regiment cleared debris, patrolled the streets to prevent looting, and directed traffic caused by the "hundreds of sight-seers visiting the stricken area," according to a report in the *Capital Times*.[47]

Economic unrest during the Great Depression triggered further deployments. In 1933, for example, Wisconsin dairy farmers staged "milk strikes," blocking roads and stopping trucks in a desperate effort to keep milk off the market and hike prices. In response, Governor Albert Schmedeman mobilized more than one thousand National Guard troops, deploying them to eight counties to help local law enforcement keep the roads open and the milk flowing. Guard troops in Waukesha County forcefully broke up a group of striking farmers in an incident dubbed the Battle of Durham Hill by the *Milwaukee Journal*'s Herbert Jacobs. "After a barrage of gas," Jacobs wrote, "the seventy-five guardsmen pushed the farmers over the hill at bayonet point, and the unbelieving pickets kept looking around to see if they were really being prodded with cold steel." The soldiers appeared "equally nervous, and looked as if they would have been glad to drop their guns and run too."[48]

In Michigan, Red Arrow troops found themselves enmeshed in one of

Wisconsin National Guard soldiers break up a group of farmers protesting near Shawano, Wisconsin, during the 1933 milk strikes. WHI IMAGE ID 73633

the most significant labor strikes in American history. On December 30, 1936, the United Automobile Workers (UAW) occupied a crucial factory building at the General Motors complex in Flint, in a bid for recognition as a bargaining unit. The strike took a violent turn on January 11, 1937, when company police stormed the plant, prompting Michigan governor Frank Murphy to mobilize two thousand National Guard troops to restore order. The sight of soldiers and machine guns in the streets of Flint rattled residents, but Murphy insisted that the soldiers would not "take sides." One striker, a member of the union shop committee as well as the 125th Infantry Regiment, got his mobilization notice while he was occupying the plant. "When he received a telegram notifying him to report to duty," reported the *Chicago Tribune*, "the shop committee held an emergency meeting and gave him permission to leave," noting its "great respect for law and order and the Michigan National Guard."[49] The "sit-down strike" ended on February 11 with the UAW gaining the recognition it sought.[50]

President Franklin D. Roosevelt's New Deal relief and recovery programs provided long-needed improvements to armories and camps. For example, workers from the Civil Works Administration (CWA) repaired twenty-one armories around Wisconsin. At Camp Williams, the CWA improved roads and buildings, and the Public Works Administration constructed fourteen "combined bath houses and latrines" connected to a newly built sewage disposal facility. "The improvements," noted Wisconsin's grateful adjutant general, were sufficient "to take care of any possible expansion of camp areas including war-time enlargement."[51] Camps Grayling and Williams also hosted the Civilian Conservation Corps (CCC), a military-style workforce of young men and war veterans tasked with reforestation and the improvement of public lands. CCC workers constructed ten buildings at Camp Williams and were "engaged in the work of clearing, tree trimming, and planting on the Military Reservation." Herbert M. Smith remembered the "paved streets, new mess halls, [and] modern bathhouse/latrine facilities" at Camp Williams, "all of which were morale boosters."[52]

The National Guard not only received aid during the Depression but also dispensed it. "During the past two years," reported the Wisconsin adjutant general, the National Guard "has cooperated with all municipal and charitable organizations in supplying blankets and cots to care for homeless people as a result of the present economic condition," and "acted as an agent of the Federal government in supplying municipal, charitable, and military organizations with serviceable items of clothing made available by the federal government from surplus stocks. This has entailed considerable clerical work which has been absorbed without any increased cost to the State."[53]

The lean years of the Depression also led to an uptick in National Guard enlistments. A teenager at the time, Roland Stoelb of Sheboygan, Wisconsin, worked on a dairy farm, taking pay in the form of milk and cream for his family, and drove a coal truck. "Any money we could make helped out at home," Stoelb remembered. "We heard the Sheboygan Guard Unit was looking for recruits to fill the ranks, [and] a bunch of us thought joining the National Guard was a good way to earn some extra money."[54] In Oshkosh, Wisconsin, Clarence Jungwirth also signed up for financial reasons. In 1940, Jungwirth was twenty-one years old, with no steady job. He later recalled "a warm summer evening when a few of us young men were sitting on our front porch talking and 'horsing around' when somebody casually mentioned that the National Guard Companies were looking for new recruits." Jungwirth and his friends heard a rumor that "the local guard units were going to Kentucky for the annual summer maneuvers for three weeks at $1.00 per day." He and his friends made quick calculations and realized that "$4.00 per month for being in the guards, plus $21.00 for three weeks at summer camp added up to more money than any of us had ever had in our whole lives." They promptly walked down to the armory. "We were given a sales pitch that convinced me and several of my friends to sign up on the spot," Jungwirth recalled. "The general attitude of the National Guard was, if the body was warm, we'll take it."[55]

Other reasons attracted Red Arrow recruits as well. "They told me there was a swimming pool at the armory," recalled Steve Janicki of Grand Rapids, "and if I signed up or got in, I could use the swimming pool anytime I wanted."[56] Amos Truckey of Oconto, Wisconsin, bowed to peer pressure to join after "some of my friends kept bugging me about it," and he "finally decided to give it a try."[57]

Underage enlistment was common. Ervin Sartell Jr. of Janesville joined at age sixteen. His father, Ervin Sr., served in the service battery of the 121st Field Artillery and often brought his young son with him to drills. "I became a mascot," the younger Sartell remembered, serving the troops food. "I used to get a lot of tips from the soldiers," he recalled, and "every time I went home the mess sergeant always gave me a big ham to take home to my mother, and of course, during the Depression days, that was quite a treat." Sartell played high school football, and on the last day of the 1938 season he and some teammates "went down to the armory and enlisted." When asked his age, the sixteen-year-old added two years. "They knew me," Sartell recalled, "but I said I was eighteen and they marked it down."[58]

These Red Arrow recruits joined up as another world war brewed. The militarist leaders of Japan were escalating their nation's expansionism in Asia. In 1931 Japan seized Manchuria from China, and in 1937 full-scale war broke out between the two nations. In Europe, the fascist regimes of Italy's Benito Mussolini and Germany's Adolf Hitler were growing increasingly aggressive. World War II began in Europe on September 1, 1939, when German tanks and mechanized infantry rolled into Poland and Stuka dive bombers screeched down from the skies above. The press dubbed the fast-paced and mobile style of war "blitzkrieg" (lightning war), and it sent shock waves through military establishments around the world.

In Wisconsin and Michigan, a few young men joined the National

Guard in anticipation of war. Erwin Pichotte of Menominee Falls remembered that a high-ranking leader in the Wisconsin National Guard urged him to sign up "because there was going to be a war."[59] But many new recruits gave little thought to overseas developments. "As young men, we did not pay much attention to the war raging in Europe," wrote Jungwirth. "It was far away and we never gave a thought to the possibility that we could get caught up in it. Making money was our primary concern." Family members, though, often had a different reaction. Jungwirth recalled the evening he told his mother that he had signed up. "She started to cry and asked me why I had done this," Jungwirth remembered, and at the time he was mystified by her response. "It was no big deal," he thought. "I was just joining the National Guard to get a little spending money." It was only later that he remembered that his father had been drafted in World War I and "was gone for a whole year. . . . She knew what could happen when one was in the Army."[60] As Roland Stoelb later reflected: "When you're 19 years old you sometimes make a spur of the moment decision that has far reaching consequences."[61]

As the world again went to war, the United States retreated deeper into isolationism, hoping that the oceans would insulate it from the rest of the world's problems. However, global events sparked a lively debate among Americans about military preparedness, and the readiness of the National Guard was an important part of those discussions. The training the National Guardsmen received was grossly inadequate. Their only instruction came during weekly drills and summer camps. "At the Armory it was pretty basic stuff," said Amos Truckey, "how to march, how to shoulder your rifle, lectures on Army regulations, stuff like that."[62] Their equipment remained substandard as well. Clarence Jungwirth recalled that on his first drill night at the armory he received a uniform of "heavy woolen khaki material, woolen wrap around leggings, woolen shirt, [and a] campaign hat," nearly identical to the uniform issued to doughboys a generation before. "The rest of our equipment was also from World War I," he noted, "such as canteen equipment, Springfield .03 rifle and many other items." Jungwirth "had taken a typing course in High School," which apparently was enough qualification to become the company clerk.[63] "Back then we really didn't think too much about preparing for war," remembered Red Lane of Oconto, "it was almost more of a social thing."[64] Grand Rapidian Erwin Veneklase recalled that on drill nights he and his comrades would "just kind of goof off for two hours."[65]

But beyond the world of local armories, great changes were stirring in the army. General George C. Marshall, one of the nation's most respected officers, became the US Army chief of staff on September 1, 1939—the same day World War II broke out in Europe. Based on his work at the Infantry School at Fort Benning, Marshall immediately began to reorganize the army. One of his top priorities was to reform the way divisions were organized. He reduced the number of infantry regiments from four to three: one regiment to attack an enemy force and hold it in place, a second regiment to outflank that force, and a third to remain in reserve. A regimental combat team was then to be built around each regiment, attaching artillery, machine guns, and support units depending on the needs of any given situation. This "triangular" structure was designed to be simple and flowed down the chain of command all the way to the company, platoon, and squad level. Marshall quickly converted regular army divisions to the triangular format. He decided to keep National Guard divisions "square" with four infantry regiments for the time being, but he ordered them to hold more drills and field training.[66]

In 1940, events overseas dramatically shifted the preparedness debate. That spring, Germany unleashed its blitzkrieg on Western Europe: France fell in June, and the Luftwaffe (the German air force) subjected Great Britain to fierce aerial attacks in preparation for a cross-channel invasion. As a result, the United States experienced that summer "a severe emotional trauma," in the words of historians J. Garry Clifford and Samuel R. Spencer Jr.[67] Fears of militarism and involvement in another European war remained high, but increasing numbers of Americans now supported defensive military preparations. President Roosevelt found ways to aid Great Britain, and Congress increased appropriations for defense as army officials began the daunting task expanding the service. Aside from replenishing massive shortages of weapons, particularly tanks and aircraft, it simply needed bodies in uniform. The regular army stood at just 190,000 soldiers, augmented by another 200,000 troops in the National Guard. Reservists, mostly officers, numbered 120,000. In June

1940, preparedness advocates introduced a conscription bill in Congress designed to expand national forces quickly. The bill elicited fierce debate. Marshall favored conscription but worried about how to train the potential flood of draftees. The regular army alone did not have the facilities or the instructors to accomplish such a gargantuan task, so Marshall warily turned his gaze toward the National Guard. "Guard divisions could absorb thousands of selectees who would otherwise swamp the nine regular infantry divisions," explained historian Christopher Gabel, "and undo the modernization process entirely."[68] The problem, Marshall believed, was that the National Guard was simply not up to the task. He needed the Guardsmen, but before they could train recruits effectively, the Guardsmen needed more training themselves. Thus, during the summer of 1940, Marshall called not just for conscription but the mobilization of the National Guard as well. President Roosevelt supported the proposals.

Marshall laid the groundwork for an army of more than one million soldiers. In July, he activated the General Headquarters (GHQ) to train combat units. Marshall himself served as its head, but day-to-day operations fell to its chief of staff, Brigadier General Lesley J. McNair. A staff officer in France during World War I, McNair served as commandant of the Command and General Staff School in the 1930s and became a leading voice for modernization, earning him the moniker "brains of the army." Marshall and McNair needed to assess the readiness of the soldiers they already had. They planned extensive field maneuvers in each of the country's four army areas during the summer of 1940. In all, more than three hundred thousand soldiers, from both the regular army and the National Guard, went to the field that summer.

The Red Arrow Division participated in the Second Army maneuvers in the area around Camp McCoy, under the supervision of Lieutenant General Stanley H. Ford. By mid-August 1940, the woods and fields and towns of west-central Wisconsin quickly filled up with sixty-five thousand troops, the largest military concentration ever in the Badger State. "Tomah, Sparta, Tunnel City, and surrounding small towns in the area are jammed beyond capacity," reported the *Eau Claire Leader-Telegram*, and "merchants have raised prices to take advantage of the 21-day 'boom.'"[69]

The forces there were an odd assemblage of an army in transition. In the wake of the German blitzkrieg a few tanks were brought in, but so were

General George C. Marshall (far left), US Amy Chief of Staff, observes the "Battle of Wisconsin" near Camp McCoy, Wisconsin, in August 1940. WHI IMAGE ID 164238

horses. The fleet of new B-17 bombers at Truax Field in Madison attracted big crowds.[70] The M1903 Springfield remained the standard infantry rifle, though for the first time Red Arrow troops saw the incoming M1 Garand semiautomatic. Robert C. McCoy, now a captain, recalled that the maneuvers marked the first time he used the portable radio devices dubbed "walkie-talkies." "They were just starting to come in," he said, and "they didn't work too good."[71]

Once at Camp McCoy, soldiers began a three-week training program. For the first five days, they focused on military fundamentals at the platoon, company, and battalion level. Higher-ranking officers were busy as well. "First full day of work," Tracy Hale, now a lieutenant colonel and executive officer of the 127th Infantry Regiment, wrote in his diary. Hale endured what he called a "paper barrage," and "looked wise, supervised or slept until orientation talk by Gen Ford."[72]

After the first week of training, the troops moved on to simulated battles of ever-increasing size and complexity, pitting regiment vs. regiment, division vs. division, and culminating in corps vs. corps. The goal of the field exercise was to simulate real-world battle conditions as closely as possible. Riflemen and artillerists fired blank rounds. "During the day the hills re-echo the sound of machine guns, the roars of field artillery and machine gun squads," reported the *Eau Claire Leader-Telegram*, while "an army bomber drones overhead."[73] Umpires monitored the mock battles. "By means of colored flags," explained the *Capital Times*, "the umpires indicate areas under artillery fire, heavily mined, or out of the combat area."[74]

The main event, dubbed the Battle of Wisconsin, began on August 24. General Marshall himself flew in to observe the action. The event pitted the V Corps, dubbed the blue force, against the VI Corps, or the red force. The V Corps was under the command of Brigadier General Campbell B. Hodges and consisted of the Thirty-Seventh Division from Ohio and the Thirty-Eighth Division from Indiana, Kentucky, and West Virginia. The VI Corps was made up of the Thirty-Second and Thirty-Third Divisions, as well as the Fifth Division of the regular army. General Fish, commander of the Red Arrow Division, received the honor of leading VI Corps. Walter Choinski, Fish's aide, recalled that his appointment did not sit well with regular army officers, most of whom were Southerners. "Tension within the staff was deep," Choinski remembered. "The Regulars considered themselves superior tacticians and always above us guardsmen in every respect. They were officers and gentlemen; we were damned Yankees and uncouth."[75]

Under the battle scenario, V Corps had invaded Wisconsin from the east while VI Corps closed in from the west to meet them. The two forces collided along a twenty-mile front in and around Camp McCoy as a cold, drenching rain enveloped the battle area. The Red Arrow was on the right flank of the VI Corps line and battled just north of Highway 16. "We 'fought' vigorously for various Hill Masses and for Tunnel City," wrote Tracy Hale. The latter village, according to the *Chicago Tribune*, changed hands three times during the fighting.[76] On August 26, just as V Corps was about to launch an armored strike at VI Corps lines, the Battle of Wisconsin came to a sudden end. "The problem was declared completed, with the rival troops in such relative positions that further maneuvering was impossible," reported the *Chicago Tribune*, also noting that the soldiers were "soaked to the skin."[77] As historian Thomas Doherty put it, "the battle was called on account of rain."[78]

During the maneuvers, troops quickly learned the difficulties of extended time in the field. They slept on the ground, ate from field kitchens, and endured ferocious mosquitoes. The persistent rain made conditions all the more miserable. "Last night it peppered troops on both sides," noted the *Chicago Tribune*, "and they plodded over the roads in tactical problems, their wet slickers making them ghostly figures in the gloom."[79] As Tracy Hale remembered, "troops from other states who took part in the maneuvers departed singing, as a result of the weather, 'God Bless America, less Wisconsin.'"[80]

The field conditions hardened both Guardsmen and regulars, but poor equipment—and at times the lack of proper equipment at all—hindered their training. Trucks rumbled across battlefields with labels designating them as tanks. Drainpipes served as antitank guns. Heavy rain kept the B-17s at Madison grounded much of the time, but horses took to the field. Richard Van Hammen of Grand Rapids recalled an incident reminiscent of the Civil War. While in the field he and his company began to hear "rolling thunder," and horse cavalry soon appeared. "They came through with swords," he recalled, "and the [umpires] came along and said, 'you've been wiped out.'"[81] Hale commented that "the first truck movement . . . to Black River Falls was fantastic in its inefficiency, but we did learn a lesson."[82]

In his assessment of the Wisconsin maneuvers, General Ford noted many problems, but the most significant was a distinct lack of competent leadership, which he thought was "due to lack of training." He was especially hard on the National Guard. "The time has come for the National Guard to submerge itself in a common military purpose and not be required to carry the handicap of home-State influence whenever in Federal service. . . . The idea of one army means just that."[83]

The 1940 summer maneuvers did not go any better in other parts of the country. *New York Times* war correspondent Hanson W. Baldwin spoke with many officers who painted a grim picture of army readiness, particularly that of the National Guard. "Many of the Guardsmen," Baldwin wrote, "had never been under canvas [and] many had never fired a rifle." Guard units were understrength, full of "soft" new recruits in need of physical conditioning, and "less than 50 percent equipped." Baldwin concluded that although "none of the Regular Army divisions could be considered qualified troops in less than three to six months," National Guard troops "will fully require [a] year's training before they can be considered fit for the modern battlefield."[84]

Back at GHQ, the 1940 maneuvers disturbed McNair as well, and his report identified numerous problems: Troops lacked adequate training in small arms and tactics; there were problems with reconnaissance and liaison between units; regimental combat teams had been poorly employed in the field; and communications, supply, and medical evacuation was faulty. He even criticized umpires for "unreal situations." McNair did not spare the regulars in his criticisms, but he too thought the National Guard divisions were far more deficient, particularly their officers. "The 1940 summer encampments demonstrated beyond dispute," concluded historian Christopher Gabel, "that, in terms of ground forces, the nation was virtually defenseless."[85]

Thus, as the Red Arrow and other National Guard divisions packed up their gear in the sodden Wisconsin countryside and prepared to head home, they learned that their military education was just beginning. The shaky performance of National Guard units in the summer maneuvers not only alarmed military officials but also prompted congressional action. On August 27, Congress authorized the president to mobilize the National Guard for one year. All of the citizen-soldiers could not be absorbed at once, so the Guardsmen entered federal service in four phases. The first contingent would report for duty on September 15. The Red Arrow was to mobilize during the second phase, on October 15. News of the activation hit Wisconsin and Michigan papers in early September. Wisconsin Adjutant General Ralph Immell reshuffled state units in anticipation of the mobilization, converting cavalrymen to artillerymen and bringing all quartermaster soldiers into the structure of the Thirty-Second Division so that "all Wisconsin units, with the exception of the 135th Medical [Regiment], would belong to the same division."[86]

Rumors circulated about their training destination, but by mid-September it was revealed to be Camp Beauregard outside of Alexandria, Louisiana. Those under the rank of captain for whom active service posed an undue economic burden could resign, but few did. In fact, many welcomed the mobilization. "I was thrilled at the prospect of being in the Regular Army," declared Jungwirth, "and to be able to see new places and having new experiences. I wanted to get out of Oshkosh and the drab unrewarding life I was leading."[87] After long and bitter debate, Congress also passed the Selective Service Act of 1940, and President Roosevelt signed it into law on September 16. Under the law, men age twenty-one to thirty-six were required to register on October 16. Local draft boards would then select those to enter the service.

The onset of the draft spurred many last-minute enlistments. "I decided to beat the draft by volunteering in order to choose my branch of service," wrote Robert J. Bable of Detroit, who joined the Red Arrow's signal company and served in the message center. In case of war, Bable thought himself in a good position, as he understood the company to be "a non-combat outfit."[88] Benjamin Winneshiek of Clark County, Wisconsin, and seven of his friends—all members of the Ho-Chunk Nation—signed up just before federalization. "Might as well put in a year," he thought.[89] Eau Claire's Roy Campbell remembered the day he enlisted. Campbell had not thought much about events overseas. "It was too far away to really worry about," he believed. Then one day he and a friend went to the movies. "The news reel before the show was mostly about two aggressive armies overseas," he recalled, "one killing Chinese, the other attacking other countries in Europe." After the movie Campbell and his friend were discussing the upcoming deer-hunting season when they ran into another friend on the street who suggested they join the National Guard. "We'd spend a year in Louisiana," he explained, "get some great duck hunting and fishing in, *and* get paid for it!!" Campbell liked the idea. "A year in uniform," he thought, meant "free meals, good exercise and guns, plus some of the best duck hunting in the United States." Campbell speculated that he "might even get the chance to shoot one of those machine guns" he had seen in the movies. Campbell signed up later that day. When he told his parents, he remembered that "tears started to flow" from his mother's eyes, though Campbell also sensed that "she was very proud." "Your family has always served proudly for their country," said his father, a Great War veteran.[90]

As the day of mobilization approached, the members of the Red Arrow Division—old hands and new recruits alike—prepared for their year of training. Morale was high. The Red Arrowmen were proud of their division's distinguished history and were confident in their soldiering abilities, though behind the bluster stood very real questions about their readiness. Few thought they were heading off to war. "This is a pretty big step to take, going into the Army right now," a friend warned Campbell, "with those goofballs overseas doing those bad things."[91] But Campbell was unconcerned. Little did he and his fellow citizen-soldiers of the Red Arrow Division know that their military odyssey was just beginning.

Wisconsin National Guard soldiers depart for Camp Beauregard, Louisiana, in October 1940. WISCONSIN NATIONAL GUARD

CHAPTER 2

OUR KINDERGARTEN

On October 15, 1940, the members of the Thirty-Second Division reported to their local armories, from which they would depart for their year of federal service. "Most of them were clad in army khaki," observed Madison's *Capital Times*, though some were "last minute enlistments in civilian garb."[1] Governor Julius Heil bid farewell to the Badger State contingent. "Wisconsin is proud of the accomplishments of its soldiers," Heil said, and "wishes you God speed." The soldiers received a printed message of encouragement from the Red Arrow staff, with a proud reminder of the unit's stellar reputation during the Great War: "The 32nd never failed in any attack against the German lines in France," and now "the Red Arrow division is starting out again!" But the road ahead was uncertain. The part-time soldiers soon discovered they were not as well prepared as they had imagined. Moreover, draftees entered the ranks, bringing new people into the tight-knit local companies. Mobilization created opportunities to see new places and meet new people, but it also posed great challenges to division morale and often strained the soldiers' intimate connections to their home communities. These experiences foreshadowed the turbulent years of war still to come. Looking back at the Red Arrow's eighteen months of training in Louisiana, Herbert M. Smith described the period as "our kindergarten."[2]

T he Red Arrow Division began its federal service at Camp Beauregard, Louisiana, five miles north of Alexandria in the central part of the state. Founded to train recruits during World War I, the facility once again drew the attention of the army as World War II approached. Training maneuvers occurred at Camp Beauregard in the summer of 1940, just as the Battle of Wisconsin had been staged at Camp McCoy. The army found central Louisiana an ideal place to train soldiers. The state offered vast stretches of federal land, including the Kisatchie National Forest; Louisiana's woods, fields, hills, and bottomlands were comparable to the landscapes the army expected to fight on in Europe; and the climate allowed for year-round training. As the military buildup proceeded, the US government worked to convert central Louisiana into a vast training complex of camps and maneuver grounds. Beauregard was to be a temporary home for the Red Arrow. Its eventual destination would be Camp Livingston, which was still being carved out of the pinelands five miles to the north. Also under construction was Camp Claiborne, fifteen miles south of Alexandria, and Camp Polk, fifty miles west of Claiborne near Leesville. Alexandria's prewar population of twenty-five thousand more than doubled as workers poured in and feverishly got to work constructing the new camps.[3]

Before they arrived in Louisiana, Red Arrow members spent several days in their home communities preparing for departure. Each officer and enlisted soldier was required to undergo a physical examination. Clarence Jungwirth recalled being "stripped naked so the Doctor could check for any physical defects." When the doctor noticed varicose veins on Jungwirth's right leg, Jungwirth's "heart sank as I thought the Doctor would flunk me out," and he "pleaded with him to check the leg over again." The physician was apparently "impressed with my eagerness," and passed him.[4] According to Amos Truckey, seven or eight soldiers failed their physicals and "some of those guys actually cried, they were so disappointed."[5] Several high-ranking officers failed their physical exams as well, including Colonel Forrest Himes, commander of the 127th Infantry Regiment. As a result, executive officer Tracy Hale soon found himself promoted to full colonel and in command of the regiment. In total, according to the

Wisconsin National Guard Review, seven officers and 565 enlisted soldiers from the Badger State were rejected on physical grounds.[6]

Some communities gave the departing Red Arrowmen elaborate send-offs. Port Huron, Michigan, for example, staged a parade through the center of town, followed by a military ball at the local high school. "The gymnasium was resplendent with patriotic decorations," reported the *Port Huron Times Herald*. "Two huge American flags flanked the stage and two other flags were suspended at the east and west walls of the gymnasium," while "constantly changing red, white, and blue lights streamed on a revolving reflectorized ball, suspended over the center of the dance floor." World War I veterans joined the National Guard soldiers on the gymnasium stage for a flag salute ceremony. "As the Guardsmen and veterans marched out of the gymnasium at the end of the ceremony," recounted the *Times Herald*, "onlookers applauded enthusiastically in a blood-tingling demonstration of approval."[7]

Some ceremonies were more somber. In Clark County, Wisconsin, Benjamin Winneshiek and seven other members of the Ho-Chunk Nation participated in a war bundle ceremony, in which the departing soldiers danced, prayed, offered tobacco, and received sacred tokens to protect them from harm. Winneshiek received a buffalo tail that he wore throughout the war. "That gave you strength," Winneshiek remembered, "that gave you confidence."[8] Other soldiers spent their last days at home in quiet moments with family, friends, and loved ones. The evening before his departure, Art Kessenich of Madison and his fiancée, Dora, drove to a spot in Madison known as Sunset Point for some time alone. "It was a beautiful moonlit night," he recalled, "the rays of the moon coming through the half leafless trees. I shall never forget that scene."[9]

Most Red Arrowmen would be traveling to Louisiana by train, and patriotic displays continued as the division members made their way to their local stations. In Holland, Michigan, Gordon Zuverink remembered a parade through downtown in which "thousands of people lined the streets to send us off."[10] In Eau Claire, Wisconsin, Roy Campbell and his cohort also marched through the city streets to the train station as a high school band played. "Some men were in step with the band," he wrote, "some were attempting to get in step, and some were just walking along. . . . Young girls were cheering, and some older women and men who remembered the first war stood silently, while young boys looked [on] with awe-filled eyes. The WWI vets held their hats over their hearts with thoughts of what they had been through."[11] As the trains pulled out of the stations, there was a mix of sadness and excitement. "The pattern of departing troop trains hasn't changed any down the years," opined the *Detroit Free Press*. "It's a pretty grim business whichever side of the platform you happen to be on."[12]

Others went south in motor convoys. The 121st Field Artillery left the armory in Whitefish Bay, Wisconsin, on Saturday, October 19, on a five-day voyage through the Mississippi Valley. The first night "we bivouacked at La Salle, Illinois," wrote George C. Eilers, the battery chaplain. After a predawn religious service in a schoolyard illuminated by the vehicle headlights, the battery ate breakfast in local restaurants and then continued its journey, stopping in Vandalia and Cairo on successive nights. On Monday the convoy arrived at Memphis and "rolled through the city under motorcycle escort," as Eilers recounted, and that evening "dined in real fashion in the ballrooms of the Chiska hotel." From there it was a drive through the Mississippi delta and on to Camp Beauregard. "Not an accident during the trek," wrote Eilers, "and not a man lost."[13] Not all motor convoys were so fortunate. At Ripley, Tennessee, on October 22, Private Donald G. Henry of the 120th Field Artillery, a native of Wisconsin Rapids, was "fatally injured when the motorcycle he was riding was run into by an automobile, said to be driven by a drunken driver."[14]

The 107th Observation Squadron flew from Detroit to Camp Beauregard, but the army soon separated aviation units from the National Guard divisions. It also detached Janesville's Thirty-Second Tank Company from the Red Arrow. In response to the German blitzkrieg, the army was building up and reorganizing armored forces. Instead of going to Camp Beauregard, the Janesville tankers went to Fort Knox, Kentucky, and became Company A of the 192nd Tank Battalion.[15]

The first members of the Thirty-Second Division, consisting of Michigan infantry and service units, arrived at Alexandria by rail in the early morning hours of October 21. More trains and truck convoys, brimming with soldiers, arrived over the next week. Leaving the crisp autumn air of the Upper Midwest, the soldiers immediately noticed the change in climate. "Boy was it hot!" declared Roy Campbell of his first day at Camp Beauregard.[16] Upon their arrival, soldiers endured hours of in-processing.

The army issued them a mountain of new clothing—dress and fatigue uniforms, various kinds of headgear, overcoats, socks, shoes, and underwear. Herbert M. Smith remembered "shots and more shots," as well as receiving his dog tags. "Orders were given to go into the tin building and take a test," recalled Campbell. "No word on what the test was about, just orders to take it." Campbell answered what he thought to be "a bunch of foolish questions" and then went off to the mess hall. Only later did he realize that it was an aptitude test that could determine his future. Campbell claimed he scored well enough to become an officer but admitted that he "would have done better" had he "known what it was for. Many men said the same."[17] The last contingent arrived on October 28. By that time, there were twelve thousand Red Arrowmen in camp.

Shortly after his arrival, Tracy Hale told the Alexandria newspaper *Town Talk* that the troops were "pleased with every phase of life at Camp Beauregard."[18] But in fact, complaints about "Camp Disregard" and "Lousy-Ana" began immediately. "It was a tent city," recalled Jungwirth, that was "hastily erected in 'mud.'"[19] The only permanent structures, according to Herbert M. Smith, were "kitchens and mess halls, latrines and bathhouse, a headquarters office, and a building for supplies."[20] Otherwise the camp was a sea of tents, each housing up to eight enlisted men or four to five junior officers. The tents made for miserable accommodations, particularly once winter came and the rains set in. "When it rains in this country," wrote Orville Suckow of Menomonie, Wisconsin, "you half [sic] to hang on to your beds so you don't float away."[21] Soldiers slept on canvas cots with just two blankets during the increasingly chilly nights. "We were required to put newspaper on the canvas to keep warm in the cold, damp Louisiana nights," wrote Art Kessenich. "Comforters, pillow cases, and sheets are coming," insisted the *Town Talk*, and when they finally did Kessenich remarked that it "pleased everyone."[22] Perhaps the soldiers' biggest complaint was the Sibley stove—a conical wood- or coal-burning sheet-iron heating device designed before the Civil War. The ancient heaters needed to be fed constantly and were a fire hazard. "Sparks would go straight up and fall down on the tent," wrote Campbell.[23] Many tents burned down.

Camp Beauregard held other miseries. The latrines were wood-frame huts covered in burlap. Fifty-gallon garbage cans were sprinkled across the camp for those who had to urinate after dark, and as Amos Truckey recalled, "every night somebody would kick that thing over."[24] The camp crawled with insects and other pests unfamiliar to the midwesterners. "A number of men showed up with tiny red bumps and reported for 'sick call' thinking they had contracted some kind of fever," noted the *Town Talk*. "Investigation revealed they had been bitten by 'redbugs' [chiggers] and there was nothing to worry about."[25] William Sikkel of Holland, Michigan, once "sat right on a scorpion," but fortunately a "doctor was right there" and rendered immediate aid.[26] The medics of the 127th Infantry Regiment had "a large black widow spider . . . on display," and the *Town Talk* reported that "men who have not seen a speciment [*sic*] of this type of spider are invited to [stop in] to see it."[27] Walter Choinski was "quartered with a trillion mosquitoes" who "resent my intrusion into their quarters and for two nights laid siege." Orville Suckow claimed that "the bugs almost carry you away," and he also noted that "we have the nicest little snakes down here 5 and 6 feet long."[28] More familiar creatures could pose problems, too; for example, according to the *Town Talk*, goats wandered through the grounds at one point and "were eating the insulation off the 127th Infantry's communication lines."[29] Herbert M. Smith saw the facilities at Beauregard as "a fitting introduction to military life," and later reflected: "Had we known what the future held for us, we would not have been so critical."[30]

For many Red Arrowmen, one bright spot was the food. Though the crude mess hall left much to be desired, the food itself was plentiful—or, as Herbert M. Smith put it, "the only item not in short supply."[31] Many GIs quickly put on weight, as Chaplain Eilers noted, "and that's not a matter of a pound or two, but often goes as high as eight, ten, and even fifteen pounds in individual cases."[32] Tracy Hale boasted that many of the Red Arrow cooks were "former hotel chefs and cooks from the Civilian Conservation Corps," and told the *Town Talk* "that the men are saying they're eating better than ever before in their lives."[33] The abundance was indeed a godsend to many who had survived the hungry years of the Depression. Not all were pleased, of course. In a letter home to Oshkosh, David Post Smith bluntly dismissed the press reports about the high quality of Beauregard's provisions. The milk, Smith wrote, was "varnish remover" that "comes from tin cans and [is] cut (and I do mean cut) with good old Louisiana water" and the toast was "scorched bread." He railed against "army slum soup" and complained that the army "does not issue fresh vegetables." Smith conceded that "we didn't join to go to a tea party," but resented what he felt were inaccurate reports about the quality of the food: "Does the army have to resort to lies like that to induce men to accept their conscription more or less willingly?"[34]

The Guardsmen had a lot to learn in their thirteen weeks of basic training, which began October 29. The *Town Talk* outlined what riflemen did in the first week of training:

> Training in military courtesy and discipline, two and one half hours; sanitation, first-aid and hygiene, one hour each; chemical warfare defense, two hours; air and mechanized attack, three hours; marches on bivouacs, two hours; close order drill, five hours; elementary knowledge of rifle, six hours; care of clothing and equipment, one hour; packs and tent pitching, two hours; interior guard training, two hours; group games and athletics, six hours.[35]

Trainers placed a great emphasis on physical conditioning. The typical day began with calisthenics before breakfast and almost always included road marches. Gifford Coleman of Rice Lake, Wisconsin, remembered "a lot of marching on the country roads with full steel packs and getting in physical shape."[36] Marches got progressively longer and often involved military problems. Herbert M. Smith recalled a twenty-mile hike: "The forenoon portion was to be conducted under combat conditions, protection of a regimental column on a road march; machine guns, vehicle-mounted, some in the column, others leap-frogging along the route to afford anti-aircraft protection." After lunch, a rest, and a change of socks, "the afternoon march was non-tactical, just slogging."[37] Training continued in the classroom, taught by regular army troops. "There are hours when the regiment looks like a big school with teachers here and there instructing their classes," reported the *Wisconsin National Guard Review*.[38]

Inadequate equipment, especially early on, hobbled training effectiveness. "Most of the equipment," claimed Art Kessenich, "had 1918 labels on it."[39] Some improvements occurred over time, as the nation's war production ramped up. On November 18, Tracy Hale noted in his diary the arrival of "approx. 400 M-1 (Garand) rifles to the Co's of the Regt. This is the first issue of this weapon to the regt. More will be issued later, no doubt."[40] Yet, dated and simulated equipment did not dampen the GIs' enthusiasm. "One day," wrote Roy Campbell, "wonder of wonders, the company received three new 30-caliber, air-cooled light machine guns and three 60-millimeter mortars, and a weapons platoon was soon formed." Campbell became a mortarman and studied the manual until he "had it down pat," and when he went to the range, his squad was "the first to set up, fire and hit the target." Campbell's enthusiasm and skill eventually led to his promotion, and he was put in charge of a mortar squad.[41] Even in the evenings, when the training day was over, Kessenich recalled that many would "practice things they were taught that day.... With the world situation as it was, everyone knew there was a possibility that our country would be plunged into a war."[42]

Within weeks, the physiques of the soldiers began to change. "One of the most notable improvements is that of the Guardsmen's posture," reported the *Town Talk*. "The humped backs which came from leaning over desks and work benches are gone; today they are straightened and rigid. The first month's training has put weight on the men who needed it and taken it off those who had too much."[43] Wisconsin Adjutant General Ralph Immell visited Camp Beauregard and observed that "the change in the appearance and carriage of the enlisted men was most marked. In fact, the improvement was so noticeable that one could easily close his eyes and hear the marching feet of their fathers in the 32nd Division a generation ago."[44] Their mindsets began to change, too, as the realities of full-time military life were sinking in. "We thought we knew something," Ervin Sartell later confessed, "until we were down there being trained by the Regular Army, we found out we didn't know as much as we thought."[45] Herbert M. Smith thought that Camp Beauregard was where the Red Arrow had truly been "introduced to army life. Summer encampments had offered hints as to the professional military life, but the first exposure to reality posed serious consideration."[46]

In January 1941, the Red Arrowmen moved five miles up the road to Camp Livingston. The new four-thousand-acre facility, carved out of the Kisatchie National Forest, represented a significant improvement over Camp Beauregard. It had paved streets and walkways made of crushed stone or oyster shells, minimizing the problem of mud. Troops still lived in tents, but they were much more comfortable, with wooden floors and walls, sealed against the wind and rain, resting upon wooden foundations to keep them off the ground. Each tent had electricity, and gas heaters had replaced the hated Sibley stoves. One engineering report called them "cottages with canvas tops."[47] "Never in the history of the National Guard or volunteers in Federal service," opined the *Wisconsin National Guard Review*, had any soldiers "had sleeping facilities that are now furnished with iron cot, thick mattress, pillow, pillow slips, sheets, blankets, and comforter in a gas heated tent. It is difficult for an old timer to comprehend that."[48] Jungwirth remembered that "each company had a large bath house with modern toilet facilities, and were equipped with washing machines for doing laundry. There was hot and cold running water, a real luxury in an army camp."[49]

Camp Livingston held still other advantages over Beauregard. Its hospital could accommodate more than a thousand patients, quartermaster troops now worked in rows of warehouses, and little luxuries abounded. "In each regimental area is a post exchange, with not only drinks, [but

Soldiers at Camp Livingston, Louisiana. On the far left is Gerald Endl, who would posthumously receive the Medal of Honor for valor at Aitape, New Guinea, in 1944.
GERALD ENDL COLLECTION, WISCONSIN VETERANS MUSEUM

also] tobacco, cigarettes and the other articles a post exchange generally carries," noted the *Wisconsin National Guard Review*. Post exchanges also offered "coffee, sandwiches, etc.," as well as "a two-chair barbershop, a shoe shine stand, and a tailor shop all under one roof." Beer was available in some portions of the sprawling camp, but because part of Camp Livingston was located in a dry parish (the Louisiana equivalent of a county), the "men from the dry section [had to] buy it by the case from the wet area."[50] The dining experience improved as well. "The mess halls are as fine as most college boarding clubs," wrote Chaplain H. J. Rasmussen of the 107th Quartermaster Regiment, "and a good deal better than some I have seen." The chaplain noted that "morale has taken a decided upturn" after moving into the new camp and believed that "the training and operation of the division will be greatly enhanced."[51]

After the move to Camp Livingston, training became more intense. The division spent increasing amounts of time in the field simulating combat problems. Troops were expected to deploy at a moment's notice, day or night. During a night alert described in the *Town Talk*, the Red Arrowmen "quickly donned steel helmets and 55-pound packs, shouldered arms, tumbled into trucks with dimmed blue headlights, and sped away into the darkness" and "within a few minutes battle lines were formed."[52] Mock battles broke out across the Louisiana countryside. At dawn on March 28, for example, the 125th Infantry Regiment defended a stretch of land along the Red River as the 128th attacked. "Throughout the night, patrols from each regiment were out trying to 'locate' the other," reported the *Town Talk*, and "the 'battle' occurred on a 2,000-yard front somewhere between the little towns of Dry Prong and Colfax."[53]

Draftees joined the Red Arrow at Camp Livingston in March and April. To maintain the regional character of National Guard divisions, the army assigned conscripts to the divisions that had originated in their home states. In turn, Red Arrow officials made every effort to assign the draftees from Wisconsin and Michigan to units from their own hometowns. "A selectee from Juneau County, Wisconsin, would be assigned to the Tomah company," explained the *Wisconsin National Guard Review*, "and a selectee from the City of Milwaukee, as far as practicable, would be assigned to a Milwaukee company or battery." Elvin Ball, a draftee from a farm family in Langston, Michigan, sent a letter back home after he arrived at Camp Livingston: "We got in the Thirty-Second Division after all. It's called Michigan's Own Army. It's the best in the World War according to the guys down here."[54]

Draftees may have come from the same cities and towns as the original National Guard contingent, but their attitudes toward military service were often different. They were conscripts, not volunteers. "Before I was shanghaied into the army," wrote Lawrence Thayer of Palmyra, Wisconsin, "I went to my local draft board, hoping to convince them my educational training as an engineer would be more useful to the war effort than my being dumped into the infantry as cannon fodder. But my words fell on deaf ears."[55] Others accepted their fate. "I just thought it was a year's training," said Martin Bolt of Grand Rapids, "and in the event we did get into a war, we would be experienced enough to fight the battle."[56]

Unlike the National Guard troops who came to Louisiana with some semblance of military training, the draftees started from scratch. The Red Arrow formed training teams, composed of three officers and eight to thirteen noncommissioned officers, to introduce the conscripts to military life, even though the Guardsmen had only recently trained themselves. One draftee, Paul Rettell from Romeo, Michigan, recounted:

> The things we were taught was how to pack your pack; how to take your rifle apart and clean it and put it back together again; how to throw grenades and practice throwing them; how to use a gas mask by putting it on and going through a tent full of tear gas; practice marching in step, the usual right face, left-face, about-face, and other steps until you got quite proficient at it. We had bayonet drills and calisthenics with rifles.

Rettell also remembered time at the firing range. "I had no problem because I lived on a farm," he wrote, "and learned to shoot . . . when I was ten years old. I could hit a hickory nut at thirty yards."[57] Individualistic young Americans sometimes chafed at army discipline. "It soon became apparent that the main objective of the army brass was to make us realize that we were just slaves subject to rigid discipline," wrote Lawrence Thayer, "and that we must obey any order without question no matter what." Thayer recalled with resentment "a long list of things we must not do. Every no-no was ended with the statement that if the rule was disobeyed we would be punished by court martial."[58] The training course lasted six weeks, and then the draftees joined their units. National Guardsman Steve Janicki saw some familiar faces among the new members of his company. "I knew them from Grand Rapids," he recalled; "they lived on the west side where I lived."[59] In a few cases, the old hands and the new arrivals did not mix well. "The National Guards were all friends and knew each other," recalled Martin Bolt. "They had been down there from [October] and they kind of stayed together in one area."[60] Red Lane recalled that "there were 84 of us from Oconto" in his company, but "then they brought in some new recruits, mostly from Detroit," and that was when "the fights started."[61]

National Guard traditionalists resented any intrusion from the regular army or reserves into the division. Officers were a particular source of friction. "I believe a National Guard division should be self contained and officered from top to bottom with National Guard officers," wrote Adjutant General Ralph Immell, "until it is demonstrated that the institution of the National Guard does not have within its organization the raw material that can be trained for every responsibility." Regular army and reserve officers, he claimed, deprived the Guard the chance to develop its own leaders. Immell was a political ally of Wisconsin's former Progressive governor Philip F. La Follette, a prominent isolationist. "I do not believe America is going to war," Immell wrote, claiming that "when the National Guard returns to its several states, these officers of the regular establishment will not come with them. The division will, therefore, be incomplete."[62]

Some enlisted men rose through the ranks and gained commissions, but by mid-1941 reserve officers began to appear in the Red Arrow uniform.[63] One was Oliver O. Dixon, who recalled the division's "clannish atmosphere" and that his new colleagues were "not kindly disposed" to reservists.[64] The reserve officers also left some enlisted men unimpressed. One day Paul Rettell, now a driver, picked up a group of arriving officers at the train station. "I heard their conversation," he wrote, and was shocked that "they didn't even know the ranks of some officers we passed." He also thought that their "training was nil" and that they "followed the sergeants like puppy dogs." Rettell claimed that bringing in these "90-day wonders" was "the biggest mistake the army ever made," though he also questioned the abilities of National Guard officers, describing them as "weekend soldiers" who were "too old for fighting."[65]

In addition to their field training, Red Arrow soldiers participated in various specialized training schools. Chaplain Rasmussen, writing in the *Wisconsin National Guard Review*, noted classes in "gas, typing, and shorthand, defense against mechanized attack, driver's schools, motor transport, Military intelligence, cooking, and . . . Spanish." Not all schools took place in camp. "The most enticing form of school assignment is of course that which sends one to a distant city," wrote Rasmussen. "Both officers and enlisted men have been given these assignments by the scores. Every week someone checks out or in from such points as Baltimore, San Antonio, Philadelphia, and Fort Leavenworth."[66] Bernd Baetcke, a lawyer and longtime member of the Michigan National Guard, attended both the Infantry School at Fort Benning and the Command and General Staff School at Fort Leavenworth. "The way they pound us along makes law school seem like a walk," he wrote from the latter location, but he was "very glad of the opportunity to come here as it is the top school in the army."[67] Indeed, so many were away from the division that it affected everyday operations. "All organizations at Camp Livingston have been handicapped on account of lack of officers," noted the *Wisconsin National Guard Review* in May 1941. "Some companies have at times only one officer on duty."[68]

American Indian soldiers participated in a project to use their own languages to transmit secure radio messages. "The 32nd Division," according to one news report, "has armed 17 Michigan and Wisconsin Indians with microphones and worked out a radio communications code that the enemy will probably never crack." The program harkened back to World War I when American Indian members of the Thirty-Sixth Division successfully used their Native languages to transmit secure messages. One Red Arrow "code talker" was Benjamin Winneshiek of the Ho-Chunk Nation. "We all had radios to talk back and forth," he remembered. Many military terms had no equivalent in the Ho-Chunk language, so participants had to get creative. "Tanks, we called them turtles," Winneshiek recalled. One officer who trained the Red Arrow code talkers noted that "a by-product of the project has been that the Indians have written home encouraging members of their tribe to intensify teaching of their own language so that other members may make a contribution to national defense." The army largely abandoned its code talker program by 1943, though the Marines took a much greater interest and recruited from the Navajo Nation. In all, fewer than seven hundred American Indian GIs took part in code talker programs during World War II (420 from the Navajo Nation alone), but they represented thirty-three nations, including the Ho-Chunk, Menominee, Ojibwe, and Oneida.[69]

When they weren't training, GIs frequently were assigned to various fatigue details. "We sodded some places around camp and the ammunition storage," wrote Elvin Ball in a letter home. "There were twelve of us to do what two could have done. They just try to keep us busy."[70] Early one morning Ball served on a detail guarding prisoners from the camp stockade as they were cutting weeds. "We carried loaded rifles with live ammunition," he wrote. "It was just like a chain gang." He further noted that "if one tries to get away, our orders are to call out halt three times, and then if he keeps going, shoot, and shoot to kill." Ball was aghast when the officer in charge said they could "say halt three times pretty fast. He told us this right in front of the prisoners. I sometimes wonder if I could shoot a fellow soldier."[71] Perhaps the most dreaded fatigue detail was working in the kitchen, an assignment dubbed the "kitchen police," or simply KP. "Washing dishes and peeling potatoes, that was the worst job," said Erling Smestad of Grand Rapids, Michigan.[72] "My turn for KP came up," wrote Byron Gibbs of Clare, Michigan. "We were up at 2:30 a.m. and put in a 17-hour day. At this time we had the dishes of 170 soldiers to wash plus the pots and pans and clean up in the dining area and kitchen."[73] Commanders often used KP duty as a punishment. One day a lieutenant asked Steve Janicki when he had last shaved. "I busted out laughing," Janicki remembered, because he had never shaved before. The officer "called me a few choice words and he put me on KP for a week."[74]

As the weeks turned into months, army life became routine. The GIs endured inspections, parades, fatigue duties, and more training. "It was getting kind of monotonous," remembered Hans Sannes of Stoughton, Wisconsin, "the same kind of drilling."[75] Ernie Long of the 126th Infantry Regiment wrote in a letter to an acquaintance, "I've been in camp two months, and it seems like a year."[76]

In July 1941, the Thirty-Second Division was officially redesignated the Thirty-Second Infantry Division, though most of its members were far too busy to notice the change. The summer and fall of 1941 brought field exercises for nearly every soldier in the United States Army. The largest and most significant exercises took place in Louisiana, and among the participating divisions was the Red Arrow. The Louisiana Maneuvers were the largest field exercises the US Army has ever conducted. In all, four hundred thousand troops played war games in the woods and fields of the Pelican State. The maneuver area spanned roughly thirty thousand square miles, from East Texas to the Mississippi River, and from Shreveport to Lake Charles. Participating in the exercises were a number of army leaders who would later play major roles in the American war effort, including Dwight D. Eisenhower, Omar Bradley, George S. Patton Jr., and Mark W. Clark. General McNair, the GHQ chief of staff, ran the show. All the proceedings occurred under the concerned and watchful eye of General Marshall.[77]

Like the maneuvers the previous summer, the exercises began small: division vs. division, then corps vs. corps, culminating in army vs. army maneuvers in September. McNair wanted to test his officer corps, find talent within its ranks, and weed out the incompetent. In light of Hitler's blitzkrieg across Europe, McNair was especially keen to test antitank capabilities. "We are definitely out to see," said McNair, "if and how we can crush a modern tank offensive."[78] Armored warfare may have been on McNair's mind, but all of the army's elements took part in the maneuvers: infantry, artillery, air forces, paratroopers, cavalrymen on horseback— even messenger pigeons.

McNair designed the exercises to resemble actual battlefield conditions as much as possible. Rather than relying on heavily scripted scenarios, he expected commanders to improvise based on battlefield situations, and he ordered his operations officer, Brigadier General Mark Clark, to "[k]eep the directive as simple as possible." The exercises assessed the readiness not just of combat soldiers, but also of critical support troops. "McNair wanted to test the soundness of our logistical doctrines in large-scale maneuvers," recalled Clark, "where men could sleep and live and work as near as possible to combat conditions."[79] Troops stayed in the field for extended periods—in rain or shine, in daytime heat and nighttime cold, in forests and swamps, and with all the wildlife that rural Louisiana had to offer. Where bridges did not exist, engineers had to build them.

On maneuvers in Louisiana in 1941. KENNETH GRUENNERT COLLECTION, WISCONSIN
VETERANS MUSEUM

Everything the troops might need—from ammunition to food—had to be transported to the front amid the constantly changing conditions of their simulated war. McNair trucked in mountains of blank rounds and even played recorded battle noises to foster realism, although no exercise could completely simulate combat. Aircraft dropped bags of flour instead of bombs, for example, and the bridges the umpires declared destroyed actually remained standing. Civilians, who would normally flee the battlefield, instead watched the maneuvers with great interest along country roads and city streets, and even from the comfort of their own front porches. Equipment shortages still hindered training. The *New York Times* featured a photograph of three soldiers with a simulated antitank gun made of sticks. The "soldier at the left waves a flag to denote that the gun has been 'fired,'" read the caption.[80]

The Red Arrow Division participated in these maneuvers as part of the Third Army, under Lieutenant General Walter Krueger. Born in Flatow, Germany, in 1881, Krueger arrived in the United States as a boy. He enlisted for the Spanish-American War in 1898 and afterward decided to make the army his career. He gained a commission as a lieutenant in 1903, and by the end of the 1930s he had pinned his first general's star on his collar. By working his way up from a private soldier to a general officer, Krueger earned a reputation as the friend of the enlisted man. "Krueger made the conditions and well-being of the troops under his command a high priority," noted his biographer, Kevin Holzimmer, and in turn "received the respect and admiration of many of those who served with him."[81] During the summer maneuvers of 1940, Krueger became known as an aggressive commander who favored fast, relentless strikes. His performance in the 1940 maneuvers led to his assignment to the Third Army in May 1941 as the Louisiana Maneuvers approached. Krueger soon brought in Colonel Eisenhower to serve as his chief of staff.

The Third Army consisted of three corps, IV, V, and VIII, comprising a mix of regular army and National Guard divisions. The Thirty-Second Division was assigned to the V Corps under Major General Edmund L. Daley. Red Arrowmen began the division vs. division exercises in June 1941 with a series of tussles against other V Corps divisions. The pretend battles "involved long stays in the field," Tracy Hale wrote, "and took place during some very wretched weather."[82] In a letter home to his family, Elvin Ball described one overnight operation: "We were on the go from 11:30 p.m. until about 9:00 the next morning. We walked nineteen 'army miles' through swamps, creeks, rivers, barnyards, and mud" with "just a small flashlight for each squad." Later that day his company was on the move again, and some soldiers struggled with the extreme heat—Ball noted that "it was 102 degrees in the shade by a little pencil thermometer one of the boys had.... A lot of the old company men had to fall out, even some of the noncoms, and boy did we give them the business. We called them tender feet and candy-asses."[83] Krueger, for his part, was quite pleased with his enlisted men that summer, calling them "the finest lot by far of any bunch of men I have ever seen.... I love them, and I am proud of them."[84]

Corps vs. corps maneuvers began in mid-August. When the Red Arrow left Camp Livingston for those war games on August 11, the division would stay in the field for nearly two months. Shortly after leaving, National Guard soldiers received unwelcome news. Earlier that summer, President Roosevelt and General Marshall had proposed an eighteen-month extension of the National Guard's active service. "The National Guard was looking forward to completing their one year of service in a couple of months and going home," wrote Byron Gibbs. But on August 18, Congress approved the extension, and General Irving Fish, the Red Arrow commander, broke the news to his troops. The announcement "didn't raise the morale of the boys very much," Elvin Ball dryly observed.[85] Some GIs threatened to desert and go "over the hill in October," commonly abbreviated as OHIO. "Soon there appeared the word 'OHIO' being inscribed on billboards, signs nailed to fence posts [and] chalked on the sides of army vehicles," remembered Clarence Jungwirth.[86] Ball wrote, "I pity some of those senators that passed the bill if the boys ever catch up with them in Washington."[87]

Most Guardsmen, however, begrudgingly accepted the change, and the intensity of the corps vs. corps maneuvers kept them occupied. In one simulated battle, V Corps drove north from Lake Charles after a hypothetical amphibious landing along the coast, and VIII Corps drove south to stop them. Here for the first time the Red Arrow Division encountered tanks—specifically, Patton's Second Armored Division—near Rosepine. "Upon contact," reported the *Wisconsin National Guard Review* of the encounter, "the reconnaissance troop, by radio, notified the advance units of the impending tank attack." Then the division's antitank troops, only recently organized and "heavily armed with 37 mm and 75 mm guns, scurried ahead and to the sides and literally saved the day."[88] In another operation, V Corps staged crossings of the Red River. "This morning we practiced going across rivers in assault boats," wrote Elvin Ball. "These little boats carry eleven men [and] weigh two hundred pounds. They are really built solid."[89] As the Red Arrowmen traversed the Louisiana countryside, they noticed more and more military assets descending on the region in preparation for the big September maneuvers. "We have antiaircraft guns, heavy artillery, and airplanes that drop sacks of flour instead of real bombs," observed Ball, who mused: "If everyone dropped flour instead of real bombs, wouldn't that be something[?]"[90]

September's army vs. army maneuvers occurred in two phases, pitting Lieutenant General Benjamin Lear's Second Army (the red force) against Krueger's Third Army (the blue force). With McNair's demand for simplicity in mind, his operations officer, Mark Clark, got to work on planning. Using an ordinary highway map, Clark "drew a big goose egg in the Shreveport area" where Lear was to assemble his troops, drew another one south of the Red River for Krueger's forces, and then gave "each army a mission that would bring them into contact."[91]

The first phase of the maneuver was scheduled to begin at 5:00 a.m. on September 15. In the days before the "war" commenced, a tropical storm in the Gulf of Mexico lashed the maneuver area with high winds and heavy rain. "From low, darkening clouds," reported *LIFE* magazine, "the drops splattered on the State's good highways, on its hundreds of marshy and mud roads, on its pine forests, and on its deep swamps full of quicksand."[92] The soldiers and the staging areas were drenched. Many of the planes at Lake Charles assigned to Krueger's blue force had to be flown to safer locations outside of the maneuver area and would not be at his disposal for the operation.

Despite the foul weather, the first maneuver kicked off as scheduled. Red forces crossed the Red River near Shreveport and Natchitoches and drove southward. Lear hoped to drive his armored forces around the western flank of the blue army, sweeping as far west as the Sabine River, but he was slow to get his tanks into position, which allowed Krueger to deploy his troops in a line from the Sabine to the Red River to block the red force's advance. While the main action occurred on the blue army's western flank, the Thirty-Second Division was far away on the eastern flank. On that first day, the Red Arrow advanced northward from Oakdale toward Alexandria, its mission to secure the south bank of the Red River and seize the bridge between Alexandria and Pineville. The Red Arrow reached Alexandria late in the afternoon and "after a night battle in the city streets," secured the Alexandria waterfront. The Thirty-Second Division "dug in . . . on the Red River levee [and] held their line," reported the *Town Talk*, "even during one artillery bombardment when an umpire rang a cow bell while waving a red flag with a white spot on it, indicating the artillery attack."[93]

On September 18, elements of the 127th Infantry Regiment crossed to the north side of the river in pursuit of retreating red forces, advancing twenty-five miles northwest of Alexandria to Colfax, where the Thirty-Seventh Infantry Division then picked up the pursuit. "The 32d was now strung out over a wide front," reported the *Wisconsin National Guard Review*, "to secure the Red River against a possible Red counter attack."[94] When McNair halted the first exercise on September 19, the Red Arrowmen "washed grime from their bodies and uniforms," reported the *Town Talk*, and made their way into Alexandria "searching for entertainment, steaks, and rest."[95]

The second phase, nicknamed the Battle of the Bridges, commenced on September 24 with another drenching storm. In this scenario, Lear's forces defended Shreveport from Krueger's forces attacking from the south. Lear retreated northward up the Red River valley, destroying bridges (in simulated fashion, of course) to slow down Krueger's advance and force his engineers to construct hundreds of pontoon bridges. Little fighting occurred, much to McNair's consternation. The second phase of the maneuvers was not without excitement, though. Avoiding the Battle of the Bridges altogether, Patton swept his armored forces around the western edge of the battlefield into East Texas, getting behind Lear and approaching Shreveport from the north. But there was no such drama for the Red Arrow. Starting out again from the Oakdale area, the Red Arrow advanced northward to Alexandria, then along the south bank of the Red River, encountering "blown up bridges by the score," noted the *Wisconsin National Guard Review*, but "only minor clashes."[96]

Tracy Hale characterized the operation as a "rat race." At one point, Red Arrow engineers had to build a bridge across the Cane River northwest of

Alexandria. "The foot soldiers went across it," Hale wrote, but "the first jeep to try to cross it went to the bottom of the River amid cheers from all the soldiers." Near Natchitoches, blue forces discovered a bridge that the red forces had failed to destroy but could not exploit the find. "Units of many divisions of the blue forces were trying to cross the bridge at the same time," Hale wrote. "The result was that all of our troops were stalled [and] sitting for miles down the road waiting to cross."[97] The *Wisconsin National Guard Review* reported that by the end of the Battle of the Bridges, "sweat-grimed 32d Division soldiers had advanced some 120 miles as far north as Hanna."[98]

Red Arrowmen found life in the field challenging. Detroit's Richard Correll wrote to his wife, Elizabeth: "Had a bath yesterday and another today. Of course, it wasn't exactly in the tub; was in the middle of a very clear and cute little creek. Was the water cold!!"[99] Meals were unsatisfying and unappetizing. Lunches often consisted of jam sandwiches wrapped in wax paper and an apple or an orange. "Ants could always seem to somehow get at the sandwich," wrote Byron Gibbs. "A jam and live ant sandwich is hard to eat unless you are pretty hungry."[100] Soldiers were constantly subjected to "the heat, dust, rain, grime, mosquitoes, bugs, and the billions of chiggers that left nasty bites on your legs," wrote Jungwirth.[101] At one point, Jungwirth's company "attempted to bivouac [set up a temporary camp] in a pine forest, but were driven out by hundreds of pygmy rattlers. . . . Some of us were driven to sleeping on the hoods of trucks instead of sleeping on the ground."[102] As Ervin Sartell succinctly put it, "We thought war couldn't be any worse than this."[103]

But simulated war did not have the intensity of the real thing, and some soldiers did not take the maneuvers very seriously. As regimental mail sergeant, Sartell was tasked with picking up the incoming mail at Lake Charles and bringing it to soldiers in the field. On one such trip, he saw a store advertising "Jean Lafitte Whiskey . . . fifty cents a pint." Sensing an opportunity to make a little money, Sartell bought thirty dollars' worth of whiskey and headed toward the front. Along the way he came across a rural tavern and decided to stop in for a beer. Sartell was wearing the blue armband that identified him as a member of the blue force. He walked through the tavern door only to find that "everyone had a red arm band on." Thinking fast, Sartell shouted, "You're all captured!" and "everyone just laughed and screamed." Two hours later, he "staggered out of the place, didn't spend a dime, [and] made a lot of friends." Sartell finally arrived at the regiment and delivered the mail. He sold his whiskey for a dollar a bottle but had many dissatisfied customers who complained that it "was seasoned with wood chips and tasted like hell." On a later mail run, Sartell bought higher-quality booze but "didn't make any money."[104] Other soldiers distracted one another with pranks. "One morning I was sleeping with my feet sticking out of the recon car," wrote Paul Rettell, "when a couple of my buddies stuck a book of matches on the edge of my shoe [then lit the matches] and gave me a hot foot." Rettell soon got his revenge. "I found a big Louisiana moccasin snake [and] killed it with my bayonet," he wrote. Rettell than put the dead snake between his two friends while they slept and when "they woke up and saw this snake they almost died of fright."[105]

The lackadaisical attitudes of some soldiers contributed to poor discipline and lapses in military bearing. Hanson Baldwin of the *New York Times* observed that "the appearance of the men is too often sloppy" and reported many other unmilitary-like behaviors: "Hitchhiking is prevalent. Officers and men sometimes drink together. Saluting is done on duty, rarely at other times." Baldwin found these problems especially prevalent in National Guard units. "Top sergeants of the old Army," Baldwin claimed, "are said to be in despair."[106] Captain Frederick R. Stofft, a member of Krueger's staff who later would command the 127th Infantry Regiment in the Philippines, inspected the V Corps on September 27 and identified numerous problems of efficiency and military courtesy: "Very little consideration given to cover and concealment. . . . Men all over the area with shirts off. . . . Trucks not properly marked . . . 128 Infantry, Service Company, Private Huberman driving truck 50 miles an hour on Highway 20 going south."[107]

Reports of soldier morale varied. National Guard troops resented the recently announced extension of their service, and many draftees did not want to be there at all. Colonel Jim Dan Hill, commander of the 120th Field Artillery, remembered one "homesick Selectee from the Paul Bunyan country of Northern Wisconsin" who said he could "get on stilts with my morale on my back and walk under a sleeping snake's belly without waking him up."[108] Another soldier claimed that reports of low morale were just "idle rumor."[109] "The men are willing and eager in the field," Baldwin wrote, "yet they have little real interest in the Army. They have one compelling desire, to get out and get home as rapidly as possible."[110]

The Louisiana Maneuvers ended on September 28, and the soldiers of the Thirty-Second Division gladly returned to Camp Livingston. All told, the Red Arrow Division spent seven weeks in the field—far beyond any summer encampment or even the Wisconsin maneuvers of the previous summer. The *Wisconsin National Guard Review* calculated that during those seven weeks the Red Arrow had "moved between nine hundred and a thousand miles making a total of between *sixteen* and *seventeen million miles* covered by the combined personnel." In addition, the division suffered three fatalities as a result of accidents in the field.[111]

Assessments of the exercises began immediately. "The lack of practical experience was particularly evident," noted Eisenhower, though he also saw encouraging signs. "The stamina of the officers and men and their ability to take care of themselves in the field increased," Eisenhower observed, and "Louisiana's sticky heat sharpened their willingness to endure."[112] Soldiers expressed a range of opinions on whether the exercises had been useful. Robert Bable called them a "half-assed façade."[113] Some found them valuable, such as Erwin Veneklase: "You got to know the guys you're with, and they become like family and secondly, you learn to take orders and follow orders."[114] Meanwhile, others, like Gifford Coleman, suspected the exercises were "more for the officers."[115]

Coleman's observation was astute. Army brass closely scrutinized the performance of officers, from the lowliest lieutenants to the top field commanders. "After each stage of the maneuvers," wrote Eisenhower, "we tried to assemble the principal officers for a critique. In these morning chats we emphasized everything that went right [while] at the same time, we had to uncover and highlight every mistake, every failure, every foulup that in war could be death to a unit or an army."

Eisenhower believed that the maneuvers and critiques improved the officers' self-confidence. The Red Arrow's Walter Choinski agreed. "All are beginning to look around and assess the officers with whom we are working," he wrote to his wife, Marion. Choinski himself "came to Louisiana somewhat doubting my capabilities," but "ended with an assurance that come what may I could and would cope with that problem which confronted me."[116] Historian Geoffrey Perret observed that "some men's reputations were made in Louisiana," while "others were ruined, just as surely as if it had been a real campaign."[117] Eisenhower himself came out as one of the shining stars, and he became a brigadier general shortly afterward. Krueger was another officer who burnished his reputation in Louisiana. He out-generaled Lear; showed a knack for the effective deployment of tanks, aircraft, and airborne infantry; and proved his skill at conducting operations on a shoestring. "The woeful shortage of weapons and equipment of all kinds," Krueger later reflected, "taught my staff and me how to do much with little and get along with what we had."[118]

But many more officers performed poorly, setting off a panic inside the army. "The manoeuvres [sic] were full of examples of officers who not only knew little," wrote Hanson Baldwin, "but displayed no initiative and common sense." Though McNair publicly denied that a "drastic purge" was on the horizon, many officers soon lost their jobs. "The commander also needed iron in his soul," Eisenhower wrote, "for one of his chief duties was to eliminate unfit officers, some of whom were good friends."[119] The performance of National Guard officers worried Marshall and McNair most of all. Indeed, McNair was so thoroughly unimpressed with the National Guard that he suggested demobilizing it altogether. The army dismissed scores of Guard officers after the maneuvers. By the end of October, ten of the eighteen National Guard division commanders who participated in the Louisiana Maneuvers had lost their jobs and were replaced with regular army officers. Removals cascaded down the chain of command, and the Red Arrow felt the pinch. "So many officers left at this time that it is impossible to mention them all," lamented Tracy Hale.[120] General Fish, the Red Arrow commander, kept his job for the time being.

In November 1941 the army staged more maneuvers, this time in the Carolinas. These war games pitted the First Army under Lieutenant General Hugh A. Drum against Major General Oscar W. Griswold's IV Corps. Though the Red Arrow was still resting and reorganizing from the Louisiana affair, the army asked the division to provide a combat team for the Carolina Maneuvers. The task fell to the 128th Infantry Regiment under Colonel William A. Holden. The combat team departed Camp Livingston in a motor convoy on October 31, set up a command post near Columbia, South Carolina, on November 4, and joined Griswold's forces. The regiment spent the better part of November participating in another pretend war. "Our big battle is on now," wrote Archie Van Gorden, a supply officer from Neillsville, Wisconsin, to his parents on November 17. "We have men to ration on a 60 mile front, guarding bridges and communications. We have a guard around our area with rifles, afraid some parachutist will drop and take over our gas and ration dump and take our trucks."[121] The cool late-autumn weather stood in stark contrast to the sticky heat of the Louisiana Maneuvers just two months before. Herbert M. Smith remembered that the "nights were frosty," so when the regiment departed the Carolinas on December 1, it took a southerly and much warmer route along the Gulf of Mexico on its way back to Camp Livingston.[122] General Griswold later characterized the regiment's performance as being "of the highest order" and complimented Holden for his "personal enthusiasm, good judgement and tactical knowledge."[123]

Training and field maneuvers kept the Thirty-Second Division busy while in Louisiana, but its members got some time for rest and recreation, too. Getting away from camp whenever possible was a top priority. Soldiers acquired weekend or three-day passes without much difficulty. "Huge buses streamed to and from Camp Beauregard throughout the afternoon," noted the *Town Talk* of one November Saturday in 1940, "and each was loaded upon its arrival in Alexandria."[124] Most Red Arrowmen had never traveled much beyond Wisconsin and Michigan before, and in their forays away from Beauregard and Livingston they often acted like tourists, seeing the sights, snapping pictures, and buying souvenirs. "Alexandria postcard scenes are going like hotcakes," noted the *Town Talk* soon after the division's arrival.[125] Most soldiers went to Alexandria for entertainment, like bowling, shooting pool, or seeing a movie. Particularly popular were taverns, dance halls, and nightclubs where one could have a drink and socialize—and where love (or at least something like it) might bloom. As Gifford Coleman recalled, "we'd . . . hit the bars and look for the girls or go to a movie, typical GI stuff."[126] The *Milwaukee Journal* reported that "officers have taken almost all rail space at swanky bars," while "enlisted men crowd other drinking and dancing places, theaters, and cafes. They rub elbows with the carpenters, masons, cementers, roofers, architects, engineers, bookkeepers, clerical help, and camp followers."[127] The *Town*

Talk noted that local merchants welcomed the soldiers, who had "pockets full of cash," and that "cash registers in cafes, drug stores, and night clubs were kept ringing far into the night."[128] Each weekend the streets of Alexandria filled up with so many khaki-clad young men that before long those hoping to escape the army milieu found the city a disappointing extension of camp.

At first, the Yankees from Wisconsin and Michigan were unsure how they would be received in the Deep South. Southern whites were "still fighting the Civil War," warned the *Wisconsin National Guard Review*, and "tell atrocity stories of the Northern Armies."[129] For most Red Arrowmen such fears were quickly allayed. "The people are so nice," reported Detroit's Marvin Van Horn, "they make you feel right at home."[130] The midwesterners could not always understand the Southern accent and were sometimes puzzled by the slower pace of life, but they quickly became enmeshed in the social fabric of Alexandria.

The *Town Talk* recognized its vast new readership and began reporting on Wisconsin and Michigan news. It also introduced a column called Beauregard Notes, and later Camp Livingston Notes, reporting about happenings in camp—transfers and promotions, visitors and furloughs, gossip and factoids. Chaplain Randolph Evjen of the 128th Infantry Regiment arranged for soldiers to attend services in local churches. "Last Sunday all of the rolling stock of the regiment was needed to transport the boys to Alexandria, where they worshipped in the churches of their own choice," noted the *Town Talk*.[131] In a special report to the *Milwaukee Journal*, Southern journalist Ralph Brewer wrote: "The planting of the youth of Wisconsin in the heart of Louisiana will cement the friendship of these states and the two sections. The boys here are finding that we have many things in common, but the greatest of these is America."[132]

Some Southerners resented the new Northern invasion and wanted the "Yankee bastards" to leave.[133] "I recognized early on that there were two types of Southerners," wrote William Sikkel, "the rebel Southerners and the Southern genteel."[134] Of course the Red Arrow Yankees went South with their own cultural expectations and ignorance. The midwesterners commented frequently on the region's intense poverty. To them, many poor white people were "hillbillies"—a "shiftless, drunken, promiscuous, and bare-footed people, living in blissful squalor beyond the reach of civilization," as historian Anthony Harkins described the stereotype.[135] "This is 'Cracker' county for sure," Bernd Baetcke informed his parents.[136] Byron Gibbs recalled that while on maneuvers he came across a shack in the countryside, home to an elderly couple, with "a hand split shingle roof, no regular windows, just openings with doors. The chimney was clay stones and sticks."[137] Red Arrow troops observed that Black Southerners generally lived in more extreme poverty than white Southerners. "You should see the houses the people live in down here, especially the colored people," wrote Elvin Ball. "Hardly any of them have windows, just a place for them to eat and sleep. Most of them have just one room. It makes me feel lucky to have a good old farmhouse to grow up in."[138]

Most Red Arrowmen had little personal experience with the Jim Crow system of racial segregation that reigned across the South. Byron Gibbs was mystified to see "two identical drinking fountains several steps apart, one with a sign for whites only, the other for colored only," even though they "were connected to the same water supply." Observing Jim Crow firsthand prompted Gibbs to reflect on the state of race relations in the North and his own experiences as a young man in Detroit before mobilization. "There were colored beauty shops, restaurants, and other small colored businesses," he wrote, while "the Polish . . . lived in Hamtramck and had their own shops and small businesses but this was the way things had always been. We did not look at it as segregation, it was considered a matter of choice, that people would live with their own group."[139]

In their interactions with Southerners, Red Arrowmen dealt mostly with white people, though some soldiers took tentative steps across the racial divide. "The colored people are treated pretty badly by the [whites]," Elvin Ball told his parents, "so when soldiers talk to them, they are tickled to death."[140] Art Kessenich remembered that "one evening, a group of us were in town walking down a street [and] came upon a Baptist church where the black people were having a revival meeting." Kessenich and his friends "watched for awhile" and then the worshipers "invited us to participate." For a devout Roman Catholic like Kessenich, going into a Baptist church "just wasn't done," but a few in his party accepted the invitation and, as he remembered, "the black people were very pleased."[141] Few Red Arrowmen condemned Jim Crow openly; most seemed to accept racial segregation as a fact of Southern life.

Alcohol created problems in civil-military relations. Soldiers frequented Alexandria's drinking establishments mostly without incident, but drunkenness, testosterone, immaturity, and scads of young men being loosened from the social restraints of their home communities led some GIs toward unseemly and unruly behavior. Local residents increasingly complained of "drunkenness and indecency" near bars, as well as "drunken men and women engaging in public fights."[142] The *Wisconsin National Guard Review* reported that "unsuspecting persons, including soldiers, had been 'doped and robbed' by women at two places." In July 1941, a member of the 121st Field Artillery was beaten to death after an altercation outside a local tavern between some soldiers and cab drivers. Compounding the tragedy was the fact that the soldier who was killed was not even involved in the scuffle but was, according to the *Town Talk*, "an innocent bystander."[143] Tracy Hale, commander of the 127th Infantry Regiment, recounted another incident at "a low dive where some of our men got in trouble." Exactly what transpired Hale did not know, but "the proprietor and the bartender came out shooting." One Guardsman was wounded, and the soldiers decided to exact their revenge. "A group of soldiers . . . marched up to the Club in formation as if under military orders," Hale wrote, and "took the entire club building down, covering the slot machines and bar equipment, and piled up the lumber from the building." Two months later the regiment received a bill for the damages and the men had money docked from their pay. The troops, Hale recalled, groused about the reduction of pay, but some commented: "It was worth it, sir."[144]

Prostitution thrived in Alexandria. Art Kessenich recalled that there were "two houses of 'ill-repute' in the area," and "on payday, there would be a lineup a couple of blocks long outside."[145] Concerns about the morals around the camp grew, including amongst the soldiers' families. "Telegrams and letters have been pouring into the war department and to the Wisconsin senators from wives and mothers of the 32nd Division," noted the *Wisconsin National Guard Review*, "about the immoral conditions . . . at Alexandria."[146] Prostitution and promiscuity contributed to an increase in sexually transmitted infections, known then as venereal disease, or VD. "As a naïve small town Catholic boy, I was scared—scared of V.D. and scared of committing a sin," Clarence Jungwirth later wrote. "Occasionally you would see a G.I. in the latrine, grimacing in pain, as he tried to urinate and could not without great difficulty. This was the result of a 'good time' a few days before."[147]

The army educated soldiers about sexually transmitted infections and required every soldier with a day pass to also carry an army-issued condom. Army camps also had prophylactic stations, or "pro stations." "There was a medical tent set up in selected areas in the camps with a red light bulb," recalled Jungwirth, where, after a "night on the town," soldiers were told to stop in for a "preventive treatment."[148]

Although soldiers might receive minor punishments through the army disciplinary system for contracting an infection or patronizing sex workers, they were rarely prosecuted; the heavy hand of the law fell almost exclusively on the women involved. Historian Marilyn E. Hegarty pointed out this double standard. "It valorized a militarized type of masculine sexuality," she wrote, "reinforcing a persistent notion that 'manly' soldiers would regularly seek out women for sex" while "the same process operated to cast female sexuality as threatening not only to the war effort but to the larger society."[149]

Thus, the warm welcome the Red Arrow soldiers initially received cooled over time. "The people down here seem to be getting more of a dislike for the soldiers, and it's hard to say why," wrote Elvin Ball. "I know a few of the men get wild, but for the most part we are pretty well behaved when in town."[150] Military police, working in tandem with local law enforcement, patrolled Alexandria, as well as the roads between the city and the camps, on the lookout for unseemly or illegal activities. "I made an inspection Saturday night," Colonel William Hones, the acting division chief of staff, told the *Town Talk* in December 1940, "and with the exception of a few isolated areas, the men of the 32nd Division were extremely well behaved."[151]

Many soldiers opted to spend their off-duty hours in camp. "It didn't pay to go into Alexandria on a pass," thought Roland Stoelb. "There were too many soldiers there and it was real easy to get into trouble without even looking for it."[152] Some stayed in camp for financial reasons, likely caused, in part, by the near-constant gambling. "Most of the boys seem broke all the time," observed Elvin Ball.[153] Rather than go into town, some soldiers held parties in camp. "Everyone in the company gave 50c for the refreshments," Ball wrote of one get-together, and "we had about $75 for beer, soft drinks, cheese, pretzels, cold meat, and peanuts."

Keeping animals as pets and mascots offered another amusement. Art Kessenich recalled that while still in Madison, a fellow soldier "picked up a mutt dog on the street" and "smuggled him on the train" to Camp Beauregard. The soldiers named him Rochester. He "never had to worry about food or water," according to Kessenich, "with 85 guys trying to take care of him."[154] Jungwirth's company adopted a dog named Smokey, "a mixed breed that one of the men had somehow gotten hold of." Smokey was "spoiled rotten," Jungwirth remembered, and "everywhere the company went, Smokey went."[155] In November 1940, the *Town Talk* reported that "since its encampment here, the 127th Infantry has acquired 12 pooches as mascots."[156]

Alexandria's civic leaders did their best to improve the recreational opportunities for soldiers visiting from camp. "Guardsmen . . . are 'slickin' up' with hair oil and talcum powder today in preparation for a dance at which they will have the honor of inaugurating a civilian-sponsored recreation program for soldiers," announced the *Town Talk* in January 1941. Soldier participants, "chosen by officers on a merit basis," will "meet young ladies of Alexandria's first families." Participants could select their own partners, but "no couple will be permitted to leave the auditorium during the dance."[157]

Alcohol and vice problems cropped up at other training camps too, and the morals of the soldier became a national concern. In April 1941, six of the country's most prominent service organizations gathered in Washington, DC, to address the problem: the International Committee of Young Men's Christian Associations, the National Board of Young Women's Christian Associations, the National Catholic Community Service, the Salvation Army, the National Jewish Welfare Board, and the National Travelers Aid Association. Together, they formed a new entity called the United Services Organization (USO), designed to work closely with the military to provide soldiers with wholesome recreational activities. State and local chapters of the USO emerged in Alexandria just weeks after the national organization was founded.[158] The USO quickly became famous for its "camp shows" featuring some of the nation's most popular celebrities, and offered other activities as well, including dances, games, sporting activities, tours and travel services, and many others.

The army undertook its own efforts to keep the soldiers entertained and out of trouble. At Camp Livingston, each Red Arrow regiment had a recreation hall, which doubled as a church on Sundays, as well as two service clubs. "Paul and I are going up to the service Club for a while tonight," wrote Elvin Ball. "We can read, write, play Ping-Pong, or dance. They also have a soda fountain and a restaurant there."[159] At Livingston, a soldier could see a movie, check out a book in the library, join a musical or theater group, or peruse the camp newspaper, the *Communique*. Morale officers—typically unit chaplains—organized scores of recreational activities. "There is now forming a 600 voice chorus for an Easter sunrise service," reported the *Wisconsin National Guard Review*.[160] The division held a motor show, in which GIs competed in such categories as "Best Turned out Vehicles," "Purring Motor," and "Course Driving."[161] Chaplain Andrew C. Boe of the 127th Infantry Regiment organized a "pet show" for the various unit mascots that included "a wooden walk for the animals to go down."[162] One soldier even started a hiking club. The *Town Talk* reported that twenty-two men participated in its inaugural two-hour excursion.[163]

The army strongly emphasized athletics, not only to keep soldiers busy but also to promote physical fitness, competition, and teamwork. Camp Livingston had a gymnasium, a swimming pool, and playing fields. Each regiment had its own football team; there was also one for artillerymen and another for soldiers in service units. The first division championship went to the 128th Infantry Regiment, after it defeated the Fifty-Seventh Field Artillery Brigade with a final score of 6–3. "It was a swell game all the way," reported Chaplain Eilers, "good interference, good blocking, good tackling, and spectacular passes and runs."[164] There also were basketball, softball, table tennis, and volleyball teams. The Thirty-Second Division's teams often competed with teams from other divisions in nearby training camps, including the Thirty-Fourth Division at Camp Claiborne and the Thirty-Seventh and Thirty-Eighth Divisions at Camp Shelby in Mississippi. They even took on local college teams.

Recreation budgets were tight, however, and morale officers struggled to obtain enough equipment. "We lacked everything for recreation," remembered Tracy Hale, but Chaplain Boe "suggested that if he could get

The 127th Infantry Regiment football team at Camp Livingston, 1941. In the front row, fourth from the left, is Kenneth Gruennert, who would posthumously receive the Medal of Honor for valor at Buna, New Guinea, in 1942. KENNETH GRUENNERT COLLECTION, WISCONSIN VETERANS MUSEUM

a truck and a few men for a few hours, he might be able to secure some athletic equipment." The chaplain returned with a boxing ring, football uniforms, and sundry other items for use in mess and recreation halls. "He had found a C.C.C. camp that was being abandoned," Hale wrote, "and begged every bit of equipment it had. . . . He turned up so much plunder that I ceased to call him 'Padre' and named him 'The Thief of Bagdad.'"[165]

The army and service organizations also used tourism to boost the soldiers' morale. The Thirty-Second Division sponsored excursions to the Civil War battlefield of Vicksburg, Mississippi, as well as the site of the 1814 Battle of New Orleans. "Officers said the trips were planned not only as recreation," pointed out the *Town Talk*, "but as demonstrations in connection with the troops' study of military strategy." During these trips, GIs learned about "the disposition and placement of troops, development of attack and action as it occurred, mistakes and bad guesses of military commanders of a by gone era."[166]

In April 1941, the army established recreation areas along the Gulf Coast, from New Orleans to Mobile, Alabama. "All troops have been instructed to carry full equipment," noted the *Town Talk* as one batch of soldiers departed Alexandria, "including fishing poles, tennis and badminton rackets, and a good pair of shoes. . . . Highlights of the maneuvers will be a series of engagements during which civilians will escort the troops on motor sightseeing trips in nearby towns, baseball games, [and] counter-battery action against some fried chicken that has to be disposed of." It was also noted that "young ladies residing in the combat area" would be attending a dance.[167]

The most popular tourist destination for soldiers was New Orleans, two hundred miles southeast of Alexandria. Chaplain Eilers led a group to the Big Easy in December 1940. The men slept and messed at a local high school and "had the opportunity to see this historic city at their leisure," the chaplain reported.[168] Later the army set up a recreation camp near a beach and amusement park on Lake Pontchartrain on the north side of New Orleans. Elvin Ball visited in July 1941 and described his experience in a letter home. He arrived at the recreation camp on a Friday evening, where an officer gave a quick briefing and then said, "I am just going to turn you fellows loose to have a good time. See all you can, go easy on the drinks in the hot sun, and be back here by ten o'clock Sunday morning." Ball and several friends then "started for town at 12:30 a.m. . . . and never went to bed." He marveled at the architecture of the French Quarter, noting that "all the houses have balconies with steel grillwork, and in the back they have courtyards." He also noted how "the cemeteries are all made of cement just like houses," explaining that "water is only three feet underground there, so they can't dig graves." He attended a "shrimp and crab boil on the lawn of the city hall," sponsored by the American Legion, and toured local breweries. "Anyone in uniform that went through [the breweries] could have all the beer they wanted," he boasted. Ball also went to the amusement park, where he rode what he called "the fastest roller coaster in the world. . . . I swear it left the track part of the time."[169] New Orleans was also a place where one could explore seamier forms of recreation. "They told us what places were 'off limits,'" recounted Roland Stoelb, "and those would be where most of us headed for to have a good time."[170] Jungwirth complained that New Orleans "catered to the weakness of the flesh."[171]

Other Red Arrowmen hunted or fished for fun. "A number of Wisconsin duck hunters," wrote Tracy Hale, departed camp and headed for local waterways "as frequently as possible." One officer was so successful, Hale recalled, that he "furnished our officers with several duck dinners."[172] Roy Campbell and a friend walked the ten miles from Camp Livingston to Catahoula Lake. "The next night the cooks roasted close to 40 ducks," he wrote, "and all that was left was a pile of bones."[173] One weekend, "four duck hunters from the 107th quartermaster regiment succeeded in 'bagging' thirty-eight ducks," reported the *Town Talk*. "Captain Veeser, reputed to be the crack shot of the quartet, only brought down two 'birds' and blames his luck on the alibi that his brother officers tampered with the sights on his gun."[174]

Homesickness was ever-present for many soldiers. It was mitigated by the fact that they were sometimes serving alongside relatives, friends, and neighbors, but it was painful nevertheless. "Down one company street there was banjo music and a tune which sounded like Suzannah [sic]," observed the *Town Talk*, "and the words ran something like this: 'Oh, Suzannah, don't you cry, I'm bound for Louisiana with my banjo on my knee, oh my true love in Wisconsin it will be a long time before I see.'"[175] The troops spent much of their free time writing letters and delighted in receiving them, too. "Mail sure is a nice thing to get down here," Orville Suckow told a class of schoolchildren back in Menomonie, "it's the only thing we have to look for from up home."[176] Soldiers could send and receive telegrams and radiograms (a telegram sent by radio). On his first day at Camp Beauregard, Art Kessenich received a telegram from his fiancée, Dora. "I shall never forget how happy I was when the commanding officer called my name and told me I had a telegram," he wrote.[177] Phone calls could be prohibitively expensive. Richard Correll told his wife about a friend who had called home to Detroit. "Do you realize," he wrote, "that he spent approximately eighteen dollars on two phone calls? Wow!!"[178] A few found more creative solutions to keep in touch with the folks back home. "Corp. Kuczynski, Med. Dept. Det., 127th Infantry, has a voice recording device," reported the *Town Talk*, and "many men are sending home voice records instead of letters."[179]

In addition to weekend and three-day passes, soldiers could request ten-day furloughs, which allowed for trips back home to Wisconsin or

Michigan. Clarence Jungwirth found a "quirk in Army Regulations" when he discovered the army would authorize a three-day pass at the beginning and end of a ten-day furlough, affording even more time away. "I was the company hero," he remembered.[180] In late December 1940, more than 70 percent of Red Arrowmen went on furlough and headed back to the Midwest. "Seeing the home town at Christmas . . . is the best present we want now," wrote Art Kessenich in a letter to the *Capital Times*.[181] Special trains left Camp Beauregard on December 21, and jubilant soldiers chalked slogans onto their train cars reading "Heading home," "Hi ya, Gals," or "Merry Christmas, Everybody." Two days later, a crowd of more than five hundred met a train of soldiers arriving in Green Bay. As the train pulled into the station, the troops were "crowding out of the coach windows," reported the *Green Bay Press-Gazette*, "waving their hats and shouting to the massed crowd, much like the soldiers of the famed World war Red Arrow division." Soon afterward, the paper noted, downtown streets "were dotted with khaki-colored soldiers with the familiar red arrow sewed on their right shoulder sleeve . . . engaged in a belated Christmas shopping spree."[182]

For the soldiers who stayed behind in Louisiana, it was not a happy holiday. "This was the first of many Army Christmases away from home and family," wrote Detroit's Edgar Connor. "I can't remember one damn good thing about it."[183]

Family members occasionally traveled to Louisiana, too. "My dad drove down," wrote Art Kessenich, "and lived on the company street." He recalled that his father "fit in very well with the guys. He enjoyed a beer, stories and a good time." Kessenich was even more delighted when his fiancée, Dora, visited.[184] Many families even took up residence in Louisiana. Accompanying Archie Van Gorden from Neillsville, Wisconsin, was his wife, Hazel, who rented a room in Pineville, just across the river from Alexandria. The Van Gordens' children came too, though "the boys are getting restless," Archie complained in one letter to relatives back in Wisconsin, and he threatened to "ship them home."[185]

The influx of soldiers' families, combined with Alexandria's burgeoning population of military personnel and war workers, exhausted the city's housing stock. "If you are planning on taking your family with you and have not made a reservation for their quarters," warned the *Wisconsin National Guard Review*, "it is suggested that you wait until you get

Local businesses catered to the influx soldiers. TOP: A woman works at a new café near the entrance to Camp Livingston. BOTTOM: On the highway leading to Alexandria, shops like this one advertised rooms for rent and hung signs in the windows proclaiming, "soldiers welcome." LIBRARY OF CONGRESS, PHOTOS BY MARION POST WOLCOTT there and look over the available places, if any." There wasn't even "a dog house vacant," complained Bernd Baetcke.[186] One group of soldiers' wives camped in the Louisiana countryside. "Four trailers, four women, four children, and one dog were found at one tourist court," reported the *Town Talk*.[187] Housing prices rose dramatically, quickly followed by accusations of price gouging. "These bastardly natives are hoisting the rents to terrible heights," complained Madison's William Lorenz Jr., "because they have army personell [*sic*] where the hair is short."[188]

The mobilization stressed some marriages and romantic relationships and prompted others to march down the aisle. Captain Elmer D. Kobs of Merrill, Wisconsin, married his girlfriend, Burdette Nelson, in an Alexandria church decorated with "potted palms and baskets of gladioli," reported the *Wisconsin National Guard Review*, while "a saxophone sextette of the 120th Field Artillery band . . . played the wedding marches."[189] Others returned home to tie the knot. Art Kessenich and several friends from his company drove north to Madison for his wedding to Dora. "Since this was a marriage during my stint in the Army, I felt it appropriate to be married in uniform," he wrote, though his brother, serving as best man, "stole the show . . . in his colorful Marine uniform." After a brief honeymoon in Chicago, Kessenich returned to camp and Dora found a room and a job in Alexandria. "Needless to say," Kessenich wrote, "we were blissfully happy and laying the groundwork for our future marriage."[190] However, not all adventures in wedlock were so harmonious, and spontaneous or hastily arranged nuptials could be troubled ones.

As 1941 drew to a close, the members of the Red Arrow Division bided their time and waited for their service terms to expire so they could go back to their civilian lives. October 15 came and went with no desertions—"OHIO" proved to be an empty threat. "We all felt we were in 'Limbo,'" wrote Jungwirth.[191] Furloughs were plentiful and many headed north whenever they could. Elvin Ball raced home for the hunting season that autumn. "Tell Bill to get my shotgun oiled and ready to go," he wrote his parents.[192] The Red Arrowmen had learned a lot about being soldiers and had grown as people during their year in Louisiana, but they were still innocently playing war. That was about to change.

A postcard showing the barracks at Fort Devens, Massachusetts. BOSTON PUBLIC LIBRARY, TICHNOR BROTHERS POSTCARD COLLECTION

CHAPTER 3

WAR FOR SURE

Like other Americans, the GIs of the Red Arrow Division remembered where they were and what they were doing when they first heard of the Japanese attack on Pearl Harbor on December 7, 1941. Martin Bolt was in New Orleans with friends on a three-day pass and walked into a restaurant for coffee and doughnuts but found the counter eerily abandoned. "We hollered, 'Where are you?'" Bolt recounted, and an agitated, disembodied voice responded, "I'll be right out." When the man appeared, he told Bolt and his friends that Pearl Harbor had been attacked, to which the soldiers responded, "Where is Pearl Harbor?"[1] Roy Campbell and a friend were walking back to camp from a duck-hunting excursion when a man offered them a ride. "They sunk our hull God dammed Navy and kilt lots of people," he remembered the man saying. "It'll be all out war for sure."[2] Indeed it was. Congress declared war on Japan the next day, and three days later Germany declared war on the United States. American entry into World War II sparked immense changes to the Red Arrow Division. Scores of soldiers left, many new members joined, and the Upper Midwestern character of the division began to fade. The division was also on the move, quickly becoming one of the army's most-traveled units. Within months of Pearl Harbor, the Red Arrow was poised to become one of the first American combat divisions to head overseas.

Pearl Harbor was just one part of a massive Japanese offensive across East Asia and the Pacific. Japan hoped to eject Western powers from the region and create what it called the Greater East Asia Co-Prosperity Sphere, a euphemism for Japanese domination. Japan particularly coveted Southeast Asia for its rich supplies of rice, rubber, tin, and oil. French Indochina (Vietnam, Cambodia, and Laos) was already under Japan's control. The Dutch East Indies (present-day Indonesia) was under the tenuous colonial hold of the Netherlands, whose government was in exile after the Nazi conquest in May 1940, while Hong Kong, Malaya, and Singapore were held by the British, who were preoccupied with European affairs. To the Japanese, the riches of what Japan called the Southern Resource Zone seemed ripe for the picking. The United States was the only nation standing in their way. The US colony of the Philippines lay astride the shipping lanes that Japan would need to use to transport any resources from Southeast Asia. The American fleet at Pearl Harbor also worried Japanese leaders. Admiral Yamamoto Isoroku, the architect of the December 7 strike on Pearl Harbor, once described the US Navy base there as "tantamount to a dagger pointed at our throat." Destroying the fleet at Pearl Harbor, the Japanese believed, would give them a free hand across East Asia and the western Pacific. To protect its newly won riches, Japan planned to build an impenetrable chain of island fortresses—from the Kurile Islands in northeast Asia, through the Marshalls and Gilberts, down to New Guinea—to prevent the United States from reentering the region.

Thus, as Japan bombed Pearl Harbor it simultaneously struck Western holdings across Asia and the Pacific. On December 8 (across the International Date Line), Japanese planes hit the American possessions of Guam, Wake Island, and the Philippines, where General Douglas MacArthur (son of Wisconsin's Civil War hero Arthur MacArthur) commanded US and Filipino forces. After learning of the Pearl Harbor attack, MacArthur weighed the possibility of bombing Japanese bases on Formosa (Taiwan); but as he dithered, Japanese planes from that island swooped in and caught his aircraft on the ground, destroying half of them and dispersing the rest.

Japanese infantry was on the move as well. Soldiers under Lieutenant General Yamashita Tomoyuki waded ashore on the Malay Peninsula hours before the Pearl Harbor attack and raced toward strategic Singapore. Japanese troops also attacked Hong Kong on December 8. The South Seas Detachment (*Nankai Shitai*) under Major General Horii Tomitaro invaded Guam on December 10 and the island fell in a day. Japanese forces attacked Wake Island on December 11, but the US Marine garrison there stubbornly held out. In the Philippines, the first Japanese units came ashore on northern Luzon on December 10, but the main force hit the beaches of the Lingayen Gulf on December 22 and headed for American bases in the Luzon's Central Valley and the capital of Manila. On January 4, 1942, Japanese planes first struck the Australian base at Rabaul on the island of New Britain, part of the Bismarck Archipelago off the northeast coast of New Guinea. The Japanese were everywhere—and they seemed unstoppable.[3]

Events in the Pacific immediately changed the atmosphere at Camp Livingston. "The guards now carried live ammunition," wrote Archie Van Gorden, "and everything is more serious and more business."[4] Steve Janicki noticed a "quiet" and "somber" mood. "Maybe a lot of guys were in deep thought," he later speculated.[5] Roy Campbell observed that as the news of the Pearl Harbor attack spread, "some men were standing in groups, some were running, others were walking slowly, but all looked very grave and serious." After lights out that night, Campbell lay down in his cot and listened to the bugler blowing "Taps." He had ended his day to that tune before, but this time, "for the first time," he wrote, Campbell "felt a twinge of sadness." As he lay there, Campbell pondered the combat that was likely to come and assured himself that he would "not be a coward."[6]

The division members expected to move out, though their destination remained unclear. "We glued our ears to the radio, and read the newspapers diligently each day," wrote Art Kessenich. "We were certain our unit would be shipped out soon."[7] There was wild talk that the Red Arrow was headed to Africa or Alaska or California. Campbell remembered one rumor that "the Japanese have invaded the Hawaiian Islands and we are going by submarine to push them out." Such rumors "were coming and going so fast," he wrote, "it took time to sort them all out."[8]

Some troops were on the move almost immediately. By 10:15 p.m. on December 7, members of the 126th Infantry Regiment had boarded trucks and rolled out of Camp Livingston and into the dark night, assigned to guard highways, bridges, railroads, utilities, and critical industrial facilities. Martin Bolt hurried back from New Orleans that evening only to be told to "load up" and head back to the city to guard bridges. "They were afraid of sabotage," he recalled, and troops pulled over cars "if they were suspicious of anything."[9] By the morning of December 8, members of the 126th Infantry Regiment were guarding facilities from Vicksburg, Mississippi, to Orange, Texas.[10] "We work guard duty four hours then we have eight hours off," Elvin Ball wrote his family. "The people around where we work give us coffee at night, and it tastes pretty good when it gets real cold. . . . They send us magazines, candy, cigarettes, and give us things to eat." Recalling the strained relations between soldiers and civilians before Pearl Harbor, Ball remarked, "The people have sure changed here since war has been declared."[11]

The troops were on high alert amid the fearful and uncertain atmosphere after Pearl Harbor, and in some cases they even discharged their weapons. On the night of December 12, for example, near Sterlington, Louisiana, an unidentified motorboat on the Ouachita River "flashed light onto the sentry," according to a report in the regimental journal. The vessel failed to stop, so the soldier "fired over the bow of boat & immediately the boat turned and went down river."[12] Three nights later, near a natural gas facility at Sterlington, a sentry "fired several shots at 5 men on levee after ordering them to halt. The men disappeared."[13]

The day after the Pearl Harbor attack, the army alerted the 125th Infantry Regiment of an impending move to California, and within days the regiment packed up and headed out. "A large number of the wives of the officers and soldiers were out at the camp this afternoon," wrote Dr. Harry Heiden, a longtime Wisconsin National Guard physician from Sheboygan, "saying farewell to those leaving. . . . Reminds me of the last war—Here today, gone tomorrow."[14] The GIs joked that they were off "to guard Hollywood," recalled Tracy Hale, and they were at least partially correct.[15] The regiment first set up headquarters in Los Angeles, but by Christmas found itself spread across the American Southwest. After New Year's Day the regiment was back in Los Angeles, based at one point in the city's Griffith Park, where—according to the regimental history—some soldiers "made several movies of tactics of small infantry units" to train recruits. "These were nervous times in California," noted Edgar Connor, "because it was thought the Japanese might make a landing there."[16] An example of just how tense things were in California was the Battle of Los Angeles in February 1942, when antiaircraft batteries fired wildly into the night skies after false reports of a Japanese air raid.

Despite invasion fears—which dissipated as the weeks and months passed—most GIs enjoyed their duty in Southern California. "Vic's Palace, Hollywood, Paris Inn, and Chinatown gave the men the gayest night life since entering the Service," noted the regimental history. By April, the 125th Infantry Regiment was on the move again, this time farther north. Based at Gilroy, the regiment had detachments posted widely across the central part of the Golden State, from Oakland to Fresno to San Luis Obispo.[17]

Back in Louisiana, and barely one month after Pearl Harbor, the Thirty-Second Military Police Company became enmeshed in an ugly racial incident in Alexandria. Although many white Louisianans welcomed (or at least tolerated) the influx of white soldiers, they often viewed Black soldiers with fear and hostility. Segregationists particularly targeted Black troops from Northern states who were unaccustomed to Jim Crow practices and deeply resented them. Discrimination was rampant within the military as well. Black troops served in segregated units under white officers who were typically from the South. According to Truman K. Gibson, an advisor to the War Department on race relations, this arrangement "condemned thousands of black servicemen to the mercy of white officers reared on notions of white supremacy, schooled in the practices of racial oppression, and determined to keep the Negro 'in his place.'"[18]

Like their white peers, Black soldiers sought entertainment in Alexandria. But unlike white soldiers, who had free rein in the city, Black troops were confined to the area around Lee Street, a segregated business and entertainment district that was dubbed "Little Harlem" in the press. White MPs (military police officers), including the Thirty-Second Military Police Company, patrolled the whole city, but the army limited Black MPs to Lee Street. Black troops reported hostility and harassment not just from local whites, but from white MPs as well. "Negro soldiers from the North

In Louisiana, Red Arrowmen trained alongside Black soldiers, like the men pictured here watching a boxing match at Camp Claiborne in 1942. The army segregated Black units, and Black troops often faced abuse from white civilians and fellow soldiers. NATIONAL ARCHIVES

stationed here," wrote journalist Penn Kimball of the New York newspaper *PM*, "say they don't mind the insults from civilians half as much as being pushed around by white MPs wearing the same uniform as theirs."[19]

Alexandria's simmering racial tensions boiled over about 8:00 p.m. on Saturday, January 10, 1942, in front of Lee Street's Ritz Theater. Accounts of how it started varied widely. According to the *Town Talk*, the incident began when an unnamed Thirty-Second Division MP arrested a Black soldier for disorderly conduct. The newspaper reported that a group of Black soldiers "swarmed around the white M.P. and his prisoner," and the MP called the local police station to ask for help. Penn Kimball of *PM* investigated the incident and reported a different story: "People who were there told me that the fight began when a white MP, roving in the Negro section of Alexandria, tried to take custody of a drunken Negro soldier away from a Negro MP who had made the arrest. The fighting took place after an argument between the two MPs and after the white MP had struck the arrested Negro soldier with a club."[20] Black journalist James B. LaFourche, vice president of the New Orleans Press Club, also investigated. According to LaFourche, the incident began when a white motorist on Lee Street honked her horn at a Black soldier in the street, who responded: "Would you run over a soldier?" Angered, the woman summoned a nearby white city police officer who, using "vile and unnecessary language," took the soldier into custody. Then, LaFourche wrote, "a group of Negro soldiers milled around the police and the apprehended soldier threatening to release the prisoner," and "quick as a flash," white MPs rushed in and "joined the melee."[21]

Alexandria police and Louisiana state troopers soon arrived, as did sixty members of the Thirty-Second Military Police Company from Camp Livingston. Police used tear gas and billy clubs to break up the growing crowd, while Black troops fought back with bricks, rocks, and sticks. Police cordoned off the area and moved through the district, closing businesses and, according to some eyewitness accounts, indiscriminately beating Black civilians and soldiers. Police also fired into the crowd. One Black soldier from Pennsylvania was standing on a street corner when he noticed white MPs "coming down the block" accompanied by "civilian policemen with shotguns." A civilian officer pushed him out of the way and called him a racial epithet, and then the police "opened fire point blank into the soldiers."[22] As another Black soldier recalled, "It looked like an army of policemen were pumping lead at us. I was going about in a daze simply because I could not believe I was actually seeing what was taking place. My mind kept saying, 'This can't be true. These are United States soldiers. They can't do this to us.'"[23]

The violence lasted about two hours, leaving local hospitals filled with the injured and Lee Street strewn with broken glass. The Lee Street incident was "Alexandria's Little Pearl Harbor," one eyewitness told the

Louisiana Weekly, adding, "Now I don't have to go to war to find out what it's like. I already know."[24] It left the morale of Black troops deeply shaken. A few days after the incident, one soldier at Camp Claiborne wrote the National Association for the Advancement of Colored People (NAACP) that he would "almost rather desert and be place[d] before a firing squad and shot down before fighting for America."[25]

The violence on Lee Street received national attention and sparked widespread calls for an investigation. "It is contradictory and hypocritical," declared the NAACP, "to fight Fascism abroad and at the same time allow it to be practiced within our own territorial boundaries, when it is the avowed national policy to carry the 'four freedoms' into every nook and corner of the world, including the reactionary south."[26] Initial reports claimed that nearly thirty Black soldiers were injured—three critically—and that Black civilians were wounded as well, including a twenty-two-year-old woman who was shot in the hip. Penn Kimball reported that several of the injured people had been struck with .38-caliber bullets—the same caliber used in Alexandria city police pistols. There was only one reported injury among the police, a state trooper who cut his hand on the broken glass from the flashlight he was using to beat a Black woman over the head.

One of the biggest controversies surrounded the question of who had done the shooting. State troopers claimed they had not discharged their weapons at all, while the local police department claimed their officers had only fired warning shots into the air. Shifting the blame for gunshot wounds onto Black residents, Alexandria's police chief explained that "some of the soldiers may have been hit by stray shots fired by negro civilians." Army officials insisted that MPs did not carry live ammunition, "not even blanks," and although three riot guns (firearms that shoot projectiles designed to incapacitate rather than kill) had been issued, "none had been fired."[27] Rumors swirled through Alexandria that several people had died. "On the streets, in buses, at churches and in homes," reported the *Town Talk* of the Sunday after the incident, "Alexandrians . . . discussed various rumors, some of them to the effect that as many as 18 had been killed." The newspaper dismissed the rumors as "erroneous and exaggerated."[28]

The army investigated, and General Walter Krueger flew in to supervise, but many residents soon suspected it was more of a cover-up. Police kept the Lee Street district closed, the army temporarily confined Black troops to camp, and civil and military officials shared precious little information with the public or the press. The army insisted that no deaths had occurred. In all his reporting, Penn Kimball, who was white, said he found no evidence that anyone had been killed. But skepticism of the army's claims abounded, particularly in the Black community. James LaFourche of the New Orleans Press Club told NAACP executive secretary Walter White that he believed at least ten Black troops had been killed, and sent him statements from two soldiers attesting to the deaths.[29] One soldier, in a letter LaFourche had obtained, wrote to his friends that "four or more soldiers were killed" that night.[30] Another soldier told LaFourche that "city police and white M.P.s were shooting up all the Negro soldiers" and that "there were several soldiers killed but the war department don't want people to know about it."[31] In early February, Leon Lewis, another official with the New Orleans Press Club, wrote to the office of the US Secretary of War, stating that he had gathered "signed statements from persons who swear to be willing to testify before a board of inquiry that Negro soldiers were killed."[32]

Given the army's tight control of information, the public has never received a full accounting of the role the Thirty-Second Military Police Company played in the Lee Street violence. There is little doubt that some of its members participated in the violence. One Black woman was coming out of a show when, as she later described, "a white M.P. struck me and I fell down on the front steps. I landed on my mouth and knocked some of my teeth out. He kicked me in the side before I could get up."[33] Many witnesses claimed to see MPs firing guns. One Black soldier recalled that a Black MP was directing people to safety when he suddenly "bawled bloody murder as a white M.P. seemed to deliberately shoot him in the foot."[34] Penn Kimball interviewed several people who claimed they saw MPs firing weapons, including, as Kimball reported, a barbershop manager who "showed me the hole in his ceiling [that was created] when a white MP came in, ordered everybody out, and fired his riot gun into the air for emphasis."[35] Though the army insisted that its MPs had not been issued live ammunition, officials conceded to Kimball that "it might have been possible for MPs to come by unauthorized ammunition."[36] In a letter to the War Department, General Krueger wrote: "Investigators have had considerable trouble in determining the identity of the persons who did the shooting," but added, "one white M.P. admitted to me that he had obtained a riot gun from the civil police and shot a colored soldier."[37]

Two months after the incident, the NAACP received a letter from a Pullman porter who reported a recent conversation with a Wisconsin soldier on a train. According to the porter, the soldier said it was "terrible how they treat the colored down in Louisiana" and claimed he had taken part in a riot where people had been killed. The soldier recounted how he and a few others "went into a pool room and got cue sticks" with which to beat people, and then "shot up the Harlem." Finally, the soldier told the porter that the army had "striped [sic] him of his insignia" and that he "didn't know what they was going to do to us—meaning I supposed the ones that taken [sic] part in the Riot."[38]

On January 23, the War Department issued a statement about the Lee Street incident. It contended that while force may have been necessary to disperse the crowd and restore order, "civilian policemen and one military policeman indulged in indiscriminate and unnecessary shooting." The army promised to continue the investigation and correct "deficiencies in military police control," but then quietly dropped the matter, despite the Black community's outrage. Government officials never admitted that any deaths had occurred.[39]

The violence on Lee Street was the first substantial racial disturbance in the United States after Pearl Harbor, though it would not be the last. According to historian Matthew F. Delmont, at least 240 incidents occurred in the summer of 1943 alone, most notably in Detroit, where nine white people and twenty-five Black people were killed.[40] "By the summer of 1943 racial turmoil had intensified across the nation, diverting attention from Alexandria's Lee Street riot," wrote historian William M. Simpson, and by the end of the war the incident "was but an obscure footnote in the nation's hectic war years."[41] But it was a footnote in a profoundly important story. For Americans, the World War II fight against fascism abroad, the wartime rhetoric of fighting for freedom and democracy, and the racial tensions both in the military and among civilians, drew national attention to the deeply racist and unjust practices in their own society—foremost among them Jim Crow and the violence that buttressed it. The Lee Street incident was one of many violent incidents during the war years that led many Americans to examine their own attitudes about race and question long-held practices. World War II proved to be a catalyst for the revitalized civil rights movement that transformed the nation in the decades after the war.

With the coming of war, the structure of the Red Arrow Division underwent massive changes. Soon after Pearl Harbor, the army began converting the "square" National Guard divisions of four infantry regiments into "triangular" ones built around three. The army also added different kinds of units based on the critiques of the summer maneuvers and observations of the war in Europe. The Thirty-Second and Thirty-Seventh were the first National Guard divisions to undergo the triangularization process. The 125th Infantry Regiment, on duty on the West Coast "guarding Hollywood," remained in California—separated forever from the Red Arrow. With the reduction to three infantry regiments, the Sixty-Third and Sixty-Fourth Brigades disbanded. The Fifty-Seventh Field Artillery Brigade was rebranded as the Thirty-Second Division Artillery, and its three constituent regiments were converted into four battalions—the 120th, 121st, 126th, and 129th. To add even more firepower, the brass in Washington added a cannon company to each infantry regiment. Engineer, medical, and quartermaster regiments were also converted into streamlined battalions. The new Thirty-Second Cavalry Reconnaissance Troop formed with the mission of patrolling behind enemy lines to gather intelligence. Each infantry regiment also had a mechanized intelligence and reconnaissance platoon for further information-gathering capabilities.

The smaller triangular division needed fewer people, and the downsizing led to a great reshuffling of personnel. Soldiers who were squeezed out of their original units often transferred to other parts of the division. Men from disbanded brigade headquarters, for example, composed the core of cavalry reconnaissance troop. Many who had served with the Red Arrow Division for decades found themselves transferred out of it entirely. The army sent displaced Red Arrowmen to other divisions, like the

Twenty-Eighth, recently arrived at Camp Livingston; or to newly formed organizations, like the 173rd Field Artillery Battalion, made up of remnants of the 121st and 126th Field Artillery Regiments. Soldiers could volunteer for transfer, but, as company clerk Clarence Jungwirth explained, "the selection process eventually ended with companies sending 'trouble makers' and 'misfits'" out of the regiment.[42] Jungwirth recalled the triangularization period as "a time of feverish activity."[43]

The massive expansion of the army offered Red Arrowmen promotions and other opportunities. Some enlisted soldiers applied to become officers. Others transferred to noncombat jobs or joined formations that offered more prestige, glamor, and extra pay. Lieutenant Archie Van Gorden lost about ten men from his company to the Army Air Forces. "A lot of them figure it will be safer and they won't have to cross the ocean," he surmised.[44] The army created or expanded elite fighting forces, such as the rangers, or mountain and airborne divisions, and needed experienced soldiers to join these outfits. One day Stoughton, Wisconsin's Hans Sannes and some friends were "walking down the company street" at Camp Livingston when someone noticed an announcement on a bulletin board. "They wanted people for the paratroops," Sannes recalled. Bored with the routine of the infantry, he transferred to the 101st Airborne Division and later jumped into Normandy on D-Day.[45]

The army continued its rigorous and often brutal evaluation of officers. Classification boards rated many National Guard officers as unfit to serve overseas. "I am too old," wrote a chagrined Archie Van Gorden, "so when this outfit goes overseas I will be thrown out and have to take some warehouse or camp job." He and several others dubbed themselves the "rocking chair gang."[46] In the end, Van Gorden kept his job in the Red Arrow, but many others were forced out, replaced with an influx of new officers. For example, the 367th Infantry Regiment, a Black unit at Camp Claiborne, was dismantled and reorganized in the wake of the Lee Street incident, and more than thirty of its all-white officers were transferred to the Thirty-Second Division. One of them was Benjamin McKnight of South Carolina, a product of the ROTC program at Clemson University. McKnight welcomed the change. "I think I'm going to like it fine, as I'm glad to be with white troops," he wrote to his family. McKnight was not the only Southerner assigned to a northern outfit. Indeed, a disproportionate number of the Red Arrow's new leaders hailed from the South. Graduates of southern schools like the Citadel, North Carolina State, Presbyterian College, and Wofford College took command of many companies and platoons in the Red Arrow.[47]

Changes occurred farther up the chain of command as well. As the new triangular division took shape, the army removed nearly all of the National Guard's senior officers. Some had served in the Red Arrow since its inception in 1917. They had attended decades of drills and summer encampments and knew their men well. Among those forced out was Colonel William A. Holden, commander of the 128th Infantry Regiment. Archie Van Gorden attended a dinner in Holden's honor. "It was rather sad," Van Gorden wrote of the event, "as it was hard for Colonel Holden to talk and say what he wanted to say."[48] Most of the dismissed officers "were veterans of World War I and had served continuously since," observed Tracy Hale, who was dismayed by what he called the army's "purge." Among all Wisconsin officers, Hale was one of only eleven World War I veterans who remained. Hale took command of the 128th Infantry Regiment. A few other National Guard officers remained in key positions. Robert C. McCoy (another Great War veteran) took command of the First Battalion of the 128th, while Herbert A. Smith remained in charge of the Second Battalion. Herbert M. Smith moved from Wisconsin's 128th Infantry Regiment to become the executive officer of Michigan's 126th.

The National Guard establishment decried what it viewed as a hostile takeover. "Tradition is unquestionably the biggest word in the military vernacular," wrote Byron Beveridge, editor of the *Wisconsin National Guard Review*, in an open letter to Colonel Ben Stafford, the new commander of the 127th Infantry Regiment. Beveridge had served with the regiment in France and with the Wisconsin National Guard since 1896, and in a tone both angry and melancholy, he argued that the dismissal of National Guard officers threatened the regiment's traditions and capabilities:

> Wisconsin is very jealous of the reputation of its troops, from the days
> of the Iron Brigade of Civil War fame, the old Second [Wisconsin]
> Infantry of Spanish-American War days and the tough, hard fight-
> ing 127th of the World War. . . . Politics has remained completely
> divorced from the Wisconsin National Guard, and military merit

alone has governed the selection of officers and non-commissioned officers. . . . The Review feels that the first politics to reach in and clutch at the military heart of the 32nd Division . . . occurred when its battle-tested commanders from civil life were replaced by the untried ambitions of men from the Regular service.

As the 127th Infantry Regiment embarked on another war, Beveridge implored Stafford to remember the regiment's distinctive heritage: "If the tradition of the regiment and Division is lost, then the men we left in France died in vain."[49]

The Red Arrow's commander, General Irving Fish, had survived the purge of National Guard division commanders immediately following the Louisiana Maneuvers. But in early 1942 the army declared the sixty-year-old too old for combat service and pushed him into a desk job. "General Fish's summary dismissal," wrote his aide, Walter Choinski, "was a blow to his ego from which he never recovered."[50] Fish's replacement was a rising star from the regular army, fifty-five-year-old Major General Edwin Forrest Harding, an Ohioan and 1909 West Point graduate. Known for his affable personality, Harding also loved history and literature. While in China during the 1920s, he published a book of poems about army life that was sold in the post exchange. Fans of his work included his friend and colleague, Lieutenant Colonel George C. Marshall.[51] In 1934, Harding edited a book on small unit tactics titled *Infantry in Battle*, based on seminars he had taught at Fort Benning. According to Harding's biographer, Leslie Anders, the volume became "the talk of military circles around the world."[52] Harding also edited the *Infantry Journal* and convinced some of the planet's most respected military thinkers to contribute to its pages, transforming it from a poorly written and little-read periodical into a leading professional publication. Harding became a general in October 1940 and the following year became assistant commander of the Ninth Infantry Division at Fort Bragg, North Carolina. General McNair then picked Harding to command the Thirty-Second. George C. Marshall, now US Army chief of staff, thought the Red Arrow was inadequately trained and riven with small-town politics, and advised Harding to turn down the job. "This is going to be your downfall," Marshall warned him. "You're going to have many friends and you're going to get relieved from command."[53]

General Edwin Forrest
Harding. WISCONSIN
NATIONAL GUARD, US
ARMY PHOTO

Harding took over the Red Arrow Division on February 9 and made a good first impression. "We had an honor guard to welcome him on his arrival," recalled Tracy Hale, who thought that "one evidence of his ability to lead is demonstrated by the act of shaking hands with every man in the Honor Guard."[54] In his remarks to the men now under his command, Harding called the Thirty-Second "as fine a division as any that ever marched under the American flag into battle."[55] Harding quickly impressed upon the men the seriousness of their endeavors, Hale remembered. "The idea of being killed or killing had been rather soft-pedaled up to that point," Hale wrote. By contrast, Harding spoke bluntly. "I know that when the time comes you will be killers," Harding said, "killers of the enemies of this country—and that is our job, to kill all the Japs and Germans that we can."[56] He concluded by saying: "An Infantry man can always take one more step and fire one more shot." At that, Hale recalled, the assembled troops erupted in "thunderous and enthusiastic applause."[57] Harding impressed the National Guard establishment as well. Wisconsin Adjutant General Ralph Immell praised Harding as a "fighter" who "shows an interest in the enlisted men," and was gratified to see that he appreciated the history of the division. "The citizens of Wisconsin," Immell stated, "can have confidence in Major Gen. Edwin Forrest Harding."[58]

As the Red Arrow Division went through its great reshuffling, world events made the United States' position more precarious. German submarines lurked off the East Coast and took a heavy toll on Atlantic shipping. In the Pacific, Allied holdings fell to Japan rapidly: Wake Island on December 23 and Hong Kong on Christmas Day. General Horii's South Seas Detachment took Rabaul, New Guinea, on January 23, 1942, and the Japanese quickly converted it into an anchor of their Pacific defense perimeter, basing scores of ships, hundreds of planes, and thousands of troops there. General Yamashita defeated a numerically superior British and Indian force at Singapore, which earned him the nickname "the Tiger of Malaya." Prime Minister Winston S. Churchill called the surrender of Singapore on February 15 "the worst disaster and largest capitulation in British history." For Singapore's large ethnic Chinese population, it was even worse. Japan's secret military police, the Kempeitai, began killing tens of thousands of Chinese in Singapore and Malaya, in a ruthless purge called the Sook Ching ("purge through cleansing") to root out any potential resistance to their occupation. In January, the Japanese invaded the oil-rich Dutch East Indies—the biggest prize of the Southern Resource Zone—and completed the conquest in early March.

The last Allied holdout in Southeast Asia was the Philippines. On paper, MacArthur had 150,000 soldiers available to him, but most were service troops or Filipino reservists and recent recruits. In reality, his combat-ready soldiers barely numbered ten thousand. In the event of an attack on the Philippines, the army had long planned to pull back to the Bataan Peninsula, which separated Manila Bay and the South China Sea, and to Corregidor Island, which guarded the entrance to the bay, where they would await reinforcements. But MacArthur was confident he could hold the archipelago. Rather than reinforce Bataan, MacArthur deployed his soldiers to defend the beachheads where the Japanese might land. When the main Japanese invasion force landed at the Lingayen Gulf on December 22, MacArthur's army—thinly spread, ill-supplied, and devoid of air cover—soon crumbled. MacArthur ordered a phased withdrawal to the Bataan Peninsula on December 23, but by then he had lost scores of soldiers and tons of equipment and supplies that he should have stockpiled at Bataan. Through the early months of 1942, US and Filipino troops fought valiantly on the Bataan Peninsula, but they quickly ran low on food and ammunition. The United States rushed what meager forces it could to Australia in the hopes of sending MacArthur some relief, but the Japanese navy blocked any realistic way for additional troops and supplies to reach him. Allied forces in the Philippines, as they would soon learn, were doomed. Nonetheless, back home MacArthur became a hero. He was the only Allied commander still fighting in the Pacific, and in those dark days when the war's outcome seemed in doubt, MacArthur's defense of Bataan and Corregidor became a symbol of American defiance and resolve.

As the war news grew ever more ominous, the Red Arrowmen detected signs they were about to be on the move. On January 2, the 107th Engineers hastily prepared to ship out from Camp Livingston. Tracy Hale recalled that "25% of [its] people were on leave at home," so the division transferred soldiers from the 127th Infantry Regiment to join the engineers. "This occurred between sunset and sunrise," recalled Hale, and when the engineers on leave arrived back at Camp Livingston, they were "amazed to find the camp site of the 107th Engineers deserted" and that they were now members of the 127th Infantry Regiment. "I have heard of some men leaving home," Hale joked, "but never heard of a home leaving the man."[59]

The purpose of the engineers' deployment was to set up a new camp for the Thirty-Second Infantry Division in Northern Ireland. The engineers traveled by rail to Fort Dix, New Jersey, and prepared for overseas movement as part of Force MAGNET, the leading edge of American combat troops in Europe. Their deployment occurred during the triangularization process, so the engineers were reorganized at Fort Dix. The regiment shrank to a battalion, with the First Battalion becoming the 107th Engineer Combat Battalion and the Second Battalion redesignated as the 131st Engineer Combat Battalion and separated from the division. The reformulated 107th departed from the Brooklyn Navy Yard on February 18, landed in Belfast on March 3, and deployed to a series of small towns outside the city. "We were at Ballyclare, Cookstown, Moneymore, Belfast, and

Hollywood," recalled Lester Doro of Appleton, Wisconsin. "The 107th was initially engaged in various construction projects," noted one history of the battalion, including a "massive" depot near Moneymore that "consisted of railroad tracks and sidings, warehouses, living quarters, [and] mess halls . . . everything required for a complete base."[60]

Official word came in late February that the rest of the Red Arrow was leaving Camp Livingston. "Our orders to move came very suddenly this afternoon at 2 o'clock," Robert C. McCoy wrote to his wife, Alberta. "I had my Bn. [battalion] in the Rec. Hall for a lecture when I was called to Hq [headquarters] and told that we would at once prepare to be ready to move. I went back and explained to the men all that I knew which was almost nothing. We haven't any idea where we will go or when, but I imagine it will be soon."[61]

Word of the departure evoked a mix of emotions. "We were all excited by the new adventures ahead of us," wrote Clarence Jungwirth. "We were young men, full of energy and enthusiasm. We were eager to participate in the illusion of the 'Glory of War.'"[62] For others, the gravity of going off to war began to set in. "Please darling, be brave and take this on the chin as you have taken all the other blows so far in our life," McCoy wrote to Alberta.[63] "It was hard to say good-bye to Dora," recalled Art Kessenich. "She had advised me that she was pregnant and would now be required to be separated from me while our first child was growing in her womb."[64]

The army pointed the Red Arrow in the direction of Fort Devens, Massachusetts, thirty miles northwest of Boston, a staging area for troops on their way to Europe. Most moved northeast by rail, and as the trains rolled out of Louisiana, the Red Arrowmen settled in for the three-day journey to New England. They rode in Pullman cars, the epitome of luxury rail travel of the day. "Now this was class," thought Roy Campbell. The soldiers gambled, talked, and watched the American landscape roll by. "The countryside was changing continuously," remembered Campbell, from "flatlands" to "heavily wooded mountains." He also noted a lot of military rail traffic: "These trains usually had flat cars loaded with trucks, tanks, half-tracks, jeeps, airplanes that looked half finished—one or two even had what looked like boats with flat ends." Campbell reflected that the rail trip "was the first time in a long time" that he "could just sit and daydream," and he fondly remembered a moment lying on the "smooth, soft mattress" of his sleeper car and watching "the countryside glide by," thinking that it was "as close to heaven" as he "would ever get."[65]

Other Red Arrowmen transported the division's vehicles to Fort Devens in a ten-day road excursion. Their journey was not as pleasant. GIs slept on the floors of armories and military bases along the way, and the weather grew colder as they progressed northward. "No heaters in trucks," Archie Van Gorden complained. In letters home, Van Gorden recounted other problems along the way. In the Carolinas the convoy hit a major snow-storm. "We sure worried last nite as it snowed very hard," he wrote, "and we had to park on the street near the depot . . . as every street and driveway was blocked." Van Gorden's convoy experienced only one minor accident and a single attempted desertion. As they were passing through Washing-ton, DC, an assistant driver jumped out of the truck, and Van Gorden "had him put under arrest."[66]

The journey was not without its pleasures. "The people along the way . . . came out and they had cookies and milk and coffee," recalled Steve Janicki.[67] One night, while camped outside of Washington, Paul Rettell and a couple of friends visited the US Capitol. "There wasn't anyone there but us," he remembered. They passed through Philadelphia, and Rettell recalled that the police there "would stop traffic and block off intersec-tions with their sirens blowing. It was like getting the VIP treatment." In Connecticut he ate pizza for the first time. "They put lots of peppers on it," Rettell wrote, and "it tasted good."[68]

The Red Arrow arrived at Devens in the snows of early March and oc-cupied the barracks that the First Division had just vacated when it left for Europe. "The area we moved into was filthy," recalled Art Kessenich. "Kitchens were so bad that we were not allowed to use them so we set up field kitchens in the company street. Barracks had to be fumigated."[69] But once the troops got their facilities in order, most were pleased with their new home. After living in tents for more than a year in Louisiana, they were happy to have heated wooden barracks—particularly in the late winter of New England. Duties there were light. "Two weeks went by with only a few small exercises and the usual close order drills," remembered Campbell. "The company was very good at those now; each man in step and lines straight, they looked like a real fighting force. The men even felt they were ready to meet the enemy."[70] Frigid weather hampered training.

"It's been snowing all day, so we had it pretty easy," Elvin Ball reported to his family. "I hope it snows tomorrow too."[71]

The northern scenery pleased many of the Wisconsin and Michigan soldiers. "We have a beautiful snowstorm today," wrote Archie Van Gorden, and "it made me think of home and the children making snowmen." The landscape stirred other emotions in him. "The country air and the pretty homes make one long to live," he wrote, and "as I look out of the trailer window and gaze at the bluff in the background dotted with pine, white birch and oak with leaves still on, I long to go hunting, to get out in the wide open spaces."[72] For Van Gorden, the New England countryside brought back schoolboy history lessons, evoking a strong sense of patriotism. "The stone fences make you think of the Revolutionary War days," he wrote, "like we saw at Concord where the embattled farmers stood and fired the shot heard round the world."[73] Boston was the nearest big city, and frequent trains made it easily accessible. Campbell and a friend went to a USO show there. Unimpressed with the USO in Louisiana, Campbell did not expect much, but he was pleasantly surprised once the show began:

> The curtain parted and out stepped Jimmy Durante and Eddie Jackson! It was great; the crowd roared with laughter for half an hour at those two. They tried to call them back for an encore, but they wouldn't come. The curtain closed and then opened again and Ina Rae Hutton's band was on, and she was a doll. The crowd loved it. Her band played for thirty minutes, then the curtain closed and when it opened, out stepped Jimmy Durante again—this time with a baby grand piano that he proceeded to wreck, all the while singing, dancing, and making believe that he was mad at the piano.

More acts and more bands followed. "The show went on until one o'clock in the morning," wrote Campbell, "and as long as it was, nobody wanted it to stop."[74] Family members showed up at Fort Devens to send off the soldiers, and a few GIs managed last-minute trips home.

As the officers and men of the Red Arrow awaited movement to Ireland, General Harding was in Washington putting together his leadership team. For his artillery chief, Harding tapped Brigadier General Albert W. Waldron. A West Pointer from New York State, Waldron had served under

General John J. Pershing during the 1916–1917 incursion into Mexico, then in France during the Great War. Herbert M. Smith recalled the time he first met Waldron while at Fort Devens. "I was checking vehicle space in our area when a jeep bearing the flag of a Brigadier General arrived," he wrote. Smith introduced himself to the general and found Waldron "a very friendly officer [who] impressed me very much."[75]

Harding brought in several other regular army officers he had known over the years. Colonel Lawrence A. Quinn, a Great War combat veteran with the Second Division, took over the 126th Infantry Regiment. Major Clarence M. Tomlinson, a native of Superior, Wisconsin, who had once served under Harding, "jumped at the chance" to join him again.[76] Tomlinson took command of the Third Battalion of the 126th Infantry Regiment. Major Alexander MacNab, an acquaintance from Fort Benning, became Colonel Hale's executive officer in the 128th Infantry Regiment.

Harding also brought in a lowly private named E. J. Kahn Jr., son of a prominent Manhattan architect. Kahn was a Harvard-educated journalist and rising star at the *New Yorker*, one of America's top commentary and literary magazines. Kahn was drafted in July 1941, but induction did not still his pen. While training at Camp Croft, South Carolina, Kahn wrote a piece for the *New Yorker* titled "The Army Life—My Day," which was published in November 1941. "One of the questions frequently asked of the selectee," Kahn wrote, "is 'Well, what do you *do* all day, anyway?'" He then walked the reader through the typical training routine, sprinkling his observations with humor and sarcasm. "From eight-fifteen until nine o'clock we are occupied with close order drill," he wrote, "without which we would never be able to give a decent account of ourselves in a Fifth Avenue victory parade." After that came a five-mile hike "with our rifles slung by their straps over our shoulders and our packs, like overweight jockeys, riding high on our backs." More articles followed, and Kahn's work appeared on newsstands just as the United States entered the war. Unlike most draftees, Private Kahn received fan mail, speaking requests, and letters from publishers. "Your articles on Army Life in the *New Yorker* have been a source of great entertainment to me," wrote one young man, "particularly since I am probably about to make my debut there myself."[77] Some praised his realism, others thought him a snob, and one army nurse questioned "whether you are really a soldier at Croft."[78]

Kahn eventually left Camp Croft and went to the Ninth Infantry Division at Fort Bragg, where he came to the attention of its literary-minded assistant commander, General Harding, who also understood the value of good publicity. "He had read some of my stuff in the *New Yorker*," Kahn later wrote, "and he got me transferred to the division headquarters, in public relations."[79] After Harding took command of the Red Arrow, he arranged for Kahn to become his secretary. In November 1942, Simon & Schuster published a collection of Kahn's essays under the title *The Army Life*. Harding wrote the forward, praising Kahn's gentle humor. "Don't read him if you are looking for belly laughs," Harding wrote. "He appeals only to that part of the anatomy above the neck."[80]

While the Red Arrow prepared for deployment to Europe, circumstances in the Pacific deteriorated even further for the Allies. Infected with what was later called "victory disease," Japanese military leaders, in the words of historian Ronald Spector, "began to search for new worlds to conquer."[81] Imperial Army commanders urged preparations to attack Siberia should Germany defeat the Soviets in Europe. The Imperial Navy sent a fleet into the Indian Ocean to harass British forces in the region. But Japan's most important security concerns lay in the Pacific. Admiral Yamamoto still saw the US Navy in Hawaii as a threat, particularly the American aircraft carriers, which had not been at Pearl Harbor on December 7. Yamamoto proposed the occupation of Midway Island, at the extreme western end of the Hawaiian chain, to draw out the remains of the US Pacific Fleet and complete its destruction. Yamamoto's superiors at the Naval General Staff were more concerned about Australia, which could serve as a rich and massive Allied base of operations against the Greater East Asia Co-Prosperity Sphere. Planners soon tabled proposals to invade Australia as unrealistic and instead advocated for a push into the islands of the South Pacific—the Solomons, New Caledonia, Fiji, Samoa—to cut Australia's links with the United States. To neutralize Australia, no place was more important than New Guinea, a large, rugged island hovering above the north shore of the continent. The Japanese had seized Rabaul in January, and by March they had occupied the villages of Lae and Salamaua on New Guinea's northern coast. But to truly isolate Australia, the Japanese needed a presence on

New Guinea's southern coast, and soon they turned their attention to Port Moresby, the island's most important harbor and administrative center.

Defending Australia fell on the shoulders of General MacArthur. Hope of reinforcing Bataan and Corregidor had waned, and in late February 1942 Roosevelt ordered MacArthur to leave the Philippines. Lieutenant General Jonathan M. Wainwright was left behind to direct the defense, while MacArthur, his family, and a coterie of high-ranking staff members boarded patrol torpedo boats (popularly known as PT boats) and departed the Philippines on March 11. When they arrived in Adelaide, South Australia, a week later, MacArthur told a group of reporters, "I came through and I shall return."

Soon after Pearl Harbor, Allied leaders hammered out global command arrangements. The war against Germany was to receive top priority in troops and resources. The United States assumed the primary responsibility for fighting the Japanese in the Pacific, but furious debate erupted between the army and navy about which service should take the leading role. Unable to resolve the dispute, Washington split the Pacific into separate domains. The US Navy's Pacific Ocean Area (POA), under Admiral Chester A. Nimitz, encompassed the lion's share of the Pacific and was further subdivided into north, central, and south areas. MacArthur took command of the South West Pacific Area (SWPA), which included Australia, New Guinea, the Solomon Islands, most of the Dutch East Indies, and his personal primary objective, the Philippines. MacArthur and Nimitz essentially ran separate campaigns, coordinated through the Joint Chiefs of Staff. Because SWPA responsibilities involved Australia as well as British and Dutch colonial territories, General Marshall urged MacArthur to appoint a multinational staff. Instead, top leadership positions went almost entirely to Americans—and particularly to a small group of MacArthur loyalists who had served under him in the Philippines. Among this "Bataan Gang" was his chief of staff, Major General Richard K. Sutherland, and his head of intelligence, Colonel (later General) Charles A. Willoughby. The only Australian in a high position in the SWPA was General Sir Thomas Blamey, head of SWPA's Allied Land Forces. Two other outsiders were Lieutenant General George Brett, chief of Allied Air Forces, and Vice Admiral Herbert F. Leary, head of Allied Naval Forces—both Americans.

As MacArthur planned Australia's defense, he was disturbed by the continent's vulnerability. The nation of seven million people had loyally gone to war alongside Britain in 1939, and its four combat infantry divisions were all overseas. The Australian Eighth Division had been chewed up by the Japanese onslaught into Southeast Asia, while the other three (the Sixth, Seventh, and Ninth) were fighting the Germans in the Mediterranean. The Australian government called up its militia, but these troops lacked sufficient training and suffered equipment shortages. Australian prime minister John Curtin demanded the return of his nation's infantry divisions, and the Sixth and Seventh Divisions began their long trek home.

MacArthur and other leaders also recognized the importance of New Guinea, which could be a launching pad for attacks on Australia, or a shield defending it. MacArthur reinforced the island with what forces he could, but he did not have much. American engineers got to work at Port Moresby and at Milne Bay, on the southeastern tip of the Papuan Peninsula, building airfields from which Allied planes launched sorties against Japanese positions. American antiaircraft units rushed in, too, but most Allied soldiers on New Guinea were Australian, and all the infantry was ill-prepared Australian militia. The meager Allied forces on the island were designated the New Guinea Force under the command of Australia's General Basil Morris.

MacArthur needed troops—and fast. As the Australian divisions from the Mediterranean were en route home, the US Forty-First Infantry Division, a National Guard outfit from the northwest training at Fort Lewis, Washington, began its movement to Australia in March 1942. With Axis forces driving across North Africa toward the Suez Canal, Churchill resisted the return of the Australian Ninth Division, so to placate him the United States agreed to deploy a second infantry division to Australia. As Washington searched for a suitable candidate, the Thirty-Second Infantry Division climbed to the top of the list. It was already poised for overseas movement, but Atlantic shipping bottlenecks had delayed its departure for Europe until July. Thus, Washington changed the trajectory of the Red Arrow, pointing it toward Australia instead of Ireland.

Word of the new assignment reached Fort Devens in late March. Because they were on the East Coast awaiting a transatlantic voyage, their redirection to the Pacific came as a great surprise. Even more surprising was the timetable: the division was to be in San Francisco by April 15. Roy

Campbell remembered that his company was in the barracks "playing poker, shooting craps, and writing letters" when another soldier came bursting into the room telling them that "General MacArthur had ordered their division to the Pacific and they were to leave soon." Someone commented that it was "the stupidest rumor they had ever heard," and Campbell agreed that "it was a hard one to believe."[82] At first the GIs were not told their ultimate destination, but as Clarence Jungwirth wrote, "we soon found out that it was to be Australia."[83] However, the Red Arrow's engineers had already deployed to Europe. Since it was not practical to recall them, the army detached the 107th Engineers from the Thirty-Second Division. The ex–Red Arrowmen went on to fight in Normandy and the Battle of the Bulge and finished the war in Czechoslovakia. To replace its original engineers, the army hurriedly brought in the 114th Engineer Combat Battalion, a National Guard unit from Massachusetts that claimed a lineage stretching back to 1636, which recently had been split off from the Twenty-Sixth Division during its triangularization.

Preparations for movement to the West Coast began in earnest. On the eve of departure, Colonel Quinn addressed the 126th Infantry Regiment, preparing its members for what likely lay ahead. "We are about to depart on a most important mission," he told them:

> Our path will not be smooth. On the contrary it will be beset with many obstacles; we shall suffer many hardships; we shall face many grave dangers. Many of us will pay the supreme sacrifice. Such is the duty of a soldier; such is the responsibility and privilege of every citizen. . . . At this moment we [are] not a perfect organization; not a perfect war machine; not a perfect team—but rather a diamond in the rough . . . but what we lack in perfection we more than make up in espirit de corps, determination, team play, loyalty, devotion to duty and country, and plain, unadulterated intestinal fortitude. . . . As we approach closer and closer to the sound of the guns we must develop that killer instinct, which is so necessary to success on the field of battle. Should you experience difficulty developing this desire to kill— you have but to recall what we are fighting for—our homes, our loved ones, our freedom, our right to live as we please.[84]

In a letter to his fiancée, Dorothy Cox, Madisonian Adrian Stransky wrote: "We have packed our barracks bags, loaded all of our supplies and equipment, cleaned out all the barracks and office buildings and are just waiting for the time to come to go."[85] A few soldiers panicked at the thought of deployment. Elvin Ball told his family of one soldier who went AWOL, or absent without leave. "I'll never know what he was thinking when he got married," Ball wrote, and speculated that "he will probably go to prison for a while."[86]

The Thirty-Second Infantry Division began its trek to the West Coast in early April. "We moved out so fast," remembered Tracy Hale, "that one of our dental surgeons . . . delayed to kiss his wife so long that he didn't catch up with us until we got to St. Louis."[87] E. J. Kahn thought the departure notably unceremonious. "Nobody waved any flags at us," he wrote, "there was nobody around except a few railroad men, who were too busy to take any special notice of us. We stood in a driving rain for two hours, wishing, as our feet got wet and cold, that we hadn't put our overshoes in our barracks bags and that we could board the train and get going."[88] The trains carrying the Red Arrow Division snaked their way across the United States in a transcontinental odyssey that took nearly a week. "The people of North Platte, Nebraska . . . were sure good to us," wrote Elvin Ball. "They brought us bushel baskets of popcorn balls, candy, cookies, and cigarettes. They gave us plenty of magazines too."[89] The GIs were instructed not to tell civilians their unit or destination, which Tracy Hale thought presented opportunities for humor. "At one stop," he wrote, "a civilian asked one of the cooks, who was leaning out of the baggage kitchen car door: 'What outfit, Buddy?'" The cook told him that "we're the 192nd Underground Balloon Battalion." In another encounter, a "kindly Red Cross lady" asked a soldier how long they had been traveling. "We have been on this train for ten years," came the reply. "The army has forgotten us completely."[90]

The journey was a scenic one. "I would go to the baggage car at the front of the train, open up the sliding doors, pull up a folding chair and watch the scenery go by," wrote Jungwirth. "It was like watching a travelogue on a movie screen."[91] The midwesterners were particularly fascinated by the scenery of the American West. "I saw a few cowboys and lots of sheep and cattle and some wild mustangs," wrote Elvin Ball, as well as "dude ranches near Reno" and "a mining operation in the Sierra Mountains."[92] The vastness of the basin and range landscape impressed many. "I've heard people tell of the wide open spaces," wrote Ball, "and now I know what they mean after coming through Wyoming and Nevada."[93] But the mountain vistas of the Rockies and the Sierra Nevada made the biggest impression. "Saw Pike's Peak, & the Rockies," wrote Robert C. McCoy, "which are beyond description. The gorges, the tunnels . . . the stone formations which in places were just beside the tracks and went straight up for 100s of feet."[94] Ball wrote to his family that "we came across Great Salt Lake on a railroad bridge thirty miles long. We crossed the bridge at sunrise, and it sure was a pretty sight. First, I could see the moon and one bright star, then the sun broke over the mountains. It really made the snow on the peaks sparkle."[95] Many pondered the gravity of going off to war. "As the miles rolled by," Roy Campbell noted, "the men aboard the train were subdued and were wearing more serious looks."[96] As they chugged across the Great Plains of Kansas, Adrian Stransky wrote to his fiancée, Dorothy: "I'm thinking of you now. It is hard to imagine that I am going away from you again, and so far. I haven't stopped hoping that it will be over soon."[97]

The Red Arrow Division arrived on the West Coast at different destinations. Many trains, including those hauling the 127th and 128th Infantry Regiments, pulled into Fort Ord on the Pacific coast near Monterey. California was a big change from cold and snowy New England. "A very fine camp overlooking Monterey Bay," thought Tracy Hale, "warm, green grass, flowers, mountains all around."[98] Art Kessenich recalled that as soon as they could, "most of us took off to see the Pacific Ocean. It was a beautiful sight, and of course, the first time most of us had seen this great body of water. Little did we realize that we would spend many days on ships going to and around the Southwest Pacific area."[99] The 126th Infantry Regiment ended its transcontinental journey in San Francisco and camped at the city's new livestock exposition center known as the Cow Palace. The facility did not inspire rave reviews. Herbert M. Smith thought it "a concrete monolith as drafty as the North Pole."[100]

Once in California, the Red Arrowmen spent much of their time preparing to ship out. "We are busy drawing equipment," wrote Robert C. McCoy, including the new M1 helmet, which replaced the World War I–era wide-brimmed headgear. "They look just like the German helmet," McCoy wrote, "but I think they will be comfortable."[101] The troops managed to get a little bit of leisure time. At Fort Ord they went swimming in the Pacific. "Soldiers who were not used to the big breakers try to swim past the first big wave," Roy Campbell observed, "and then try to get back to shore after finding themselves in big trouble from the undertow."[102] The Cow Palace may have been uncomfortable, but it offered easy access to the city. "San Francisco is laid out among hills," Richard Correll wrote to his wife, Elizabeth, "with streets on them that appear to run straight up." He was particularly fascinated with the "old fashioned" cable cars. "Bells clang, groans from underneath, and the thing moved almost straight up the hill," he described, and "when you start to go down you think [the conductor will] never get it stopped, but he pulls back hard and lo and behold it stops."[103] Elvin Ball was enamored with Chinatown. "They have lots of chop suey joints and curio shops," he reported. "All of them speak Chinese when talking to each other. . . . I couldn't understand a single word."[104] Paul Rettell also enjoyed Chinatown, particularly a "dim and hazy" rooftop bar where "girls were strip dancing. What was interesting was the exotic. . . . We didn't know anything about the Far East. Japan, Singapore, China and other exotic places were just names. Oriental names for drinks were something we never heard before. It was fascinating for us."[105]

The division arrived in California with nearly four thousand vacancies, all of which needed to be filled before heading overseas. Infantry replacement training centers were cropping up across the United States to support the nation's military buildup. Camp Roberts near Paso Robles, California, supplied the Red Arrow with the bulk of its new members. They were a mix of volunteers and draftees, mainly from western states, and had been inducted just a few months before. One was Raymond Dasmann, a student at San Francisco State University and budding naturalist, who had vacillated between pacifism and interventionism before Pearl Harbor. The Japanese attack settled the argument in his mind. "The 'bad guys' had hit my home country," he wrote, "and were rumored to be headed for San Francisco." The navy and marines rejected Dasmann for poor eyesight, so he enlisted in the army, but soon questioned his decision. "I discovered that none of my friends who had talked about enlisting had [done it]," he noted. "When the gate closed behind me in late December 1941 at the Monterey Presidio," Dasmann wondered if he had "rushed to sign up for an indefinite stay in federal prison."[106] Howard Kelley of Los Angeles received his draft notice about two weeks after Pearl Harbor and reported for induction at Fort MacArthur in San Pedro on New Year's Eve 1941. "I got up early and rode the city bus," he recalled, and wondered: "Would this be a one way trip for me?"[107]

After only the most rudimentary basic training, groups of recruits at Camp Roberts got word that they were leaving. "One bright morning," remembered Thomas R. "Ozzie" St. George, a draftee journalism student from Minnesota, "fifty-seven average young men were routed out of their West Coast barracks at the brutal hour of 5 A.M., pushed into the semblance of a straight line, and informed by a captain . . . that they were on for shipment."[108] After being informed of their departure, the troops collected their gear and loaded onto trucks bound for the rail station. Most assumed they were off for more training. St. George heard—and believed—a rumor that they were off to Fort Leonard Wood, Missouri, "to form the nucleus of a new division." He and his comrades were "firmly convinced that they would arrive . . . in time for a weekend pass, and two had laid exhaustive plans as to what they would do first chance they got home to Des Moines."[109]

The trainees were surprised to find they had been assigned to a combat division heading overseas. After his train came to a stop, Howard Kelley "pulled back the blackout curtain and saw a sign that read 'Fort Ord, California.'" Soon "trucks began arriving and we were all loaded into them and taken to some barracks housing the 32nd Division." Kelley wrote that the recruits had breakfast and then "began to get acquainted" with the GIs in their new outfit, the 127th Infantry Regiment. "Most of them were older and had been in the division for a year or two," Kelley remembered. He thought them "good natured boys but some of them had long Russian names that ended with 'ski.'" His new company commander informed Kelley that the names were Polish, and that "large numbers of Polish and German people lived in Wisconsin and Michigan."[110] Old-timers like Roy Campbell noticed new soldiers "filling the streets" of Fort Ord "from almost every state in the nation."[111] Robert C. McCoy reported to his wife, Alberta, that his "Bn is now up to full strength," and that the "2 & 3rd" battalions "will be filled next week."[112] The recruits looked around their new environment with trepidation. "We 'new men,' who still figured our service in weeks, felt out of our depth," remembered Ozzie St. George. "They couldn't send *us!* We weren't ready!"[113]

But a handful of new members had considerable combat experience. The Spanish Civil War of the 1930s had offered a ghastly preview of World War II, as Spain's left-wing Republic fought a fascist rebellion led by Generalissimo Francisco Franco. Western democracies did not aid the Spanish Republic, but idealistic antifascists—often but not always communists—volunteered to fight for it. These volunteers served in "International Brigades" composed of people from their own country of origin; Americans made up the Abraham Lincoln Brigade. The *brigadistas* were poorly trained and poorly armed, but they fought with commitment and zeal. The brigades disbanded as Franco gained the upper hand, and the Spanish Republic fell in 1939, but a burning hatred of fascism remained in the hearts of the brigades' veterans.

One American volunteer in Spain was an Oregonian named Robert G. Thompson, who joined the communist movement during the Depression. After attending a communist youth conference in Moscow in 1935, Thompson traveled to Spain, fought with the Lincoln Brigade, and was wounded near Jarama. Upon his return to the United States, Thompson became the secretary of the Young Communist League in Ohio, and ten days before Pearl Harbor he volunteered for the US Army hoping to continue his fight against fascism in an American uniform.[114]

Thompson was not the only Spanish Civil War veteran to join the Red Arrow in California. Herman Johann Friedrich Bottcher was born in Landsberg, Germany, in 1909. He witnessed the rise of fascism in Germany and as a teenager joined the burgeoning communist movement to fight against it. Bottcher left Germany in 1928, heading first to Australia and then to the United States, where he settled with his aunt in San Francisco. There he worked as a cabinetmaker and joined a carpenter's union. He also applied for American citizenship, but in 1936 his hatred of fascism drove him to Spain. "Many stories are told of his efficient and responsible service," the Veterans of the Abraham Lincoln Brigade later noted. When one commander was shot standing beside him, "Bottcher, himself wounded, carried the dying [man] to a dugout through heavy enemy fire." In another instance he and some other *brigadistas* were "forced to requisition two burros" to transport communication equipment to the front. Bottcher "refused to rest with the other men at the end of the march but tramped back 10 miles to return the burros to their owner."[115] Bottcher returned to the United States in 1938 and renewed his quest for citizenship, but his politics and his time in Spain complicated the matter. His virulent hatred of fascism continued, though, and soon after Pearl Harbor the German immigrant showed up at a US Army recruiting office.

The four months after Pearl Harbor were heady ones for the Thirty-Second Division. The whirlwind of activity following the attack brought thousands of new faces into the Red Arrow and took its members to new places as well. In a few short months, the Red Arrow was whisked from the segregated South to the snowy woods of New England to the breakers of the California coast. "I never realized how large this country is," an astounded Robert C. McCoy told his family.[116] But the personnel changes and lengthy travel disrupted the Red Arrow's training. The division's old guard, whose abilities were already suspect in the eyes of army brass, now absorbed thousands of recruits barely trained at all. But ready or not, the Red Arrow was heading overseas—and closer to the fighting.

The *S.S. Monterey*, pictured here in 1932, was used to transport Red Arrowmen and other troops across the Pacific during World War II. HISTORY AND HERITAGE COMMAND, US NAVY

CHAPTER 4

VOYAGE DOWN UNDER

Bataan fell to the Japanese on April 9, 1942, but for the American and Filipino troops who surrendered, their ordeal was just beginning. The victors marched their captives from Bataan to prison camps in the interior of Luzon. Despite the blazing tropical sun, the Japanese offered no sustenance, and they beat, shot, and sometimes beheaded those who fell out. Among those who endured the Bataan Death March were members of Company A, 192nd Tank Battalion—formerly the Thirty-Second Tank Company out of Janesville, Wisconsin—which the army had dispatched to the Philippines months before Pearl Harbor. "The guards put us on the road and double timed us," remembered Janesville's Forrest Knox, and when prisoners lagged behind "you could hear the shooting start at the tail of the column." Roughly one thousand Americans and nine thousand Filipinos died before ever reaching the camps, where the brutalization continued.[1] The news of such horrors created an ominous atmosphere as the Thirty-Second Infantry Division shoved off into the Pacific. After sailing more than eight thousand miles to the opposite side of the world, the Red Arrowmen arrived in Australia, where they were welcomed exuberantly as protectors at a moment of great vulnerability. The Red Arrow GIs enjoyed their sojourn there, exploring a land at once exotic and familiar, but shuttling from camp to camp limited their training time, leaving them dangerously unprepared as they stood on the threshold of combat.

Roughly a week after arriving in California, the Thirty-Second Division received orders to ship out. "Most of the men breathed a sigh of relief," wrote Roy Campbell, as "the waiting was over."[2] Trucks and buses carried GIs from Fort Ord or the Cow Palace to the San Francisco waterfront, where they met the ships that would carry them to war. Among the ships were three luxury vessels of the Matson Line, the *Lurline*, the *Matsonia*, and the *Monterey*, which had delivered well-heeled tourists to Hawaii and other Pacific destinations before Uncle Sam turned them into troop transports. Four others were converted ocean liners, the *Ancon*, the *Argentina*, the *Hugh L. Scott*, and the *Mount Vernon*.

Loading the soldiers onto the ships took days. Ozzie St. George recalled "stumbling through the blacked-out freight yard at one A.M. with my arms full of barracks bag and rifle belting me across the back of the neck at every third step."[3] Officials at the foot of the gangplanks checked in each soldier before they could board. "The gangplank was at a fairly steep angle," recalled Campbell. "It was a hard climb, but grunting and puffing, all the men made it safely without falling over the side."[4] After boarding the *Mount Vernon*, Tracy Hale surveyed the harbor. "Everything looks so beautiful and calm," he wrote in his diary, "from Fort Mason to the Golden Gate Bridge, gee it looks swell."[5] Howard Kelley, also on the *Mount Vernon*, had different thoughts. "I wonder how many spies were also watching," he asked himself, and whether "there was a fleet of Jap submarines lying in wait for us."[6]

The convoy of transports and two freighters departed San Francisco on the afternoon of April 22, escorted by the heavy cruiser USS *Indianapolis*. As the ships pulled away, the GIs watched San Francisco's landmarks pass by, including Alcatraz and the Presidio. The city's signature landmark was the Golden Gate Bridge. Passing under it evoked a deep emotional response from practically every Red Arrowman, as it symbolized their departure from the United States. "Everyone was very quiet," wrote Art Kessenich, "and I'm sure many prayers were being said."[7] Howard Kelley noticed "an old gray-haired officer up on the ship's bridge crying. I suspected that he had probably been in WWI and knew what lay ahead."[8] Claire Ehle remembered being "a little emotional. It didn't really hit till I went under that bridge."[9] Ozzie St. George claimed that "never, in fifteen minutes, have I ever become so attached to anything as that bridge," and after it had faded from view he felt—despite the throngs of GIs along the railing—"suddenly, utterly, and completely alone."[10] It was a sobering moment. "A lot of us watched the coastline get smaller and smaller until gone," recalled Roland Stoelb. "There was no turning back."[11]

A few hours after clearing the Golden Gate, the convoy hit a terrible storm that lasted several days. "The sea is really seething and boiling," wrote Harry Heiden, "the waves mountainous. In the distance the white caps maketh the surf look as though it were covered with snow. . . . The waves shoot over the bow of the boat, and tons of water flow off the deck."[12] An epidemic of seasickness ensued. "Most of us had never been to sea before," explained Clarence Jungwirth, and "soon vomit began to run down the decks as most of the 5000 men aboard the ship all got sick at once."[13]

Eventually the storm let up and most Red Arrow soldiers soon became accustomed to the motion of the waves, though some had more trouble adjusting. "I was flat on my back for about almost two weeks," remembered Claire Ehle. "Couldn't eat, couldn't get up."[14] Kenneth Springer recalled one GI who claimed: "I'm not going back . . . until they build a bridge over the Pacific!"[15]

As the convoy cruised the open ocean, the GIs scanned the waters for Japanese submarines. "An efficient anti-submarine lookout is an 'all hands' job," noted the *Lurline's* daily bulletin, and "everyone must participate." Upon spotting a periscope or oncoming torpedo, soldier-passengers were told to "give the alarm in a loud voice" and "report the news immediately to the nearest telephone operator. . . . Don't be bashful about sounding off—remember, it's still a long swim!"[16]

To evade detection, the ships were blacked out at night and changed course frequently. The troops were required to wear lifebelts and attend lifeboat drills. "Alerts were called periodically," remembered Art Kessenich, but he seldom knew whether they were "for training or the real thing."[17] Soldiers tried not to dwell on the potential consequences. "We took interest in these precautionary procedures," wrote E. J. Kahn, "but somehow we rarely stopped to think about whether we would ever be called to use them in order to save our lives. Our attitude was not callous, indifferent or frivolous; it was simply fatalistic."[18] Some thought the convoy was particularly vulnerable. "Each day we could see our navy escort, which seemed to be a single cruiser," wrote Raymond Dasmann. "We were sure there must be more somewhere, just over the horizon?"[19] Ozzie St. George noticed that church services on Sunday mornings "were well attended, there being an amazing number of young men who became deeply and suddenly religious on finding the nearest land two miles away, straight down."[20]

The quarters for the enlisted GI were close and uncomfortable. The *Monterey* "was a former luxury liner," wrote Raymond Dasmann, "but the luxury had been removed" as soldiers were "stacked on bunk beds, six to a cabin."[21] Other soldiers were crammed into cargo holds, ballrooms, and other large spaces in the bowels of ships where there was no natural light and the ventilation was poor. "I was quartered in a large room," recalled Raleigh Sill, "completely filled with isles of hammocks" arranged "six high, with only six or eight inches between them." Sill added that "the room reeked with the smell of body odor" and the inhabitants dubbed it "stinking sock alley."[22] Roy Campbell found the conditions so appalling that he and a friend grabbed their blankets and pillows and slept on deck at "the very prow of the ship."[23] The officers were crowded, too, but they were housed in staterooms located in the ships' upper reaches. Herbert M. Smith recalled being billeted with five other majors, but at least his room had a "veranda . . . from which to watch the sky and the sea."[24]

Rank also determined the quality and quantity of food. Enlisted men lined up outside the dining hall twice a day, mess kits in hand. "It took three to four hours to get your food, eat, then stand in another long line to wash your dishes," recalled Jungwirth.[25] "The food on the ship was horrible," claimed Campbell, "boiled eggs and thick pieces of bread with cheese, and sometimes dehydrated potatoes."[26] For officers it was an entirely different experience. They selected their meals from the same sumptuous menu given to peacetime cruise passengers, as Matson Line stewards tended to them. "So far it has been just like a pleasure cruise," wrote Benjamin McKnight, "as the officers travel first class."[27]

For most soldiers on board, their only duties were to appear for daily musters, lectures, lifeboat drills, and calisthenics. The rest of the time was their own. "Life on board a troopship is inevitably monotonous," wrote E. J. Kahn, "but soldiers are perhaps better equipped to adapt themselves to it than civilians would be, since a large part of their lives is spent on doing the same things over and over again."[28] Morale officers organized various activities. On the *Lurline*, for example, soldiers could participate in a talent show, tour the ship's ice cream plant, or enter an essay contest based on the question, "What are we fighting for?" General Edwin Forrest Harding personally read all 118 entries and proclaimed himself "proud of the showing made by the men." The winner, Eugene Wasserman, wrote: "We are fighting for freedom, security, and a hopeful future for ourselves, our children, and the world's captive people, but also we are keeping faith with those soldiers before us, from the scrappers of Bataan to the minute men of Concord and Lexington."[29] Soldiers also wrote letters and caught up on their reading. "This long ship trip has given me the chance to complete the New Testament," Archie Van Gorden told his mother.[30] The passengers "talked endlessly," observed Ozzie St. George, "about what combat would be like, what home had been like, what was wrong with the Army (a subject too big for adequate discussion . . .), and what we had heard or overheard during the past twenty-four hours."[31] Gambling was probably the most common pastime. Art Kessenich recalled that card and dice games "with thousands of dollars involved" could go on "twenty-four hours a day."[32]

The GIs spent as much time as possible on deck. Many, coming from the Midwest, found the ocean environment fascinating. The soldier-passengers spotted flying fish, dolphins, sharks, and whales. Roy Campbell marveled at the vastness of the ocean itself, describing it as "a beautiful blue sheet of glass stretching from horizon to horizon."[33] Not all were so impressed. "Lovers of the sea can say what they want to about its 'ever-changing aspects,'" claimed Ozzie St. George. "It always looked the same to me."[34] Nature's highlights often came after dark. "Evenings were especially beautiful when the moon was full," thought Jungwirth. "The moon light would catch the glow of the phosphorescence in the water. One could see ten miles in each direction." He also noted that "as we headed farther south, we began to lose sight of the North Star and began to view the beautiful constellation of the Southern Cross."[35]

For centuries, sailors crossing the equator for the first time have endured a hazing ritual known as a line-crossing ceremony. In the American tradition, mariners who have previously crossed the equator, called "shellbacks," dress in elaborate costumes as King Neptune and his Court, and then subject first-timers, nicknamed "pollywogs," to a wide range of humiliations—sometimes rather sadistic and violent ones. Afterward, the pollywogs become shellbacks and are admitted into the "Order of Neptune." The Thirty-Second Division's convoy reached the equator on April 30, but on troopships with thousands of pollywogs, it was impractical to initiate everyone. "If every man on board . . . had taken his turn at being dunked into a barrel of water, sprayed with a hose, paddled, and subjected to various other forms of good-natured abuse, the ceremonies would have lasted several days and concluded at some latitude far from the equator," wrote E. J. Kahn.[36] Instead, each unit selected an unfortunate few by lottery to endure the hazing, while the rest became interested spectators. Sheldon Dannelly, one of the unfortunate, remembered being "soaked in water, shocked by an electric fork, [and] paddled."[37] At the end of the ceremony, observers and participants alike received certificates proclaiming their shellback status.

As the Red Arrow steamed toward Australia in early May, the war took dramatic turns. First, Corregidor fell to the Japanese on May 6. Then, as that news broke, the GIs learned that a major naval engagement was taking place hundreds of miles to their north, in the Coral Sea between Australia and New Guinea. American cryptographers had discovered that a Japanese invasion force of five thousand soldiers was heading for Port Moresby, New Guinea, accompanied by an aircraft carrier task force. The US Navy raced some of its own carriers to the Coral Sea to intercept the Japanese, and by May 7 each side was pounding the other's ships by air. Word of the battle spread among the Red Arrow and "the mood aboard ship immediately took on a more serious tone," recalled Roy Campbell, as soldiers "no longer thought about weekend passes, poker games, women, and whether or not they were going to get promotions."[38] The war no longer seemed an abstraction but a very real threat, and some worried the Japanese force was headed for their convoy. This caused lifeboat drills to take on new urgency. "The troops reacted as if it had been serious," wrote Herbert M. Smith, "and under pressure, they performed as veterans, no confusion, no jitters and no wisecracks."[39] The Battle of the Coral Sea was the first major battle in history between fleets of aircraft carriers. In a tactical sense the engagement was a draw; but the forceful American presence in the Coral Sea compelled the Japanese to call off the Port Moresby invasion, saving the critical harbor for the time being.

After nearly three weeks at sea, the passengers began to detect signs that they were approaching land. Herbert M. Smith noticed "floating bits of debris" and "graceful flights of birds," and then "as we were about to enter the Tasman Sea . . . several Aussie corvettes [small warships] came out to greet and escort the convoy."[40] The first sighting of land created great excitement. "It happened at four o'clock one afternoon," wrote Ozzie St. George. "Somebody mooning along the rail snapped his spine like a jitterbug hearing the call of Benny's clarinet, bugged his eyes like a Ripley Odditorium character, gurgling 'LAND!' Two thousand guys said, 'WHERE?' and jammed the rail till the rivets cracked."[41]

The Red Arrow Division arrived at Port Adelaide in South Australia on May 14, 1942. As the troopships pulled into the harbor, the GIs pressed against the railings to get their first glimpse of the Land Down Under. They disembarked to find an enthusiastic welcome. "Our first acquaintances were a few of the local soldiers," wrote E. J. Kahn, "who, we soon learned, should informally be called 'diggers.'" Kahn found them "affable" and "eager to exchange souvenirs."[42] Civilians were there to greet them too. "Young girls were throwing flowers and blowing kisses at us," remembered Raleigh Sill, and "the older ladies were waving handkerchiefs, some were crying."[43] From the port, trucks and trains carried the soldiers across the pastures and farmlands of South Australia. "It's a steppe region," as Jack Williams described it, "strangely beautiful with its gnarled eucalyptus trees, grass, and black earth."[44] To Roy Campbell, the country looked "like a giant artist went crazy with his green paint."[45] It was late autumn in the southern hemisphere. After escaping the snows of Massachusetts, the Red Arrow now entered the bone-chilling winter rains of South Australia. "It was not so cold as Michigan in winter, but cold enough for winter woolens and jackets," recalled Detroit's Kenneth Springer.[46] "This was the year that we had to endure two winters," noted Clarence Jungwirth.[47]

The Red Arrow made its new home in two camps east of Adelaide. One was Camp Woodside, which failed to impress the new arrivals. Roland Stoelb described the place as "just a bunch of tin shacks and warehouses with canvas roofs and no insulation," and where "our beds were burlap bags filled with straw."[48] Veterans of Camp Beauregard had experienced adverse conditions before, but for those who had joined the division at Camp Livingston or in California, Camp Woodside was a shock. Ozzie St. George was "mildly stunned. . . . We were accustomed to living in barracks with insulation over our heads, thermostats at our beck and call, hot showers under the same roof, and fancy iron cots." St. George was also surprised to share his quarters with avian roommates. "If the windows were open," he observed, "anything up to the size of a large duck could—and sometimes did—fly in and out."[49] The cold, drizzly weather and the close quarters of camp life "produced numerous cases of acute pharyngitis and tonsillitis," noted one medical report, "which soon became popularly known as Woodside Throat."[50] Conditions were even more spartan at Camp Sandy Creek, located in a sheep pasture thirty miles to the north. There, the new arrivals had to pitch their own tents and stuff their own bedding. Howard Kelley took the conditions in stride. "Anything was better than that crowded ship," he believed. Life at both Woodside and Sandy Creek soon improved. "Crews of carpenters from Adelaide built flooring for tents," Kelley recalled, and "we only had to sleep in our pup tents for about a week."[51]

However, complaints about the food were endless. South Australia was sheep country, and mutton was the main protein on the menu. Few GIs had ever tried it—and when they did, they did not like it. To Ozzie St. George, for example, mutton stew was "like cold glue, full of unidentifiable vegetables, with all the delicious appeal of a soggy snowbank."[52] Soldiers frequently complained about the pungent smell of mutton, which, wrote Archie Van Gorden, inspired some men to "start bleating like sheep."[53] GIs turned to other food sources whenever they could. "The country was teeming with wild rabbits," wrote Roy Campbell, and every evening after drill he and a friend "would have a rabbit to cook over an open fire behind [the] barracks."[54]

Within a few days of arrival, the Red Arrow resumed its training. Many soldiers had joined the division mere days before its departure for Australia and had received only the most rudimentary introduction to military life. The troops had to get back into shape after their rail odyssey and sea voyage. Mornings of drill and long afternoon hikes quickly brought the men back into shape. They spent many hours at the rifle range and participated in increasingly complex field maneuvers. Adrian Stansky described the experience as being "the same as the Louisiana maneuvers, only the climate was just the opposite."[55] The 128th Infantry Regiment conducted a three-day field exercise, during which the troops "experienced for [the] first time overhead artillery fire," according to one report.[56]

As the Red Arrow Division resumed its training, the momentum of World War II in the Pacific began to shift. In early June, a fleet of Japanese ships headed for Midway Island at the extreme western end of the Hawaiian chain, intending to draw the US Pacific Fleet into battle. But American code breakers once again discovered the Japanese plans. In the ensuing Battle of Midway, the US Navy consigned four Japanese carriers and scores of Japan's best pilots to the deep. It was the first decisive Allied victory in the Pacific.

Soon after, the US Joint Chiefs of Staff began laying the groundwork for a Pacific counteroffensive. On July 2, the joint chiefs adopted a plan to target the Japanese base at Rabaul. The plan was divided into three phases, or tasks. Task One, tentatively set for August 1, was an amphibious operation to neutralize the Japanese base at Tulagi in the southern Solomon Islands. Though Tulagi lay within MacArthur's SWPA, the navy insisted on commanding the operation, prompting the joint chiefs to shift the boundary between SWPA and the POA, thereby bringing Tulagi into the realm of the navy. The remaining tasks were for MacArthur. Task Two involved the seizure of the northern coast of New Guinea and the Solomons north of Tulagi. Task Three was to take Rabaul itself. MacArthur immediately began reorganizing his command and redeploying his forces. Within weeks he moved his headquarters from Melbourne to Brisbane and ordered the two US Army infantry divisions in Australia, the Thirty-Second and the Forty-First—composing the American I Corps—to move northward as well.

Thus, the Red Arrow Division's stay in South Australia lasted a mere two months. In mid-July, the troops boarded trains and headed north to establish a new camp in Queensland, a thousand miles away. An advance party from the 114th Engineers and the 126th Infantry Regiment went first. Their final destination was Logan Village, thirty miles south of Brisbane. The party arrived there on the morning of July 19 but, as the 126th Infantry Regiment journal recorded, "found no guides or anyone here to meet us."[57] A call to MacArthur's headquarters produced trucks to take them to the camp site. The advance group found the location exotic and forbidding. Herbert M. Smith remembered "a wilderness, where semi-tropical vines had to be cut to erect tents and cut pathways."[58] Located halfway between Logan Village and the little town of Tamborine, the site initially took the name Camp Tamborine.

The rest of the division arrived during late July and early August, and the camp quickly expanded. "Even after you've been in the army for more than a year," observed E. J. Kahn, "you are still impressed by the way a military organization is able to move into a previously unsettled area and within a relatively few short weeks turn it into a place which, if not equipped with all the comforts, can be called home."[59] Most supplies and equipment arrived by rail, but a good deal of it came north by sea. This led to the Thirty-Second Division's first combat death of the war. Corporal Gerald O. Cable of Bedford, Michigan, volunteered to serve on the gun crew of the Liberty Ship *William Dawes* as it departed Port Adelaide for Brisbane, loaded with vehicles and ammunition for Camp Tamborine. It was a dangerous job. Japanese submarines menaced the Australian coast, sinking ships and occasionally lobbing artillery ashore. In the early morning hours of July 22, the Japanese submarine *I-11* spotted the *Dawes* about twelve miles off Merimbula, New South Wales, surfaced, and fired a torpedo. According to one account, Cable spotted the torpedo as it headed for the ship and "less than ten seconds before his death he sought to warn the other men on board of their imminent danger."[60] The alarm sounded just as the torpedo slammed into the ship. It hit the stern, instantly killing Cable and the rest of the gun crew. A second torpedo then hit the middle of the ship, triggering massive explosions and ultimately sending the *Dawes* to the bottom.[61]

The news of Cable's death hit the Red Arrow hard. The division held a memorial service for him on August 30. Lieutenant Colonel Lester Doerr, division chaplain, called Cable "a true soldier and a real American" and recounted the many positive comments his comrades said about him: "One of the finest fellows I ever met. . . . Had a lot of fun out of life. . . . Went to church as often as his job permitted."[62] General Harding also spoke:

If we need anything more to bring home to us the fact that we are engaged in a serious business, this memorial service in commemoration of the death of the first soldier to lose his life by enemy action would bring it home to us. I sometimes think of this division's Red Arrow as one of fateful lightning, and this division as one of the terrible swift swords that will cut down the enemy and leave him powerless to rise against the world again for generations to come.[63]

Cable posthumously received the Purple Heart and the Silver Star, and Camp Tamborine was renamed Camp Cable in his honor.

As the troops settled in at Camp Cable, training resumed in earnest, though perhaps not the kind the division needed. It was now clear that the Red Arrow was destined for jungle warfare somewhere in the South Pacific, but the division had received little training for such combat. Indeed, the US Army had very little experience with it. The army's field manual for jungle warfare, FM 31-20, warned soldiers that, "in [the] jungle . . . the soldier fights two enemies, man and nature, [and] of the two, nature is often more formidable." To prepare for jungle operations, the manual advised extensive physical conditioning and cautioned that soldiers would "require a period of physical adjustment to the increased heat and humidity and the greater power of the sun's rays." That conditioning period, according to the manual, "is usually from 6 to 8 weeks for seasoned troops and a correspondingly longer time for recruits." The Thirty-Second Division had virtually no specialized jungle equipment—nor did the army generally. "The woolen olive-drab shirt, regulation khaki trousers, canvas leggings, and field shoes are suitable for jungle service," claimed FM 31-20, though "a heavy, loosely woven cotton shirt, when issued, may be used instead." The manual also instructed that "before beginning jungle operations men should be provided with new shoes that have been well oiled to protect them against wet rot."[64]

Based on these guidelines, Red Arrow's training program emphasized activities that would build the troops' stamina. Daily conditioning marches grew progressively longer. "We practiced marching from the camp to the coast," recalled Clarence Jungwirth, a twelve-hour, thirty-mile excursion that soon became "a weekly affair."[65] By mid-August the Red Arrow spent an increasing amount of time in the field—the most since the Louisiana Maneuvers the previous year. The 128th Infantry Regiment, for example,

Red Arrow troops on a training march in Australia. WHI IMAGE ID 164223

conducted a "jungle march" in the mountainous Lamington National Park area south of Brisbane, during which Roy Campbell remembered "sweating and swearing profusely."[66] Californian Raymond Dasmann, who worked as a firefighter for the US Forest Service before the war, observed that "climbing mountains was old stuff for me," but "most of the others in my regiment were flatlanders from Michigan and Wisconsin who were more used to cornfields or factories."[67] The troops lived off the land during the march, though not in the way the army might have liked. Dasmann recalled that he and a group of GIs found a small village and "it seemed reasonable to us that we should liberate it." There they were delighted to find "a pub and a party going on," so Dasmann and his cohort went in "with our backpacks, rifles, steel helmets, and all, and were given an enthusiastic welcome and provided with all the food and beverages we could handle."[68]

In anticipation of beach landings, some Thirty-Second Division troops received amphibious training. The Americans and Australians established the Joint Overseas Operational Training School at Port Stephens in New

South Wales, 125 miles up the coast from Sydney. Construction began early September—and with Red Arrow labor. "We were dumped out of [the] trucks and told to clear out trees and brush and build a camp," wrote Howard Kelley, and "after a day or two we had our tents up, latrines dug, and mess kitchen operating."[69] The Allies established a second amphibious training facility at Toorbul Point, forty miles north of Brisbane. At Port Stephens and Toorbul Point, the troops learned the techniques of beach landings. "Amphibious training consisted of lectures, landings with small craft, landing formations with assault boats with and without full field equipment from transports," noted one report of the 128th Infantry Regiment's training at Toorbul Point.[70] "It was impressed upon us that too often [beach landings] were accomplished under trying circumstances," wrote Herbert M. Smith, "which was proven to us the following day when we went over the side . . . on a stormy day." He recalled that "the rain, choppy waves and the bouncing pontoon boat in which we were towed to shore certainly demonstrated the points which we heard in the lecture."[71]

Ultimately, however, the training the Thirty-Second Division received in Australia left it unprepared for combat. General Harding later lamented that his division was "almost continually preparing to move, on the move, [or] getting settled after a move," all of which interrupted their dedicated training time; but the problems went beyond that.[72] The field marches physically conditioned the men and familiarized them with the tropical environment but failed to teach them how to fight in the jungle. Harding placed little emphasis on crucial topics like patrolling, camouflage, and fire discipline, and he rarely conducted live fire exercises. "It was true that we were all newcomers," wrote Major General Robert L. Eichelberger, a West Point classmate of Harding's who arrived in early September to take command of I Corps, "but I had expected to learn lessons on jungle training in Australia. And it seemed to me our troops in training were just being given more of the same thing they had had back home."[73]

On or off duty, the troops of the Thirty-Second Division formed impressions of the Land Down Under. For most, Australia was the first foreign land they had ever visited. The geography lessons from their youth suddenly came to life. Kangaroos are the continent's most iconic creatures, and the members of the Red Arrow Division were thrilled to see them. On the train ride between South Australia and Camp Cable, "shouts of laughter erupted at the first sight of a big red kangaroo bouncing in the outback," recalled Roy Campbell, who described the voyage as "hundreds of miles and thousands of kangaroos."[74] The animals even appeared on the grounds of Camp Cable. "Now and then a kangaroo came hopping down the company street," wrote Ozzie St. George, "hotly pursued by half a hundred of yelling soldiers with some pretty far-fetched ideas about catching and eating this native Australian."[75] Soldiers could not resist shooting them. "It sounded like the first day of deer hunting season here the other day," wrote Elvin Ball to his family, "until soldiers were told to stop." Many kangaroo sightings were probably wallabies, the kangaroo's smaller and more common cousin. Camp Cable, carved out of wallaby habitat, was crawling with them. According to Clarence Jungwirth, wallabies "roamed at night thru the camp, scaring the day-lite out of the armed guards."[76] The creatures were so common that Jack Williams suggested a new name for the facility: "Camp Wallaby."[77]

Kangaroos and wallabies were just the tip of Australia's zoological iceberg, and Camp Cable sometimes resembled an open-air zoo. Although human activity drove out some animals, E. J. Kahn observed that others "stood their ground, no doubt as curious about our intrusion as we were about their unfamiliar antics."[78] A group of Red Arrowmen once noticed pellets dropping from the forest canopy as they sat around a campfire. Looking up, they saw a group of brush-tailed possums. "Apparently," observed Raymond Dasmann, "they were defending their space by shitting."[79] Given the GI penchant for acquiring pets, some hoped to domesticize the wild creatures. Kenneth Springer and friends were returning from a movie one night "when a koala ran across the path and climbed a tree. We caught him by cutting off the limb on which he was clinging." Springer's group "kept him a few days, then let him go."[80] There was exotic bird life, too. Elvin Ball was thrilled to see parrots but disappointed that they did not talk "like you see in the movies."[81] As Howard Kelley recalled, "we began to hear [what] sounded like a flock of chickens cackling," and "we asked an Australian what kind of birds they were and he said they were 'Kookaburras,' but we call them Laughing Jacks."[82] Kahn noted "numerous spiders and fantastic insects beyond our powers of description," as well as a lizard called a goanna, "which, if photographed against a background that gave no indication of scale, could be passed off as a dinosaur."[83]

Australia's wildlife may have been exotic, but for most Americans its culture was not—often to their disappointment. "Many of the soldiers in our expeditionary force arrived in Australia expecting to be met at a primitive wharf by aborigine porters on kangaroos," E. J. Kahn wrote. "We had dwelt on its more unusual features, talking expectantly of boomerangs, platypuses, and the like, and never bothering to take into serious consideration that we might encounter a substantially familiar civilization."[84] Many soldiers were struck by the similarities between Australia and the United States. Passing through Port Adelaide, Roy Campbell thought the people "looked exactly like those at home. They wore the same clothes and worked in the same large buildings."[85] Despite the cultural similarities, the GIs were aware that they were in a foreign land. Kahn recalled a confusing incident at the end of a movie, when the Americans "stood up respectfully upon hearing the first chords of what they assumed to be *America* and were taken aback to find the music illustrated on the screen by a picture of George VI. A couple of Australian soldiers whispered informatively, '*God Save the King.*'"[86]

GIs were often anxious to explore the areas outside of their camps. Nearby small towns were the easiest and most common destinations: Gawler, Sandy Creek, Williamstown, or Woodside in South Australia; Logan Village or Tamborine in Queensland. Raymond Dasmann found Woodside to be charming, with "many of the characteristics of an Agatha Christie English village."[87] Cities offered far more excitement. While in South Australia, soldiers packed the trains and streamed into Adelaide every weekend. From Camp Cable, "we quickly made our way to the railroad into Brisbane," wrote Raymond Dasmann, "or found rides on supply trucks going that way."[88] Even Sydney was within reach. Usually the first destination in a city visit was a service club for soldiers. The USO had not yet arrived in Australia in force, but organizations like Salvation Army and Australia's Cheer Up Society offered substitutes. "Adelaide had a 'cheer up House' like our USO," remarked Byron Gibbs, with "a cafeteria, billiard tables, reading room and hot showers."[89] The clubs offered meals and lodging for GIs, though competition for a place to sleep could be fierce. "All the beds having been taken long ago," Ozzie St. George recalled of one evening, "we usually settled for the top of a pool table."[90]

Americans and Australians shared a common language, which helped soften the GIs' culture shock. But the dialects were not the same, and Australian English could cause confusion for American soldiers. Ozzie St. George, a journalism student before the war, recounted what happened when a GI asked an Australian soldier for the location of the nearest latrine. At first the Australian seemed confused: "'Oi!' said the Digger, a great light breaking over his face. 'You means the bloody lavatory! Down the street, Mite, roight to the end, an' acrosst the paddock. You'll see 'er. She's a little 'ut, wit pipes on. An' 'ere, Mite . . . you better tike me newspiper.'" GIs also noted the differing vocabularies. A gas station "wasn't a gas station at all," St. George learned, "but a 'petrol bowser.'"[91] Paul Kinder explained in a letter home:

> When they meet you on the street, they say "Good Day" or "Good Night" in place of "Hello." On the telephone they answer, "Are You There?" They say "ite" for "eight," "diy" for "day," etc. They call a streetcar a "tram"; a tavern is a "pub"; (Yes, I would know that); a train is "the cars"; a barber is a "hairdresser"; and they have many other odd expressions.[92]

Australia's British heritage was evident in many ways. As in Britain, vehicles in Australia traveled on the left side of the road, leading to some close calls for the Yanks accustomed to traveling on the right. E. J. Kahn recalled that on road marches "our jeeps clattered up the roads, the drivers swerving self-consciously as they suddenly remembered that they were driving on the wrong side."[93] GI pedestrians had to be mindful of the traffic, too. Archie Van Gorden wrote of one American killed in Adelaide on the very first weekend that passes to the city were authorized. He "looked to the left expecting traffic coming from that side," Van Gorden recounted, "and seeing none he stepped into the street just as a car came on his right."[94]

Australian money also confounded the Red Arrowmen. "When we asked how much," recalled Howard Kelley, the merchant "began saying something that sounded like this, 'Quid, hupennie, three pence' [and] we didn't know what he was talking about."[95] Many soldiers, Kahn observed, "would simply extend a handful of Australian coins . . . and trustingly invite the countermen to remove as much as they wanted," though he also noted that soldiers quickly learned the system.[96] "They do take an unfair advantage of us in raising prices," wrote Paul Kinder, "but we had become quite used to that back in the States, and most of us say nothing."[97] Americans pressed their economic advantages, too. "There was a terrible shortage of nylons," noted Art Kessenich, "and a few enterprising young soldiers had them sent to Australia and commanded quite a profit. The same was true of cigarettes."[98]

Food and drink also showed British influence. GIs discovered, for example, that a "spot of tea" was not just a drink but a late afternoon meal with scones and small sandwiches. They also enjoyed fish and chips, but, according to E. J. Kahn, "our favorites among all the Australian delicacies were meat pasties, which, once we had determined that they were not typographical errors, we accepted as tasty local versions of chop suey, enveloped in a pie crust."[99] For the most part, though, GIs found Australia gustatorily inadequate. Wartime rationing limited food options, and the country did not have the fast food joints that young Americans craved. "The nearest approach to our twenty-four-hour wonders," wrote Ozzie St. George, were "various milk bars serving a limp sort of milk shake that always tasted like discouraged vanilla."[100] Without access to familiar soft drinks, Kahn wrote that "we turned to ginger beer and lemon or orange squash, sold for sixpence in quart bottles with rubber stoppers."[101] Australian attempts to imitate American fast food usually fell flat. "Certain sharp operators around the town alleged that they were selling 'Real American Hamburgers,'" recalled St. George, but "being just a little too sharp, they tried to slip a certain amount of mutton between their buns," a practice he thought "a cruel blow to international friendship. . . . In the end, we readily admitted something we had never so much as dreamed of back in the States—camp chow was better than town chow. Much better."[102]

Going into town often meant a search for alcohol, but the Yanks found that the locals had different drinking habits. "Australians mostly drank socially, for the companionship it offered," observed Ozzie St. George, whereas the GIs "went to the pubs and drank because we wanted to get drunk." An Australian pub had a different atmosphere than an American tavern. "This was a small room," wrote St. George of a pub in one South Australian town, "flanked by a bar that had no stools [and] with a fire-place instead of a juke box."[103] The GIs poured into the pubs nonetheless, though pub hours were brief and spotty. "The trouble was that these places were so crowded," wrote Lawrence Thayer, "and the length of time allowed for drinking so short, that it was hard to gulp down enough to get a buzz on."[104] Australian beer—ales rather than lagers, served at room temperature—failed to satisfy American tastes. "We succeeded, finally, in obtaining a glass of something . . . the label insisted was 'XXXX Bitter Beer,'" wrote St. George. "I decided it certainly was bitter if nothing else, and went off in search of some ice cream."[105] The XXXX brand became notorious in the ranks of the Red Arrow. "It was known to the local G.I.'s as 'Green Death,'" remembered Clarence Jungwirth. "It delivered a 'hard hangover' and among the G.I.'s it was believed you could commit suicide by drinking enough of it."[106]

The American soldiers often viewed Australians as backward and out-dated, particularly in rural areas. "Those towns were like something out of an old western movie," thought Amos Truckey. "They have wooden sidewalks, dirt streets, covered wagons."[107] For the Red Arrowmen, per-haps nothing symbolized Australian "backwardness" more than the nation's rail system. Because Australian states had different rail gauges, cross-country trains had to stop at state borders and then transfer their cargoes and passengers onto another train before continuing the journey—a time-consuming process that meant backbreaking work for GIs. Train cars and engines seemed antiquated, too. "The cars were the original old-fashioned English type," wrote Lawrence Thayer, "which were made up of separate small compartments with a bench on either side," and "with all our packs, rifles, equipment, there wasn't enough room for all of us to lie down at once."[108] Ozzie St. George quipped that one train he rode was "on loan, I think, from the National Museum."[109] The train between Camp Sandy Creek and Gawler was so slow that the GIs dubbed it the "Gawler Crawler." "On the return trip it would be loaded with troops and could never make the incline," Jungwirth recalled. "It became the practice to have a number of troops get off the train at the bottom of the incline and help push the train up."[110]

Whatever the Red Arrowmen thought of the progress of Australian civilization, they were grateful for the hearty welcome they received. The Americans arrived at a time when Australia was practically defenseless, and the GIs' presence offered hope in an otherwise dark time. "Approaching the railroad station . . . for the first time," remembered Jungwirth of his arrival in Gawler, "we saw the station platform filled with local citizens" and "getting off the train the G.I.'s were swamped with requests to come and be a guest in their homes. It was overwhelming."[111] Claire Ehle remembered that "you'd go to town and you'd stand on a corner and somebody would stop and ask you if you knew where you were going, and invite you to their home for meals."[112]

US popular culture was pervasive in Australia, through movies, music, fashion, and more. This fed the local perception of Yanks as glamorous, and many GIs reported feeling a kind of adulation usually reserved for celebrities. "We must have looked like Hollywood stars," thought William T. King, "as the kids stopped us everywhere we went for autographs."[113] In 1942, "this GI infatuation reached near epidemic proportions," claimed historian John Hammond Moore, "and helped a frightened people forget their problems."[114] Paul Kinder told his family that "they treat us more like kings than soldiers."[115]

Many Yanks admired the way Australians faced the war with grit and determination. Australia had been at war since 1939 and for years its people had endured sacrifices most Americans were only beginning to appreciate. "Nowhere did we see any men," remarked Ozzie St. George, "except a few old codgers and one Minister of the Gospel."[116] The Japanese threat to the US West Coast was largely hypothetical, but for Australians it was real and immediate, with enemy submarines lurking off the nation's coast and planes striking its northern shore. Robert Hughes described Australia as "a nation under the gun." He remembered frequent brownouts, in which cities dimmed their lights at night, as well as alerts that would prompt immediate blackouts.[117] In a letter to his wife, Elizabeth, Richard Correll emphatically wrote that "the people of Australia are working very hard, devoting every possible spare minute to work of some nature in war defense. It's vital, this work they're doing, and it must inevitably come to the states. So if you can help, do!"[118] According to Archie Van Gorden, "these Aussie soldiers, especially these boys who spent 2 years in Pallestine [sic], Crete, Libbia [sic] are a fine, hard-working group. I have never seen a better bunch of men in my life."[119]

Countless sexual liaisons occurred between GIs and Australians. Prostitution was legal in Australia, and as historian John Hammond Moore wrote, the American soldiers were "eager, affluent clients." Beyond commercial sex, many GIs struck up casual relationships with local women. "This was a dream come true for a generation of Australian females nurtured on Hollywood legends," wrote Moore, and "with the cream of Australian manhood overseas, the GI was here in the flesh, both available and willing."[120] Robert Bable wrote that "wartime love affairs abounded and free sex was running rampant. In retrospect, we knew we were going into combat soon. Most of us were apprehensive and, perhaps, afraid, so we all tried to bolster our macho images by living each day as though it was our last."[121] Lawrence Thayer observed that "those who were married [also] searched for sexual satisfaction,"[122] while Ozzie St. George noted simmering resentment on the part of Australian servicemen who were returning from the Mediterranean. "They were understandably burned to find the female population gone 'Yank crazy,'" he wrote, "but what could they do?"[123] The army once again hoped that condoms and camp prophylactic stations might curb the rising rates of sexually transmitted infections. It also tried moral persuasion. "One time at Camp Cable the Regimental Chaplain called for an assembly," recalled Roland Stoelb:

> He scolded us for our behavior when we were in Adelaide. He said there were over 700 pregnant Australian girls who identified their fathers as soldiers of our regiment. The chaplain said he was shocked at the possibility that a lot of soldiers may not have used their real name. One of the guys got up and yelled, "Sorry, chaplain, we could have done better, but the officers keep us so busy we don't get to town much." Everyone broke out laughing and we were dismissed.[124]

It was not all commercial or casual sex. Clarence Jungwirth went on a blind date with a woman named Valda. "For the both of us, it was 'love at first sight,'" he remembered, and "we dated as often as possible, going to the movies, visiting her friends and relatives." Jungwirth struck up a friendship with Valda's aunt, and he and friends spent weekends at her home. "When I and my friends got up in the morning," he wrote, "we would find that Aunt Molly had pressed our clothes and had shined our shoes and had a healthy breakfast waiting for us."[125] Some Red Arrowmen married Australian women. As the Thirty-Second Division prepared to move to Camp Cable in July, South Australian newspapers reported several marriages between American men and Australian women. "Following a meeting in a train travelling to a military camp some weeks ago," reported the *Mail* of Adelaide, "an American soldier and a private of the Australian Women's Army Service were married in Glenelg today." The bride wore "her trim khaki uniform" and "a diamond wristwatch, the gift of the bridegroom."[126] Less than a week later, a GI from Superior, Wisconsin, married a celebrated local equestrian in Adelaide. The couple met "while she was out riding in the city," reported the *News* of Adelaide. "She was astride one of her own mounts, and leading the other. The enterprising American suggested that he should ride the lead horse, and that's how the romance began."[127]

Despite the warm reception they received in Australia and the excitement of seeing a new country, the homesickness many soldiers felt upon entering the service only intensified once they were half a world away. "Most of our soldiers were very young," recalled Lawrence Thayer, "and being so far from home, and not having enough work and recreation to keep them occupied, [they] became homesick and depressed."[128] Jungwirth, who left Oshkosh enthusiastically, nevertheless felt the tug of home after being away for months. One weekend he went to Brisbane and noticed a theater showing the American film *Holiday Inn*, starring Bing Crosby. "I went to the theater at 1.00 PM and stayed till 10.00 PM," Jungwirth said. He watched the movie three times in a row "to alleviate the home-sickness."[129]

Before September 1942, the war had seemed like a grand adventure for the Red Arrow Division. In just the first eight months of that year, its members had traveled more than most Americans would in a lifetime. But very grim business lay ahead. In September 1942, MacArthur ordered the Thirty-Second Division forward yet again, this time to New Guinea to meet the Japanese.

Red Arrow soldiers make their way through the jungles of New Guinea, November 1942.

CHAPTER 5

Green Hell

In July 1942, Allied planners pored over maps of New Guinea's northern coast, searching for potential bases to support their anticipated counter-offensive against the Japanese. Scouts zeroed in on the area around the coastal village of Buna, one hundred air miles northeast of Port Moresby, on the island's Papuan Peninsula. Unfortunately for the Allies, Buna also caught the attention of their adversaries. On the night of July 21, Japanese troops came ashore near Buna, initiating a six-month-long struggle for control of Papua. That struggle, along with the concurrent battle at Guadalcanal in the Solomon Islands to the east, would determine control of the South Pacific.[1] Perhaps no place had a greater impact on the history of the Red Arrow Division than New Guinea. Members of the division would serve and fight there on and off for two years. The leading elements of the division arrived in September 1942, yet before the Red Arrowmen ever met the Japanese, they struggled mightily with the island's formidable wilderness of jungles, mountains, and swamps. Many Wisconsin and Michigan soldiers were experienced woodsmen, but few had ever seen anything quite like this—what Paul Lutjens of the 126th Infantry Regiment called a "green hell."[2] Traversing the wilds of Papua—a land devoid of roads or almost any touches of the modern world—proved tremendously challenging and left the poorly prepared Red Arrow exhausted, diseased, and ill-supplied on the eve of its first encounter with the Japanese.

New Guinea is the second largest island in the world. Measuring one thousand five hundred miles from east to west, it spans roughly the distance from New York City to Dallas. Surrounding New Guinea are scores of islands of varying size, including the Bismarck Archipelago off its northern shore, site of the great Japanese base at Rabaul. A spine of rugged mountains runs through the center of the island, with many spurs branching outward. Some peaks rise more fourteen thousand feet—as tall as the Rockies and the Sierra Nevada in the American West. Located just south of the equator, New Guinea is covered with lush tropical vegetation. Vast tidal swamps dominate the coastal regions, patrolled by swarms of mosquitoes and merciless crocodiles. On higher ground, vast open areas teem with kunai grass that can grow as high as ten feet and have edges sharp enough to slice through human skin. Heat bakes the coastal areas year-round, with high temperatures averaging near ninety degrees Fahrenheit. Heavy rains can occur at any time but are most intense during the monsoon season, which runs from November through March. Rivers cut their way from the mountain spine down to the coast and fluctuate from dribbles to raging torrents depending on the season.

New Guinea is part of the ethno-cultural region known as Melanesia, and its people are referred to today as Papua New Guineans. The first humans arrived on the island perhaps fifty thousand years ago, making it one of the longest continually inhabited places on the planet outside of Africa. Over thousands of years, New Guinea developed a vast array of cultures. During the midtwentieth century there were as many as one thousand different languages spoken on the island. Traditionally, Papua New Guinean societies were organized tribally, with different peoples living in distinct territories they often guarded jealously. Most Papua New Guineans lived in small villages and survived by hunting and gardening. Europeans first arrived on the island during the seventeenth century. Portuguese mariners called it *Ilhas dos Papuas* (Island of the Papuans)—the word *Papuan* was derived from Malay words meaning "frizzy haired" due to the physical appearance of its people. Spanish sailors noted the island's similarities to the Guinea coast of West Africa and dubbed it "New Guinea."

European empires divided the island in the nineteenth century. The

Papuan Peninsula, New Guinea

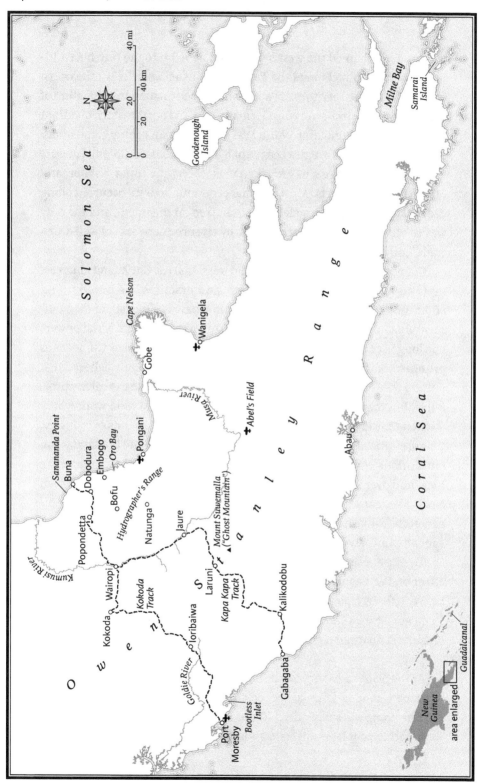

Netherlands claimed the western half and added it to the Dutch East Indies. Great Britain claimed the Papuan Peninsula and the southeastern coast, called it the Territory of Papua, and passed on the administration of the colony to Australia in 1906. Germany took the northeastern quadrant of the island, though after World War I the German colony came under Australian control through a League of Nations mandate. Colonial powers established plantations to grow bananas, coconuts, copra, rubber, and other tropical products. Most colonial economic activity occurred along the coast. By 1942, few modern roads existed on the island, and the only way to move through the interior was by rivers or networks of well-worn trails, commonly known as tracks.[3]

Colonization also brought Christian missionaries. Christianity increasingly supplanted traditional religions, and practices like headhunting and cannibalism that had existed on some parts of the island died out. Australian officials embraced the racist stereotypes that imperial powers had long used to justify colonialism. They viewed Papua New Guineans as primitive, warlike, and lazy. Australian authorities not only believed that putting the "natives" to work on plantations would make the colony profitable, but they also argued paternalistically that plantation work would "civilize" the Papua New Guineans and teach them the habits of industry. Colonial officials portrayed their policies as benevolent and humanitarian, but working conditions were in fact quite harsh. Pay was low, hours were long, and overseers frequently beat their workers. According to historian Noah Riseman, "employers justified violence on the grounds that indigenes' child-like nature required beatings, or because as 'warrior cultures' Papuans and New Guineans would respect violent employers more."[4]

The Japanese invasion and the coming of war in 1942 had a profound effect on the peoples of New Guinea. Their land became a battleground between foreign powers, with the island's residents caught in the middle. One Papua New Guinean man described the scene when the Japanese attacked the Australian government station at Buna in July 1942:

> As the plane came very low it started to fire its machine gun and went ta-ta-ta-ta-ta-ta-ta, like coconuts falling from the tree, and everything was smashed. . . . There was no time to go to your village to gather your family or collect your valuable belongings. Wife ran

naked without her husband and children. Husband ran naked without wife and children. . . . All ran in different directions into the bush
[and that night] the soil was your bed and the rotten logs your pillow.

People found their villages blown up, burned, or occupied by foreign soldiers. Dead bodies and shell craters littered their gardens and their forests.
As historian John Waiko wrote, Papua New Guineans "felt like refugees in
their own land."[5] The war stimulated great social changes. People from
around the world suddenly converged on the island—Americans, Australians, Chinese, Dutch, Filipinos, Formosans (Taiwanese), Japanese,
Koreans—bringing Papua New Guineans into sustained contact with
people of many different cultures. By the end of the war, perhaps a million Americans, half a million Australians, and three hundred thousand
Japanese had passed through New Guinea. The foreigners brought tons
of military hardware and supplies, as well as consumer goods. They built
roads, airfields, harbors, and other engineering works. Papua New Guineans watched with interest as the Japanese (at first) routed their colonizers
in battle. Australian dominance suddenly seemed breakable. During the
war some Papua New Guineans sided with the Japanese, others with the
Allies. Most simply tried to survive and remain neutral. World War II left
a political mark on the island as well. As historian Jonathan Ritchie wrote,
the war led Papua New Guineans to "foster a sense of common identity and
even an early form of nationalism, especially among [those] whose lives
were most affected by the conflict."[6]

   During the war years, the Australian New Guinea Administrative Unit
(ANGAU) managed the civil, economic, educational, legal, and medical
affairs of Papua New Guineans on the Australian side of the island. The
Royal Papuan Constabulary—the territory's police force—came under
the authority of ANGAU, as did New Guinea's militia, the Papuan Infantry
Battalion (PIB). But ANGAU's main wartime function was to provide labor,
especially to support the efforts of the Allied troops. The construction of
much of the island's new infrastructure was done with Papua New Guinean hands. In combat areas, they carried supplies, served as guides, and
evacuated wounded soldiers. Australian wartime propaganda portrayed
the relationship between the Australians and the Papua New Guineans
as a partnership against the Japanese invaders. The realities were more

Allied forces in Papua relied on the hard work of Papua New Guineans, who served as laborers, stretcher bearers, guides, and soldiers. Hundreds of Papua New Guineans eventually received medals for their service at ceremonies like the one pictured here in March 1943. LIBRARY OF CONGRESS

complicated. Some young Papua New Guinean men volunteered for the constabulary, the PIB, or ANGAU labor, motivated by pay, adventure, hatred of Japanese invaders, or loyalty to Australia. Most workers were conscripted—not unlike the soldiers they served alongside. As Australian demands for labor increased, more and more young men were swept up into ANGAU labor organizations, leaving scores of villages inhabited only by women, children, and the elderly. As on prewar plantations, ANGAU officials subjected Papua New Guinean workers to harsh physical discipline. "They were always hitting us and knocking us over," said one Papua New Guinean laborer.[7] Anti-Australian sentiment was high, and disaffected workers sometimes turned to the Japanese (who also exploited Papua New Guinean labor) or more commonly escaped. In all, about fifty thousand

Papua New Guineans worked in ANGAU labor units. Forty-six died as a result of combat, and about two thousand died of other causes.[8]

As confrontation with the Japanese loomed, MacArthur grew dissatisfied with the lack of aggressiveness and efficiency of many top SWPA leaders, and he shook up his command. Major General George C. Kenney replaced Lieutenant General George Brett as head of Allied Air Forces. A former World War I flier with an outsized ego, Kenney had a personality strong enough to stand up to the Bataan Gang, and MacArthur gave him free rein to run his command as he saw fit. Vice Admiral Arthur S. Carpender became the new head of Allied naval forces, while Australia's Major General Sydney F. Rowell took over the New Guinea Force. The Australian Seventh Division, under General Arthur "Tubby" Allen, had recently returned from the Mediterranean. To beef up Rowell's troops with more battle-hardened soldiers, Allen's men were hurriedly dispatched to New Guinea. Two of Allen's battalions went to Port Moresby and one went to Milne Bay.

Two thousand Japanese troops came ashore in the Buna area on July 21–22, led by an engineering officer, Colonel Yokoyama Yosuke. Yokoyama had two missions. The first was to establish a Japanese base on the north shore of the Papuan Peninsula. Most of Yokoyama's soldiers were engineering specialists, and they got right to work building things. Yokoyama set up headquarters at Giruwa, a shoreline village just to the east of Sanananda Point. To the west of the point, at the docks of a rubber plantation, his engineers constructed a naval facility. To the east, at Buna, they took control of an Australian government airstrip and converted it into their own combat air base.

Yokoyama's second task was to lay the groundwork for an overland attack across the Owen Stanley Range to Port Moresby, as its harbor was still very much on the minds of Japanese planners. From the Sanananda docks, a crude corduroy road (a type of road made from logs, commonly used in swampy areas) known as the Sanananda Track led fifteen miles inland. Where that road ended, a trail continued to the village of Kokoda. From the village, a jungle path called the Kokoda Track snaked southward through the mountains to Port Morseby. Almost immediately upon landing on July 21–22, a Japanese force of nine hundred infantrymen marched toward Kokoda. Defending the village was Australia's five-hundred-member Maroubra Force. Outnumbered and lightly armed, the Australian forces had few options. They destroyed the wire rope bridge across the swift Kumusi River at Wairopi ("wire rope" in the local pidgin) hoping to slow the advance, but Japanese engineers soon built another bridge and continued. By August 13, the Japanese were firmly in control of Kokoda and the northern end of the Kokoda Track.

Japanese commanders then prepared to move on Port Moresby—and indeed take the entirety of the Papuan Peninsula. General Horii Tomitaro's South Seas Detachment—which had already conquered Guam and Rabaul—was to land in Papua and press inland over the Kokoda Track to Port Moresby. Meanwhile, another force, the Kawaguchi Detachment, was to establish a base on the island of Samarai, a trading center on the eastern tip of New Guinea, and from there, in coordination with Horii's overland assault, move on Port Moresby by sea. But as the Japanese prepared their attack on Port Moresby, the Americans made a move of their own. On August 7, US Marines invaded Tulagi and an island thirty miles to the south of it—Guadalcanal, the site of a Japanese airfield. Task One of the American counteroffensive in the South Pacific had begun.[9] The growing fight at Guadalcanal forced the Japanese to divert resources to the Solomon Islands, but they still considered New Guinea the key to isolating Australia and expanded their base in Papua. More Japanese engineers arrived there on August 12, and the main body of the South Seas Detachment came six days later. By the end of August, Horii had more than eleven thousand troops on the northern coast of the Papuan Peninsula, including elite infantry and engineering units. The Japanese also brought in hundreds of conscripted Chinese and Korean laborers.

Japan's discovery of the Allied base at Milne Bay also complicated their plans. Canceling the attack on Samarai, Imperial forces targeted Milne Bay instead. The Japanese landed along the northern shore of Milne Bay on August 25, then drove along the muddy shoreline track toward the main Allied base. With the help of a few tanks, Japanese troops brushed aside the Australian militia guarding the track, but their momentum stopped when they reached an airstrip along their line of advance, where the open, level ground gave the Allies clear fields of fire. Japanese commanders at Rabaul sent in reinforcements, but the Allied line held. With the battle at Guadalcanal intensifying, Japan had no more soldiers to spare and withdrew from Milne Bay in early September. This little battle had big consequences. Allied control of the eastern tip of New Guinea effectively blocked any further Japanese attempt to take Port Moresby by sea. The Allies greatly expanded their presence at Milne Bay, transforming the coconut plantation into an airfield complex and major supply base, and giving them a potential stepping-stone to the northern shore of the Papuan Peninsula.

Despite the Guadalcanal and Milne Bay setbacks, Horii began his ascent of the Kokoda Track on August 26. Japanese commanders had a poor understanding of the New Guinea interior and began their attack without properly assessing the feasibility of moving troops across the peninsula. The Kokoda Track was a narrow, winding path that rose and fell precipitously, reaching heights of seven thousand feet, and was hemmed in by thickly jungled mountains. Japanese troops paid a heavy price for their leaders' ignorance and impatience. They had to carry everything they needed for the operation—every round of ammunition, every artillery piece and shell, and every morsel of food. It was exhausting and backbreaking work on top of the combat.

The Australians on the track—the much-depleted Maroubra Force, elements of the Papuan Infantry Battalion, and the troops of Allen's newly arrived Seventh Division—also suffered great privation. They fought with bravery and skill, but the Japanese continually seized the ridgelines above the track, outflanking them and forcing their withdrawal. Horii's troops steadily advanced, crossed the mountain divide by September 1, and began their descent toward Port Moresby. By September 9, the Japanese had two full infantry regiments on the Kokoda Track. The Australians had only three battalions (slightly more than half as many soldiers as the Japanese). By September 16, the Japanese reached Ioribaiwa, less than thirty miles from Port Moresby. The Australians dug entrenchments on nearby Imita Ridge and prepared to counterattack. From Ioribaiwa, Horii and his men could hear the faint sound of airplane engines from the Port Moresby airfields and glimpse the Coral Sea sparkling in the distance. Their objective was in sight.

Back in Brisbane, MacArthur grew alarmed at the developments on the Kokoda Track. He knew that if Port Moresby fell, the defense of Australia and the South Pacific might crumble. MacArthur's well-known vainglory no doubt amplified his fears as well. The fall of Port Moresby would not look good in newspaper headlines, and, on the heels of MacArthur's ouster from the Philippines, the fall of Papua might well lead to his dismissal. His poor understanding of exactly what was happening on the Kokoda Track also hindered his assessment. The Americans were just as ignorant of the rugged geography of the Kokoda Track as the Japanese, and MacArthur did not go to Papua at this critical moment to assess the conditions for himself. Instead, he relied on Colonel Charles Willoughby's intelligence assessments.

At first Willoughby assured MacArthur that the Japanese only planned to establish an air base at Buna, and when that proved incorrect, Willoughby grossly and consistently underestimated the number of Japanese soldiers in Papua. Based on these inaccurate assessments, MacArthur believed the Australians possessed a manpower advantage, when in fact the opposite was true. MacArthur concluded the Australian forces were inept and poorly led. He ordered Blamey to Port Moresby to take command of the New Guinea Force and pressured him to relieve commanders in the field. With Port Moresby under threat, MacArthur needed more soldiers. Elements of the Australian Sixth Division arrived at Port Moresby in mid-September. MacArthur also had two untested American divisions in Australia to draw upon. The Thirty-Second Division got the call.

As the Japanese pressed toward Port Moresby on the Kokoda Track, Allied planners in Brisbane organized a counterattack. Under the plan, which MacArthur adopted on September 11, the Australians would push the Japanese northward back up the track, while an American regimental combat team would somehow cross the Owen Stanley Range and outflank the Japanese—though where the GIs would cross the mountains was yet to be determined. MacArthur immediately issued orders for the Thirty-Second Division to move to New Guinea. Not every element of the Red Arrow was to leave Australia immediately, though. Combat teams formed around the 126th and 128th Infantry Regiments, but the 127th Infantry Regiment stayed in Australia in reserve. The division's artillery battalions would remain Down Under as well. SWPA planners questioned the effectiveness of artillery in the dense jungle environment, and General Kenney had assured MacArthur that his planes could furnish the infantry with all the fire support it needed. "The artillery in this theater flies," Kenney boasted. The division was so unprepared for combat that it had no camouflage uniforms, so their workaday denim fatigues were sent to a Brisbane laundry shop where they were hurriedly dyed green. When the uniforms came back "the men put them on," Kenneth Springer wrote, although "they were still damp and stiff."[10]

The choice of the Thirty-Second Division was a peculiar one. The Forty-First Infantry Division at Rockhampton was closer to New Guinea and arguably had a better training facility for jungle warfare. In a September 6 memo, General Robert Eichelberger, I Corps commander, described the Red Arrow as "a fine looking body of men," but argued that the "frequent movements of this division, both before and after its arrival in Australia, have hindered its training" and that "aggressive leadership seems lacking."[11] Eichelberger's chief of staff, Colonel Clovis E. Byers, took a dimmer view. "March discipline bad," Byers recorded in his diary after one inspection, "and basic training in general didn't look too good. Their chief concern seems to be to get settled in a comfortable camp and to this end they are working hard."[12] "I told Generals MacArthur and Sutherland that I thought the 32nd Division was not sufficiently trained to meet the Japanese veterans on equal terms," Eichelberger wrote after the war.[13] Byers flatly stated later that "we recommended to General MacArthur that the 41st Division, not the 32nd, be sent into combat," calling its officer corps "a scrub team."[14] MacArthur inspected the Red Arrow just once, in early September. "The last time I saw your outfit was on the battlefields of France," he told the assembled troops, and "I took a particular pride in it because at that time half of it came from my beloved section of the country." As the Red Arrow was poised to begin fighting in another world conflict, MacArthur told the division: "I have every confidence that in this war . . . you will carry out in full the old traditions."[15] As General Edwin Forrest Harding, the Red Arrow commander, remembered it, MacArthur told him that a "unit can go just so far in its training before experiencing combat. It takes battle to make men susceptible to acquiring the additional training they need and your men seem to be at that point."[16]

On September 12, a small group of officers flew from Brisbane to New Guinea to prepare for the division's arrival and determine a route through

General MacArthur (center) visits the Red Arrow at Camp Cable, 1942. WHI IMAGE ID 3827

the Owen Stanley Range. Leading the detachment was a logistics officer from MacArthur's headquarters, Brigadier General Hanford MacNider. The Iowa native had fought on the western front during the Great War and was a rising star in the Republican Party, serving as assistant secretary of war under President Calvin Coolidge and ambassador to Canada under President Herbert Hoover. Some Republican leaders had promoted MacNider as Hoover's running mate in 1932, and even as a potential presidential nominee in 1940. Though MacNider was an ardent isolationist, he lobbied to get back in uniform after Pearl Harbor. He was given a colonelcy and sent to Australia, where he detested staff work. MacNider told his wife, Margaret, that he could "never get used to fighting a war in a blizzard of paperwork," and he thought most of his colleagues were "bozos" who "like this kind of an assignment." MacArthur rescued MacNider from his deskbound world, gave him a general's star, and sent him to New Guinea. "Praise the Lord and the star spangled fellow himself," MacNider crowed.

He reveled in being back in the field and assured his nervous spouse that "general officers die of nothing but old age."[17]

Accompanying MacNider to New Guinea was Lieutenant Colonel Joseph Bradley, the Thirty-Second Division's chief logistics officer, as well as three members of the 126th Infantry Regiment's staff: Major Bernd G. Baetcke, Colonel Quinn's executive officer; Captain William F. Boice, intelligence officer; and Captain Alfred Medendorp, assistant logistician.[18]

Getting the division to New Guinea quickly was imperative, but transporting the troops by ship was likely to take two weeks. With the Japanese on Port Moresby's doorstep, the Americans might not get to New Guinea in time to make any difference. General Kenney proposed a novel solution—transport by air. Never before had American infantry been delivered to a combat zone by airplane. MacArthur's staff "didn't like the idea at all," Kenney recalled. MacArthur himself expressed doubts and asked Kenney how many men might be lost in such a movement. He "hadn't lost a pound of freight yet on that route," Kenney replied, adding that "the airplanes didn't know the difference between 180 pounds of freight and 180 pounds of infantryman." Though MacArthur "hated to hear his doughboys compared to freight," he authorized Kenney to send one company to Port Moresby by plane so they could "see how long it took and how the scheme worked out."[19]

General Harding chose Company E of the 126th Infantry Regiment, from Big Rapids, Michigan, to be the first to fly to New Guinea, along with an assortment of attached medical and engineer troops. The party gathered at Amberley Field, outside Brisbane, in the early morning hours of September 15, 1942. The troops, carrying small arms, mortars, and field packs, quietly milled around on the tarmac. "Nobody knew what to say," recalled Paul Lutjens, until someone started whistling the "old cavalry bugle call" and that "broke the tension." Harding addressed the company, calling it "the Spearhead of the Spearhead of the Spearhead," and told its members: "You have been picked to go first because you are the best company in this outfit."[20] Company E then boarded "a mixed collection of Douglas and Lockheed transports," as Kenney recalled, and took off. "We didn't know where we were going," commented Lutjens, but "it wasn't hard to guess it was north." The planes stopped to refuel at Townsville and

Cooktown on Australia's York Peninsula, then headed out over the Coral Sea. They touched down at Port Moresby late that afternoon, roughly ten hours after leaving Brisbane. "Landed Port Moresby, New Guinea, September 15, 1942," Lutjens recorded in his notebook. "Temperature 115°. Japs twenty miles away. New Guinea is hotter than the lower story of hell."[21]

Company E was the first American infantry unit to set foot on New Guinea, though its first task wasn't combat but road construction. MacNider was still searching for a way to get troops across the Owen Stanley Range, and two possibilities had emerged. The first was an eighty-five-mile track from the coastal village of Gabagaba, forty miles east of Port Moresby, to Jaure, near the headwaters of the Kumusi River on the north slope of the island. From Jaure, trails led down the Kumusi Valley to Wairopi, where Allied troops might cut off the Japanese on the Kokoda Track and ultimately move against Buna itself. The Americans mispronounced Gabagaba as "Kapa Kapa" and called this proposed route the Kapa Kapa Track. But the route crossed mountains of more than nine thousand feet, and nobody was known to have crossed the track in decades.

The Australians believed the Kapa Kapa Track was impractical and instead suggested a second, longer route from the coastal village of Abau, more than one hundred miles east of Port Moresby, to Jaure. They called this route the Abau Track, and although it would require a longer march, it traversed mountains of a mere five thousand feet.

Two parties would be sent to assess each route. The Red Arrow's Captain Boice led one party to explore the Kapa Kapa Track, while Colonel Leif Sverdrup, an SWPA engineering officer, led another to reconnoiter the Abau Track. Regardless of which route was chosen, troops and supplies would have to move from Port Moresby to staging areas to begin the march. Company E—except for a detachment assigned to Boice's reconnaissance party—joined the US Ninety-First Engineers in linking up the fragments of existing roads and building new ones to create a coastal highway suitable for jeep and truck traffic.

When Kenney received word of Company E's safe arrival, he "rushed up stairs to MacArthur's office to give him the good news" and asked him to send the remainder of the division by air. MacArthur had already issued orders for the 126th Infantry Regiment to move by ship, and his staff opposed any more air transport, "a little more forcefully this time," Kenney recalled, "afraid this foolishness might get out of hand." Undeterred, a persistent Kenney promised MacArthur that he could deliver the 128th Infantry Regiment "ahead of this gang that goes by boat," and MacArthur agreed to let him try. Kenney quickly rounded up any aircraft he could find that was capable of carrying troops. "All bombers overhauled anywhere in Australia from then on until further notice would assist in hauling troops to New Guinea," Kenney wrote, "and any planes coming in from the United States would be commandeered, civilian ferry crews and all, to help out."[22]

The first planes carrying the 128th Infantry Regiment took off on September 21, and two days later the entire regimental combat team had reached New Guinea. The GIs flew over Australia's Great Barrier Reef, and a few got a glimpse of it. "There were all the colors of the rainbow in the many tiny coral islands," remembered William Thackston.[23] "I wriggled my way to a piece of floor where I could stand right behind the pilot for a bird-eye view of the flight," wrote Lawrence Thayer. "There was a beautiful coral encrusted ocean below, but the pilot's eyes were constantly searching all over the sky for enemy planes."[24]

The beauty of the Great Barrier Reef belied what lay ahead for the regiment on New Guinea. It had entered a war zone. "Rumor had it that Jap patrols had reached the airstrip," recalled Art Kessenich, and "we wondered if we might be fired upon before we got out of the aircraft."[25] Roy Campbell recounted how, as his plane approached the airfield, orders were "to jump from the plane as soon as it stopped, and run for the jungle." Japanese bombers frequently attacked Port Moresby's airfields. "That night they bombed the Air Corps," remembered Herman Owen of his arrival, "and we were just far enough away that we got shook up a little bit, but not any direct bombing right on us."[26]

Soon the 128th Infantry Regiment marched into the jungle, with Papua New Guinean guides in the lead, and took up positions along the Goldie River, near the southern terminus of the Kokoda Track. "The trail wasn't difficult," as Campbell remembered it, "and the line of men looked like a giant snake as it wound up, higher and higher into the mountains."[27] Should the Japanese break through the Australian position on the Imita Ridge, the Red Arrowmen would become one of Port Moresby's last lines of defense.

Fortunately for the newly arrived GIs, the Japanese were no longer marching down the Kokoda Track to meet them. After taking Ioribaiwa on September 16, Horii's advance ground to a halt, and when the Australians counterattacked on September 27, they found Japanese positions at Ioribaiwa abandoned. Ever-increasing supply problems, combined with General Kenney's unceasing air raids on the Japanese column, had exacted a heavy toll. Furthermore, the intensifying battle at Guadalcanal continued to drain Japanese resources away from New Guinea and made any reinforcement of Horii impossible.

While the Japanese situation deteriorated, that of the Australians only improved. They steadily brought reinforcements up the trail—including combat veterans from the Mediterranean—and their communication lines grew shorter. The tide of the fight on the Kokoda Track had turned. Unable to advance any further, Horii retreated toward Buna, with the Australians now in pursuit.

The main body of the 126th Infantry Regiment departed for New Guinea by sea September 18, but their trip took ten days rather than ten hours. At Brisbane, the troops loaded their equipment onto awaiting Liberty Ships, including their trucks and jeeps (plus those of the 128th, which could not be sent by plane), barrels of gasoline, and tons of ammunition. "We worked all night," noted Herbert M. Smith. "It was amazing to me the volume of cargo that a Liberty Ship could hold."[28] Upon landing at Port Moresby on September 28, the 126th Infantry Regiment traveled to Bootless Inlet southeast of town and became the New Guinea Force reserve. "It's pretty hot here," Elvin Ball told his family, "even worse than Louisiana. My nose is very sunburned and has peeled three or four times already."[29] It was so hot, according to Paul Rettell, "we had to get up before daylight to train in the cool of the early morning."[30] Japanese planes appeared often. "I remember a Japanese reconnaissance plane we called 'Photo Charlie' that flew over after dark on many nights," wrote Byron Gibbs. "The search lights of the Australian antiaircraft battery would come on and brightly light the plane which seemed rather low as I could see each rivet in it and could plainly see the pilot wearing the leather helmet inside the canopy."[31] Then the rains set in, turning the camp into a sea of mud.

Whether on the Goldie River, at Bootless Inlet, or while building the coastal highway, the GIs took stock of their strange new environment.

Riding a truck down the newly built road east of Port Moresby, E. J. Kahn passed through a variety of landscapes. "We rolled up and down some of the countless hills," Kahn wrote, "through patches of jungle with vines hanging down to lash at the heads of tourists who forget to duck, through coconut-palm groves and banana plantations, through tall, wavy fields of grass, and past clumps of rubber trees and other vegetation peculiar to this outdoor hothouse."[32] The dense, dark tropical rain forest fascinated the GIs the most. Trees reached heights of more than 150 feet, creating a vast canopy above the dimly lit forest floor. "The roots seemed to start some thirty feet up the tree," recalled Roy Campbell of one massive specimen he inspected, "then curved down to make it look like a huge Christmas stand. The roots went out at angles from the main trunk, creating spaces between where two dozen men could sleep totally hidden from view."[33]

For some soldiers, the palm-lined shores and dense jungles of New Guinea evoked popular culture images of a tropical paradise. For others, the island appeared far more ominous. "As soon as we landed I was looking over those God forsaken jungles," remembered Herman Owen, "and thought, 'Let the Japs have them.'"[34] No jungle creature fascinated the GIs more than the crocodile. Kenneth Springer recounted an incident when he and those on his roadbuilding crew were on break and swimming in a river. "Shortly a man yelled out, 'Crocodile!' The men got out of the water at once [and] there was no more swimming that day."[35] Art Kessenich recalled that "out in the marshlands that surrounded Moresby, some of our goofballs used to hunt crocodiles in native canoes."[36]

Port Moresby was the only place resembling an urban center on the entire island. Though its harbor held immense strategic significance, the GIs arrived to find a bomb-damaged town "with rusty corrugated tin-roofed buildings," recalled Robert Bable, who thought Port Moresby was "surprisingly small considering it was the seat of government and the hub of commerce for the second largest island in the world."[37] Moreover, the town's only residents were Allied military personnel. The Papua New Guinean population lived in small villages, often little more than collections of huts, scattered across the island. In the village of Gabagaba, for example, Bable saw "bamboo-and-palm-frond huts constructed on platforms raised about five-feet above a coral reef." In a seaside village down the road, Bable noted that residents "lived in individual family compounds that were raised on stilts and surrounded by a 15-foot bamboo fence lashed together with bamboo fibers" to protect against the "large man-eating estuary crocodiles."[38] And E. J. Kahn recalled passing through another village composed of "a half-dozen thatched huts on stilts clustered about a relatively substantial church with an English name over its door."[39]

Most American troops arrived in New Guinea without any prior knowledge of the island. Based on images gleaned from popular magazines and movies, they expected to find an island of primitives and cannibals. Upon their arrival, the sight of bare-breasted women and men dressed only in loin cloths reinforced these crude expectations, and a good many GIs never got past the colonial or Hollywood stereotypes. But for many others, interaction with Papua New Guineans quickly challenged their beliefs. "The natives we met at first were very friendly," wrote E. J. Kahn.[40] Elvin Ball reported home that many Papua New Guineans "speak English nearly as good as we do." When the local population did not speak English, the Red Arrowmen could usually communicate through the New Guinea pidgin language spoken across the island, called Tok Pisin. If all else failed, hand gestures usually worked.

Trade quickly flourished between the Papua New Guineans and the American soldiers, often fueled by the GIs' constant search for souvenirs. "I had a chance to buy some beads from one of the natives today," Ball told his family. "They are made out of seashells and are very pretty."[41] The Red Arrowmen also wanted local foods like coconuts and bananas to add some variety to rations. In exchange, bits and pieces of army uniforms, and other kinds of military goods, found their way into the hands of islanders. Papua New Guineans often wanted salt and, perhaps more commonly, tobacco. Kahn recalled that some Papua New Guineans he encountered knew very little English "except for the words 'smoke' and 'cigarette,'" and "as we rode past settlements in our trucks, we tossed cigarettes down to the natives, and they occasionally offered us coconuts in return."[42]

Papua New Guineans, for their part, had mostly positive views of American troops. Trade boosted local economies and people began to produce grass skirts, model canoes, necklaces, and other such trinkets for the GI souvenir market. The GIs also gained a reputation for generosity. In their study of wartime Melanesia, anthropologists Geoffrey White and Lamont Lindstrom found that in many cultures "giving out food, cigarettes, clothing, and military supplies accrued considerable prestige to the givers." Papua New Guineans often thought Americans were friendly and more open than the Australians. Whatever pejorative views some GIs may have held about "the natives," Papua New Guineans often found Americans comparatively kinder and more respectful; more willing to engage in conversation, share food, and offer medical care; and less likely to be violent toward them. American soldiers "had less commitment to maintaining prewar relations of inequality between metropolitans and locals," wrote White and Lindstrom.

Australian authorities fretted about social interactions between GIs and Papua New Guineans.[43] "If you spoil them," an Australian officer warned Alfred Medendorp almost immediately upon his arrival, "they'll expect it every time."[44] Australians sometimes went so far as to confiscate goods Papua New Guineans obtained from Americans to discourage commerce. Later, in February 1943, SWPA would publish a pamphlet titled *You and the Native*, urging soldiers to treat Papua New Guineans kindly and respectfully but also to act as their superiors. "Don't deliberately descend to his level," the authors warned, but "always, without overdoing it, be the master. The time may come when you will want the native to obey you. He won't obey you if you have been in the habit of treating him as an equal."[45]

Almost immediately upon landing on the island, GIs began to experience problems with food and disease that would plague them throughout their time on New Guinea. In a land with little transportation infrastructure at the end of a thousand-mile communication line, and with little ice or refrigeration, the soldiers could only dream of fresh meat and vegetables beyond those purchased from Papua New Guineans. The mainstay of their diet was an Australian concoction called bully beef: minced corned beef and gelatin packed into a tin. Roy Campbell described how he opened a tin, "smelled it, spooned out a bit of fat, greasy meat, tasted it" and declared it "the foulest mess [I have] ever been faced with."[46] Dysentery frequently broke out among the troops, from rations spoiling in the hot sun or poorly washed food obtained from the Papua New Guineans. With no reliable source of treated water, soldiers drank from rivers and streams, using chlorination pills or iodine drops as their only protection against the countless microorganisms swimming in it. Flies swarmed around the camps. Mosquitoes and the diseases they carried, especially malaria, posed the greatest threat of all. The GIs slept under mosquito bars when possible, but during the day they were exposed to the multitudinous stinging pests. Quinine pills offered some protection from malaria, but the troops hated them. "I . . . still have a bitter taste in my mouth," wrote Elvin Ball after taking a dose, "but it's better than a case of malaria."[47]

With Port Moresby out of immediate danger, MacArthur unveiled a plan to push the Japanese out of Papua. Adopted on October 1, it was largely a revision of his earlier plan to halt the Japanese advance, adapted to the evolving situation. MacArthur envisioned a three-pronged convergence on Buna. First, the Australians would continue driving the Japanese over the Kokoda Track toward Buna. Second, a combat team built around the 126th Infantry Regiment would cross the Owen Stanley Range, secure the Kumusi River valley between Jaure and Wairopi, and harass the Japanese communication line between the Kokoda Track and Buna. Third, Allied forces would secure the north coast of the Papuan Peninsula. The Australians were to take Goodenough Island in the D'Entrecasteaux chain that paralleled the coast. Then—somehow—the 128th Infantry Regiment would secure the coastline south and east of Buna. All three forces would then converge on Buna and drive the Japanese from the peninsula.

How to get the 126th Infantry Regiment across the Owen Stanley Range remained a question, but as MacArthur planned his counterattack, the reconnaissance reports on the two tracks across the mountains came in. Colonel Sverdrup concluded that the Abau Track was impractical for moving large bodies of troops. Reports from the Kapa Kapa Track, by contrast, were positive. Captain Boice's patrol arrived at Jaure on October 3, finding no sign of the Japanese. "The trail is well defined all the way," one patrol report stated, and "getting lost is next to impossible in the day time." The mountaintop village of Laruni, just before the crest of the range, and Jaure at the trail terminus, offered good spots for resupply by airdrop. Jaure, Boice believed, might even host an airfield. The patrol conceded that the track was "difficult in spots," but stated that modest engineering improvements could facilitate movement. Reports also suggested that the challenge of crossing the crest of the mountains "has been overestimated." The patrol reported few problems with mosquitoes, particularly at higher elevations, but noted that "villages are flea infected" and that soldiers should keep out of them. "There should be ample first-aid facilities along the track," Boice wrote, and suggested that "kitchens could be set up along the track to feed [the soldiers] en route." He advised the marchers to cut the weight of their packs to the bare minimum (sweaters and blankets for the higher elevations could be dropped at Laruni) and that hobnail boots would be best for the wet and rugged pathway, asserting that "rubber heels are of no value." "Do not plan on parties moving against traffic unless vitally necessary," Boice advised. "These tracks are one-way."[48]

The Australians still warned that the Kapa Kapa Track was impractical. But to MacArthur's staff in Brisbane—relying on two-dimensional maps, ignorant of the New Guinea interior, and anxious to attack the Japanese (not to mention eager to secure a victory before the Marines at Guadal-canal)—the Kapa Kapa Track looked promising, and based on the Boice patrol reports, New Guinea Force authorized the 126th Infantry Regiment to proceed over it. By early October the Company E roadbuilding crew had established a camp at the base of the track, on the grounds of a rubber plantation near the village of Kalikodobu, six miles inland from Gabagaba. The Michigan soldiers, proud and homesick and unsure how to pronounce Kalikodobu, called their base camp "Kalamazoo." There, the Second Battalion gathered to ascend the Kapa Kapa Track. Leading the way were roughly 250 soldiers from the 126th's antitank and cannon companies under the command of Captain Medendorp, accompanied by one hundred Papua New Guinean workers (and their ANGAU overseers) who would carry supplies. The Medendorp Force was to identify drop zones and river crossings, establish supply and medical bases, and be on the lookout for any Japanese presence. Medendorp departed Kalamazoo on October 6. He reached Laruni on October 13, established a drop zone, then pressed on, crossing the crest of the Owen Stanley Range and arriving at Jaure on October 20.

The Second Battalion began its climb on October 14. Company E, the "spearhead of the spearhead of the spearhead," went first, with the other companies of the battalion departing at one-day intervals. The battalion commander, Colonel Henry A. Geerds, was a forty-eight-year-old Great War veteran from Holland, Michigan. He suffered a heart attack three days out, so Colonel Quinn dispatched the regimental executive officer,

Major Herbert M. Smith, into the jungle to catch up and take command. Engineers and medical personnel—the Nineteenth Portable Hospital, as well as twenty medics from Company A of 107th Medical Battalion—accompanied the march. So did a chaplain, Father Stephen J. Dzienis. The battalion traveled as lightly as possible, although the marchers carried rifles, machine guns, and mortars as they marched into the unknown and toward the Japanese.

The trek across the Owen Stanley mountains took the Red Arrowmen across territory as remote and forbidding as any in the world. "Nothing in their training," claimed journalist James Campbell, "no twenty-five-mile hike through the tablelands of Australia, no Louisiana Maneuvers . . . could have prepared them for the strain of it."[49] The first days out were deceptively easy. "The trail was beautiful," Alfred Medendorp later reflected, "and the hills were not too high."[50] Most of the trail passed through dense jungle, which shaded the marchers from the blistering sun, and through open grasslands. They crossed numerous rivers, some too wide and fast to wade through. "Those that could swim took off their clothes and equipment," Medendorp wrote of one difficult crossing, and "placed them in a native canoe," then "swam across the swift and treacherous stream. It took a strong swimmer. By dark everybody was over."[51]

As the Red Arrow troops reached the Owen Stanleys, however, the topography became increasingly rugged and varied. "The hills reached up into the clouds, then dipped down into the valleys, where we could sometimes see the clouds high above masking the top of the next hill," Medendorp wrote.[52] Captain Bernard Friedenthal, commander of the Nineteenth Portable Hospital, described "a typical day's march":

> We started the day climbing a steep hill. . . . In climbing these hills we found it necessary to stop every five minutes or so for what we called "breathers". This consisted of a 10 or 15 second break for the purpose of getting our breath. Our marching breaks were taken at about 40–50 minute intervals and were for 10 minutes. We found as the days progressed that the number of our breaks became more frequent and for longer periods. . . . After reaching the top, often after climbing 1000–2000 feet, we marched along a ridge for about 1–2 hours. The walking was difficult because of the many roots on the trail. . . .

We had to keep our eyes glued to the track. After the ridge came the descent which often was more hazardous than the ascent. There was plenty of slipping, sliding, and falling. . . . But the most disheartening factor was that after climbing and descending we would begin another climb.[53]

Every now and then, wrote Herbert M. Smith, "the trail would break out of the jungle clutter on to a bare rock outcropping," from which "we could count ridge after ridge of jungle" through which they yet had to cross. Smith thought it "awesome" and "terrifying" to be in such a "huge, unmapped wilderness."[54] In some places, the trail was so narrow that the soldiers had to walk single file. At times, wrote Paul Lutjens, "the company would be stretched out over two or three miles."[55] Progress was slow. "Sometimes in twelve hours marching we would make three miles," remembered Herman Bottcher, "some days only a mile."[56]

The rugged landscape was only part of the problem. The jungle vegetation contained all manner of misery-inducing plants. Kunai grass cut and stung. Clouds of insects—fleas, chiggers, and mosquitoes—harried them constantly. "We all were full of fleas," remembered Alfred Medendorp, and "singing blankets and hunting through the seams of our clothing was all commonplace."[57] The riverbanks and muddy ground were a haven for leeches. "The best procedure to get rid of them," wrote medic Kenneth Springer, "was to place a lighted cigarette against the creature and it would drop off."[58] The terrific heat caused the troops to perspire almost constantly, contributing to overpowering thirst. Desperate marchers drank from rivers and streams, sometimes careless about water purification. Rain came "every afternoon almost without fail," Medendorp remembered. "Clouds from the sea piled up against the mountains all during the day, and as they cooled with the lowering sun, the rain fell."[59] But, rather than offer relief from the heat, the rain made the trail slick and muddy, compounding the soldiers' misery. "All you could see was the mud and the guy's feet ahead of you," recalled Lutjens.[60] "Once in a while when we got muddy we'd just jump into a stream and wash what we had on," recalled Francis Walden.[61]

Each day began and ended with meals, and sustenance was a constant concern. The marchers departed with rations for six days, which Paul Lutjens recorded as "one pound of rice, one handful of green tea, a little sugar and two cans of bully beef."[62] But for active young men on a grueling trek, it was not nearly enough. The bully beef was sometimes spoiled or laced with maggots. Because of the late-day rains, they had a hard time starting fires for cooking. "Our matches were usually wet," remembered Francis Walden, "so we had to find a dry spot on our uniform, then rub the heads of the matches real easy until they were dry enough to strike."[63] Sometimes the marchers simply ate their meal uncooked. Food supplies quickly dwindled, and when camped, the soldiers talked excitedly and longingly about food. "We discussed what we had at Christmas two years ago, and every other kind of meal imaginable," recalled Lutjens, and "we'd lie there and think if we ever came back we'd devote the rest of our lives to eating."[64]

Beset with hunger, heat, rain, and insects, the marchers struggled to carry their packs. "Our packs weighed fifty pounds apiece when we started," said Herman Bottcher, but after being soaked with days of rain "they must have weighed twice that much."[65] The GIs solved the problem by jettisoning unneeded or unwanted items. "The trail was strewn with cast off articles," Medendorp observed. "Leather toilet sets, soap, socks, towels and extra underwear told a tale of exhaustion and misery."[66] The Papua New Guinean carriers bore the heaviest loads. In addition to hauling supplies, the carriers taught the Americans how to survive in the jungle mountains. "The natives showed us how to find dry wood by sounding trees," said Herman Bottcher, "and from then on we managed a little better." Carriers also helped the soldiers find foods to supplement their meager rations. "The natives would bring in some squash and green bananas," Bottcher recalled. "We roasted these in a fire, and I remember one of the fellows saying, 'Boy this sure is good! When I get home, I'm going to go on a picnic and roast squash.'"[67]

The Papua New Guinean carriers on the Kapa Kapa Track suffered every bit as much as the soldiers. "Our natives sweated under their loads," wrote Alfred Medendorp. "Their shoulders became sore, and their legs and feet were cut and bruised." Unrest brewed amongst them. Papua New Guineans of one ethnic group were reluctant to pass into the territory of another. "These natives were coastal people," observed Medendorp, "and they were getting more and more nervous as we got into the hills." He also noted that "as far as they were concerned, we were marching straight into starvation." The harsh treatment of ANGAU overseers made their conditions even more miserable. "An Australian sergeant was arranging the loads for . . . twenty natives," Medendorp noted one day, when "for some offense he cuffed two of them smartly," then explained: "You gotta treat them with a firm 'and or they'll run all over you." Many Papua New Guinean carriers fled at the first opportunity. One night Medendorp was "awakened by a wild pattering of feet and a crashing headlong into the brush," then "a frightened shriek" that "sounded through the night." In the morning he learned that a band of escaping carriers had caused the commotion. The ANGAU overseer "was angry because our guards had not shot the deserters," Medendorp wrote, but "I had given no orders to shoot runaway natives, and would have been reluctant to do so anyhow." In subsequent days more carriers fled, "plac[ing] us in a desperate situation," Medendorp conceded. "We were almost entirely on our own, and all the rations the troops had was what they were carrying in their packs." He reluctantly gave the order to shoot any further deserters, but "eight more faded into the jungle the next night."[68]

Dysentery ravaged the column. As Stanley Jastrzembski recalled, "I had 'jungle guts' so bad I could scrape the crap off my legs with a tin ration can. Some guys had to go thirty times a day and all that came out was blood." Some marchers simply cut out the seats of their pants so that their frequent bowel movements did not slow them down as they plodded forward. Malaria was common, too. Jastrzembski noted that "the guys with quinine pills were popping them like gumballs," and as the march went on supplies of the drug ran low.[69] Physical injuries abounded as well: sprained ankles, cuts and bruises, and blistered feet that quickly became infected. Troops suffered from pure exhaustion. "We walked as much as 14 hours a day," Earl Anderson wrote in a letter home. "We got so tired it just seemed impossible to take another step."[70] Medendorp wrote that "stragglers were left panting along the trail," and he recalled one soldier "who could sometimes only moan when his buddies roused him from the rest periods to go on. His gaunt and tired face haunts me. He traveled for days on courage alone." For the Papua New Guinean carriers, the sick and injured added yet another burden.[71]

Medics patrolled the line of marchers and set up aid stations along the way. Evacuating sick or injured soldiers to the rear was only possible at the very beginning of the trek, and by the time they were a few days into the march, as Russell Buys put it, "It was walk or die."[72] Medics rounded up stragglers and brought them into bivouac areas. "They came in at night with their flock of 'cripples.'" wrote Medendorp. "Sometimes they took care of those stragglers all night. They made camp and cooked not only for themselves, but for their patients." Medical personnel worked around the clock, "helping the sick, bandaging sores (especially on feet), and encouraging the exhausted. It was no easy job," Medendorp wrote. He conceded that "we infantry had it hard crossing the mountains on the hellish trail, but the medics had it harder."[73]

For most of the trek, the only way to receive additional food, medicine, and other supplies was from C-47 cargo planes that dropped supplies along the trail. The marchers laid out identification panels to mark their location. When the pilot flying overhead spotted the panels, crewmen (often Red Arrow band members and service troops) kicked the packages out of the plane's side doors. The GIs on the ground then scrambled to locate them. The sound of a C-47 was a welcome one. "Whenever we heard a transport," claimed Paul Lutjens, "our mouths began to water."[74] The planes dropped a lot of bully beef and rice and occasionally a few luxuries. "The greatest treats," Herman Bottcher noted, was "the few times when the planes dropped B-ration chocolate bars."[75] But there were few open spaces in the thick rainforest to use as drop zones. In addition, airdrops were a new thing in warfare and Kenney's airmen experimented with the best elevation from which to release the goods. "Dropping from a low enough altitude to ensure accuracy imparted such a velocity to the bundles that they were smashed upon landing," noted one report, but "dropping from a high altitude in the very broken mountainous terrain resulted in bundles going over a sharp ridge or into the jungle and not being recovered at all." The air crews found that "dropping from four to five hundred feet gave the best results," although "an average of fifty per cent loss was still encountered."[76] Stormy weather and Japanese air activity frequently prevented the C-47s from delivering supplies at all.

As the trek dragged on, the marchers took on an ever more bedraggled appearance. Their uniforms wore away to little more than rags, their shoes and boots disintegrated in the sodden environment, and the marchers lost weight. Paul Lutjens remembered, "All the men were gaunt. We were down to a shadow. Our eyes were sunk deep in our heads. We looked like a bunch of wolves."[77]

It came as a great relief when they reached the supply base at Laruni, thirty air miles north of Kalikodobu, at an elevation of six thousand feet. The village was located on the top of a hill, near a large and barren slope that offered an ideal drop zone. Cargo planes rained down packages and, according to Herbert M. Smith, Laruni soon had "a well-stocked inventory."[78] Soldiers received food, medicine, new uniforms, blankets, sweaters, and even mail. Perhaps most importantly, Laruni meant a few days' rest. Those unable to continue stayed at Laruni to operate the supply base. Medendorp's second in command, Captain Roger Keast—a star athlete at Michigan State University before the war—sprained his knee a week into the trek. "His march over the mountains was an epic in endurance and fortitude," Medendorp wrote admiringly. "Often in the night I would hear Keast cry out in pain, whenever he moved in his sleep."[79] Medendorp placed him in command of the supply base until he was able to continue the march.

Upon leaving Laruni, the Red Arrow troops headed into the most difficult portion of the march: crossing the crest of the Owen Stanley Range beneath Mount Suwemalla, which the GIs ominously dubbed the Ghost Mountain. "On the morning of the second day from the dropping zone we found ourselves confronted by the dreaded 'Ghost Mountain,'" Alfred Medendorp wrote:

> It towered high in the clouds before us. We got an early start and tackled it. This was the worst day's march of the entire trip. Until the middle of the afternoon we climbed grasping with our hands and digging with our toes, then for four more hours skidded downward on our [heels] and the seats of our pants. At one place we right-stepped over the face of a stone cliff with our bellies pressed against the stone and our arms outstretched like Moses in prayer so that we could get a grip without pushing ourselves outward and off balance. It is still a miracle to me that all of our men got over that point safely.[80]

Constant rain added misery and danger. "I think the day we went over the mountain it rained for eighteen straight hours," recalled Francis Walden, "a slow, steady drizzle" so cold that "we could see our breath."[81] The cold rain was especially brutal for the Papua New Guinean carriers, who marched barefoot and bare-chested. Eventually, the marchers reached an elevation of more than nine thousand feet. "We would walk along a hog's back," recalled Paul Lutjens, "straddling the trail, with a sheer drop of thousands of feet two feet on either side of us."[82] Exactly when the troops crossed the divide they did not know. "There was no signpost," wrote Herbert M. Smith, and "if there had been, we would have burned it to keep warm."[83]

Soon after descending the divide the Red Arrowmen entered a cloud forest, an unusual climactic zone found only in high elevations in the tropics. Here the Red Arrowmen were awestruck by the strange scenes that appeared before them. "The trees were enormous and grew close together," wrote Herbert M. Smith, "their limbs were nearly hidden by vines, vines more profuse than anywhere draped by more vines; moss covered the tree trunks, boulders, and any other available area."[84] Indeed, moss defined the environment. "The trees and vines were everywhere covered with a greyish brown moss," noted Alfred Medendorp, and "no bark could be seen anywhere; there was no grass, no earth showing, everywhere moss."[85] It not only covered the trees but also blanketed the forest floor. "We could thrust a stick six feet down through the spongy stuff we were walking on without hitting anything real solid," recalled Paul Lutjens.[86]

Rain frequently pelted the marchers in the cloud forest, and the persistent fog condensed on the trees and the moss. "Between showers we could hear a constant drip of water off the spongy moss overhead," wrote Alfred Medendorp. Paul Lutjens recalled an eerie muffled silence and noticed that "there wasn't a sign of life. Not a bird. Not a fly. Not a sound. It was the strangest feeling I ever had. If we stopped, we froze. If we moved, we sweated."[87] According to Herbert M. Smith, "there was a ghostly semidarkness glow punctuated by an eerie phosphoresce, which added to the spookiness."[88] Despite their sickness and weariness, many found Mount Suwemalla mesmerizing, though most were just glad to have passed. "The men were too exhausted to build fires after crossing this mountain," recalled Medendorp. "They ate their rations cold, and crawled under a shelter half to get out of the rain." According to Medendorp, they nevertheless felt a sense of accomplishment.[89] "We were over the Owen Stanley Range," he explained, "and easier marching lay ahead—also the Japs."[90]

The march did not get easier, though—at least not immediately. "We were happy to be going down the mountain," wrote Herbert M. Smith, but he found that the descent "was more difficult as well as more dangerous," as "a slip in the mud here meant the speed would be increased" and "controlling the fall more difficult and chances of being torn by the briars and needles at trail side much increased."[91] As the Red Arrowmen headed down the mountain, the temperature rose and they began to encounter villages again. Medendorp regularly asked the people in the villages they passed through if they knew where Japanese troops were located. "In every case," he wrote, "the answer was 'Plenty far', with hand gestures to indicate distance." Medendorp was careful to maintain good relations with the villagers they encountered. "It would be a simple matter for them to tell the Japs of our whereabouts," Medendorp believed, "and it was our hope that we could make friends with them so that they could tell us where the Japs were."[92]

The marchers pressed on to Jaure, and the miseries of the Kapa Kapa Track continued. "Our strength is about gone," wrote Paul Lutjens. "Most of us have dysentery. Boys are falling out and dropping back with fever. Continuous downpour of rain. It's hard to cook our rice and tea. Bully beef makes us sick. We seem to climb straight up for hours, then down again. God, will it ever end?"[93]

Jaure marked the end of the Kapa Kapa Track. Herbert M. Smith thought Jaure a "metropolis" compared to the villages and wilderness they had passed through along the track, "with a drop ground, ample bivouac area, food and limited equipment supply."[94] As Herman Bottcher remembered, "We made our first comfortable camp, and the natives gathered coconuts, green bananas, squash, taro roots, sugar cane, paw-paws, [and] limes." One officer even shot "a scrawny wild pig" and as Bottcher described it, "we had an orgy of eating" while the Papua New Guinean carriers "stayed up all night, dancing and beating their tom-toms."[95] The Jaure interlude was brief. Within days, Medendorp led his force—now dubbed the Wairopi Force and down to 190 effectives—to the northwest into the Kumusi River valley toward Wairopi. Smith's Second Battalion headed northeast to Natunga, in a two-day march through the belt of mountains called the Hydrographers Range, to establish a base camp and staging area for the coming assault on Buna. Smith reached Natunga on November 2. "A campsite was laid out," Smith wrote, "a camp guard was established and the battalion was given a few days to rest and relax, which I am certain they appreciated."[96]

Medendorp's force and the Second Battalion had gone through one of the most difficult noncombat trials of World War II. Hanson Baldwin of the *New York Times* called it "one of the great marches of American history."[97] It was also a terrible mistake. "The fiasco of the Kapa Kapa Track," wrote historian Lida Mayo, "stemmed from impatience and ignorance." Captain Boice's wildly optimistic reports of the trail's suitability for moving troops, Mayo argued, were "probably inspired by the urge—common in all armies—to tell generals what they wanted to hear" and the "generals had believed it because they wanted to believe it."[98] Alfred Medendorp called the trek "a futile task well done."[99] Disease, malnutrition, and pure exhaustion diminished the participants' fighting effectiveness as they closed in on the Japanese. Some battled its effects for the remainder of their lives. Perhaps miraculously, only two soldiers perished. "Dysentery and fever," wrote Paul Lutjens in his notebook about one of those who died. "A damn good man. The trip was a little too much for him."[100]

As the Medendorp Force and the Second Battalion of the 126th Infantry Regiment struggled on the Kapa Kapa Track, the 128th Infantry Regiment began its move to the north shore of the island. Getting them there posed great challenges too. Japanese planes patrolled the coastline, threatening any Allied ships venturing into those waters. MacArthur had no fighter bases on that side of the Owen Stanleys, so any Allied planes that came up to challenge Japanese air power had to operate out of airfields south of the mountains, limiting their range and effectiveness. In addition, the waters off the Papuan Peninsula were largely uncharted and strewn with dangerous coral reefs. Experienced navigators in shallow-draft ships could slowly make their way through the treacherous waters, but the larger ships that would be needed to sustain a military campaign risked running aground or having their hulls ripped open on the jagged reefs. Limited resources and interservice rivalry further handcuffed MacArthur. The navy was focused on Guadalcanal and dispatched vessels to SWPA reluctantly and parsimoniously. Admiral Carpender, MacArthur's naval commander, hesitated to send his limited number of ships north of Milne Bay at all.

MacArthur simply did not have enough water transportation to take the Thirty-Second Division to Buna by sea, the combat ships to protect them, or the landing craft to stage an amphibious assault.

Once again, General Kenney's planes offered a solution. A few months earlier, in July 1942, the Australians had carved a crude airstrip in the jungle near Wanigela Mission, at the base of Cape Nelson on Collingwood Bay, eighty miles southeast of Buna. Beginning on October 5, a detachment of US and Australian troops flew into Wanigela and began improving the airstrip and building a wharf along the nearby shore to bring in supplies by sea, while the Australian navy charted a route through the reefs. In about a week the Allies had an airfield capable of handling C-47s, and MacArthur ordered the 128th Infantry Regiment—the first to fly to New Guinea the month before—to be airlifted to Wanigela. Joining them was the Australian 2/6 Independent Company, a commando unit trained in jungle warfare. The first C-47s took off from Port Moresby on October 14 and the airlift ended four days later. "We flew over the mountains so low, the wingtips appeared to shake the top of the trees," Marvin Langetieg said.[101] As they prepared to land at Wanigela, "the plane nosed down at a steep angle," remembered Roy Campbell, and "seemed to be diving into the ground." The plane then "flattened the descent and soft-landed in what had been a field of kunai grass" stopping "just yards from the trees." After disembarking, the soldiers watched the planes lift off to return to Port Moresby. "A different feeling came over the men," Campbell recalled. "They knew now that they were on the Japanese side of the line and there was nowhere to go but war and hell."[102]

The troops at Wanigela became known as the Hat Force. They came under the command of General MacNider (Colonel Tracy Hale, commanding officer of the 128th Infantry Regiment, was livid about being passed over for the job). MacNider's mission was to build up sufficient troops, establish resupply bases, and move on Buna. From Wanigela, MacNider planned to march to Pongani Mission, fifty miles up the coast and thirty miles from Buna, and there prepare a marshalling area for the attack. Intelligence indicated an inland trail from Wanigela to Pongani across the neck of Cape Nelson. The lightly armed Australian 2/6 Independent Company led the way, starting out on October 14. The Third Battalion of the 128th, under Lieutenant Colonel Kelsie E. Miller, followed the next day. "We slogged through dense jungle," wrote James Kincaid, "seeing only glimpses of sunshine at a time through the overhanging canopy of trees" and "fields of shoulder high kunai grass which was sharp enough to slice skin."[103] Marvin Langetieg remembered crossing rivers nearly every day and that some watercourses were "so swift we'd have to form a line of men hanging on the other one to get across." Langetieg did not know how to swim, but that didn't matter much "because, with all that equipment over your head, it's not like there was much of a chance of swimming anyway."[104]

Hat Force increasingly received materiel deliveries by sea thanks to the Combined Operational Service Command (COSC), a joint Australian-American logistical organization. The successful Australian invasion of Goodenough Island on October 22–23 gave the Allied ships a little more security, but the uncharted shoals still limited the size of vessels that could move along the coast. To ship goods to Wanigela, the Red Arrow depended on one of the most unusual outfits in the US Army—the Small Ships Section of COSC, founded by two maritime adventurers and brothers from New York, Adam Bruce and John Sheridan Fahnestock. The pair had gained fame with their 1938 book *Stars to Windward*, which described their 1934–1937 voyage across the Pacific, sailing from French Polynesia to New Guinea and then on to China, collecting specimens for New York's Museum of Natural History. The book led to another South Pacific expedition in 1940, and then a third to the Dutch East Indies the following year.[105]

With the onset of the war, the Fahnestocks' knowledge of Pacific waters, as well as their maritime connections in the region, proved invaluable to the Allies. Bruce and Sheridan Fahnestock each received US Army commissions—Bruce as a lieutenant and Sheridan as captain—as did many of their closest associates, a group known as "the Originals." The brothers scoured the ports of Australia, New Zealand, and the South Pacific, and soon acquired a diverse array of vessels, including fishing trawlers, freighters, pleasure craft, tugboats, and even captured Japanese barges. Though the ships were technically commissioned by the US Army, the Fahnestocks hired civilians to operate them, including many Dutch and Filipinos, but mostly Australians. "Adventurers, chronic jobless, charlatans [and] bums, filled applications," recalled Ladislaw Reday, one of the Originals, "along with patriotic ex-engineers, skippers and mates wanting to fight for the cause."[106] The drive toward Buna was the first major operation for the

Small Ships Section, and as more and more Red Arrow troops arrived at Wanigela by air, the ragtag fleet gathered at Milne Bay to sustain them.

On October 15 two of the small ships, the *King John* and the *Timoshenko*, departed Milne Bay for Wanigela. On the trip was Bruce Fahnestock and the Thirty-Second Division quartermaster, Lieutenant Colonel Laurence A. McKenny of the Michigan National Guard. Arriving the next morning, Fahnestock and McKenny expected simply to unload their goods and return to Milne Bay, but they found that their mission had changed. They were now to carry infantrymen—and all the way to Pongani. The reason for this change was MacNider's realization that the overland route was not as simple as it first appeared. The Australian commandos had successfully reached Pongani as planned, but the Third Battalion—larger and more heavily laden—experienced insuperable problems. When Miller reached the banks of the Musa River on October 16, he found it swollen and flowing brisky. Unable to cross, Miller set up camp in what he called "the most filthy, swampy, mosquito infested area we were to cope with in all of our New Guinea experiences." The troops then built a twenty-man raft out of local materials, but patrols could find no discernible trail on the far bank. Next, engineers proposed a 350-foot bridge at a point farther downstream. Planes dropped steel cable for the bridge, but as Miller recalled, "no clamps, tools, or tie wire were included" in the delivery. The engineers made do with what they had, and according to one report their bridge was "90% complete" when word came that the trail further down the line was under seven feet of water and impassable. Stymied in each attempt to cross the Musa, Miller marched his men northward to the mouth of the river at the coastal village of Gobe, where they awaited the Small Ships Section to transport them to Pongani.[107] The remainder of the regiment would travel by boat as well.

The seaborne movement began on the afternoon of October 17, when the *King John* and the *Timoshenko* took on one hundred GIs and shoved off for Pongani, sailing through the night to avoid being sighted by Japanese planes. Joining Fahnestock and McKenny on the voyage was Byron Darnton of the *New York Times*, a reporter after more than just a good scoop. Originally from Adrian, Michigan, Darnton fought with the Thirty-Second Division during World War I and was anxious to see his old unit go back into battle. The *King John* and the *Timoshenko* chugged their way up the palm-lined coast as dawn broke. They arrived at Pongani just before 8:00 a.m., but as passengers and crews prepared to move ashore, an airplane appeared in the distance. Tensions rose aboard the ships as the unidentified plane drew closer, and Darnton wrote in his notebook the question on everyone's mind: "Ours, or theirs?" It was an American B-25 bomber, but its pilot and crew were unaware that friendly forces had moved into the area, and mistaking the small ships for Japanese, they attacked. The first two bombs missed. Machine-gun crews on the ships opened up on the plane. The B-25 then looped around and dropped two more bombs, hitting the *King John* before flying off. The friendly fire attack wounded eighteen and killed two: Fahnestock and Darnton. McKenny, slightly wounded, soldiered on, offloading the vessels and setting up the base. Despite the tragedy, the seaborne movement of the Hat Force continued. McKenny established a chain of makeshift ports along the coast and shuttled increasing loads of men and materiel to Pongani.

By the first week of November, Allied forces were across the Owen Stanley Range. The Australians continued their relentless drive northward, driving the Japanese back toward Buna. The bulk of the 128th Infantry Regiment was camped at Pongani and surrounding villages, sustained with a tenuous but functioning supply line, and in liaison with Major Herbert M. Smith's Second Battalion of the 126th Infantry Regiment at Natunga, less than twenty miles to the west. Captain Medendorp's Wairopi Force occupied the Kumusi Valley.

It was at this time that Major Smith's Second Battalion witnessed a tragedy that shook the entire 126th Infantry Regiment—the death of its commander, Colonel Lawrence Quinn. On November 5, three planes appeared over Natunga to drop supplies. By this time crews had begun attaching parachutes to the cargo packages to slow their descent. "When the lead plane circled our panels," wrote Herbert M. Smith, "a parachute billowed out of the cargo door dragging a very heavy machine gun repair kit." Unfortunately, the chute wrapped around the plane's tail. Smith remembered that the aircraft "lurched and it appeared that the pilot had regained control," but then "nose-dived into a hillside near the camp." All nine aboard were killed, including Quinn, who was observing supply

Pongani Village, where the Red Arrow gathered and prepared for its attack on the Japanese at Buna. WHI IMAGE ID 45243

operations. Smith's soldiers salvaged what supplies they could from the wreckage and prepared a cemetery for the dead. Colonel Clarence Tomlinson, the Third Battalion commander, assumed command of the regiment.

With the successful aerial movement of the 128th Infantry Regiment to the north shore of the island, MacArthur authorized the First and Third Battalions of the 126th Infantry Regiment to be flown over as well. Troops at Pongani had constructed a new landing strip there, allowing the 126th to fly directly to the marshalling area. Once the First and Third Battalions landed at Pongani, MacArthur wanted them to march to a new marshalling area at Bofu, thirty miles away in the foothills of the Hydrographers Range. The regiment's Second Battalion, ten miles south of Bofu at Natunga, was to pack up and join them there.

The airlift of the remaining 126th Infantry Regiment personnel began on November 8, with the First Battalion in the lead.[108] Pongani was deluged with rain that day, leaving its new airfield inoperable, so the first planeloads—three companies and portions of two more, as well as the battalion commander, Lieutenant Colonel Edmund J. Carrier—landed at another recently built airstrip called Abel's Field, on the upper reaches of

Red Arrowmen offload equipment at Pongani. Because New Guinea had few roads or port facilities, soldiers found it challenging to transport equipment and supplies to the battle area. WHI IMAGE ID 45242

the Musa River near the village of Fasari. For the 590 men under Carrier's command, that meant a forty-five-mile jungle march just to get to Pongani, then another thirty to Bofu. The rest of the First Battalion, as well as the Third, landed at the Pongani airfield beginning on November 9. Like the Kapa Kapa veterans and Colonel Miller's Third Battalion of the 128th before them, the First and Third Battalions of the 126th quickly came to appreciate the rigors of the jungle while en route to Bofu. Paul Rettell compared the hot, steamy jungle to a sauna, but one with "vile odors [and] the stench of rotting wood and growth." He also remarked on "fleas, biting ants, chiggers, poisonous spiders, and brilliantly colored enormous insects, that just love to feast on you." Rettell called the jungle "hell on earth. I had a hard time convincing myself how a human being would be subject to such torture."[109] Conrad Drescher offered perhaps a more poetic take:

> Despite all these hardships we endured we were able to enjoy the beauties of the deep steaming jungles, great hanging vines that hung from great 100 ft tall eucalyptus trees, aireal [sic] roots that hung [from] the great trees many feet in the air, beautiful waterfalls, native villages, and an occasional . . . hibiscus bush and orchids. These things all helped make our swollen feet sweat soaked clothing and complete fatigue indurable [sic].[110]

As the Red Arrow got into position, the Australians continued their advance down the Kokoda Track. By the end of October, they had pushed their way back across the crest of the mountains; but when they reached the north slope, they met intensified Japanese resistance. General Horii conducted a holding action, buying time to allow the bulk of his forces to reach Buna, receive reinforcements, and build up defenses around the Buna perimeter. As the Australian advance slowed, MacArthur renewed his criticism of Australian fighting prowess. Blamey, succumbing to Mac-Arthur's pressure, replaced General Allen as head of the Seventh Division with Major General George A. Vasey. Despite dogged Japanese opposition, the Australians pressed forward. They recaptured Kokoda on November 2, in an achievement that was more than symbolic. Improvements to the airstrip there allowed C-47s to bring in food and weapons without having to lug them over the wet and winding overland track. Heavy fighting broke out at Oivi and Gorari two days later and lasted more than a week. As the Australians drove toward the Kumusi River, ragged and starved Japanese troops pulled back across it toward Buna. Allied planes had destroyed the bridges across the river, making the crossing difficult. Late in November, General Horii drowned in the Kumusi when his raft overturned and the raging waters carried his body away. He was never seen again.

On November 6, as Allied forces closed in on Buna, MacArthur moved from Brisbane to Port Moresby. He took over the Government House, the home of the Australian colonial governor. Set among swaying palms and overlooking the harbor, the airy one-story building featured a wide veranda, screened in to keep out the mosquitoes. Complete with colorful gardens and indoor plumbing, the house was the most luxurious structure on the island. To MacArthur's subordinates, it became known as the "Ivory Tower."

On November 13, Harding moved his headquarters to Mendaropu, a small village on a hill overlooking the Solomon Sea near Pongani. Among those accompanying Harding was a new member of his staff, Major Philip F. La Follette, the former three-term governor of Wisconsin.[111] La Follette relished being with Wisconsin troops. "I know some of them by name [and] many more by their home towns," he wrote to his brother, Senator Robert M. La Follette Jr., shortly before departing for New Guinea.[112] However, Philip La Follette failed to impress at headquarters.

Soldiers of the 107th Medical Battalion board a transport plane at Port Moresby bound for the battle zone, November 1942. US ARMY SIGNAL CORPS

E. J. Kahn wrote that when La Follette learned he was headed for combat, he "gulped" and "one sensed that he would rather take his chances on swimming back to Australia, crocodiles or no crocodiles." Kahn dismissed La Follette as "inept" and quipped that he made "most deskbound officers look like Tarzan."[113] After just one day in New Guinea, La Follette received orders to return to Brisbane.[114]

Meanwhile, the camp at Bofu grew as the 126th Infantry Regiment filtered in. MacNider's Hat Force pushed northward from Pongani along the coast. The First Battalion of the 128th Infantry Regiment reached Oro Bay on November 11, where Red Arrow engineers began construction on wharves where ships could bring in supplies. By November 14 the battalion reached Embogo—less than ten miles from the Japanese lines. Patrols fanned out to locate trails and scout Japanese positions.

Harding was anxious to attack Buna and urged an early November strike. Morale was high in the Red Arrow, and Harding believed his troops were ready. The rainy season was just getting underway, and Harding worried wet weather would make field operations more difficult the longer the Allies waited. He also thought that after the exhausting Kokoda Track campaign, the Japanese would not be able to put up much of a fight. "Things look pretty favorable now for a quick conquest," Harding told Sutherland, arguing that Buna would be "easy pickings." General Kenney concurred with Harding's assessment. But Blamey rejected the proposal (MacArthur concurred with Blamey) and ordered Harding to wait for the Australians to cross the Kumusi before advancing. The decision led to an explosion of anger at Harding's headquarters, where accusations of alliance politics flew hotly. Blamey "naturally wanted to see his Australians get in for the kill," wrote Kenney, and "he probably thought they had earned something besides watching the Americans rush in and reap the glory."[115]

In truth, there were good reasons to wait. The Allied supply line remained tenuous. Until MacArthur could build more airfields on the north shore of the island, the operation depended either on airdrops or the limited capacity of the Small Ships Section, which was vulnerable to Japanese interdiction. Even once the airfields became operational, planes could not carry heavy equipment like trucks and tanks. To bring in heavier weapons, not to mention the sheer volume of supplies needed to sustain a major combat operation, the seaborne supply link needed bigger ships and better docking facilities. Allied commanders did not even know how many Japanese they were facing. On November 10, Colonel Willoughby estimated about four thousand Japanese in the Buna area, but just a few days later he cut that figure in half. Vasey also estimated about two thousand, while Harding thought the Japanese had a mere battalion there—no more than a thousand soldiers. Finally, the Thirty-Second Division itself was a cause for concern. Blamey, who had endured MacArthur's blistering and unfair criticism of Australian troops, had serious questions about how well the ill-trained and unblooded Red Arrow would perform in its first combat operation.

The Australians reached the Kumusi River at Wairopi on November 13. By mid-November, the Allies controlled a line from Wairopi to Bofu to Embogo on the Solomon Sea, and were poised to strike at Buna. Allied patrols skirmished with Japanese outposts and patrols. The fight to take Buna and Sanananda was about to begin.

CHAPTER 6

BAPTISM OF FIRE

On November 14, 1942, General MacArthur ordered his soldiers forward to attack the Japanese. Two full years after the Thirty-Second Infantry Division was mobilized for federal service, it was finally going into battle. "We thought it was going to be a snap," recalled Ernest Gerber. "We were just going to walk up the trail and take things over. . . . Hell, we were whistling on the approach march."[1] The Red Arrow Division pierced the Japanese lines as they had the German lines a generation before, but the triumph at Buna came at an enormous cost that brought the division to the verge of collapse. In military circles, a soldier's first combat experience is known as the "baptism of fire," and it is always painful and shocking. Soldiers, and sometimes entire divisions, often struggle in their first fight, but the Red Arrow's baptism was among the most troubled and traumatic in US history. Confident but inexperienced, the division was thrown into a major engagement against a veteran adversary. The jungle, swamps, rain, and mosquito-borne diseases undermined the soldiers and complicated the conduct of modern battle. Poor decision-making, miscalculation, infighting, and egotism at the top of the command structure further hobbled the Red Arrow's efforts. The division's ultimate fate lay with the ordinary foot soldier. At first the Red Arrowmen stumbled, but they overcame these obstacles to achieve one of the first Allied ground victories in the Pacific—and helped change the direction of World War II.

FACING: Lieutenant Colonel Herbert A. Smith ("White Smith") leads the Second Battalion of the 128th Infantry Regiment toward Buna, November 15, 1942. WHI IMAGE ID 54359

When the Buna campaign began, Japanese forces held a sixteen-mile stretch of coastline along the north side of New Guinea's Papuan Peninsula, with troops concentrated in three pockets. The Gona pocket, on the far west, was the smallest of the three. The Sanananda pocket, in the center, contained the largest concentration of troops, as well as the Japanese headquarters at Giruwa, the port facility at Sanananda Point, and the terminus of the Sanananda Track leading inland. The Buna pocket, on the far east, was the third and geographically largest of the three, and it was subdivided into several distinct sections. On one end was Buna Village, on a point of land along the coast formed by the confluence of the Girua River and Entrance Creek. The creek spilled into a tidal lagoon east of the village, with two sandspits separating the lagoon from the sea. Northeast of the lagoon, on a point of land, was Buna Government Station, commonly (though mistakenly) referred to in most US records as Buna Mission. From there, the Buna pocket extended roughly three miles east to Cape Endaiadere, where the coast hooked southeastward. South of the cape, the Duropa Plantation hugged the shore with its long, graceful rows of coconut palms. To the west of the plantation were the two airstrips, the "Old Strip" and the "New Strip," with Simemi Creek running between them. A bridge spanned the creek between the strips; downstream from the bridge the creek turned northwesterly, meandered along the north side of the Old Strip, and then emptied to the sea.

The Japanese reorganized their South Pacific forces in mid-November. New Guinea and the Solomons came under Eighth Army Area, based at Rabaul and led by Lieutenant General Imamura Hitoshi. The Eighteenth Army under Lieutenant General Adachi Hatazo (then also headquartered at Rabaul) was responsible for operations on New Guinea. Colonel Yokoyama Yosuke took charge of the Gona and Sanananda pockets, while Captain Yasuda Yoshitatsu of the Imperial Japanese Navy commanded at Buna. The Allies' estimate of two thousand weary and diseased Japanese soldiers proved wildly inaccurate. In fact, there were six thousand Japanese troops in the area, and although many indeed suffered from hunger and malaria, reinforcements arrived in mid-November—veterans of the fighting in China, Hong Kong, and Java under Colonel Yamamoto Hiroshi.

Buna Battle Area

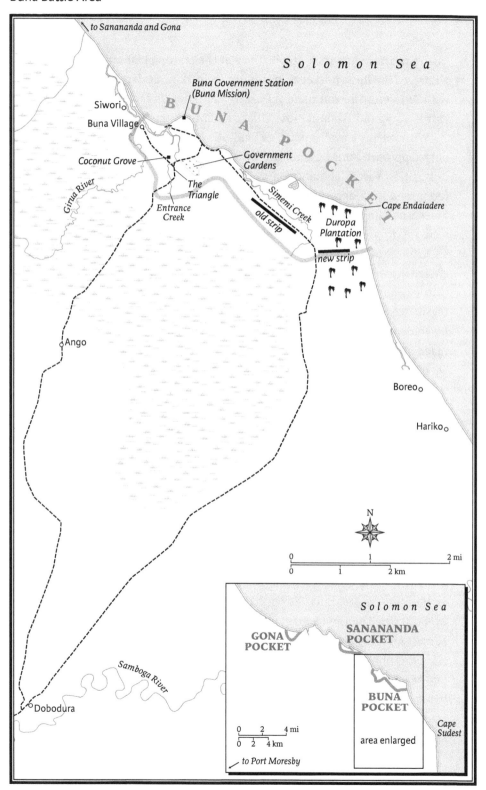

to Sanananda and Gona

S o l o m o n   S e a

Buna Government Station
(Buna Mission)

Siwori

Buna Village

B U N A   P O C K E T

Government
Gardens

Coconut Grove

Girua River

The
Triangle

Entrance
Creek

Simemi Creek

old strip

Cape Endaiadere

Duropa
Plantation

new strip

Ango

Boreo

Hariko

N

| 0 | | 1 | | 2 mi |
| 0 | 1 | | 2 km |

Samboga River

Dobodura

GONA
POCKET

Solomon Sea

SANANANDA
POCKET

BUNA
POCKET

area enlarged

Cape
Sudest

| 0 | | 2 | | 4 mi |
| 0 | 2 | | 4 km |

to Port Moresby

The reinforcements took up positions at the Duropa Plantation and the airstrips. The Buna pocket alone now contained 2,500 Japanese fighters, with Yamamoto in command at Duropa Plantation and the airstrips in the east sector, and Yasuda at Buna Village and Mission to the west.

Without any naval support or landing craft, the Allies had no choice but to approach Buna by land, but the terrain and climate posed enormous difficulties. Vast tidal mangrove swamps dominated the coastal plain, interspersed with occasional high ground clogged with brush and kunai grass. The rainy season was underway, and the swamps and watercourses were full to overflowing. The Japanese took every advantage the terrain and climate offered them. The swollen Girua River and Entrance Creek anchored the west end of their defensive line. To the east, the airstrips and the Duropa Plantation offered excellent fields of fire against oncoming infantry. In between, the tangled mangrove swamps served as a massive moat. Japanese engineers built hundreds of interconnected bunkers typically made of strong and fibrous coconut logs—some of them one foot thick. Oil drums filled with sand offered further protection, and some bunkers even had steel or concrete reinforcement. The Japanese camouflaged the bunkers by covering them in earth and planted vegetation, making them difficult to spot from the air or on the ground. The Japanese studded the Duropa Plantation and the airstrips with these bunkers and concentrated them along the trails leading through the swamps to the coast, transforming the jungle pathways into killing zones. Snipers hid in the trees above or in spider holes below ground. General Robert Eichelberger, I Corps commander, later described the Japanese defenses as "brilliant" and "perfect."[2]

Australian Lieutenant General Edmund F. Herring, the head of the Advance New Guinea Force, commanded the operation. Allied forces were divided into two groups, one on either side of the Girua River. To the west of the river, the Australian Seventh Division, under General George Vasey, would attack Gona and Sanananda. To the east of the river, General Edwin Forrest Harding's rookie Red Arrow Division was responsible for Buna. Harding split his troops into two strike forces. The first was General Hanford MacNider's Hat Force, now renamed the Warren Force after Harding's home county in southwestern Ohio. The Warren Force's mission was to advance along the coast toward Buna. The First Battalion of the 128th Infantry Regiment, under Colonel Robert C. McCoy, was to drive through

This is one of hundreds of camouflaged Japanese bunkers the Red Arrow encountered during the Papuan Campaign. WISCONSIN NATIONAL GUARD, US ARMY SIGNAL CORPS PHOTO

the Duropa Plantation to Cape Endaiadere. The Second Battalion, under Colonel Herbert A. Smith, and the Third Battalion, under Colonel Kelsie E. Miller, were to move inland toward a large, flat kunai patch at Dobodura, which the Americans had identified as a potential site for building an airfield complex. From Dobodura, Miller's Third Battalion would move down a trail that paralleled Simemi Creek and attack the airstrips. Meanwhile, the Second Battalion would be held in reserve at Dobodura, working alongside engineers to construct the airfields. The Australian 2/6 Independent Company, still at Pongani, prepared to move up to join the Warren Force. The 126th Infantry Regiment, under Colonel Clarence Tomlinson, would compose the second strike force. Its mission was to attack the western end of the Japanese pocket, marching through the jungle from Bofu to Dobodura, and from there attack Buna Mission and Buna Village.

The first Allied attack forces marched out to meet the Japanese on November 16. To the west of the Girua River, the Australians of the

To aid Red Arrow soldiers in their attack, a Papua New Guinean guide draws a diagram in the dirt showing Japanese positions near Buna on November 15, 1942. WISCONSIN NATIONAL GUARD, US ARMY SIGNAL CORPS PHOTO

Twenty-Fifth Brigade moved toward Gona under Brigadier Kenneth W. Eather, while the Sixteenth Brigade headed for Sanananda under Brigadier John Lloyd. The Warren Force moved out that day too. The Third Battalion of the 128th Infantry Regiment reached Dobodura midafternoon, then headed down the trail toward the Buna airstrips, tangling with small Japanese patrols along the way. The Second Battalion followed the Third and got right to work on airfield construction. Colonel McCoy's First Battalion marched up the coast. General MacNider, in dramatic fashion, moved on ahead of his ground troops by boat. Colonel Tracy Hale dismissed it as a publicity stunt. "The 128th Inf. was assigned four places on the boat," he recalled bitterly, but there were "four war correspondents on board!" Rounding Cape Sudest, MacNider's flotilla came within sight of the Japanese on Cape Endaiadere. Hale thought it an egregious act of recklessness to move under potential enemy observation "in broad daylight . . . in a small unarmed boat!" As MacNider passed the infantrymen marching along the shore, McCoy tried to warn him there were no friendly troops ahead. McCoy "ran out into the surf and waived [sic] his shirt rearward," Hale wrote, to convince MacNider to turn back. MacNider proceeded anyway, landed at Hariko, and set up his headquarters. When McCoy arrived at Hariko, MacNider "took him to task pretty sharply," as Hale remembered it, "because the Bn. was so slow!"[3] By late afternoon McCoy's troops had reached Boreo, about a mile north of Hariko, where they exchanged fire with a Japanese outpost and then halted.

The ragtag fleet of the Small Ships Section usually operated at night to avoid Japanese planes, but on November 16 it sailed up the coast in broad daylight. American fighter planes, based on the south side of the Owen Stanleys, afforded some protection, and the belief that the Japanese at Buna were weak and starving boosted American confidence all the more. Harding was anxious to get to the front. He boarded the lugger *Minnemura*, which joined the *Alacrity* and the *Bonwin* bound for Hariko. The ships brought a wide array of supplies: ammunition, gasoline, machine guns, medical supplies, mortars, rations, and the records of the 128th Infantry Regiment. Bringing up the rear was a captured Japanese barge carrying two Australian twenty-five-pound artillery pieces, ammunition for the guns, their crews, and the Red Arrow artillery chief, General Albert Waldron. Unfortunately, the overconfident Americans had let their guard down, and they paid for it dearly. The ships reached Hariko late that afternoon, within sight of the Japanese on Cape Endaiadere. By this time, American planes had returned to their bases and the ships were unprotected. As the GIs began to unload their supplies, Japanese Zero fighter planes came streaking in. Reporter Robert Doyle of the *Milwaukee Journal* was already ashore. "About 6:45," he recorded in his diary, "at least 18 Jap [planes] came over flying high along the coast from the Buna direction."[4] Also ashore were Benjamin Winneshiek and George Green of the 128th Infantry Regiment Service Company, digging foxholes along the beach. "Hey," Green joked as the planes swooped in, "I'm digging my grave."[5]

The Zeroes made several passes at the ships, spraying them full of lead. Ammunition on the ships exploded and gasoline caught fire. Lieutenant Colonel Laurence McKenny, the Thirty-Second Division's quartermaster, was incinerated on the bridge of the *Bonwin* when it burst into flames. The Americans fired back with machine guns and rifles, including General

Harding, who took a few shots with his M1 from the deck of the *Minnemura* before the flames forced him to abandon ship. Those already ashore rushed into the water to save their comrades, as the ships burned and Japanese bullets rained down on them. George Green was among those who went out into the water to bring in survivors and was killed. The attack lasted about twenty minutes and then the planes disappeared. Harding and Waldron both washed ashore, alive but drenched. As dusk descended, the survivors picked up the pieces. "What few medics there were," noted Robert Doyle, "pitched in with flashlights to help the survivors and give first aid," their work partially illuminated by the burning hulks offshore.[6]

The attack killed twenty-four men and destroyed precious materiel. Most of the ammunition was lost. The two artillery pieces sank to the bottom, as did food and medical supplies. Even the records of the 128th Infantry Regiment were lost. Japanese planes returned early the next morning and hit the fleet again, before American fighters could arrive from Port Moresby, and incapacitated two more luggers. For an army already on a shoestring, in a land without modern infrastructure, and poised to launch an offensive, the losses were incalculably devastating.

The Hariko disaster forced Harding to delay his attack, but on the morning of November 19, he ordered the Warren Force forward to the Duropa Plantation and Cape Endaiadere. McCoy's First Battalion jumped off at 7:00 a.m. in a soaking monsoon rain. Because of the attack on their ships, the GIs had only one day's worth of rations and ammunition. Japan's main line of resistance lay about 750 yards south of Cape Endaiadere and ran across the plantation all the way to the airstrips. In front of the main line, the Japanese had installed scores of well-concealed machine-gun outposts and sniper positions. As the Red Arrowmen marched confidently through the jungle toward the southern edge of the plantation, Japanese machine-gun fire suddenly erupted. "Men fell all around," wrote Roy Campbell, "many mortally wounded; some with legs riddled with bullets sank to the ground crying and moaning. The guns kept firing, and many of those who had fallen were hit again, killing them."[7] The Red Arrowmen received minimal artillery support and no air support at all because of the rainy weather. Their mortars and grenades proved almost useless against the Japanese bunkers, which were so well hidden that the GIs could rarely detect them anyway. Major David B. Parker, an engineer liaison officer observing the operation, noted the "deadly accuracy and strength of the enemy MG [machine gun] and rifle fire. . . . It was dangerous to show even a finger from behind one's cover, as it would immediately draw a burst of fire."[8] McCoy's men advanced only a few hundred yards and no more.

Colonel Miller and his Third Battalion set out that morning too, also short on rations and ammunition, and headed for the airstrips. Miller fared no better than McCoy. To reach the airstrips, the Third Battalion passed down a rough jungle trail that narrowed as the troops moved ahead. "The whole area," recalled Percy Hiatt, "was a mixture of tall grass, jungle, and tide-controlled streams and swamps."[9] Here, too, the Japanese had excellent fields of fire. "The Japanese let the lead men come within a few feet of their camouflaged pill boxes," recalled James Kincaid, "and then opened fire on them, pinning them down [and then] they started dropping mortar shells and grenades from grenade launchers."[10] Crossing the bridge over Simemi Creek proved impossible. "Anytime we tried to cross that bridge," recalled Hiatt, "they zeroed in on us with everything they had." Troops deployed into the surrounding swamps, but sloshing through the waters— sometimes chest deep—slowed them down. "Bullets zinged all over the place," remembered Robert Freese, "and when the [mortar] rounds impacted the swamp around us, shock waves went through the water and stunned us." Freese recalled being "trapped in an open swamp about hip or chest deep, while the Japanese were on solid ground, safely in the pillboxes, which were hidden in the vegetation. We didn't have a chance."[11]

Harding ordered more attacks in the following days but made little progress. On November 21, American planes joined the fight, but their actions were poorly coordinated with ground troops—and often were inaccurate. "One flight of A-20's dropped their complete string of anti-personnel bombs two miles at sea," wrote David Parker, and "another flight dropped several heavy bombs on our own forward positions, killing 6 men."[12] Another attack on November 23 yielded a little more progress. Harding shifted the bulk of his forces to the right, reinforcing the First Battalion in a concentrated push across the Duropa Plantation. He sent his trusted friend, Alexander MacNab, executive officer of the 128th Infantry Regiment and now a lieutenant colonel, to coordinate the attack.

With a little more artillery support, the GIs reached the Japanese main line but could not punch through. Among the casualties that day was

General MacNider. Never one to shy away from battle, MacNider went forward to observe. At about 6:30 p.m, he noticed an infantryman abandoning the front for the safety of the rear. MacNider raced out into the open to get the GI back into the fighting when there was a sudden explosion, damaging MacNider's left hand and eye and forcing his evacuation. "The general's audacity finally caught up with him," wrote MacNab. "He was without fear and believed that exposing himself cooly inspired his troops. Many of us tried to reason with him, but without results."[13] Percy Hiatt had a somewhat different perspective. "He strolled up there like he was going to win the War single-handedly," as he remembered it, and "I think it surprised him when he found out he was at the front."[14]

Harding appointed Colonel Hale the new Warren Force commander, but little changed. "Three more days and nights passed without food, officers, or information," wrote Roy Campbell, "just rain and bugs at night and sweltering heat in the daytime."[15] Day after day, wrote Percy Hiatt, "we'd make fifty yards [but] couldn't hold it. . . . Then we'd move back fifty yards . . . to the same old hole and try again the next day."[16] Buna was not going to be the "easy pickings" Harding had imagined.

Just as Harding dispatched the Warren Force, he received some devastating news. Brigadier Lloyd's Sixteenth Brigade, en route to Sanananda, had crossed the Kumusi River on November 16 and fought its way along the Kokoda Track toward Soputa. But the weeks of combat on the Kokoda and Sanananda Tracks had taken a toll and reduced Lloyd's brigade to a third of its original size. Three days out, its advance ground to a halt north of Soputa, just south of the juncture of the Sanananda and Killerton Tracks, heavily defended by the Japanese. Lloyd's men, reduced in size and strength, could not break through. Because the Sanananda pocket held the greatest concentration of Japanese forces, General MacArthur believed the strongest effort needed to be made there. So, on November 19, MacArthur redirected Colonel Tomlinson's 126th Infantry Regiment from the Buna pocket to assist Lloyd and his men. It was a devastating blow for Harding, who had expected to have two regimental combat teams for his attack on Buna.

Further complicating matters was the fact that the 126th was still scattered in various places. Much of it was at Natunga and Bofu preparing for its move to Dobodura. The portion of the First Battalion under Colonel

Gona and Sananda Battle Areas

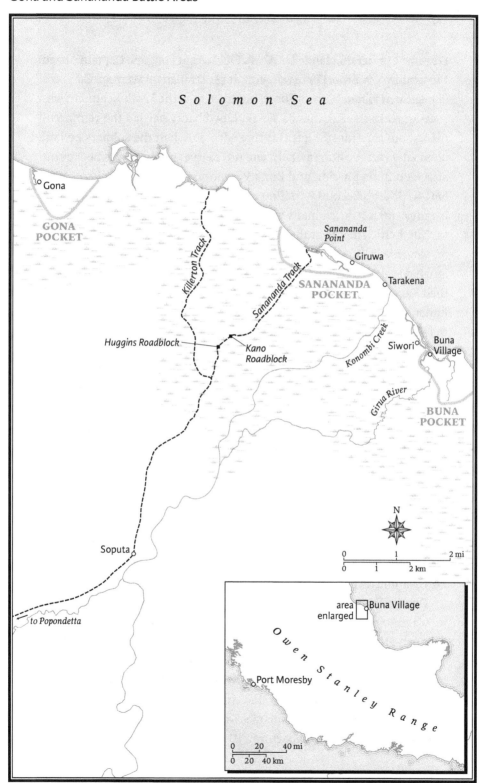

Solomon Sea

Gona

GONA POCKET

Killerton Track

Sananda Track

Sananda Point

Giruwa

Tarakena

SANANDA POCKET

Huggins Roadblock

Kano Roadblock

Konombi Creek

Siwori

Buna Village

Girua River

BUNA POCKET

Soputa

to Popondetta

N

0   1   2 mi

0   1   2 km

area enlarged

Buna Village

Owen Stanley Range

Port Moresby

0   20   40 mi

0   20   40 km

MAPPING SPECIALISTS, LTD.

Edmund Carrier that landed at Abel's Field was at Pongani. Captain Alfred Medendorp's Wairopi Force was with the Australians at Wairopi. Carrier's detachment joined Warren Force, but the rest of the 126th Regiment was reassigned to the Sanananda Track. Lloyd badly needed the reinforcements, but the transfer left Harding with only half the soldiers he had planned on for the Buna assault, and no reserve. All that remained for his attack on Buna Mission and Buna Village was Lieutenant Colonel Herbert A. Smith's Second Battalion of the 128th Infantry Regiment—one battalion for a task originally assigned to an entire regiment.

The first elements of the 126th Infantry Regiment arrived at Soputa on November 21, with plans to attack the following day. Tomlinson designated Major Herbert M. Smith's Second Battalion (still exhausted from their Kapa Kapa Track misadventure) as his reserve, but the Third Battalion under Major George Bond prepared for action. Tomlinson faced a front that looked rather like a horseshoe with its wings pointing northward. To take the junction that lay behind it, Tomlinson planned a double envelopment. The detachment of the First Battalion, under Major Richard D. Boerem, was to attack the main Japanese line. Then, Bond's Third Battalion would make wide sweeps around the right and left flanks, get behind the Japanese, and seize the junction. Companies I and K would move to the left, while Company L would join two companies of Australians already in position on the right. Once the Japanese were significantly broken up and confused, Smith's Second Battalion was to push up the Sanananda Track and take control of it. But the night the regiment arrived, the units were reshuffled yet again. Harding had lobbied furiously for the return of at least one battalion of the 126th. Herring relented and transferred Major Smith's Second Battalion back to Buna. Harding had won a victory, but now Tomlinson had lost his reserve on the eve of an attack.

Despite this setback, Tomlinson's troops daubed camouflage paint on their faces and moved out at 11:00 a.m. on November 22. On the right, Company L took up positions at the extreme end of the Australian line, on the grounds of a derelict banana plantation, and advanced about two hundred yards until heavy Japanese fire stopped them. Company L and the Australians then endured a fierce nighttime counterattack but held their ground. On the left, Companies I and K met Japanese patrols almost immediately upon their departure. "There was lead flying everywhere," noted the Company K journal, "and everyone seems pretty scared."[17] Steve Janicki remembered that "in three or four minutes we lost quite a few guys. There was no screaming, no hollering, we were just dumbfounded."[18] The troops attempted to move forward through swamps sometimes chest deep. They had no accurate maps, and communication with headquarters was spotty. By the end of the first day, Companies I and K had advanced just 350 yards. The following days saw little improvement on either flank. Major Bert Zeeff, the Third Battalion executive officer, took command of US troops on the right wing, while Bond moved forward to take personal charge on the left. Tomlinson launched another attack on November 26— Thanksgiving Day. Zeeff advanced about three hundred yards, while Bond consolidated his forces on a patch of high ground about seven hundred yards from the Killerton Track. Meanwhile, Medendorp's Wairopi Force arrived at Soputa. Tomlinson allowed the men a day of rest and then sent them to reinforce Bond on the left wing.

Tomlinson launched yet another push on November 30. The right and center of the line made little progress, but forces on the left achieved a breakthrough. The attack began at 9:00 a.m. with Bond in command. His 265-man force was made up of Company I, the antitank company, communications troops from Third Battalion headquarters, and a detachment of machine gunners from Company M. Remaining behind in support was Company K and the cannon company, which were under the command of Major Bernd Baetcke. Just four hundred yards out, Bond reached a flat expanse of kunai grass where the Japanese were waiting. Japanese forces unleashed a heavy fusillade of rifle, machine-gun, and mortar fire on Bond and his men. Bond was severely wounded and at first the attack faltered. But the Americans regrouped under the command of Captain John D. Shirley of Company I, cleared the flat of Japanese, and continued on, passing through more jungle, knee-deep swamps, and Japanese machine-gun fire. At about 5:00 p.m. they came to a Japanese bivouac on relatively high ground along the Sanananda Track. Shirley's troops charged it, bayonets affixed to their rifles, driving out its shocked Japanese occupants. Then, as dusk fell, Shirley established a perimeter 250 yards long and 150 yards wide, encompassing land on both sides of the track. From this position, Shirley now controlled movement along the Sanananda Track, hindering Japanese communications with their rear. However, he was also sandwiched between the Japanese first and second defensive lines. The Japanese lobbed mortars into Shirley's roadblock and launched concerted ground counterattacks, but the GIs held their ground.

Linking the roadblock to Baetcke's force proved difficult. On December 1, a party from inside the roadblock under Captain Roger Keast probed beyond its perimeter, searching for weak spots in Japanese positions through which they might open a communication line to Baetcke. Instead they ran into an ambush. Keast and an Australian artillery observer were killed, and the remainder, including nine wounded, pulled back into the roadblock. On December 2, a party led by Captain Meredith Huggins fought its way through to the roadblock, bringing in badly needed ammunition and rations. Just minutes after Huggins arrived, Shirley was shot and killed by a Japanese sniper. Huggins, as ranking officer, now took command. "I ordered the establishment of a double perimeter," Huggins later said, "two men to a foxhole."[19] The Japanese kept the roadblock under near-constant attack—artillery and mortars, infiltration, ground assaults, and snipers high in the trees. A sniper shot Huggins in the head on December 5. "Luckily, I didn't have any brains," he later quipped, "so I wasn't badly hurt."[20] In fact, Huggins was seriously wounded, but he remained in command. The troops' position became known as the Huggins Roadblock.

During the first week of December, the Allies reorganized their forces. Herring transferred Tomlinson and the 126th Infantry Regiment headquarters to Buna, where its Second Battalion and a portion of the First were fighting. Major Baetcke assumed command of American forces on the Sanananda Track, but malaria forced him to the rear just two days later, leaving Major Boerem in charge. On December 7, the Australian Thirtieth Brigade under Brigadier Selwyn H. Porter, fresh but untested in battle, arrived to relieve the exhausted Australian Sixteenth Brigade. Porter assumed command of the Sanananda front, put his own troops on the front line, and pulled Boerem's worn-out Red Arrowmen back into supporting positions. Porter then ordered a frontal assault to muscle through the Japanese lines. Once again, inexperienced troops—this time Australian—floundered in their first fight. More than two hundred of Porter's men were killed, and the Australians made no appreciable gain.

As Allied forces struggled to reach Huggins, conditions inside the roadblock grew increasingly desperate. Constant Japanese attacks depleted

their ammunition stocks. Sleep was impossible. There was no way to properly dispose of human waste. Mosquitoes plagued the GIs and malaria
burned through the ranks. Medical supplies ran low, and the troops had
to bury the dead within their small perimeter. Food dwindled to almost
nothing, and captured rainwater or groundwater (contaminated by filth
and dead bodies) was their only source of drink. By December 8, there were
approximately 225 men in the roadblock, down from the original force
of 265. Barely half of them were in fighting shape. Several attempts to
reinforce and resupply the roadblock had failed, but on December 8 Lieutenant Peter L. Dal Ponte led a party that finally broke through. The badly
wounded Huggins returned to the rear, and Dal Ponte now took command.
Medic Kenneth Springer was part of Dal Ponte's group. "I learned several
things in a hurry," Springer wrote, one being "to keep your head down."
Springer vividly recalled his first night inside the roadblock: "Darkness fell
and I heard the distant boom of the Aussie 25 pounders and the almost
simultaneous whistle and then an explosion as the shells fell around the
perimeter." With each blast "the shrapnel would ricochet through the
trees" and "I did not rest too well or close my eyes."[21]

Another supply party reached the roadblock on December 10, and a
few more broke through in subsequent days. Communicating with the
roadblock was difficult. Radios performed poorly. The GIs laid down a
telephone line, but the Japanese repeatedly cut it or tapped into it to eaves-
drop. In telephone conversations the Red Arrowmen sometimes spoke in
Dutch—a language familiar to a good many from western Michigan—to
prevent English-speaking Japanese from understanding them. The supply
situation was always precarious, and casualties mounted. According to
Kenneth Springer, those in the roadblock nicknamed their tenuous link
to the outside world the "Track of Dead Men's Bones."[22]

On November 21, as Tomlinson's troops prepared to join the fight along
the Sanananda Track, and as the Warren Force tried to break through the
Japanese line on the Duropa Plantation, Lieutenant Colonel Herbert A.
Smith's Second Battalion of the 128th Infantry Regiment marched from
Dobodura to attack Buna Mission and Buna Village. Its first objective was
to secure a fork in the jungle trail; to the left the trail led to Buna Village,

and to the right it led to Buna Mission. The GIs dubbed this track junction "the Triangle." Here, the Japanese had built a particularly dense array of bunkers and machine-gun nests to block any movement toward the village or the Mission. When Smith's battalion reached a point just south of the track junction in the early afternoon, heavy fighting erupted and Colonel Smith organized a flanking movement, sending Company F to the left and Company G to the right. Company F ran into swamps and Japanese bunkers, but it also found a patch of relatively high ground. On the right, Company G plunged into swamps that got continually deeper, where the GIs spent a wet and uncomfortable night. "Some men were able to climb up on the roots of trees," Colonel Smith later wrote, "but the majority merely stood in the water from waist to neck deep." In the morning, Company G reached an unoccupied patch of kunai grass that could serve as a launchpad for an attack on the Triangle. Smith doubted he could supply and hold the position due to the dense swamps, but Harding ordered him to hold it.

The Second Battalion of the 126th Infantry Regiment, under Major Herbert M. Smith, arrived from the Sanananda Track on November 23. The combined battalions took on the name Urbana Force, after the Ohio hometown of General Eichelberger. Harding was grateful for the reinforcement, but it presented complications. Not only did each unit bear the designation Second Battalion, but each was commanded by a Wisconsin National Guard officer named Herbert Smith. To simplify communications, Harding dubbed Colonel Smith "White Smith" and Major Smith "Red Smith." As the senior officer, White Smith was in command. The two Smiths developed a plan of attack for November 24, striking the right and left flanks of the Triangle and probing to find a way around it. The plan was much the same as the earlier attack, but now with more troops.

The attack began with an air bombardment, but it was weak and ineffective. The first airstrike missed Japanese targets. The second accidentally strafed the Urbana Force command post. The GIs jumped off at 2:30 p.m. On the left, Company E of the 126th Infantry Regiment proceeded along the west bank of Entrance Creek. The men waded through swamps and then neared a footbridge across the creek, where they began taking heavy Japanese fire. They had unknowingly walked into a massive bunker complex that the GIs dubbed the Coconut Grove. The company took cover for the night and, after dark, some of the soldiers lit cigarettes. "It was the worst thing we ever did," wrote Paul Lutjens. The cigarettes gave away their positions, and Japanese bullets filled the air all around them. The company spent several days pinned down with meager rations.[23]

On the right, Company E of the 128th Infantry Regiment waded through swamps and joined Company G on the kunai flat. While Company E and the Company G heavy weapons platoon remained in place, the main body of Company G probed to the northwest. Before long, they ran into a group of Japanese soldiers building an antiaircraft gun emplacement on a second kunai flat. A fierce firefight ensued. Company G, quickly finding itself outgunned, pulled back to one end of the second kunai flat. The sounds of the battle alerted the Japanese to the American presence. Late that afternoon, Japanese forces attacked Company E and the heavy weapons platoon on the first kunai flat, screaming as they rushed toward the Red Arrowmen. The GIs fired back, but their weapons often failed. "Mortars did not fire because they were improperly packed," recalled Ernest Gerber. "They were totally saturated with water, and the ammunition was damp. The round would fire, plop out twenty feet in front of the mortar, and that was that."[24] White Smith later wrote that "machine guns jammed because the web belts were wet and dirty and had shrunk." He also noted that "Tommy Guns and BARs [Browning automatic rifles] were full of muck and dirt," and even the M1 rifles jammed "because clips were wet and full of muck from the swamp."[25] As the Japanese charged at them, the Red Arrowmen abandoned the flat of high ground and took refuge at the edge of the swamp, leaving many of their machine guns and mortars behind.

In the face of the attack, White Smith told E and G Companies to "remain where they were," and that he "would join them as soon as possible after daylight." Then the phone line went dead, and what happened next is murky. Whether through miscommunication, misinterpretation of orders, sheer panic, dereliction of duty, or some combination thereof, word spread among companies that they had been ordered to return to the battalion command post. When they arrived, White Smith was surprised to see them. "Most of them were utterly exhausted," he recalled. He realized "it would be necessary to give them food and rest before any other action could be taken." And what action to take? Smith's choice was to send the men back into the deep swamps to the right, or concentrate his efforts on the left. "I realized that I stood less of a chance of being personally criticized if I selected the first," he wrote, but Smith believed the swampy terrain on the right was too deep and dense to launch an attack. "My decision was to abandon, for the time being, any action on the right and concentrate on the left."[26]

White Smith's decision proved controversial. "What he should have done was kick their fannies right back to the forward positions," Red Smith later wrote.[27] Harding agreed with White Smith's assessment but also suspected Smith was not pushing his men vigorously enough. So Harding sent in his chief of staff, Colonel John W. Mott, to assess the situation. Mott had a reputation for being bombastic and abrasive. Harding later described him as "an intelligent, forceful, and capable officer with a notable talent for antagonizing superiors, subordinates, and contemporaries."[28] Years later, White Smith reportedly remarked that Mott was "the one man whom he would knock cold" if he ever saw him in civilian life.[29] Mott assumed command of the Urbana Force and relieved the commanders of Companies E and G. He then sent the companies back into the swamp to retrieve the weapons they had left behind. "This was done by sundown," Mott recalled, although "Company E, which was the first to return, was without one of its mortars and had to be sent back a second time."[30]

Mott then developed his own plan of attack. Like White Smith had planned to do, Mott focused his efforts on the left, but his attack would be done at night. Mott planned to sweep west and move directly toward Buna Village on the coast. One force, built around Red Smith's Second Battalion of the 126th Infantry Regiment, would move onto the patch of high ground between the Triangle and the Girua that earlier patrols had reported. Little was known about the area. Patrol reports and aerial photographs obscured by cloud cover identified some open grassy areas, as well as some "trails above the high water mark," recalled Red Smith, "and those had to be the axis to follow."[31] Several companies of the Second Battalion of the 128th Infantry Regiment, supplemented with some troops from regimental headquarters, would protect Red Smith's right flank, cut the track between Buna Village and the Triangle, and take the Coconut Grove. Company F of the 128th Infantry Regiment would cross the Girua River, make a wide sweep to the west, and take Siwori Village on the coast, cutting the Buna-Sanananda coastal trail. Mott relegated White Smith to a marginalized role, giving him a company to protect the rear areas and guard against a Japanese counterattack.

Mott scheduled his attack for just after midnight on November 30, but the GIs struggled in the darkness as they tried to reach their jump-off point. "We floundered through the jungle in mud nearly up to our hips," remembered Herman Bottcher, "hanging onto each other in the pitch darkness."[32] The confusion delayed the attack until 4:00 a.m. They had advanced only a few hundred yards when Japanese machine-gun tracers lit up the predawn sky. Robert Odell remembered a "solid sheet of flame" as "everywhere men cursed, shouted, or screamed. . . . Brave men led and others followed [while] cowards crouched in the grass." Some units got lost in the confusion and darkness. Despite all the problems, the night attack caught the Japanese off guard. "We were all scared," claimed Odell, "but we scared the Japs more."[33] As dawn lifted the darkness, Red Smith's forces neared Buna Village, but their advance stalled about three hundred yards short of the village as Japanese resistance stiffened. Meanwhile, the Second Battalion of the 128th Infantry Regiment had successfully severed the track between Buna Village and the Triangle and reached the south bank of Entrance Creek, though it was unable to penetrate the Coconut Grove. And Company F of the 128th Infantry Regiment had successfully reached the coast at Siwori Village and cut the land link between Buna and Sanananda.

In the morning, the Red Arrowmen mopped up snipers and stragglers, and in doing so gained an appreciation of Japanese strength. "Along the edge of the field were strongpoints built with large tree trunks as supports," noted Robert Odell. Red Arrow engineers tried to blow them up with dynamite, but "one was so well constructed," Odell recalled, "that six sticks merely collapsed a bit of the roof." Urbana Force had also captured an important Japanese headquarters replete with barracks, a hospital, and warehouses full of foodstuffs and ammunition. Some of the buildings were linked together by underground tunnels. Odell marveled at an officer complex with a "floor and a roof" that was "completely outfitted with large mosquito nettings, blankets, pillows, bed rolls, [and] 14 rolls of toilet paper under lock and key—a prize of prizes." (The "prize" was in fact writing paper, rolled up in the Japanese fashion.) The capture provided an intelligence bonanza, including "maps, code books, diaries, everything that any military force would hate to have fall into enemy hands," recalled

Red Smith. They also found "American cigarettes and whiskey taken from a hotel in Manila," Smith later wrote. "All except one bottle was stored in the Bn. Aid Station" for medical use, though Smith later admitted that he "kept one bottle" for himself.[34]

Although Mott's attack did not accomplish all of his ambitious goals, it did achieve much. The GIs were on the doorstep of Buna Village and had severed a vital Japanese communication line between Buna and Sanananda. Though the Coconut Grove remained in the hands of their adversaries, the GIs had enveloped it on three sides—north, south, and west. It was the most ground the Red Arrow Division had yet taken in the campaign.

On December 1, in the wake of Mott's attack, White Smith sent Staff Sergeant David Rubitsky and Captain Joseph Stehling to a remote outpost east of the Triangle to lay a communication wire. When the two men arrived there, they found an unmanned .30-caliber machine gun. Rubitsky and Stehling claimed that while they were at the outpost, several hundred Japanese soldiers suddenly converged on them. Stehling left the outpost just before dark to get help from the battalion command post, leaving Rubitsky to face the onslaught alone, armed with only a carbine, an automatic rifle, and the machine gun. Rubitsky held off the Japanese through the night, and when Stehling returned in the morning, he saw "more than 500 Japanese killed or wounded."[35]

White Smith arrived at the scene later that morning. He estimated that Rubitsky had "killed more than 600" Japanese troops, blunted a major counterattack, and "saved both battalions from being wiped out."[36] Smith recommended Rubitsky for the Medal of Honor, but Mott mocked the proposal. As Smith remembered it, Mott scoffed and said, "You mean a Jew for the Congressional Medal of Honor?"and then Mott "laughed and walked away."[37] The paperwork Smith submitted for Rubitsky's decoration disappeared. Anti-Semitism was prevalent in the army, and Rubitsky was frequently the target of slurs. Even Smith confessed his own prejudice. He later wrote that he should have made Rubitsky a lieutenant but did not because of his "ethnic background," adding, "Lord forgive me for what I have done."[38]

Rubitsky never received the Medal of Honor, but after the war he fought to obtain it. In the 1980s, the Pentagon began reviewing the denial of awards of valor for reasons of racial and ethnic prejudice. The government conducted a two-year-long investigation of Rubitsky's case, which had attracted the support of a congressional delegation led by US senators Robert Kasten (R-Wisconsin) and Herbert Kohl (D-Wisconsin), and representatives Les Aspin (D-Wisconsin) and Nita Lowey (D-New York). However, in December 1989, the Pentagon issued a report concluding that Rubitsky's claims were unsubstantiated. Official American and Japanese records made no mention of the attack, investigators noted, and Japanese forces in the area at that time were in a defensive posture with no more than five hundred effective troops. The report questioned whether Rubitsky would have had enough ammunition to continue firing for such a long period of time, or whether he would have been able to keep up such a heavy volume of fire by himself with so many opposing troops firing back at him. In the end, the report did not claim that Rubitsky had fabricated his account, and indeed suggested he likely had engaged Japanese forces. But investigators determined there was "incontestable evidence" that "no major attack took place" and thus concluded that the Medal of Honor was not warranted.[39] Rubitsky's congressional supporters accepted the Pentagon's findings. "What we are dealing with here is not a lie," they said in a statement, but "simply the unfortunate result of the passage of many years, the fogging of many memories and the reliving of many difficult memories from a war long past."[40]

"My country has let me down," Rubitsky said in response to the report. He continued his quest for the decoration until his death in 2013.[41]

Harding kept up the attacks on both the Urbana and Warren fronts as November came to an end, but the Thirty-Second Division still marked most of its gains in mere yards. The Red Arrow commander knew he didn't have the tools he needed to break through. Despite General George Kenney's boastful optimism about air power, planes had proven no substitute for artillery. As the campaign continued, the Allies' artillery force grew steadily, and by November 27 General Waldron was operating an artillery base at Ango, about three miles behind the front lines. Of Waldron's eleven guns, two were 3.7-inch mountain guns that dated to the early twentieth century. All but one—a 105-millimeter howitzer of the Red Arrow's 129th

Field Artillery—were Australian. While the Red Arrow infantry slugged it out on New Guinea, all but one of its artillery pieces remained in Australia. Harding had requested tanks, which he thought would smash through the Japanese line on the Duropa Plantation. "We begged for them," claimed Alexander MacNab, but Herring flatly rejected Harding's request, stating there were no watercraft capable of transporting tanks to Buna. He offered Harding a substitute: Bren machine guns mounted atop armored vehicles. But the vehicles failed to arrive. The Red Arrowmen were left deeply frustrated, as the lack of artillery and armor meant they were risking their lives in attacks that had little chance of success. "We knocked heads, on orders, against a line that we knew was impregnable to our present weapons," a frustrated MacNab later wrote.[42]

Supply problems also hindered operations. During the day Japanese planes roamed the coast, hitting the small ships and their coastal supply bases. Japanese dive bombers sank an Allied barge at Hariko on November 21—five days after the first attack at Hariko that killed twenty-four men and sank ammunition, artillery, and supplies. On November 27, four Zeroes attacked the *Timoshenko* and *Morton*, as well as a dinghy in the harbor at Oro Bay, killing one Australian and injuring three Americans.[43] Quartermaster troops bravely unloaded their cargoes even as Japanese planes bore down on them. "Many men would still be here," wrote supply officer Maxwell Emerson, "if they had gone over the side and made a swim for shore."[44]

The troops at the front felt the impact of the logistical problems. Food seemed in particularly short supply. Roy Campbell claimed he once got so hungry that he abandoned his foxhole and went back to the company command post, where he spotted "a large stack of Bully Beef." Campbell "picked up a box under each arm," headed back to the front, and passed the rations "on down the line."[45] Uniforms and footwear disintegrated, through a combination of heavy use and constant exposure to the wet, humid conditions of the jungle. "It was common to see infantrymen going down the trail barefoot, with their bare buns showing out of what was left of their pants," recalled Robert Bable.[46] One bright spot was the continuing expansion of the air base at Dobodura, though here, too, as one report put it, "the detachment lacked men and equipment to function smoothly."[47]

Casualties weakened the ranks, but Harding only received a handful of replacements. Vincent Riddle, for example, was working at a motor pool in Sydney when "we were told to pack up and be ready to move out the next morning."[48] James Myers, a musician who hailed from a family prominent in Philadelphia's entertainment scene, was also in Sydney. "A buddy and I were assigned to guard a warehouse full of fine foods consigned for the American army officers in Australia," he wrote, when he learned he was heading to New Guinea. Riddle and Myers both joined Company K of the 128th Infantry Regiment, where the veterans welcomed them with gallows humor. "Don't worry if you have two left feet—one of them will soon get shot off," one old-timer joked with Myers, who, upon hearing that, "felt like throwing up."[49] The dribble of replacements could not come close to meeting the division's needs. Harding wanted the 127th Infantry Regiment brought up as soon as possible, but Herring continually denied the requests.

The army brass had long been skeptical about the abilities of the Thirty-Second Division's officers. Once in combat, that criticism came not just from above, but also from below. Sergeant Gifford Coleman described the lieutenants and captains above him as "very poor" leaders. "They were trying to lead from behind," Coleman claimed, and were "passing the buck down the line and letting the enlisted men do it."[50] "Most of the noncoms were better than their officers," thought William De Mers. "I saw a co. commander hiding behind a tree while his unit was being desimated [sic]."[51] The problem appeared to go even higher up the chain of command. Alexander MacNab, Hale's executive officer who coordinated the fighting on the Warren front, recalled one battalion commander who MacNab was "never able to get . . . away from his slit trench," and another who stayed behind the front "except on one occasion, when he couldn't stand my needling any longer."[52] As Warren Force commander, Colonel Hale kept his headquarters well behind the front. "Yes, my C.P. was 4½ miles to the rear," he later told Harding, but noted that in addition to the fighting at the Duropa Plantation, he was also responsible for "guarding Dobadura [sic] air strips many hours march away and could only communicate with them with great difficulty." Hale also told Harding that "had we been closer to Cape Endiaderi [sic] the Japs could have spit in our mess kits," and, in reference to the November 16 air attack at Hariko, wrote, "I am sure you will not forget swimming ashore."[53]

Back at the Ivory Tower in Port Morseby, MacArthur was growing increasingly frustrated and angry with the Thirty-Second Division's lack of progress. MacArthur had imagined a quick and triumphal march into Buna—and the headlines back home that would follow. Perhaps above all, MacArthur was personally embarrassed. After he had unfairly disparaged the fighting abilities of Australian troops on the Kokoda Track, now his Americans were the ones advancing slowly. At a meeting on November 25, MacArthur suggested bringing up the US Forty-First Division. But General Blamey said he preferred Australian troops, as he believed they were better fighters. "I think it was a bitter pill for General MacArthur to swallow," wrote Kenney, who was present at the meeting.[54]

As was the case with the Kokoda Track, MacArthur never visited the front to inspect the conditions personally. On November 27, he sent his operations officer, Lieutenant Colonel David Larr, to visit Buna, and upon his return, Larr was highly critical of Harding's generalship. MacArthur then dispatched his chief of staff, General Richard Sutherland, to meet with Harding on November 30. Once again, Harding pleaded for more troops. "I expressed the belief that the Japs did not have enough men to protect the perimeter of their beachhead at all points," Harding later wrote, and he argued they had "an excellent chance if we struck with fresh troops." Sutherland denied the request, citing supply problems, and instead was more concerned about the Red Arrow's lack of aggressiveness—from both officers and soldiers. He recounted Blamey's criticisms of US fighting prowess and singled out Colonel Hale—a National Guard officer—in particular. Sutherland's suggestion that his troops lacked courage startled Harding. Although Harding conceded that he, too, had questions about Hale's abilities, he believed that Hale was "doing fairly well in the only chance he had had to show his stuff."[55] Sutherland returned to Port Moresby and shared his critical assessment of Harding with MacArthur.

MacArthur summoned the I Corps commander, Robert Eichelberger, to the Ivory Tower. When Eichelberger and his chief of staff, Clovis Byers (recently promoted to brigadier general), arrived at Government House late in the afternoon on November 30, they found MacArthur, Sutherland, and Kenney on the veranda. "Kenney was calm," Byers recorded in his diary, "but not the other two!" Sutherland sat behind MacArthur's desk, while MacArthur "paced back and forth across the floor."[56] MacArthur got right to the point. Eichelberger was to relieve Harding and take command at Buna. "I want you to remove all officers who won't fight," MacArthur told Eichelberger. "Relieve regimental and battalion commanders; if necessary, put sergeants in charge of battalions and corporals in charge of companies—anyone who will fight." As the emphatic SWPA commander paced across the veranda, he related stories of soldiers retreating and abandoning their weapons on the battlefield. "Never did I think I'd see American troops quit," Byers remembered MacArthur saying. Though MacArthur acknowledged the Red Arrow Division's shortcomings in training and supply, as well as the difficulties of the battle area, he insisted that strong leadership could rescue the situation. Fearing Japanese reinforcement, MacArthur told Eichelberger that "time is of the essence" and ordered him to fly to Buna the next day. "All during this tirade," wrote Byers, "Sutherland's eyes nervously followed the Chief as he paced back and forth. They were a desperate pair."

MacArthur then shared with Eichelberger his final instructions: "I want you to take Buna or not come back alive." After a brief pause, MacArthur pointed a finger in the air and added, "And that goes for your chief of staff too."

"That was our send-off," wrote Eichelberger, "and hardly a merry one."[57]

Eichelberger arrived at Buna the next day and immediately sensed the difficulties that lay before him. "When the stink of the swamp hit our nostrils," he wrote, "we knew that we, like the troops of the 32nd Division, were prisoners of geography."[58] As corps commander, Eichelberger was the ranking officer at Buna and assumed command. Despite MacArthur's harsh words, Eichelberger claimed to have an open mind about retaining Harding as division commander, but Harding resented Eichelberger's presence and the two former West Point classmates soon clashed. Eichelberger talked of relieving officers. "Nobody should be relieved," Harding responded. "Everybody should be decorated. They are doing superhuman acts."[59] Eichelberger spent a day conferring with staff officers. Too many of them, he believed, "had never been up to the front with the doughboys."[60] Yet, he saw encouraging signs too. "There is no lack of fight in anybody I have seen out here," Eichelberger reported to Sutherland, and requested that portions of the 127th Infantry Regiment be brought to Buna as soon as practicable.[61]

Eichelberger grew far more critical the following day after he and his staff inspected the front lines. He dispatched two of his staff members, Colonel Clarence Martin (his operations officer) and Colonel Gordon Rogers (intelligence) to report on the situation at the Warren front. Eichelberger went to the Urbana front himself, Harding in tow. As the two generals drove over a rough corduroy road, Eichelberger complained about the sight of engineers resting. Then the party descended the "torturous and poorly marked footpath" that led to Mott's command post. Along the way, they saw apparently uninjured soldiers at an aid station, which further annoyed Eichelberger. "Undoubtedly some of these men had been sent back for a rest," he later wrote, but suspected that others "had left the front without permission."[62] They reached Mott's command post at midday, and after about an hour, Eichelberger wanted to see the front line. That morning "the fire from the Japanese, particularly snipers in trees, was somewhat intense," Mott later wrote, but "by the time they started out all firing had ceased." As Eichelberger got closer to the front, his displeasure intensified. In the forward area he saw unconcealed machine guns. His perturbation mounting, Eichelberger asked a machine-gun crew to scout Japanese positions down a nearby trail, and even offered to decorate any soldier who would do so. None did. "I suspect the men did not consider the remark to be [an] actual offer," surmised Harding, or "may have felt that the posthumous award of a piece of ribbon was not such an alluring bait."[63] Eichelberger sent his aide, Captain Daniel K. Edwards, forward instead. Edwards crawled through the jungle, came within sight of Buna Village, and returned without being fired upon. "It was evident," claimed Eichelberger, "that a very pallid siege was being waged."[64]

Eichelberger had still more complaints. As Red Smith recalled, Eichelberger "raised particular hell" about a wide range of topics: "the men's appearance, both clothing and personal, lack of military courtesy, lackadaisical response."[65] Eichelberger wrote to Sutherland with his concerns: "The rear areas are strong and the front is weak. Inspired leadership is lacking. In a circuit of Buna Village I found the men hungry and generally without cigarettes and vitamins. Yesterday afternoon the men immediately in contact with the Japanese had had no food since the day before...."

The units have been scrambled like eggs."[66] By the time Eichelberger and Harding reconvened at Mott's headquarters late that afternoon, Eichelberger was visibly angry. "Most everything he said was critical," claimed Harding, and "his criticisms had much of the flavor of those designed to bolster a preordained decision." Harding and his staff grew particularly angry when Eichelberger "made a sweeping assertion that the men had not fought." Harding, smoking a cigarette, listened as "Mott flared up" and defended his soldiers "in no uncertain language." Harding then took the cigarette out of his mouth and angrily threw it to the ground for emphasis, writing in his diary that he "approved of every word [Mott] said and the vehemence with which he stated his case."[67]

At the Warren front, Martin and Rogers were equally unimpressed. Just the act of getting there was difficult. After a short jeep ride, the road ended, so Martin and Rogers continued on foot along "a muddy foot trail to Hariko" and another jungle path, before reaching the frontline positions. "When we arrived at the front," Martin recalled, "the area was as quiet as the inside of a church." Martin and Rogers spoke with several soldiers over the course of the day. Most soldiers asked them when they would be relieved, leading Martin to detect a "feeling sorry for ourselves" attitude that was "not only depressing, but to my mind contagious." Martin and Rogers noticed discarded equipment strewn across the area, including empty ration cans covered with flies. "The troops are deplorable," Rogers reported. "They wore long dirty beards. Their clothing was in rags. Their shoes were uncared for, or worn out." Rogers also disapprovingly noted that Hale rarely left his headquarters. Indeed, Hale apparently was unaware that Martin and Rogers even visited the Warren front that day. "As far as I know," Hale told Harding a few years after the war, "neither Col. Martin nor Col. Rogers visited the front line on the 2nd of December 1942."[68]

Eichelberger did not wait for Martin and Rogers to give their report. Even before the colonels had arrived back at headquarters, Eichelberger had decided to dismiss Harding. "I received nothing but excuses," he wrote to Sutherland. "Harding is ready to fight for his men and his men had nothing to offer."[69] Samuel Auchincloss, Eichelberger's signal officer, wrote that "it was easy to see that Harding was about as sick as many of the men, and a very tired man."[70] About 8:00 p.m. on December 2, Harding went to Eichelberger's quarters to discuss his plans for another attack, but Eichelberger instead turned the conversation to his criticisms of the Urbana front.

"You are probably here to get some heads," Harding told him. "Maybe mine is one of them. If so, it is on the block."

"You are right," Eichelberger replied.

Eichelberger placed General Waldron in command of the Red Arrow, and Harding boarded a plane for Port Moresby the next morning. Colonel George DeGraaf, Eichelberger's supply chief, remembered that Harding departed "a bitter and depressed person."[71]

Harding's head was not the only one to roll. Eichelberger also removed Hale and Mott from their commands. Martin now assumed command of the Warren Force, while Colonel John E. Grose, the I Corps inspector general, took over the Urbana Force. In the days and weeks that followed, other commanders down the line lost their jobs. "We were swarmed with inspectors wanting to know why we weren't going forward," recalled Robert C. McCoy. "The regular army came in there and they were after promotions. They didn't give a damn—we were just National Guard and they were looking for their own glory."[72] Within weeks of Eichelberger's arrival, McCoy was out as commander of the First Battalion of the 128th Infantry Regiment, replaced with Major Gordon Clarkson, a West Pointer.

Eichelberger was determined to make more progress than Harding had. He launched his first attack on December 5. On the Warren front, Eichelberger planned another push to take Duropa Plantation and the airstrips—this time with the Bren gun carriers and their Australian crews that had finally arrived. On the Urbana front, he moved yet again against Buna Village.

The attack on the Warren front opened with airstrikes and artillery, followed by Martin's ground assault, which began about 8:00 a.m. Martin hoped that the five Bren gun carriers, driving northward along the coast, held the key to finally punching a hole in Japanese lines. "We were excited because for the first time we had armor supporting us," recalled Percy Hiatt. Other GIs were skeptical that the Bren gun carriers could accomplish the job. Lawrence Thayer described them as "nothing more than Jeeps with a large automatic rifle mounted in the back and protected somewhat by thick steel plates, waist high, fastened to the sides."[73] Robert Bable wrote that "we didn't think they had a prayer of a chance, but I said a silent one for them."[74] Roy Campbell remembered that "a flare went up, a whistle blew," and the attack began. The Bren gun carriers moved forward, lumbering across the uneven ground of the plantation, studded with shell holes and the fallen logs and battered stumps of coconut palms. The Japanese fired on them immediately with their machine guns and tossed hand grenades into their open tops. "It seemed like the world blew up," wrote Campbell, and "the hail of bullets was so intense that [I] swore it was a gray sheet of lead screaming over." Within twenty minutes all five carriers had been destroyed, and as Campbell described it, the "Aussies fell like wheat from a mower."[75] The Bren gun carriers were no substitute for tanks, and the attack failed. To the west, fighting raged across the New Strip, but gains were minimal. By the end of that day, the Warren Force under Martin fared little better than it had under MacNider and Hale.

On the Urbana front, Eichelberger, Waldron, and a host of other brass went up to supervise the attack on Buna Village. Given Eichelberger's criticism that previous commanders were too far behind the lines, he believed it was important for troops to see him at the front. "I was glad on that particular day that there were three stars on my collar which glittered in the sun," he later wrote. "How else would those sick and cast-down soldiers have known their commander was with them?"[76] Despite such bravado, gains at Buna Village that day were minor and expensive. Troops managed to knock out some bunkers and penetrate to within fifty yards of the village until withering Japanese fire stopped them.

Dissatisfied with the effort and the results, Eichelberger personally took charge of a second attack on Buna Village, using the soldiers held in reserve. Grose objected to using up the reserves. "You will attack," Eichelberger thundered, and the colonel did as he was ordered. The second attack fizzled and "cost us a bunch of casualties which we could not afford," remembered Herbert M. Smith.[77] Grose was equally bitter. "They are courageous fine men and all of them gave me the utmost cooperation," he wrote in his diary, "but they have been pushed almost beyond the limit of human endurance."[78]

Eichelberger's hubris did not just have consequences for the ordinary soldier. That day General Waldron was shot through the shoulder and evacuated—his tenure as Red Arrow commander lasting just three days. He joined General MacNider in the hospital, while General Byers assumed command of the division. Later that afternoon, Eichelberger's aide, Captain Edwards, took a bullet through the abdomen. Stretcher bearers rushed Edwards to the rear but "the carriers were shot at so frequently," wrote Byers, "that they dropped him three times."[79] Eichelberger accompanied the stretcher party to the rear, and Gordon Rogers recalled seeing him "fuming with rage and stricken with grief."[80]

There was one bright spot that day—the heroics of Staff Sergeant Herman Bottcher of Company H, 126th Infantry Regiment, the German-born Spanish Civil War veteran who had joined the Red Arrow back in California. A platoon from Bottcher's company, attached to Company G, attacked Japanese forces from the far right of the American positions at Buna Village. At first the attack went nowhere. "We got only 25 yards through the swamp when the attack bogged down," Bottcher noted, adding, "you feel so futile sloshing around in the mud." Bottcher then conferred with his company commander, Captain Harold Hantleman, who "suggested we drive to the beach on the right flank of the village." Bottcher then led the platoon across the creek and drove toward the shore, knocking out several bunkers along the way. When the platoon reached the beach that afternoon, the Japanese "opened up with enfilading fire and within five minutes we had seven casualties," remembered Bottcher.[81] Despite the heavy opposition, the troops dug themselves into foxholes so they could hold the ground they had taken. Bottcher set up machine guns to cover both flanks and opened up a communication link to bring in supplies and reinforcements. The Red Arrowmen held off several counterattacks and "the next morning," according to Gordon Rogers, "the beaches were covered with dead Japs in both directions." Rogers wrote that "Sgt Bottcher fought his company like a tiger" and was "the epitome of an aggressive leader, spurring men on and setting a personal example of daring and drive."[82] The salient became known as "Bottcher's Corner" and it effectively severed the trail link between Buna Mission and Buna Village.

In the following days, Bottcher's Corner endured numerous counterattacks. "Tomorrow is the anniversary of Pearl Harbor and the Japs are sure to have a go at us," Bottcher wrote. Just as he anticipated, Japanese forces came in that morning from both sides. Bottcher skillfully used his machine gun to blunt attacks from the Mission side of the salient, then the village side. "A piece of shrapnel got me in the right hand," he wrote, but he dismissed the injury as "nothing serious" and kept firing.[83] That evening the Japanese attempted to reinforce Buna Village from the Mission by barge, but Bottcher set the vessel ablaze with his machine gun. Holding the salient took an emotional and physical toll on the soldiers inside. "We were all pretty jittery," wrote Robert Odell. "I remember at one stage I simply shook all over and try as I did it wouldn't stop."[84] But Bottcher's Corner held firm.

Nevertheless, progress on the Urbana front remained slow, painful, and bloody. By December 9, the Second Battalion of the 126th Infantry Regiment—survivors of the Kapa Kapa Track and the withering combat at Buna Village—had dwindled to about 250 soldiers, and its ranks grew smaller by the day. On December 7, Red Smith went forward to "check conditions at . . . Bottcher's Corner" when "a Jap mortar shell landed in a tree overhead, showering fragments down on us." Smith remembered that initially he "experienced no pain; maybe something resembling a pat of the hand," but soon "felt very weak and tired" and realized he "had more than a flesh wound."[85] Red Smith was evacuated to Australia, leaving only one Herbert Smith at Buna. Paul Lutjens was wounded by a Japanese grenade. "It tossed me around a couple of times," he remembered, and the force blew the "tommy gun right out of my hands and bent the barrel." At first, Lutjens thought his legs had been blown off. "I finally got enough guts to reach back and feel my legs. They were there, but kind of wet." Then the Japanese poured gunfire on him. "One bullet went through my shirt," he remembered, "and another creased me under the eye. I think another bullet went through my thigh, but I never could be sure, because there was so much metal of all kinds in me."[86] The Japanese left Lutjens for dead, but he somehow crawled to an aid station. Smith and Lutjens lived to tell their stories. Many others did not.

By the second week of December, the Allied situation in Papua brightened. Australian forces took Gona on December 9. After launching a fierce artillery and mortar barrage, the diggers then moved in, destroying bunker after bunker until they finally overran Japanese positions. Absorbing more than seven hundred casualties, the Australians paid a steep price for a small piece of land, but the first of the three Japanese pockets had been eliminated.

At Buna, the arrival of the 127th Infantry Regiment greatly boosted Allied prospects. An advance party flew from Port Moresby to Dobodura on December 4, and the first contingent of combat troops—elements of the Third Battalion—arrived two days later, destined for the Urbana Force. On December 9, Companies I and K moved up to Buna Village, and on December 11 they relieved elements of the battered and bruised 126th Infantry Regiment at Bottcher's Corner. The new arrivals entered the fight immediately. "Companies I and K were slowly consolidating small gains and exerting constant pressure on the village," noted one report. "These companies had suffered a few casualties and were inflicting a proportionately bigger percentage of casualties on the enemy."[87] More companies soon followed, and by Christmas the entire regiment was at Buna.

The supply situation was improving steadily. By the latter half of December there were four airstrips in operation at Dobodura, a network of supply dumps nearby, and a salvage yard where serviceable clothing and equipment could be cleaned and stored for reissue. Dobodura even had a post office.[88] Another airfield opened at Popondetta on the Sanananda Track. Seaborne supply markedly improved too. Mariners had charted a path through the coral reefs of the northern Papuan coast, allowing larger supply vessels to reach Oro Bay. Meanwhile, Kenney's fighters had gained the upper hand against Japanese planes, making the supply line less vulnerable to aerial attack. By late December, Oro Bay had been transformed from a small coastal relay site into a major supply base, where a growing number of ships could bring more and more supplies to the battle area. The ragtag fleet was ragtag no more. Between November 16 and December 20, 1942, Captain Maxwell Emerson of the 107th Quartermasters estimated his unit had moved 760 tons of goods along the coastal route. Between December 20, 1942, and January 28, 1943, that figure rose to 7,800 tons, not including vehicles.[89] The 114th Engineers built a network of roadways connecting Oro Bay with Dobodura and with the fighting front. By contrast, Japanese reinforcements had largely dried up by mid-December. "There was never enough food, water, ammunition, guns, and medical supplies," recalled Clarence Jungwirth, but "the only saving grace was that the Japanese had less than we had."[90]

The Thirty-Second Division employed new weapons and tactics to dislodge the Japanese from Buna, some more successful than others. One new weapon was the portable flamethrower—a device consisting of fuel tanks strapped to the back of a soldier, connected to a hose that shot a stream of fire toward the opponent. Though flamethrowers dated to World War I, Buna marked the first time the US Army had ever used one in combat. It was an inauspicious beginning. When an E1R1 flamethrower (E stood for "experimental") arrived from Australia, the GIs tested it and then brought it up to the front on December 8 to take out a Japanese bunker near Buna Village. Wilbur G. Tirrell of the 114th Engineers had the honor of leading the attack. According to the plan, riflemen would fire on the bunker to distract its occupants while Tirrell—his experimental weapon concealed in a burlap bag—advanced toward the bunker. Tirrell was to release the flame about thirty yards from the bunker, then keep going as fire immolated its defenders. The flamethrower "worked well behind the lines," recalled Raymond Dasmann, but it malfunctioned in combat. Tirrell ran toward the bunker and activated the weapon as planned, but "instead of being protected by a wall of flame as he ran forward," Dasmann observed, "his device simply piddled out a stream . . . that did not come close to the bunkers."[91] Tirrell advanced nevertheless, trying to ignite the device as hail of lead came toward him from the bunker. He got within fifteen feet of the bunker when a bullet grazed his helmet and knocked him unconscious. Tirrell survived and the GIs recovered the flamethrower a few days later. Subsequent flamethrower attacks fared little better. "Half the time they malfunctioned," recalled Ernest Gerber. "You rarely got close enough to use them" before "the Japanese would shoot you."[92]

The Red Arrowmen improvised other ways to reduce bunkers. Raymond Dasmann attended an Australian guerrilla warfare school where he learned "how to increase the damaging power of a grenade by placing it in a jam tin packed around with gelignite [a highly explosive jel]." Dasmann could find no such tins at Buna, so he improvised. "We packed dynamite around a hand grenade in a 10-inch length of drain pipe," he wrote, to create a device that could then "be thrown like a football for an effective distance."[93] Similarly, Red Arrowmen also used a weapon called a "pole charge," which Howard Kelley described as "a six foot length of pipe filled with explosives and tied to a long pole used to push it into place."[94] Percy Hiatt remembered that "we [used] a five-gallon can of gasoline that we'd pour into a bunker, then throw in a grenade."[95] But, according to Ernest Gerber, "the thing that eventually worked best was sheer guts." As Amos Truckey described it: "Sometimes guys would move up just to draw fire and get a better idea of where the shooting was coming from." Once the location was fixed, "the squad in the middle would fire on it, while the other squads would send guys around the sides" and "drop grenades through its windows. Nobody thought about being brave. You just thought that with every bunker knocked out, fewer of our guys would get killed."[96]

Indeed, the Thirty-Second Division soon became wise to the ways of battle. Like most soldiers entering combat for the first time, the Red Arrowmen naively believed that their skill and training—and perhaps a little luck—would guarantee their survival. The realities of combat came as a deep, injurious shock—philosophically, morally, and psychologically. The diarist of Company K, 126th Infantry Regiment, initially sounded optimistic on the move up to meet the Japanese on the Sanananda Track. "Men are getting haggard looking," he wrote, "but in good spirits." After a few days of combat, his tone had changed. "I pray to God this ends pretty soon," he wrote, "it's really horrible, words can't express it."[97] No two individuals are affected by combat in quite the same way, but it leaves a profound, lifelong mark on virtually everyone who survives the experience. "Few other human activities are as certain as combat to alter substantially those who participate," wrote historian Gerald F. Linderman, "and American soldiers who survived more than a brief span of the fighting found themselves propelled through changes overthrowing, one after another, propositions that they had regarded as both fundamental and assured."[98] For the Red Arrowmen at Buna and the Sanananda Track, the innocence of their precombat world—the weekly drills at the local armory, war games in the Louisiana countryside, dates with their Australian girlfriends—was obliterated. It was a brutal epiphany.[99]

Combat stirs up a range of emotions in its participants—from hatred to pathos—but none are stronger than fear, which comes in many forms: fear of being a coward, fear of letting down comrades, fear of breaking the biblical commandment, "thou shalt not kill." But the most primal fear of all is the fear of being killed. "I remember lying in the foxhole night after night with my finger on the trigger and sweat running down my back in little rivulets and wondering if I would be alive to see the sun come up the next morning," wrote Howard Kelley.[100] Artillery barrages made GIs feel particularly helpless. "The shells were coming in strong," wrote Paul Rettell, and "the noise was hell on your nervous system. You felt like screaming or beating on something. It was awful."[101] It was gut-wrenching to watch comrades die, and in National Guard units like the Red Arrow, many soldiers were longtime friends, neighbors, or even relatives. Death often came randomly and unglamorously. "One man from another platoon couldn't seem to crap in his hole," recalled Roy Campbell, "so he crawled out into the brush. A rifle barked and the man died in his own feces, shot in the spine."[102] Gruesome sights and smells elicited horror. "The worst wound from a rifle bullet I have seen was one which a soldier received between the shoulder blades," recalled Alfred Medendorp. "The bullet tore away the section of the spine between the shoulder blades, as well as the skin and the fat and some sections of the muscle. The white spinal chord [sic] lay exposed; the muscles could be seen and their contractions watched, the lungs were torn open in spots and with every exhalation of the breath several fine sprays of blood shot up for almost six inches."[103] Percy Hiatt remembered how "a dead body in New Guinea lasted about three days. Then there'd be nothing left but clothing and bones, or just a pile of maggots."[104]

Soldiers learned to control their emotions in combat. Their lives—and those of their comrades—depended on it. "I couldn't let certain things bother me," Hiatt said. "I didn't think about the ramifications of combat."[105] Religion gave succor to many. Campbell recalled one night, after weeks of frustrating combat, when he was trying to sleep in a trench and his "knees starting shaking," his "arms and hands shook violently," and he began he to feel "completely out of control." But then Campbell "felt something like a soft, warm hand or breeze" pass over him, "sort of like a warm breath," and "a voice seemed to say, 'Be calm, my son. All is well and you will be fine.'" Campbell recalled that "a supernatural calm" came over him and "immediately the shaking subsided." It was at that moment that Campbell "knew, absolutely, that there was a God," and he was able to "sleep peacefully."[106]

No story of faith in combat was more tragic and heartbreaking than that of Lieutenant Hershel Horton of Company I, 126th Infantry Regiment, who was wounded outside the Huggins Roadblock on December 1. Rescue parties reached him twice, but Japanese snipers drove them away. Horton spent many days wounded and alone. On December 11, he wrote a letter to his family in his prayerbook:

> I sit here and lay in the terrible place, wondering not why God has forsaken me; but rather why He is making me suffer this terrible end? It is true I understand life and its reasons now, but why should He send it to this terrible grave with me? Why not let me live and tell others? I am not afraid to die although I have nearly lost my faith a couple of days here. I have a pistol here, but I could not kill myself; I still have faith in the Lord. I think He must be giving me the supreme test. I know now how Christ felt on the cross. . . . God bless you my loved ones. Keep the faith, don't worry. I shall see you all again some day. I prepare to meet my Maker.

Red Arrowmen discovered Horton's remains on December 21, about fifty yards from the roadblock perimeter. Horton's family received his prayerbook, and his letter was published in newspapers across the United States.[107]

After witnessing days and weeks of killing, and with no end in sight, some soldiers grimly accepted the inevitability of their own deaths. "I had stopped thinking of the past and couldn't believe I had any long-term future," wrote Raymond Dasmann.[108] One night on the Sanananda Track, Byron Gibbs looked back at his life. "I could see the moon up through the trees," Gibbs wrote, "and wondered if mother and Gertie were looking at the same moon. I could see well enough to look at their pictures in my billfold. After that time I felt rather resigned with the feeling we were not going to get out of this and I was ready to go."[109] A few men resorted to injuring themselves to escape combat. "I knew a captain, a company commander, who shot himself through both hands," claimed Henry Dearchs, "because he couldn't send his men forward, boys he had trained for years, out to die."[110]

The medics of the 107th Medical Battalion accompanied the infantrymen into battle. Armed with sulfa powder, tape, gauze, bandages, and

Papua New Guinean stretcher bearers evacuated soldiers wounded on the front lines. Here, stretcher bearers pause to let injured Red Arrowmen rest in the shade of a coconut grove before continuing on to a field hospital in the rear. LIBRARY OF CONGRESS

morphine syrettes, the medics crawled out under fire—through brush, jungle, and swamp—to reach the wounded. As the battle raged around them, they had to make snap decisions about who might survive their injuries and who might not, patch up wounds as best they could, and evacuate casualties to the rear. From the battlefield, wounded soldiers then passed through a chain of progressively larger medical facilities that, depending on the severity of wounds, led soldiers either back into combat or to a hospital in Australia.

Battle injuries were not the only reason for a medical evacuation. Disease took an even greater toll than fighting. Soldiers suffered from heat stroke, dehydration, and dysentery. Skin conditions abounded, exacerbated by the constant wetness and the organisms that thrived in the damp jungle environment. Medic Kenneth Springer recalled one soldier in the Huggins Roadblock "covered from the waist down, including his genitalia, with hundreds of small ringworms. It looked like his body was covered with one complete uniform tattoo."[111] The mosquito remained the greatest problem, and malaria could strike at any time. "I was sitting around stuffing high explosives into drainpipes when I realized I was very ill, shaking all over with chills," wrote Raymond Dasmann.[112] Because of the lack of replacements, Red Arrowmen had to keep fighting even when sick. "Not sending any man in [to the aid station] unless he has a fever of a 106 for 24 hours," noted the journal of Company K, 126th Infantry Regiment, "and by that time they carry them in."[113]

Even harder to treat were the unseen wounds of the mind. Many soldiers struggled with the sights, sounds, and stresses of combat, and some experienced mental breakdowns. During World War II, this phenomenon was known as "battle fatigue." "Boys were sitting around trees crying," remembered Henry Dearchs. "Their buddies had fallen on both sides right and left." Medic Fred Johnson recalled:

> Three guys came back, threw down their weapons, and said they were sick and couldn't fight. We checked them out, and couldn't find anything wrong with them. They said they had dysentery and all kinds of things. Well, a hell of an argument ensued. No matter what the doctor said, the men refused to go back. So finally the doctor gave up. In his diagnosis that the men carried to the rear he wrote "scared shitless." Off they went.

John Augustine of the Red Arrow military police escorted soldiers suffering from battle fatigue to the rear. "If you tried to do anything for them they'd break down and cry," Augustine remembered. "Some cursed themselves for cowardice and called themselves worthless. It was so sad."[114] Lawrence Thayer reflected on the cumulative psychological toll of sustained combat. "Battle fatigue in some of the officers and men took a few away," he wrote. "Some men resorted to shooting themselves in the foot, and others simply disappeared, never to be seen again. I, myself, even resorted to prayer."[115]

The GIs of the Thirty-Second Division were among the very first Americans to fight the Japanese, and they had little knowledge of their adversaries beforehand. After just a short time in combat, the Red Arrowmen developed a begrudging respect for the bravery and tenacity of the Japanese forces. Gifford Coleman thought that "as troops, they were tops."[116] The Japanese sometimes staged human wave assaults, shouting the battle cry "banzai" (a phrase wishing long life to the emperor) as they rushed Allied positions. "They'd kick it off with an officer waving a samurai saber," recalled Robert Hughes, "and come screaming out of the night."[117] But the GIs were also appalled by what they saw as Japanese cruel and wanton disregard for the rules of war. They shot at medics and attacked hospitals. Particularly vexing was the Japanese soldier's refusal to surrender, even when faced with insuperable odds. The Japanese also routinely killed Allied soldiers who fell into their hands rather than taking them prisoner—sometimes in remarkably horrific ways. The writings and reminiscences of Red Arrowmen at Buna—and indeed throughout the division's entire time in the Pacific—are replete with grisly stories of Japanese brutality toward prisoners. Going into combat, James Myers was "still not quite resolved to kill anyone in cold blood," but "had no further trouble shooting live targets" after seeing the corpse of an American soldier who had been tied to a tree and bayoneted to death.[118] "We came across an American GI the Japanese had tortured and killed," recalled Roland Stoelb. "They had his legs tied to two trees that bent over like spring poles and then cut the ropes."[119] Ernest Gerber arrived in New Guinea believing that "this would be a war fought by gentlemen [but] that's not how it was."[120]

Wartime propaganda, racial stereotypes, and decades of hackneyed Hollywood movies have depicted Japanese soldiers as mindless killing automatons willing to die unquestioningly for their emperor. Such wooden portrayals obscure the complicated reasons for their behavior. Like European fascism, Japanese militarism was infused with extreme nationalism in which traditional concepts of patriotism and national identity were exaggerated and perverted. One such concept was the philosophy of *bushido* (the "way of the warrior"), descended from the samurai warrior class of feudal Japan. *Bushido* stressed strict discipline and unquestioning obedience to superiors. Surrender was the ultimate transgression, bringing such shame and dishonor that no true warrior would ever consider it.

Even as the samurai lost their status during the late nineteenth century, the modern Japanese armed forces consciously retained the *bushido* ethic, and indeed romanticized and popularized it to fit its nationalist narrative. *Bushido* spurred the Japanese soldier to fight to the death and view any opponent who surrendered as dishonorable. Religion further amplified their ultranationalism. Purity is a key concept in Japanese Shinto. Militarists urged the Japanese people to purify their culture of corrosive Western values, such as materialism and individualism, and by extension serve in a divine mission to expel Westerners and their influence from Asia. Japanese propaganda dehumanized Western soldiers, depicting them as demons, ogres, and other malevolent creatures worthy only of death. According to historian John Dower, "the Japanese were indoctrinated to see the conflict in Asia and the Pacific as an act which could purify the self, the nation, Asia, and ultimately the whole world."[121]

Though appalled by Japanese behavior, the Red Arrowmen quickly adapted. As the Japanese would not surrender, the GIs rarely induced them to do so, despite the obvious value of prisoners for gathering intelligence. Allied soldiers routinely stripped dead Japanese troops for souvenirs— flags, money, weapons, or the swords that officers carried as an homage to the samurai of the past. Allied soldiers dehumanized the Japanese too. "It is easy to forget the visceral emotions and sheer race hatred that gripped virtually all participants in the war," wrote historian John Dower.[122] Some GIs became more than just hardened to battle. Combat had warped their minds and souls. Paul Rettell remembered one soldier who "got the urge to kill; it was like a drug to him. . . . His eyes were wild, and he would laugh crazily."[123] Robert Odell remembered that "some men took gold teeth as souvenirs," and "in one case at least one man a pair of ears."[124] Despite the surreal brutality in which he found himself, the typical Red Arrowman held on to his basic sense of humanity. "When I killed my first Japanese soldier I went through his clothing," recounted Roland Stoelb. "I found his wallet and inside was a picture of a young woman and a baby—I knelt there and cried."[125]

Buna Village finally fell to the 127th Infantry Regiment on the morning of December 14. It happened with surprising ease. Companies I and K pushed forward "steadily and cautiously," as one regimental report described it, and "fire from the Village was very light." The two companies secured the village by 10:00 a.m. Bottcher's Corner had made the Japanese position in the village untenable, causing them to withdraw. American casualties were light. "One man of the 126th CT, souvenir hunting, was the only casualty during this operation," noted the report.[126] MacArthur cabled Eichelberger: "My heartiest congratulations. Under your magnificent leadership the 32nd Div. is coming into its own."[127]

Attention now turned to the dreaded Coconut Grove—the last Japanese position on the west bank of Entrance Creek. General Byers ordered Colonel Smith's Second Battalion of the 128th Infantry Regiment to attack on the afternoon of December 15. The assault gained no ground and Byers joined the casualty list. "Near the edge of a clearing I stretched out on a leaning palm tree chin in my hands to observe," he recorded in his diary. "Thought I saw a sniper, lifted my head to ask for a gun and 'ping' someone else got me in the right hand."[128] Byers was the third general officer from the division wounded at Buna, joining MacNider and Waldron in a hospital in Australia. Buna was "a bad spot for generals," quipped MacNider upon hearing the news.[129] Eichelberger was now the last US general officer in Papua.

Smith attacked again the following day. This time, troops under his executive officer, Major Roy F. Zinzer, knocked out a key bunker. First, Zinzer's men marked it with a smoke grenade, which also reduced the visibility of its occupants. Then a corporal named Daniel F. Rini, covered with an automatic rifle by his comrade Bernardino Y. Estrada, raced to the top of the bunker and "pushed hand grenades through the firing slits." After explosions tore through the bunker, Smith ordered a push across his front. "Freed from the flanking fire of the key bunker," he wrote, "we were able to move without too much difficulty and were soon mopping up."[130] Zinzer later claimed that the battalion took the grove "through guts, grenades, and small arms."[131] Sadly, both Rini and Estrada were killed later that day, the former shot by a wounded Japanese soldier to whom Rini was giving medical aid.

In addition to clearing the Coconut Grove, the battalion won another prize. "The Japs for some unknown reason left a bridge intact across Entrance Creek," recalled Major Zinzer, "and we at once pushed a force including machine guns, across to occupy the base portion of the triangle."[132]

The Red Arrow now controlled the entire west bank of Entrance Creek, as well as a bridgehead on the other side. Eichelberger praised the battalion to Sutherland. "I took General MacArthur's name in vain in telling the 2nd Battalion . . . how ashamed he was of them," Eichelberger wrote, but "they redeemed themselves . . . and are now high in my favor." Colonel Smith, once on the verge of being relieved, "has developed into quite a fighter," Eichelberger wrote, and expressed his satisfaction that Smith's battalion "has found its soul."[133]

Meanwhile, the Warren Force had changed its approach to the strong line of Japanese bunkers. Rather than stage frontal assaults, the troops now focused on patrols and infiltration, targeting specific bunker complexes for destruction and softening up the battlefield for the expected arrival of tanks. And those tanks, which Harding adamantly requested but never received, finally came. In all, eight M3 Stuart tanks from the Australian 2/6 Armored Regiment were spirited up the New Guinea coast and hidden in the jungle. Coming with them were two infantry battalions from the Australian Eighteenth Brigade. The attack was scheduled for December 18 and would be under Australian command. Indeed, Brigadier George F. Wootten took command of the entire Warren Force; Colonel Martin now served as his deputy.

Wootten's plan was simple: push six of the tanks through the Japanese line along the coast on the Duropa Plantation and drive northward to Cape Endaiadere. The Australian 2/9 Battalion would accompany the armor, and the Red Arrow's Third Battalion of the 128th Infantry Regiment was to follow behind and mop up remaining pockets of resistance. Upon reaching the cape, the formation was to turn west toward Buna Mission, three miles away. Meanwhile, Australians of the 2/10 Battalion, with two tanks and Clarkson's First Battalion of the 128th, would attack the New Strip. On the far left of the Allied line, the First Battalion of the 126th would take the bridge between the airstrips. On the evening of December 17, the tanks moved up to the front, a mortar barrage masking the sound of their engines.

The action on December 18 began with an air attack and artillery barrage on Japanese positions. Then, at 7:00 a.m., the Australian tanks rolled onto the battlefield, followed closely by infantry. For a month, Red Arrowmen had advanced yard by bloody yard, but this time the Japanese front

Australian tanks crash through a chain of heavily fortified Japanese pillboxes during the attack on Buna. LIBRARY OF CONGRESS

gave way, as tanks blasted through and rolled over their carefully prepared bunkers. As Dick Randall remembered, the tanks "went through those pillboxes in almost no time."[134] They advanced 750 yards through the rows of coconut palms on the Duropa Plantation and reached Cape Endaiadere in an hour, losing two vehicles, one to enemy action and the other to mechanical problems. The remaining tanks then pivoted westward, but after about five hundred yards encountered a line of bunkers undamaged by the air and artillery preparation. They could not punch through.

The attack on the New Strip encountered much more difficulty, as Japanese forces put up concerted resistance, but by nightfall the Allies had reduced a bunker complex and taken the east portion of the airstrip. The First Battalion of the 126th, with no tank support, was unable to reach the bridge between the strips. As the Allied troops mopped up the territory they had taken, their commanders inspected the blasted bunkers that had stymied them for so long. "We found concrete pill boxes with steel doors," Eichelberger told Sutherland, "interlocked in such a way that it would have been almost impossible for doughboys unassisted to get across."[135]

After a one-day pause to reorganize, the Warren Force resumed the attack. By the end of December 20, the 2/9 and the Third Battalion of the 128th had advanced more than a mile and pushed to the north bank of Simemi Creek, threatening an encirclement of the Old Strip from the north. A couple of days later, the Allies controlled the entire north bank of the creek. Continued attempts to take the bridge between the strips proved costly and unsuccessful, but on December 20, the Australians of the 2/10 Battalion forded the creek four hundred yards north of the bridge. Then, on December 22, elements of the 114th Engineer Battalion repaired and reinforced the bridge while under heavy Japanese fire. By midday, Allied tanks and infantry began to cross. "Morale has improved during the pas[t] seven days," observed the diarist of the First Battalion of the 128th, "as a result of advances of Bn against enemy and as a result of deliverances of mail."[136] Christmastime saw a bloody battle for control of the Old Strip, but by December 28 it was in Allied hands.

The Urbana Force was on the move as well. Repeatedly rebuffed in his attempts to take the Triangle, Eichelberger now chose to bypass it. On December 21–22, Companies I and K of the 127th Infantry Regiment crossed Entrance Creek north of the Triangle and established a bridgehead in an open, level grassland called Government Gardens. Then, on December 24, they pushed from that bridgehead northeastward toward the sea in an effort to sever the link between Buna Mission and the Triangle. The GIs passed through the clumps of kunai grass in the Government Gardens, then about 100 yards of swamp, and then through a coastal coconut plantation—all of it studded with bunkers and snipers. One platoon came within sight of the ocean, but intense Japanese fire forced its withdrawal.

Two Red Arrowmen received the Medal of Honor for their actions that day, both posthumously. Thirty-four-year-old Elmer J. Burr of Neenah, Wisconsin, had been a Wisconsin National Guard member since the late 1920s. Burr and his company were under enemy fire in the Government Gardens when a Japanese grenade landed in their midst. To protect his comrades from the blast, Burr threw himself on the grenade just before it detonated. He died from his wounds on Christmas Day. Twenty-year-old Kenneth Gruennert of Helenville, Wisconsin, in Jefferson County was the former captain of his championship high school football team and had joined the Wisconsin National Guard at sixteen. On December 24, Gruennert was just 150 yards from the seashore when his company encountered two Japanese bunkers. With remarkable aim, Gruennert knocked out one of the bunkers by throwing grenades through its firing slits, despite having been wounded in his shoulder during the attack. Undeterred, Gruennert bandaged his wound—while still under fire—and then moved toward the second bunker. He threw more grenades and skillfully hit the second bunker. Fleeing Japanese troops were shot down by GIs, but then a Japanese sniper shot Gruennert dead.[137]

The attack resumed on December 25. A party consisting of troops from Companies A and F of the 127th once again came close to the shore, but then the Japanese counterattacked. "Bullets whizzed through the air and shrapnel from grenades was flying everywhere," remembered Roland Stoelb.[138] The GIs near the shore were cut off from their comrades by the counterattack, and they spent Christmas Day surrounded and under intense Japanese fire. A rescue party broke through to them the next day, and thanks to the leadership of Major Edmund R. Schroeder—First Battalion commander and Wisconsin National Guard officer from Oconto—Urbana Force reinforced the salient and held it after two days of hard fighting. By December 28, Stoelb and his comrades had been relieved, the wounded evacuated, and the GIs were in sight of the Solomon Sea. The Triangle was cut off from Buna Mission, and the Warren Force was pressing in from the east. The Japanese suddenly found their position in the Triangle unsustainable, and they withdrew. After more than a month of bloody and futile attempts to take the Triangle, now the Red Arrow walked in. "The area was extremely strongly fortified," observed a 127th Infantry Regiment report, "and consisted of 14 major bunkers and numerous secondary positions all connected by a pattern of communication trenches. Sniper positions covered all possible approaches to the area."[139] Eichelberger reported to MacArthur: "I walked through there today and found it terrifically strong. It is a mass of bunkers and intrenchments [sic] surrounded by swamp. It is easy to see how they held us off so long."[140]

By New Year's Eve, the fate of the Japanese at Buna had been sealed, though the last of the fighting was among the most bitter of all. The Warren Force relentlessly pressed eastward from the Old Strip toward Buna Mission. As the Warren Force closed in, the Urbana Force planned to attack Buna Mission on December 31. It was to be a double envelopment. On the

Two members of the 127th Infantry Regiment lay communication wire between the regimental command post and the Fifth Portable Hospital on December 25, 1942.
US ARMY SIGNAL CORPS

right, Major Schroeder was to lead a collection of companies toward the Mission from the south and east. On the left, two companies (Company E of the 127th Infantry Regiment in the lead, with Company F of the 128th close behind) were to attack from the direction of Buna Village, crossing the shallows between the sandspits at the mouth of Entrance Creek to gain a foothold on the Mission side of the creek. Once on the Mission side, Company E would hook right and establish a bridgehead across the creek, allowing two more companies to cross to the Mission side. As Company E secured the riverbank, Company F would drive along the coast toward the Mission, augmented by the companies expected to cross from the Company E bridgehead. With forces converging on them from two directions, the Japanese at the Mission would then be trapped, with nowhere to go but the sea.

The New Year's Eve attack got underway at 4:30 a.m. when Company E, followed by Company F, began quietly crossing the shallows between the sandspits. The troops were under strict orders to remain silent and hold their fire. At first the Japanese did not detect their movement, and the lead elements reached the spit closest to the Mission. But, just as the lead elements began heading inland, some of the soldiers still crossing the shallows threw grenades into a collection of wrecked barges just offshore, alerting the Japanese to their presence. The Japanese launched flares and lit up the predawn sky with flickering red and green light. The GIs still crossing the sandspits were completely exposed. Japanese troops fired on them with machine guns and rifle grenades. Suddenly men were falling, killed and wounded, including the Company E commander, who was hit in the legs and incapacitated. His successor, a young lieutenant, "became panic stricken," as Colonel Grose described it, "and ran to the rear, followed by most of his company."[141] Grose confronted the lieutenant, "pistol in hand," and ordered him back onto the spit.[142] When the lieutenant refused, Grose had him arrested. Company F did not break and run, and along with returning Company E troops, they held the Mission end of the spit, but they could not establish the bridgehead as planned. Major Schroeder kept steady pressure from the south and east but could not reach the Mission either. Meanwhile, to the east Urbana Force patrols came into contact with those of the Warren Force, and Japanese vessels appeared offshore after dark. "During the night time hours we could see occasionally a lone Japanese submarine surface to take out their wounded," wrote Clarence Jungwirth. "We would call for some mortar fire . . . but it was difficult to determine the range at night."[143]

New Year's Day 1943 saw more hard fighting. On the Urbana front, Buna Mission remained just out of reach. On the Warren front, tanks and infantry pushed forward and isolated a pocket of Japanese at the mouth of Simemi Creek. Urbana Force troops could see the Warren Force tanks operating just five hundred yards in the distance, but stiff Japanese resistance prevented liaison that day. In the newly taken territory, Warren Force troops rooted the remaining Japanese out of their bunkers by throwing grenades into the bunkers and then setting them ablaze with gasoline. As their territory shrank to nothingness, some Japanese troops took to the sea, hoping to swim to Sanananda to fight another day. "Out on the water were dozens of Japanese soldiers swimming for their lives," recalled Roy

Campbell. "No one seemed to want to fire at them," but then Campbell "fired a burst at one of the bobbing heads and soon everyone was firing," and "the heads disappeared" beneath the waves.[144]

January 2 proved to be the day for which every GI and digger at Buna had been waiting. The Warren Force reduced the Japanese pocket of resistance at the mouth of Simemi Creek. "Spirits were high," wrote Alexander MacNab, "as we were putting on the finishing touches to a most unpleasant job."[145] James Myers was with the party that followed behind an Australian surge, mopping up. "We walked forward but the Australians ran," Myers wrote, "shouting and making a lot of noise." Myers found it a surreal experience. "I was awed by the activity in front of me and gave no thought to any danger to myself," he wrote. "I just looked at what was taking place in front of me and occasionally firing my tommy gun whenever I found a target to shoot at." Myers compared the experience to "standing in a theater watching a carefully rehearsed play unfurl before my eyes."[146]

The Urbana Force attack focused on the eastern coastal route. At first the advancing Red Arrowmen encountered only scattered opposition, though the fighting claimed the life of Major Schroeder, who was shot through the head. Artillery pounded the Mission, using incendiary white phosphorus shells that set the grass and huts afire. Resistance grew stiffer as the GIs approached the Mission. By 2:00 p.m., Company C had crossed Entrance Creek and was attacking from the south. "We would all form a scrimmage line and sweep through," recalled Howard Kelley. "An officer told us to walk slowly and keep a sharp look-out for booby traps, trip wires, and land mines." Once again, the Japanese tried to escape by sea. "We could see heads bobbing up and down in the surf," wrote Kelley. "We all lined up and began firing at them from the beach." Even General Eichelberger, who came up to supervise the fall of the Mission, fired at his swimming adversaries. Soon about a dozen Allied planes arrived to attack the Japanese in the water. "They started forming a wide circle," Kelley recalled, and "one plane at a time would go into a long strafing dive and when he had completed his run and pulled up, another plane would start his dive with all guns firing."[147]

For the Japanese, the end was at hand. Colonel Yamamoto and Captain Yasuda committed ritual suicide in the traditional samurai way—by plunging blades into their intestines and disemboweling themselves. Those still in bunkers resisted to the very end, some killing themselves when they could fight no more. Dick Randall watched a Japanese soldier end his life with his own grenade. He was "very weak," remembered Randall. "He kept tapping it, trying to activate the fuse. . . . Finally, he got it going and blew his guts out."[148]

By 4:30 p.m., the Urbana Force had overrun the Mission area. "Dead Japs were everywhere," noted one report, and "the last point of resistance on the Mission, excluding a stray here and there, was wiped out at 1700."[149] As all this was going on, elements of the Urbana and Warren Forces drove toward each other, fighting their way through still more bunkers. At 7:30 p.m., Companies B and C of the 127th Infantry Regiment coming in from the west linked up with the Australian 2/12 Battalion driving from the east. The Urbana and Warren Forces were finally joined. After six weeks of fighting, Buna was finally in the hands of the Red Arrow Division and its Australian allies.

With the end of organized Japanese resistance, the American and Australian troops set up beach defenses to guard against a possible seaborne counterattack. Surviving Japanese fled into the jungles and swamps. A few stubbornly remained in bunkers or sniped at the Allied troops. Japanese planes from Lae occasionally raided Buna as well. "Mopping up continued in all areas," noted one report on January 3, "and the 7 barges beached on the Mission were cleaned of a small group of Japs who had taken refuge in them."[150] Now able to walk around freely, the GIs inspected their devastated surroundings. "The area was pitted with bomb craters that were half filled with water, some as large as 30 feet in diameter," wrote Clarence Jungwirth. "The craters were littered with the remains of dead Japanese, [and] the smell of rotting bodies filled the air."[151] Dead Japanese lined the beach as well. Robert Bable remembered that "several hundred or perhaps close to a thousand corpses had washed up on the shore as far as Cape Endaiadere." They were "horribly distorted and hideously grotesque in their animated poses," Bable noted, including one corpse that "twitched and rippled," because "the body cavity was completely filled with maggots."[152] Indeed, the Red Arrowmen called the shore between Buna Village and Cape Endaiadere "Maggot Beach." Crews gathered up the dead from both sides. The bodies of Japanese soldiers were thrown into mass graves or burned. Allied dead were laid out in a cemetery in long, neat rows, which some dubbed "Eichelberger Square."

Allies captured a handful of Japanese who were too injured to offer resistance and questioned them for intelligence information. One prisoner told interrogators that "he was determined to die because he did not wish to be a P/W [prisoner of war] and that he could no longer face his family and friends in Japan." He added that he would "kill the enemy radio operator if he should transmit news of his capture by the Americans" and that "he intended to take his own life before he could be sent back further behind our lines."[153] The Chinese and Korean laborers the Japanese forced into service were happy to surrender. A group of Koreans brought to Buna to construct the airfields told their American liberators that "they had not eaten for eight days." The interrogation report also noted that "many of them had skin eruptions showing signs of pellagra. Most of them were suffering from fever. They were extremely filthy, poorly clothed and emaciated." The Koreans "showed their happiness in being taken prisoner," noted the report, and "some stated they would 'work hard and long for us for they knew we would feed them well.'"[154]

With the fighting over, some semblance of military routine returned. "We had a lot of paper work to be done," wrote Jungwirth, the company clerk. "I had my portable typewriter brought up and began typing the necessary reports." GIs got a little leisure time too. Roy Campbell fashioned a hammock out of items he salvaged along the beach. He enjoyed swaying "gently, between two coconut trees, and [sleeping] soundly for the first time in months."[155] The Red Arrowmen also swam at Maggot Beach. It "was a great relief from the heat and humidity," Jungwirth noted, but "we had to watch out for the many dead Japanese floating in the waters of the Bay. When they floated too close to shore, they were dragged in, searched for information and souvenirs, and then buried in a shallow grave."[156]

Three Japanese pockets existed when the campaign began. With the fall of Buna, only Sanananda remained. As the final act at Buna played out, the agony of the Americans inside the Huggins Roadblock finally came to an end. An advance force of the Australian Seventh Division Cavalry arrived at Soputa on December 15, and three days later the cavalrymen fought their way through to the roadblock, where American soldiers had been stranded since November 30. On December 19, Brigadier Porter launched another aggressive attack on the Japanese at the Sanananda-Killerton Track junction. While the Allies were unable to break the Japanese line, the Australian Forty-Ninth Battalion swept around the right side of it and reached a position just outside the roadblock. The Australians reached the beleaguered Americans the next day and opened a supply line to them.

Meanwhile, the Seventh Division Cavalry set out northward from the Huggins Roadblock, bound for Sanananda Point. The cavalry never got past the Japanese second defense line, but established another blocking position on the track, this one dubbed Kano, four hundred yards north of Huggins. On the evening of December 22, the Australian Thirty-Ninth Battalion arrived at the Huggins Roadblock and took over from the Americans. After twenty-two days of hellish fighting against great odds, the survivors of the roadblock finally marched to the rear. "Christmas packages were received by the troops," recalled Kenneth Springer, "with raisins and other goodies as well as greetings from folks back home."[157] Wellington Homminga recalled that "we had hot rice [and] corned beef," but the sudden intake of food shocked their digestive systems and "everything we ate, we threw up."[158]

The relief of the Huggins Roadblock was good news for the Allies, but the fighting along the track remained a bloody stalemate. The main Japanese line in front of the Sanananda-Killerton Track junction still held, as did Japan's secondary line north of the Kano position. The Sanananda Track in between the two lines resembled pearls on a necklace, with Allied and Japanese positions interspersed along the route.

With the fall of Buna on January 2, General Herring could now focus all his efforts on Sanananda, but before he could take any action there, he needed more troops. The Australian tanks and infantry battalions of the Eighteenth Brigade that had fought on the Warren front in the last days at Buna crossed over to the Sanananda Track. American soldiers from the 163rd Regimental Combat Team of the Forty-First Infantry Division, under the command of Colonel Jens Doe, relieved the exhausted remnants of the 126th Infantry Regiment. Elements of the 126th had first entered the fight along the Sanananda Track on November 22; when the regiment finally stepped off the line on January 9, it was down to a mere 158 effective fighters.

On January 4, Herring convened a conference of his top commanders, among them General Eichelberger, to plan the final elimination of the Sanananda pocket. One complication was that the Allies were unsure how many Japanese soldiers they were facing. As Eichelberger wrote to Sutherland, the Allies had no idea if "there were one thousand Japs in Sanananda or five thousand."[159] Under the plan Herring and the others eventually devised, Allied forces would move toward the remaining Japanese positions from two directions. Colonel Grose's Urbana Force, consisting mostly of the 127th Infantry Regiment, would attack along the narrow coastal route from Siwori toward Sanananda. Herring hoped that the Japanese would assume the Urbana Force was the primary assault force; in reality, Herring planned for a second group to stage the main attack from the Sanananda Track to the south. The Australian Eighteenth Brigade and the 163rd Infantry Regiment of the Forty-First Division were to clear the Japanese off the track and then move northward to the coast and overrun the remaining Japanese positions.

As the Allies' plan got underway, command arrangements suddenly changed. On January 8, MacArthur departed the Ivory Tower in Port Moresby and returned to Brisbane. He issued a communiqué declaring the fight in Papua all but over. "The Sanananda position has now been completely enveloped [and] faces certain destruction," MacArthur announced.[160] His early declaration of victory surprised and angered his field commanders back in New Guinea who were about to take on thousands of Japanese. Two days later, Herring assumed command of New Guinea Force and moved to Port Moresby. Eichelberger took the job of commanding the advance force and oversaw the assault on Sanananda.

On January 5, the Urbana Force began its march along the coast toward its first target, the village of Tarakena. Allied artillery had blasted the area between Siwori and Tarakena the night before, but when the infantry moved out, it encountered stiff Japanese resistance. When they reached Tarakena on January 7, that resistance strengthened even further. Lieutenant Powell A. Fraser positioned himself on the sandbar that paralleled the coast and used a 37-millimeter gun to blast away at the Japanese in the village, firing antipersonnel canister rounds that sprayed little steel balls through the air like a shotgun. The Japanese held. The American attack continued on January 8. Grose positioned more guns on the sandbar, and late that afternoon he sent Companies A and C to push through to the village. By the end of the day, Tarakena was finally in GI hands.

Just beyond Tarakena was Konombi Creek, fast moving and forty feet wide. The Japanese controlled the bridge spanning the creek, but Urbana Force had two collapsible canvas boats, and Grose ordered Company C under Lieutenant Tally D. Fulmer to use them to cross the creek. Fulmer's first attempt came in the wee hours of January 10, but as soon as the boats hit the water, the swift current carried them downstream. Fortunately, the boats and the GIs aboard were all recovered. Just before daybreak, two soldiers, Private First Class Jack K. Cunningham and Staff Sergeant Robert Thompson, swam through the current and attached a cable to the far shore to guide the boats across the creek. Unfortunately, soon after Fulmer began the second crossing, the cable came loose. That afternoon Fulmer made a third and even more dangerous daytime attempt. While Allied artillery and mortar fire rained down on the Japanese—including the guns of Lieutenant Fraser on the sandbar—Thompson, a Spanish Civil War veteran, swam across the creek yet again, this time with four others, and reattached the cable. Then Thompson, who was "clad only in shorts, armed with a pistol and three hand grenades," as Fulmer recalled, remained on the "hostile bank, in order to direct the crossing of his platoon." The third crossing succeeded. With the Red Arrowmen now on the far bank, Thompson led an attack on "two dominating pillboxes," as Fulmer described them, "thereby securing a small bridgehead, and Company A crossed over immediately afterward."[161] Fraser, Fulmer, Thompson, and the four others who swam the river—Raymond R. Judd, Raymond Milby, Marvin M. Peterson, and Lawrence F. Sprague—each received the Distinguished Service Cross for their actions. Soon afterward, a war correspondent asked Thompson about his peacetime occupation. "An organizer of the Young Communist League for Ohio," he responded.[162]

Once across the Konombi Creek, the Urbana Force encountered still more bunkers and more fighting. The troops approaching along the Sanananda Track faced opposition that was just as strong. On January 11, the Australians hit the Japanese on the track with artillery and then launched an attack with two battalions and the tanks from Buna.

Commanders hoped this attack would be a repeat of the Duropa Plantation triumph, but it was not. The Japanese mined the road, and antitank guns, which the Allies hadn't realized the Japanese possessed, knocked out the tanks in short order. Without armor to push through the bunkers, the infantry stalled. The Australians took 142 casualties and made no appreciable gains.

Despite the strength of their troops' resistance, the Japanese high command understood their position in Papua was untenable. By early January, their forces had effectively run out of food and ammunition, with no realistic hope of reinforcing them in a meaningful way. The situation was no better at Guadalcanal, where US Marines and a growing army contingent had successfully rebuffed all Japanese attempts to force them off the island, and by the New Year were outnumbered, outgunned, and hungry. In early January, Imperial Headquarters in Tokyo ordered a withdrawal from both Papua and Guadalcanal. Japanese troops on Guadalcanal pulled back into the northern Solomons. On New Guinea, they withdrew to Lae and Salamaua, about 150 miles up the coast. Japanese barges evacuated the sick and wounded, traveling at night to avoid Allied planes, while able-bodied soldiers marched through the jungles and swamps along the coast, bypassing the Australians at Gona as best they could.

Nevertheless, when the final Allied push at Sanananda came on January 16, the fighting was as brutal as ever. The 163rd Regimental Combat Team launched yet another attack on Japanese positions along the Sanananda Track near the old Huggins Roadblock site. The Australians bypassed the track and pressed north to Cape Killerton. Then they turned east and moved through dense swampland to close in on Sanananda Village. The Urbana Force moved forward too, now under the command of Lieutenant Colonel Merle H. Howe (Eichelberger had pulled Grose off the line for a rest, much to Grose's consternation). As the Red Arrowmen pressed up the coast toward Sanananda, the Japanese still challenged them, but the GIs could tell that the condition of their adversaries was rapidly deteriorating. "Co I has killed 7 Japs and Co K 5," noted the Urbana Force journal. "Uniforms, ragged; weapons were rusty and bodies in poor condition."[163] Within days, Japanese troops had been reduced to several widely separated pockets: two on the Sanananda Track, including one near the old Huggins Roadblock site; one along the coast northwest of Sanananda Village; and another—facing Howe—along the coast to the east, at their headquarters at Giruwa.

Howe reached Giruwa on January 21 and linked up with the Australians coming in from the west. Japanese troops battled to the very end, even when they were sick or wounded. Robert Hughes encountered Japanese patients "all packed up on bunks" when his unit took over a military hospital. "They didn't give up," Hughes recalled. "Even then they'd have a grenade or pistol with them [and] attempt to use it."[164] Amos Truckey remembered one patient who "pulled out a knife and brought it up to throw." Truckey quickly shot the patient, and the knife "landed right between my feet."[165] According to one report, "20 Japs were killed resisting capture in the Giruwa hospital area."[166] But most patients were simply too weak to resist. "Very few were able to walk because of beriberi, physical exhaustion or wounds," noted another report.

Some Japanese soldiers had become so desperately hungry that they even turned to cannibalism. One report of the 127th Infantry Regiment documented "evidences of cannibalism amongst the enemy in several instances" at the Japanese hospital at Giruwa. Mopping-up operations in subsequent days around Giruwa revealed more evidence of cannibalism. One patrol led by Lieutenant Kenneth Virch followed a Japanese telephone line to a communication center. "At one point I saw a Jap not long dead with his right arm missing," wrote Virch. "His thigh appeared as if steaks had been cut off. His intestines were also disturbed. Some of his internal organs seemed to be missing."[167]

The Papuan campaign officially ended on January 22, though the Red Arrow encountered Japanese stragglers for weeks afterward. "Shot 1 Jap in poor condition," noted the Urbana Force journal entry for February 1.[168] The Papuan campaign, along with the simultaneous battle at Guadalcanal that concluded on February 9, were the first major Allied land victories of the Pacific War. The two campaigns—which are perhaps more properly viewed as one—were a major turning point of World War II. The Allies had effectively halted Japan's advance into the South Pacific and secured the sea links between Australia and North America. Papua and Guadalcanal, along with the battles at the Coral Sea and Midway, severely damaged Japan's offensive capabilities. The Allies now could begin the long and arduous process of rolling the Japanese back across the Pacific. In the United States, Guadalcanal is remembered as a glorious triumph, where the tough and plucky US Marines held off the battle-hardened Japanese and turned the tide of the war. The same could be said about the Thirty-Second Division at Buna. But in the American mind, the Papuan campaign is barely remembered at all.

And yet, the Allied casualty rate in Papua was six times higher than at Guadalcanal. Between July 1942 and January 1943, the Allies in Papua took 8,546 casualties—3,095 dead and 5,451 wounded. The Australians suffered the brunt of these losses, but the toll on the Red Arrow was heavy too. A total of 707 Red Arrowmen were killed, 1,680 were wounded, and 62 were missing in action. Disease exacted an even heavier cost. The Red Arrow Division recorded 8,286 disease casualties, including 5,358 recorded cases of malaria, though many cases originally marked as "fevers of unknown origin" turned out to be malaria as well. Disease was not limited to frontline troops. More than one thousand cases of malaria and other diseases were recorded among rear echelon troops in places like Port Moresby and the supply base at Milne Bay.

In all, including non-combat-related injuries and neuropsychiatric cases, the total number of recorded casualties in the Red Arrow during the Papuan campaign was 11,022—or nearly 90 percent of the division's original strength when the campaign began.[169] The 126th Infantry Regiment was the hardest hit of all. It began the campaign with 3,171 troops. By the time it left Buna in late January, the regiment had shrunk to just 611. In the words of historian Samuel Milner, "the regiment as such had ceased to exist." The full extent of Japanese casualties in the Papua Campaign remains unknown. But, of the perhaps 17,000 Japanese troops who took part in the campaign, an estimated 12,000 died and just 350 were taken prisoner. "The conclusion is inescapable," wrote Milner, "that the fighting in Papua . . . proportionate to the forces engaged, had been one of the costliest of the Pacific war."[170]

Though Buna was a significant victory, the rookie mistakes of the campaign and the high casualty count left a bitter aftertaste for American leaders. MacArthur pledged there would be "no more Bunas," and the army studied the Papuan campaign carefully for lessons that would inform future Pacific operations. MacArthur seemed not to consider how his own actions may have contributed to the challenges at Buna, although many historians since have been highly critical of his leadership. Historian Richard Frank called MacArthur's "Buna or die" remark to Eichelberger "the absolute nadir of his generalship."[171] Instead, MacArthur and his circle fully blamed the Red Arrow Division for the difficulties at Buna—and as a National Guard division already suspect in the eyes of army professionals, the Red Arrow was an easy target. Despite its hard-won victory, the Thirty-Second Division came away from Buna with its reputation sullied rather than enhanced. Eichelberger, for one, objected to such criticisms. "A great deal has been said and whispered about the 32nd Division," Eichelberger wrote in his memoir, "and much of it makes no sense. The 32nd which 'failed' at Buna was the same 32nd that won the victory there. No one else did."[172] As for the Red Arrowmen themselves, they were relieved the battle was over and proud to have prevailed. As James Myers wrote: "We fought the Japs. We fought the jungle, the rain and mud, the insects, swamps and diseases—and we won."[173]

Red Arrow soldiers march down Queen Street in Brisbane, Australia, during the Allied Flag Day parade on June 14, 1943. WISCONSIN NATIONAL GUARD, US ARMY SIGNAL CORPS PHOTO

CHAPTER 7

REBUILDING THE RED ARROW

After its victory at Buna, a battle-weary Red Arrow returned to the relative comforts of Australia. As his troopship sailed along the Australian coast, Lawrence Thayer glimpsed "a little old farmhouse . . . near the shore" and felt "almost as though I was home again." Crowds cheered wildly as the troopships sailed up the Brisbane River to the docks, and Red Cross workers met the arriving soldiers at the foot of the gangplank. "They had prepared a huge pile of steaks for us," Thayer remembered, and "we sure gobbled up that marvelous treat."[1] Every Red Arrow soldier was relieved to be away from the green hell of New Guinea. However, 1943 would bring the division many changes and challenges. New troops came by the thousands to replace the Red Arrowmen who were lost in Papua. Among those replacements was a new commanding general. Training grew more intense and comprehensive, informed by the hard lessons learned in the jungle. As the Red Arrow trained and absorbed new members, more and more US fighting units arrived in Australia and the South Pacific. Also streaming across the ocean were more ships, planes, and better, more plentiful equipment. By the end of 1943, the rested and rebuilt Red Arrow would find itself back in New Guinea, poised to make its return to the terrible world of war.

The GIs of the Thirty-Second Division—exhausted, ragged, hungry, and diseased but victorious—arrived in Australia in scattered fashion over the course of January and February 1943. Upon their arrival, many Red Arrowmen went to rest camps along the Queensland coast to unwind from their battle experiences. Some, like Robert Bable, recuperated at Burleigh Heads. "It was a small hamlet of about 200 residences nestled in a secret cove," Bable wrote, "high on the escarpment that rose behind a lovely white sand beach. The surf was superb."[2] Others went to Coolangatta. "The beach was long and wide with beautiful white sand," Vincent Riddle remembered. "The salt water and sunshine was good for our sores and ulcers. We spent a lot of time in the surf and enjoyed every minute of it."[3] Raymond Dasmann "organized a water soccer game to be played in the surf, and of course volleyball and table tennis."[4] The usual gambling occurred as well. "We have five months pay coming," Elvin Ball wrote home, so "there have been plenty of crap games going on the past few days."[5] Whatever their recreational choices, the soldiers were temporarily free from duties. "We lived like what we thought was kings," said Marvin Langetieg.[6]

GIs spent much of their newfound free time in search of food. "I went [to Buna] weighing 186 pounds," remembered Robert Hughes, "and came out . . . weighing 120."[7] Hughes and the others went about gaining back their lost poundage as quickly as possible. Elvin Ball told his family of a woman near the camp who sold roasted chickens to the soldiers. "They were stuffed with a dressing that had onions and dill in it," Ball wrote. "That chicken just melts in your mouth."[8] Dairy was among the most common cravings. "Every morning," recalled Lawrence Thayer, "an old farmer came by with a horse pulling a two-wheeled cart loaded with eight-gallon cans of milk for sale by the cup. It was certainly a great pleasure to gulp it down."[9] The GIs also welcomed the opportunity to drink alcohol. "The first night most of the troops went into town to get roaring drunk and to try to forget what they had been thru," remembered Clarence Jungwirth. He noted that "Australian liquor joints were selling bottles of booze at $20.00 a bottle, quite a sum of money in 1943," but "the G.I.'s exhausted their stock [and] there were a lot of big hangovers the next day."[10]

Many other Red Arrow soldiers returned from Buna with injuries or diseases and were hospitalized in the Brisbane area, sometimes for extended periods. Herbert M. Smith, wounded at Bottcher's Corner on December 7, 1942, had several operations to remove shell fragments from his body and remained hospitalized until April 1943. Percy Hiatt remembered that "I was [in] the hospital for about four months." He endured several surgeries on his ankle and was treated for malaria and "jungle sores and ulcers."[11] Recuperating soldiers passed the time playing cards and games. "I've taken up chess," reported Archie Van Gorden, who contracted malaria at Milne Bay. "It takes a lot of thought, and takes one's mind away from all worries."[12] They also spent a lot of time immersed in conversation. Soldiers scattered by the vagaries of battle were often reunited in hospital wards. Herbert M. Smith visited with several people he had not seen since Buna or the Kapa Kapa Track, including Henry Geerds, Harold Hantleman, and Paul Lutjens. Alfred Medendorp, being treated for malaria and dysentery, fondly recalled a visit from General Edwin Forrest Harding, the former Red Arrow commander who was about to depart for the United States. (Harding soon would be assigned to command the Panama Mobile Force, guarding the canal and training GIs for jungle warfare.) "He walked right up to my bed and called me by my first name," Medendorp wrote. "The last time I had seen him was when he gave instructions just before crossing the mountains," and Harding "wanted to know all about the trip across, every detail."[13] As Herbert M. Smith recovered, "soon I was using a wheel chair [sic], then able to take short walks," he recalled. Once ambulatory, Smith remembered, "the hospital was very liberal on [its] pass policy," affording him a visit to the Queensland beaches. Hospitalized soldiers received their Purple Heart—the US military's decoration for those wounded in action. "There was no formation," Smith wrote of one presentation ceremony, "as many of the honorees were in wheelchairs."[14]

The GIs who were too sick or injured to resume their duties were separated from the division. A few took up noncombat duties in SWPA, like Herbert M. Smith, who became the executive officer of a supply base in Melbourne after his release from the hospital.[15] Most returned to the United States and were discharged from the service. Some of the first returnees arrived at the US Army's Percy Jones General Hospital in Battle Creek, Michigan, in March 1943. "Like the boys of '17 who turned back the Germans," proclaimed the *Battle Creek Enquirer*, "the young Wisconsin and Michigan men of today—nearly all former national guardsmen— overcame almost insurmountable obstacles to push the Japs out of New Guinea."[16] Others went to the Milwaukee Veterans Hospital. The first to arrive was Norman Cuff, who the *Milwaukee Sentinel* described as "29, unmarried, tall, handsome, brown eyed." But the reporter's celebratory coverage of Cuff's return took a somber turn:

> Sgt. Norman Cuff of Rio, Wis., sits in a wheel chair in the sunny re-ceiving ward at the Veterans hospital at Soldiers home. He is the first battle casualty of World War II to arrive here for treatment. Sgt. Cuff doesn't say much, answers mechanically, dully. His words have no en-thusiasm, no color. He doesn't mean to be rude or surly, but there is no use trying to make a reporter understand the Buna jungle swamps unless he's been there.[17]

Robert Thompson, who fought fascism in Spain and then the Japanese in New Guinea, also returned to the US in March. Thompson's heroics at Konombi Creek in January 1943 had kept the Urbana Force driving toward Giruwa in the late stages of the Papuan campaign. While at Buna, he wrote a primer on jungle warfare tactics and afterward published an article in *Infantry Journal* about sniping. Few could match Thompson's enthusiasm for fighting fascism, but he could not beat malaria.[18]

By March, the Red Arrow's rest period came to an end, and able-bodied members returned to Camp Cable, south of Brisbane. They did so in the midst of great changes in the South West Pacific Area. In January, Gen-eral MacArthur activated the Sixth Army to accommodate the growing number of fighting units that would be joining the Thirty-Second Di-vision in SWPA. To command the Sixth Army, MacArthur passed over General Robert Eichelberger (who basked in public acclaim after Buna, angering his boss) and brought in Lieutenant General Walter Krueger—a familiar face to many Red Arrowmen from the Louisiana Maneuvers. At sixty-three, Krueger was rather advanced in age to command a field army, but he seemed a perfect fit to MacArthur. According to historian Kevin C. Holzimmer, "Krueger's performance in the GHQ maneuvers of 1941 and subsequent training with the Third Army most likely cemented in MacArthur's mind that Krueger was a first-rate commander, one who could successfully take his army back to the Philippines."[19] Given MacArthur's intoxication with publicity, there is also no doubt that he sought a commander who—unlike Eichelberger—would not seek public attention for his achievements on the battlefield. As historian Stephen R. Taaffe put it, "MacArthur wanted a capable officer with whom he was familiar, with sufficient seniority to outrank any Australian generals who might otherwise claim authority over American troops, and with enough perspicacity to stay out of the limelight."[20] Eichelberger remained in command of I Corps, now under Krueger.[21]

The Red Arrow Division also got a new commander: Major General William H. Gill. A 1907 graduate of the Virginia Military Academy, Gill received a Silver Star for action with the Fifth Division during World War I. During the army's rapid expansion after 1940, Gill took on several training assignments and earned a reputation as a stern disciplinarian. In 1941, he led a brigade of the Twenty-Eighth Infantry Division (Pennsylvania National Guard) in the Carolina Maneuvers. In May 1942, Gill was promoted to major general and the following month went to Camp Carson, Colorado, to assume command of the Eighty-Ninth Infantry Division. In February 1943, Gill received a phone call from Washington, ordering him to take command of the Red Arrow in Australia. Gill was crestfallen. After having trained the Eighty-Ninth Infantry Division for the better part of a year, he strongly desired to lead it into combat. "I said I didn't want to go," Gill recalled, "and they said that doesn't have anything to do with it."[22] He soon found himself on an airplane scudding across the Pacific.

Gill arrived in Brisbane on February 27 and reported to MacArthur the next morning. "He was nice and very kind," Gill recalled, although his new boss painted a grim picture of the task before him. "The main thing I remember about our conversation," Gill later reflected, "was that he tried to explain to me the many problems I would face because of the poor condition of the outfit."

As the Red Arrow reassembled at Camp Cable in March, Gill quickly came to agree with MacArthur's assessment. "It's an odd sort of thing to say," Gill later commented, but he thought the Red Arrow troops were "only part men." He observed that "their morale was low, their equipment was low, many men were sick with malaria, and they didn't know which

Milwaukee Journal reporter Robert Doyle (center) talks with General William H. Gill (left) and General Robert Eichelberger. Doyle joined the Red Arrow in Australia in October 1942 as a civilian war correspondent, and he reported from the South Pacific until early 1944. Doyle's writings and photographs helped Wisconsinites back home better understand the lives and war-time experiences of soldiers. WHI IMAGE ID 99496

way to turn." Gill decided that "a complete reorganization had to take place," a process that "had to be done carefully," he said, "because you are dealing with people: dealing with soldiers, dealing with officers, many of them were sick and disheartened. It had to be definite; it had to be sympathetic; it had to be intelligently applied."[23]

However, the Red Arrowmen did not consider themselves broken or defeated and were rankled by Gill's appraisal. One anonymous soldier described the first time Gill addressed his regiment. The general was scheduled to speak at 10:00 a.m. but showed up an hour and a half late. "With the hot sun beating down," the soldier recalled, "the morale of the men had not changed for the better." When Gill finally spoke, he assured the regiment that he would "make a good division out of the 32d." The troops were offended by Gill's implication. As the anonymous soldier wrote, "the men having just returned from a successful engagement with the enemy . . . felt that they had done a good job and were members of a good division." As Gill continued speaking, "there was whispering going on throughout the regiment," and one soldier, in an apparent show of his contempt, "held a newspaper up in front of his face." The conclusion of Gill's speech, the soldier reported, was greeted with "a mixture of handclapping, yelling and some boos."[24] Considerable tension also existed between Gill and his officers. "He was very unhappy with the Guard unit that he inherited," Herbert A. Smith explained. "I think initially he was very prejudiced against Guard officers."[25]

Gill was just one of many new faces to join the division after Buna. Replacements arrived to fill out the ranks, though at first their numbers were small, as stateside training camps were just beginning to produce new soldiers. By March 1943 the Thirty-Second Division had received fewer than five hundred of the six thousand replacements it had requested. Replacement depots, nicknamed "repple depples," sprang up at Melbourne, Sydney, and Brisbane to funnel troops into depleted army units, and gradually more and more new soldiers entered the rolls of the Red Arrow.[26] One was a medic from Iowa named Dean Andersen, who arrived at Brisbane in March 1943. Andersen was unimpressed with his repple depple—a racecourse converted into an army camp. Soldiers lived in tents, slept on bales of hay, and according to Andersen, "the bathroom facilities were not as good as we had on the boat."[27] Arkansan Jesse Coker arrived in Brisbane in May. "Our mess hall was located in the stable area," he recalled, "and we were housed in a number of structures which had been hastily constructed."[28] The replacements were trucked from the repple depples to Camp Cable, where they received a meal, had their paperwork processed, and were classified for assignment. "The 32nd Division was fast being brought back up to full strength," remembered Buna veteran Howard Kelley, "with replacements arriving every day."[29]

Replacements came from across the United States, further diluting the Upper Midwestern character of the division. "The men with whom

I was placed were a group of the most ignorant hillbillies from Tennessee," recalled Andersen. "All they talked about was fishing, hunting, and farming with mules. In about a week I was fed up with their stories."[30] Gifford Coleman, a National Guardsman since before mobilization in 1940, thought some of the new men "were educated much better than the original people." Others viewed the newcomers with skepticism. "There was a very young man in my squad," remembered Vincent Riddle, "who had been in an Army prison in the States [and] was released because he agreed to join an infantry combat outfit."[31] Whatever their circumstances, the veterans were grateful for the reinforcements. "I could not have received a warmer welcome," wrote Jesse Coker.[32]

There were new officers as well, but they were not nearly as well received. Veterans were wary of the graduates of officer training programs who had never been in combat. Paul Rettel wrote of "a new second lieutenant fresh from the states who was going to teach us how to cook and eat in the jungles. That was like the patient telling the doctor what to prescribe."[33] In some cases, skepticism turned into outright hostility. "We were assigned a new Company Commander," recalled Clarence Jungwirth, who described the new officer as "a real (*###*@ SOB)." This "90 day-wonder," he wrote, was "mean-spirited" and "flaunted his authority in an abrasive manner." Fortunately for the company he did not last very long—the officer was arrested for drunkenness and put before a court-martial. "Before the trial he called me," wrote Jungwirth, "and asked if I would be a character witness." Jungwirth refused. "I told him . . . that I was a Catholic" and "could not take an oath and swear to what was false," then "hung up on him."[34] Some officers took the time to learn from their combat-hardened subordinates. "Our new Lieutenant Griffin came over to where I was and began asking me about the Battle of Buna," recalled Howard Kelley. "We talked for more than an hour."[35]

The turbulence and turnover in the Thirty-Second Division after Buna provided opportunities for advancement. Herman Bottcher received a promotion to captain after his heroics at Buna and took command of Company A, 127th Infantry Regiment. In April 1943, Art Kessenich's company commander urged him to apply to officer candidate school, an opportunity Kessenich welcomed. His wife, Dora, had just given birth to their first child back home in Madison, and the pay hike that came with the promotion would help him support his growing family. "I felt the war would last a long time," he wrote, "so I had better accept a progression in rank." After passing the three-month officer training program in Brisbane, Kessenich became a personnel officer in the Forty-First Infantry Division. "Both the 32nd and 41st were in Australia," he pointed out, "so those of us who were enlisted in the 32nd went to the 41st and vice versa."[36] Charles Brennan, a longtime member of the Massachusetts National Guard, was part of a contingent from the 114th Engineers who went to officer candidate school. "We . . . had just finished a long and bitter campaign," Brennan remembered, and "the instructors had never seen combat." He thought the program "a piece of cake" and became an officer in the Ninety-First Engineers.[37]

The sick and wounded from Buna filtered back into the division as soon as they were cleared for duty, though sometimes they had difficulties reintegrating themselves, particularly the officers. "After four months in various hospitals," Alfred Medendorp was "anxious to get back" to the Red Arrow, but the division personnel office was not anxious to see him. "We have no vacancies," he was told flatly. Medendorp was crushed. "While I was recovering in the hospital," he lamented, "the jobs, and the promotions that went with them, had been given to those that were on their feet at the time. The payoff for being battered in hell was to be left out." The veteran of the Kapa Kapa Track who had fought outside the Huggins Roadblock now drifted from position to position in the Thirty-Second Division. Medendorp described himself as a "Malarial Orphan" but still considered himself lucky, commenting that "the dead and the maimed are not being given jobs either."[38] As the formerly sick and wounded were discharged from hospitals, many were sent to repple depples for reassignment and never returned to the Red Arrow.

Training resumed in March 1943. Eichelberger came down from his Rockhampton headquarters and visited Camp Cable frequently to supervise. Some at Sixth Army headquarters wondered if the division could be salvaged at all. The new soldiers and officers had no combat experience, and the veterans still suffered mightily from diseases and injuries. In March, General Clovis Byers (still Eichelberger's chief of staff) flew from

Rockhampton to Brisbane to confer with Krueger's chief of staff, Brigadier General George Honnen. They discussed a variety of issues, but the condition of the Red Arrow was at the top of Honnen's agenda. "He is worried about the 32 Div.," Byers recorded in his diary, and added: "Who isn't?"[39]

Incorporating lessons learned at Buna, the Thirty-Second Division's training became more comprehensive and rigorous. The enhanced training curriculum included topics neglected in the division's pre-Buna instruction. One report noted instruction in "scouting, patrolling, cover and concealment, night operations, combat firing, amphibian landings, grenades and smoke, sniping, swimming, and hand-to-hand combat."[40] Troops also received better and more plentiful equipment. "We were issued jungle boots," remembered Claire Ehle. "They were canvas boots made like tennis shoes [with] rubber bottoms and they'd come up about mid-calf. They were so much lighter and they would dry out sooner."[41] Vincent Riddle wrote that "we drilled with all the weapons: [the] '03', Garand and Carbine rifles, Browning 30 caliber air-cooled machine guns, Bren-guns, and 60 mm mortars and hand grenades," and "we were given written tests on all the weapons and on all the actions of an infantry company."[42] According to Jesse Coker, "our combat-experienced officers and sergeants worked diligently at all times to prepare us for every aspect of combat," and "each training exercise was conducted as realistically as possible." Coker remembered "crawling with our rifles for quite a distance under barbed wire while machine guns fired live ammo over our heads" and one particular sergeant who "delighted in tossing TNT charges near us at night in an effort to simulate incoming artillery rounds."[43] James Myers recalled that "every time we practiced, someone would wind up in the hospital with a broken arm or something."[44]

The Red Arrowmen spent increasing amounts of time on field maneuvers and long conditioning hikes. Jesse Coker recalled a "hundred mile hike carrying full-field equipment weighing approximately 75 lbs." His battalion commander, Herbert A. Smith, "marched along beside us, constantly whistling 'Waltzing Matilda.' Though not always on key." Smith was "not the kind of field commander who rode in a jeep," Coker wrote admiringly. Halfway through the march Coker injured his ankle while climbing a hill but limped back to camp despite the pain. "We were ashamed to fall out," he explained, "so I gritted my teeth and hobbled along on my aching feet. . . . There were many other times in the future when I would need to call on that inner strength."[45]

Amphibious training, spotty and incomplete before Buna, now became standard and more comprehensive. Preparations began at Camp Cable. "A high board wall, with a wide rope ladder secured to the top, was constructed to represent the side of [a] ship," remembered Coker. "We continually practiced going up and down the rope ladder, first, without our rifles, and later with cumbersome rifles and heavy packs."[46] Then the soldiers went to the amphibious training centers at Port Stephens or Toorbul Point, where they boarded transport ships and practiced getting into landing craft. "The small boat at the bottom of the ladder would bob up and down and away from the ship in the choppy water," recalled Coker, "creating a hazardous situation where sometimes we would be thrown with force against the side of the ship."[47] The troops then simulated beach landings. Vincent Riddle wrote of a training in which "[we] climbed down the cargo nets into the Higgins boats and headed for shore where we beached, jumped into the surf, and waded ashore. It went off like clockwork."[48] Coker remembered one exercise in which his cohort was to paddle a rubber raft from the beach to a ship in the harbor. "Nine men had much trouble launching a rubber raft into a strong wind which produced some very high waves," he wrote, and "the force of the wind and the stinging salty spray would drive us and our unwieldy craft back upon the sandy beach. It took a lot of coordination and brute strength to launch our raft and row out over the waves to a large ship, but with persistence we finally succeeded." Making it all the more difficult was Australia's late-autumn weather. "Our bodies turned blue," recalled Coker. "I have never been so cold in my life."[49]

At first, the rebuilding of the Red Arrow did not go very well. In April 1943, I Corps put the division through a series of tests. One inspection of the 126th Infantry Regiment characterized its readiness status as "rather unfavorable, due to improperly trained replacements, sickness, and the generally poor physical condition of the veteran men."[50] General Byers wrote in his diary that "we must indicate to the high command the time it will take to prepare 32d Div for combat. It will make them mad but that can't be helped."[51]

Medical problems significantly hindered the training. "The total number of men in the hospital," noted one report of the 127th Infantry

Regiment for the second quarter of 1943, "has never come below 360 and has reached a peak of 587." Malaria remained the biggest culprit. During the second quarter of 1943, the 127th Infantry alone experienced an average of 13.12 daily hospital admissions for malaria.[52] The microorganisms that cause malaria remain in the victim's liver long after initial infection. Changes in climate or environment can trigger relapses, as might any episode that lowers the body's immune response. The resumption of rigorous training and the onset of the Australian winter seemed to stimulate many malarial episodes in the Buna veterans. Clarence Jungwirth remembered one relapse while lying on his cot in which the chills and tremors were so intense that "the floor vibrated from my shaking."[53] Robert Bable remembered that he and others suffered from "successive attacks of malaria, which caused us to go to the hospital for about ten days. Our fevers would break in three days, then we would loaf around for a week, eating better food [and] sleep as late as we wanted in addition to having no responsibilities." Bable admitted that "most of us enjoyed our life-style."[54] One medical report complained that "too many men were losing the opportunity to get Amphibious training because of malaria."[55] Eichelberger recalled one meeting in which MacArthur ranted extensively against "babying malaria cases."[56]

To suppress malaria, the army pinned its hopes on a new drug, quinacrine hydrochloride, better known by the trade name Atabrine. Perhaps no unit in the entire US Army suffered more from malaria than the Thirty-Second Division, and its members were among the first to use the drug. They hated it. Atabrine's side effects included nausea, vomiting, diarrhea, and yellow-tinged skin. It was also rumored to cause sexual impotence. Many GIs evaded taking it or refused altogether. However, Major Herbert C. Wallace, chief surgeon of the 128th Infantry Regiment, noted "a marked drop in the incidence of malaria" when Atabrine was administered to the troops.[57]

To confirm the drug's efficacy, and to determine the proper dosage and regimen, doctors needed more information. In August 1943, the army established the Sixth Army Training Center near Rockhampton, where army physicians, under the direction of Lieutenant Colonel G. G. Duncan, administered Atabrine to soldiers with recurrent malaria, then monitored their responses and analyzed the results. "We were to be 'guinea pigs,'" wrote Jungwirth resentfully, and the GIs derisively called the Sixth Army Training Center the "Fox Farm" or the "Malaria Concentration Camp."[58] The facility had "all the malarial patients from the entire division," said Robert Hughes, who thought that "there must have been a couple thousand of us."[59]

The doctors divided the "guinea pigs" into four battalions of four companies. Each group received a different dosage given at a different interval. To determine the best dose and schedule, doctors then gave their patients increasingly intense duties. At first, wrote Duncan, the troops received "light camp fatigue, calisthenics, drill, and games not involving violent exercises." By the end of the program one battalion was subjected to "intensive physical training from eighty to eighty-four hours per week for two consecutive weeks, with a final forced march of 25 miles." All the while, patients received "exceptionally liberal" amounts of food and had their blood tested constantly. Duncan's work indicated that Atabrine was indeed effective in suppressing malarial symptoms. His study guided the army's malaria suppression protocols throughout the war.[60]

Buna veterans suffered many other lingering medical problems. Analysis of stool samples from the 127th Infantry Regiment revealed 15.96 percent had pathogenic intestinal infestations, while another 5.53 percent had parasites classified as nonpathogenic. More than half were hookworm cases, though testing revealed the presence of ten other organisms, and some patients were infected with more than one type of parasite.[61] Roy Campbell was at a rehabilitation facility, recovering from a wound to his ankle, when he realized he "wasn't feeling that great." After doctors looked Campbell over, he learned he not only had malaria but also "hookworm and roundworms" and amoebic dysentery, which made him feel "as weak as a kitten."[62] Some medical officials even questioned the fitness of the replacements. "It has taken considerable time and effort to examine many of these men who are unfit for field duty," claimed one report, "a task that should have been done prior to their movement overseas."[63]

Mental health problems also plagued the division. Raymond Dasmann experienced depression on his return from New Guinea. "My friends were being scattered," Dasmann wrote, and "some were dead. The war seemed without end. . . . I had truly hit rock bottom emotionally."[64] Kenneth Springer recalled an incident he witnessed at a camp on his way back from New Guinea. "There was gunfire and all of us hit the floor," Springer wrote. "It turned out it was a sergeant who had fired the shots. He was apparently suffering from a war neurosis, and was quickly subdued."[65] Lieutenant Colonel Simon Warmenhoven, the Red Arrow's chief surgeon, witnessed the heartbreak and madness of war at Buna and Sanananda, where he saved as many lives as he could from a surgical tent just behind the fighting. Warmenhoven returned to Australia with malaria and hookworms—and signs of depression. "Sure had the 'blues' here for a couple of days," he wrote his wife, Henrietta, on May 3, 1943. "I often don't allow myself to get that way but after all, when one is away from his best friend in the world you my wife, away from such grand children, you just can't help it." A couple of days later, Warmenhoven put a gun to his head and pulled the trigger.[66]

In the months after the Red Arrow returned to Camp Cable, medical boards declared many members unfit for combat duty and removed them from the division. In April 1943, Alfred Medendorp's recurring malaria led to his reassignment to an amphibious warfare training center in Australia. Medendorp found that being "kicked out of the division" was "hard to take," but the dedicated soldier was nevertheless grateful to remain in the service. "It was a job," he wrote.[67] Others returned to the United States and were discharged. Archie Van Gorden's malaria forced his return to the US in July 1943. He traveled on the USS *Monterey*, "the same ship I had come over on one year and 2 months before," he noted. When the *Monterey* stopped at the Panama Canal Zone, where General Harding had recently been assigned, Van Gorden and two other Red Arrow officers met Harding for dinner. Harding even arranged a chauferred tour of the canal zone for them. "It was a great experience," Van Gorden remembered. "The General was one of the finest officers I met in the service."[68]

By mid-1943, the health and readiness of the Red Arrow had improved. For many GIs the frequency and severity of their malaria attacks diminished over time, and the chronic cases had departed. Replacements learned the ropes and integrated themselves into their units. The brass now sounded more confident about the Red Arrow's training. On June 22, Byers wrote in his diary: "Up at 5:00 saw 3 Bn 126 make a dawn landing. Men showed fine spirit."[69] He later noted that "Gill's gripes are quite strong over many small things so he must feel the training is shaping up well."[70] Eichelberger visited Camp Cable in June and wrote an encouraging report to Krueger. "I saw some of the housekeeping this time as well as a night problem," he wrote. "We also watched a battalion come in and during a halt I was able to look them over and talk to a good many men. They all seemed hard and there was not the slightest indication of a hangdog or resentful attitude." In another letter he wrote: "There seems to be fine morale and a lot of enthusiasm on all sides. I thought the work of certain companies in night attack with accompanying night reconnaissance work was unusually good. The work of other companies in defense accompanies with infiltration and night withdrawal was not as good." Eichelberger thought that "there is no question that Gill is doing a grand job" and assured Krueger that "the 32nd will give a grand account of itself."[71]

Throughout their intensive training, Red Arrow troops occasionally enjoyed some time off. Weekend passes and furloughs returned, and division members once again gravitated to cities like Brisbane and Sydney. For the replacements, this was their first chance to see a kangaroo or navigate their way through the strange-yet-familiar Australian culture as their comrades had done a year before. "I enjoyed listening to the 'Aussies' [sic] beautiful dialect," wrote Jesse Coker. "They frequently called us 'Bloody Blokes.'"[72] James Mayo, a replacement from Tennessee, informed his family that "I have learned more about this place in the length of the time I have been over here than all that time I went to school."[73]

For a soldier with a pass, finding female company was a high priority. According to James Myers, the GIs went to town with "two things on their minds—drinking and women."[74] Many veterans reconnected with the girlfriends they'd had before going to New Guinea. "I figured my unit was being trained for more combat and I would, undoubtedly, not survive the next campaign," wrote Kenneth Springer, who went to Adelaide to see his girlfriend. It was a long journey and he returned to Camp Cable five days late. As punishment, Springer was reduced in rank to private, confined to the company area for thirty days, given KP duty, and made to "regularly clean the open seat outhouses and burn the pits."[75]

Australian girlfriends likewise tried to find their GI beaus. One Australian woman who had been dating a Red Arrow officer before Buna grew alarmed when she didn't hear from him upon the division's return. She took her search all the way to MacArthur. "I know I am just one of many," she told the SWPA commander, "but not hearing from the one you love makes you think that something has happened to him. . . . I know that you have a terrible lot of work on your mind, and I would even understand if my letter was just put aside, but if you only knew how much I think and pray, an[d] lay awake, night after night, with the vision of his face before me." MacArthur's staff located the young officer in a US military hospital.[76] Many new romances bloomed. Raymond Dasmann met Elizabeth Sheldon, an artist, on a blind date in Sydney. "We sat around talking, joking, drinking a bit of beer as though we were old friends," Dasmann recounted. More dates followed. When he was with Elizabeth, Dasmann claimed, "the war and the army seemed far away." The pair soon decided to marry.[77]

Many more soldiers weren't looking for long-term relationships. In Sydney, James Myers met a woman at a party and ended up spending the night at her apartment. "I didn't even know her name," Myers wrote, "so I didn't know what to say in the cold light of dawn." The following day he returned to his hotel and struck up a conversation with a server at the bar. "I invited her to join me for a drink and before we knew what was happening she was in bed with me. I was sure making up for lost time."[78] Not all division members approved of the sexual behavior of their comrades. "On Mondays much bragging was heard relative to the experiences with the girls," wrote Jesse Coker, and "these conversations left little to the imagination." Coker, a married man, was shocked to find that "the married G.I.'s were just as boastful as the single guys." He also noted that "occasionally, at mail call one of the fellows would receive a 'Dear John' letter from his spouse. Apparently, there was also some infidelity going on back in the States."[79]

The Red Arrowmen still found Australia hospitable, but the dynamics of Australian-American relations had shifted while the division was in New Guinea. The growing number of GIs in the country increased tensions and resentments. "Aussie vets were returning home from Africa," remembered Erwin Pichotte. "We then had problems with these vets because of women."[80] Brawls broke out between Allied troops. James Myers walked past an Australian armed forces canteen in Brisbane when three Australian soldiers, "slightly inebriated," shouted (as he remembered it): "There goes another one of those damned Yanks that's drinking up all our booze and taking our girls." They chased after him. "The first one I kicked in the balls," Myers recounted, "the second got kicked in the shin; and the third I ran at with my head down and caught him squarely in the chest."[81] Many soldiers preferred to stay in camp. "We have an out-door movie every night," wrote Paul Kinder. "Although the pictures would be old to you, they are new to us." As in all army camps, soldiers gambled, held parties, and wrote home. Jesse Coker wrote letters for illiterate soldiers and read "to them the letters they received from home. I found it many times painful to read their very intimate letters that were filled with love and concern."[82]

In September 1943, the Red Arrow Division returned to the national spotlight. That month, First Lady Eleanor Roosevelt toured the Pacific and made a stop in Australia. Ten thousand people turned out to greet her when she arrived in Sydney on September 8. General Eichelberger escorted her to a local Red Cross Club, where he introduced Roosevelt to two Red Arrow veterans sitting at a lunch counter, Captains Herbert G. Peabody and Herman Bottcher. "They chatted for some time," reported the *New York Herald Tribune*, "an uneaten apple pie a la mode in front of Mrs. Roosevelt."[83] The First Lady visited hospitals at Sydney and Brisbane and proceeded to Camp Cable on September 9. Her visit created numerous chores for the troops there—and some resultant grumbling. "In addition to painting the stones that lined the drive into camp," recalled Robert Bable of the Thirty-Second Signal Company, "we painted the termite hills as well." Bable also noted that the GIs had to build a "private toilet for Mrs. Roosevelt," and that "a detachment from General Headquarters in Brisbane arrived with all manner of sports equipment. They set up a ping-pong court—complete with canvas canopy, a basketball court, a badminton court with nets and birdies, and baseball equipment." The headquarters detachment also "left complete instructions to have personnel participating in these activities" when Roosevelt arrived. According to Bable, "no stone was unturned to stage this asinine performance."[84]

Roosevelt arrived at Camp Cable at midday with Eichelberger and Byers, as well as Red Cross representatives and a gaggle of reporters. After making a brief address to the assembled troops, she joined the

First Lady Eleanor Roosevelt visited the Red Arrow at Camp Cable in September 1943. LEFT: Roosevelt tours a tank destroyer. BELOW: Roosevelt eats lunch with soldiers. WISCONSIN NATIONAL GUARD, US ARMY SIGNAL CORPS PHOTOS

Thirty-Second Signal Company for lunch. Roosevelt then visited with soldiers from the 126th Infantry Regiment who were dressed "in jungle suits and equipment." (Paul Rettell claimed that a few days before the visit the division "borrowed a couple hundred camouflage uniforms for the occasion," and returned them after Roosevelt's departure. "Throughout the war we never wore camouflage," he pointed out. "It was the same old green denims.")[85] By 4:00 p.m. the First Lady was off to Rockhampton to inspect more troops and more hospitals. Roosevelt had won over the acerbic Robert Bable, one of the soldiers with whom she had lunch. "I became so intrigued by her magnetic personality that I forgot to remain angry," he wrote, though his ire soon returned. The headquarters detachment, he observed, "disassembled all the athletic equipment before the dust had settled from Mrs. Roosevelt's departing motorcade." He surmised that "they wanted to re-assemble it at her next stop."[86] A few days later, Roosevelt mentioned the Camp Cable visit in her "My Day" newspaper column. "I lunched in one of the messes with the men and talked with some sergeants who had been through the hardest fighting," she wrote. "They were men from Michigan, Wisconsin, and Illinois" who "were not trained then for jungle warfare," but "fought with magnificent courage and won." Roosevelt reported that "they looked fit" and that "nobody out here has any pity for the Japanese," explaining that "they have seen them do too many things which we consider beyond the pale of civilized practice."[87]

Also in September 1943, memoirs by two former division members hit the bookstores. Simon & Schuster released *G.I. Jungle* by E. J. Kahn, the former *New Yorker* staff writer and aide to General Harding. That same month Thomas Crowell published *C/O Postmaster*, a humorous look at military life in Australia written by Thomas R. "Ozzie" St. George, the former member of the 128th Infantry Regiment who had found his way onto the staff of the popular army magazine *Yank*. Orville Prescott of the *New York Times* reviewed both works in the same column, not mentioning (and probably unaware) that the authors had served in the same division. Prescott thought St. George's book "cheerful, foolish, and merry," and "filled with laughter and zest for an experience that may be dull and trying much of the time." Prescott found humor in Kahn's *G.I. Jungle* as well but thought it a deeper and more serious work. He proclaimed it "entertaining and informative reading."[88] *C/O Postmaster* was featured in the October

1943 Book of the Month Club, and by the first week of December it was the second-best-selling nonfiction book in the Detroit and Los Angeles markets.[89] Another *New York Times* reviewer called it "one of the best and funniest soldier books ever written."[90] Kahn's book was less successful commercially but found a receptive audience hungry for insight into the battles of the South Pacific. "My brother, Lt. V.O. Fryer, was killed in action at Buna Mission," one admirer wrote Kahn. "Knowing how impossible it must have been for the boys to write, your book fills in so many gaps that we probably never would have understood."[91] Kahn also published several articles about the Thirty-Second Division at Buna in the *Saturday Evening Post*, including a profile of journalist Byron Darnton (the *New York Times* reporter and World War I veteran of the Red Arrow who was killed in the accidental bombing of supply ships off Pongani, New Guinea, in October 1942) and a two-article series on the travails of Company E of the 126th Infantry Regiment on the Kapa Kapa Track and at Buna.[92]

LIFE ran several features on the Red Arrow Division at Buna over the course of 1943 that reshaped the government's policy on censoring battle-field images. George Strock, a staff photographer for the magazine, was among the journalists accompanying the division to Buna. A collection of Strock's photos from Buna—of General Eichelberger, Herman Bottcher, Maggot Beach, and the destruction at Buna Mission—appeared in *LIFE*'s February 15, 1943, issue. The following week some of Strock's more whimsical photos appeared in a piece titled "Booty and Buna." One featured two happy-looking GIs from Manitowoc, Wisconsin, gloating over some captured Japanese items.[93]

The February 22 issue also contained an article titled "How the Heroic Boys of Buna Drove the Japs into the Sea." In it, the magazine told the story of a soldier identified only as Bill. "He loved the blue lakes of Wisconsin, the cool winds, the bright farmlands," wrote the author. "That was where his folks belonged—and his girl." The article went on to describe how Bill and his comrades surged to the sea during the last days of the battle. "He charged through, emerging onto the smooth white beach, chasing a bunch of Japs, hot and tired and blazing mad. And it was right there that he got hit. . . . It was the first rest he had had in a long time. But he would never go back to his girl in the farmlands of Wisconsin." Strock had photographed Bill's lifeless body, along with two others killed nearby, but *LIFE* could not print it because the US government forbade the publication of images of American war dead—a policy to which the editors of LIFE objected. "We think that occasional pictures of Americans who fall in action should be printed," declared the magazine.

> We think Bill would want that. Maybe some of our politicians would think twice about their selfish interests if they could see him lying there in the white sand. Maybe some of our absentee workers in war plants would make more of an effort to stay on the job if they could have a look at Bill. Maybe some industrialists would be more progressive if they had Bill in their minds. Maybe some housewives wouldn't be in such a hurry to raid grocery stores, and maybe John L. Lewis wouldn't feel so free to profiteer from the war if they could see how Bill fell. Why should the home front be coddled, wrapped up in cotton wool, protected from the shock of the fight? If Bill had the guts to take it, we ought to have the guts to look at it, face-to-face.[94]

The editors of LIFE were not alone. President Roosevelt had also grown concerned that the American public was not prepared for the hard sacrifices to come. "The home front had no firsthand knowledge of the war," wrote historian Peter Maslowski, "unlike the people of Poland, France, Britain, Russia, Germany, China, Burma, and elsewhere," so "to both inspire and embarrass civilians into complaining less and sacrificing more, Roosevelt decided that the home front should have a more accurate picture of the hardships endured by soldiers, sailors, airmen, and Marines."[95] Slowly and tentatively, harsher images appeared in American popular culture. A photo essay in the August 2, 1943, issue of LIFE, for example, showed a dead GI on a stretcher in Sicily, covered with a blanket and lying on a beach. Only the dead man's elbow and boot peeked out beneath the blanket.[96]

Strock's image of Bill and his dead comrades was finally published in the September 20, 1943, issue of LIFE and was the starkest yet released to the public. It came with an editorial titled "Three Americans," retelling Bill's story with a kind of maudlin Americana. The GIs, as the editors described it, ran toward the Japanese "almost like a halfback carrying the ball down the field." Their sacrifice protected "a stout, gray-haired woman

This photograph by George Strock shows three dead Red Arrow soldiers on the beach at Buna. The image sparked debate about wartime censorship and was eventually published in *LIFE* magazine on September 20, 1943. GEORGE STROCK/THE LIFE PICTURE COLLECTION/SHUTTERSTOCK

pulling out of the oven an American apple pie . . . a road leading around the wood lot under the big harvest moon . . . the pool hall where the guys get the baseball scores" and the "minister in his pulpit pointing upward to where he thinks God is." *LIFE* called the dead men "three units of freedom" and reminded readers that "this is the reality that lies behind the names that come to rest at last on monuments in the leafy squares of busy American towns."[97] Strock's photograph created a national sensation. One angry reader accused *LIFE* of "masking morbid sensationalism with talk about the necessity."[98] Many more drew inspiration. "Maybe you think there's too much noise about bond drives, too many speeches, too many requests," opined the *Atlanta Constitution*. "Well, none of it will wake from death any man who has died for you and the rest of us. Maybe you saw that picture of the American soldiers, dead on the beach at Buna."[99] Strock's photo was not as gruesome as war photography can be—the faces of the dead were not shown and their bodies were intact. Many news outlets still avoided publishing images the editors felt were too shocking for their readers. Nevertheless, the publication of Strock's photograph of the dead Red Arrowmen marked an important shift in US government censorship policy and the way the American public perceived the war.

As the Red Arrow Division recuperated from its harrowing experiences at Buna, the fighting in the Southwest Pacific raged on. Over the course of 1943, more US fighting units arrived in the South Pacific to join Krueger's Sixth Army. The Twenty-Fourth Infantry Division arrived in Australia in May, followed by the elite First Cavalry Division a few months later. The army also dispatched several separate regiments to MacArthur, including the 158th Infantry Regiment, the 112th Cavalry Regiment, and the paratroopers of the 503rd Parachute Infantry Regiment. The First Marine Division, recovering at Melbourne after its own ordeal at Guadalcanal, temporarily came under MacArthur's command as well.

In mid-1943 the Allies began to implement Task Two of the joint chiefs' July 1942 directive—the counterattack through the Solomons and New Guinea toward Rabaul. The plan was codenamed Operation Cartwheel. It was to be a joint army-navy operation, initially composed of thirteen subordinate operations but later reduced to ten. Admiral William F. Halsey Jr., head of the US Navy's South Pacific Area, would move northward through the Solomon Islands. Simultaneously, MacArthur's SWPA forces would advance along the northern coast of New Guinea. The admiral and the general would essentially run two separate campaigns, though under MacArthur's overall direction.

Cartwheel began on June 30, 1943. That day MacArthur launched Operation Chronicle, the 112th Cavalry Regiment's invasion of the unoccupied islands of Kiriwina and Woodlark in the Solomon Sea. MacArthur staged a simultaneous landing at Nassau Bay, south of Salamaua on New Guinea's northern coast, with a force of American and Australian troops, as well as the Papuan Infantry Battalion. Also on June 30, Halsey commenced Operation Toenails, the seizure of New Georgia and nearby islands. On August 15, Halsey sent US Army troops and New Zealanders farther north to nearby Vella Lavella, bypassing and isolating the Japanese strongpoint of Kolombangara. Halsey's troops secured the central Solomons by October, and he then struck in the northern portions of the archipelago, hitting the Treasury Islands (Operation Goodtime) on October 27, Choiseul Island (Operation Blissful) on October 28, and Bougainville (Operation Cherry-blossom) on November 1.[100]

As Halsey ascended the Solomons, MacArthur focused on New Guinea's Huon Peninsula, jutting into the Solomon Sea north of Salamaua. An extension of the forbidding Finisterre Range, the peninsula resembles a human nose. At the base of the nose was Lae, on the shores of the Huon Gulf. The port of Finschhafen, an old German colonial town, sat at the tip of the nose, sixty miles east of Lae. Madang was at the bridge of the nose, 170 miles up the coast to the northwest of Finschhafen. The island of New Britain hovered above the Huon Peninsula, and separating them was the Vitiaz Strait. From Lae, the Markham River reached deep into the interior, draining the south slope of the Finisterre Range. From the headwaters of the Markham, a trail led to the Ramu River, which then flowed northward to the coast. Defending the area was the Japanese Eighteenth Army under the command of General Adachi Hatazo, who now made his headquarters at Madang. In mid-1943, Adachi had roughly fifteen thousand personnel in the Lae-Salamaua-Finschhafen area. Madang hosted another twenty thousand, and the Ramu-Markham corridor provided an inland communication line between them. From Madang westward, more Japanese bases dotted the northern New Guinea coastline all the way to the Vogelkop Peninsula, including Wewak, Hansa Bay, and Hollandia.

MacArthur launched Operation Postern on September 4. Allied forces—mainly Australian ground troops—pressed in toward Lae and Salamaua from three directions. The Australian Ninth Division under George Wootten (one-time leader of the Warren Force at Buna, and now a major general) landed on the south shore of the Huon Peninsula east of Lae. The following day, US paratroopers of the 503rd Parachute Infantry dropped into the Markham River valley at Nadzab, twenty miles west of Lae. The paratroopers secured the airfield there, then scores of C-47 transport planes brought in General George Vasey's Seventh Australian Division. Meanwhile, Allied troops from the south pressed up from Nassau Bay. With Allied forces converging on Lae and Salamaua from the east, west, and south, the Japanese withdrew from Lae and Australian troops took it on September 16. The fighting now shifted to Finschhafen, which the Australians captured on October 2, although bitter clashes occurred in the hills outside of the port for weeks afterward.

As Cartwheel proceeded, Washington shelved Task Three of the original directive—the seizure of Rabaul—and chose to bypass and isolate Rabaul instead. With Europe receiving priority for troops, planes, and materiel, the Pacific commanders simply would not have the forces necessary to take on the massive Japanese fortress directly. MacArthur angrily and vehemently objected but followed his orders and shifted his planning to the encirclement and neutralization of Rabaul. The objective of his next attack, Operation Dexterity, was to seize the western half of New Britain and build air and naval bases there—the first of many that would eventually ring Rabaul. Slated for sometime in November, it was originally to consist of two steps. The first was to seize the Japanese air base at Gasmata on New Britain's south shore, roughly halfway across the island's southern coast. This task fell to a combat team built around the 126th Infantry Regiment of the Red Arrow. Then, six days later, the First Marine Division was to land at Cape Gloucester on the western tip of the island.

Back at Camp Cable, the 126th Infantry Regiment's members learned they were headed back into battle. To train for the Gasmata operation, the regiment departed Australia and sailed for Milne Bay. The First Battalion landed there during the very last days of September, and the rest of the regiment arrived throughout October and early November. The return to New Guinea generated dark thoughts among the troops. Paul Rettell served on guard duty along the Australian coast. "It was dark and you could hear the ocean," Rettell wrote. "It was a peaceful sound, but it brought back memories of New Guinea, the misery, the hardships, the almost inhuman possibility of making it back alive. I wondered, 'Can a person go through that again and live?'"[101]

The members of the 126th Infantry Regiment found that much had changed in New Guinea since they left more than eight months earlier. Milne Bay was no longer a small collection of makeshift buildings, but a sprawling and ever-growing port and staging area. Malaria control units now drained swamps and sprayed insecticide around the camp to manage the mosquito population. "There was a detachment of Seabees building simple roads, bridges, and boat docks near our camp," noted medic Dean Andersen.[102] Milne Bay even offered entertainment, and the GIs were both surprised and thrilled to see Hollywood stars there. "Gary Cooper is on tonight's program (in person)," Andersen wrote his parents, and added: "Did I tell you that Lanny Ross . . . is with us[?] He is a lieutenant in the special services and instructs group singing." But Milne Bay was not all recreation. The regiment was there to train. "We spent most of our time on long hikes along trails in the terrible jungles," wrote Andersen.[103]

But the Gasmata operation never happened. MacArthur's subordinates, including General George Kenney (the top SWPA air commander) and Krueger, argued that Gasmata was too far east and would be too hard to defend. On November 22, MacArthur changed the invasion site to Arawe, fifty miles to the west of Gasmata. Krueger believed a smaller force would be better suited for the operation and sent in the 112th Cavalry Regiment instead. MacArthur also had to adjust his timetable. He originally hoped to strike in November, but marshalling all the troops, supplies, and equipment by that early date proved too optimistic. The Arawe landing took place on December 15. The First Marines landed at Cape Gloucester on December 26.

During the last months of 1943 the remainder of the Red Arrow Division went north as well—and this time there would be no return to Australia. "We began making preparations to make the move which we had anticipated with apprehensions," wrote Jesse Coker. "I kept telling myself that the sooner we defeated the Japs, the sooner we would get to go home. I found some consolation in this litany, but it did not erase the cancerous anxiety that was growing."[104] The 127th Infantry Regiment arrived at Milne Bay in November. Buna veterans again noted the improvements. "Conditions up here are incomparably better than we experienced," Herman Bottcher wrote his old friend Harold Hantleman, now in a deskbound job due to his Buna injuries. "Just imagine regular roads, decent tents and extraordinarely [sic] good food. We hardly ever get bully beef, only twice a week C-ration. The remaining meals consist of various canned or dehydrated vegetables, Spam, hot dogs and twice weekly fresh meat (frozen of course)." Bottcher also commented on his return to the jungle. "Whereas it was a formidable obstacle and a horrifying place for us last year," he wrote, "it has now become a friendly place with a beauty and charm all its own," assuming it was not "permeated with and polluted by the enemy."[105]

At the same time, the 128th Infantry Regiment sailed north to Goodenough Island off the north coast of the Papuan Peninsula. The 114th Engineers arrived on Goodenough Island as early as September 1943 to build a camp for the division. From September through early January 1944, the Red Arrow engineers constructed office buildings, officers' quarters, shower and water facilities, thirty-seven mess halls, ten bridges (the longest span fifty feet), seven miles of roadways, improvements to the island airport, five jetties totaling three thousand feet, and loading platforms at the port. For construction materials, they operated a saw mill that produced 163,563 board feet of lumber and a stone crusher that produced 7,848 cubic yards of fill.[106] The ever-expanding base at Goodenough was not just the home of the 128th Infantry Regiment, but also became a major staging area for operations in the Southwest Pacific. The 112th Cavalry prepared for the Arawe operation there. General Krueger moved his headquarters to Goodenough on October 21. Not long after the 128th Infantry Regiment arrived, the 126th moved there from Milne Bay.

Away from the Allied military base, Goodenough Island was hardly touched by the modern world and even had a little air of danger, with rumors of hostile Papua New Guineans and Japanese soldiers lurking in the higher elevations. There were no hostile encounters with either, but the GIs found the island's wildlife menacing. Some of its insects were enormous—and poisonous. Robert Bable was serving as sergeant of the guard one night when a young lieutenant came to him, pale and in pain, and reported being bit by a giant centipede. "I could see five saucer-sized welts," Bable wrote, each "chalk white and hard as clay," and "two fang punctures appeared in the center of each welt." Bable called the hospital and spoke with an Australian doctor. "It was the Great Blue Centipede," the doctor told him, and "extremely poisonous." He said the victim could expect pain, muscle spasms, and hallucinations before adding: "If he lives until morning, he will probably pull through." The lieutenant "sweated, jerked, shook, puked, and was off his nut" all the following day and through the next night, but pulled through and "after a week of light duty Larry was back to normal."[107] Raymond Dasmann wrote of an encounter with stick insects "9 or 10 inches long, ½ inch across, and armor plated" crawling across his cot. He attacked them with a machete, "strewing insect parts around the tent." He also recalled "a fair number of big pythons" that grew "12 feet or more in length and were quite formidable in appearance."[108]

Further adding to the miseries of Goodenough was the rain—it was the New Guinea monsoon season again. "The water ran through our tents just underneath our canvas cots," wrote Jesse Coker. "We had to wade through the rushing water before we could get our mud slicked bodies into bed." Malaria had been brought under control here too, but Goodenough Island posed numerous other health risks. Rashes and other skin conditions plagued many GIs. More seriously, there was an outbreak of typhus—a bacterial disease spread by mites, fleas, and lice that first bite infected animals (typically mice and rats) and then bite humans. Typhus can cause chills, fever, rashes, and head and body aches, and it can be fatal. "We lost several men because of this dreadful disease," recalled Coker.[109] Attempts were made to eliminate the disease-carrying rodents. "With the help of the natives we tried to cut down and burn the grass, which grew as high as a man's head," wrote medic Dean Andersen, "but we did not get rid of the rats."[110]

Some Red Arrowmen nonetheless found beauty on Goodenough. The huge volcano in the center of the island lured many GI explorers like Robert Bable. "Beautiful orchids, bougainvillea, and dewy spider webs sparkled in the morning sun," Bable wrote after a climb up the mountainside, where he "passed green iguanas warming themselves in the morning sun" as "giant bird-wing butterflies flitted through the numerous sundogs that

Red Arrowmen enjoy a brief respite from the heat, thanks to this mountainside swimming hole on Goodenough Island. This was one of hundreds of images by Robert Doyle documenting the lives of Red Arrow soldiers during World War II. WHI IMAGE ID 99742

sent brilliant spears of light through large overhead trees."[111] Andersen and a friend also took a walk into the jungle. "As we left our camp and native villages we came to more and more rare wildlife," Andersen wrote. "Birds seemed to be following us as we climbed. We saw large yellow birds and large birds that looked like eagles but were darker in color."[112] Paul Rettell remembered finding "a beautiful waterfall like you see in the movies. It was nice and cool. I dove in and swam around for a while," though he later "got a terrible earache."[113]

Red Arrow soldiers hit the beach from an LCI (Landing Craft, Infantry) in a training exercise in New Guinea, November 1943. WHI IMAGE ID 99998, PHOTO BY ROBERT DOYLE

In mid-December, Goodenough Island attracted some of the army's top brass. MacArthur arrived on December 13. "While we were on the main highway one afternoon," Jesse Coker recalled, "we saw a jeep with four stars on the placard conspicuously placed on the front end." He spotted MacArthur inside the jeep, "sitting erect with that famous corn-cob pipe in his mouth." Coker was thrilled to see the famous general, but he also sensed trouble. "I knew that General 'Mac' had not come to Goodenough to plan a celebration," he wrote. "Something big had to be brewing."[114] Two days later an even greater personage arrived: US Army Chief of Staff George C. Marshall. MacArthur had long criticized Marshall for allegedly failing to support him, either with men and materiel for SWPA or in negotiations with the navy. Given MacArthur's litany of complaints, Marshall thought it wise to visit MacArthur and reassure him of his support, so after attending a conference at Cairo, Marshall returned to Washington via the South Pacific.

Marshall and his entourage arrived at Goodenough Island on December 15 and met with MacArthur over the course of two days, along with a host of army, navy, and air force brass also in attendance. By most accounts, their sessions were cordial but tense; Marshall and MacArthur did not know each other very well, and MacArthur's criticisms of the chief of staff had been rather biting and personal. MacArthur yet again asked for more soldiers and supplies for SWPA, and he came away from the meeting at least partially mollified. SWPA remained low on the Allies' priority list, but after the meetings MacArthur was left with the sense that Marshall now appreciated the challenges he faced, and would back him up in his ongoing competition with the navy. "From that time on," MacArthur later wrote, "Washington became more generous to the SWPA."[115] Historian D. Clayton James wrote that Marshall's visit to Goodenough Island "boosted the morale . . . of MacArthur and his SWPA personnel."[116]

Though the Red Arrow was rebuilt, rested, and ready for combat, the division remained in the Sixth Army reserve throughout the Cartwheel operations. But as 1943 drew to a close, General Wootten's Ninth Australian Division was back on the offensive, pushing the Japanese from Finschhafen westward along the northern coast to the village of Sio on the Vitiaz Strait, and from there toward Saidor—where the Thirty-Second Division was about to reenter the fight against the Japanese.

The Third Battalion, 128th Infantry Regiment, near Aitape, July 1944.
WISCONSIN NATIONAL GUARD, US ARMY SIGNAL CORPS PHOTO

CHAPTER 8

LEAPFROGGING

During World War II, the Allied practice of bypassing some Japanese-held islands while skipping ahead to others became known as "leapfrogging." In Operation Cartwheel, for example, Allied forces leapt past Japanese strongholds, attacking weaker targets and bypassing Rabaul altogether. By 1944, leapfrogging was standard practice, allowing the Allies to cover vast stretches of the Pacific and position themselves ever closer to the Philippines and to Japan. MacArthur was at first bitterly critical of leapfrogging but by 1944 had changed his tune. He wanted "no more Bunas" and ached to return to the Philippines, and leapfrogging provided him a way to do both as quickly and inexpensively as possible. In later years, he even implied that he'd invented the practice. "I intended to envelop them," MacArthur wrote in his memoir, "incapacitate them, apply the 'hit 'em where they ain't [and] let 'em die on the vine' philosophy."[1] MacArthur's leapfrogging across the northern coast of New Guinea in 1944 brought the rebuilt Thirty-Second Infantry Division back into combat. The battles at Saidor and Aitape were smaller in scale than Buna—though they occurred in the same muddy rain-soaked jungle environment, and their adversaries were as tenacious as ever—but the Red Arrow was now better trained, better equipped, better supported, and battle hardened.

I n January 1944, the Thirty-Second Division returned to combat at Saidor on the Vitiaz Strait, one hundred miles northwest of Finschhafen. The site had an airfield and seemed to have a serviceable harbor (though SWPA planners had little information beyond aerial photographs), and only a small Japanese detachment guarded them. An American air and naval base there would add another brick in the wall MacArthur was building around Rabaul, while also supporting future operations farther west along the New Guinea coast. An Allied presence at Saidor also might block the Japanese forces retreating from Sio as the Australians chased them westward. MacArthur envisioned a small campaign—an add-on to Operation Dexterity—and created the Michaelmas Task Force for the job. The Michaelmas force consisted of just one combat team built around the 126th Infantry Regiment. It was led by Clarence Martin, the one-time Warren Force commander at Buna who was now a brigadier general and Red Arrow assistant commander. MacArthur wanted to strike fast, and the Saidor operation was hastily organized. Vice Admiral Daniel E. Barbey, head of the US Navy's VII Amphibious Force assigned to SWPA, remembered that "the Navy plans were written between Friday noon and the following Monday morning."[2] General Walter Krueger, Sixth Army commander, begged for more time, but MacArthur insisted on a strike as soon as possible. He set the date for January 2, 1944.

For the Red Arrowmen, Christmas 1943 was far more festive than the one at Buna the previous year. Dean Andersen told his family of his Christmas dinner that consisted of "turkey, mashed potato, carrots, peas, dressing, cake, pie and cranberry sauce."[3] And in Elvin Ball's Christmas letter home, he noted that "the Red Cross gave us each a box of candy, sewing kits, razor blades, a little stationary, and a few other items." Though the army had tried to promote the holiday spirit, "it still doesn't seem like Christmas," Ball wrote. "You can never feel too comfortable with the enemy out there."[4]

Within a week of the Christmas festivities, the Michaelmas Task Force was loading onto ships for the journey to Saidor. Unlike Buna, where the Red Arrow approached the Japanese by land, this would be an amphibious

The Thirty-Second Division sails toward Saidor on December 31, 1943, on an LST (Landing Ship, Tank) packed with soldiers, vehicles, artillery, and supplies. As 1944 dawned, the Red Arrow was much better trained and equipped than it had been at Buna a year earlier. WHI IMAGE ID 100058, PHOTO BY ROBERT DOYLE assault. The troops "were in excellent spirits," observed Admiral Barbey. "They were fresh, and with new equipment."[5] Barbey's convoy was a far cry from the ragtag fleet that had ferried portions of the Red Arrow to Buna little more than a year before. It contained APDs (destroyers converted into troop carriers), LCIs (troop carriers holding about two hundred soldiers that could move right onto the beach), and LSTs (versatile, beachable vessels that transported men and materiel), among others. As the convoy sailed through the Solomon Sea, the GIs took in the ocean views. "We watched the dolphins jumping and playing in the wake of our ship," recalled Andersen, and "frigate birds and sea gulls were flying about," but despite the picturesque views, Andersen's anxiety was growing. "This was my first combat," he wrote, "and I was scared as hell."[6]

Dawn broke over Saidor on January 2, 1944, with gray, overcast skies and misty rain. The landings were to occur on three beaches, designated Red, White, and Blue. The first wave was scheduled to land at 6:50 a.m., but poor visibility forced a delay. To soften up Japanese forces before the landing, navy guns laid down a twenty-minute barrage. Then rockets hit the beach, "making a spectacular display," according to the Michaelmas Task Force diary, and the concussions from the blasts could be felt "on board ship 1000 yards at sea." As naval gunfire bombarded the beaches, "solemn-faced boys, men but for their age, lowered themselves over the side of the ship, into the landing craft," wrote Edward Nyenhuis. "Helmets on, rifles ready, and with a prayer on their lips, they crouched in the Higgins boat[s]" and then ploughed toward the shore.[7] The first wave hit the beach at 7:25 a.m., unopposed. More troops followed, and the GIs quickly moved inland. The Second Battalion reported "very light" opposition. Meredith Huggins recalled encountering "a few Japs wandering around in shell shock."[8] The invaders found the remnants of Japanese camps and outposts, one with warm food still on the tables. The Red Arrow seized the airfield, set up its artillery on the beach, and began unloading supplies. One Japanese soldier, the task force diary recorded, "walked into the Shore Bn area with a white flag and surrendered to the Service Company."[9] Japanese bombers attacked that evening, but as Admiral Barbey observed, "by the time the planes arrived the targets were few. The ships were long gone, and most of the equipment and supplies had been dispersed into the jungle."[10]

Saidor Battle Area

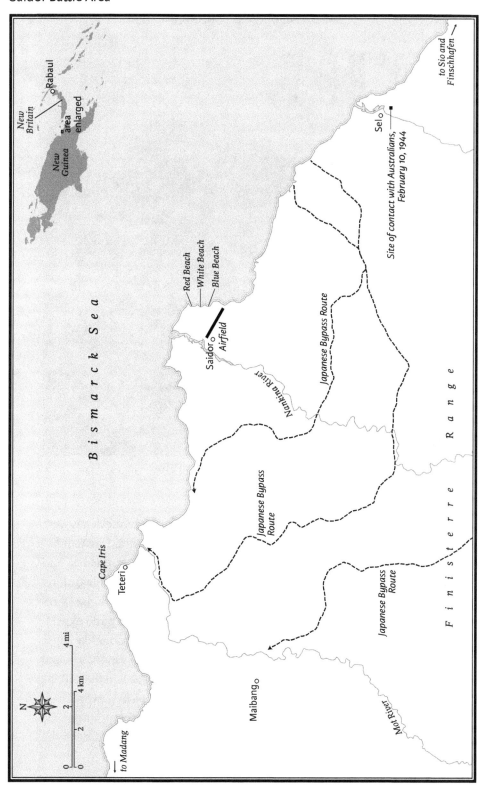

Troops unload an LST (Landing Ship, Tank) on the beach at Saidor, January 2, 1944.
WHI IMAGE ID 100068, PHOTO BY ROBERT DOYLE

By the end of the first day, more than seven thousand Americans were ashore at Saidor. "What a contrast from the days at Buna and Sanananda," recalled Huggins, where "we were fighting with rifles, grenades, and rocks!"[11] Only one Red Arrow soldier was killed on that first day, along with two sailors who drowned. Admiral Barbey called the landing "a resounding success" and wrote that "the speed of the planning and expertness of its execution could only have been possible with troops like those of the 126th Regimental Team who had become thoroughly indoctrinated with every detail of Seventh Amphibious Force technique." In the end, he claimed, "the whole operation was just too perfect to be newsworthy."[12]

In the days that followed, General Martin set up defensive positions. He placed the Third Battalion on the west flank, the Second Battalion on the east, and directed the First Battalion to patrol the gap in between. Within a week, Martin expanded his beachhead to encompass fourteen miles of shoreline. Engineers immediately got to work improving the airfield, building a base for PT boats, and laying down roads. ANGAU brought in Papua New Guinean workers and recruited among the local population. Heavy rain hampered American efforts, as did Japanese bombing raids. Their planes hit the division command post on the night of January 3, wounding four. Two more Japanese air raids came on the night of January 5, and five air raids followed on January 7, causing no damage or casualties but resulting in many hours of lost sleep.[13]

Task force soldiers patrolled beyond their beachhead in search of the Japanese. Indeed, for the Red Arrow infantrymen, Saidor was a battle of patrols. Martin established observation posts deep in the jungle and staged amphibious landings beyond his flanks, from which the troops then penetrated inland. Observation planes also flew above the vast stretches of jungle. At first the Michaelmas patrols found few Japanese. One patrol captured a pair of Japanese soldiers on January 3. "Both Jap prisoners indicated that the morale of the Jap forces in this area was low," noted the task force diary, as "rations in the vicinity of SIO were insufficient." GIs killed a lone Japanese soldier on January 4 who "wore no shoes, one sock, and carried no weapon but an old machete." The following day, a patrol "was attacked by approximately thirty Japs armed with rifles and two machine guns. The Japs staged a bayonet charge with which our patrol met with automatic fire. Three Japs were reported killed and the attack repulsed. Our patrol lost one man killed." Another patrol came across five dead Japanese troops and a wounded soldier who later died. "It was noted that all dead men were freshly shaven and had had recent haircuts," and while they had rifles and mortars, they carried "no packs or canteens," which suggested "a base camp in the immediate vicinity."[14]

Martin and Krueger worried the Japanese were planning a counterattack. As they saw it, the Saidor beachhead was vulnerable from two directions. To the west loomed Madang, where, Krueger wrote, "the Japanese were in considerable strength."[15] But the east worried them more. The Australians were driving the remnants of two Japanese divisions—about twenty thousand fighters—directly toward them. Martin wanted more troops to defend Saidor, and he advocated a push to the east to trap the

Japanese between his forces and the Australians. Krueger hesitated. In addition to the threat from Madang, Krueger oversaw the ongoing operations at Arawe and Cape Gloucester, and in January the fighting had reached a critical point in both places. In the end, Krueger assented to the eastward move and authorized more troops for the Michaelmas Task Force. With the arrival of the First and Third Battalions of the 128th Infantry Regiment during the third week of January, command of the task force passed from Martin to General William Gill, the Red Arrow commander.

Japanese intentions became clearer in the days and weeks that followed. Intelligence gleaned from patrols indicated that no counterattack was imminent. Instead, it appeared the Japanese intended to bypass Saidor and make their way to Madang. Lieutenant John L. Mohl led a patrol to capture Japanese prisoners for interrogation. He selected a trail he knew the Japanese frequented, and in the early morning hours of January 25, he set a trap. From one position, behind a fallen tree and stump, GIs lay in wait to grab two prisoners. A fire position nearby would kill the rest of the patrol. The wait was "tedious," Mohl wrote, "and, as the minutes dragged into hours . . . it seemed as if time had dropped an anchor." By midmorning a six-man Japanese patrol ambled down the trail, and although it came from a direction Mohl had not anticipated, the operation "proceeded exactly as planned." One Japanese soldier offered little resistance upon being tackled. Another, whom Mohl wrestled to the ground personally, put up "quite a struggle, screaming and yelling at the top of his voice." The soldier bit Mohl on the hand, but Mohl knocked him unconscious with the butt of his pistol. During the interrogation, Mohl noted that "both prisoners talked freely" and conceded that their comrades planned to bypass Saidor.[16]

To reach Madang, Japan's Twentieth and Fifty-First Divisions had to march through the high, rugged, and jungle-clad Finisterre Range. This was a daunting route anytime of year, but particularly during the rainy season when cliffs and rock outcroppings became slick and jungle trails dissolved into mud. Severe shortages of food and supplies, as well as exhaustion after weeks of combat against the Australians, added to the miseries. The arduous march tested the dedication and endurance of each of the twenty thousand Japanese soldiers who embarked on the trek.[17]

General Adachi, commanding the Japanese Eighteenth Army in New Guinea, sent several companies to harass the Red Arrow beachhead at

Saidor while their comrades marched around it. Some encounters between the GIs and the Japanese were sharp and deadly. On January 28, a forty-three-man patrol from the First Battalion of the 128th Infantry Regiment crossed the Mot River, then the western extreme of the Red Arrow beachhead, to scout for Japanese near the village of Teteri on Cape Iris, and "take prisoners if possible." As the patrol moved westward the Japanese spotted it and got behind it, blocking the patrol's escape route back to the river. A force of sixty Japanese converged on the Americans, who quickly split into three groups, each racing back to the Mot separately. Two groups made it across, but the third—carrying three wounded men—moved more slowly. As the third group reached the riverbank, Japanese grenades and machine-gun fire blocked their crossing. Word of the trapped patrol reached battalion headquarters, which sent a small party to the river to help it get across. Among those heading out was the battalion commander himself, Lieutenant Colonel Gordon Clarkson. Only after nightfall could the survivors return to the American side of the river. At least ten GIs were killed, including Clarkson, struck down in the middle of the river helping his troops to cross.[18]

The Thirty-Second Division continued to expand its beachhead, and on February 10, Michaelmas troops came into contact with Australian forces near Sel, fourteen miles east of Saidor. Unfortunately, Krueger's hesitation in authorizing Martin's eastward push had allowed thousands of Japanese to escape into the Finisterre Range. To interdict the bypassing Japanese, Red Arrow patrols went deep into the rugged mountains. The Michaelmas Task Force "tried hard to block these escape routes," wrote Krueger, "but torrential rains, the ruggedness of the country with its impenetrable rain forests and jungles and impassable rivers, and the resistance of enemy troops pushed forward from Madang to guard the trails, made this effort fall short of success."[19] Rather than send large forces into the interior, the Red Arrow instead pushed its forces farther to the west of Saidor, hoping to control the coastal plain and block the reemergence of the Japanese divisions from the mountains. By the first week of March, the Red Arrow had reached Yalau Plantation, thirty miles west of Saidor.

The environment at Saidor was every bit as challenging as Buna had been the year before. The coastal plain was less swampy, but the rains were just as heavy and the jungle was every bit as thick. "Most of the time we had

Milwaukee's Ed Gigowski plays the accordion for his comrades during a break in the action at Saidor. WHI IMAGE 100156, PHOTO BY ROBERT DOYLE

to cut our way through with machetes," wrote James Myers.[20] Jesse Coker spent two months at a mountain outpost. During one patrol, Coker and other soldiers had to "climb up an almost vertical bank covered with rocks and boulders." The rocks "cut my hands with each precarious movement," Coker later described, though soon he faced an even greater danger:

> The men above me were jarring loose some of the rocks. I looked up to see a large boulder coming down rapidly and directly toward me. I acted quickly, out of instinct; I leaned as much as I could in the opposite direction. In a moment, the thundering boulder brushed my left leg without knocking me off balance. It hit the bottom of the stream with an intimidating explosion that sounded as if a bomb had been dropped.[21]

Japanese aircraft continually harassed the American beachhead. As at Buna, sometimes just a single, older-model plane flew over, usually for reconnaissance. The GIs variously referred to these planes as Milk Run Charley or Washing Machine Charley. Some raids were a nuisance. "We get an air raid nearly every night now," Elvin Ball wrote to his family on January 31. "I guess the Japanese don't want us to get too much sleep."[22] Other raids were more serious. Robert Bable described an attack on division headquarters in which a newly arrived draftee was "buried from his hips up to head with dirt, while laying face down at the edge of a bomb crater." Fellow soldiers frantically dug him out and asked why he made no effort to extricate himself. "It never occurred to me," the soldier replied. "I thought I was dead."[23] Japanese infiltrators also launched attacks on rear areas. Writing a letter home, Ball told his family: "I think a bullet just sailed past my ear, so I had better hunker down for a while."[24] The threat from the Japanese left American troops constantly on alert. "Some snipers would kill six or eight of our people before they were eliminated," medic Dean Andersen wrote, and "it took a lot of automatic guns spraying into the tree tops to get them. It became clear that we were on the offense in the daylight, but the Japs would attack us at night."[25]

At Saidor, the Thirty-Second Division received support it did not get at Buna. The navy brought in a steady stream of supplies and evacuated the wounded. PT boats patrolled the shores and transported troops. Some elements of the Red Arrow had seen little or no action at Buna but participated fully at Saidor, most notably the artillery. The Thirty-Second Cavalry Reconnaissance Troop, under Captain George Bowles, had remained in Australia during the Papuan campaign, but at Saidor it ranged deep into the New Guinea interior searching for Japanese and gathering information. One patrol lasted two weeks and reported numerous encounters. "On the morning of 27 February, I requested artillery fire on the village of MAIBANG as well as on the trail leading from the MOT RIVER," Bowles wrote in one report. "I found that the artillery bursts had perfectly bracketed the entire trail. Two freshly killed Japs evidently killed by the artillery were found dead along the trail. In MAIBANG itself 24 Japanese were found on the outskirts of the village." On March 1, the patrol "shot a Jap officer and two enlisted men," and captured an "enemy machine-gun, three rifles, sixteen hand grenades, regimental records, pay books, maps, officer's insignia, [and] money from the Phillipines [sic]." Three days later the patrol "killed 2 Japs at an old bivouac area [that] consisted of a large headquarters, officers' mess, corrals, hospital, much abandoned equipment consisting of saddles, bridles, bags of oats, etc."[26]

Patrols also searched for downed planes and fliers in the trackless New Guinea jungle. The Thirty-Second Cavalry Reconnaissance Troop sent out a patrol to find a lost Piper Cub artillery spotter plane. The patrol didn't find the spotter plane, but it did happen to witness an Allied B-24 Liberator crash into the jungle. Troopers and their Papua New Guinean guides searched for two days before finding the wreckage. "Apparently the plane came down with terrific force," noted the patrol report, "as wings and fuselage were shattered, all four motors were torn out and wrecked, all guns were broken and twisted." They found "no evidence that [the] plane was occupied when it crashed," and began searching for the airmen who may have bailed out. A few days later, Papua New Guinean villagers discovered three airmen who were "weak and hungry but all right physically." The patrol located four more members of the ten-man crew and evacuated them back to Saidor by PT boat.[27]

For many Red Arrowmen, Saidor was their baptism of fire. Inexperienced troops engaged in indiscriminate firing, even in rear areas. "Although the area was secure by day," wrote Buna veteran Robert Bable, "many of the green troops were very nervous by night and it was not really wise to be moving too far from your own bailiwick after dark."[28] Buna veterans had learned about the true costs of war; now the newcomers learned them too. Dean Andersen recalled the first time he attended to a soldier—an Iowan like himself—who was riddled with machine-gun bullets. "The blood was a bright red like an arterial and I knew I was not going to get it and stop it even with lots or pressure," Andersen wrote. He comforted the dying man as best he could. "He talked about his home life on a farm in northwest Iowa," Andersen remembered, and "about his family and his loved ones. He asked me to talk with his family when I was home again [and] he died while I was holding him."[29] Percy Hiatt recalled that some soldiers "went off the deep edge" and had to be evacuated to the rear. "One of them started collecting ears," he recalled, and another "gold teeth." Hiatt also recalled an incident in which he and another soldier brought a Japanese prisoner back to battalion headquarters. As they passed an aid station, a doctor became enraged at the sight of the Japanese man and "came out of the operating tent and shot him dead." Hiatt reflected that "this type of brutality took place on both sides, though I don't think we ever tied anyone up and bayoneted them like they did to our people."[30]

The Red Arrow's ongoing expansion of the Saidor beachhead drove the escaping Japanese farther and farther inland. Reports on their condition varied. Japanese troops "were in high spirits and fought aggressively," noted one report. "They are reported as having yelled 'Give up' to our troops [and were] well equipped and had plenty of ammunition."[31] Most reports, however, painted a far grimmer picture. Patrolling GIs often found trails littered with the graves of Japanese, or with bodies lying where they'd fallen and in various states of decomposition. "Hundreds of Jap bodies and skeletons were counted along each of the escape routes as they fell into our hands," wrote James Myers. "Thousands died, victims of disease, starvation and the weapons of the 32nd Division."[32] Edward Nyenhuis recalled one spot "where they were forced to scale a cliff by means of a rope, at least 60 to 80 dead Japs were found in one pile. They had been too weak to scale the precipice."[33]

On March 21, Australian forces from the Ramu Valley linked up with the Thirty-Second Division soldiers west of Yalau Plantation. The Australians drove on and took Madang a month later. The Saidor operation was at an end. The Michaelmas Task Force had accomplished much. The Allies now had an airfield and PT boat base on the strategic Vitiaz Strait to support the neutralization of Rabaul and future operations along the northern coast of New Guinea. "Saidor had become like a huge city with a large supply depot, a base hospital, a naval base for PT boats, army landing crafts, and the air force bomber base," wrote Dean Andersen, "supported by a tent city with thousands of Army, Navy, and Air Force troops."[34] In a letter to his alma mater back in South Carolina, Powell Fraser noted how Saidor was "much different from Buna. The equipment and support we have from the Navy and Air Corps has made the going very easy for us." He compared the Saidor campaign to "just another Saturday afternoon game with the other side being the underdog getting a thorough whipping."[35]

However, the Michaelmas Task Force was not able to destroy the two Japanese divisions bypassing them. Of the twenty thousand Japanese troops departing from Sio in January, roughly half made it around Saidor to fight another day. The Australians expressed frustration—verging on apoplexy—that Krueger had failed to crush Japanese forces in eastern New Guinea. According to historian Peter Dean, Krueger had grossly overestimated the capabilities of the Japanese forces and concluded that he "timidly let some thirteen thousand Japanese troops escape." Dean also faulted the Thirty-Second Division, citing a "lack of aggressive patrolling" and characterizing its performance as "lackluster."[36] For those who still harbored doubts about the fighting abilities of the Red Arrow, Saidor did not erase them. In the end, the Americans simply did not attach a high priority to the Saidor operation. The Sixth Army seemed more focused on Arawe and Cape Gloucester, as well as charting a pathway to the Philippines. Krueger later wrote that in pushing westward from Saidor, the Michaelmas Task Force "did not press its advance too far on receiving my instructions not to get seriously involved. Its troops were needed for other tasks."[37] Gill later described the Saidor operation as "not a very important one."[38] The Australians later had to face many of the very same Japanese soldiers who made their way around Saidor. So did the Red Arrow.

Saidor was the last attack of Operation Cartwheel, although fighting continued on Bougainville and New Britain until the end of the war. MacArthur moved into the Admiralty Islands west of Rabaul in February 1944. General George Kenney's Fifth Air Force bombers pounded the Japanese fortress incessantly. Rabaul remained formidable, but by mid-1944, it was effectively isolated and neutralized.

As the Red Arrow expanded the Saidor beachhead and Operation Cartwheel drew to a close, American leaders began their drive toward the western Pacific, and as they did, the army-navy rivalry continued. Once again, there would be two separate offensives, though this time the navy received top priority. Beginning with the bloody battle at Tarawa in November 1943, the navy and marines leapfrogged through the Gilbert and Marshall Islands and closed in on the Marianas. To the south, MacArthur and SWPA drove along the northern coast of New Guinea. Although MacArthur's campaign was to be secondary, the two-track movement westward nonetheless gave him the opportunity to beat the navy to the western Pacific via a southern route. "New Guinea," wrote historian Stephen R. Taaffe, "was now more than just a road to the Philippines; it was a racetrack as well, with the Navy running hard on a parallel road to the north."[39] During 1944 MacArthur conducted a series of brilliant flanking movements across northern New Guinea toward the Vogelkop Peninsula, bringing him ever closer to his promised return to the Philippines.

As MacArthur looked westward from Saidor, the next logical targets on the New Guinea coast were the Japanese naval base at Hansa Bay, 120 miles west of Saidor, and the airfields at Wewak, another 100 miles farther west. In the areas surrounding Hansa Bay and Wewak, General Adachi had fifty-five thousand troops, roughly ten thousand of whom had survived the march around Saidor. But instead of hitting these obvious targets, MacArthur went around them, leaping all the way to Hollandia in Dutch New Guinea, nearly five hundred miles west of Saidor. Today known as Jayapura, Indonesia, Hollandia had an excellent harbor and important air bases. Control of Hollandia would allow MacArthur to dominate western New Guinea and would provide an important staging base for the invasion of the Philippines. The Japanese garrison at Hollandia consisted mostly of service troops and was lightly defended. The operation to take Hollandia posed risks, of course. MacArthur needed air support for the invasion, but with no airfields in the vicinity and the ongoing campaign in the central Pacific, the navy was reluctant to give him any. Admiral Chester Nimitz, the US Navy's top commander in the Pacific, finally agreed to send a limited number of carriers to MacArthur—but only for three days. To provide sustainable air power, MacArthur decided that simultaneously with the Hollandia attack he would also seize the Japanese airfield at Aitape, 120 miles to the east. Control of Aitape had the added benefit of protecting Hollandia's eastern flank from Adachi's Eighteenth Army near Wewak.

MacArthur organized two task forces, the Reckless Task Force and another codenamed Persecution, for his westward leap. The Reckless Task Force, composed of the Twenty-Fourth and Forty-First Infantry Divisions, invaded Hollandia on April 22. Persecution landed at Aitape that same day. Aitape lay on a broad coastal plain covered in swampland and dense jungle. About five miles east of Aitape, at the village of Tadji, was a large coconut plantation, and near to that was the airfield MacArthur wanted to seize. The Torricelli Mountains ran parallel to the coast about ten miles to the south. Just east of Aitape, several important rivers and streams flowed

Aitape Battle Area

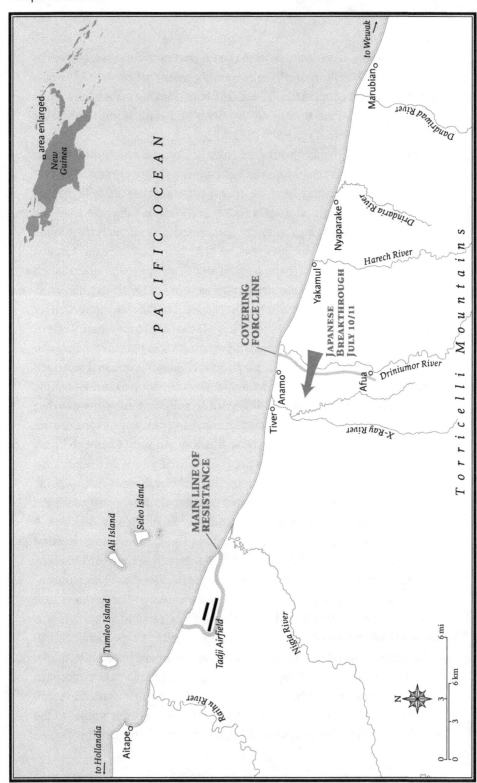

MAPPING SPECIALISTS, LTD.

from the mountains northward to the coast, including the Nigia, the X-Ray, the Driniumor, the Harech, the Drindaria, and the Dandriwad.

The Persecution Task Force consisted of two regimental combat teams from different divisions. The lead element was the 163rd Regimental Combat Team of the Forty-First Division under Brigadier General Jens Doe, who commanded the operation. The Second and Third Battalions of the Red Arrow's 127th Infantry Regiment under now-Colonel Merle Howe—which had not seen action at Saidor—composed the second element. Doe's team went in first. As at Saidor, it was overcast the morning of the invasion. Red Arrowman Howard Kelley watched the 163rd's landings from offshore. "Just at daylight navy guns began shelling the beach," he wrote. "Next the Navy dive bombers began dropping bombs into a coconut grove. I could see the concussion wave of the powerful explosions above the trees. Then a Navy destroyer went in close to the beach and began machine gunning the bushes."[40] Smoke and fog obscured the beach, and the assault troops landed in the wrong spot, but, as at Saidor, they were met with little opposition. Doe's invaders quickly took the airfield at Tadji, established a defensive perimeter, and patrolled for Japanese. Howe's troops went ashore the following morning. Two companies (F and G) landed on small Japanese-held islands immediately offshore. They met little opposition as well, though a Japanese sniper killed one Red Arrowman on the island of Tumleo.[41] The remainder of Howe's soldiers joined the 163rd Regimental Combat Team at Tadji. Howe put some troops to work offloading supplies in the rough surf, while others joined the 163rd Infantry Regiment in patrolling. The First Battalion of the 127th Infantry Regiment arrived on April 26.

Doe and Howe built up the base around Aitape as fast as they could and expanded their patrols around the area, mapping trails and searching for Japanese stragglers. They understood that Adachi's Eighteenth Army lurked somewhere to the east, so they concentrated patrols in that direction to learn more about his forces and intentions. Howe established patrol bases at Anamo, ten miles east of Tadji near the mouth of the Driniumor River, and at Afua, six miles upstream from there. On April 28, Company C of the 127th Infantry Regiment, reinforced with a contingent from Company D, traveled even farther east by boat to Nyaparake, at the mouth of the Drindaria River, twenty miles east of the airstrip. The force, dubbed the Nyaparake Force, was under the command of Captain Tally Fulmer.

Reckless and Persecution had gone well. In early May, the 126th Infantry Regiment arrived at Aitape, and Doe's 163rd Regimental Combat Team withdrew. Krueger then brought in the 128th Infantry Regiment, and with the entirety of the Red Arrow at Aitape, Gill took command of the Persecution Task Force. Guarding the airfield seemed easy duty, even pleasurable, though Dean Andersen did not see a tropical paradise. He admired the long beach, but also noted "coconuts laying everywhere [and] the ground crawled with land crabs, turtles and other beach creatures. Dead fish, seaweed, decaying wood and rotting coconuts left an unpleasant odor."[42] When not on duty, the GIs took to beachcombing. "We enjoyed looking for shells," wrote Andersen. "Several of my friends started making jewelry, combining the beautiful shells with mountings made from Australian coins." Division leaders took a dim view of such careless behavior. "Numerous instances have been observed of Allied personnel wandering about alone and in small groups in areas not definitely clear of Japanese," noted the division bulletin for May 31. "The purpose of this is apparently souvenir hunting. This practice will cease."[43]

With Hollandia and Aitape under his control, MacArthur then leapfrogged even farther west, seizing more Japanese airfields along the coast. The 163rd Regimental Combat Team attacked the Wakde Islands and nearby Sarmi, more than one hundred miles west of Hollandia, on May 17. Ten days later, the Forty-First Division—with the Red Arrow's 121st Field Artillery attached—invaded the island of Biak, another 180 miles farther west, along the northern neck of the Vogelkop Peninsula. Once again, intelligence failures led to the deaths and dismemberment of many foot soldiers. MacArthur's intelligence chief, General Charles Willoughby, estimated five thousand Japanese on the island. The number was more than double that. Moreover, the Japanese burrowed themselves into caves and tunnels deep into the coral cliffs overlooking the airstrips. The Japanese did not contest the landing as it happened, but instead attacked in force once all the Americans were ashore—a practice used in later operations to devastating effect. Japanese commanders, wrote historians Waldo Heinrichs and Marc Gallicchio, were not so much interested in a decisive victory at Biak as "stringing out the battle, denying the airfields, and weakening the Americans by attrition."[44] Consequently, the fighting at Biak was slow, painful, and bloody. The 121st Field Artillery was in continuous action from the commencement of the campaign. "C Battery set up on the beach," noted one report, "for direct fire into the coral cliffs about 250 yards inland." On another day, in support of an infantry assault, the Red Arrow artillerymen "definitely knocked out one AA [antiaircraft] gun, neutralized the fire of others, and had excellent results. . . . Over 2000 rounds were fired during the day." Darkness did not stop the battle from raging as the battalion launched shells nightly. The Red Arrow artillerymen also endured infiltrators and counterbattery fire. Japanese resistance at Biak weakened after a month of heavy fighting, but the battle went on for another two. The 121st Artillery fired its last shot on Biak on July 18.[45]

Back at Aitape, Gill and his commanders worried about Adachi's Eighteenth Army to their east. Adachi was outflanked and isolated, but he was also an unusually aggressive officer who, as historian Edward J. Drea wrote, "wanted to go down fighting, and dying, for the emperor."[46] Rather than wither away in the stifling New Guinea heat, Adachi personally led a force of twenty thousand from Wewak on a one-hundred-mile trek westward toward Aitape. "Adachi concluded that if he could not recapture Aitape or Hollandia by counterattack," wrote historians Waldo Heinrichs and Marc Gallicchio, "he could at least use his army to slow the American advance."[47] Among his troops were members of the Twentieth and Fifty-First Divisions who had bypassed Saidor just months earlier. The Japanese soldiers under his command, underfed and under-supplied, had to lug their equipment over primitive jungle trails. Adachi inspired his troops through his willingness to endure the same hardships and privations as the men he led, moving alongside them through the jungle, despite suffering from the excruciating pain of a hernia. Historian Stephen Taaffe characterized Adachi's move toward Aitape as "an army-wide banzai charge."[48]

By early May, the Allies had detected the Japanese approach toward Aitape, due in large part to advances in cryptanalysis. By 1944, the Allied code-breaking program, known as ULTRA, provided MacArthur with a steady and reliable stream of information about Adachi's plans, movements, and supply woes. Information obtained from Red Arrow patrols east of Aitape, as well as aerial reconnaissance, confirmed the ULTRA decrypts. Fulmer's Nyaparake Force reported increasing clashes with the Japanese to its west as well as to its east. Fulmer pushed his patrols east of the Dandriwad River, eight miles farther east of Nyaparake, and during the second week of May became involved in a pitched battle near the village of Marubian. As the fight intensified, Gill sent Company A of the 127th Infantry Regiment under Captain Herman Bottcher to reinforce Fulmer. Gill, however, grew concerned that he did not have the troops or the boats necessary to sustain a larger operation that far east and feared the fight at Marubian might detract from the priority mission of airfield protection. Thus, on May 19 Gill moved Fulmer's force back to Nyaparake. He also reshuffled his lineup, replacing Companies C and D with the Thirty-Second Cavalry Reconnaissance Troop and putting Bottcher in command of the cavalry troop and the Nyaparake Force.

Evidence that a substantial Japanese force was heading toward Aitape mounted. Medic Dean Andersen accompanied one reconnaissance patrol. His party reached a rock outcropping overlooking a coastal plain. "We stayed behind rocks and took turns looking with binoculars," he remembered. Peering through the lenses, Andersen saw "hundreds of Japs milling around in the area that was close to the ocean. We were so far away they looked like ants, even with the glasses."[49] Patrol reports suggested that the Japanese had ample supplies. "Japs appear to have plenty of ammunition and grenades," noted one report, and "there is no apparent shortage of food at this moment."[50] Another report suggested that the "movement of troops in our direction, coupled with their aggressive patrolling, seems to indicate the intention of moving toward TADJI."[51]

Surrounded by Japanese on three sides, Bottcher withdrew from Nyaparake to a more defensible position at Yakamul, three miles to the west. Toward the end of May, clashes became more frequent and the Japanese seemed markedly stronger. Sensing a threat to Aitape, and given the changing conditions, Gill reshuffled his forces at the eastern outpost yet again. He withdrew Bottcher's cavalry troops and replaced them with the First Battalion of the 126th Infantry Regiment under Lieutenant Colonel Cladie Bailey, along with some additional infantry and artillery. The Japanese buildup continued, and during the first week of June Japanese troops struck the Red Arrowmen at Yakamul, threatening to drive them into the sea. The First Battalion withdrew. Andersen remembered seeing Gill upon his return to Aitape. "His question was not how many casualties we suffered," Andersen remembered. "He wanted to know how many guns had been abandoned and if they had been destroyed. . . . This is the military mentality. Guns are more important than people."[52]

As Adachi's forces closed in, the GIs at Aitape spent a lot of time digging fighting positions into the jungle floor. Gill ringed the airfield with defensive fortifications, his main line of resistance. He also dispatched two battalions under General Martin to the banks of the Driniumor River. Martin's covering force stretched for six miles, from the mouth of the river to south of Afua. The purpose of the covering force was to slow down any Japanese attack coming in from the east. Should the line prove untenable, Martin was to withdraw his forces to a secondary line along the X-Ray River, then to a tertiary line at Nigia River, ultimately falling back on the main line of resistance around the airfield, if necessary.

Supply and communication between the main defensive line and Martin's covering force proved difficult. The wide beaches made vehicle traffic possible along the coast, but dense jungle hindered movements in the interior. "The jungle trails were muddy to start with," wrote Dean Andersen, "but after thousands of troops marched single file through the quagmire, the mud became deeper and deeper."[53] In addition, Japanese patrols slipped behind the Driniumor line and attacked supply and communication lines. Papua New Guinean carriers brought supplies to the covering force, but often hesitated to enter the combat zone. There were also reports of Papua New Guineans cooperating with the Japanese. On May 31, for example, the Japanese ambushed a supply train of ANGAU carriers, but an American officer who witnessed the attack noticed something unusual. The Japanese initially "fired up in the air," he recalled. The Papua New Guinean carriers then "dropped rations and ran into the bush," and "Japs did not fire directly after us until natives were off the trail." Around dusk he observed that "an enemy party came up the trail and picked up rations" and "saw at least two natives with Japs."[54] The army airdropped supplies to Martin's troops, but with opposing forces intermixed, recovering the items posed dangers. Kelley recalled an incident as part of a detail to recover some dropped packages. "We had all unloaded our supplies and were standing there talking when a mortar shell exploded about 20 feet away," he wrote. The detail jumped into a ditch but one man dropped his helmet and tried to retrieve it when there was another explosion, "ripping open his whole stomach allowing all his intestines to fall out."[55] Maintaining communication was also problematic. Radios often failed and telephone lines were vulnerable. "Telephone wire cut by japs [sic]," noted one report, and when a crew came out to repair the break, the "wire section [was] fired on by two light machine guns and some riflemen. . . . One of our men wounded."[56]

Adachi's advance caused great consternation at all levels of American command. MacArthur wanted no distraction from his goal of getting back to the Philippines. For him "Aitape was a backwater inconvenience," wrote Heinrichs and Gallicchio. "Now he was having to redirect his forces to meet that threat instead of leaping farther ahead."[57] Krueger beefed up his forces at Aitape even more. The 112th Cavalry Regiment under Brigadier General Julian Cunningham arrived on June 28. Smaller than a standard infantry regiment to begin with, the cavalry troopers were still recovering from operations at Arawe and only at 85 percent strength. Cunningham took up positions along the southern flank of the Driniumor covering force near Afua. On July 3, the unbloodied 124th Infantry Regiment of the Thirty-First Infantry Division arrived. The Forty-Third Infantry Division, beat up on New Georgia and recovering in New Zealand, was hastily ordered to Aitape as well, but aside from a few advance elements the division would not arrive for weeks. American strength at Aitape had now reached the equivalent of two divisions. On June 28, Krueger passed the Persecution Task Force to the operational control of XI Corps under Major General Charles P. Hall, a West Pointer and a veteran of the North African campaign. By the first week of July, Hall had six infantry battalions of the Thirty-Second Division at the main line of resistance around the airfields, along with a reserve of three recently arrived battalions of the 124th Infantry Regiment. Martin's Driniumor covering force now consisted of three battalions of the Red Arrow (Third Battalion of the 127th Infantry Regiment and the First and Second of the 128th), as well as the 112th Cavalry Regiment.

To locate the Japanese and discern their intentions, American patrols increased precipitously. The jungles around Aitape were crawling with patrols, both American and Japanese, of various sizes and for various purposes. Smaller, lightly armed reconnaissance patrols only sought information and avoided combat except when necessary. More heavily armed combat patrols went out to break up and destroy opposing forces. "For over a week," wrote Henry Zabierek of the 127th Infantry Regiment, "I Company had sent daily patrols across the river to check on possible enemy activity. . . . The incursions over the river usually penetrated as much as a mile [but] they encountered no sign of enemy activity."[58] Coker suspected the Japanese allowed many patrols to pass by. "The Japs did a great job of hiding from us," he thought. "They watched us and knew exactly where we were located."

Other patrols encountered the Japanese, whose presence along the Driniumor seemed to be on the rise. Howard Kelley went out on a three-man patrol "to scout out the enemy's rear." The patrol proceeded down "a dim trail" when a storm set in. "It began to thunder and lightning and the rain got real heavy," he wrote. Unable to get back across the river, the patrol decided to spend the night in the jungle, building small shelters just off the trail with logs and banana leaves. Kelley woke up in the middle of the night. "The rain had stopped and the moon was shining and it was a fine night," he recalled, and he could "hear hundreds of crickets making a rasping sound." After about twenty minutes the sound of crickets abruptly stopped. "I knew what that meant," wrote Kelley. The alerted patrol "parted the bushes just enough to see the trail and watched as a whole company of Jap soldiers walked by. Their equipment was slapping against their legs and jangling. There were about 200 soldiers in the company."[59] Machine gunner Percy Hiatt recalled talking with riflemen who patrolled east of the Driniumor. "They'd come back saying, 'God, there's a lot of Japs over there,'" Hiatt noted. "I don't think they were believed, but I knew these rifle company people . . . and I knew what they were saying was true. . . . They just kept saying that and we just kept digging deeper."[60]

Despite the mountain of evidence that Adachi was about to strike—from decrypted communications to ground patrols—there was still considerable disbelief at the top. At SWPA headquarters, Willoughby still failed to grasp the Japanese military mentality. According to historian Drea, Willoughby's "ethnocentrism and tendency to superimpose his own rationality onto his opponents" blinded him to the obvious.[61] To Willoughby, Japanese complaints about lack of food and information were evidence that any attack would be little more than a diversion to cover their withdrawal, making it ineffective and manageable. A major attack, in his mind, made no sense. Historian Gerhard Weinberg went so far as to suggest that Willoughby was "the stupidest intelligence chief of

World War II."[62] General Hall, inexperienced with ULTRA, distrusted the information he received. "He could not conceive," wrote Heinrichs and Gallicchio, "that the enemy could gather a force 20,000 strong in the impenetrable jungle without being detected."[63] Gill recommended the withdrawal of the Driniumor covering force, arguing that it was too thin and too difficult to supply. Krueger understood the ULTRA intelligence, and additionally was under great pressure from MacArthur to finish the operation quickly. He wanted strong patrols to march east of the Driniumor and break up Japanese forces before they could strike. "I directed General Hall to strengthen the covering force on the Driniumor," Krueger later wrote, and "take steps to meet the expected enemy attack with a powerful counteroffensive."[64]

Krueger harangued Hall to strike eastward and break up Adachi's forces, and on July 10 he finally sent strong reconnaissance-in-force patrols across the Driniumor. The Second Squadron of the 112th Cavalry moved out from Afua while the First Battalion of the 128th Infantry Regiment moved along the coast. The two forces were to proceed inland, then link up at the Harech River, roughly ten miles east of the Driniumor. The troops for the patrols came out of the covering force, substantially weakening Martin's defenses along the river. No reinforcements came from the main line of resistance around Tadji to replace them. With the departure of the First Battalion eastward, the Second Battalion of the 128th had to stretch its line all the way to the coast, making it responsible for a front more than three miles long with just seven hundred troops. "This was an impossible defense situation," reflected Jesse Coker, "especially at night in a jungle."[65] Patrols that day indicated increased Japanese activity, suggesting an imminent attack. Persecution Task Force headquarters remained skeptical.

As the American commanders argued among themselves, Adachi prepared his soldiers to strike. He planned to punch through Martin's covering force at several places and drive toward the Tadji airfield. A coastal attack force was to strike toward Anamo, threatening the artillery base there. The main force was to fall near the center portion of the covering force—where the Red Arrow's defenses were the thinnest—at a wide, rocky spot in the river with an island in the middle defended by the overstretched Company E of the 128th Infantry Regiment. After crossing the Driniumor, Japanese soldiers would then split in two—one group heading northwest toward Anamo and the other driving west toward Tadji. Just to the south of the island, yet another force was to push its way across the river and then split, with one wing driving on Tadji and the other hooking south to secure Afua before moving toward the airfield. Adachi understood precisely the weaknesses of the covering force. His soldiers had scouted the American positions well.

The Japanese struck ten minutes before midnight with a brief artillery barrage. Then they charged across the Driniumor River, smashing into the thin American line. "I was awaked from my pup tent by the sound of bullets flying just above me," recalled Jesse Coker of Company E, 128th Infantry Regiment, and "in the background I could hear blood-curdling screams emitting from hordes of Japs." Coker remembered that "fear engulfed every fiber of my being. . . . I knew I must calm and control myself." American machine guns mowed down the attacking Japanese. "Every fifth round was a tracer," wrote Coker, "but they were firing so rapidly that it looked as if each round was a tracer." Percy Hiatt called it "a field day for a machine gunner!"[66] Flares went up to illuminate the battlefield, and American artillery rained down on the Japanese. "The river was lighted with the clarity of a modern baseball stadium," thought Henry Zabierek.[67] The bodies of dead and wounded Japanese piled up in front of American bunkers. They piled up in the river too, in one place creating a dam that emitted a flow of bloody red water downstream. "The aggressiveness of the Japanese was awesome," wrote Coker. "Wave after wave of fanatical, screaming Japs attempted to cross the river during the first hour of battle. . . . The air became saturated with the smell of cordite" and "the smoke over the river hung low like a dense fog."[68]

The American line held for a time, but the Japanese kept coming. By 2:00 a.m. on July 11, Japanese forces overran Company E of the 128th Infantry Regiment, opening a two-thousand-yard gash in the Driniumor line, through which the Japanese poured into the rear of the Red Arrow. "Uncertainty now reigned in Company I ranks," recalled Zabierek, who was on the Driniumor line to the south of the gap. "Now every noise was suspect and anyone who appeared on the trail was a potential enemy."[69] Zabierek also noted that "practically all our communications were out, and it was impossible for our organization to find out what the other had done or what the situation was."[70] Casualties mounted on both sides. Though the Japanese had punctured the American line, the enormous casualties they took weakened their assault, and Adachi did not have the power to sustain the drive to Tadji. The attack caused tremendous chaos among the Americans, though. "Friendly and enemy were merged in the darkness in a very dense jungle," wrote Coker, "full of hostilities."[71]

General Hall immediately withdrew his patrols east of the Driniumor and pulled the covering force back to the secondary line of defense along the X-Ray River. The First Battalion of the 128th Infantry Regiment received word to withdraw around 2:00 a.m. on July 11 and reached Anamo at dawn. Soon after their arrival, Martin ordered the battalion onto a trail from Anamo to Afua to help close the gap in the US line. They proceeded little more than a thousand yards when Japanese machine guns opened fire from the far bank of a creek that crossed the trail. Thick vegetation obscured the Japanese positions, and their fire was intense. The Japanese then converged on the trail from both sides, and in the process threatened to cut off a group of wounded GIs. Staff Sergeant Gerald Endl of Fort Atkinson, Wisconsin, jumped into action, charging at the Japanese. His fierce, one-man onslaught bought time for others to move forward and evacuate most of the wounded men. As the battalion withdrew, Endl rescued four more wounded men along the trail and was carrying one man in his arms as Japanese fire finally cut him down. Endl received the Medal of Honor for his actions—the first for the Red Arrow since Buna, and the second from Jefferson County, Wisconsin, to receive the decoration. After the skirmish, Martin ordered the First Battalion back to Anamo and then to join the secondary defensive line from the village of Tiver southward.

Back at headquarters, the Japanese attack led to a lot of finger-pointing and prompted Hall to shake up his commanders. He relieved Martin of command of the covering force and replaced him with Gill. Meanwhile, Krueger was extremely unhappy that the covering force had been withdrawn, as he believed that Hall had sufficient forces in place to handle the onslaught. Krueger flew to Aitape to assess the situation. Upon his arrival, Hall presented him with plans for a counterattack that would seal the gap in the Driniumor line. Hall divided Gill's forces into two sections. The North Force, under the command of Brigadier General Alexander Stark (assistant commander of the Forty-Third Infantry Division), consisted of the First Battalion of the 128th Infantry Regiment, as well as the First and Third Battalions of the 124th Infantry Regiment. The Red Arrowmen of the 128th would drive from Tiver along the coast to the mouth of the Driniumor, then push south along the river. At the same time, the soldiers of the 124th were to secure the trail that led southeast from Anamo to the Driniumor, then link up with the 128th along the river. The South Force, under General Cunningham, was composed of the 112th Cavalry and the Third Battalion of the Red Arrow's 127th Infantry Regiment. Cunningham was to return to his previous position on the Driniumor. Inspired by Cunningham's notable male-pattern baldness, the South Force assumed the nickname "Baldy Force." Once reestablished on the Driniumor, the North and South Forces were to link up along the river and close the gap.

The First Battalion of the 128th Infantry Regiment pushed out along the ocean shore with the help of the 632nd Tank Destroyers on July 13. Remnants of the Japanese coastal attack force held up the Red Arrowmen for a time, but skillful artillery dispersed them. With the aid of a rolling artillery barrage, the battalion reached the mouth of the Driniumor early that evening. As planned, the battalion then hooked south along the west bank of the river. That same morning, the two battalions from the 124th Infantry Regiment took inland trails to the river. Japanese patrols held up their progress several times, but the 124th also reached the banks of the Driniumor that evening. Unfortunately, its members had become disoriented in the thick jungle. They were not as far south as they thought and reported their positions incorrectly. Meanwhile, Cunningham's Baldy Force proceeded as planned, reaching the Driniumor, but its patrols could not locate the 124th. The gap in the line remained. A frustrated Cunningham sent a troop of the regiment northward and guided the rookies into position. The Japanese tried to keep the gap open at the island in the Driniumor and a sharp fight ensued there, but the GIs closed it on July 18. The First and Second Battalions of the 127th Infantry Regiment, released from the main line of defense at the airstrips, mopped up straggling Japanese forces that remained west of the river.

Though the gap in the line had been closed, the aggressive Adachi had not given up on crossing the Driniumor. On July 15, Baldy Force detected the Japanese moving to their south, attempting to outflank them. The

The 632nd Tank Destroyer Battalion moves along the beach at Aitape, July 1944.
NATIONAL ARCHIVES

Japanese force, led by General Miyake Sadahiko and known as the Miyake Force, numbered some two thousand soldiers. On July 18, Miyake attacked the 112th Cavalry positions at Afua and seized the village, though Cunningham took it back the following day.

Miyake struck again on July 21. This attack forced Cunningham to shorten his lines and abandon Afua once more, but also left Troop C of the 112th Cavalry stranded behind Japanese lines. To rescue them, Cunningham sent two platoons from Company I of the 127th Infantry Regiment to break through. One platoon reached the trapped cavalrymen, but heavy fire forced the other to turn back, and then that platoon found its retreat line blocked by a Japanese machine gun. It, too, was cut off and surrounded. Private Donald R. Lobaugh of Freeport, Pennsylvania, volunteered to knock out the gun position blocking their retreat. To reach it, he had to traverse thirty yards of open ground, but he went forward anyway. Once Lobaugh got close enough to the machine gun he stood up and threw a grenade at it, but in doing so he also exposed his position and the Japanese sent a hail of bullets in his direction. Though wounded, Lobaugh still rushed forward, firing as he went, until the Japanese finally shot him down. However, as the Japanese focused their attention on Lobaugh, the rest of the platoon continued the attack he had started, knocking out the gun and making it back to American lines. Lobaugh received a posthumous Medal of Honor for his actions.

On July 23, Gill sent the First and Second Battalions of the 127th to the South Force, reuniting the entire regiment and placing it under Cunningham's command. Troop C (as well as the Red Arrow platoon trapped with them) endured three days of Japanese attacks until soldiers from the 127th fought their way through to them.

On July 31, Hall sent elements of the 124th Infantry Regiment, known as the Ted Force, east of the Driniumor to break up remaining Japanese forces. Fighting raged around Afua until the first week of August, as the Japanese staged increasingly desperate and suicidal attacks on the South Force. "In the jungled, broken terrain near Afua," wrote historian Robert Ross Smith, "operations frequently took a vague form—a sort of shadow boxing in which physical contact of the opposing sides was oftentimes incidental."[72] A Japanese attack on August 4 proved to be the last in the

Afua area, offering cover as Adachi gathered up the remnants of his army east of the Driniumor and withdrew his forces.

The Forty-Third Infantry Division began arriving during the second week of August and relieved the Red Arrow troops from combat duty. Roy Campbell described the new GIs as "light skinned, new uniforms, new guns, and anxious looks in their eyes."[73] Aitape and the Driniumor had been the toughest fight the Red Arrow had seen since Buna. "I was lucky enoufe [sic] not to get hit this time," wrote James Mayo after his first combat operation, "and I sure do hope the next time I will be just as lucky."[74]

The Red Arrow Division received a steady stream of replacements throughout the Aitape campaign. By early 1944, stateside training camps had turned millions of draftees and volunteers into soldiers, and the rapid development of infrastructure allowed the army to ship those men virtually anywhere in the world. As MacArthur's armies advanced, replacement depots cropped up across New Guinea and nearby islands—Goodenough Island, Oro Bay, and even Buna. The influx of replacements continued to dilute the Upper Midwestern character of the Red Arrow Division, although some of the new men hailed from the Badger and Wolverine States. One Wisconsin newcomer was John Walters, a school principal from Eau Claire. Thirty years old, married, and with a ten-month-old daughter, Walters thought he "probably wouldn't be called for a while" and was "shocked" when he received a draft notice in 1943. After basic training at Fort Bragg, Walters arrived at rainy, typhus-infested Goodenough Island. "For us Goodenough was hell enough," he complained to his wife, Jewell, in a letter home. From there Walters went to Finschhafen, where he found the conditions even worse. "There is absolutely more mud here than can be imagined," he wrote, "but I guess the closer one gets to the front the worse living conditions are." Walters then boarded a transport bound for Aitape.[75]

Walters was one of many new faces in the division. "We reached Aitape the first day of July," recalled Texan Robert S. Hiatt (no relation to Percy Hiatt). "It was dusk as we drifted slowly to a standstill in the bay. . . . Most of the boys were both excited and nervous at the same time."[76] Despite the publicity the Red Arrow had received the previous year, some newcomers were not sure what to make of the division. "At first I was disappointed the 32nd was a National Guard Div—not a regular unit," wrote Edward Guhl, but "I soon got over that."[77] Veterans scrutinized the replacements. Roy Campbell thought many "looked like they had just graduated high school." Racial tension sometimes flared, as when an influx of Mexican American soldiers arrived. Campbell recalled that among one batch of replacements were "some fifteen or so 'zootsuiters' from California," whom he thought were "cocky" and lacked military bearing, though he later conceded "they turned out to be good combat men."[78] Whatever misgivings the veterans may have had about the replacements, they welcomed them. As Newman Phillips remarked, "soldiers are always happy with new blood."[79] Newcomer Whayland Greene was "nervous" about meeting combat veterans, "but pleasantly surprised at how concerned older personnel were for the younger guys."[80]

Replacements entered the fighting at Aitape almost immediately. "When we landed," recalled Walters, "we were just given packs and I was given a rifle, and into the jungle we went."[81] Buna veteran Marvin Langetieg remembered that "they just dropped these guys into battle with no experience and no time to get accustomed to the climate or anything." Langetieg reflected on one particular replacement: "I don't think he was even 18. It was pitch dark and he hung close for a few days until he got used to things. . . . All of the replacements had a bad time with their introduction to combat under those conditions."[82]

Replacements at Aitape learned from veterans, though their learning curve was quite steep. Even minor slip-ups or chance could quickly lead to tragedy. Henry Zabierek recalled a patrol with three replacements that set out to find a Japanese machine-gun nest. The squad leader gave the rookies a crash course in survival. "Make as little noise as possible," he told them. "Have your weapons ready. Drop to the ground at the first shot. Wait for orders. Don't get yourselves killed. We need you." But when a Japanese machine gun fired on them twenty minutes into the patrol, one of the replacements took a bullet immediately. "Hit in the neck, he died without a murmur," lamented Zabierek. "His war lasted less than a week."[83] Newman Phillips thought that "after the first few days" in combat, replacements were generally "as good as the veterans."[84]

There were replacement officers too. "It always amazed [me] that after every main battle, all the officers disappeared and new ones took over," wrote Roy Campbell. "My company fell out one morning and was faced with all new officers—all second lieutenants fresh from the states." Their inexperience could have grave consequences. Campbell watched one day as a platoon, "headed by a newly arrived second lieutenant, cross[ed] the river into Japanese territory." In a short time Campbell heard the sounds of battle in the jungle, and then saw the lieutenant return without his men. "He had no gun and no helmet," Campbell recalled, "his hair was disheveled and he had a wild look in his eye." The lieutenant said that he had run into an ambush and that "all of his men had been killed." But shortly after the lieutenant's return, several soldiers from his patrol came back across the river. "The first men back reported that the lieutenant had ordered them to fire when he thought he saw a Japanese soldier," wrote Campbell, but they had instead "fired on a patrol of Americans coming down the river." Campbell recalled that "it took hours to bring back all the wounded and dead," and the lieutenant later went "completely off his rocker."[85]

New soldiers meant more baptisms of fire. "I will always remember the first night," commented John Walters. "A Jap sniper knew where we were and kept firing at us. Although he did not hit any of us, he kept us awake all night." Soon after, his patrol was "pushing the Japs through the jungles" when a machine gun opened up on it. Walters dove behind a large treetrunk, then looked up to see that "chips were coming off the top of the old tree."[86] Returning from the mission, Walters noted that the ranks of his platoon had thinned. "It seems hard to know that some of the fellows I knew so well are gone," he wrote to his wife, Jewell. "It just don't seem possible."[87]

Veterans were hardly immune to the emotional traumas of war. Paul Rettell had fought at Buna and Saidor, yet an incident in a foxhole near Aitape profoundly affected him. He was alone in the foxhole ("my buddy said he had to go to the toilet," he remembered) when a Japanese soldier jumped in. "I didn't have a chance to fire my gun," he wrote. "I had to use my knife." It was a hand-to-hand struggle, but Rettell stabbed his attacker to death. "I was sticky with blood and didn't realize blood had such an odor," he reflected. The incident rendered him speechless; when his buddy returned "all I could do was point my finger at the dead Jap that I had laid on the edge of the hole" and "I couldn't wash the blood off because I didn't have the means to do it." The incident affected him long afterward. "I kept looking at my hands," he wrote. "I had a feeling there was still blood on them. My buddy said I didn't hardly speak to anyone for a couple of days."[88]

The Aitape campaign took an immense psychological toll on nearly everyone involved. "The dark, desolate nights and the rain kept us constantly jittery," wrote Jesse Coker. "Everywhere around us we thought we heard the footsteps of our enemy. They were in front of us—behind us—we couldn't escape them physically or even in our dreams."[89] In a medical history of the Pacific War, author Mary Ellen Condon-Rall noted that "the psychoneurosis rate rose sharply during and just after combat, especially among replacements newly arrived from the United States."[90]

Although disease rates were nowhere near as high as at Buna, malaria and other fevers still posed a significant problem. "Atabrine discipline has been rigidly enforced," proclaimed one medical report, and "all possible breeding places of the mosquito have been oiled or drained."[91] Many Buna veterans suffered malarial relapses. In the midst of the Aitape fight, Roy Campbell still had "the usual chills and fever," he later wrote. Campbell also noted stomach pains, which meant he had "not gotten rid of the pestilence of hook and roundworms."[92] The 128th Infantry Regimental surgeon reported "one death from spontaneous rupture of the spleen following chronic malaria."[93] Aitape had its own disease challenges. By one estimate, 85 to 90 percent of all combat troops at Aitape suffered from some kind of skin disease.[94] In the third quarter of 1944, the 107th Medical Battalion recorded nearly 150 cases of scrub typhus, with a mortality rate of six percent.[95] At Afua, medic Dean Andersen became the patient. "I was not feeling well," he wrote, and "couldn't eat without vomiting." The doctor at Afua diagnosed Andersen with hepatitis and sent him to the rear. But when Andersen arrived at the clearing station, the doctor there questioned the severity of his illness. "The top brass are after us for sending too many men to the hospital," the doctor told Andersen, "but I will have you on the next plane out." He spent a month at a hospital in Finschhafen.[96]

Replacements came in not just for the sick, dead, or wounded. Veterans began returning to the United States. By April 1944, many Red Arrowmen had been overseas for two full years. Army brass recognized that keeping soldiers in combat units indefinitely was bad for morale, both in the ranks and on the home front. The army began serious discussion of a rotation policy in 1943, and Congress kept up the pressure on military leaders so soldiers could finally come home. The War Department issued a directive on rotation in June 1943, leaving policy specifics up to theater commanders. MacArthur, perpetually complaining of manpower shortages, stated flatly that he could not spare a single soldier. In December 1943, the War Department initiated a policy that would begin rotating 1 percent of soldiers per month as of March 1944. MacArthur once again protested, but SWPA reluctantly developed a rotation policy. To qualify, a soldier needed to have served overseas for at least eighteen months, and preference went to those with six months or more in tropical areas like New Guinea. Soldiers would not be discharged from the army but would be reassigned to stateside duties.[97]

Splashed across the front page of the January 28, 1944, edition of the *Milwaukee Journal* was the headline: "Men of the 32nd Division Scheduled to Start Journeys Home in March." The announcement was enthusiastically received on both sides of the Pacific. "This is the biggest news the Red Arrow soldiers have heard since they were sent overseas," reported the *Journal*'s Robert Doyle. "From morning until night they talk of little else.... Some soldiers are afraid to believe it."[98] Many were eligible, but only a few at a time could go home. "Each man ... was told to reach into a glass jar and take out a piece of paper with a number on it," wrote Howard Kelley. "The lowest number meant that you would be the first to go home on a rotation plan. I think my number was 17 so I had a long wait."[99]

But some won the lottery. The first contingent of about sixty Red Arrowmen, mainly Michiganders, arrived at Fort Sheridan, Illinois, in March 1944, and in April they began to reach their hometowns. The *Detroit Free Press* proclaimed them "home from hell" in a story that portrayed them in highly idealized terms. "They came back looking like athletes in pink," wrote the reporter. "These veterans of New Guinea readily admit that their Army service has changed them, but the change appears—on the surface, at least—to have put them far ahead of the average citizen, morally and physically. Nothing in their behavior suggests the brutality of the deeds to which a treacherous enemy forced them." The veterans were amazed to be home. "I want to get out and look around," Walter Putt told the *Detroit Free Press*. "I want to see the country and find out why it and the people I've met since my return seem so strange to me."[100] Men came back to the Badger State too. "Sergt. Pawlowski got the surprise of his life," reported the *Milwaukee Journal*, "as he strode along Lincoln av. at S. 5th st. on his way home when his sister, Eunice, stepped off a bus and into his arms." Pawlowski said that "she was crying and I guess maybe I was too, a little."[101]

As the Aitape campaign dragged on, a small but steadily growing number of Red Arrow soldiers received word they were going home. "On the 21 May Captain Roeder of Company D and sixteen (16) enlisted men, the May Rotation Quota departed this station," noted one 107th Medical Battalion report, adding, "the morale was high because of the apparent functioning of the Rotation Plan."[102] Robert Bable got orders out of the blue to "board ship the next morning," he later wrote. "We were all happy and laughing like giddy kids. We congregated in groups on the wide expanse of the beach, waiting to be ferried out to a liberty ship anchored outside the reef in the harbor."[103] In a letter home, Elvin Ball told his family that "some of the boys here are getting ready to catch a boat for home, and they sure are a happy bunch if ever I saw one. I can't blame them either. I hope to be home at least by Christmas if nothing happens to change the current plans [but] right now I'm sweating out the days until I can catch a boat."[104]

Those Red Arrowmen who stayed behind relished being away from combat and back in camp. "Our training routine has become a bit G.I.," John Walters wrote, "but it's heaven compared to those damn jungles."[105] Jesse Coker thought "it felt good to shave, take a bath, [and] wash our filthy clothes."[106] The army tried to keep the GIs entertained. Movies were popular, even if they were not Hollywood's latest releases. Roy Campbell enjoyed watching them "on a small screen, with coconut logs to sit on," and found it amusing to "look around at the grizzly combat soldiers watching movies, and marvel at the way some of them seemed to be mesmerized." The troops gave some films bad reviews. "One movie had John Wayne playing the part of a sergeant in the jungle," recalled Campbell. "When his best little buddy was killed, old John got mad, grabbed a light machine gun and running through the jungle, firing as he ran, he wiped out the whole Jap army!" At that, wrote Campbell, "the audience of combat men laughed so loud it took the rest of the movie to quiet them down." One GI shouted, "Hey John, get the hell over here, we need you!" and "the audience roared with laughter and went back to their tents fully entertained."

Bob Hope arrived at Aitape in September on a USO tour of the Pacific. Campbell remembered how Hope "walked out with his cocky strut and his first words were, 'Welcome to New Guinea, where they have hot and cold running malaria.'" Joining Hope onstage were other "well-known actors and performers such as Frances Langford, Lanny Ross, Jerry [Colonna], and a dancer named Patty Thompson," as well as "Judith Anderson and a company of performers." Campbell remembered that "the crowd roared when the girls sang and danced, and all were sad when Bob sang 'Thanks for the Memories' to end the show."[107] Not everybody clamored to see Hope. "Hell with it," thought Benjamin Winneshiek. "We used to see him in the movies."[108]

The combat survivors found other ways to amuse themselves. They caught up on their correspondence and their reading. The gambling wave continued. "We went down to the beach this afternoon for a couple of hours," wrote John Walters, "the whole company. Some swam, others played ball . . . and took a good sun bath. Seemed good to relax again."[109] James Myers remembered that "several men from the hills of Kentucky and Tennessee were able to set up stills to make 'white lightning,'" while "others stole raw alcohol from the medics, adding four parts water, some concentrated lemon extract and whatever else was handy."[110] According to Paul Rettell, "the Navy sailors who came ashore were looking for souvenirs" and "we got ten dollars for every Jap rifle we sold." Not every souvenir the sailors picked up was genuine. Rettell recalled that one GI "got the idea of using the silk from the parachute flares" to make counterfeit Japanese flags. He enlisted the help of a "Chinese-American soldier with us who could write Japanese," and "by painting the rising sun and writing some Japanese words on them they could sell them as souvenirs. They got twenty-five dollars for each one."[111]

As the Red Arrowmen rested at Aitape, MacArthur continued leap-frogging westward across New Guinea, seizing airfields and bases for the invasion of the Philippines. On July 2, US forces invaded the island of Noemfoor, sixty miles west of Biak, and on July 30 came the invasion of Sansapor near the eastern tip of the Vogelkop Peninsula. At the same time, Admiral Nimitz moved across the central Pacific. On June 15 Nimitz invaded Saipan in the Marianas, and a few days later the US Navy laid waste to the Japanese carrier fleet at the Battle of the Philippine Sea. From the Marianas, American forces were just two thousand miles from the Japanese home islands. Encouraging news came from Europe as well. On June 6, 1944, the Allies landed on the shores of Normandy, France. By September nearly all of France had been liberated and some predicted an end to the war in Europe by Christmas. Allied leaders increasingly turned their attention to the Pacific. MacArthur's long-awaited return to the Philippines seemed at hand.

General Douglas MacArthur (center) wades ashore at Leyte, October 20, 1944.
US ARMY SIGNAL CORPS

CHAPTER 9

I HAVE RETURNED

In July 1944, General MacArthur received an urgent message from General Marshall, ordering him to attend a conference at Pearl Harbor. "No intimation was given as to the identity of the personage with whom I was to confer," MacArthur later wrote, though he suspected it was President Roosevelt.[1] He was right. MacArthur arrived on July 26, and over the course of two days he made a fervent pitch to the president for paving the road to Japan through the Philippines. "Give me an aspirin," Roosevelt said after the first day of meetings. "In fact, give me another aspirin to take in the morning. In all my life nobody has ever talked to me the way MacArthur did." But MacArthur's dogged insistence on an invasion of the Philippines ultimately paid off. Three months later, MacArthur splashed ashore on the Philippines' Leyte Island and, echoing the promise he made in 1942, proudly proclaimed, "I have returned." The land and sea battles at Leyte during the last months of 1944 reestablished the American forces in the Philippines and changed the course of the Pacific War. It was here that the Thirty-Second Division entered its most significant fight since Papua. Leyte also ushered in a period of near-constant fighting for the Red Arrow that would last until the very end of the war—perhaps the most difficult phase of the division's Pacific experience.

The Pearl Harbor discussions were part of a larger debate amongst the Joint Chiefs of Staff during mid-1944 over what course to take in the Pacific. The army and the navy both agreed that cutting Japan's shipping links with the riches of Southeast Asia was crucial to an Allied victory, but debate raged about how best to achieve that goal. Chief of Naval Operations Admiral Ernest J. King wanted to bypass the Philippines entirely and press on to Formosa (Taiwan) and the port of Amoy (Xiamen) on the Chinese mainland. Such a move, King argued, would sever Japan's connection to Southeast Asia and put American forces at Japan's doorstep. US air bases in southern and eastern China could support the Formosa invasion, King believed. General MacArthur argued that control of the Philippines, and particularly the main island of Luzon, would block the sea lanes just as effectively. In addition, MacArthur made a moral case for returning to the Philippines, arguing that the United States had an obligation to liberate its colony, which was scheduled to gain its independence in 1946. Bypassing the islands, MacArthur believed, could lead to starvation for the people of the Philippines and continued suffering for prisoners of war. "I felt that to sacrifice the Philippines a second time could not be condoned or forgiven," he later wrote. MacArthur developed a plan, dubbed Reno V, to liberate the archipelago by invading the southern island of Mindanao first, then leaping to Leyte Island in the central Philippines, and finally moving to Luzon.[2]

Many in Washington initially favored King's Formosa proposal, but by late summer 1944 the joint chiefs had gravitated toward MacArthur's point of view. Formosa was farther distant from existing American bases than the Philippines. Taking and holding it meant maintaining a supply line across more than a thousand miles of open ocean. Moreover, Formosa, a Japanese colony since 1895, was well defended and invading it would require more men and materiel than were available. Hopes for a quick victory in Europe after D-Day faded as German resistance stiffened late that summer, and with the European war dragging on, soldiers and supplies from that theater could not be transferred to the Pacific anytime soon. In addition, Japan's ongoing Ichi-Go Offensive in China threatened the American air bases there, and they would not be able to support a

Formosa invasion. An invasion of the Philippines would involve shorter supply lines. The islands also appeared to be less well defended, so invading them would require fewer troops. President Roosevelt seemed to favor the Philippine route, though he did not directly influence the deliberations of his commanders. By early September MacArthur's views had won over most of the joint chiefs, though Admiral King still favored the Formosa proposal. On September 8, the joint chiefs issued a directive for the invasion of the Philippines, implementing much of MacArthur's Reno V plan. The invasion of Mindanao would begin on November 15, followed by Leyte a month later. However, they deferred for the moment whether to move to Luzon or Formosa after Leyte.[3]

To prepare the way for the Philippine invasion, MacArthur and his naval counterpart, Admiral General Chester Nimitz, staged simultaneous landings on September 15 on islands that guarded the approaches to the islands. The marines, under Nimitz, invaded Peleliu in the Palau Islands, five hundred miles east of Mindanao. MacArthur's forces took Morotai in the Molucca (Maluku) Islands, four hundred miles southeast of Mindanao. Morotai lies to the north of the larger island of Halmahera, where the Japanese concentrated their forces. By September 1944, Halmahera hosted an estimated thirty thousand Japanese soldiers, as well as several airfields. Morotai, by contrast, was only lightly defended with no more than five hundred troops, mostly Formosans under Japanese commanders. The egg-shaped island, fifty miles long and twenty-five miles wide, has a mountainous, jungled interior, a craggy coastline, and scores of offshore islands. Jutting from the southern tip of the island was the Gila Peninsula, and just to the north of the peninsula was an airfield. The goal of MacArthur's operation was to capture the airfield, improve it, and establish a naval base on Morotai to support ongoing operations on the Vogelkop Peninsula as well as the impending invasion of the Philippines.

The invasion of Morotai, dubbed Operation Tradewind, came under the direction of General Charles P. Hall and his XI Corps. The Thirty-First Infantry Division would be the main force. The 126th Regimental Combat Team, which had seen comparatively little action at Aitape, was the Tradewind reserve. The invasion of Morotai went off as scheduled on the morning of September 15. Navy guns bombarded both Halmahera and Morotai. At 8:30 a.m., the Thirty-First Division landed at two beaches on the western shore of the Gila Peninsula: Red Beach just north of the Japanese airstrip, and White Beach to the south of it. To maintain an element of surprise, American planners had done very little reconnaissance of the area, assuming the beaches would be suitable for a landing. This proved to be a mistake. Sharp coral reefs prevented landing craft from getting close to the shore, and they were forced to dump the troops out in five feet of water. The terrain beneath the water was not sandy as expected, but sticky clay. Vehicles and other equipment offloaded from the ships got stuck on the coral. "The beach conditions in the landing area were the worst we had ever seen in our operations," wrote General Walter Krueger in his memoir, "and that was saying a lot."[4] Fortunately, Japanese opposition to the landing was sporadic to nonexistent, and by the end of the day the Thirty-First Division had established a defensive perimeter well inland.

The 126th Infantry Regiment landed at 9:30 a.m. the following day between the Red and White Beaches. The Red Arrow troops endured the same poor landing conditions. "They put us on small landing barges and started toward the beach," wrote Whayland Greene. "They could not get us close to shore, so they had to let us off in about 5' of water. It sure was hard trying to move our feet in the water thinking any minute the machine guns would open up on us, but they didn't."[5] Dean Andersen swam in water he estimated to be ten feet deep. "A sailor had to swim ashore with a rope and tied it to a tree," he wrote. "We then used this rope to pull ourselves with our packs and equipment to the shallow water."[6] The Red Arrow established a base camp on the peninsula and planned its next moves. The task force expanded its perimeter and got to work making the airfield serviceable. MacArthur came too, stared longingly across the ocean toward the Philippines as cameras clicked, then departed.

On Morotai, the mission of the 126th Infantry Regiment was to establish observation posts and patrol bases, and to protect radar installations. On September 17, the Red Arrowmen moved out over water, by company and platoon, to six locations along the island's coastline, staging their own mini-D-Days, although the landings were all unopposed. In the coming days the number of US bases along the shoreline only grew.[7] In their search for Japanese troops, the GIs usually had the cooperation of the local population, whom the Japanese had brutalized since their arrival in 1942. As Red Arrow patrols fanned out across the island, they located Japanese entrenchments and equipment but found their adversaries reluctant to engage, though a few fights occurred. At Cape Wajaboela, for example, patrols located a concentration of Japanese soldiers on a prominence dubbed Hill 575. Company K attacked on September 23. "Naval gun fire was placed on the hill with remarkable accuracy," stated the after-action report, but "the terrain was difficult because of the lack of trails and its steepness [and] it was hard to place mortar fire because observation was almost impossible." The company was unable to break up the Japanese concentration that day and two of its members were killed, though in subsequent days the company successfully cleared the area.[8] Such engagements were rare. On Morotai the Red Arrow endured numerous Japanese air raids but saw little ground fighting. Richard Van Hammen later called it "the easiest campaign I was in."[9] The experience of the Tradewind Task Force stood in sharp contrast to what was happening on Peleliu, where the marines suffered through one of the most brutal island battles of the war. The brass declared Morotai secure on October 4, although small pockets of Japanese fighters would remain until the end of the war.

As September turned to October, the rest of the Red Arrow Division departed Aitape bound for Hollandia, which had become an important and ever-growing American base. MacArthur even made his headquarters there. The Red Arrowmen settled in camps and began an intensified training program. "New war tactics were the topic now," wrote Jesse Coker, "because we would be fighting over terrain which was different in a number of ways from that we had experienced in New Guinea."[10] They would have access to more advanced weaponry as well. "Flame thrower and rocket launcher operations will be trained in each rifle platoon," noted one training memo.[11] The troops also conducted patrols searching for any Japanese forces who might still be in the area. "Daily local security and reconnaissance patrols radiated in all feasible directions from each company outpost," noted one report. "It is estimated that this entire patrol system covered daily an area of approximately 30 to 40 square miles," but "there were no Japs contacted nor confirmed reports of recent signs of Japs."[12]

In off-duty hours, the GIs talked, gambled, or went swimming. "We have movies every night," wrote John Walters, who noted that "the food has been good lately and yesterday we even had fresh potatoes." James Myers remembered that "the beer was always hot, but by putting the cans in a helmet and wrapping a wet towel around them, the sun would cool off the beer by fast evaporation of the water."[13] Ernest Montoya remembered listening to Tokyo Rose—the nickname the GIs gave to Japan's women propaganda broadcasters. "We'd go to the mess hall and they'd be playing music and she'd be on the radio," Montoya remembered. "She knew the divisions and some of the officers' names. She was the one who told us we were going to the Philippines."[14]

Replacements arrived at Hollandia and Morotai, like Californian Monte Howell, whose assignment to the 114th Engineers filled him with anxiety. "A nineteen-year-old kid who has never been away from home before needs all the help he can get," Howell wrote. "I had no idea what I was supposed to do, or how to do it. . . . There were a lot of things they don't teach you in Twelve weeks basic training."[15] Rotations home picked up, too. Howard Kelley got the word he was going home while at Hollandia. "A truck came over to take three of us down to the docks," Kelley wrote glee-fully. "Look at me," he said as he departed. "I'm yellow as a pumpkin from taking atabrine, I'm 30 pounds underweight. I have recurring malaria. My shoulders are stooped and I have the slow reflexes of an old man. I've done my time in hell and now it's your turn."[16] One historical report of the 127th Infantry Regiment noted "that of the officers and enlisted men who came overseas with the Regiment, only 49 officers, 5 Warrant Officers, and 635 Enlisted Men entered the Leyte Campaign."[17]

For those who remained in the Red Arrow, anticipation of the next mis-sion grew. "You could feel something big was going to happen," claimed Monte Howell.[18] Jesse Coker noted that "ships were being loaded with various types of combat equipment, ammunition, and supplies of every description," and "the hurried activities at the recently constructed docks indicated that an important move would be made in the near future."[19] A new crop of Red Arrowmen was about to face its own baptism of fire. "I had never killed anyone," wrote Howell. "I had never even pointed a gun at anyone, except a cap gun when I was playing cowboys and Indians as a kid with my playmates."[20] Veterans like John Walters felt the stress too. "If for any reason I shouldn't come home," Walters wrote to his wife, Jewell, "you'll know that it wasn't because I didn't want to—and that some where—some place—I'll always be waiting for you."[21]

The Red Arrow's next rendezvous with the Japanese came sooner than expected. Two days before the landings at Peleliu and Morotai, Admiral William Halsey, commander of the US Navy's Third Fleet, sent an urgent cable to his boss, Admiral Nimitz. Halsey's aircraft carriers had been raiding the coasts of Mindanao and Leyte and reported weak resistance from the Japanese. In his September 13 cable, Halsey urged the cancellation of the Mindanao invasion and the preparatory operations in the Palau Islands, and instead recommended moving directly to Leyte. Further, Halsey wanted to speed up the timetable for the Leyte invasion to October 20.

MacArthur and Nimitz understood that the Japanese were not nearly as enfeebled as Halsey portrayed them. ULTRA intelligence indicated the Japanese had simply withdrawn much of their air forces north to Luzon to keep them out of the range of American planes. Intercepts further showed that the Japanese were building up ground forces in the Philippines in anticipation of an American invasion. But the confident US commanders were anxious to strike, and Halsey's report fit the narrative they wanted. Nimitz mostly concurred with Halsey's recommendation, though he still wanted the Peleliu operation, and sent the proposal to the joint chiefs, who in turn queried MacArthur for his views. The SWPA commander was on his way to Morotai and was incommunicado, but General Richard Sutherland, MacArthur's chief of staff, knew his boss's thinking and eagerly gave assent in MacArthur's name. A little more than a month later, MacArthur would make his much-desired return to the Philippines.

Japan planned to make the American return to the Philippines as bloody as it could. The Japanese fully understood the threat that US control of the islands posed to their supply line from Southeast Asia. In addition, they saw the opportunity for decisive battles, both on land and at sea, that might halt the American drive toward the home islands. During mid-1944, the Japanese shifted more of their attention to the Philippines. Field Marshal Terauchi Hisaichi, head of Japan's Southern Expeditionary Army Group, moved his headquarters from Singapore to Manila. Defending the Philippines was the Fourteenth Army Area, under the command of General Yamashita Tomoyuki, who had gained fame as the "Tiger of Malaya" for his rapid conquest of Malaya and Singapore back in 1941–1942. By October 1944, Yamashita had more than two hundred thousand troops in the Philippines, most on the main island of Luzon. The Japanese initially kept very few troops on Leyte, but as the American invasion approached, they dispatched increasing numbers there, most notably the Sixteenth Division, veterans of the Bataan campaign. By October, there were perhaps twenty-one thousand Japanese on Leyte. They brought tanks with them and had as many as five airfields in operation. The Japanese Thirty-Fifth Army, under Lieutenant General Suzuki Sosaku, was responsible for the defense of Leyte and the central Philippine islands. Suzuki's troops got to work constructing defensive positions and awaiting their US adversaries.

By the early fall of 1944, the forces under MacArthur's command had grown substantially. Krueger's Sixth Army had been the workhorse of the SWPA command since 1943, but with the activation of the Eighth Army in June 1944, MacArthur now had two field armies at his disposal. The Eighth Army was under the command of a familiar face: General Robert Eichelberger, with whom MacArthur had a long and fraught relationship. Eichelberger's Eighth Army took command of Allied forces on New Guinea in September 1944, freeing up Krueger's Sixth Army for the Leyte operation. Krueger had two corps available for the invasion of Leyte. The X Corps, under Major General Franklin Sibert, consisted of the First Cavalry and Twenty-Fourth Infantry Divisions. The XXIV Corps, under Major General John R. Hodge, consisted of the Seventh and Ninety-Sixth Infantry Divisions. The Red Arrow Division at Hollandia and Morotai, as well as the Seventy-Seventh Infantry Division at Guam, made up the Sixth Army reserve. With the exception of the Ninety-Sixth, every one of these units had seen action in the Pacific. In all, MacArthur and Krueger had more than two hundred thousand troops for the Leyte operation, with more on the way.

The island of Leyte runs 110 miles north to south and is loosely shaped like a figure eight, with a bulbous protrusion on its northwestern coast. The island of Samar hovers above Leyte to the northeast, just across the San Juanico Strait, while the northern tip of Mindanao juts up from the south. To the east is Leyte Gulf, an arm of the Pacific, and to the west is the Camotes Sea. Leyte's interior is covered in lush jungle and mountains that reach as high as four thousand feet. Indeed, the southern half of the island was so mountainous and sparsely populated that the Japanese based no troops there at all. Tacloban, a city of thirty thousand people on the northeast tip of Leyte and within sight of Samar, was the largest city

Leyte Battle Area

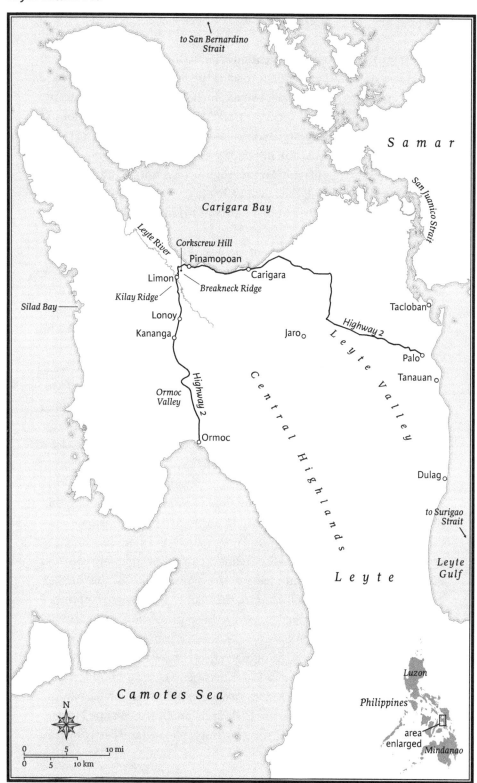

to San Bernardino Strait

Samar

Carigara Bay

San Juanico Strait

Leyte River

Corkscrew Hill

Pinamopoan

Carigara

Limon

Breakneck Ridge

Kilay Ridge

Tacloban

Silad Bay

Lonoy

Kananga

Jaro

Highway 2

L e y t e   V a l l e y

Palo

Tanauan

Ormoc Valley

Highway 2

C e n t r a l   H i g h l a n d s

Ormoc

Dulag

to Surigao Strait

Leyte Gulf

L e y t e

C a m o t e s   S e a

N

0   5   10 mi
0   5   10 km

Luzon

Philippines

area enlarged

Mindanao

and administrative center on the island. Between Tacloban and the town of Carigara on the island's north coast is the fertile Leyte Valley, where farmers grew a great variety of produce, including rice, corn, sugarcane, and bananas, with carabao (water buffalo) serving as the primary beasts of burden. On the northwestern shore lies the port of Ormoc. From there, the Ormoc Valley runs to the north, tapering off in the rugged central highlands toward the village of Limon. Highway 2 connected Tacloban and Ormoc, running through the Leyte Valley to Carigara and Pinamopoan, then hooking southward into the mountains to Limon and then down the Ormoc Valley.

In the early morning hours of October 20, a flotilla of more than seven hundred Allied ships entered Leyte Gulf. After a massive bombardment, Krueger's Sixth Army landed at 10:00 a.m.: X Corps just south of Tacloban, and XXIV Corps ten miles farther south. Japanese opposition was surprisingly light. As the GIs pushed inland, cargo ships bellied up to the beaches to disgorge tanks, trucks, and tons of supplies. Early that afternoon, the beaches were secure enough to allow MacArthur to wade ashore, the sounds of battle booming in the distance as he announced his return. By nightfall American troops had penetrated as far as two miles inland and had reached the outskirts of Tacloban. In the following days the Sixth Army expanded its beachhead. The X Corps took Tacloban on October 21, then advanced through the northern Leyte Valley toward Carigara. Some troops even crossed the San Juanico Strait to Samar. XXIV Corps pressed into the southern Leyte Valley, the site of several Japanese airfields. Elements also drove toward the remote southern part of the island.

MacArthur expected a quick and easy victory on Leyte, but American planners had underestimated the Japanese capabilities and misread their intentions—on both land and sea. Admiral Nimitz believed that the Japanese would not risk the remnants of their devastated fleet to halt the US invasion. In fact, the Imperial Navy sought confrontation. Soon after US troops landed on Leyte on October 20, three Japanese naval task forces steamed toward Leyte Gulf. A southern fleet, under Admiral Nishimura Shoji, approached the Surigao Strait between Leyte and Mindanao. A central fleet, under Admiral Kurita Takeo, headed to the San Bernardino Strait between Samar and Luzon. Nishimura and Kurita planned to converge on the American landing forces in the Leyte Gulf and destroy them.

Meanwhile, a third fleet of aircraft carriers under Admiral Ozawa Jisaburo descended from the Japanese home islands to the north. The carriers had few planes and instead were intended as a decoy to divert US naval forces northward, allowing Nishimura and Kurita a freer hand to destroy the landing force. During the night of October 24–25, Rear Admiral Jesse B. Oldendorf blocked Nishimura from entering Leyte Gulf at the Surigao Strait. However, the situation at the San Bernardino Strait was far more perilous. Admiral Halsey took the bait and headed north to meet Ozawa, leaving the San Bernardino Strait unguarded. During the night of October 24–25, Kurita sailed through the strait, then turned southward toward Leyte Gulf. In the early morning hours of October 25, fierce fighting erupted off Samar between Kurita's force and the US Navy ships guarding the landing force. Here the Japanese introduced a fearsome new tactic— the kamikaze attack. Suicidal pilots intentionally flew their planes into American ships, sacrificing themselves but taking the lives of many more US sailors. Kurita landed some hard punches on the American ships, but believing himself outnumbered and outgunned, he reversed course and slipped away through the San Bernardino Strait, leaving the US fleet damaged but intact.

The Battle of Leyte Gulf, as the engagement became known, was the last great fleet action of World War II. For Japan, it was a crippling blow. The Imperial Navy lost nearly thirty ships—including four aircraft carriers and three battleships—and its offensive capabilities had been destroyed. The Allies lost just seven vessels. But Japanese commanders did not immediately understand the gravity of their losses. Based on the false and questionable reports of their pilots, the Japanese thought they had broken up the American landing force, leaving MacArthur's ground troops on Leyte unsupported and vulnerable. In reality, Allied navies now sailed the Pacific virtually unimpeded, and MacArthur's buildup on Leyte continued.[22]

MacArthur made some miscalculations of his own. One of his top priorities on Leyte was to establish airfields to lessen his dependence on navy carriers. Unfortunately, the invasion corresponded with the arrival of monsoon season, and near-constant heavy rains quickly transformed the airfields into seas of thick mud. Rains also made things nearly unbearable for the infantry. Muddy roads made the resupply and reinforcement of frontline soldiers difficult, and soldiers on both sides of the line suffered

through a world of clinging muck and constant wetness. Typhoons occasionally lashed Leyte as well, adding high winds and more misery. At the
same time, Japanese planes menaced American land and sea forces, and
the dreaded kamikazes continued their attacks, including on troop carriers
headed to the island.

MacArthur anticipated that the Japanese would make their stand on
Luzon. Yamashita believed Luzon was the proper place for a decisive battle
too, but General Terauchi disagreed. Believing the exaggerated reports of
Japan's naval victory at Leyte Gulf, Terauchi poured reinforcements onto
Leyte to make his stand there. The reinforcements usually arrived during
the night and evaded American observation. By early November, Terauchi
had increased the number of his troops on Leyte to thirty-four thousand,
including Japan's elite First Division under Lieutenant General Kataoka
Tadasu, arriving from China.

By November 2, Krueger had taken Carigara on the north coast of the
island, effectively completing the liberation of the Leyte Valley. Krueger
now planned a pincer movement to crush the Japanese in the Ormoc Valley, with X Corps pressing down from the north and XXIV Corps taking
Ormoc and moving up from the south. An optimistic MacArthur believed
the Leyte campaign was all but completed; an SWPA press communiqué on
November 3 talked of mopping up the remnants of Japanese on the islands
and claimed that "the end of the Leyte-Samar campaign is in sight." But
General Suzuki had ideas of his own. From Ormoc, he planned to ascend
the Ormoc Valley, cross to the north coast at Carigara, then press on to
Tacloban and drive the Americans into the sea. Thus, on November 3 two
advancing armies crashed into each other west of Carigara along the coast
road. The following day Krueger was able to advance to the point where
Highway 2 turned into the mountains, but then found Kataoka's First Division digging into the hills above.

Here Krueger made one of his most controversial decisions. He might
have pressed up Highway 2 and attacked before the First Division had arrived there in force. However, after learning of Suzuki's planned offensive,
Krueger feared a Japanese amphibious landing along the coast—a move
they were in fact considering. Krueger had no reserves. "A more aggressive
commander might have ignored the seaward threat to Carigara . . . and
thrown everything into seizing the crucial ridges and hills before the Japa-

nese could secure them," wrote historian Stanley Falk, but "Krueger was not by nature inclined to take such a gamble."[23] Krueger later defended his decision: "Although I was anxious to gain early possession of the hills north of Limon which controlled access to the Ormoc Valley, I could not ignore the possibility of such a landing."[24] Thus, rather than advance into the hills, Krueger prepared for an amphibious assault on his forces, blunting his forward momentum. The delay gave Kataoka the opportunity to fortify the ridgeline.

When the Twenty-Fourth Infantry Division, under Major General Frederick A. Irving, finally began its move into the hills along Highway 2 on November 6, it faced a dazzling array of Japanese bunkers and fighting positions on the high ground, which quickly became known as Breakneck Ridge. Fighting raged there for more than a week. Americans repeatedly moved forward only to be pushed back. Incessant wind-driven rain knocked down trees and turned the ground slick and unstable. Combat was sometimes hand-to-hand. After nearly a week of this, Irving sent two forces behind Japanese lines, hoping to cut the communication line between Ormoc and Breakneck Ridge and compel their retreat. One battalion set up roadblocks three miles south of Breakneck Ridge. Another fought its way onto high ground west of the highway at a spot dubbed Kilay Ridge, named after a deceased Filipino guide. Both battalions faced heavy opposition and, although they held their ground, could not sever the highway. Irving's division clawed its way forward and reached the crest of Breakneck Ridge but had suffered such devastating casualties that it could proceed no farther. Meanwhile, the XXIV Corps's drive to Ormoc had stalled as well, and Krueger found himself bogged down in a protracted struggle he did not expect. Fortunately for Krueger, reinforcements were on the way, including the Thirty-Second Infantry Division.

During the second week of November the Red Arrow began its movement north to the Philippines. Nearly a dozen ships departed from Hollandia. "It was a beautiful day when [we] finally left New Guinea," wrote Roy Campbell. "The sun shined brightly and the weather stayed perfect as the big assault boat plowed its way to the islands where the Japs had started this whole mess."[25] Nine more ships departed Morotai. The two convoys converged at sea on the morning of November 12 and headed north to Leyte. As they sailed toward their next battle, the Red Arrowmen received lectures on the land and people of the Philippines. Japanese planes attacked the convoy on November 13. It was "just at sundown" when Robert Hiatt heard the warning bell. "The guns were manned," Hiatt wrote, "and the troops were in their quarters when the first of five Jap torpedo planes hovering over the clouds above dove screaming shrilly upon the fourth ship in our convoy, just to our rear, and let go a torpedo." The torpedo missed, and the attacking plane "burst into flames and crashed into the sea," as American P-38 fighters "came out of nowhere."[26]

The Red Arrow convoy arrived at Leyte the morning of November 14, landing between Tanauan and Tacloban. "I remember so clearly the brightness of the sun that morning," wrote Hiatt, "the fluffy, scattered bits of clouds and wettish sort of atmosphere, rather instilled in me a depressed sensation, and yet a careless gaiety."[27] As the convoy approached the shoreline, Roy Campbell was amazed to see "hundreds of boats of all sizes—great battle wagons, cruisers, destroyers, landing craft, and smaller craft moving about from ship to shore. Until [I] actually saw the great battle fleet [I] never would have believed there were such monsters moving about on the oceans." But when Campbell looked out across the distant hills, he spotted three Japanese planes approaching his convoy. "In a split second the air was filled with shells, and every gun in the harbor and on the boats was firing at the three planes," he wrote. Gunners shot down two of the planes but the third kept coming, flying just above the water until it too was hit. "Dipping its right wing," Campbell recalled, "it touched the water and flew end over end for many yards, exploding into bits."[28]

Once ashore, some GIs got the onerous task of unloading the ships. Robert Hiatt recalled doing such work "in the blistering sun," which "constituted a reason for much griping and we used our tongues relentlessly for it."[29] Most of the division moved inland to a bivouac near the town of Jaro, in the foothills of the central mountain range. The Red Arrowmen expected to be put in reserve, but instead they were headed for Breakneck Ridge, and on the rainy morning of November 16 they loaded onto trucks and moved toward the front. "When an infantry soldier is put into a truck you know you are not going to mail call or the chow line," Whayland Greene wrote. "Someone needed us bad and quick or we would be walking."[30]

On the trip to Breakneck Ridge, the Red Arrowmen got their first glimpse of the Philippines and realized they were in a land quite different from the one they just left. Amid its jungles and mountains, Leyte was a land of highways, farmlands, cities and towns, shops and churches. "I remember what an impression it made on me," wrote Dean Andersen, who passed through Tacloban. "We had left the jungles of New Guinea where cities marked on a map turned out to be only groups of primitive native housing. Here was a town with a main street with stores and shops. It was not an American city, but better than anything we had seen since leaving Australia." Rural scenes differed from what they had seen in New Guinea too. "Rice fields were overflowing with muddy water," Andersen noted, and "we could hear chickens clucking."[31] The Philippines had been a Spanish colony for four hundred years, then an American colony since 1898, so its culture and landscapes did indeed seem comparatively familiar to American GIs. Many Filipinos spoke English, and some Red Arrow troops talked of being back in "civilization." Leyte was also an impoverished place, distant from the political center at Manila, subjected to centuries of colonial rule and then three years of Japanese occupation. "The people living there didn't have very much," observed Paul Rettell.[32]

The Filipino experience during the Japanese occupation was complex. Some Filipinos, particularly among the economic elite, collaborated with the Japanese. Many others held back and calculated which side best served their interests, Japan or the Allies, or accommodated both sides in an effort to survive. But anti-Japanese sentiment dominated on Leyte and across the Philippines. Japan's rhetoric of ejecting whites from Asia rang hollow in a country that was largely self-governing and already on the road to independence. Exploitative and extractive Japanese economic policies only increased the hardships of the population, much of which already lived in dire poverty. The brutality of the Imperial Army and the Japanese secret police, the Kempeitai, further promoted anti-Japanese sentiment. "The Filipino people," wrote historians Ikehata Setsuho and Ricardo Trota Jose of the occupation years, "were forced to suffer loss of jobs, starvation, lack of basic necessities of life, forced labor, torture, insult, plunder, violence, and deprivation of life." Few Filipinos wanted to go back to US colonial rule, but for most Filipinos the return of American forces meant liberation from Japanese occupation and the reopening of the road to independence.[33]

Guerrilla groups sprang up across the archipelago during the occupation to continue the fight against Japan, many of them led by American troops and Filipino military personnel who had evaded capture or escaped from Japanese prison camps. By 1944 there were hundreds of guerrilla organizations: the Fighting Bolo Battalion, the Fil-American Yay Regiment, the Hunters ROTC, and the Philippine Chinese Anti-Japanese Guerrilla Force, just to name a few. Popular support for the guerrillas led to harsh Japanese reprisals against civilians. MacArthur coordinated guerrilla operations through SWPA's Allied Intelligence Bureau, spiriting weapons and equipment to underground forces by air drop or submarine. The guerrillas lacked the training, equipment, and discipline of regular soldiers and could not dislodge the Japanese on their own, but they applied constant pressure on Japanese forces, ambushing patrols, blowing up bridges, and severing communication lines. They inflicted an estimated 13,500 casualties on Imperial forces during the occupation. Guerrillas also provided MacArthur with valuable intelligence and aided American aircrews shot down over the islands.[34]

With the return of American forces to Leyte in October 1944, at least 3,200 guerrillas under Lieutenant Colonel Ruperto Kangleon linked up them. Kangleon's guerrillas fought alongside GIs, served as guides, provided security behind the lines, and recruited laborers to serve as carriers or perform other tasks for American forces. Over the course of World War II, at least 260,000 Philippine men and women took up arms against the Japanese, substantially bolstering Allied forces in the islands. "Without the guerrillas," concluded historian James Villaneuva, "the Philippines campaign would have been much more difficult for Allied forces and would have consumed greater amounts of time, resources, and manpower."[35] Red Arrowmen encountered Philippine guerrillas and workers almost immediately upon landing on Leyte. In a letter home shortly after his arrival on the island, Dean Anderson remarked that Filipinos "volunteer to work for us, and they help a lot."[36]

The civilians of Leyte greeted the Red Arrow with hearty enthusiasm as well. "The children raised their fingers in victory signs and screamed at us with glee," wrote Robert Hiatt. "We returned the greetings, and tossed gum, chocolate, or anything else at hand to the children, and they would run screaming to retrieve the presents."[37]

Others noted ominous sights. In the distance "you could hear machine

gun fire and rifle fire and also artillery," recalled Whayland Greene.[38] The
landscape bore the scars of battle. Roy Campbell saw "trees blown to bits,
huts burned, shell holes, and everything that goes with man's destruction."[39] The impact of the war on civilians was obvious and heartbreaking.
"Shelling and bombs had destroyed much of the towns," wrote Robert
Hiatt.[40] Rettell was horrified by evidence of Japanese atrocities. "There
were women and children tied to the trees and left to die," Rettell wrote.
"All that was left of them were skeletons and rags on their bodies."[41] The
brutality of the Japanese occupation steeled the Red Arrowmen's determination. "After you see how they were treated," Dean Andersen wrote to
his fiancée, Marie Gleason, "it creates a greater hatred for the Japanese."[42]
Greene noticed a US cemetery on the route toward Breakneck Ridge. "I
did some thinking as we passed . . . all those rows of neat graves and white
crosses," he wrote. "Those graves didn't look too old. I also looked at those
rows of new graves already dug."[43]

The Red Arrow set up base camps in the Pinamopoan area, along the
shores of Carigara Bay. Robert Hiatt was near an artillery base, and he remembered that "the guns were shelling targets over the mountains."[44] The
divisional camps received fire too. "Every night the Japanese would shell . . .
our headquarters," recalled Monte Howell. "We finally figured out that they
had zeroed in on a tall tree that was standing in our area," and once they
chopped it down, "the shelling stopped."[45] Highway 2 was a vital lifeline
for the operations at Breakneck Ridge, but the road was in poor condition.
"The road was very muddy," wrote Andersen, "and trucks with winches
were stationed in places to pull each vehicle along and out of the deep mud."
Impassable sections led to detours along a coral beach, which "worked out
all right when the tide was out," according to Andersen.[46] Maintaining this
lifeline posed a great challenge for the 114th Engineers, a task made more
difficult by the constant Japanese sniping and shelling. Supply convoys
over the highway were in great danger too. "One day the Japs were shelling
the entire length of the road," wrote truck driver Rettell. He took refuge in
a ditch with members of a chemical unit that had recently arrived at the
front. A shell then made a direct hit on four members of the chemical unit.
"All you could see was pieces of hands, eyeballs, mouths, jaws, arms—all
kinds of body parts and blood," Rettell remembered. At that, the remaining

Unlike New Guinea, much of Leyte was laced together with highways—though heavy traffic, frequent rains, and Japanese attacks often made transporting men and materiel incredibly difficult. NATIONAL ARCHIVES

members of the chemical unit went "running down the road as fast as they could go—the whole bunch—colonel, captain, lieutenant, sergeants. . . . It was like a stampede you would see in a western movie."[47]

Veterans and rookies alike anticipated the fight ahead. Greene had been on a few patrols at Aitape and Morotai, but Leyte felt different. "I thought I was nervous when I walked up the gang plank to get on the ship," Greene wrote, but "there was no comparison" to the anxieties he now felt.[48] Robert Hiatt remembered that "the older men took a fatalistic attitude. . . . That is, to enter calmly, though fear be present in the heart, for it is our fate."[49]

Upon the arrival of the Thirty-Second Division at Breakneck Ridge, the Red Arrow's commander, General William Gill, assumed control of the US troops there, including the Twenty-Fourth Division troops who remained at the roadblocks along Highway 2 and on Kilay Ridge. The Red Arrow entered the fight at midday on November 16—nearly two years to the day since they first engaged the Japanese at Buna. As at Buna, the 128th Infantry Regiment went in first, now under Colonel John A. Hettinger, a Great War combat veteran and protégé of Gill. Hettinger attacked with two battalions abreast. On the left, the First Battalion's assignment was a prominence known as Corkscrew Hill. On the right, the Third Battalion was to move south along Highway 2 and take the Japanese-occupied village of Limon, fifteen hundred yards south of Corkscrew Hill.

At Corkscrew Hill, the First Battalion met a brick wall. On the right of the battalion front, Company A made no forward progress. On the left, Company B advanced about two hundred yards, reaching two fingerlike ridges before it too was stymied. The Japanese had been on Corkscrew Hill for some time and had prepared their battlefield well. "The enemy were in extremely deep spider holes on the reverse slopes of the maze of ridges," noted one report. "Heavy jungle vegetation limited observation of enemy positions, and the Jap had cunningly placed his many automatic weapons so that the only routes of approach were directly uphill [sic] into the face of his fire."[50] Mother Nature also hampered the American advance. "The weather," noted the battalion operations report, "seemed to be perversely working against us. It rained almost every day without fail and usually three or more days in succession with a high wind accompanying the rain, which did nothing to lessen the discomfort of the men." The fighting on Corkscrew Hill was reportedly even more savage than that at Buna. "For the next two or three weeks the Battalion was engaged in the fiercest fighting at close range ever experienced by the unit," noted the battalion operations report. "Many men, veterans of Buna, stated that the Buna 'Show' was a 'Picnic' compared to this one."[51]

One of those Buna veterans was Roy Campbell of Company B, who recounted many assaults against Corkscrew Hill. Campbell wrote of his captain who ordered a platoon to attack a ridgeline, a move Campbell thought foolish.

"They have that hill covered," Campbell told him, "and you can dang well bet they'll be waiting."

"I'm running this outfit," the captain replied, "so *you* shut up!"

Campbell watched as the platoon "moved along the face of a ridge" when "suddenly guns fired and the first four men went down. The guns raked back and forth across the platoon and more men fell." The attack failed. The captain ordered more attacks in subsequent days, leaving more men dead, little ground gained, and the captain himself "badly shaken."

Days later Campbell led an assault launched from a position dubbed Maggot Ridge, named for the maggot-filled corpses left behind after earlier fights. Campbell thought this attack futile too, but "said a silent prayer" and prepared his men. They descended Maggot Ridge in the early morning darkness, and as dawn broke Campbell and his men found themselves "in a deep, brushy ditch" between two ridges. To attack, Campbell wrote, the GIs had to "climb straight up a steep bank strewn with wire and brush some twenty feet high." As they prepared to jump off, Campbell heard the sound of Japanese soldiers arming their grenades, and he knew he and his men were "about to catch hell." Machine-gun fire then roared down on them, along with a hail of grenades. Campbell lobbed his own grenades up the hill. As he watched his "last grenade fly," Campbell "saw a hand reach up, catch his grenade and throw it back all in one motion." The explosion hit Campbell in the foot. Judging the attack a failure, he ordered his men back to Maggot Ridge. Despite his injuries, Campbell carried an injured friend on his back as the Japanese fired on them. He "could feel the adrenaline take over" as he "almost ran up the trail."[52]

The Third Battalion, on the right, met considerably less resistance in its November 16 attack. Companies L and K moved along Route 2, reaching a ridgeline dubbed Hill 13 at about 2:00 p.m. But with the First Battalion unable to move forward, the Third Battalion stopped its advance to wait for them, dug in, and poured fire onto Japanese-occupied Limon. The following day their objective was another prominence, known as Hill 19. They reached it before noon and were now within five hundred yards of Limon. There they halted again, waiting for the First Battalion to come abreast. The Third Battalion had taken only small losses and claimed to have killed eighty-seven Japanese. "During the next three days," noted one historical report, the Third Battalion kept Limon "under constant small arms, artillery, and mortar fire."[53] The Japanese attempted to infiltrate the battalion's positions. "I spotted about fifteen Japs crossing an open field below us and to our left," wrote James Myers. "They were covered in branches and leaves. They would move forward a few feet, then stop."

Artillery hit the Japanese attackers, but about six of them worked their way to "where some shelter was provided by the slope of the hill." Myers and a small group got orders to go in and kill them. "They opened up on us with rifle grenades," Myers recalled, injuring several men, but Myers and his cohorts "eliminated them."[54]

Hettinger now opted to seize Limon without waiting for the First Battalion on Corkscrew Hill to catch up. His objective was a bridge over the Leyte River on the south end of the village. On the morning of November 22, while attacks continued on Corkscrew Hill, the GIs laid down an artillery barrage on Limon. Then the Third Battalion—now reinforced with the Second—moved out to take it. "The air was hot and humid, almost suffocating," wrote Jesse Coker. Opposition was light at first. Coker recalled that "a solitary Jap soldier in the base of a dead tree, by firing at us intermittently, had detained our company most of the morning," but a GI finally killed him with a grenade, and the battalion moved on. By midday, Coker stood on a ridge overlooking Limon. "I scanned the village," he wrote, and saw a few buildings "constructed of bamboo poles and grass or palm leaves."[55] Fearing a trap, the Red Arrowmen proceeded carefully. They occupied the village and moved toward the bridge on its southern end. Mindful that the span might be mined, the troops waded across the shallow river instead. They proceeded about two hundred yards south of the river and then, according to Myers, "we were then told to hold up our advance to wait for our communication and support lines to catch up with us."[56]

Late that afternoon the battle took a turn. Heavy rain began, and the lazy river quickly developed into a flooded torrent. It was at that moment that the Japanese launched a fierce counterattack. For those Red Arrowmen on the south bank of the river, the raging waters blocked their retreat as the Japanese charged toward them. Coker found himself pinned down out in the open. "The enemy soldier firing at me would get close to my head," he wrote, "the bullet often kicking mud into my face, or the bullet would land near my side or at my heels. . . . Men began running for their lives and were instantly killed [and] the moans and groans of the wounded and dying were almost unbearable." Many of the GIs who tried to recross the river were shot or drowned. "The sound of dying men mixing with the roar of the river created a macabre sound," Coker wrote, and decades later he was still horrified at the memory of "those poor guys going under the violent, blood-red waters of the river." Coker got up and found his company commander lying in a "congealed pool of his own blood," immobilized with a shattered spine. He also found a friend whose "leg was soaked in blood, and he had a large, gaping wound in one of his thighs." Both men begged Coker not to leave them on the field. "Even the bravest and largest men," he recalled, "feared the wanton acts of torture to which the bastard Japs subjected prisoners."[57]

Despite the heavy rain and hail of bullets, small groups of survivors began to gather and organize. James Myers and a band of about thirty-five men took refuge behind a creek embankment. They followed the creek bed westward toward the Company I position on the ridge above the village. To reach the ridge, Myers and his cohort had to cross an open field. Myers raced across the open ground, zigzagging to thow off the aim of any Japanese gunman, when a rifle bullet ripped into his thigh. "My right leg felt like it was hit with a baseball bat just as hard as someone could swing it," he remembered later. Myers bandaged his wound and hobbled "with the help of a stout stick" several hundred yards "to a native hut that several medics had taken over as an aid station." Gathering as many wounded as they could, Coker and his band crossed the bridge after dark "without a single shot being fired by the enemy. I can only explain our successful escape as a miracle."[58]

The fight at Limon was a tough one, but the Red Arrow now controlled the village. "I was exhausted and overwhelmed by sorrow for my fellow soldiers," wrote Coker. "My clothes were soaked through and my body caked with mud [but] the physical pain I was enduring was nothing compared to my tormented emotions."[59] Over the next several days, the Red Arrow consolidated its positions around the village and patrolled aggressively. The Japanese made clear they did not intend to let the Red Arrow advance any farther. "A banzai charge was made in an attempt to drive us from our positions," recalled Coker. "We counted 52 dead Japs after a brief fire fight," and "after the battle was over, we recovered cigarettes, pictures, watches, etc., from the dead Japanese soldiers. They had taken these from the dead Yanks who were killed in the trap across the river." Japanese artillery harassed American lines and infiltrators got behind them. Myers, injured in the Limon bridge fight, was loaded onto one of two jeeps evacuating the wounded to the rear. "After we had gone several

Red Arrow soldiers receive incoming Japanese artillery fire at Limon. NATIONAL ARCHIVES

miles," he wrote, "we heard a Jap machine gun start chattering." Bullets ripped into the jeep behind him, and "no one in the other jeep escaped alive."[60] Patrols even spotted Japanese tanks coming up. The 127th Infantry Regiment, in reserve at the beginning of the fighting, joined the 128th Infantry Regiment at Limon. Elements of the 632nd Tank Destroyer Battalion and the Forty-Fourth Tank Battalion also arrived. The fight at Corkscrew Hill continued unabated.

By the last days of November, Kataoka's First Division held the ridges running east-west south of Limon, commanding Highway 2—the road to Ormoc—with his elite troops occupying the trenches and spider holes now so familiar to the Red Arrow veterans. Division artillery blasted the ridges for days, then Gill sent in the infantry. The Third Battalion of the 127th Infantry Regiment drew what may have been the toughest assignment: a ridge overlooking the Limon bridge known variously as Bridge Ridge or Bloody Ridge. The attack began on November 29. "There were no dramatic flourishes to launch the attack," remembered Henry Zabierek. "No bells were sounded, no starter's gun fired into the air, no horns tooted," just "a mere wave" of his company commander's arm. There was little opposition at first but his company still advanced slowly over the brushy, uneven ground. Then, "in what seemed only a flash," Zabierek recalled, "enemy rifle fire filled the air. Their machine guns then chattered their deadly melody. Mortar shells whined before inflicting their damage. The carnage was immediate." The fire was so intense Zabierek's company was forced to withdraw, but it renewed the attack the following day—this time preceded by an artillery barrage. The Japanese responded with a banzai charge. "They waved their arms and shouted," he recalled. "Most of the enemy had guns, but some who led did not. They would sacrifice themselves so that others could break through." Zabierek remembered that "bodies began to pile up on bodies," and "parts of bodies lay apart from the torso." Once again, the GIs were forced to pull back. Gains were minimal.

It went on like that for more than a week, the Red Arrowmen slowly inching forward. "One day seemed to blend into another," wrote Zabierek, "first the shelling, then the advance, another bunker or machine gun nest, a suicidal attack, attempted infiltration of the perimeter at night, and always a steady hail of rifle bullets. Only the intensity seemed to increase." One day Zabierek's company encountered a Japanese tank. The GIs knocked out its treads with grenades, and as soon as the crew opened the hatch to escape, a GI lobbed a well-aimed grenade inside the vehicle. The blast "almost lifted the tank into the air," Zabierek remembered, as "the store of ammunition was being blown up" and "machine gun shells scattered . . . in all directions."[61] The Red Arrow finally reached the crest of the hill on December 6. Among those killed at Bridge Ridge was James Mayo, a farmer from Robertson County, Tennessee, who joined the Red Arrow after Buna. "There is a chance that I may not get home," Mayo wrote, in a letter home several months before his death, "for you know some of the boys must stay on this side of the ocean. I think I will be able to go throw [sic] this thing and returne home when this war is over. But there is a chance I may be one of the boys to stay. All I know to say is if it is God's will for me to returne I will so say a prayer for me."[62]

The Red Arrow seizure of Limon and its environs came at a critical moment in the battle for Leyte. "The 32nd Division," wrote historian Stanley Falk, "had all but turned Kataoka's western flank." As Falk noted, "although the distance actually gained was small, the territory won was important." One Japanese commander described the moment as "one of the most disastrous for the First Division."[63] It was a great achievement and hard-won victory. The Red Arrow did not do it alone, of course. The roadblocks that the Twenty-Fourth Division and the position on Kilay Ridge overlooking the highway to its west hindered Japanese movements. The Japanese launched fearsome attacks to push the Twenty-Fourth Division troops off the Kilay Ridge, and the position barely held on, but on November 30 the Second Battalion of the 128th Infantry Regiment reached the site, relieving the exhausted soldiers of the Twenty-Fourth Division. In subsequent days the Second Battalion solidified its hold of the ridge. Coker remembered that "this campaign would take a long time and be at great cost," but Coker and his comrades held Kilay Ridge, allowing the Red Arrow to observe and harass Japanese movements along Highway 2.[64]

Meanwhile, American pressure also built on Kataoka's eastern flank. The First Cavalry Division, reinforced with the 112th Cavalry Regiment, pressed into the central mountains toward the Ormoc Valley. On November 20, the Red Arrow's 126th Infantry Regiment entered the battle as well. Its mission was to drive inland to the south and east of Corkscrew Hill, cross the central mountain range, and reach the high ground above Highway 2 south of Limon. The job posed many challenges. The route took them through mountainous jungles with primitive trails and no accurate maps to guide them. Communications would be difficult and resupply would come only by airdrop or over twisting and muddy mountain trails. The First and Third Battalions led the way, but their attack did not start out well. Japanese troops harassed their rear areas as well as their front. The battalions failed to keep in contact with each other as they advanced. General Gill grew frustrated with the lack of progress, and on November 25 he replaced the regimental commander. Four days later, the regiment crossed the Leyte River, and by the first week of December it had established roadblocks along Highway 2 to further hinder Japanese movement along the route.[65]

As December began, the Red Arrow Division stood near the head of the Ormoc Valley, poised to drive south and clear it of Japanese. Only a few miles of jungle separated them from the valley plain. To their south, the Seventy-Seventh Division landed near Ormoc on December 7, and three days later, the city was in American hands. The Americans now controlled all of the island's major ports and both ends of the Ormoc Valley. Krueger's planned pincers were finally beginning to close. As the Seventh and Seventy-Seventh Divisions drove northward up the Ormoc Valley, the Red Arrow moved south to meet them. Gill assigned the 126th Infantry Regiment to drive along the east side of the highway, while the 127th Infantry Regiment cleared the west side. Meanwhile, the 128th Infantry Regiment would reduce the remaining Japanese forces in the hills east of Limon. At the same time, other American divisions also pressed in from the mountains to the south of Red Arrow positions. In all, two corps converged on the Japanese in the Ormoc Valley.

Ormoc was a mere fourteen miles to the south of the Red Arrow's forward positions, but it might as well have been Milwaukee or Detroit. The weeks ahead were some of the toughest in the history of the Thirty-Second Division. The hills lining both sides of Highway 2 were rugged and jungle-draped, and the GIs sometimes battled nature as much as they did the Japanese. Robert Hiatt remembered his company advancing "down steep crevices, through swamps, [and] jungles," when the GIs "began cursing and blaspheming the infantry, the Army, and every patriotic instinct that may have at one time been part of their thinking."[66] Percy Hiatt thought the soldiers in his outfit were "the bravest people on the face of the earth," but one day a group of them came running toward the rear. "It must be the whole Japanese army after them," he thought, until someone shouted, "Snake! Snake!" It was a large boa constrictor. "Those Company L boys fought Japs all day long, but by golly, they weren't going to fight that damned snake!"[67]

The Leyte campaign occurred in near constant rain and mud. "Foot travel, even on level terrain, was laborious," wrote medic Dean Andersen, "because of the heavy, sucking, clinging, knee-deep mud."[68] Robert Hiatt recalled that "water pockets formed in our shelter halves and had to be pushed up from within to drain the water," and "by morning the downpour of the night had mastered our shelters, and we lay in the mud."[69] Frequent storms made conditions even worse. "It was heard over the radio that a major storm was coming," wrote Roy Campbell. "First the wind came, blowing harder and harder until the large jungle trees were bent the way a field of wheat bends when the wind hits. Soon the rain came at high speed—limbs from brush and trees flew through the air and nothing loose was safe from the storm." Foxholes filled with rain and "mud moved down the mountain in streams." Campbell remembered that as "the storm slowly subsided [the] sounds of men bitching took over the roar of the wind."[70]

The constant mud and rain made supply and communication difficult. "The trails to the rear were so mud-slick and hazardous," recalled Lloyd Fish, "that our supply lines . . . were totally inadequate most of the time." As in previous campaigns, airdrops were used to deliver food supplies, but the planes could not always reach the soldiers. "The only available zones for airdrops were in valleys and only then when the clouds and fog lifted," said Fish, "and then it was questionable who would get to the drop area first, our ration parties or Japanese stragglers behind our lines. In several instances the battalion ration carriers really did have to fight for our supper."[71] Planes dropped supplies "while we sought cover from the boxes falling earthward on us," wrote Robert Hiatt. "Most infantrymen who have thus been supplied can tell of close calls when the ration boxes missed them by inches or worse."[72] Whayland Greene remembered a period when the Japanese cut their supply line "and the whole 126th Infantry Regiment had to do without food for 5 days."[73] Andersen claimed that he went without food for ten days while at a roadblock. "The hunger pains were bad at first, but after two days they subsided." The hungry Red Arrowmen often took to foraging. "When we had time we would look through the forest for wild fruit," Andersen wrote. "We found some wild bananas and dug up some roots that looked like potatoes." Getting clean water was a problem too. "The streams were red with clay washed by the rain," recalled Andersen. "We used our handkerchiefs to strain out the larger pieces of mud."[74] "There was a water hole that had good water," recalled Percy Hiatt, "but every time we tried to get water out of it, so did the Japs. We fought them once a day to get water out of this hole. There were finally so many dead around it that we had to give it up."[75]

The same conditions made it difficult to get the sick and wounded out. The only option was to evacuate them overland, and if Highway 2 was blocked or impassible it had to be done along rugged jungle trails. Wounded soldiers often had to be transported more than ten miles through mountains and jungle before reaching a clearing station. It was a journey that could take two days. "Many places were so steep that four men could not carry a litter (stretcher) with a wounded man up the grade," medic Andersen remembered. "We had to form a chain of men on either side of the trail and hand the litter from one man to the next, then form another chain again until we reached the top."[76] Though the Red Arrow faced less disease at Leyte than at Buna, there were still plenty of evacuations for medical issues. Contaminated food and water bred dysentery, and mosquitoes still swarmed the battlefield. Mosquito control measures were impossible in the midst of the fighting, and though Atabrine suppressed many cases, malaria remained a problem. Martin Bolt had made it through Buna, Saidor, and Aitape without contracting malaria, but on Leyte his luck ran out. Bolt was hospitalized for jaundice when, as he described it, "I woke up one night with the shakes, hot then cold." The following day the doctor diagnosed him with malaria. "I've got to start spraying the whole hospital area," the doctor said, "because you got malaria right here in the hospital."[77] Greene got trench foot. "My feet were hurting so bad that I could not run fast when they were shooting at me," Greene wrote. "The medic looked at them and said I should have been in the hospital several days ago so he sent me back with the litter train." Once at the hospital the doctor "had to cut my socks off because my sock had grown to the skin on my feet and blood came off with the rotten socks."[78]

The Japanese took every advantage the landscape offered to transform Highway 2 into a shooting gallery. They filled the trees with snipers and constructed a labyrinth of bunkers, trenches, and machine-gun nests in the path of the Red Arrow. "The Japanese basic training must have consisted of nothing but digging holes," wrote Monte Howell. "[They] were very good at tunneling and digging foxholes in the sides of embankments. . . . The Japanese would dig under fallen logs, embankments; anywhere their presence would be concealed. Every square inch of the area had to be looked at. It was slow and dangerous."[79] Their positions were indeed well hidden. Greene remembered engaging in a firefight in which "[we] couldn't really see them but we could hear them talking [and] every now and then you could see a hand or a leg" or "caps and leg wrappings." Greene likened it to "shooting at phantoms."[80] The Red Arrowmen patrolled constantly to locate, isolate, outflank, and reduce Japanese positions. It was a hated task. "You do not know where the enemy is," explained Robert Hiatt, "or when or where he will strike. You do know, however, if he does, he will sacrifice his very life to destroy you . . . so you trod the trail slowly and quietly, keeping low, and watching all about you."[81]

The Japanese launched attacks too. "During the night approximately 40 Japs made several Banzai attacks on Companies A and C," noted a 127th Infantry Regiment report. "They attacked with blocks of TNT, grenade dischargers, heavy machine gun fire, rifle fire, and fixed bayonets. There was some hand to hand fighting before the Japs were repulsed."[82] An after-action report from the 126th Infantry Regiment stated that, "during the night of 13–14 December, approximately 60 Japs entered and attacked the Regimental Command Post. Hand to hand fighting took place, and the attack lasted until approximately [1:45 a.m.] when the enemy was driven off."[83] Japanese artillery could strike anywhere. Roy Campbell recalled taking a hill against fierce opposition, but then only finding five dead Japanese. Campbell advised pulling back, telling an officer that he suspected "the Japs had left early on purpose, and they probably had the ridge zeroed in with artillery."

"Are you crazy[?]" snapped the red-faced lieutenant. "We lost a lot of men taking this hill and here we'll stay."

But "the words no sooner left his mouth," Campbell later wrote, "when the whistling sound of an artillery round was heard." Campbell dove for cover, and when the barrage lifted he found the lieutenant dead.[84]

Japanese forces were formidable, but so were those of the Red Arrow. The GIs on Leyte were far better equipped than fellow Red Arrowmen had been in any previous campaign. Flamethrowers, ineffective at Buna, were now more reliable and available in greater numbers. The full weight of the Red Arrow artillery was brought to bear, pleasing many foot soldiers. "I cannot adequately praise our brilliant artillery units for doing their job even better than I anticipated," wrote Jesse Coker.[85] The Red Arrow deployed its own snipers. "During the day, Company C snipers killed 15 to 20 Japs to their North and South," boasted one report. "Several snipers posted were maintained by Company C in their rear with the hope of catching any Japs who might escape from the advance of the 126th Inf." The Forty-Fourth Tank Battalion, attached to the Red Arrow for the Leyte campaign, bolstered the GIs' firepower and aggressively eliminated many Japanese tanks and gun carriers. Rocket launchers, commonly called bazookas, served as excellent antitank weapons. At one roadblock, Tally Fulmer saw a Japanese tank coming down the road. The bazooka man "got on the edge of that road," Fulmer remembered, where it "curved a little bit just past our location, and he busted him." The tank burst into flames and blocked the road so that "no other tanks could get by him."[86]

The Thirty-Second Cavalry Reconnaissance Troop under Captain Herman Bottcher patrolled deep behind Japanese lines. Bottcher established a command post in the jungle near Agayayan and set up observation posts throughout the Ormoc Valley, gathering intelligence and harassing Japanese rear areas—often working with Philippine guerrilla groups. One post was "on the high ground immediately W of [Kananga]," Bottcher reported, and "was ideally situated. The left flank offered good possibilities for ambushing small enemy groups. Subsequently, several prisoners were taken at this position." Capturing Japanese soldiers remained challenging. On December 15 "two Japanese had approached the CP [command post] unknowingly," stated one report. "Captain Bottcher attempted to capture them. One killed himself with a grenade. The other gave himself up only after being severely wounded. He died . . . that evening." The incident drew the attention of Japanese commanders, and later that afternoon fifty to sixty Japanese troops attacked the command post. Bottcher and his men "put up a stand and during the night withdrew to a new CP about two kilometers SW."[87]

Three Red Arrow soldiers received the Medal of Honor in the fight for the Ormoc Valley—all from the 126th Infantry Regiment. The first was a young machine gunner, Private William A. McWhorter of Liberty, South Carolina. On December 5, McWhorter and another private, William D. Brooks of Alabama, were at their gun when Japanese troops charged their position. McWhorter killed several of them, but just as it seemed the attack had been blunted Brooks noticed "an object come flying through the air and land inside our position." It was a block of TNT with a fuse on it, ready to blow. "McWhorter rushed to it and picked it up," recalled Brooks. "There was no time to do anything with it [so] he hugged it to his chest and bent over and turned away from me." The explosion killed McWhorter instantly, but his actions spared Brooks and another soldier who was bringing ammunition to the position. "He had deliberately given his life for mine," Brooks remembered gratefully.

The second Medal of Honor recipient was Sergeant Leroy Johnson of Oakdale, Louisiana. On December 15, Johnson was engaged in an attack on a machine-gun nest when two Japanese grenades landed nearby.

Johnson fell on the grenades and absorbed the blast, saving the lives of his comrades.[88]

The third recipient, Dirk J. Vlug, was the only one who survived. Vlug was a twenty-nine-year-old private first class from Grand Rapids, Michigan, who had been with the division since the days of Camp Livingston. On December 15, Vlug and his First Battalion were stationed at a roadblock along Route 2. Lloyd Fish, who was present for Vlug's heroics, remembered that "the road was like a reverse 'C' with a finger ridge knoll at the top, a curve to the east, and then a second knoll." Suddenly, Japanese tanks "emerged from behind the first knoll," Fish recalled. The first tank "was laying a smoke screen to conceal their movements," remembered James J. Madigan, "and started firing at us with heavy machine guns and 37 mm cannons." Most GIs took cover, but Vlug raced toward the tanks with a bazooka and six rounds of ammunition. He knocked out the first tank under a hail of Japanese gunfire, causing the second one to stop. When crew members emerged from the second tank, Vlug "instantly killed one of them with his pistol," recalled Captain James K. Sullivan, and "forced the rest to return to the tank," which he then promptly destroyed with another bazooka round. Three more tanks came around the knoll and laid down heavy fire, but Vlug moved forward yet again, systematically knocking out the tanks with his bazooka and sending one careening down a steep roadside embankment. "When I finally looked up," recalled Fish, "there was lots of smoke, some fires and GIs running up and down the highway. The tanks were not firing anymore and several were ablaze." Vlug's actions, claimed historian Harold Blakeley, "surely ranks not only as one of the most heroic exploits of the war but also an amazing example of the efficient use of weapons under the most difficult circumstances."[89]

Slowly and relentlessly the Red Arrow pushed back the Japanese, ridge by ridge, valley by valley. But as the division slogged its way down the Ormoc Valley, MacArthur grew dissatisfied with the progress of his army. He had all but declared victory a month earlier, and the continued fighting on Leyte delayed his planned invasion of Luzon. It was also a source of embarrassment for him. Once again, MacArthur never got near the front; but from his headquarters in Tacloban, he spewed criticisms of his troops and his commanders. One target of MacArthur's vitriol was the Red Arrow. "Big Chief stated 32d had never been any good," Eichelberger recorded in his diary, also noting that MacArthur was "very disappointed over the slow progress of the 77th and 7th."[90]

As in any battle, Leyte exacted an emotional toll on the fighting men. After a long and bitter day of fighting on a hill that had exchanged hands numerous times, Jesse Coker took refuge in a foxhole anticipating a Japanese night attack, only to find that "a badly decomposed body was sharing it with me." The body had deteriorated so badly that Coker "could not distinguish if the body was American or Japanese." Trapped until morning, Coker endured "one of the longest, most miserable nights which I spent in combat."[91] Whayland Greene asked: "Can you picture burying one of your close friends who was killed near you, wrapped in a poncho and going back days after the battle digging him up and putting him on a litter and carrying him for miles on a narrow jungle trail[?] The odor was almost unbearable. When you see these war pictures you never smell that horrible odor. Be thankful you don't."[92] Greene also recalled the first Japanese soldier he killed. "I saw him about the same time he saw me," he remembered, and "I was ready to fire just a second or two before he could get ready. I shot and killed him." The incident haunted him for a fortnight afterward. "Every time I tried to close my eyes," he remembered, "I could see that Jap on his hands and knees."[93] Robert Hiatt recalled an incident when one man, a "Buna veteran, and a squad leader," had "accidentally shot himself in the ankle with a Tommy gun." Later, a group of GIs questioned whether it was accidental or purposeful. "Some said they would not blame him," Hiatt recalled; "he had seen two campaigns, and that was enough for any combat soldier." Others said that "any man who would purposely shoot himself, no matter how much he hated combat, was a bastard."[94]

Religion remained an important part of many GIs' lives. "No man in combat denies the existence of God," wrote Robert Hiatt. "I know they all prayed in combat, same as myself." Hiatt greatly admired his chaplain, who was "almost like a buddy to the men, rather than an officer." He recalled one Sunday sermon given as "lead snapped twigs in the tops of the palms." The topic was brotherly love, "an unusual subject in combat," Hiatt conceded. The chaplain urged the men: "rather than hate the humans we are fighting, we should hate the principles for which they stood and the acts they committed." Even though "at times it has been difficult not to hate the Japanese," Hiatt wrote, he "always attempted to keep those views in mind."[95] Greene recalled a conversation with God after he killed his first enemy soldier. "I said, 'Thanks for pulling me through this, Lord, but do you think you let that one get a little too close?'"[96]

But for some, war shook their faith in God. John Rawls was the son of a prominent Baltimore lawyer who graduated with a B.A. in philosophy from Princeton in 1943. Caught up in the wartime spirit, Rawls enlisted in the army and was assigned to the 128th Infantry Regiment. He had considered a future career as an Episcopalian minister, but an incident at Kilay Ridge sowed doubts in Rawls's mind about his faith. "One day a Lutheran pastor came up," he wrote, and "gave a brief sermon in which he said God aimed his bullets at the Japanese while God protected us from theirs." Rawls was outraged. "I don't know why it made me so angry," he wrote, "but it certainly did." He "upbraided" the minister "for saying what I assumed he knew perfectly well . . . were simply falsehoods about divine providence." Rawls knew the chaplain was only trying "to comfort his troops," but as an aspiring minister, Rawls believed that "Christian doctrine ought not to be used for that."[97]

Replacements came into the unit, even in the midst of combat. Roy Campbell went to the company command post one day and saw "a group of fifteen men, all with new equipment." Each was a sergeant "from the Air Force back in the States" with no infantry training. Campbell paired them up with more experienced men, but the thought of fighting with rookies "did not sit well with old boys." Inexperience could be deadly—for officers and for enlisted men. Campbell recalled a new second lieutenant who had just come to his unit. The mission was "to attack and take the big mountain in front" up a winding road. The troops jumped off at dawn, but when a scout "stepped out around the first cutback he was shot instantly." As Campbell remembered, the new lieutenant then "ran out to the scout and was shot, just above the scrotum." Campbell and his men poured fire on Japanese positions while others pulled back the two wounded men. "The medic opened the officer's pants and pulled his bloody shorts down, watching as blood filled the scrotum. It grew like a big balloon." The officer soon bled to death. "He had only been in combat a few minutes."[98]

Rotations home continued as well. Roy Campbell found it painful to watch a buddy from Eau Claire, "one of only four left from the original company," depart. The hometown contingent had "now been cut down to three," he wrote, and he watched as his friend "picked up his equipment, walking like a tired old man" and "started down the trail to freedom, turning back to wave just once."[99] Rotations picked up toward the end of December as the campaign drew to a close. "It was near Christmas time," remembered Paul Rettell, when "I received my orders to go back to the States."[100] Marvin Langetieg also got the word just before the holiday. He remembered that he was "on top of a mountain heading down the west side when I received word my rotation number was up and I could go home. It didn't take me long to do an about face and find my way back to Tacloben [sic] where the ships were."[101] Percy Hiatt remembered a difficult trip to Tacloban to catch his boat. "The first truck we saw, we flagged it down and jumped in the back," he said, but "it was full of dead GIs so we rode the fenders down to the other side of Limon." Japanese roadblocks along Highway 2 prevented travel down that route, but "we appropriated a DUKW [an amphibious vehicle commonly referred to as a "duck"] and went out into the ocean." Hiatt then hitched a ride in another truck and arrived at Tacloban on Christmas Day.[102]

On December 17, a patrol from the 127th Infantry Regiment reported an unusual sight. Emerging from "the heavily wooded and mountainous area we had been fighting in," the men suddenly found themselves gazing at "a large, rolling Kunai valley as far as could be seen to the south." They had finally emerged on the Ormoc Valley plain. "It was a red letter day for the Regiment," described one report, "because after 2½ years overseas and two campaigns, they were looking at open ground for the first time." By December 20 the rest of the regiment had pushed through and reached a ridgeline overlooking the valley. "The entire regiment was rejuvenated," claimed the report. "They had been fighting in the dark dense hilly wooded area for a month and here they were out in the wide open spaces in the sunshine. There was no holding them, they charged forward. It was a real field day."[103]

But the Thirty-Second Division would not make it all the way to Ormoc. After the bitter fight through the mountains from Limon the division was exhausted, and Krueger handed the drive south over to the First Cavalry Division and the 112th Cavalry Regiment. The Red Arrow connected with the Seventh Cavalry Regiment outside Lonoy on December 21 and halted. Later that day, the First Cavalry Division and the Seventy-Seventh Infantry

Division linked up at Kananga. Krueger's pincers had finally slammed shut, and the Ormoc Valley was in the control of US forces. In five weeks of the most bitter fighting since Buna, the Red Arrow had advanced little more than two miles but did so in some of the toughest terrain and conditions Leyte had to offer and against one of Japan's most elite divisions. As the official US Army history of the campaign noted, "the 32d Division had borne the brunt" of the campaign in the Ormoc Valley.[104]

After the fight in the Ormoc Valley, the Red Arrowmen looked forward to a hard-earned rest. According to a 127th Infantry Regiment report, "the men were at last permitted to care for their person[s], clean clothing and equipment, and rest. They were relaxed [and] happy in knowing they had done a tough job in an extremely fine manner."[105] The rain let up and the sun shone. The holidays were approaching, and many looked forward to celebrating Christmas away from combat. "Our chaplain held a meeting under a starlit sky," remembered Robert Hiatt fondly, "and we sang Christmas songs."[106]

Unfortunately for many members of the Red Arrow, it would be another Christmas under fire. After the battle in the Ormoc Valley, the surviving Japanese troops had melted away into the rugged mountains of the island's bulbous northwest peninsula. Krueger wanted to finish them off with a massive sweep across the peninsula, from the Ormoc Valley to its west coast, and drive them into the Camotes Sea. Though exhausted and understrength after the Ormoc Valley campaign, the Red Arrow was one of four divisions Krueger sent back into combat after only a few days of rest and just before Christmas. The Twenty-Fourth Division was to take the northern quarter of the peninsula. The Red Arrow Division (specifically, the 127th and 128th Infantry Regiments) would be to the south of the Twenty-Fourth and would drive toward Silad Bay. To the south of the Red Arrow would be the First Cavalry Division, and the Seventy-Seventh Division was to sweep the southern quarter of the peninsula. The 126th Infantry Regiment and other elements of the Red Arrow not participating in the westward attack were to guard and patrol Highway 2.

The Christmastime mission evoked an unusually deep and visceral bitterness in the Red Arrowmen. As Robert Hiatt wrote, "many of us felt like

A Red Arrow chaplain conducts Christmas mass for members of the 127th Infantry Regiment near Lonoy on December 23, 1944. The service was held early because the regiment was about to spend another Christmas in combat. NATIONAL ARCHIVES

the bottom had been pulled out from under us."[107] The advance stepped off on December 23. "General MacArthur announced the Leyte Campaign had been concluded except for mopping up," stated one report in an unusually critical tone for an official army document, but "for us, this mopping up meant what turned out to be an eight-day march over some of the most difficult mountain trails we had encountered since our training days in Australia."[108] At first, the advancing troops encountered only a few Japanese stragglers and minimal resistance. "We hiked slowly and cautiously all day with frequent pops of rifle fire being heard from our point," remembered Robert Hiatt, and a few minutes later the rest of the marchers would "walk by or over a dead Nip who was the source of the disturbance."[109]

As the days went on the march became more difficult. "[We] were almost crawling through the mud," wrote Roy Campbell. "It stuck to [our] boots, almost sucking them off when it got deep enough, and it had a very rotten smell, unlike any [we] had smelled before."[110] A report from the 127th Infantry Regiment described the arduous terrain they traversed on Christmas Day:

The morning was spent climbing to the top of a mountain ridge. The climbing was difficult but we later found out, the descent was to be much worse. The trail led almost perpendicularly down the side. After reaching the bottom, another ridge was encountered, this, almost straight up, everyone had to use hand holds to pull themselves up. All in all there were seven ridges from the bottom of the first descent to the first possible bivouac area.[111]

The Red Arrowmen "were so tired and disillusioned," Robert Hiatt later wrote, "that we cursed America, the Philippines, the Army, our General Gill, and MacArthur in particular."[112]

Airdrops, which had continued delivering supplies, virtually stopped around Christmas, despite the fact that "it was good flying weather," as an embittered Jesse Coker remembered it. Coker further wrote that his regimental commander radioed the Thirty-Second Division headquarters with the message "no food, no fighting," and ordered his men "to stop in our tracks in order to conserve energy." Hungry Red Arrowmen took to foraging. Coker's men traded with a farmer for some rice and chicken, but the bird escaped from their clutches. "I have never seen such a comical race in my life," wrote Coker, "as men dashed around in all directions to retrieve their luscious captive." The famished soldiers recaptured the bird and then cooked it in a steel helmet. Unfortunately, "the paint on the side of the helmet had melted and mixed with the rice and chicken, ruining the meat." On another occasion, Coker's men bartered for some carabao meat. "It had been a long time since we had eaten fresh meat of any kind. At this point, Australian mutton would have been delicious."[113] Roy Campbell's Filipino guide led a group to his own house, where his wife cooked rice and chicken for the troops. "Those without mess kits could take a banana leaf and use part of it for a dish," he wrote, and "each man received a good portion." The soldiers pooled what money they had to pay for the meal.[114]

As the troops approached the seacoast, exchanges with the Japanese increased and intensified. On Christmas Day "the 1st Bn [of the 127th Infantry Regiment] closed in on an estimated 300 to 400 Japs armed with HMG's [heavy machine guns] and LMG's [light machine guns]," noted one report. "They routed the Japs driving them to the West. Artillery fire was directed on [them], but due to the heavily wooded terrain observation was difficult." The battalion claimed that it had killed fifty-three Japanese and suffered just one fatality.[115] The Red Arrowmen reached the coast on December 29 and 30. "It was truly a lovely sight for our hungry eyes," remembered Robert Hiatt, though his elation was deflated by a gruesome discovery. "On the way we flushed several huts," Hiatt wrote, "one in which was a Filipino man, woman and child tied to chairs and bayonetted to death."[116]

Upon reaching the coast the GIs sent out patrols and sporadic fighting continued. Coker spotted several hundred Japanese in the jungle. He and a small group followed them to a farm with "a beautiful corn field, reminiscent of home," and there "a Jap soldier was waving a white flag at the far end of the fence." A replacement soldier "eagerly insisted that we go immediately to accept the surrender," but Coker was convinced "that it was a trick." The Japanese then began to fire on them, confirming Coker's suspicions. "The day-long confrontation with a stubborn enemy ended successfully for us," Coker remembered, "for we had either killed or driven them away without a single casualty on our side."[117]

After reaching the coast, the Red Arrow Division lost one of its most popular and famous members: Herman Bottcher. With the campaign in the Ormoc Valley complete, the Thirty-Second Cavalry Reconnaissance Troop transferred its operations to the mountains west of the Ormoc Valley, and by the last days of 1944 patrolled the hills and jungles in the area of Silad Bay. The troopers took a few prisoners but saw little action. On December 29, Bottcher established a command post on a knoll roughly a mile northeast of the village of Silad. With American forces on the coast, the operation seemed about to end. Bottcher received orders that day to return to base camp "on or about 2 Jan 1945." However, on the evening of December 30 "a native came running to our CP," stated one report, and "all he could say was, 'Many Japs, Many Japs!'" Bottcher was skeptical of such sightings from the local population, but he withdrew an outpost, deployed an additional machine gun, and "the patrol turned in for the night."[118]

At 2:45 a.m. on December 31, Japanese rifle fire streamed into Bottcher's camp. A Japanese force of 275 to 300 took up positions on two sides of the Americans, creating a deadly crossfire. The reconnaissance troopers repulsed several attacks but at the cost of two killed and several wounded. Rifle and machine-gun fire intensified about 3:30 a.m., and at 3:45 mortars streamed into the camp, striking the perimeter as well as the command post shack. Bottcher began organizing a withdrawal when a mortar exploded just three feet behind him at 3:55 a.m. "The Captain's leg was practically blown off," the report stated, "and fragments had wounded him in several places thruout his body." Lieutenant Royal Steele applied a tourniquet to Bottcher's bleeding leg, and a medic, Milwaukeean Tony Gaidosik, gave Bottcher a shot of morphine to numb the pain. "Leave me," Bottcher reportedly told those aiding him. "I'm done for." But the cavalry-men would not leave their leader. As the Japanese closed in, the GIs with-drew toward the lines of the 127th Infantry Regiment, carrying Bottcher on a makeshift litter made of a shelter half. The troops eventually got him to an outpost of the 127th Infantry Regiment, but Bottcher had gone into shock. A Cub plane dropped blood plasma at 8:00 a.m., but it arrived too late to make any difference. "An incision had been made in order to locate a vein and inject the plasma," noted one report, but "all efforts failed" and as the light of day came in "wounds were discovered that had been hidden by the darkness that must have bled profusely." Bottcher died at 8:10 a.m. Steele took command of the troop.[119]

Just as Bottcher's heroics at Buna had made the national news, so did his death. *Yank* published a feature about him titled "From German to American," which read in part: "His men later said that they couldn't be-lieve their captain could be killed by the Japs. They didn't talk much about it. They just sat around and stared wearily at the constant drizzle."[120] Red Arrowmen who had returned to the United States were equally saddened by the news. Raymond Dasmann had befriended Bottcher and when he heard the news, "for the first time in the war, I broke down and cried."[121]

Several months after Bottcher's death, he was honored by the Veterans of the Abraham Lincoln Brigade at a tribute event in New York City. "It is natural that a hero in the war to save Spain from fascism should have been ready to agree to continue the fight in the World War," New York City coun-cil member Stanley M. Isaacs told the gathered crowd. "After all, the con-flict in Spain, in reality, was basically the same as the world-wide conflict which followed."[122] Gustav Faber of the German-American Trade Union Committee also spoke. "We German-Americans are especially proud of Boettcher [sic] because he was born in Germany," Faber said, "because his deeds have proven to the world that there are other Germans besides Nazis."[123] Other speakers included former Cuban president Fulgencio

Batista (who would later return to power only to be ousted by Fidel Castro in 1959) and US Representative Emanuel Celler (D-NY). Not attending the event but sending his sentiments was noted physicist Albert Einstein, who had escaped Nazi Germany. In a letter to the Lincoln Brigade veterans, Einstein called himself "one of the most unheroic and unmilitary people imaginable," but felt compelled to express his "strong feeling of admiration" for Bottcher and his sacrifice. "He gave himself in the cause of freeing men from their chains," Einstein declared.[124]

On January 1, 1945, the day after Bottcher's death, the Seventy-Seventh Division assumed responsibility for the Silad Bay area and the Thirty-Second finally left the fighting. In all, the Leyte campaign cost the Red Arrow Division 450 killed, 1,491 wounded, and eight missing. The corresponding figures for US forces overall were 1,670 killed, 5,384 wounded, and seventy-two missing. The number of Japanese killed approached fifty thousand.[125] Except for MacArthur's dramatic beach landing, historians have largely relegated the ground battle on Leyte to the footnotes, but it was a crucial moment in the Pacific War. Japan's hope for a decisive battle to stop the Allied return to the Philippines ended in disastrous failure—on land as well as at sea. While the battle tied up the Sixth Army and delayed the US assault on Luzon, it also substantially weakened Japan's ability to hold the strategic archipelago. The Red Arrow played a pivotal role on Leyte, pushing through Breakneck Ridge, wearing down the Imperial Army's elite First Division, and unlocking the northern entrance to the Ormoc Valley. Despite these hard-won accomplishments, MacArthur still viewed the Red Arrow with a jaundiced eye.

In the first days of January, the division moved into tent camps around Pinamopoan, where their Leyte combat ordeal had begun six weeks before. "They ran us through a trough full of 'sheep dip' to kill the lice and bugs," wrote Monte Howell, and "painted our underarms and crotch with some purple stuff. Some of the guys had their heads shaved."[126] The simple act of getting clean gave Jesse Coker "an ecstatic feeling."[127] The GIs conducted a little training and received a few work details, but mostly they rested. "The cooks had prepared ten-gallon boilers full of turkey," recalled James Myers. "This was the first hot food we had seen in many days and there it was laid out in front of us, all the turkey, drumsticks, etc., we could eat."[128] Mail deliveries made the soldiers especially happy. "I hit the jack pot yesterday," wrote John Walters to his wife, Jewell, "26 letters and cards." Yet Walters in his own letters hinted at trouble ahead: "If you don't hear from me for some time (more than a week) you will know that it's impossible for me to write. Seeing that another island of the Philippines has been invaded— one cannot tell what will happen to us."[129] That island was Luzon, and although the Red Arrow was exhausted and understrength, it was soon back in combat.

The Red Arrow pulls back to a rest area on January 2, 1945, after the long fight in the Ormoc Valley. NATIONAL ARCHIVES

CHAPTER 10

MOUNTAIN GOATS

In early 1945, the Thirty-Second Division began its fourth year overseas. The cumulative weight of years abroad and numerous battles took a heavy toll on the Red Arrowmen. Their families suffered too. The spouse of a Michigan GI wrote to General MacArthur in February, berating him for his overreliance on the Red Arrow. "These fellows were the 'guinea pigs' in jungle warfare and had to learn the hard way back in '42," she wrote, "and the 126th has since been through the New Guinea Campaign, the Netherlands East Indies, then on to Leyte where they were in combat for forty five days and then after a semi-rest of two weeks you've pushed them on to Luzon and into action again! Don't you think it's high time they are all sent home for relaxations from their war weary lives?"[1] Unfortunately, in 1945 the Red Arrow's tribulations only mounted. Although Japan's defeat was now all but certain, the fighting in the Pacific intensified as Allied forces inched closer to the home islands. The horrific fighting on Luzon, coming on the heels of Leyte, brought the division yet again to the brink of collapse, though also earning it the begrudging respect of its adversary. The first US Army division to go into combat against the Japanese in 1942, the Red Arrow was among the last to leave the battlefield when Japan finally surrendered in September 1945.

FACING: Two machine gunners from the 127th Infantry Regiment in position on the Villa Verde Trail. NATIONAL ARCHIVES

MacArthur chose the Lingayen Gulf as the site of his Luzon invasion—the same place the Japanese had come ashore back in 1941. The gulf lay at the northern end of Luzon's Central Valley, which stretches southward 130 miles to Manila. The broad and level valley gave MacArthur a straight shot to the Philippine capital. The valley's road and rail links—the most developed infrastructure on the island—would further aid his advance. Defending Luzon for Japan was the Fourteenth Army Area under General Yamashita Tomoyuki. Once again, American planners had widely varying estimates of Japanese strength. MacArthur's intelligence chief, General Charles Willoughby, estimated 172,000 Japanese troops on Luzon. General Walter Krueger's Sixth Army, tasked with conducting the operation, estimated 234,000. In fact, Yamashita had more than 260,000 troops under his command.

The invasion began on January 9, with two corps hitting the beaches that morning: I Corps under Lieutenant General Innis P. Swift, and XIV Corps under Lieutenant General Oscar W. Griswold. Short on armor and artillery and with no realistic hope of reinforcement, Yamashita understood he did not have the power to oppose the landings effectively. Rather than take on the Americans directly, he opted for a battle of attrition, hoping to tie down as many American units as he could, inflict heavy casualties on them, and delay the impending invasion of Japan. In the Central Valley, Yamashita planned to fight only delaying actions along Krueger's route to Manila. He sent the bulk of his infantry into mountainous regions of Luzon, hoping to lure the Americans into bloody, protracted struggles there. Yamashita divided his forces into three groups. The Kembu Group, 30,000 strong, occupied the mountains west of the Central Valley, as well as the Bataan Peninsula. The Shimbu Group, with roughly 80,000, held the highlands south and east of Manila, including the long Bicol Peninsula stretching to the southeast. The Shobu Group, with 152,000 soldiers, held the mountainous northern half of Luzon and came under the personal command of Yamashita. Two mountain ranges run north to south in northern Luzon, the Cordillera Central range along the island's west coast and the Sierra Madre along the east coast. In between lies the fertile Cagayan Valley, famed for its terraced rice paddies.

Yamashita moved his headquarters from Manila to the Cordillera Central resort town of Baguio, where American colonial officials had escaped the heat of the lowlands before the war.[2]

Within days of the invasion, Krueger had landed 175,000 soldiers with little difficulty. However, as Swift's I Corps probed into the hills on the left of the American beachhead toward the Shobu Group, it met stiffening resistance. Krueger feared a Japanese counterattack from the mountains and told MacArthur that he wanted more troops before he pushed southward. "I tried to explain," Krueger later wrote, "that a precipitate advance . . . toward Manila would probably expose it to a reverse and in any case would outrun its supply," and an "all-out drive on Manila would not be feasible until the 32nd Division and the 1st Cavalry Division had arrived."[3] An impatient MacArthur dismissed Krueger's assessment and harangued him to move toward Manila. MacArthur wanted to capture the airbase at Clark Field and the port of Manila as soon as possible—places essential to the coming invasion of Japan. MacArthur also spoke of liberating prisoners of war. Yet as historians Waldo Heinrichs and Marc Gallicchio wrote, MacArthur's desire to reach Manila "extended beyond rational objectives." Taking Manila would garner world headlines just as Eisenhower's advance on Germany had stalled, and a triumphant entry into Manila would make MacArthur "the only conceivable general to lead Allied forces in the invasion of Japan." In addition, the "recovery of Manila . . . was [MacArthur's] key to redemption for having deserted Bataan and its soldiers."[4] Krueger nervously kept some I Corps divisions near the Lingayen Gulf to guard his left flank, but dispatched Griswold's XIV Corps southward as directed.

During the third week of January, the Thirty-Second Infantry Division, along with the First Cavalry Division and the 112th Cavalry Regiment, loaded onto troopships and shoved off for Luzon. It had been a mere three weeks since their grueling fight on Leyte had ended, and the Red Arrow was four thousand soldiers understrength, but as Dean Andersen lamented, "we were again on the high seas."[5] During yet another ocean voyage to yet another battle, Roy Campbell stood at the prow of his ship and contemplated what lay ahead. The time between battles "just didn't seem long enough," he wrote, though he also welcomed the opportunity to fight in Luzon, "where the Japs had murdered thousands of American troops on the Death March." For Campbell, "it was payback time." The convoy arrived at the Lingayen Gulf on January 27. The troops debarked and set up camp a few miles inland. "The first few days were a peaceful time," remembered Campbell, as the men "just sat around writing letters home and relaxing."[6]

The Thirty-Second Division joined Swift's I Corps. The 126th Infantry Regiment went into reserve, but by the end of January the other two Red Arrow regiments had moved out to protect the flank and rear of the main force headed to Manila. Entering the front line between San Manuel and Asingan, the Red Arrow pushed northeastward during the first days of February, crossing the Agno River and then through an area of farms and rice paddies, taking numerous small towns: Batchelor, Natividad, San Nicolas, Tayug. The Japanese withdrew into the mountains as the Red Arrow moved forward. Observation posts of the 128th Infantry Regiment's intelligence and reconnaissance (I&R) platoon, based along Highway 5, noted considerable Japanese traffic heading into the mountains. One report counted four hundred northbound and one hundred southbound vehicles during a ten-hour period. The platoon called in artillery strikes. One barrage "effectively broke up a large truck convoy in the vicinity of ANABAT," the I&R platoon claimed, "destroying 14 ammunition and gas laden vehicles, damaged an undetermined number, and dispersed the convoy so thoroughly that vehicular traffic ceased for two days."[7]

The advancing Thirty-Second Division encountered some Japanese stragglers, a few snipers, and a little harassing artillery fire, but no significant fighting. "Southeast of TAYUG was a defensive position of trenches, caves, spider holes and log emplaced bunkers capable of holding two hundred or three hundred Japs," reported the 128th Infantry Regiment, but nobody occupied them.[8] "Young and old greeted us with open arms," wrote Jesse Coker. "As we passed through the villages and towns, everyone old enough to hold up their hands flashed their fingers at us, giving us the 'V' sign for victory."[9] The sun shined and the weather was dry. Good road conditions allowed elements of the Red Arrow to advance by truck. The lack of resistance surprised the GIs. Roy Campbell recalled a three-day patrol "across the rice paddies toward the mountains." He remembered it as "uneventful except on the third night the lieutenant somehow lost track of direction" and confessed, "I don't know where the hell I am."[10] But as patrols moved from the lowlands into the river valleys leading into the mountains—the Agno, the Ambayabang, the Arboredo—they began to meet more concerted resistance. The Red Arrow probed the valleys for a possible avenue through the mountains but found only Japanese soldiers and rugged terrain.

On February 1, patrols of Colonel Frederick R. Stofft's 127th Infantry Regiment reached the hamlet of Santa Maria near the confluence of the Ambayabang and Cabalisiaan Rivers. There the Caraballo Mountains rose sharply above the plain. Santa Maria was the western terminus of the Villa Verde Trail, a pathway through the mountains to the village of Santa Fe and the Cagayan Valley. It was named for Juan Villaverde, a Spanish priest who blazed the trail in the late nineteenth century to spread his faith to the mountain peoples.[11] The trail was improved for the first five miles, but after that it devolved into little more than a narrow, winding footpath that snaked up and down mountainsides, along sharp ridgelines, and through deep forested valleys. At its high point at Salacsac Pass the trail reached an elevation of nearly five thousand feet. As the crow flies the distance between Santa Maria and Santa Fe was eleven miles, but on the trail that distance stretched out to twenty-seven. Santa Maria was an entryway into the mountains, and Japanese resistance increased as the Red Arrow approached it. "Japanese ground troops never contested our occupation of the town," noted one report, but intense artillery and mortar fire killed two and wounded eleven.[12]

On February 3, the Second Battalion of the 127th Infantry Regiment began a reconnaissance in force up the Villa Verde Trail. Japanese artillery rained down on them almost immediately. On the north bank of the Cabalisiaan that morning the battalion encountered a steep ridgeline above a long, flat rice paddy. "At the top of the ridgeline extending to the north, the enemy placed its bunkers with grazing fire over the flat terrain," noted the regimental historical report. The Red Arrow blasted the ridgeline with artillery and mortars. But when the barrage lifted and the GIs moved forward, they were "repulsed by enemy automatic and rifle fire." The battalion finally broke through, though on February 7 it came to another Japanese position dug into another ridgeline, where "resistance . . . increased to such an extent that our forward elements were forced to stop their advance."[13] The battalion probed for weak spots in the Japanese lines but found none. The Red Arrow had reached a strong Japanese outpost line—the outer edge of the Shobu Group's defenses. Looking up at the ridgeline above a curve in the roadway, the GIs dubbed the area "the Bowl." The Second Battalion did not have the force to punch through, nor was Krueger prepared to attack that direction. Indeed, the reconnaissance mission had accomplished its goal of locating Japanese defenses. The battalion held its ground but proceeded no farther.

Meanwhile, Krueger's forces continued their drive south. Like a jockey whipping a horse with a riding crop, MacArthur urged his commanders forward to Manila. This time MacArthur went to the front himself, sometimes even in the midst of the fighting. The First Cavalry reached Manila's northern outskirts on February 3. The following day MacArthur announced that the liberation of Manila was imminent. He planned an elaborate victory parade through the city, though his entry turned out to be far less of a triumphant procession than he envisioned. While Yamashita had no plans to contest Manila, his naval counterpart, Rear Admiral Iwabuchi Sanji, did. Iwabuchi's sailors, as well as the remaining army troops there, barricaded themselves inside Manila's Intramuros—the old walled section of the city. The fight to root them out involved a month of some of the most destructive and vicious urban combat of World War II. By the time American troops finally secured the city on March 4, more than one thousand GIs and sixteen thousand Japanese troops had been killed. At least one hundred thousand Philippine civilians (and by some estimates far more) died at the hands of Japanese soldiers who murdered civilians on a massive scale, and by US artillery that pummeled the city's buildings and old fortifications into smoking heaps of blood-stained rubble. As the battle for Manila raged, other American forces retook Bataan by February 12 and Corregidor Island on February 26.

MacArthur's next moves are the subject of great debate. With Manila and Luzon's Central Valley secured, MacArthur had the base he needed to stage the invasion of Japan and could have chosen to bypass and isolate the remaining Japanese forces in the Philippines. Even Yamashita's formidable Shobu Group might have been left to wither away, much as Rabaul had been in 1943. Instead, MacArthur wanted to liberate the entirety of the islands from Japanese occupation. Without any authorization from Washington, he dispatched his troops across the archipelago. General Robert Eichelberger's Eighth Army launched a series of amphibious landings on far-flung beaches. "There was never a time during the action-packed interlude," wrote Eichelberger, "when some task force of my command was not fighting a battle. And most of the time, hundreds of miles apart, separate task forces were fighting separate battles simultaneously."[14] The actions ousted the Japanese from scores of islands and liberated thousands of Allied war prisoners, but they also spread American forces thinly across the islands.[15] The Eighth Army campaigns deprived Krueger's Sixth Army of any hope of reinforcement for its own campaign to eliminate Yamashita's Shobu Group.

MacArthur's drive to Manila was just one of many dramatic war events in the early months of 1945. In the North Pacific, the battles of Iwo Jima and Okinawa put American forces at Japan's doorstep. From bases in the Mariana Islands, US planes firebombed Japanese cities. One March raid on Tokyo killed as many as one hundred thousand men, women, and children. In Europe, Allied forces crossed the Rhine during the second week of March and by the third week in April had linked up with the Soviets in the heart of Germany, though not before an ailing and exhausted President Roosevelt died of a cerebral hemorrhage on April 12. In the shadow of these momentous global events, the Red Arrow began its ascent into the mountains of northern Luzon.

Once Krueger was confident that the fall of Manila was certain, he authorized the attack on the Shobu Group. His goal was to deprive Yamashita access to the Cagayan Valley, which might sustain the Japanese army there indefinitely. How to get there was the problem. Highway 5 ran from the Luzon lowlands to the Cagayan Valley, crossing the mountains through Balete Pass, where the Caraballo and Sierra Madre mountains meet. That thoroughfare offered Krueger the most direct route to northern Luzon and would give him the logistical link he needed to sustain operations there. Krueger assigned I Corps the job of punching through the mountains to the Cagayan Valley. He planned to attack with three divisions abreast. On the left, the Thirty-Third Division (originally the Illinois National Guard) was to push through the river valleys toward Baguio. On the right, the Twenty-Fifth "Tropic Lightning" Division, a battle-tested outfit that had been fighting in the Pacific since Guadalcanal, got the tough task of

Villa Verde Trail

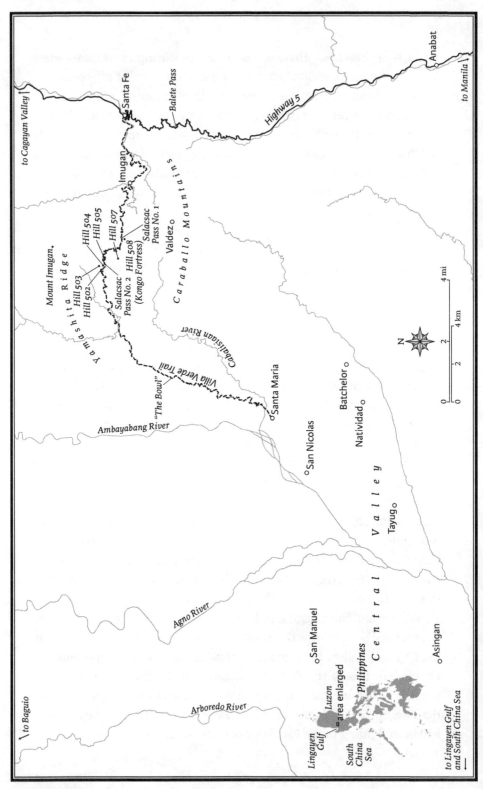

Santa Fe
Balete Pass
Highway 5
Anabat
to Manila

to Cagayan Valley
Imugan
Hill 504
Hill 505
Hill 507
Salacsac Pass No. 1
Salacsac Pass No. 2
Hill 508 (Kongo Fortress)
Valdez
Caraballo Mountains

Mount Imugan
Yamashita Ridge
Hill 503
Hill 502

Cabalisiaan River

"The Bowl"
Villa Verde Trail
Santa Maria

Ambayabang River

San Nicolas
Batchelor
Natividad
Tayug

Agno River

Central Valley

San Manuel
area enlarged
Philippines
Asingan
Luzon
Lingayen Gulf
South China Sea

Arboredo River

to Baguio

to Lingayen Gulf and South China Sea

N
4 mi
4 km
2
2
0
0

moving up Highway 5 through Balete Pass. In the center, the Red Arrow Division was assigned to take the Villa Verde Trail.

As Krueger envisioned it, the Tropic Lightning and Red Arrow Divisions would converge on Santa Fe, a village on Highway 5 one mile north of the pass. He anticipated that the Twenty-Fifth Division would have the toughest fight, but if the Thirty-Second could reach Santa Fe first, it could turn and attack Balete Pass from the rear, trapping the Japanese who were defending it. On the Red Arrow's front, the 126th Infantry Regiment was to probe into the river valleys to the left of the trail, while the 128th Infantry Regiment was to guard rear areas and patrol in the hills and valleys to the right. The 127th drew the task of ascending the trail itself.

On February 22, Stofft's 127th Infantry Regiment began an attack to puncture the outpost line it had discovered at the Bowl two weeks earlier, pushing up the trail and wrestling the Japanese off the high ground overlooking it. By 3:00 p.m. that day the regiment had "secured and consolidated on a series of 6 hills and reported 152 Japanese KIA [killed in action]," according to the regimental history, and then began "cleaning out scattered Japanese pockets of resistance."[16] The following day Company G got behind the Japanese line and set up a roadblock along the trail to the Japanese rear. A platoon of Company K, consisting of just nineteen soldiers, reached the crest of one hill and also got behind the Japanese. Over the next six hours the platoon engaged in heavy fighting. "Individual acts of heroism were numerous," claimed the citation the platoon received afterward, "as man after man charged the enemy in his deep positions, frequently engaging in hand-to-hand combat [and] the battle ended only when every single defender lay dead."[17] Recognizing their position as untenable, the Japanese withdrew from the Bowl on February 24. In the days that followed, "it was mostly just walking up a trail," recalled John Walters, "subject to Japanese artillery," but "we pushed on and pushed on."[18]

As the Red Arrowmen climbed ever higher into the mountains, whether on the Villa Verde Trail itself or through the hills and valleys along its flanks, they noted a changing environment. James Myers commented that "it was the first time [the members of] the 32nd Division, many of them natives of the forests of Wisconsin and Michigan, had smelled the pungent odor of pine in the more than three years they had been overseas."[19] Most approved of the change. Roy Campbell thought it good to be "out of the rotting damp jungle. It was clean, mountain air so the dead wouldn't rot in a matter of hours."[20] While on patrol near the village of Valdez, Jesse Coker came across "a small thicket of pine trees" and "took a break under familiar boughs of needles." He noted that "until now I had not seen any pine trees since leaving South Arkansas," and "the respite made me homesick."[21] Sheldon Dannelly quipped that "we were once known as jungle veterans [but] now they'll have to call us mountain goats."[22]

In early March, the 127th Infantry Regiment entered the Salacsac Pass—the highest segment of the trail. The pass was divided into two sections. The western part, from which the Red Arrow approached, was called Salacsac Pass No. 2. Roughly two miles to the east (air distance) was Salacsac Pass No. 1. From there, the trail began its descent to the village of Imugan and then on to Santa Fe. Dominating the landscape between Passes No. 1 and No. 2 were rugged wooded hills identified on US military maps simply by number, starting with Hill 502 at the western end. The terrain was ideally suited for defense, and the Japanese studded every hill and valley with mutually supporting artillery pits, machine-guns nests, and sniper positions. Japanese troops dug deep caves into the hills—some underground bunkers were capable of holding hundreds of soldiers. Tunnels led from the subterranean bunkers to camouflaged fighting positions on the surface, which peppered the hills and valleys. Six-thousand-foot-high Mount Imugan towered north of the pass, affording the Japanese excellent observation of the trail, as did a series of hills between the mountain and the Villa Verde Trail that the GIs dubbed "Yamashita Ridge." As the Red Arrow approached Salacsac Pass No. 2, Yamashita rushed in reinforcements, including the Second Tank Division, sans tanks and fighting as infantry, under Lieutenant General Iwanaka Yoshiharu, who took command of the Salacsac Pass defenses.

Thus, when the 127th Infantry Regiment began its attack on Salacsac Pass No. 2 in early March, its slow but steady progress ground to a crawl. Bitter fights now broke out over every hill and valley. The regiment seized Hill 502 by March 7 but at a steep cost. American patrols went out to locate Japanese positions and found them in great abundance and very formidable. "The Japanese were dug-in to deep caves immune to mortars, grenades, and small arms fire," noted the regimental historical report. They also raided the American positions, especially after dark. "During the

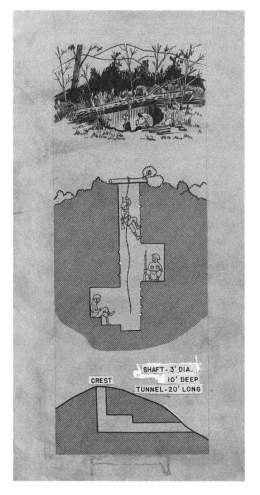

Japanese soldiers dug elaborate fighting positions and underground bunkers along the Villa Verde Trail. These sketches show how some of the bunkers were configured. They were drawn by Joseph E. Ash, an artillery liaison officer for the 126th Field Artillery on the Villa Verde Trail. The sketches appeared in Harold Blakeley's 1957 book, *The 32nd Infantry Division in World War II*. Ash, a long-time Wisconsin National Guard officer, worked as a commercial artist in the Milwaukee area. EDWARD T. LAUER PAPERS, WISCONSIN VETERANS MUSEUM night of 8 March," stated the historical report, "a small Japanese raiding party attacked machine gun positions of Co B and with grenades knocked out the machine gun and wounded 2 of our men. The raiders escaped." On March 9 a Japanese company attacked a platoon of Company A at 8:00 p.m. "The attack lasted until daylight [with] the Japanese using grenades, TNT, and land mines. The Co A platoon held its position and at daylight 40 dead Japan[ese] were counted."[23]

General William Gill, the Red Arrow's commander, tried to outflank the pass. The Third Battalion of the 127th swept through the valley south of the pass to Valdez, then climbed north into the mountains and struck Salacsac Pass No. 1. The battalion got to within a thousand yards of the trail, between Hills 507D and 508, but could advance no farther. The Second Battalion of the 128th Infantry Regiment near Valdez went in to reinforce the Third Battalion on March 15. Coker recalled "two weeks of intense, severe fighting. . . . They attacked us relentlessly, day and night," and infiltrators "crawled into the foxholes in our perimeter to kill quickly and quietly with their knives."[24] This attack was halted as well.

Although moving at a glacial pace, the Red Arrow slowly took the hills, eliminated scores of caves and bunkers, and inflicted heavy casualties on its adversaries. Gill had the 127th Infantry Regiment in a good position to cut off Salacsac Pass No. 2, but in the process his own ranks were becoming dangerously depleted. The regiment had gone into the fight there substantially understrength after the bloody Leyte campaign. The Villa Verde battles only weakened it further. After two weeks on the trail, more than one hundred members of the 127th were killed, twice that number were wounded, and roughly five hundred went to the rear because of disease or battle fatigue. The entire regiment was reduced to as few as fifteen hundred effective troops. For those heavy casualties, the regiment had gained little more than one thousand yards. The supply situation became critical too. This portion of the Villa Verde Trail was incapable of supporting significant vehicular traffic, so everything the regiment needed—ammunition, mortar shells, food—had to be brought up the winding trail by human power. Thus, as historian Robert Ross Smith wrote, "with its forces spread thin and its strength dwindling, the 127th was in no state to exploit its apparently advantageous position. . . . Immediate relief was an obvious necessity."[25]

Finally, Gill replaced the 127th Infantry Regiment with the 128th. First to arrive was the First Battalion on March 23, and the weary survivors of the 127th walked back down the trail to a rest area near Asingan. "It's wonderful to be out of that hell," John Walters wrote to his wife, Jewell.[26] The 128th Infantry Regiment now endured the same kind of grueling combat their predecessors had. "Received a heavy volume of enemy fire during the day and was unable to advance down the forward slopes of Hill 504," noted one report of the First Battalion's first full day of combat. "During the night, a heavy barrage of enemy artillery fell in the vicinity of Hills 502 and 504 and strong enemy counter-attacks were unsuccessfully launched against elements of the First Battalion on Hill 504."[27] Roy Campbell remembered that "the infantry would fight and die for weeks to take one mountaintop [only] to face another one just as strongly defended as the one they just fought for."[28]

On March 27, combat claimed the regimental commander, Colonel John Hettinger, who had just arrived at the front after a conference with General Gill. James Myers witnessed the tragedy. "The Jap artillery opened up and a shell landed right in the hole where the Colonel and his driver were standing," Myers wrote. "We looked and saw arms, legs, and other parts of their bodies flying into the air in all directions."[29] Gill replaced Hettinger with Colonel Merle Howe, the one-time commander of the 127th Infantry Regiment who was then leading the 126th probing the river valleys to the left of the trail. With his new assignment, Howe earned the distinction of having commanded all three of the Red Arrow's infantry regiments.

Within two weeks, the 128th Infantry Regiment was in much the same shape as the 127th had been. It suffered hundreds of casualties (including eighty-five killed), was more than one thousand understrength, and was unable to push through the pass on its own. Moreover, the onset of monsoon rains made the conditions on the Villa Verde Trail all the more miserable. "Clouds and heavy fog obscured vision throughout the day," noted the regimental historical report, "while torrential rains made the steep supply trails muddy and most difficult to negotiate."[30] By the first week of April the 126th Infantry Regiment appeared on the Villa Verde, relieved of its river valley patrol duty. On April 5, Gill launched an attack with his two regiments abreast. As the 128th continued to fight on the trail, the 126th moved through the hills just to the north of it. The 126th faced relatively light opposition at first, apparently catching the Japanese by surprise. As one report noted, "3rd Bn moved off to secure ridge N of Hill 503, was met with 3 or 4 bursts of MG fire but secured objective without casualties." The regiment cut an important Japanese supply trail running from Mount Imugan, but then Japanese resistance stiffened considerably, and the 126th experienced the same grueling conditions as the other two regiments.[31]

Although the process was desperately slow and bloody, the Red Arrowmen nevertheless inched forward, and General Iwanaka, commanding Japanese forces on the trail, recognized that Salacsac Pass No. 2 faced envelopment. He beefed up defenses at Salacsac Pass No. 1 but continued his stubborn and murderous defense of Pass No. 2 to inflict as many casualties on the Americans as he could. By April 10, Salacsac Pass No. 2 was finally in the hands of the Red Arrow Division, though clearing the Japanese out of ruined bunkers and caves took another week.

As the fighting ground on, Gill grew alarmed about the rapid attenuation of his ranks. By mid-April all three of his infantry regiments were exhausted, and he queried General Swift about reinforcements. "His reply was very definite," Gill recalled. "There were no reinforcements available. . . . There was very small chance of getting anything and I would have to use what I had to accomplish the mission."[32] Gill had no choice but to reshuffle his regiments continually, taking them off the line for brief periods only to feed them back in weeks later. The 127th Infantry Regiment returned to the Villa Verde on April 17, and the 128th Infantry Regiment took its turn at the Asingan rest area. During the first week of May, the 126th Infantry Regiment finally left the fighting, replaced with the 128th after just two weeks to recover from its own ordeals.

The fight for Salacsac Pass No. 1 was just as slow, difficult, and bloody. Dominating the trail there was Hill 508, dubbed "Kongo Fortress," which the Japanese studded with caves and artillery pits and honeycombed with tunnels. American guns and planes blasted the hill for weeks, then during the last week in April the Second Battalion of the 127th Infantry Regiment began to claw its way up the slopes. Japanese fire from nearby hills (which also had to be taken) harried the Red Arrow advance, as did counterattacks, infiltration attempts, and artillery from Yamashita Ridge. The fighting around Kongo Fortress went on for weeks, but by early May the GIs established a roadblock on the trail to the east of it, severing the Japanese communication line. Then "aircraft, self-propelled guns, mortars, and machine guns lacerated the slope," as Technician Fourth Class Charles P. Murdock of the Red Arrow's public relations office wrote in the *Saturday Evening Post*, and "not a square yard escaped pounding." Infantrymen then "had to haul themselves along by roots and vines," wrote Murdock, and "the struggle raged among the charred stumps and burned underbrush."[33] Finally, on May 19, the First Battalion of the 128th Infantry Regiment cleared the "remaining maze" of bunkers on the hill.[34]

After the battle, John E. Jones of the *Pittsburgh Post-Gazette* surveyed the ruins. The "barren knob" was "littered with shell shattered trees, with trenches and with stinking bodies of Jap defenders," he wrote. Jones also inspected the "labyrinth" of underground tunnels. "This intricate design included a devious arrangement of upper and lower passages and off-shooting lanes and slots," he wrote. "This cave fortress ran zig-zag 150 feet through the hill, with entrances on each side. A third escape route was dug straight up to the top of the ridge." He also noted that "there were separate quarters for Jap officers and enlisted men, and a complete kitchen department. There were sabers, pistols, and maps which gave evidence that Kongo fortress was at least a battalion command post, with a Jap major and captain recognized among the dead."[35]

The Red Arrow received replacements for those killed and wounded, but there were never enough of them. Most often the replacements came during rest periods, but some arrived during the fighting. William Painter boarded a truck at a replacement depot near Manila and headed north, though he wasn't told where he was going. Hours later Painter stood near the base of the Villa Verde Trail, where he met a sergeant who "started calling off names for different companies." That was when Painter learned he had joined Company C of the 127th Infantry Regiment. The sergeant "had a bullet hole right through the center of his helmet," Painter recalled, and said that the helmet once belonged to his best friend. "I'm wearing it because he's dead," the sergeant said, adding, "this is what you can expect when you get up there." Even more unsettling was the fact that after Painter and the other replacements got off the trucks, "they put the dead on those trucks. Their feet stuck out the back, and there were three levels—one group in the bed, a second layer, and a top layer." The sight of "many pairs of shoes sticking out the back" haunted him, and "the smell was awful." From there the sergeant marched the replacements up the Villa Verde, continuing their orientation. "He talked to us all the way," Painter recalled, "but there was a kind of indifference. Like, you don't make friends in the military. That's how he was treating us. It was not patronizing. He was pretty cold about it."[36]

Ready or not, the replacements went into combat as soon as practicable. "We had to start fighting [with them] before I even learned their names," lamented Whayland Greene.[37] It was the same for replacement officers. "I came . . . into the hills for the first time," wrote Jerry Angel, "and within an hour was ordered to take out a patrol to look for snipers. I was totally unprepared mentally and by experience for it."[38] In combat "the replacements looked around in awe and amazement," observed Henry Zabierek. "It was not like the movies. No one acted like John Wayne. He remained in Hollywood. No wonder he always survived." Zabierek recalled two replacements on their first combat operation who spotted what they thought were ruined Japanese tanks and "walked toward [them] as carefree as if this was a picnic." Then "out from nearby holes emerged several enemy riflemen" and as Zabierek put it, the newcomers "were rendered 24-hour heroes."[39] Greene remembered a patrol during which "one of the new guys came right up over a Jap in his hole. Sgt. Sullivan said, 'Shoot him, that's what you were sent over here for.' He said, 'I can't.'"[40]

The Red Arrow worked extensively with guerrilla organizations on Luzon. Soon after the Sixth Army landings at Lingayen Gulf on January 9, Krueger began to supply and train guerrilla units and even integrated them into his command structure. Operating north of the Villa Verde Trail was the United States Army Forces in the Philippines–North Luzon, or USAFIP (NL), under Colonel Russell W. Volckmann, a West Pointer who had evaded capture at Bataan. Numbering ten thousand at the beginning of the campaign, Volckmann's command swelled to more than twice that number by mid-1945—a force larger than a standard US infantry division. Major Robert Lapham, a US officer in the Philippine Scouts when the war broke out, commanded the Luzon Guerrilla Armed Forces (LGAF) in the northern reaches of the Central Valley. Lapham dispatched an entire LGAF regiment to fight with the Red Arrow. It was led by Captain Ray C. Hunt, an ex–air force sergeant who had escaped the Japanese during the Bataan

Death March. The Thirty-Second Division trained and equipped yet another guerrilla unit, the Buena Vista Regiment, based at Valdez. The guerrillas also organized the local Igorot peoples to supply the Red Arrow. The term *Igorot* (from Tagalog for "mountaineer") refers to the diverse array of ethnic groups residing in the highlands of northern Luzon, such as the Bontoc, Ibaloi, Ifugao, and Kalanguya. Igorot carriers—women as well as men—lugged goods up the Villa Verde Trail to the frontline troops, and the Red Arrowmen developed a particular affection for them. "They had negotiated the hills, overcame the effects of the monsoon-like rain, and handled the deep ravines," wrote Zabierek, who always found their arrival a "welcome sight" as "they brought something for everyone: food, ammunition, supplies, even mail."[41] Igorot civilians also served as scouts and guides. They too fought and died alongside the Red Arrowmen.[42]

The members of the Red Arrow Division's 114th Engineers were assigned the arduous task of transforming the narrow and crooked footpath that was the Villa Verde Trail into a roadway capable of sustaining major combat operations. It was by far the biggest challenge they had yet faced. The engineers' key tool was the bulldozer, which they used to plough through earth and rock to widen the trail. In many places, work crews had to carve the roadbed into near-vertical mountainsides. Once improved, the trail often had rock ledges above the roadbed, which overlooked steep wooded ravines hundreds of feet deep. The engineers widened the road to two lanes whenever possible and constructed pullouts to relieve congestion, but many stretches were just one lane wide. Road grades were sometimes as steep as 35 percent, particularly on the many switchbacks. Rockslides and accidents frequently left bulldozers tottering precariously on the edge of the road above the ravines, and in several cases they plunged over the side. Whenever feasible, engineers recovered the vehicle "by building a spur sidehill cut to it."[43]

As the engineers proceeded into the mountains, they could hear the battle sounds in the distance. Sometimes Japanese artillery reached them, causing a few injuries. Once construction crews reached the Salacsac Pass, the bulldozers were in the thick of the fight and the Japanese targeted them with snipers, artillery, and infiltration raids. Zabierek recounted one such assault when the Japanese "emerged from their hideouts and pushed their highly maneuverable 75-millimeter gun into position." Then the "firing upon the bulldozer began." Artillery knocked out the gun, but the bulldozer tumbled into a deep ravine below the trail.[44] "I heard an officer order an enlisted man to drive a bulldozer," remembered Ray Hunt, but "the man refused, saying it was suicide." Hunt noted that "for such a reply he could have been executed for disobeying orders in combat, but the lieutenant merely looked at him, climbed onto the bulldozer himself, and went to work. The enlisted man watched silently for a few minutes, then motioned to the lieutenant to stop, and the two traded places without a word."[45]

Once at the front, bulldozers also built road spurs from which tanks and self-propelled guns could fire into caves and bunkers. One spur had a 40 percent grade and took two days to construct. Building these fighting positions made the bulldozers even more vulnerable to shells and gunfire. The engineers—skilled at building things—improvised armored cabs to protect drivers from bullets. "In the face of direct fire from three enemy machine guns, the armored cab dozer opened up another firing position for the tank," noted the engineer battalion's historical report of one incident. "The operators continued despite superficial face wounds from bullet splash through the portholes until the dozer was hit in the oil filter."

On several occasions, bulldozers became weapons. One came around a bend in the road "and ran into machine gun fire from a gun on the trail only 20 feet away," noted the historical report. The driver, though slightly wounded, raised the blade of his vehicle and "charged the gun with his dozer." Bullets cut the cables to the blade, forcing it to drop and preventing the driver from moving forward, but the bulldozer backed up and gave way to a tank that "blasted out the machine gun." The engineers then repaired the cables and "work resumed in forty-five minutes." The following day the same bulldozer "unintentionally acted as the left flank of an infantry attack" as GIs pressed forward. "During this engagement" the bulldozer "buried three Japs in caves" and an engineering officer "killed one Jap in the act of shooting at the dozer and killed another with a grenade after the dozer had removed the brush from a cave entrance."[46]

For the ground soldiers, destroying the hundreds of caves along the Villa Verde Trail was their most immediate and important task. Because one cave guarded the approaches to another, outflanking them was exceptionally difficult. "It is necessary that you have a well coordinated

Bulldozers at work on the Villa Verde Trail. NATIONAL ARCHIVES

fire plan," advised a 128th Infantry Regiment report from the fighting
on Hill 505, "so that each and every position they can have can be covered by two or more of your weapons."[47] Sometimes the GIs dug trenches
toward the cave openings, burrowing through the earth with picks and
shovels as Japanese rifles, machine guns, and grenades tried to stop them.
Typically, the Red Arrowmen launched blunt frontal assaults against the
caves, which depended on sheer guts or simple desperation. Bazookas and

mortars battered the entrances, and flamethrowers shot streams of burning napalm into them. "So bitter was the fighting," wrote Zabierek, "that the horrific sight of enemy soldiers lit afire brought no gasps from the men of [our] company."[48] According to Jesse Coker, most of the GIs manning the flamethrowers were killed, "but they are to be commended for their fabulous success."[49]

Upon reaching the mouth of a cave, the GIs then tried to seal it up. Perhaps the most common method of destroying a cave entrance was the pole charge. Zabierek described the weapon as "a lethal home-made creation" that "consisted of blocks of TNT that were wired to a board from a ration box, and . . . tied to a bamboo pole." The soldier with the pole charge approached the entrance carefully as "rifle shots were fired to keep the occupants inside," Zabierek wrote. The attacking soldier would then "light the fuse and throw the bamboo bomb into the cave."[50] After the charge detonated, "the tunnels cave in," explained Julius Sakus, "and the entrance is closed forever."[51] Cave entrances that could not be sealed tightly had to be sandbagged and guarded, as the scores of Japanese soldiers buried underground often dug their way out to keep fighting. Monte Howell remembered Japanese "emerging from the ground like corpses back from the dead."[52] One report noted that "throughout the entire night digging could . . . be heard under our positions," but "the men . . . stuck to their post and fed hand grenades to the Japs down under their position as an opening would occur."[53] Other Japanese trapped underground chose suicide. "American troops would sometimes hear muffled explosions far underground," noted Ray Hunt. "They were set off by Japanese troops whose tunnel openings had been sealed off by American explosives and who now, sick and despairing, chose to blow themselves up with grenades."[54] As one report noted, "there was continuous firing and hand grenades going off in the Jap dugouts. After each shot there would be loud yells of pain, indicating the Japs were committing Hara Kiri [suicide]. . . . It is estimated 50 Japs committed Hara Kiri that night and as much as a week later some Japs were still trying to get out by reopening some of the holes."[55]

The GIs welcomed the appearance of the Sherman tanks and M7 self-propelled guns to blast the caves. Artillery and air power brought copious amounts of firepower too, though the close quarters of the fighting often limited their effectiveness. "I observed the action of U.S. dive bombers trying to place napalm bombs into the openings of some very large caves," wrote Coker. "I tensed as the first bomb was released far behind me and angling in a direction which I was sure would cause it to drop on my platoon. I was petrified with fear as the bomb fell, and I watched helplessly." Fortunately for Coker the bomb "sail[ed] far over my head and into a ravine in front of us. . . . The napalm really scorched those hills, and the best part was that the Japs were extremely afraid of it."[56] However, in many cases American planes accidentally bombed and strafed their own troops. "We were dug in on one side of a hill and the Japs on the other side," James Myers recalled, but the pilots "must have had their signals mixed" because instead of attacking the Japanese "they came [down] right on top of us, in strafing runs." Myers wrote that "after that episode, we did not call for any more air strikes."[57] In the fight around Hill 508, the 127th Infantry Regiment noted several friendly fire incidents. On April 25, a US plane dropped a bomb on Company A, "killing one enlisted man . . . and injuring seventeen more." In another case a bomb hit Company G as it attacked on the hill. "Damage to the personnel . . . was severe," the regiment reported, and "the forward progress of that organization became impractical."[58]

Four Red Arrowmen earned the Medal of Honor on the Villa Verde Trail. The first was Private First Class Thomas E. Atkins of Company A, 127th Infantry Regiment, a farmer from Campobello, South Carolina. On March 10, Atkins and two other Red Arrowmen were occupying a foxhole on a ridgeline when, at 3:00 a.m., two Japanese companies launched an intense attack with gunfire, grenades, and TNT charges. Atkins's comrades were killed and he was severely wounded, but he kept firing and single-handedly repulsed his attackers. The Japanese then poured machine-gun fire on his foxhole, but Atkins held his ground. By 7:00 a.m., Atkins had expended four hundred rounds of ammunition, and as a result thirteen Japanese lay dead, but all three rifles in his possession (his own and those of his dead comrades) had jammed. Atkins pulled back to get another weapon when he was instead taken to an aid station for his wounds. Even then he kept fighting. While awaiting treatment he spotted a Japanese soldier, grabbed a nearby rifle, and shot him dead. While being evacuated to the rear, Atkins spotted more Japanese and—sitting up on his stretcher—opened fire, forcing them to withdraw.

The other three recipients were Californians, all awarded post-humously. Private First Class William R. Shockley of Company L, 128th Infantry Regiment, had migrated from Oklahoma to the farming community of Selma in California's San Joaquin Valley. On March 31, Shockley poured machine-gun fire into a group of advancing Japanese to cover the withdrawal of his comrades, telling them he would "remain to the end." He held off one attack, but a second outflanked and killed him. Through Shockley's sacrifice, the remainder of his squad escaped.

The two other Californians served in the 127th Infantry Regiment. The first was Staff Sergeant Ysmael Villegas of F Company, a native of Riverside County who was known as "Smiley" for his affable personality. On March 20, Villegas led his men in an attack on a cave complex. As his squad reached the crest of a hill, they suddenly faced the intense fire of Japanese troops concealed in nearby foxholes. Villegas charged one foxhole, "running like a football player," recalled Lieutenant William Newburn, and shot a Japanese soldier dead. Then "all enemy weapons were brought to bear on him," Newburn recalled, "causing dirt to spurt up at his feet," but Villegas "whirled and headed for another foxhole, stood over it, killed the Japanese rifleman, and then headed for another." He attacked five Japanese foxholes in all, but by the time he headed for a sixth "every Jap on that hill" had "a bead on him," as Newburn described it, and Villegas "went down in a tornado of fire." "The men were so incensed at his death," recalled Lieutenant William Zahnizer, "they charged the position and couldn't be stopped," and "when the charge was over, 75 Japanese lay dead in their foxholes."

The final recipient was Private David Gonzalez of Pacoima. During a firefight on April 25 a bomb went off inside the Company A perimeter, burying five men alive in a mound of rock and sand. Gonzalez and his company commander immediately rushed forward to dig them out. Machine-gun fire killed the officer, but Gonzalez kept digging, using an entrenching tool and even his bare hands as bullets snapped around him. Gonzalez pulled three men out before Japanese fire finally struck him down. "It was the bravest thing I have ever seen a man do," claimed one eyewitness. The other two men were extricated as the firefight subsided. All five of those buried survived.[59]

The Thirty-Second Division's fight for the hills and caves of the Villa Verde Trail took a tremendous toll on the Red Arrowmen—both physically and mentally. No battle since Buna had shaken the division so deeply. There was a constant flow of wounded from the battlefield. The medical chain of evacuation led from the mountains down to the lowlands of Luzon's Central Valley. As in all earlier engagements, the members of the 107th Medical Battalion remained the heroes and saviors of the wounded. As journalist John Carlisle of the *Detroit News* observed: "The medical aid men, the litter bearers, and the ambulance drivers are close to every infantryman's heart."[60] Jesse Coker was severely wounded in an artillery barrage in April. Shrapnel ripped into his chest and arm and knocked him flat on his back. "I was immobile and breathing with much difficulty," he remembered, "but I was still clutching my trusted M-1 rifle between my legs." At first Coker felt numb, but "by the time the medics put me on a stretcher, the severe pain hit me and I could feel the blood flowing down my leg. I worried that I was losing too much blood, but I trusted those young, able medics whom I had seen in action many times before."[61] Those medics gave him blood plasma and a shot of morphine before carrying him to an aid station.

Getting the wounded like Coker away from the battlefield could be an arduous process. Stretcher bearers had to carry the wounded under fire while crossing a landscape of clogging brush, charred stumps, slippery hillsides, deep mud, shell holes, cave remnants, and the general detritus of war. "It took our litter team four hours to bring one rifleman in," medic Gideon Millar remembered. "It would have taken 25 minutes to walk by yourself." In the most remote areas evacuation took even longer. "All evacuations from Valdez were accomplished by Filipino carriers back to Batchelor at the foot of the mountains," noted the medical battalion's historical report. "This took nine (9) hours." For the 126th Infantry Regiment patrolling the river valleys to the left of the Villa Verde early in the campaign, "litter hauls were long and over rough terrain sometimes taking as long as twenty (20) hours." As in previous battles, the Japanese targeted medical personnel. "Sometimes the Japs let you get through to the wounded," noted medic Harold Beauregard, but "as you start out with your litter their snipers open up and pin you down."[62] Danger lurked farther down the evacuation chain too. At one point "Battalion Aid Stations were under constant artillery fire," noted one report.[63] Dean Andersen recalled an attack on a collecting station well behind the lines. "One morning at first light a machine gun opened up from the top of a peak," he wrote. "I was asleep on a litter [and] I dived for the sandbags. When I looked back there were two holes in the litter where I had been sleeping."[64]

Fortunately, Red Arrow doctors and medics on Villa Verde Trail had a few more tools than in previous campaigns, such as motorized ambulances, which had been of limited use in the jungles of New Guinea and Leyte. As "the Engineers pushed forward very rapidly in the construction of the road," noted the medical battalion history, "the ambulances followed them [and] cut shorter the hauls of the litter bearers." In some cases ambulances could drive right up to frontline aid stations. It was often a dangerous ride, though. Japanese shellfire or infiltrators "slowed evacuation considerably," noted the battalion history, and "night runs to the rear by ambulances were extremely hazardous because of the narrowness of the road, sharp curves, and in places was complicated still further by a steep grade which made backing and turning doubly difficult." At times other vehicles served medical purposes. "Because of heavy machine-gun fire on open spots on the trail," noted the battalion history, "armored half-track Reconnaissance vehicles were used for evacuation of battle casualties, and ran the gauntlet through dangerous areas. The 32nd Cavalry Reconnaissance personnel operating these vehicles are to be highly commended for this fine job."[65]

Air evacuation had improved as well. On Luzon modified Cub planes transported the wounded to hospitals in the rear. "Wounded are brought down the trail in ambulances to an airstrip," observed journalist John E. Jones, where "the patients are loaded into the planes and flown back to base or evacuation hospitals." Jones noted that "bed-ridden patients are placed on litters in the specially constructed fuselage of the cub plane, while the able-to-walk wounded sit in the plane behind the pilot."[66] By air the wounded could get to a base hospital in fifteen to twenty minutes—a trip that might take an entire day by ground transportation. Coker went to the hospital by Cub plane, remarking that it was his "very first plane ride," though hardly a pleasant one. By the time Coker's plane landed, the doses of morphine administered to him had worn off, and "when that little plane touched down it began to bounce, I had to grit my teeth to keep from crying out from the terrible pain."[67] Elsewhere in the Philippines, medical crews experimented with a new aerial vehicle to evacuate the wounded: the helicopter.

Illness afflicted frontline troops. "The increase in respiratory diseases was somewhat new to this Regiment," noted the history of the 127th Infantry Regiment. "While in New Guinea this disability did not give us any great deal of trouble," but the weather on Villa Verde Trail was "cold, foggy, and misty" and "troops were not at first properly clothed to withstand cold and moisture."[68] The ever-present malaria problem continued, with both new and recurring cases. "I was hit again with a bad case of malaria," wrote Buna veteran James Myers, "and was carried back down the trail to an ambulance." Once in the hospital the doctors suspected that he might also have worms, so they gave him three pills "the size of a small egg," and after swallowing them he promptly vomited into a pan. "I looked into it," he wrote, "and there, swimming around, were a half dozen worms that were like small snakes."[69] In one report, a frustrated medical officer asked rhetorically: "In general, what is the general condition of the troops? Poor. These boys are worn out and exhausted from 54 days of continuous combat. And it wasn't long since they went through a similar period. If they can now get adequate rest and relaxation the general health will increase markedly."[70] As Edward Guhl described it, "we were worn out, used up, and diseased."[71]

The grinding, continual combat affected the emotions of the fighting man in numerous ways. John Walters's separation from his young daughter weighed heavily on him—even in battle. "I am sorry to hear that Jane awakens at night and cries for her daddy," he wrote to his wife, Jewell. "I really feel hurt because I know how hard it is when one misses another." He added that sometimes "I cry too when I think of you and Jane."[72] Watching friends die, and the randomness of so many deaths, played upon the minds of soldiers. John Rawls, now a member of the 128th Infantry Regiment's I&R platoon, had become friendly with a man named Deacon. "One day the First Sergeant came to us looking for two volunteers," Rawls wrote. One was to scout Japanese positions with the regimental commander, Colonel Hettinger, while the other was to "give blood badly needed for a wounded soldier." Who did what, remembered Rawls, "depended on who had the right blood type." As it turned out, Rawls gave the blood and Deacon went with the colonel; Deacon and Hettinger were killed minutes later. Rawls was "disconsolate" over the loss of his friend and wrote that he "couldn't get the incident out of my mind." His emotions puzzled him. "I don't know why his death so affected me," Rawls wrote, "as death was a common occurrence."[73] The near-constant combat led many GIs down the road to despondency. As Guhl remembered: "I just gave up and decided I would be killed."[74]

In their world of brutality and carnage, most GIs somehow maintained their moral compass and their humanity. Robert Foist was guarding ration trains when "we had a Japanese truck driver surrender to our outfit." As Foist recalled, the man "said he was born in Oakland and was drafted on a visit to Japan." The GIs treated their captive well, he remembered, "although some of the New Guinea vets were for shooting him on the spot—they were stopped by the captain."[75] William Painter remembered one soldier who had been "knocking the gold teeth out of those Japanese mouths," until his company commander put a stop to it. "If I ever see you doing that again," the officer said, "you're going to be court-martialed." Painter remembered that he "liked the guy for that. At least he kept some semblance of civilization there."[76] As the fighting raged around him, John Walters kept Jewell and Jane in the front of his mind. "I'm still clinging to the side of this mountain," he wrote, "and able to look longingly at the roads that may sometime lead to home—even tho' the roads are far below."[77]

The Thirty-Second Division experienced an unusually high number of neuropsychiatric cases on the Villa Verde Trail. Between April 17 and April 27, thirty-four soldiers from the First Battalion of the 127th Infantry Regiment were hospitalized for psychiatric issues—7.1 percent of the entire battalion strength. "The symptoms exhibited by these casualties were varied but certain signs and symptoms were common to all," noted Major Louis A. Sass, surgeon of the 127th Infantry Regiment. "They exhibited extreme nervousness, anxiety, generalized weakness, some weeping, depression and in a few cases, hysteria conversion symptoms."[78] Those suffering from psychological trauma could endanger themselves and their comrades. "Some of them left their posts and ran off until one of their friends caught them," wrote medic Dean Andersen, and "by the time they came to us, they were out of control." Andersen also noted that "some of the worst cases did not make it to the medics. They exposed themselves to enemy fire and were killed." Officers suffered as well as enlisted personnel, and not just those on the front line. "One of the worst cases was a medical captain," Andersen recalled. "He was different because we didn't know what medicine he had given himself before he went out of his head. He was hysterical and it took several of us to keep him quiet."[79] The cumulative stress of successive grueling campaigns apparently reached the apex of the Red Arrow command structure. In a February letter to his wife, Emmaline, Eichelberger intimated that General Gill had been hospitalized after "he pushed some of his enlisted men and officers around physically." A few days later Eichelberger told her: "I have not heard from Bill G since he went into the hospital except one of the doctors told me that he made quite a hit when he was interviewed."[80]

Doctors evacuated severe battle fatigue cases to the rear. "About 50% examined," reported Dr. Sass, "were placed on phenobarbital and returned to duty." Sass observed that "a few adjusted and were able to perform efficiently" while "the remainder cowered in their fox-holes, trembling and in fear that they were unable to control until they were returned to the aid station by their officers as no use to the company and a demoralizing influence on the other men in the line." Sass believed that replacements were more likely to break down than veterans. "The majority of these men were 18–20 years of age," he wrote, "an age where even in civilian life governments do not consider them to be sufficiently stable emotionally to entrust them with adult decisions and situations." Combat then "subjected them to heavy punishment for which they had not been psychologically prepared." However, Sass also noted that amongst the afflicted "a substantial number of men had seen previous combat. Here the additional strain of numerous campaigns, previously being wounded, long years overseas, lack of adequate rest periods between campaigns, etc., played a part."[81] In Andersen's observation, battle fatigue "was more prevalent among infantrymen who had been in combat for over three years."[82]

Medical officers across the world witnessed individual combat soldiers breaking down and losing their effectiveness as the war dragged on. "Over the course of time," wrote historian Albert E. Cowdrey, "reliable soldiers, well led, and adequately supplied, were observed to fail at a fairly predictable rate."[83] Army doctors offered varying estimates of how much fighting a soldier could endure, ranging anywhere from one hundred forty to two hundred aggregate days of combat. By 1945, many Red Arrowmen had reached that point or pushed beyond it. At the beginning of the Villa

Verde campaign, about 30 percent of the division had spent three years overseas, and many had experienced heavy combat on and off since Buna back in 1942.[84] In the Philippines the Red Arrow experienced its longest duration of combat. With the exception of a three-week break between Leyte and Luzon, the division had been on the line almost continuously from November 1944 through May 1945—and it was involved in some of the most relentless fighting seen on any World War II battlefront. A handful had been with the division since its initial mobilization in 1940, such as Gifford Coleman of Rice Lake, Wisconsin, who saw action at Buna, Saidor, Aitape, Leyte, and then Luzon. On the Villa Verde Trail Coleman felt the accumulated weight of his many campaigns. "You can only take so much of that and you start worrying and cracking," he said. "I was at that point."[85]

Veterans like Coleman commanded great respect in the division, and they continued to fight and die. "It's hard to watch old timers get it after going through so much," Walters told his wife, Jewell. "It makes one wonder just how long one is going to last and also how fortunate some of us are."[86] Others finally got their chance to rotate back to the United States. Lieutenant Colonel Herbert A. Smith had been in the Wisconsin National Guard since the Roaring Twenties, took command of the Second Battalion of the 128th Infantry Regiment during the 1930s, and fought in every major Red Arrow campaign. While on the Villa Verde Trail, Smith left the front line and began his long journey back to Oshkosh. "The war had not lessened his essential humanity, so he wanted to go to the front lines to bid his men farewell," observed Ray Hunt. "Col. Smith shook hands with some of his [men] in their foxholes. After goodbyes we went back to the command post down in the foothills, got into a jeep, and started off. Smith's eyes were moist, more at the thought of leaving his men than with joy at the prospect of going home."[87]

The war in Europe finally came to an end on May 8, but it meant little to the Thirty-Second Division on the Villa Verde Trail. "V-E Day came," reported Charles Murdock, but "nobody got excited. The trucks were still coming down out of the mountains with bodies lashed to stretchers."[88] Walters told his family that he was glad to see Germany's fall but added that "as we move closer to Japan the fighting is becoming more severe."[89] Throughout May the fighting around Salacsac Pass No. 1 continued. The 128th Infantry Regiment had finally secured the pass by May 24, but the regiment was so wrung out that it could not continue the three miles to Santa Fe. However, the Twenty-Fourth Infantry Division, after its own hellish fight at Balete Pass, found a gap in the Japanese lines in their sector and pushed through. With the Twenty-Fifth Division advancing northward along Highway 5, I Corps adjusted the divisional boundaries. The battered Thirty-Second Division now had the more modest goal of taking Imugan, while the Twenty-Fifth would take Santa Fe. To add heft to the Twenty-Fifth Division's attack, General Swift attached to it the Red Arrow's 126th Infantry Regiment—ten days rested and replenished with more than one thousand replacements. The 126th secured the high ground west of Highway 5. It set up a roadblock north of Santa Fe, patrolled for Japanese concentrations, and drove toward Imugan to link up with its Red Arrow comrades. With the Villa Verde Trail all but lost and US troops driving up Highway 5, General Iwanaka withdrew the remnants of his forces toward the Cagayan Valley to fight another day.

Members of the 126th Infantry Regiment patrol along the Villa Verde Trail near the village of Santa Fe. NATIONAL ARCHIVES

On May 28, patrols from the 128th Infantry Regiment and the Thirty-Second Cavalry Reconnaissance Troop linked up with those of the 126th Infantry Regiment near Imugan, and the Buena Vista Regiment moved into the remnants of the village itself. The long, grueling fight for the Villa Verde Trail was finally over. The toll on the Red Arrow was immense. In all, the fighting on and around the Villa Verde Trail left 825 Red Arrowmen killed and 2,160 wounded, with an additional 6,000 evacuated due to disease or combat fatigue. Japan lost an estimated 5,750 killed out of the nearly 9,000 troops it committed to the Villa Verde. The battles at Iwo Jima and Okinawa that occurred concurrently with the Villa Verde fight grabbed US headlines, while the Red Arrow's experience—as well as that of the other army divisions in the mountains of Luzon—was just as horrific yet went largely unnoticed. "All the adjectives in Webster's dictionary won't describe the action," John E. Jones told the readers of the *Pittsburgh Post-Gazette*, "'incredible' and 'impossible' don't cover it. You simply can't believe that men have to fight under such conditions until you see it."[90]

Between stints on the Villa Verde Trail, the Red Arrowmen went to a rest area near Asingan. At the conclusion of the campaign, the division settled into rest camps along the Lingayen Gulf. At the rest areas the troops lived in tents and slept on cots rather than hunkering down in foxholes. It was a welcome change. "Our tent is rounding into pretty good shape," John Walters wrote to Jewell from Asingan. "We have bamboo lattice work around the sides of the tent with a door at the front and rear. Seems homey." The tents even had electricity. Food was plentiful. "Just finished a nice supper of steak, dehydrated potatoes, green onions, gravy, fruit salad and a fresh bun," Walters wrote, "also coffee. The steak was well received by all." Walters felt particularly fortunate to be in the rest area for Easter Sunday, April 1. "Like a good boy I attended church," he reported home. "I enjoyed the service . . . simple but nice." He also remarked that he had just received "four Xmas cards. . . . They were sent in Dec but arrived on April Fool's Day."[91]

While in the rest camps, the soldiers spent time at the rifle range to keep up their marksmanship skills and took part in various kinds of training exercises. They also patrolled the surrounding areas, as the problem of

Japanese snipers and infiltrators persisted. At the conclusion of the Villa Verde Trail campaign, the Red Arrowmen also experienced the unwelcome return of inspections and other "spit and polish" dimensions of military life that had disappeared during combat. They did not like it. William Painter recalled "a new lieutenant who joined our outfit at Lingayen" and was a "pretty brash guy. . . . He had the first sergeant call reveille, and we were all going out to do calisthenics." When Painter's company commander got wind of the young officer's practices he gathered the troops and informed them that the lieutenant "is going to demonstrate calisthenics for the next forty-five minutes! Everybody find a seat!" Painter watched gleefully as the officer did push-ups, sit-ups, and jumping jacks, and remarked that "he never pulled that on us again."[92]

Rest camps offered numerous recreational opportunities. The GIs went swimming and fishing. Beer was available. "Occasionally our company headquarters in Tayug had a party," recalled Dean Andersen, where "grapefruit juice was mixed with medical alcohol."[93] Gambling continued, as did the adoption of pets, though often rather different ones than at stateside training camps. "We have a little monkey," John Walters told his family, that "acts almost human sometimes [and] rides around on our shoulder[s]."[94] Morale officials labored to keep men entertained and out of trouble. Soon after James Myers received a promotion to second lieutenant, his battalion commander "learned that I had some show business experience" and made him the morale officer, though the battalion had very little recreational equipment. "I borrowed a covered pick-up truck from the motor pool," he wrote, "and, with a few Jap war souvenirs, swords, etc., set off for Manila." At a Red Cross center Myers scrounged "quite a load of ping-pong balls, nets, cards, books, checkers and other things to keep the boys back in camp happy." He then went to Army Special Services where he obtained "footballs, baseball equipment, soccer balls, volley balls, nets and enough things to fill the truck to the top." He also picked up a gas generator and a refrigerator, though when Myers passed through regimental headquarters "the brass decided they could make better use of the refrigerator than a mere battalion." The rest areas had movies and USO shows, and the Red Arrowmen sometimes organized their own productions. "We were able to build a stage, using tarpaulins for backdrops, and a roof for a stage," wrote the ever-resourceful Myers, and after holding auditions he "wrote a musical review around the talent available" entitled "Got You Covered." The show featured "vaudeville and burlesque bits," and bawdy poems and lyrics that were "well-received by the men in the audience. There were no women." Indeed, the show proved so popular that "we had to put on a number of additional performances in the area for other units and regimental headquarters."[95]

Luzon offered the Red Arrowmen numerous opportunities to interact with Philippine civilians and their culture. Hungry GIs savored the flavors of the tropical east. "The wife of a Filipino major who was serving the Guerrilla Forces brought us some candy which she made from coconuts," remembered Jesse Coker. "The candy tasted sweet and exotic; so much better than those concentrated chocolate bars that we had eaten for so long."[96] John Walters visited with an ethnic Chinese family and described the feast he enjoyed with them. "We had chop suey in the raw instead of being cooked," he wrote, and "several kinds of vegetables that really hit the spot. Meat (something like our farmer sausage), potatoes, fresh lettuce, and fresh cucumbers—plus several kinds of greens. Our dessert was made of avocadoes, bananas, papau, and some other kinds of fruit. Also cream on it. It was a wonderful meal."[97] As on Leyte, the GIs noted intense poverty. "All of the people's clothes are tattered," Andersen wrote, and "we gave the Philippine people burlap from our sandbag sacks in our supply. They used the burlap to create shorts and shirts."[98] Some dismissed the Filipinos as beggars. Donald Dill, a newly arrived replacement, thought that the local population was "always looking for hand-outs."[99] Others noted an enterprising spirit. Selling food to GIs was one way to make money. Others produced souvenirs for the GI memento market. "Just saw some nice rings made by Filippinos [sic] of silver and gold," wrote Walters, which "cost anywhere from $15 to $20 or $25."[100] Many took jobs servicing the American military. "On Luzon there were a lot of Filipino women who would wash your clothes for a [peso] or two," wrote Monte Howell. "We would give them a bar of Lye soap and they would take the clothes down to the local river and beat them against the rocks until they were clean."[101]

The GIs' search for sex continued, and the rest camps of Luzon presented them with many more opportunities than they had found on Leyte or New Guinea. "I assume that it is natural to expect men who have been . . . for many years without female companionship in any form or manner," wrote Monte Howell, "to be very eager to seek out women once we arrived in a more civilized area."[102] True romance sometimes bloomed between American men and Philippine women, but sexual contact was usually commercial. Poverty, exacerbated by long years of war, drove many women into sex work. Days after coming ashore Jesse Coker saw "a line of men . . . at the front door of a house" and discovered that a local man "was collecting money from [them] for an act of prostitution with his wife."[103] Dean Andersen recalled that "prostitutes traveled from camp to camp." At night, traffickers sneaked women into camps, where "as many as fifty men might line up to be served"—a sight that, Andersen wrote, "made me sick."[104] Not all Red Arrowmen participated in such lewdness. As Donald Dill commented, "those V.D. films did me in."[105]

Sexually transmitted infections—particularly gonorrhea—rose dramatically. "It became an epidemic," claimed Howell. "At one point in time fifty percent of the men in my company had a venereal disease."[106] Hospitalizations for sexually transmitted infections affected readiness and took infantrymen off the front line. Army efforts to control the rate of infection, while not entirely fruitless, barely dented the problem. "Contraction of venereal disease is a manner of service which is not honest and faithful," one memorandum told the troops, and it warned them that if they became infected they might have their good conduct medal suspended, be reduced in rank, or—the greatest threat of all—be placed "at the bottom of the rotation list." Medical officers issued condoms to soldiers when they left camp and reminded them that "Prophylactic Stations are in constant operation at all Battalion Aid Stations, and will be utilized by personnel even though the protection appliance has been worn."[107] Doctors tried other methods to control infection. "The officers in charge formed a special unit to treat these women," remembered Andersen, and "a task force was sent out to round up as many as possible for testing and treatment."[108] The introduction of penicillin offered an effective weapon against gonorrhea, though as one report noted, multiple courses of the drug were often necessary "to insure cessation of symptoms."[109] The Red Arrow also set up treatment stations close to the front to keep infected men fighting. "I was sent to work at one of these new units," wrote Andersen. "I had a ward tent with twenty patients. I had to sterilize needles and syringes, and sharpen needles for injections every three hours. This wouldn't have been so bad, but we were set up beside the artillery's eight-inch guns. Every time one of those guns went off it would nearly knock you off your feet."[110]

GIs highly prized furloughs to Manila. After the terrible battle that took place there in February and March, the "Pearl of the Orient" was little more than rubble. "Everything was in ruins," wrote journalist John Carlisle. He thought it particularly sad "that the once magnificent Roman Catholic Cathedral of Manila, first built in 1581 and five times destroyed by fire and earthquake, was again in ruins."[111] But the city healed. On his second visit to Manila, Myers noted that "quite a number of changes had taken place. Much of the rubble had been cleaned up and much building was going on."[112] Visiting GIs complained of Manila's sky-high prices. "We couldn't buy anything because the prices were out of this world," wrote Andersen.[113]

Nevertheless, the lure of Manila was too powerful to resist. Though war-torn and inflationary, it was the first major city the Red Arrowmen had visited since they left Australia two years earlier. In Manila they could go to clubs and restaurants, shop for souvenirs, or just explore. For some, Manila's pagodas, mazelike back streets, gardens, and cuisine satisfied their expectations of the East. At the same time, the city offered a sense of familiarity to the homesick soldier. "In the evening we walked up a sidewalk and were amazed at the neon lights and modern store fronts," wrote Andersen. "Theaters were open and people were lined up to see a show. Peanut vendors and popcorn stands lined the streets. Stands sold ice cream, ice cold root beer and orange drinks. It was the closest thing to home I had seen in two years." The army maintained a recreation center for the flood of GIs that inundated the city. "It is a nice clean camp," Andersen thought, "with wood floors in the tents and a nice large mess hall and shower. Philipino [sic] boys keep the place clean and wait on us."[114] The Red Cross and the USO had a strong presence too. By the end of 1945 Manila had six USO clubs. Some "were windowless and doorless with walls pock-marked by shell-fire," noted one USO report, but "at least there were chairs, coffee, hot dogs, some ice cream and movies."[115] Like peacetime tourists, GIs could even enjoy guided tours. "Trucks made a tour of the city so that we can see everything," Andersen wrote, and "a sight-seeing party took us to Corregidor."[116]

The attraction of Manila was so strong for the Red Arrow troops that while fighting on the Villa Verde Trail, the division offered a case of beer and a three-day pass there to any soldier who took a Japanese soldier alive. Sergeant Willie Brown of DeWitt, Arkansas, accomplished the task four times. "He is not much of a garrison soldier," claimed Carlisle, but at the front this grizzled veteran was "one of the best front-line platoon sergeants in the Southwest Pacific." Brown "doesn't care much for medals [or] citations," wrote John E. Jones, "except that beer and a three day pass." The first prisoner he took was playing dead in a cave after an attack. "I kept talking to him, telling him to come out, but he just lay there," Brown told Jones, "so I dug him a little in the leg with a knife and he opens one eye. . . . Jez, how I wanted to plug him. But then I kep' thinkin' about that beer and Manila." As Carlisle told the story, Brown offered the Japanese soldier "a piece of chocolate, a leftover from a K ration," a "drink out his canteen," and even "a lighted cigaret." The Japanese soldier finally "handed over his rifle and his saber," and "Willie got him to his feet and took him out of the cave." After his return from Manila, Brown took another prisoner. "The guys in my patrol tell me to bump this Nip off," Brown said, "but I know what Manila's like so I go in the cave and get him." In subsequent days he took two more prisoners, making him a darling of the press and a Red Arrow legend. "I don't want to hurt nobody," Brown told Jones. "All I want to do after this war is to go back home, get me a store and mind my own business."[117]

As the Thirty-Second Infantry Division recuperated on the shores of the Lingayen Gulf in June, the Japanese position in northern Luzon deteriorated rapidly. Krueger hoped to deal Yamashita and his Shobu Group the coup de grâce, and he developed a two-pronged campaign to do it. The main effort targeted the Cagayan Valley. The Thirty-Seventh Infantry Division, followed by the Sixth, was to advance up Highway 5 into the Cagayan Valley. At the same time, a force of eight hundred soldiers under Major Robert V. Connolly of the Thirty-Third Division was to press up the west coast of Luzon toward the port of Appari on the northern tip of the island. Dubbed the Connolly Task Force, it was made up of fragments from many

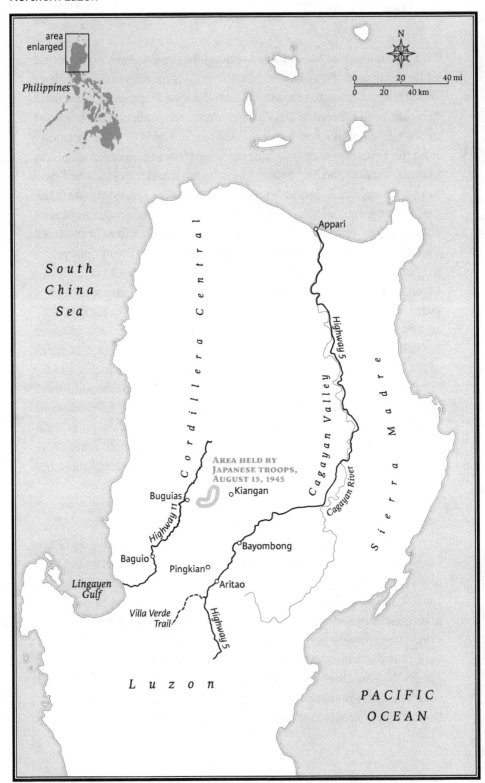

different units, from US Army Rangers to guerrilla forces. Among its constituent parts was Company G of the 127th Infantry Regiment, reinforced with a mortar platoon from Company H.

As the Thirty-Seventh Division surged forward on May 31, the Twenty-Fifth Division, as well as the members of the 126th Infantry Regiment still attached to it, set up checkpoints along Highway 5 to secure the communication line for the attack and sent out patrols to root out any Japanese remaining in the area. The GIs of the 126th Infantry Regiment found a few Japanese stragglers and called in artillery barrages on suspected concentrations. A few fights were sharp ones. On June 16 Companies E and F attacked a Japanese force on the Aritao-Pingkian Road, "killing 44 Japs," according to one report. The Red Arrow "suffered 9 killed and 11 wounded," and recovered "2 enemy HMG's, 6000 rounds of MG ammunition, 2 knee-mortars and 3 carbines abandoned along the road." The Japanese occasionally attacked as well. At 4:00 a.m. on June 4 "Japs made a banzia [sic] attack on Co C position," noted one report, killing four GIs. Most patrols reported meeting only small numbers of Japanese and many none at all. "A 1st Bn patrol killed three Japs and found a large quantity of rice," noted one report for June 23. "One Jap walked into the CP of Co C and surrendered. 2nd Bn patrols reported no enemy contacts."[118]

The Thirty-Seventh Division reached the heart of the Cagayan Valley by mid-June, and the Connolly Task Force took Appari on June 21. Reinforced with a contingent of paratroopers, Connolly then drove southward and on June 26 linked up with the Thirty-Seventh Division driving northward. American forces had now surrounded Yamashita in the Cordillera Central, but the Tiger of Malaya had no intention of surrendering. Instead, he planned to make a suicidal last stand in the mountains to occupy and chew up as many American units as he could. As Krueger's forces closed in on him, Yamashita reinforced strategic mountain passes and his men stripped the Cagayan Valley of food and materiel, even herding live carabao into their mountain redoubt. By early July Yamashita had an estimated fifty-two thousand fighters in the Cordillera Central and another thirteen thousand in the Sierra Madre on the other side of the valley.

On July 1, operations on Luzon passed from Krueger's Sixth Army to Eichelberger's Eighth, as the former prepared for the upcoming invasion of Japan set for November 1.[119] At the same time, the brass transferred the

Captain Stanley Pinomar of the 120th Field Artillery debriefs members of the 126th
Infantry Regiment and Filipino guerrillas after patrol in the Cagayan Valley, July 1945.
NATIONAL ARCHIVES

Thirty-Second Division from the Sixth to the Eighth, and Eichelberger
immediately put the Red Arrow back into action. It joined a collection
of units tasked with closing the ring around the Shobu Group. The Sixth
and Thirty-Seventh Divisions, along with Colonel Volckmann's guerrillas,
pressed in on Yamashita from the north. The Red Arrow took up positions
on the southern section of the pocket. The 126th Infantry Regiment remained along Highway 5. To their north, the 128th Infantry Regiment
operated out of Bayombong, while the 127th Infantry Regiment focused
on Highway 11 northeast of Baguio. The Red Arrow's mission was to locate
Japanese positions, destroy whatever troops and supplies they found, and
investigate civilian reports of Japanese activities. As combat operations resumed, yet another crop of replacements went into battle for the first time.
Donald Dill thought his reception by the division's veterans was "fine on
the surface" but understood that they viewed rookies like him "with cau-

tion or reservations until they found out what kind of people we were. . . . We expected, as replacements, to be more-or-less on trial."[120]

The mountains of the Cordillera Central were even higher than those along the Villa Verde Trail. "Highway 11 is a scenic mountain trail which twists and turns tortuously around and over the precipitous mountains of northern Luzon which reach heights of 8000 feet in several places," noted a 127th Infantry Regiment report. "Heavy rains cause continuous landslides in many places along the road making the problems of supply and evacuation of the wounded more acute."[121] Roy Campbell went on a long-range patrol. "The platoon made its way ever upward," he wrote, "traveling up a mountain stream and walking in the shallow water. . . . The usual heat of the Philippines didn't seem to penetrate the cool umbrella formed by the trees as [we] pushed [our] bodies higher and higher." At one point Campbell reached a mountaintop. "A beautiful green valley was visible below," he wrote, "with a river winding its way down the center like a silver thread . . . and to the right was another mountain even higher than the one [we] were on." The following day Campbell's patrol "started a long hike" up "a steep, narrow, winding trail, and even though [we] were in shape," he recalled a lot of "huffing and puffing, sweating and swearing." Farther along, the patrol came to "an even higher mountain range . . . looking dark and very sinister," and subsequent days meant more mountains where "only roots protruding from the rocks made it possible to climb" and valleys that were "almost totally obscured by fog."[122]

Many patrols found no Japanese at all. "On 2 July the Co E patrol scouted from Itogon to Millsite finding an abandoned aid station, 2 dead Japs, 14 50-gallon drums of oil, but no signs of activity," noted a 127th Infantry Regiment report, while "the Co I mountain-trail patrol advanced along high ground . . . investigating caves, finding numerous Jap graves and indications of a prevalence of dysentery."[123] Others found only stragglers and small groups. "We could tell the war was beginning to wind down," wrote Whayland Greene. "The Japs we were killing were not supplied real good and we were running into fewer and fewer all the time."[124] Roy Campbell's platoon attacked a Japanese camp, but he noticed that there was no return fire. When the platoon members moved in, they discovered that they had attacked "a small casual company of wounded." The Japanese soldiers "all had bandages on their bodies," Campbell remembered, "and most of the

Japs couldn't have fought even if they did have guns."[125] Charles "Tex" Dunnam claimed that "I never did fire my rifle [more than] two or three times all the time I was up there."[126]

However, in other instances Japanese troops still fought hard, laying ambushes, infiltrating American positions at night, and staging desperate banzai attacks. "Ninety to one hundred Japs are occupying well-prepared positions in this area and are putting up stiff resistance," noted one 127th Infantry Regiment report. "Artillery and mortars were placed on these positions and one platoon of Co K made a flanking movement to the right . . . where they received intense MG fire which forced them to withdraw, suffering 1 KIA and 2 WIA [wounded in action]."[127] Indeed, the brutal pattern of Pacific War fighting continued to the bitter end. "What the enemy lacked in organization," thought Henry Zabierek, "they compensated for with fanaticism."[128] Only a handful of Japanese surrendered and "the 32nd didn't take many prisoners," noted Jerry Angel. "Our guys killed every Jap they saw."[129]

By early August the Allies had confined Yamashita to a small bean-shaped area along the Agno River between the villages of Buguias and Kiangan, the latter location now the 128th Infantry Regiment's headquarters. The end of the campaign in northern Luzon seemed at hand. As it turned out, the entire war was about to end. As the Thirty-Second Division patrolled the wilds of the Cordillera Central on the morning of August 6, a B-29 bomber named *Enola Gay* dropped the first atomic bomb ever used in combat on the Japanese city of Hiroshima. When the Red Arrowmen first got the news, many did not fully appreciate the significance of the new weapon. "We did not get excited or feel like celebrating," Dean Andersen remembered. "This was just another bomb." On August 8, the Soviet Union declared war on Japan and Soviet troops raced across Manchuria to Korea. "We heard the good news today about Russia declaring war," John Walters wrote home. "Along with the news of our new bomb, it begins to look like this war may fold any day now. . . . I can't see what will keep them fighting."[130] The following day the United States dropped a second atomic bomb on Nagasaki, and anticipation of the war's end only grew. "The events seem too far beyond imagination to be true," Andersen wrote his parents. "It seems I have been dreaming."[131] As rumors of the war's end spread, the fighting men grew more cautious. "Mostly you didn't want to get wounded or killed while rumors of the war's end were everywhere," wrote Dill.[132]

Japan announced its intention to surrender on August 15, a date Americans dubbed V-J Day. In a letter to his wife and children, James Casteel described the moment he got the news. Casteel and about fifty other GIs were coming back from a patrol when the lieutenant in charge received a message and then suddenly shouted: "The war's over." But the men misheard. "We all [thought] he yelled—'Take Cover,'" Casteel wrote. "In about nothing flat . . . we had all dived for cover—but just the day before we had been fighting them like fury—so—do you blame us?"[133] Zabierek remembered that "few could fathom the report at first. . . . First there was relief. They had survived. No more war. Now thoughts could turn to family and girlfriends."[134] Andersen wrote to his fiancée, Marie, that "the men were stunned. A common expression was, 'I'll be damned!' or 'I can't believe it.' Most men here had decided that the Japs would fight to the last."[135] Others remembered more boisterous celebrations. "They brought beer and stuff up on the line," recalled William Painter.[136] According to John Walters, "most of us felt that our prayers had been answered."[137]

Unfortunately, the end of war for the Thirty-Second Division was still tantalizingly out of reach. "For a few days we were all very happy until we learned the Jap forces we were fighting had no intention of surrendering," wrote Whayland Greene.[138] "None of the Japs surrendered," wrote James Myers. "They intended to fight until the death."[139] A few days after V-J Day, Henry Zabierek recalled "a full-throated banzai charge" in which one American and forty-nine Japanese were killed.[140] The "never surrender" *bushido* ethic that animated Japanese military thinking motivated many to fight on. In other cases, Japanese soldiers did not know the war was over. Colonel Frank Murphy, the commander of the 127th Infantry Regiment, later learned that "it was 20 August before some of the Jap Units received word of Japan's capitulation." Major General Sato Bunzo, commander of the Fifty-Eighth Independent Mixed Brigade, told Murphy that "as they had no radio communication with Gen Yamashita's headquarters, word came from that point by runner."[141] To get the word out to their adversaries, American forces broadcast the surrender news to any Japanese with a radio. "Cub planes are being employed," noted one report, "to drop leaflets which tell of the surrender of Japan and advising the Japanese troops how to effect a surrender."[142] Foot soldiers spread leaftets too. "Company L patrol scattered leaflets along the trail and on trees in this area," noted a 127th Infantry Regiment report.[143] In some cases, the Americans even released Japanese prisoners and sent them back to their own lines to convince their comrades to give themselves up. Thus, the Red Arrow Division—after having fought the US Army's first major land battle of the Pacific back in 1942—was still in battle even after Japan announced its capitulation. "All of this left the men in a state of frustration and exasperation," recalled Zabierek. "Peace wasn't supposed to be like this."[144]

After August 15, patrols took on a strange quality. "The life and death choices that the company leaders had had to make throughout the war became more difficult than ever," Zabierek wrote. "Selecting men for patrols put them in harm's way [when] just days ago the war seemed over and men had expressed gratitude for surviving it. How silly it all seemed now." One squad leader told Zabierek and his comrades that "as much as we may hate them, they should be allowed to surrender peacefully." Zabierek remembered one patrol during which the GIs surrounded a group of unarmed Japanese sitting around a campfire, who promptly threw up their hands. "They were startled, malnourished, and pitiful," Zabierek thought, "almost bringing about sympathy." A little while later the patrol located another group. "One of the enemy reached for his gun," wrote Zabierek, and the GIs responded with "a fusillade of bullets." The remainder surrendered. After taking these captives, Zabierek's company experienced a banzai attack a few nights later. "It became eerie," he wrote. "By day [we] had rounded up a group of hapless enemy soldiers. Yet at night [we] were bracing against attacks that were as fanatical as before."[145]

Japanese troops debated what to do. On August 26, two Japanese turned themselves in to the 127th Infantry Regiment. They reported that "45 of them started coming in to surrender but were fired on by a detachment of Nips commanded by a Captain. Three or more were killed and the rest fled into the hills."[146] A patrol of the 127th Infantry Regiment discovered "an undated, unsigned message written in Japanese" claiming "the Japs there could not surrender until they got authority from their CO," but once their commander could "confirm the surrender they would enter American positions waving a white flag."[147] According to Whayland Greene, one patrol went out with "a note in English and some cigarettes and candy bars" to entice the Japanese into surrendering. As soon as the patrol made contact, the Japanese began shooting at them, so the GIs left the peace offering and withdrew. The next day Greene's patrol discovered the candy and cigarettes were gone. "We were carrying a white flag," Greene recalled, and "just a little piece up the hill, we could see some heads look out around some trees. They did not fire." The GIs coaxed the Japanese out into the open. "In five minutes," Greene said, "we were smoking cigarettes, laughing, and trying to talk." The Japanese told Greene's patrol to return the next day to speak with an officer, and when they did the officer said that he and his men could not surrender "until they got direct orders from Gen. Yamashita."[148]

As these final patrols played out, Yamashita arranged for a formal surrender. Negotiations began with an American observation pilot who had been shot down over Japanese-held territory on August 8—perhaps the only American the Japanese took prisoner during the entire northern Luzon campaign. After word came of the Japanese capitulation, Yamashita sent the pilot back to American lines. That pilot then flew over Yamashita's camp and dropped a letter from General Gill suggesting that the two leaders enter surrender discussions, and panels to display in a particular fashion if he agreed to do so. The following day an American pilot saw the panels laid out as instructed and dropped a second letter from Gill telling Yamashita to send a delegation to American lines. On August 26, a Japanese officer and a small party of enlisted men delivered a message from Yamashita to an outpost of the 128th Infantry Regiment near Kiangan. In it, Yamashita said he had stopped hostile action but had not yet received surrender instructions from Tokyo. His letter was exceptionally respectful and polite. "I also wish to add at this point the expression of my heartfelt gratitude to you," Yamashita wrote, "fully cognizant of the sincere efforts and deep concern you have continuously shown with reference to the cessation of hostilities as evidenced by the various steps and measures taken in this connection." In his memoir, Eichelberger observed that "in the Japanese military character there is a combination of exquisite courtesy and utter savagery, which I understand but am at a loss to explain."[149]

Radio communication was spotty in the jungled mountains, so Gill used messages delivered by Cub planes to keep in contact with Yamashita. On August 30, one of the planes crashed, leading to the tragic death of one of the longest-serving members of the Thirty-Second Division, Colonel Merle Howe. The World War I veteran and Grand Rapids high school teacher had led a company in the Michigan National Guard when the Red Arrow first mobilized back in 1940. Howe was in the observer seat in the front of the plane, and when it crashed he took the brunt of the impact. He died instantly. After having survived combat from Buna to the Villa Verde Trail, Howe died in an accident just days before the war's official end. Yamashita informed Gill of Howe's death: "Col. Howe died in the line of duty. In view of the unchanging zeal and friendship, from start to finish, with which the late Col. Howe served and distinguished himself in the present negotiations between the Japanese and American armies, I on behalf of the entire Imperial Japanese Army and myself, express our deepest condolence."[150] Gill later said that "Colonel Howe was one of the most outstanding combat officers in the division, there's no question about that."[151] General Eichelberger shared Gill's sentiments. "The onetime schoolteacher whose blue language appalled rough-spoken sergeants, the driving leader who helped make the Buna victory possible, was not to go home to his native Middle West," Eichelberger wrote. "I never knew a more determined or courageous fighter."[152]

The Japanese formally surrendered to McArthur on the deck of the USS *Missouri* in Tokyo Bay on September 2, 1945. That same day, Yamashita and his staff appeared at a predesignated meeting point on a hilltop near Kiangan. There to meet him was a small party led by a Wisconsin man, Lieutenant Russell Baumann of the 128th Infantry Regiment—the first Red Arrow unit to go into battle against Japan at Buna on November 19, 1942. "It was entirely fitting that the 32nd Division should receive the vanquished enemy," Eichelberger later wrote. "Three years before at Buna they had won the battle that started the infantry on the jungle road to Tokyo."[153] Yamashita was "attired in a clean but worn uniform and wearing his sword and ribbons," reported John Carlisle, and "appeared to be in good health in spite of his loss of weight."[154] Baumann led the general to the Company I command post, and from there Yamashita went to a schoolhouse in Kiangan where he met Major General Robert S. Beightler, commander of the newly formed Luzon Area Command, which had taken over combat operations on the island on August 20. The next day Yamashita was in Baguio where a formal ceremony took place. In attendance was Britain's Lieutenant General Arthur Percival, who surrendered Singapore to Yamashita in 1942, and Lieutenant General Jonathan Wainwright, who gave up Corregidor months later. Not present was General Gill, who was on his way back to the United States. After having led the Red Arrow since 1943, "I was in pretty poor physical condition," he later admitted. "I'd lost an awful lot of weight" and the months of combat "had been a terrific strain."[155] Brigadier General Robert B. McBride Jr., the Red Arrow's artillery chief, assumed command of the division.

With Yamashita's formal surrender, his officers and men now laid down their weapons. When they did, the Red Arrowmen found the Japanese soldiers docile and compliant—a remarkable contrast to their battlefield behavior. Whayland Greene thought the Japanese "were very humble to the point that you could not believe the way they were just a few days before."[156] Henry Zabierek thought them stunned and disbelieving. "They had never envisioned being captured," he wrote. "Given the savage nature

General Yamashita (far left), soon after his surrender to the Red Arrow at Kiangan on September 2, 1945. WISCONSIN NATIONAL GUARD, US ARMY SIGNAL CORPS PHOTO

of the war, they fully expected to be shot."[157] Tex Dunnam remembered that the Japanese "offered no resistance whatsoever, and as they came in they threw their rifles, hand grenades, pistols, sabers, machine guns, and everything [into] a pile."[158] For some GIs, wartime hatreds dissipated. "When I finally met them," thought Donald Dill, "I found them amazingly like myself. This did not square with the propaganda we heard."[159] Dill even remembered that "Japanese officers autographed a $2.00 bill in my photo album," and he claimed he was "proud that these men had peaceably turned themselves in and had not perished in the mountains of Luzon far from their homes because of a misunderstanding." As Greene noted, "after that they weren't Japs anymore, they were Japanese soldiers. The hate was gone just that quick."[160] Not all Red Arrowmen were so forgiving. Dill recalled a sergeant he believed to be a Buna veteran who had "such bitter memories of the fighting" that he "refused to even talk with the Japanese."[161]

In the weeks following the formal surrender the number of Japanese turning themselves in grew precipitously. "From the 11th to 13th of September," noted a 127th Infantry Regiment report, "1036 Japs surrendered to the RCT [regimental combat team]."[162] The division constructed stockades for the growing number of prisoners. Dill described the Red Arrow camp at Kiangan as "lined with tents filled with surrendered Japanese stretching from mountain side to mountain side."[163] Those needing medical attention soon overwhelmed the division's doctors and medics. "There were about 50,000 to go through our hospital," recalled medic Dean Andersen, but "we could handle only so many a day."[164]

After the Japanese surrender, the 127th Infantry Regiment interrogated General Sato and his officers about their perspectives on the last months of the war. "The Japanese still thought they were fighting the 33d," noted the regimental historical report, "but were aware that a new unit had been thrown against them that was far superior in tactics to the one previously opposing them." The report further stated that "Japanese officers were aware of the 32d Division's reputation as good mountain fighters."[165] Perhaps Sato and his men were simply ingratiating themselves with their captors, but Yamashita offered unsolicited praise of the Red Arrow. "General Yamashita indicated that he considered the 32nd Division the best his troops encountered both on Leyte and Luzon," wrote General Krueger. "He also mentioned the 38th Division favorably and expressed admiration for the end run of the 1st Cavalry Division to Manila."[166] The Thirty-Second Division was not accustomed to such praise. Thrown into battle unprepared in Papua back in 1942, the National Guard division had endured years of disrespect and scorn from the leaders of its own army—including the acid tongue of MacArthur himself—despite its victory there and in every subsequent fight. But after three years of battling the Japanese, the Thirty-Second Division had gained the respect of its tough, hard-bitten adversaries—and in war, that may be the most important praise of all.

CHAPTER 11

THE RED ARROW AND THE RISING SUN

"This morning we got the wonderful news that the war was over," John Walters wrote to his wife, Jewell, on V-J Day, and although he was clearly elated, the news also left him troubled. "When will I get to go home?" he wondered, and "will I have to be one of the occupation troops?" Those two questions, Walters wrote, have "a lot of us on edge."[1] The Thirty-Second Infantry Division had been on active duty since October 1940. In five years, it had served on three continents and fought in five substantial campaigns and several minor ones. Few organizations in the US armed forces had served longer or sacrificed more. But the Red Arrow had one last duty to perform: the occupation of Japan. After the war, the US transformed Japan from a militaristic enemy into a democratic and demilitarized ally. It was surely important work, but after the long and bloody years of fighting, most Red Arrowmen had a single overarching desire: to go home. In October 1945, the Thirty-Second Division began its sixth year of active service, and its final task of World War II, in the homeland of its longtime adversary, Japan, the Land of the Rising Sun.

FACING: Albert Jackson of East Jordan, Michigan, and Michael Mikula of Detroit, in the Cagayan Valley. By the time Japan surrendered, both of these Red Arrow soldiers had served forty months overseas. WISCONSIN NATIONAL GUARD, US ARMY SIGNAL CORPS PHOTO

With combat in the Luzon mountains finally over, the Thirty-Second Infantry Division returned to General Walter Krueger's Sixth Army and gathered along the shores of the Lingayen Gulf to prepare for the movement to Japan. Before leaving the island, the division experienced an accelerated turnover in personnel. Hundreds of replacements fresh from basic training arrived as veterans went home in increasing numbers. In May 1945, the War Department implemented a uniform rotation policy. Each soldier received an Adjusted Service Rating Score based on four criteria. They received one point for every month of service after September 1940, one point for each month served overseas, and five points for every campaign credit or combat decoration. Parenthood weighed most heavily of all. Soldiers received twelve points for each child under the age of eighteen, up to a limit of three.

At first the policy applied only to soldiers in Europe, where combat had ended, and the number of points needed for rotation was eighty-five. With the end of the war in September, the army applied the policy globally and dropped the point threshold to eighty. Much to the chagrin of GIs, any service after September 2, 1945, did not apply to their rating score. "Those first to leave were loaded on trucks and freight cars and were gone so quickly we couldn't believe the army could act that fast," wrote Monte Howell, who had not yet accumulated eighty points. "No fanfare, no farewell party, no thank you for the four years out of your life. Just be thankful you lived thru it."[2]

GIs who had served together for months or years under the most difficult circumstances imaginable now parted ways. It was an emotional time as Henry Zabierek described:

> Those who had fought through the nightmare that was New Guinea, the savagery of Leyte, and the ferocity of Luzon had forged relationships that truly defined the meaning of friendship. Now they were as ill at ease as a swain on his first date in determining how they would take leave of one another. . . . They contented themselves with slaps on the back, friendly taps on the biceps, and occasional handshakes. They had seen so much of each other. They knew everything about

one another. Now they would probably never see one another again. But they didn't know how to say good-bye.[3]

Among those departing in early fall 1945 was Dean Andersen, who had joined the Red Arrow in Australia in 1943. The combat medic was glad to be going home, despite the "miserable" sixteen-hour overnight train trip to the redeployment center in Manila. "We rode in box cars," he wrote later, "packed so close that we hardly had room to sit."[4] Also leaving was Roy Campbell, one of only a handful who could still remember the days of Camp Beauregard back in 1940. Campbell had become something of a legend in the division, and as he gathered his gear he "noticed that all the men wanted to help [me] carry [my] bags." They escorted Campbell to his waiting truck, tossed the bags into it, and watched as the vehicle kicked up dust and pulled away, Campbell joyously shouting: "I'm going home." He felt proud to be "the only man to serve the whole war with Company B."[5]

In Manila, Andersen and Campbell joined thousands of others going home. "We turned in our records and grabbed a bunk," wrote Andersen. Soldiers were grouped with others headed to the same region of the United States, and not by unit. "We had to leave our company friends and be with complete strangers," Andersen later wrote.[6] The wait for a troopship could last anywhere from days to weeks, and sometimes more than a month. Before departing, Campbell caught one last USO show. "When the band started to play," he wrote, "a skinny little man in a World War I uniform came out," and when he "introduced himself as Irving Berlin" Campbell thought "it couldn't get any better than this." After the show Campbell lay down on his cot and "felt for the first time in years" that he would "live through the damned war."[7] Many GIs, according to Andersen, "talked about how anxious they were to get on their way," but he also admitted that "most of us were a little scared that we would not be the same ourselves and we were afraid of seeing the changes that we might find when we arrived home."[8]

Sooner or later the troops boarded ships and sailed back across the ocean they had traversed years before. Andersen landed in Los Angeles. "We were met in the harbor by a welcoming small craft with lights and banners and spraying water hoses," he wrote, as well as "big band music" blaring from loudspeakers.[9] Campbell, who suffered a bout of food poisoning on ship, landed at San Diego. Medics tried to load him onto a stretcher but he insisted on going down the gangplank under his own power. "I walked onto the boat when I went overseas," he said, "and I'm gonna walk onto my land coming back." Campbell "staggered like a drunk down the plank" and when he reached terra firma he "motioned for the stretcher." On the train from the docks Campbell looked out the window and saw "people leaning out of factory windows, cheering and waving handkerchiefs. The men on the train returned the waves, shouting just as loudly."[10]

From the West Coast, the returnees went to a separation center near their home of record. There the soon-to-be-ex-soldiers received a physical examination to document any service-connected medical problems. The filing of disability claims began. The army counseled soldiers on their transition to civilian life and briefed them about the benefits available to them, like the new GI Bill of Rights that offered unemployment compensation, home and business loans, and educational opportunities. Soldiers got a new uniform festooned with all the decorations they had earned during the war. At Camp McCoy, Roy Campbell's new uniform included "tech sergeant stripes, the seven overseas hash stripes for longevity, the bars for battle, and everything else . . . including the presidential citations and combat infantry badge," as well as "a large red arrow for the left shoulder." The shiny, colorful uniform hanging from his bunk attracted lots of attention in the barracks. "Soon entire groups came to stare," he recalled, "trying to figure out what all of the bars meant; Purple Hearts and Bronze Stars received the most interest."[11] Finally, the GIs endured a "departure ceremony" to mark their official separation from the army. "When the speeches were concluded and decorations issued," wrote historian John C. Sparrow, "the separatees filed past the officer in charge to receive their discharge certificates."[12] They were civilians again.

From the separation centers, the ex-soldiers received a train or bus ticket home. Iowan Dean Andersen left Fort Leavenworth and met his fiancée, Marie, in Cedar Rapids. "I took her in my arms," Andersen wrote. "This was the moment I wanted to celebrate my homecoming and the end to the awful war." By Thanksgiving he was back in his hometown of Nora Springs. "It was a real homecoming," he recalled. "We had Thanksgiving dinner with my folks. I was with my loved ones and never wanted to leave again."[13]

Roy Campbell departed Camp McCoy five years to the day after he enlisted and hitchhiked to Eau Claire. Along the way he enjoyed the landscape of his native Badger State, the "green fields, cows munching along rolling hills, the farms and cities," and thought "the scenery hadn't changed one bit." Once in Eau Claire, Campbell was walking toward his house when his niece spotted him on the street and "at the top of her lungs" announced his presence. "People suddenly appeared from the homes," he wrote, and then "aunts and uncles, cousins, and then . . . mother and father all came exploding" out the front door of his house. "Ma stood with tears in her eyes," Campbell wrote, "unable to speak. She grabbed [me] in a big bear hug and wouldn't let [me] loose" until his father, fighting back tears, joined in. Campbell walked into his house, put down his bags, and "with a plop sat down in an easy chair." He tried to control his emotions but choked up when he heard his mother "rattling pans as she started to cook for her youngest son." Campbell turned to his father and said, "Dad, it was one hell of a trip!"[14]

On V-J Day, President Harry S. Truman named General Douglas MacArthur the Supreme Commander for the Allied Powers (SCAP) in Japan, a term that also applied to MacArthur's entire command. Unlike Germany, where each of the four major victorious Allied powers controlled a portion of the country, the occupation of Japan was almost exclusively an American endeavor. Washington's instructions to MacArthur came in the form of the Initial Post-Surrender Policy, a document that outlined two main goals for the occupation: democratization and demilitarization. MacArthur arrived in Tokyo on September 8 and went right to work laying the foundations of a new Japan. He kept the existing government in place, though purged of militarist leaders and under tight SCAP supervision. Within months, two American armies totaling more than four hundred thousand troops had taken up positions around the country. General Robert Eichelberger's Eighth Army took control of Japan from Tokyo northward. Krueger's Sixth Army, which included the Red Arrow, occupied the southern part of the country. The army planned to demobilize the Sixth Army within months and turn over all occupation duties to Eichelberger's Eighth.[15]

After years of ferocious and bitter fighting across the Pacific, Americans from MacArthur on down to the ordinary foot soldier were unsure how the Japanese people would receive them. Given the *bushido* military mentality, some feared that rogue units and leaders might not accept the occupation and would fight on, or that underground resistance movements would take root. Not knowing what to expect, US forces entered Japan combat-ready, and a contingent of the Red Arrow soldiers was among the first to go in. On September 4—just two days after Japan's formal surrender—US planes flew into the Japanese air base at Kanoya on the southernmost island of Kyushu to lay the groundwork for the arrival of occupation troops. Providing security for the Kanoya Air Task Force was the First Battalion of the 127th Infantry Regiment. "Immediately on landing," noted the regimental history, "the Battalion started its assigned mission of securing and defending the Kanoya Airdrome," setting up a security perimeter around the field. "They dropped us three at a time," recalled William Painter, "out of a truck with a .30 caliber machine gun set up on a tripod at a crossroad intersection." The regimental operations report noted that "motorized patrols reconnoitered the road net from Company front to Coast for the purpose of observing any enemy troop concentrations." The battalion experienced no resistance, but its members were still uneasy. "In the daytime you saw nothing," Painter recalled, "but at night you heard cart wheels moving all the time. . . . We were scared to death."[16]

It soon became evident that there would be no resistance. American troops, many of whom expected to arrive in Japan under a cloud of hot lead, instead arrived in peace. The rest of the Red Arrow departed the Philippines for Japan during the second week of October. But before they arrived, they rolled into a typhoon en route. "The weather gods were angry," recalled Monte Howell. "Giant waves were breaking over the top deck, [and the] trucks chained down on the top deck [were] being washed away." As giant waves hit his ship, Howell noticed that "the rivets, which hold the ship together, were breaking off and exploding/ricocheting around the lower deck." He thought it ironic that "after three years of war we were all going to drown in this stupid storm."[17] But the tempest passed and the remainder of the voyage was calm. Troops received lectures on Japan, its geography, and its culture. "The obvious condition noticed aboard ship was the very high morale," claimed one report. "Many of these men had made previous boat trips and landings under enemy fire with enemy aircraft and kami-kaze planes screeching overhead. To them this trip seemed like a pleasure cruise."[18]

The convoy arrived at Sasebo, Kyushu, on October 14, and the troops got their first glimpses of Japan from the decks of their transports. Sasebo was a major Japanese naval base, and during the war it was a frequent target of American bombers. "The city had been hard hit," John Walters wrote to Jewell and Jane, "and the engineers were hard-pressed cleaning up the roadways so we would get our equipment ashore."[19] Surveying the harbor, Walters noted a once-familiar sight that now struck him as odd. "Tonight, the many lights from the city shown brightly," he wrote, "the 1st lighted city I have seen since leaving the states." The scene evoked a deep emotional response in him. "Looking shoreward at the lights made me very lonely for you and Jane," he wrote. "It seems so much like home to see a city all lighted up after so many months of darkness."[20] The GIs stayed on their ships for several days and then debarked. "The landing was uneventful, but weird," thought Henry Zabierek. "There seemed to be no Japanese in sight. Those who were seen were far away, and they quickly

The Red Arrow arrives in Sasebo, Japan, October 1945. NATIONAL ARCHIVES

scurried for cover." Zabierek's company then marched to their barracks two miles inland, a movement that apparently did not go well. "Men in battle are not judged by their marching cadence," he wrote, and "most had not paraded since basic training."[21]

The Thirty-Second Division replaced the Fifth Marine Division, which had taken up the initial occupation duties on Kyushu three weeks earlier. The 127th Infantry Regiment—less the one battalion at Kanoya—remained in Sasebo for the time being, but the other elements of the division fanned out to duty stations across northern Kyushu and southern Honshu. The 126th Infantry Regiment took up positions around the industrial city of Kokura on the northern tip of Kyushu. The 128th Infantry Regiment made its headquarters at Yamaguchi, on the southern tip of Honshu. In early November the 127th—reunited with the First Battalion from Kanoya— traveled to Fukuoka, an important port on the Tsushima Strait separating Japan and Korea.

Once at their duty stations, the Red Arrow units established outposts and sent out security patrols. "Outposts were set up in the hills," noted a report of the 127th Infantry Regiment, and "all military installations, air-fields, public utilities, communication and transportation facilities were placed under surveillance."[22] Units made their headquarters at various Japanese military bases, in factories, or in other such places with sufficient spaces for offices, barracks, and vehicles. For example, the First Battalion of the 128th Infantry Regiment moved into the grounds of the Kobe Seke Iron Works in Chofu. "The building selected for the Battalion Headquar-ters was a large, two story office building," noted one report. "It was an ideal building, that boasted of steam heat, hot and cold running water, serviceable latrines, electric lights and a sufficient number of rooms to provide both office and living quarters for headquarters company and the entire compliment of battalion officers."[23] The 107th Medical Battalion moved into a former Japanese military hospital at Yamaguchi. The medi-cal officers thought it a "splendid location," but "a great deal of work was necessary to bring the area up to our standards of sanitation and comfort. The grounds have been cleaned and rearranged, new landscaping has been done and many of the buildings have been repaired and remodeled."[24]

The new quarters offered comforts far beyond anything the Thirty-Second Division had experienced overseas. Throughout its five years of active duty, the division had rarely slept in anything other than tents and foxholes. Not since their brief stay at Fort Devens, Massachusetts, back in 1942 had the Red Arrow troops enjoyed four solid walls and a roof over their heads. "The men found the barracks to their liking," wrote Zabierek. "Sheets and mattresses had not been a staple at their recent addresses. Being told that these quarters once housed kamikaze pilots might have been numbing at first, but then came the realization that these suicide pilots received special treatment. Theirs was no ordinary housing."[25] The GIs described their new quarters in rapturous letters home. "We are in barracks, 4 men to a room," John Walters wrote from Sasebo. "We have six drawers for our clothes, toilet articles and such. We are sleeping on our cots but all in all it looks like it will be a good setup." He was especially pleased with "windows galore—sliding ones to the outside and the same kind facing the long hall that runs from one end of the building to the other end."[26]

Not all were so impressed their new digs. "We were given an old abandoned factory to live in," recalled Monte Howell. "The only problem was it had no heat, no toilets and no water or electricity and we had no blankets" and "all they could tell us was, you are engineers, get to work and build whatever you need." Howell found humor in the fact that the army had given such bad accommodations at a place named Fukuoka. "We laughed at the name," he wrote, "as we thought the army had done it to us again."[27] The 126th Infantry Regiment reported that housing "seemed to be a never ending problem," but "procurement of Japanese supplies soon made it possible for units to be equipped with hot water heaters, dish-washing sinks, built-in ranges and room-heating stoves." The report also noted that "some companies procured chinaware so that mess kits could be dispensed with."[28]

The GIs remained concerned about possible Japanese resistance—though the GIs carried their own lingering animosities as well. "After fighting the Japs for nearly four years I was in no mood to coddle them," asserted James Myers.[29] As the soldiers of the 126th Infantry Regiment were instructed, "all operations will be planned and conducted in such a manner that forces are constantly prepared for combat, in the event of resumption of hostilities, treachery, or sabotage."[30] A 127th Infantry Regiment report noted that the men "were constantly prepared for combat," and "during the initial phases of the operation care was exercised not to decentralize our force to the point that we would endanger our security in the event of attack."[31] The occupation forces were careful not to provoke any incidents. "Strict fire discipline will be maintained by commanders of all echelons," declared one field order, and "the gravity of premature use of fire power in the execution of occupation missions will be impressed upon all individuals."[32] American forces took steps to demonstrate their authority without appearing too threatening. "The strictest observance of military courtesy and discipline," noted one report, was "an absolute necessity," and "special emphasis was placed upon the treatment of the civilian population so as to develop respect for, and confidence in, the United Nations and their representatives."[33]

At first the occupation troops were surprised to find Japanese civilians largely cooperative, though aloof. "As we rode thru [Sasebo] most of the grown ups ignored us or looked at us with stone faces," wrote John Walters soon after his arrival there.[34] But before long many Japanese civilians not only appeared to accept the occupation but welcome it. "Fear of the enemy was giving way to a curiosity about the occupiers," wrote Zabierek.[35] Walters described the rail trip from Sasebo to Fukuoka in a letter to his wife, Jewell. "Every time we stopped," he wrote, the rural populace "gathered like flys—and we tossed them candy, gum, cigarettes, and C rations. They welcomed the gifts. It's probably the first candy they'd had for years."[36] Having prepared for the worst, the troops were relieved. "No evidence of sabotage or action against the occupation has come to light," noted the 128th Infantry Regiment. "All civilians have been friendly and answered questions readily." In fact, the "people in the country and the city . . . appear very cheerful," the report continued. "They teach the children to say 'Hello' and 'Goodbye' and the kids welcome a jeep with these cries."[37] Howell suspected that Japanese civilians "were glad the war was over," though he added that because of the heavy firebombing Japan endured during the war, "they hate anyone who was in the Air Force."[38]

American attitudes soon softened as well. "After watching them as we rode thru [Sasebo] it makes me feel sorry for them," Walters wrote. "They look almost as bad as the Filipinos." Children often served as the bridge between former adversaries. Walters found it touching to see "the little babies strapped on their mothers back, sleeping with their little heads & arms & legs flopping around. . . . Every time I see a little baby it reminds me of Jane when she was small—and of course I get terribly lonesome for her."[39] William Painter recalled one patrol when he and other GIs stopped for lunch outside of a small village. "We were all sitting there," he said, "and here came this little girl. She was probably four [and] wasn't a bit afraid of us." The GIs were instantly smitten. "We gave her chocolate bars" and "put a helmet on her and a gun belt" and "she was cutting up and having a good time." The GIs then noticed "about ten women" standing in the distance. "They were letting us know that they didn't want any harm coming to the little girl." The men took back their gear and sent her on her way. "She didn't want to go back, but she did," recalled Painter.[40] As one report noted, "It became apparent very early in the occupation that American troops do not harbor any deep, unforgiving hatred," and "in fact quite the contrary seems to be the case."[41]

Mistrust of the Japanese remained in some quarters of the Red Arrow, often fed by Western racial stereotypes of Asians as treacherous and deceitful. "Since it is the inborn trait of the Japanese people to conceal their

Children often bridged the gap between former adversaries. Here, Henry Meras of the 128th Infantry Regiment learns a little Japanese with the help of children in Sasebo, Japan, in October 1945. NATIONAL ARCHIVES

emotions, it is difficult to analyze their true feelings toward the occupation," claimed a 127th Infantry Regiment report. "At times these people seem over cooperative in executing orders and over generous in presenting gifts to the soldiers. They behave as though we were their liberators and not the conquerors." However, "the cooperative and pleasant attitude shown by the Japanese people may be but a mask for their true feelings," the report went on. "They may sincerely dislike the occupation but accept it as unavoidable, and their apparent docile attitude may merely be an instrument used through their own common sense for their personal well being."[42] A 128th Infantry Regiment report complained that "for the most part the average American has apparently forgotten that we was [sic] at war with the Japanese less than six months ago," arguing that "the Japanese have never become aware of the monstrous crime of which their nation is guilty. Our attitude has been such that the Japanese quite logically feel that they were the victims of some very bad luck, but that no one blames them for it."[43]

Despite worries over Japanese resistance, the Thirty-Second Infantry Division reported only a handful of threatening acts. A 126th Infantry Regiment report described one incident:

> On the 19th of November a CIC [Counterintelligence Corps] representative encountered two Japanese fishermen, one carrying a machete, on a narrow trail. . . . On nearing the Jap changed the machete from his left hand to his right hand and blocked the path. The CIC man drew his pistol and forced them to move aside. No attempt was made on his part to arrest either of them. An investigation was made by the provost marshall in the area later the same day and he found no indications of unrest evinced by the population. . . . Since the occurrence of this incident, periodic patrols have been conducted through the area with out discovering suspicious actions on the part of the Japanese.[44]

The regimental journal recorded another occasion in which a lone soldier was guarding an arsenal warehouse near Kokura when "three [Japanese] civilians attempted to gain entrance into the building." One of them "spoke good English and insulted the guard, saying that he would return later and use force to enter the building." Being alone, the soldier was unable to make an arrest. However, the jounal noted that after the incident, "the guard has now been increased to five men."[45]

Not all perceived threats turned out to be acts of aggression. For example, on the fourth anniversary of Pearl Harbor, members of the 128th Infantry Regiment responded to what they thought was a riot of "an estimated 100 Japs" on a college campus. An armed detail rushed to the scene, according to the regimental journal, and medics were "alerted to have men ready to move out in case of emergency." The precautions were unnecessary. The commotion was not a riot at all, but "students who were celebrating before going home on Christmas vacation."[46]

For Red Arrow troops, occupation duties varied. One mission was to maintain law and order. Japanese civil police conducted everyday law enforcement activities, such as traffic control and crime prevention, but they did so under the close supervision of American MPs. The 105-member Thirty-Second Military Police Platoon was so overwhelmed by the breadth of this task that it deputized soldiers from other Red Arrow units to help. Red Arrowmen also were on the lookout for Allied prisoners of war. The First Battalion of the 127th Infantry Regiment liberated scores of prisoners when it arrived at Kanoya on September 4. The physical condition of prisoners after years of brutality and deprivation shocked William Painter. "A lot of them didn't have shirts," or "one leg of the pants would be torn off," Painter remembered. He also noted that there were "sores all over them. Their ribs were sticking out. They were gaunt." Painter thought they looked like "walking dead people."[47] Most Allied prisoners had already been liberated by the time the main body of the Thirty-Second Division arrived in October, though patrols occasionally came across the graves of Allied personnel who had perished in Japan during the war. In January 1946, for example, a team from the 127th Infantry Regiment on the island of Ikishima discovered the graves of two American airmen who had been shot down.[48]

The Thirty-Second Infantry Division played an important role in the postwar repatriation of displaced peoples. By the end of the war there were approximately 6.5 million Japanese nationals scattered across Asia and the Pacific—3.5 million soldiers and sailors in faraway lands ranging from Manchuria to Singapore to New Guinea, and another 3 million civilians who had settled in parts of the Japanese empire but who now faced intense persecution at the hands of the people Japan had attempted to colonize. All were to be brought to the home islands. Meanwhile, there were more than 2 million foreign laborers in Japan—the vast majority brought there forcibly—who wanted to go home. Most of these workers, about 1.35 million, were Koreans. The Japanese government administered the repatriation effort. It mobilized the remnants of its merchant and naval fleets to transport Japanese nationals back to the home islands and established processing centers at major ports to receive them. US occupation officials closely monitored the process. The Sixth and Eighth Armies "established troop detachments at each of the reception centers," noted General MacArthur's postwar report, "so that close supervision over the Japanese could be exercised."[49]

Japanese nationals—soldiers and civilians alike—typically returned penniless, malnourished, and suffering from diseases like cholera and smallpox. Thousands died before they ever reached home. The ships that brought in the Japanese nationals then transported Korean, Chinese, and other foreign laborers back to their home countries. But the Japanese government prioritized the return of its own citizens and gave far less attention to those who were trying to leave the country. As a result, the movement of foreign nationals out of Japan was messy and chaotic. Foreign nationals flocked to the ports, but the Japanese government made virtually no provisions for their care. "The Koreans were without shelter," reported the First Battalion of the 128th Infantry Regiment at Shimonoseki. "Thousands were living in the railway station, more in an abandoned warehouse, still others under a fishing wharf, some in makeshift shelters scattered along the streets, and a large number in the streets themselves. The absolute filth in which they were living was indescribable. There were no latrines provided whatsoever. The area was literally filled with human excrement."[50] Desperate repatriates turned to the black market and petty thievery to survive. The Second Battalion of the 128th Infantry Regiment in southern Honshu reported that "five Chinese and one Korean attempted to steal stores of raw rubber and other items from an occupation force dump near Iwakuni."[51] Disturbances broke out between foreign nationals and Japanese civilians, and when Japanese police could not control the disturbances, Red Arrow MPs showed up to restore order. The First

Battalion of the 128th Infantry Regiment called the thousands of repatriates flooding into Shimonoseki "one of the single biggest problems that
confronted us."[52]

Occupation authorities stepped in and thoroughly reorganized the
repatriation system. The Red Arrow established its own processing centers
for foreign nationals across the division's zone of responsibility to gather
the repatriates and control the flow of humanity to the ports. The 126th
Infantry Regiment established a center at Tobata that could accommodate
two thousand people. "Upon arrival, the repatriates were given a physical
examination, a delousing, and immunization shots," noted a regimental
operations report, and "when a sufficient number had gathered there, they
were transported by train to Fukuoka under the guard of US Army personnel."[53] The Red Arrowmen improved conditions at the ports as well. At
Shimonoseki, the 128th Infantry Regiment ordered the Japanese "to clean
up the area, to establish medical inspections, furnish adequate food, repair
old warehouses for satisfactory shelter, and construct adequate latrines,"
and "in a few weeks, a deplorable situation was made into a very efficient
and well supervised repatriation center."[54]

By February 1946 more than 800,000 foreign nationals (630,000 of
them Koreans) had returned to their home countries, while 1.5 million
Japanese nationals had landed in the home islands.[55] The flow of repatriates peaked in 1946, but the great movement of displaced peoples across
Asia and the Pacific would continue into the 1950s. In supervising this
massive migration, Red Arrowmen witnessed many heartbreaking scenes,
though there were life-affirming moments too. At the Tobata repatriation
center "a Korean woman gave birth to a healthy son," noted a 126th Infantry Regiment report, "with an anxious Signal Corps Captain working as
head assistant to the Japanese doctor on duty at the time."[56]

The Red Arrow devoted most of its time to dismantling the Japanese
military. "The infantry regiment," noted MacArthur's postwar report,
was "the chief instrument of the disarmament program, charged with
seizing all Japanese military installations and disposing of all confiscated
material."[57] Japanese troops gathered at processing centers, where the
Red Arrowmen fed them, interviewed them, took away their insignia, and
sent them home. "In every instance encountered," one report noted, "the
Japanese military personnel were extremely eager to be demobilized."[58]

The division's main task was to locate, inventory, and destroy Japanese weapons, hardware, and other military goods. Prohibited items ranged from tanks and aircraft all the way down to rifles and binoculars. The Japanese government provided SCAP with lists of places where prohibited goods had been stockpiled, and GIs then took control of them. Occupation troops also searched for unreported items. "Every road in the battalion zone was covered by motorized patrols," noted the Second Battalion of the 128th Infantry Regiment, "and better than a third of the total battalion areas were covered by foot patrols that moved across the country in a line of skirmishers. . . . The mission of these patrols was to investigate every building and warehouse, excluding private homes, and to enter and explore every cave and air raid shelter in the assigned area."[59] Civilians were expected to turn in weapons as well.

In their sweeps across the Japanese landscape, the Red Arrowmen came across scores of defensive preparations built to thwart the anticipated American invasion. Near Shimonoseki, the 128th Infantry Regiment found one installation "which consisted of twenty-two (22) large subterranean vaults filled to capacity with artillery shells, explosives, gasoline, and oil."[60] The 127th's Third Battalion reported that "from Sasebo all the way north to Fukuoka, the preparations made by the Japanese to wage war have been outstanding. Tremendous caves were dug out of solid rock in the Sasebo area. Searchlights, 5 in. dual purpose and 20mm. AA. [antiaircraft] guns were dragged to the tops of the hills to provide protection for the harbor." Near Fukuoka, battalion patrols found a "multitude of caves that are scattered all over the countryside. Tons of projectiles and explosives have been hauled by hand into [them]." The battalion report concluded that "these caves, ammunition dumps, weapons, storehouses, and defensive constructions have impressed the patrols with one point. This would have been a tough island to invade."[61]

Occupation troops discovered tons of unreported materiel. "Patrol activity increased and 'regrettable omissions' began to appear," noted a 128th Infantry Regiment report. "A location on the island of Nagashima . . . proved to be a group of warehouses of the Kure Store Dept" that "included coal, briquettes, mineral oil, crude rubber, radio [and] radar equipment, torpedoes, mines, etc." GIs found military equipment in unexpected locations. "Late in November information gathered led us to believe that certain precision instruments, especially those used in aircraft, were being concealed in and about certain shrines and temples," noted the 128th Infantry Regiment. "Near Iwakuni over 200 bomb sights were found in the temples, a large quantity of blasting material was found in the immediate vicinity of a shrine in Bofu and the additional materials found justified our extensive check of all shrines and temples in the Battalion Zone."[62] Patrols of the 126th Infantry Regiment "found three machine guns, 55 rifles and an assortment of military training aides" in a school.[63]

In most cases omissions stemmed from misunderstandings or the disorganization of Japanese officials in the immediate aftermath of the war. On rare occasions, Japanese officers attempted to hide contraband items. "In the disarming and demobilizing of Japanese Forces in this area full cooperation and honesty were received," claimed a 126th Infantry Regiment report, "with the exception of one unit which was the Japanese 12th Flying Division . . . commanded by a sly underhanded officer who had made plans to conceal a great deal of equipment." Though the unit had turned over "large stocks of airplane parts, 109 planes, bombs, guns, and ammunition," Red Arrow inspectors thought it odd that "such a unit had no radio equipment, no gasoline, no vehicles, and no parachutes." The Red Arrow hauled the unit's officers in for interrogation, and they "gave information that revealed hidden stores of radios, signal equipment, gasoline, parachutes, and the whereabouts of some 30 Japanese Army vehicles."[64]

The contraband items were gathered up and destroyed. "The planes were demolished by saturating them in aviation gasoline and then igniting them," reported the First Battalion of the 128th Infantry Regiment, and "the motors and propellers were further destroyed by specially chosen demolition squads using Japanese Picric Acid."[65] Lower-ranking members of the Japanese military performed much of the labor. Henry Zabierek's company was assigned to supervise a group of Japanese workers tasked with demolishing aircraft engines. "The first meeting in the warehouse," he remembered, "proved to be a mixture of culture clash, misunderstanding, and resentment." He described the Japanese work crew as "a motley one composed of airmen and soldiers of various rank" who "seemed to resent the mere presence of the enemy on their land." Two GIs "armed with sledgehammers" demonstrated the task the Japanese were to perform. Then "the interpreters explained to the Japanese soldiers what to do," but in a lengthy and animated exchange the workers "seemed to argue with the interpreters." Zabierek thought the reaction "a mixture of confusion and defiance," and by the end of the day little work had been done. The following day the situation improved. "The work proceeded with an ebb and flow that produced some periods of slowdowns," wrote Zabierek, but the GIs also noted "a more intense Japanese effort." Zabierek wrote that "once our supply of plane engines was depleted, the destruction proceeded anew, now involving mortars, machine guns, and small arms."[66] Not every Japanese item was destroyed. "Small arms and binoculars are being distributed to the troops as war trophies," noted one report, while larger items like tanks and artillery guns "will be retained for war memorials and museum pieces."[67]

The Red Arrow disposed of ammunition and explosives in various ways. Most often these were detonated or dumped into the ocean. The 127th Infantry Regiment experimented with burning ammunition. On December 5, "one hundred tons of ammunition were burned by saturating the pile with oil and setting the torch." The regiment thought the technique successful, and "further increases in amounts burned reaching a climax on 10 Jan. 46, when 10,851,000 rounds of small arms ammunition, 110 LMG's, 130 HMG's, 5,605 pyrotechnics, 5,400 smoke pots, 4,000 lbs. of propellant powder, and 250 gas masks were burned in one pile. This was the largest single-burning of enemy arms, ammunition, and equipment attempted by any occupation unit in Japan."[68] Destroying weapons and ammunition was a dangerous task. On November 12, for example, the 126th Infantry Regiment tried to blow up munitions stored inside the Futamata Tunnel near Soeda. Japanese police cleared the area and the GIs lit the fuse, but there was no explosion. Red Arrowmen "remained in the vicinity," stated one report, waiting for a possible delayed detonation, but when none occurred after two hours they "returned to their bivouac." Unfortunately, shortly after the Red Arrowmen departed the munitions finally exploded, "virtually causing the entire mountain to disintegrate and causing considerable damage to the village." The regiment's initial investigation counted 121 Japanese civilians killed, 74 injured, and 9 missing.[69]

In clearing locations of contraband items, the Red Arrow rounded up nonmilitary items as well and transferred them to the Japanese Home

Ministry for civilian use. According to its operations report, the 126th Infantry Regiment handed over "more than 3,200 tons of much-needed food, 4,000 tons of coal and hundreds of thousands of pieces of clothing" to the Japanese government during the winter of 1945–1946. Scrap metal from destroyed weapons was melted down and turned over as well. During the winter of 1945–1946, the 126th Infantry Regiment destroyed "more than 6,100 machine guns, 813 artillery and coastal guns, 3,826 mortars and grenade dischargers and 247 airplanes of various types" at the Yahata Steel Works. The operation produced "1,130,521 tons of scrap steel" for Japanese industry.[70] Before destroying aircraft, the GIs removed engines and other items with civilian economic uses. Among the items the 128th Infantry Regiment turned over to the home ministry "were machine tools and small aircraft wheels and tires suitable for use on small agricultural equipment."[71] Swords had become ploughshares.

With its arrival in Japan, the well-traveled Red Arrow Division added yet another country to its impressive itinerary. After their years in the tropics, Japan's temperate autumn weather came as a jolt. "It's been bitter cold the past two days and nights," wrote John Walters soon after landing at Sasebo, "and we really don't have the equipment necessary to be comfortable." The mountainous landscape impressed many. "The terraced gardens (rice paddies) along the [hillside] are something to see," wrote Walters. "They look so miniature but look neat." He also noted the "many cherry trees along the road."[72] The soldier-travelers also found charm in cityscapes not scarred by bombing. Eloy Duran thought Kokura Castle and its mani-cured grounds in the center of that city picturesque and romantic. He passed the castle one evening while returning to his barracks. "I almost ran along the moat," Duran wrote his mother and sister, "and the pine trees standing sharp against the huge rock emplacements was reminiscent of all those old post [cards] labeled 'Old Japan.'"[73] Not since Australia had the Red Arrowmen been in an urban industrialized nation. City centers con-tained many modern buildings of glass, brick, and steel like those familiar to denizens of any US city, but the GIs thought residential areas looked cramped and shabby by American standards. "Their homes seem to be built about anyplace as they are scattered quite a bit," observed Walters. "The homes are made of boards, with tile roofs and much corrugated slate is used for siding."[74]

However, what the GIs noted most about Japan's cities was the immense devastation caused by American bombers. James Myers was part of a group traveling inland from Sasebo. "As we rode in the train," he remembered, "we passed steel mills and factories nearly completely demolished by our bombers."[75] Not far from the Red Arrow occupation zone were the ruins of Hiroshima and Nagasaki—the two cities laid waste by the US detonation of atomic bombs. The ruins left a deep impression on those who saw them. Nagasaki was supposed to be off limits, recalled engineer Monte Howell, but "one of our survey patrols sneaked into" the city. "The Atomic Bomb destruction was unbelievable," Howell wrote. "We found newspapers where all of the black print was burned out. When you held up the newspapers it looked like confetti."[76] Myers passed through Hiroshima by train and later described what he saw:

> The only thing standing for miles in any direction were high, round factory smokestacks. Everything else was obliterated. . . . Several people we passed on the train had one side of their bodies burned black from the atom bomb blast, while the other half of their bodies, on the side that had been pointed away from the blast, had their natural color. I had passed many towns in Japan where our air force bombers had dropped tons of explosives day after day, but none of those other scenes of destruction was even remotely comparable to what I saw in Hiroshima.[77]

As it became clear that the Japanese would not resist the occupation, the army allowed GIs to explore during their off-duty time. Social interactions between GIs and Japanese were initially awkward. Not only were there significant cultural and language barriers, but wartime animosities persisted on both sides. Anthony Chavez, a replacement from Milwaukee's Third Ward who joined the division just after it arrived in Japan, remembered that the Japanese were "still angry" so "you always traveled around in pairs."[78] But most GIs quickly lost such fears. Commercial activity commonly brought together the occupied and the occupier. "Direct contact with the Americans was still to be avoided," Henry Zabierek observed in Fukuoka, though "shopkeepers were the exception. Desperate for sales, they managed to transact business with the I Company men by a weird combination of hand signals, contorting body language, and the occasional recognition of basic words in one another's language." Zabierek remembered that "business was brisk, and smiles abounded."[79] Food shortages and economic turmoil limited the GIs' opportunities to sample Japan's distinctive cuisine. "All public civilian restaurants, cafes, cabarets, eating and drinking places of all types serving food from Japanese sources will be placed out of bounds to all Allied Occupation Forces personnel," one daily bulletin told the Red Arrowmen.[80] One exception was the GIs' beer ration, which came from local breweries. Zabierek thought it "begrudgingly good."[81]

Japanese culture fascinated the GIs. Howell, for example, enjoyed kabuki theater. "It was fun to watch their very animated and vocal characters with white make up on their faces," Howell wrote. Perhaps no Japanese cultural practice interested GIs more than bathing. "It is the Japanese custom to use public baths," wrote Howell. "It is not unusual to see old Japanese men in this cold weather walking down the street in shorts with a towel on their way to the public bath. When they are finished with their bath and walking home, steam is coming off their hot bodies."[82] Myers was stunned to see "men and women bathing together in the nude, several hundred of them. Later, I found out it was the custom, or a ritual, for everyone in Japan to take a complete bath every day. This was a lot more than I could say for most Americans." One day Myers received an invitation to a Japanese bath. "Each bath was like a junior-sized, tile-lined swimming pool," he recalled, "and was attended by several young and attractive Japanese girls. The girls would help one disrobe and wash him down with soap and hot water. You would then submerge yourself in the oversized bath. The girls would then rub your back and generally help you relax until you wondered why we did not have the same thing back in the States." Myers made other observations on Japanese cleanliness. "Shoes were not worn into their houses," he wrote, "but placed near the outer doorway so that germs would not be carried into the houses." He also noted that "when any Japanese have a cold, they wear surgical masks over their faces so that they will not spread cold germs."[83]

As was the case from Louisiana to the Philippines, many Red Arrowmen in Japan were preoccupied with sex. Commercial sex between GIs and Japanese women was common and began almost immediately. On the eve of American arrival, Japanese leaders feared that their conquerors would rape and abuse the nation's women—much as their own soldiers had done in the countries they occupied during the war. In the interregnum between V-J Day and the surrender, Japanese leaders recruited sex workers to serve the GIs, but the proliferation of sexually transmitted infections in these government-sanctioned brothels—not to mention the moral outrage of many American observers—soon led to their closure. The GIs were forbidden to enter the preexisting adult entertainment areas of Japanese cities, where prostitution was tolerated. "Patrols checked OFF LIMITS districts," noted a Thirty-Second Military Police Platoon report, "and military police were notified by Japanese proprietors whenever a soldier entered."[84] How many GIs sneaked into these areas anyway, and how often proprietors were willing to turn away such affluent customers, is a matter of speculation.[85]

Despite official prohibitions, the sex trade still thrived. "As the [brothels] were off limits," wrote Howell, "the men turned to geisha houses." In Japan, a geisha was a professional female entertainer who wore heavy white makeup, dressed in kimono and obi, and sang, danced, and conversed with male customers. The geisha was not a sex worker, but like most Japanese they too lived in greatly reduced economic circumstances and "they soon learned," claimed Howell, "the American soldiers put other things ahead of entertainment and they were willing to pay for it."[86] But for the lonely and amorous GI, the most common source of gratification was the *panpan*. Catering almost exclusively to Allied military personnel, *panpan* dressed in Western clothing, wore heavy makeup, smoked in public, and appeared wherever GIs congregated. It was not sex work as Americans traditionally conceived of it. "*Panpan* and their customers connected in the gray area between dating and prostitution," wrote historian Holly Sanders.[87] Some were *bataafurai* (from the English word *butterfly*) who had many clients. Others were *onrii* (only) who stayed with one soldier until he shipped out and would then take up with another. Payment might be in cash, but American goods from the post exchange often served just as well. The *panpan* were their own free agents and avoided the efforts of pimps to control them. They even formed associations and established specific territories. Due to their relationships with Allied servicemembers, the *panpan* had access to material goods most Japanese did not, but as historian Robert Kramm also reminds us: "Most of them were poor and starving, without any social security or health care, and often subject to sexual violence and harassment by police, gangsters, pimps, clients, and other sex workers."[88]

Whether relationships were commercial or romantic or somewhere in between, sex flourished between GIs and Japanese women. "Part of the guard duty was to go around and wake all the guys up and tell them to get all the girls out," remembered William Painter. "You could see them leaving in droves."[89] As historian John Dower noted, "those who chose the path of chastity during their tour of duty were by all accounts exceptional."[90] Many Japanese people objected to the relationships. Posters in the Bofu area "derided Japanese girls who associated with American soldiers," according to one report from the 128th Infantry Regiment. "Fraternization is generally disliked by Japanese young men, but they do not display their objections openly."[91] Sexually transmitted infections continued to skyrocket. "The Venereal Disease rate has been climbing steadily since the arrival of the troops of the 127th RCT in Japan," noted one medical report. "The situation has taken on the proportions of an alarming problem. Various preventative and educational measures were initiated with little apparent effect."[92] But aside from the usual lectures and graphic films, the army did little to curb GI libido. In fact, one Red Arrow Division medical officer claimed that it was the Japanese "custom of free love [that] makes V.D. a serious problem."[93] Once again, efforts to curb disease fell upon the women. SCAP authorities wanted sex workers tested for sexually transmitted infections, and both American and Japanese police periodically rounded up suspected *panpan* and carted them to hospitals for examination.

Some GIs engaged in other questionable and unseemly behaviors. "American soldiers can get pretty wild in foreign countries, and their interpretation of what is fun is to some others rather crude and rowdy," claimed Monte Howell. "One of the favorite things our group liked to do was 'Steal Street Cars.' . . . We would kick the conductor off and proceed down the line, picking up only young Japanese women. It was fun while it lasted and the MP's . . . put a stop to it."[94] Some GIs committed outright thievery. Howell and his group spruced up their barracks by confiscating goods from civilians. "We told the Japanese the United States government would pay for them," he wrote, but gave names like George Washington and Abraham Lincoln. "Eventually we got caught and this stopped." Indeed, Red Arrow MPs documented numerous alleged GI crimes against the local population, and "found that it was necessary to educate Japanese civilians to identify truck markings and remember identifying features of the soldiers robbing them. Japanese newspapers were used to effect this result." A few GIs—especially in the first months of the occupation—engaged in serious and violent crimes, including armed robbery, breaking and entering, carjacking, and rape, though Red Arrow military police records document just a handful of such incidents.[95]

Postwar Japan was rife with black market activities. "For many Japanese," wrote historian John Dower, the black market "was virtually *the* economy."[96] In the few weeks between V-J Day and the arrival of US troops, some Japanese military leaders cashed in by releasing stockpiles of goods to black marketeers. Criminal gangs, often violent, proliferated to control the trade. Law enforcement officials were reluctant to take on powerful gangs and were sometimes on the take themselves. The black market threatened Japan's economic recovery and undermined confidence in the occupation. SCAP civil government officials and the US Army Counterintelligence Corps led the fight against black market activities, but occupation troops served as their eyes and ears. In their patrols, Red Arrowmen came across numerous instances of questionable or illegal economic activities. "At the cessation of hostilities," reported the Third Battalion of the 127th Infantry Regiment, "approximately 933 naval uniforms were on hand [at a clothing factory] and . . . were turned over to Fukuma town hall to be distributed among residents of the area. This order was complied with, but the uniforms were not given, but sold to residents at a rate of 20 yen per uniform. The 18,660 yen which was collected was turned back to the manufacturer."[97] The 128th Infantry Regiment investigated the activities of an organization that "controlled the City Council of Shimonoseki and members of the gang were in many of the key positions in the city government. The machine was guilty of extortion that was carried out under the old guise of a protection association. They were diverting the already limited food supplies into machine operated black markets."[98]

American goods, including military uniforms and equipment, fetched high prices in the black market. They often entered the Japanese economy via the *panpan*, who obtained them from their paramours. However, the lure of quick profits attracted some unscrupulous GIs who learned that they could supplement their army pay by pilfering American goods and selling them. In his study of the Japanese black market, historian Owen Griffiths noted how one Japanese black marketeer obtained US goods from soldiers who brought him items like chewing gum, chocolate, and cigarettes "by the jeepful."[99] The Thirty-Second Military Police Platoon noted "a few exceptional cases of theft and larceny, committed by joint action of American soldiers and Japanese." Prosecutions of GIs were rare, though. "It was learned that it was difficult to convict a soldier of selling rations, clothing, or PX supplies to Japanese civilians," the platoon noted, "because of the absolute eye-witness proof needed. The only other alternative was to prosecute the Japanese under Japanese tobacco and [economic] laws. This was more easily done because the Japanese, when apprehended usually had the items with them. And the Japanese, knowing that they would be held and prosecuted, avoided, for the most part, this illegal trading." In one report the Thirty-Second Division MPs noted that "no large scale rings of black-market operations were found although . . . there were numerous cases of small dealings."[100] The operations report of the 126th Infantry Regiment concluded that "military police duties should be rotated among troops to prevent soldiers from becoming overly-familiar with illegal opportunities which offer themselves."[101]

Back on base, disciplinary problems ticked upward. Most GIs were draftees who, with the fighting over, grew impatient with their involuntary service. Combat veterans were anxious to get out of the army after years overseas, and they chafed at the army's insistence on military courtesies like saluting, the strict enforcement of uniform regulations, inspections, and parades—practices that had all but disappeared during combat. Officers found some of their subordinates increasingly surly and uncooperative. "I gradually worked my way up to Sergeant during my time in the Pacific," wrote John Rawls, "but was busted back to Private in Japan by a First Lieutenant whose order to punish a soldier who had insulted him I refused to obey."[102] One private in the 128th Infantry Regiment was charged with being absent without leave for three days around New Year's

1946. Once he returned to duty, he showed "disrespect" toward a superior officer by—as the charges against him read—"saying to him, 'Blow it out your ass,' or words to that effect." The soldier was convicted and sentenced to six months hard labor and forfeiture of a portion of his pay.[103]

Keeping soldiers busy and entertained seemed more important than ever. In Japan the Red Arrow enjoyed a richness of recreational opportunities not seen since the days of training in Louisiana. "The Major in charge of our battalion asked me to see what I could do to set up a nice recreation area for the men," wrote morale officer James Myers, and "gave me carte blanche" to make it happen. Myers went right to work. "I took over a large newly completed building," he wrote, and with the work of Japanese "carpenters, electricians, and laborers" built a multipurpose facility:

> We built volleyball, basketball, horseshoe courts and a latrine on the outside of the building. On the inside, we set up a post exchange (PX) and a large ballroom with a stage and traverse curtains, painting a black and white screen on the back wall of the stage. At the other end of the ballroom, we built a projection booth and made indoor basketball backboards that could be raised and lowered when necessary. We set up a kitchen to make coffee and doughnuts for the men. We also provided a reading and waiting room, a library and finally a barber shop.

Myers also arranged a film exchange with a navy supply ship, and his battalion soon had "more new movies than any other outfit in the division." On his travels around Japan, Myers was "able to pick up many nice things, such as silk kimonos, toys and other souvenirs and turn them over for sale in the PX." He even contacted local club and theater owners. "If I saw any Japanese stage shows in the area that I thought the men would enjoy, I talked to the theater managers, had the theater closed, took the cast outside the theater, still in their make-up, stopped a public bus, put off the people riding in the bus and used it to transport the entire show troupe to the club. This helped to fill the off days of the men."[104]

Athletics kept the troops both entertained and physically fit. "Basketball leagues were formed within the battalions and a RCT league was also formed," noted the 126th Infantry Regiment operations report. "The

2d Battalion won the regimental title and was invited to participate in the division tourney," the report stated, adding that "the 2d Battalion won its first game in the division semifinals by defeating the division headquarters team." After that "more than 300 of the RCT's most rabid fans accompanied the team to Oita to witness the championship playoff against the strong 126th Field Artillery team. The game was bitterly contested with the 126 FA Bn team winning the game and the championship."[105]

As their return home approached, many GIs turned their thoughts to making a living and partook in various educational opportunities. The 127th Infantry Regiment reported that "one hundred and fifty men enrolled in the schools to take following courses: Small Business Management, Farming, Bookkeeping, Algebra, Review Arithmetic, English Grammar, Motor Mechanics and Radio Procedure." In addition, "literacy courses and Basic English and Simple Arithmetic were held for those men failing to have a fifth grade education" and "U.S.A.F.I. correspondence courses were taken by many of the men who wanted courses other than those given by the unit schools."[106]

December 1945 was the first peacetime holiday season the Red Arrow had seen in five years. Indeed, the division had spent three holiday seasons either in combat or preparing for it. Though still far from home, for veteran soldiers this was a holiday season to be savored. "A real Christmas and dinner with turkey and all the 'fixin's' was enjoyed by the troops," noted a 127th Infantry Regiment report. The division and regimental commanders paid visits to the various units, and "throughout the regiment gaily lighted Christmas trees and other decorations brought a little of the Christmas spirit of home to the men."[107] It was much the same in the 128th Infantry Regiment. "Additional supplies were issued for the Christmas and New Years [sic] celebration," stated one report, "in order that the men would have meals that would include everything obtainable in the United States at such a celebration. A Christmas program which included the decoration of the barracks, Christmas parties, and allied activities aided in making the Christmas one that all would remember."[108] There was even a "photograph studio," which "produced personal portraits which the men had made and sent home to family and friends."[109]

Overall, Red Arrow soldiers were pleasantly surprised with their sojourn in Japan. "I'm glad I could come here, even for a short time," wrote John Walters, "just to see things and compare them with other places that I have seen."[110] But above all else, they wanted to go home. As the occupation proceeded, the pace of rotations to the United States accelerated further. The number of points required to return dropped to seventy by October 1, to fifty-five on November 16, and then down to fifty on December 19. Redeployment centers Yokohama and Nagoya did a bustling business. By the end of January 1946, each center had processed more than one hundred thousand returning troops, leaving MacArthur with fewer than two hundred thousand soldiers for occupation duty.[111]

For the men of the Thirty-Second Division, the constant shuffling of personnel diminished the effectiveness and readiness of their units. "So many of the older men of the organization have been going home," noted the 107th Medical Battalion, "that training of replacements has become a real problem."[112] James Myers was one of a small number of Buna veterans remaining in the division. "I had about one hundred and forty points," he recalled, "which was nearly the highest, if not the highest, in the division." Myers went to his battalion commander who "looked up my record and was surprised to see the number of points I had picked up." The major asked him to "stay on and build an officer's club," even offering him a promotion, but Myers refused. "After four years I had had it and was thinking only of home," and "two days later, my orders came through."[113]

As soldiers went home the army tried to prepare them for their return to civilian life. "Our Colonel called a meeting," remembered Monte Howell, and "explained that our vocabulary over the past several years had deteriorated to the point we were using certain adjectives to describe every item. He was of course referring to the F--- word, as well as other four letter words." Up to that time Howell had not considered his colorful vocabulary a problem. "We didn't think we were swearing," he reflected. "To us these were just 'slang' words that we had been hearing and we all picked it up."[114]

The return of the veterans from Japan did not always go smoothly. The transportation of troops stretched shipping capacity to the limit. Those eligible to go home found the wait agonizingly long, particularly combat veterans who measured their service in years. John Walters, who had joined the Red Arrow at Aitape, wanted to be home with Jewell and Jane in time for Christmas. His letters expressed his increasingly bitter and visceral frustrations. "I'm so damn mad and disgusted because nothing is being done," Walters wrote. "It seems to us that the higher officials are giving us the run around—telling lies, promising—and still doing nothing." Reports of empty ships in harbors infuriated him. "No one on this earth can tell me that there can't be transportation for us," he wrote. "I've watched thousands of ships coming over here. I know that all aren't now necessary to carry supplies and equipment to us. We don't ask to ride in luxury—we just want to get away from here." Walters singled out MacArthur and the Sixth Army brass for criticism and felt that the Thirty-Second Division was the victim of discrimination, claiming it "has taken more s__t from higher ups than any three other divisions." He added that he hated "anyone that has anything to do with demobilization—because never has such an important job been bungled. . . . No wonder so many men blow their tops & go batty. I'll probably be nuts before I get home (If I'm not already)." Despite Walters's angry screeds, his wait continued.[115]

Walters and his fellow Red Arrowmen were hardly alone. GIs in overseas locations around the world were becoming increasingly bold and vehement in their demands to return home. They wrote letters to newspapers, to Congress, and even to President Truman. In Japan, GIs working in mailrooms stamped the phrase "no boats, no votes" on outgoing mail, and one soldier in the Philippines circulated a petition based on that slogan to be sent to members of Congress. "In six days' time he had replies from twenty outfits promising to carry on the campaign," reported the *New York Times*.[116] After the cancellation of a troopship sailing from Manila, four thousand GIs marched on the headquarters of the replacement depot there on Christmas Day 1945, some carrying signs proclaiming "We Want Boats." The depot commander ordered the soldiers back to their barracks, reminding them that they were "still in the army."[117] The War Department announcement on January 4 of a slowdown in discharges led to further protests—all peaceful—in far-flung places like France, Germany, Guam, and Japan. General Charles P. Hall, now acting commander of the Eighth Army in Japan, believed the protests exposed "a general breakdown of morale and discipline," and warned that "the Japanese people are watching with interest." MacArthur called the protesters "good men who have performed magnificently under campaign conditions and inherently are not challenging discipline and authority."[118] General Dwight D. Eisenhower, now army chief of staff, echoed MacArthur's sentiments, though he banned any further demonstrations.[119]

As soldiers overseas agitated for demobilization, their families back home became increasingly active too. The slow pace of demobilization posed a great threat to the American family, they argued, as a husband's income provided an essential resource in the uncertain postwar economy. Many expressed concerns about marital infidelity—particularly given the reports of GI sexual behavior overseas. But perhaps the most "potent source of symbolic power," argued historian Susan Carruthers, was "the image of the fatherless child."[120] Bring Back Daddy Clubs sprang up across the country. "The war is over and there is no more need of holding fathers in the service any longer," two members of Madison's Bring Back Daddy Club told Wisconsin governor Walter Goodland. "The daddy's place is in the home so please see what you can do to have all fathers discharged. Please. Please."[121] Soldiers' families sent a blizzard of letters to Congress urging faster demobilization, sometimes accompanied by touching photographs of children. Others sent baby booties to further drive home their point.

Though not nearly fast enough to suit them, Red Arrow veterans eventually returned to the United States. John Walters departed the 127th Infantry Regiment in mid-November, though his frustrations continued. He boarded a train bound for the Eleventh Replacement Depot in Nagoya, but a rail accident led to lengthy delays. "Slept on a seat," Walters wrote to Jewell and Jane, and "got terribly cold—ate two cans of rations in 36 hours." He arrived at the Nagoya depot at 4:00 a.m. "in pouring rain" and then stayed in barracks he described as "colder than the dickens." Then came the long wait. Days stretched into weeks but he received no ship assignment. Walters caught a cold but suffered through it because, as he told Jane, "I don't want to mess my chance up of going home by going to the medics." His anger mounted as he calculated that he would not get home in time for Christmas. At one point he even wrote forlornly: "I believe that I have been forgotten."[122] At last Walters's day of departure had arrived. Although he did not make it back to Eau Claire for Christmas, he walked through the door and reunited with Jewell and Jane on New Year's Eve 1945.

Other Thirty-Second Division veterans made their way home, too. "I left on Christmas day," wrote Monte Howell. "Now that was my Christmas present for 1943, 1944, and 1945 all wrapped up into one." Howell had not seen his California home since being drafted in 1943. "It was quite a thrill," he recalled later, "as we sailed under the Golden Gate Bridge."[123] Also heading home was Buna veteran James Myers. Ever the entertainer, Myers "found a set of drums" aboard his ship, as well as "a few other instruments" and "put together a band." After a few rehearsals, Myers's band performed for the passengers on "the last day aboard ship." For Myers, the highlight of the concert was the show's final song, the 1944 hit "Sentimental Journey." He remembered that "everyone in the audience joined in on the words," and "after the number was finished, there was not a dry eye in the place."[124]

In the end, the Red Arrow Division's stay in Japan would be a brief one. The Sixth Army was deactivated on December 31, 1945, and the Thirty-Second Division was transferred to the Eighth Army, though it would only serve two months in that command. The Thirty-Second Infantry Division itself—on active duty since October 1940—had also been slated for deactivation. Over the course of January 1946, the Red Arrow handed over its duties to other American units, most notably the Second Marine Division, and by the end of the month the Thirty-Second Division's occupation work officially ended. "Without a tactical mission for the first time in more than 3 years," noted a 127th Infantry report, "the Regiment started inactivating."[125] Soldiers without sufficient points to return to the United States transferred to other units. "The 32nd Division split up," recalled William Painter, who came to the division on the Villa Verde Trail, "so then I was with the Twenty-Fourth Infantry Division."[126] Anthony Chavez, who joined the Red Arrow in Japan, recalled that "the 32nd Division pulled out of there, and we stayed." He too went to the Twenty-Fourth Division.[127]

The "pack out" operation began at the start of February. Troops stockpiled and inventoried their remaining equipment, which was then warehoused or shipped to other units. They gathered and boxed up sheaves of records. "The deactivation task began with the turning in of Chemical Warfare Equipment," noted the 128th Infantry Regiment. Then, "with the exceptions of certain essential items, the other classes began to be turned in: Engineer, Medical, Signal, and Quartermaster."[128] In mid-February the division gave up most of its vehicles. "A large side loading ramp was acquired near the Kashii Railroad Station for the loading of all rail shipments," reported the 127th Infantry Regiment, and "with one officer and a trained crew of five men to supervise it was possible to load 74 automotive units on 39 cars in five hours. One of the clerks was especially trained to make out shipping tickets and bills of lading." Weapons were the last items to be turned in. "The regiment maintained until the end an armed force prepared for any emergency," noted the 127th Infantry Regiment.[129] And according to the 126th Infantry Regiment, "The consolidation of companies within the Battalions continued steadily as the men and equipment was shipped out, until at last only a handful of men and machines remained of what had been one of the best-equipped, best-manned Regimental Combat Teams in the Army."[130]

Throughout February, the constituent units of the Thirty-Second Division held deactivation ceremonies. "From the farms of Wisconsin to the cities and Hamlets of Michigan, since early September 1940, the 128th Infantry has come to the end of a long road," its commanding officer, Lieutenant Colonel Alex J. Robinett, told his men. "Now our job is finished and the occupation of Japan has progressed to the successful accomplishment of nearly four years of difficult and arduous missions." The proceedings included a moment of silence for "those Officers and men who made the Supreme sacrifice in the efforts of this regiment in bringing World War II to a triumphant and victorious end."[131] The 127th Infantry Regiment held a ceremony on February 13 at Gannosu airfield near Fukuoka, with representatives of other Red Arrow units participating. "In a farewell message to every man in the Regiment," noted one account, "the Regimental Commander expressed his sincere appreciation for the cooperation and loyalty the men of the 127th have given to his predecessors and himself as their Commanding Officer. Praise for a job well done and the hope for a bright future in a peaceful world were expressed in the message." General Robert McBride, commander of the Thirty-Second Division, also addressed the assembled soldiers and after he spoke the troops "passed in review."[132]

In the final days of the Red Arrow's active wartime service, the ranks continued to shrink until just a handful remained with a Red Arrow on their shoulders. The journal of the 732nd Ordnance Company captured the unit's final days:

> 25 Feb Monday
> Cleaning up area and loading vehicles
>
> 26 Feb Tuesday
> Shipped 30 EM [enlisted men] and 1 Off to 724 Ord and 5th Ord Cos. Last meal served at noon. Messed with Hq Co for supper. . . .
>
> 28 Feb Thursday
> Remaining men transferred out except those on TDY [temporary duty] with the 32 Prov. Det, I Corps. Turned in all company records to Headquarters Special Troops. Lt. Schiff and 7 EM remaining on TDY to finish business of the company and complete shipment of equipment.
>
> <u>Finis.</u>[133]

On the final day of February 1946, "the glorious history of the 127th Infantry Regiment for World War II was brought to a close," declared the regimental operations report. "The hard earned victories at Buna, Aitape, Leyte, and Luzon, together with the successful occupation of Japan mission will live forever in the history of the regiment. In years to come veterans of the 127th will point with pride to the achievements of their regiment and use this old phrase to cinch their argument, 'Let's take a look at the records.'"[134]

Epilogue

S hortly after General Yamashita Tomoyuki surrendered to the Thirty-Second Division in the mountains of Luzon, he and his staff awaited transportation to the formal surrender ceremony at Baguio, biding their time devouring US Army rations and signing autographs for GIs. Lieutenant General Muto Akira, Yamashita's chief of staff, noticed the red arrow emblem on the shoulder of Colonel Ernest A. Barlow, the division's chief of staff, and inquired about its meaning. Barlow told him that it symbolized the fact that the Thirty-Second Division had pierced the German line during Meuse-Argonne Offensive in World War I. "Yes," Muto commented, "and the Yamashita Line in World War II."[1] The Red Arrow Division had indeed maintained the tradition the Great War doughboys had established of achieving victory in every battle, though this time on a much grander scale—in the remote jungles and mountains of New Guinea and the Philippines, and over four years of some of the most savage combat any Americans have ever endured. It accomplished several firsts in US military history: the first infantry unit to be flown into a combat zone, the first US Army division to take the offensive against the Japanese, and the first to defeat the Japanese in battle. Through most of the conflict it fought on a shoestring, at the end of a long supply line, in a secondary theater and often without the confidence of its own commanders. According to official US Army statistics, the Thirty-Second Division suffered 1,613 soldiers killed in action (the most of any infantry division in the Pacific theater), 2,002 battle-related deaths (second most in the Pacific), and 5,627 wounded (the third highest in the Pacific).[2] In all, the Red Arrow logged 654 days of fighting, claiming the distinction of more time in combat than any other US Army division during World War II.[3]

Most Red Arrow veterans were happy to put the war and military life behind them. "I didn't get a parade," Michigan's Paul Rettell wrote, "and I didn't expect one. I didn't even want one. I was glad it was over."[4] Benjamin Winneshiek returned to his home in western Wisconsin. Of the eight members of the Ho-Chunk Nation who joined the Red Arrow back in 1940, seven survived the war. "We had our ceremony," Winneshiek remembered, "put out pails, deer meat, chicken, offered to the spirits, gave them tobacco, thanking them that we . . . came back."[5] Years later, Winneshiek became chief of the Ho-Chunk Nation. Art Kessenich returned to Madison to meet his three-year-old son, born while Kessenich was at war. "I walked in with tears in my eyes and saw my son for the first time," he wrote. "He looked at me and said, 'Hi Dad.' Dora really kept him informed about his father and I was so very pleased he recognized me."[6]

Many like Kessenich returned to wives or girlfriends, while others found partners and settled into family life. A few years after his return to California, Monte Howell met "a cute little redhead" at a dance contest and they were married in 1952. "We found jobs, lived on TV dinners and had a wonderful time," he wrote.[7] Federal benefits like the GI Bill helped many fit themselves back into the economy. Donald Dill called the GI Bill "[the] best thing that ever happened to me. My subsequent education would not have been possible without it."[8] Erwin Pichotte wrote that it "helped me get a low mortgage rate on my first house," and claimed that "I would not have been able to afford it without the GI Bill."[9]

Some faced difficulties fitting back into the civilian world. "I was sort of drifting," wrote Raymond Dasmann, "with no clear goal in mind."[10] Malaria plagued many for years after discharge. "When I was a young boy I remember seeing Dad wrapped up sweating and shaking," wrote Richard Stoelb, whose father, Roland, fought at Buna and Aitape. The younger Stoelb remembered how his father's feet "bore testimony to the ordeal. His toenails were permanently discolored, deformed, and thickened due to contracting a jungle fungus infection," and added that he also "took Lithium, a mood stabilizer for 'neurosis, depression and anxiety disorder.'"[11] Roland Stoelb was hardly alone in his struggle to shake the emotional effects of combat. The killing inherent in war haunted Whayland Greene's postwar thoughts, though he found solace in the fact that millions around the world were also "put into the situation" of having to fight. Religion helped Greene, too. "If God could forgive small sins, and if God could forgive middle size sins," he reasoned, then "He could surely forgive large sins."[12] Jesse Coker wrote that he "had a rough time coping with nightmares and the hate and exasperation which I still felt," but his wife Ernestine's support carried him through. "She helped me make it through the war," he wrote, "and now she was helping me adjust to civilian life. I know this was not always easy for her and I shall always be indebted to her with gratitude for her loving care and patience."[13]

A few Red Arrow veterans went on to achieve public acclaim. James Myers, who joined the Thirty-Second Division at Buna and kept the 128th Infantry Regiment entertained as a morale officer in the Philippines and Japan, returned to Philadelphia after the war and became a music publisher, promoter, and composer. In 1953, under the pseudonym Jimmy DeKnight, Myers cowrote "Rock Around the Clock," which was recorded the following year by Bill Haley & His Comets. When the song was featured in the 1955 film *Blackboard Jungle*, it helped unleash an explosive new genre of popular music: rock 'n' roll. The hit song "became the very enactment of youthful rebellion against parental conformity," claimed the *Times* of London in its 2001 obituary of Myers, "sending the full skirts of the period twirling waist high as teenagers lost themselves in the hectic dance forms that went with the new music idiom."[14] At Myers's funeral in Philadelphia in May 2001, a high school band played the iconic tune. The *Philadelphia Inquirer* reported that mourners, despite their grief, "could not help but bop their heads to the rhythm of the song."[15]

Raymond Dasmann returned to the US in late 1944. His wife, Elizabeth Sheldon, an Australian artist whom he met and married while overseas, joined him the following year—one of more than one hundred thousand "war brides" who came to the US in the postwar years.[16] Dasmann, who had worked as a firefighter for the US Forest Service before the war, used the GI Bill to study forestry at the University of California–Berkeley, eventually receiving his doctorate. Dasmann became a leading scholar whose groundbreaking and prolific work helped create the modern environmental movement. He pioneered the concepts of biological diversity and what he called "eco-development," arguing in favor of a sustainable relationship with nature, rather than an exploitative one.[17] Dasmann's work was globally recognized, and he was lauded for his efforts to center indigenous people and cultures in conservation work. "Although not a household name such as Rachel Carson or Jacques Cousteau," noted a 2002 obituary, "he is considered a luminary in environmentalism."[18]

John Rawls returned to Princeton on the GI Bill, earned his PhD, and became a towering figure in the field of philosophy. In works like his seminal

1971 *Theory of Justice*, Rawls argued that the essence of justice is fairness and that the equitable treatment of everyone should be the organizing principle of law and government. The soft-spoken Rawls rarely discussed his wartime experiences, though they clearly influenced his thinking. Before the war, Rawls had considered a career in the Episcopal ministry, but after the violence he witnessed overseas, he admitted he no longer saw the hand of God in the world and rejected religion altogether. "To interpret history as expressing God's will," Rawls wrote, "God's will must accord with basic ideas of justice as we know them."[19] Rawls had witnessed the burned-out cities of Japan, including the devastated Hiroshima, and after the war he argued that the firebombings and the use of atomic bombs violated the concept of a just war. When fighting a dictatorship, Rawls wrote, "a democratic society must carefully distinguish between three groups: the state's leaders, its soldiers, and its civilian population." Dictators need to be held responsible for their actions and soldiers must inevitably die in battle, he believed, but civilians, "often kept in ignorance and swayed by state propaganda," should not pay for the sins of their oppressors.[20]

The Red Arrow was demobilized in Japan on February 28, 1946, but the division officially sprang back to life less than nine months later, on November 8. "Hardly had the smoke of battle of World War II cleared away," noted Wisconsin Adjutant General Ralph J. Olson, "before the War Department started making plans for National Guard reorganization."[21] Under its new incarnation, the Thirty-Second Infantry Division was entirely a Wisconsin unit. Michigan troops, including the 125th and 126th Infantry Regiments, became part of the new Forty-Sixth Infantry Division. With the onset of the Cold War, the United States maintained a large, permanent military for the first time in its history. The reconstituted National Guard was twice as large and better funded than it had been before World War II. Federal funds improved the training facilities, and the 1962 *Wisconsin Blue Book* noted that with federal help, "the state has expanded its armories very substantially."[22] As the US military changed, so did the Red Arrow. It became racially integrated, and women joined its ranks.

Washington did not mobilize the Red Arrow during the conflicts in Korea and Vietnam but called it into service during the Berlin Crisis of

Red Arrow troops on the rifle range at Camp McCoy, 1949. WHI IMAGE ID 142474

1961. Red Arrowmen reported for mobilization on October 15 of that year—twenty-one years to the day after its World War II activation—now under the command of Major General Herbert A. Smith, who had commanded the Second Battalion of the 128th Infantry Division for most of World War II. Augmented with some "filler" reservists, the division departed by rail one week later for Fort Lewis, Washington. Among the fillers were Green Bay Packers greats Boyd Dowler and Ray Nitschke. Packers coach Vince Lombardi pulled every string he could with the Kennedy administration to keep his players in Green Bay, and fans and local politicians wrote letters hoping to get the two men released from service. "If this had been a real war, perhaps the sentiment would have been different," wrote journalist David Maraniss, "but for many Wisconsin residents the Cold War confrontation in Berlin did not seem worth depleting their beloved

Red Arrow soldiers read the news of their Berlin Crisis deployment while en route to Fort Lewis, Washington, in October 1961. WISCONSIN NATIONAL GUARD

squad for the weekly football battles of the Western Conference."[23] The footballers performed their military duties, but thanks to the creative use of furloughs they continued to play as well. The Berlin Crisis abated and the Red Arrow returned home in August 1962.

The army downsized the Thirty-Second Division into a brigade in 1967 and then subjected the Red Arrow to further reorganizations in the years that followed. The terrorist attacks of September 11, 2001, and the subsequent conflicts in Iraq and Afghanistan put the Red Arrow back on the battlefield. On December 27, 2004, Staff Sergeant Todd Olson of Loyal, Wisconsin—a member of the First Battalion, 128th Infantry Regiment—became the first Red Arrow member killed in action since World War II when an improvised explosive device struck his squad while on patrol near Samarra, Iraq.[24]

The Red Arrowmen of World War II inherited a strong sense of unit pride from their World War I predecessors. Indeed, the criticism from higher-ups during the war and the lack of recognition for battlefield accomplishments only seemed to intensify it. As Charles Murdock observed in the *Saturday Evening Post* in 1945:

> These men from the 32nd have developed a strange, irreverent pride
> in their outfit. They've cursed the war. They've cursed their fate.
> They've cursed the Army. They've hated every minute in the line
> with a deep and burning hatred. . . . Yet, they're quick to take issue,
> by force if necessary, with anyone who challenges the Red Arrow's
> impressive array of claims to top Pacific battle honors. . . . Barroom
> brawls are on record as a result of conflicting claims.[25]

Red Arrowmen do "not get the credit they deserve from either the public or the army," Dean Andersen wrote to his family in September 1945, adding, "the army is rotten. It is full of politics, militarists, and scum."[26] As Edward Guhl put it, "We considered ourselves the best division in the army."[27] That pride continued long after the war. In 1961, E. J. Kahn—back on the staff of the *New Yorker*—covered the call-up of the Red Arrow Division for the magazine during the Berlin Crisis but had trouble maintaining his journalistic objectivity. "I still have an old-school-tie feeling about the Thirty-second," Kahn wrote. "To me, it will always be the finest division in the world, which is probably the way most soldiers feel about whatever division they served with in battle." He added that "one does not stop loving a woman because her outfits change."[28] Newman Phillips claimed that "of all the things I have done in my life, the one thing of which I am most proud is that I carried a rifle in 'L' Co. in the 126th Infantry. . . . [It] was the finest body of soldiers this county ever produced."[29]

As the World War II generation passes on, the war itself has taken on mythological proportions in the American mind. It was the "Good War" in which the "Greatest Generation" selflessly liberated the world. However true that may be, such simplistic portrayals—no matter how heartfelt or well intended—cloud our understanding of the conflict. Literary scholar Elizabeth Samet observed that "as the generation passes away—to be frozen within the pantheon of heroes, walled off from the present, larger than life, untouchable, not quite of this world—the real and deeply ambivalent legacies of the Second World War risk becoming lost forever."[30] One perspective at risk is that of the GIs themselves—the ones at the very heart of the mythmaking. The experience of the Red Arrow Division during World War II shows the world of the soldier to be a complicated one, and that no two soldiers saw the war in quite the same way. Yes, there was adventure, travel, and camaraderie. There was the satisfaction of defending the nation after it was attacked, and the consequent bravery, valor, and sacrifice on the battlefield unexplainable to those who were not there. But there was also wanton cruelty, racist hatred, and immoral behavior, often amplified by the loosened social restraints of the wartime world. The war brutalized the bodies, minds, and souls of its participants. Petty politics, self-dealing, incompetence, and poor decision-making in high places only accentuated the anguish and horror for those further down the chain of command. Myopic, glorified, and romanticized portrayals of the GI blind us to the actual experience of war and ultimately obscure the true nature of the sacrifices and heroism of those who served and fought. The GIs of the Red Arrow Division told us of their world in their letters, memoirs, and reminiscences. If we are to understand that world—or that of any soldier in any war—we must be willing to listen to them.

Although history often overlooks the Thirty-Second Infantry Division, its record in World War II was remarkable. The Red Arrow was not an elite fighting unit like the US Marines, or army paratroopers or rangers who received extra pay and special equipment. Indeed, it was quite ordinary: a National Guard unit, unprepared when the war began, that learned the hard truths about war, applied those bitter lessons on the battlefield, prevailed in every engagement, and earned the respect of its formidable opponent. "We were just ordinary citizens from all walks of life that were given a job to do," wrote Clarence Jungwirth, "and we did it to the best of our ability. Sometimes we liked the job, sometimes we hated it. . . . We grew up in combat. We didn't consider ourselves heroes. What we did, we did for the love of our families and our country."[31]

Acknowledgments

Books and manuscripts related to the Red Arrow Division are scattered far and wide across the United States, as well as in repositories abroad. Wherever I traveled for research, information professionals took valuable time out of their days to dig up the materials I needed, and they responded to my many queries. The COVID-19 pandemic struck in the middle of my research and threatened to derail my progress, but dedicated archivists and librarians undertook even greater labors under trying conditions to reproduce and send me materials so that I could continue working. In addition to the repositories cited in the endnotes, I would like to thank the archives and library staff members at the following institutions: the Australian War Memorial, the Croton Free Library, The Denver Public Library, the Franklin D. Roosevelt Presidential Library and Museum, the James C. Bolton Library at Louisiana State University at Alexandria, the School of Oriental and African Studies at the University of London, the University of Massachusetts at Amherst, and the Wisconsin Legislative Reference Bureau.

Funding for this work came from the Wisconsin Historical Society and a Ridgway Research Grant in Military History from the United States Army Heritage and Education Center at Carlisle Barracks, Pennsylvania. I am deeply grateful for this indispensable support.

Special thanks go to Kevin Abing, Kathy Borkowski, Bill Brewster, Mark Danley, Diane Drexler, Brian Faltinson, Xaviera Flores, Kristin Gilpatrick, Russell Horton, Frank Jacob, Douglas Johnson, Jonathan Kasparek, Carrie Kilman, Shannon Kincaid, Vaughn Larson, Eric Lent, Alfred W. McCoy, Neera Mohess, Richard Moran, John Nondorf, Thomas Pogge, Margaret and Elizabeth Rawls, Michelle Riggs-Waller, Luke Sprague, Stephen R. Taaffe, Justin Taylan, Kate Thompson, Eric Van Slander, Marc Zelcer, and the cartographers of Mapping Specialists, Ltd. All enriched this work in some important way.

NOTES

The following abbreviations are used here:

GVSU: Veterans History Project, Special Collections and University Archives, Grand Valley State University, Allendale, Michigan

MMA: MacArthur Memorial Archives and Library, Norfolk, Virginia

NARA: National Archives and Records Administration, College Park, Maryland

USAHEC: United States Army Heritage and Education Center, Carlisle Barracks, Pennsylvania

WHS: Wisconsin Historical Society Archives, Madison, Wisconsin

WVM: Wisconsin Veterans Museum Research Center, Madison, Wisconsin

Preface

1. To call the scholarship on World War II voluminous is an understatement, and compiling a bibliography of historical works on the subject is a daunting task. In *Retribution: The Battle for Japan, 1944–1945* (New York: Knopf, 2008), historian Max Hastings opted not to include a bibliography at all. "A catalogue of relevant titles," he wrote, "becomes merely an author's peacock list" (559). In this work, suggested introductory readings on specific events and topics related to the Red Arrow Division's wartime history are offered in these endnotes. In contrast to the vastness of the World War II literature, works focusing specifically on the Thirty-Second Division are rare. The historiography of the division begins with *13,000 Hours: Combat History of the 32d Inf Div—World War II* (Public Relations Office, Thirty-Second Infantry Division, 1945), compiled while the Red Arrow was still in the Philippines. In the immediate postwar years, the division's veterans association struggled to complete a history of its World War II experiences, but finally succeeded with Harold W. Blakeley, *32d Infantry Division in World War II* (Madison: Thirty-Second Infantry Division History Commission, 1957). For other general works on the division during World War II, see Joe H. Camp Jr., *32 Answered: A South Carolina Veterans' Story* (Charleston, SC: Joe H. Camp, Jr., 2015), which focuses on the experiences of Palmetto State officers, and a two-article series by Robert H. Young, "A Division at War—Part I," *Saber and Scroll Journal* 9, no. 3 (Winter 2020): 173–92; and "A Division at War—Part II," *Saber and Scroll Journal* 9, no. 4 (Spring 2021): 67–78.
2. Blakeley, *32d Infantry Division*, 279–80.
3. Young, "A Division at War—Part II," 67.
4. For an introduction to the social and cultural experiences of American GIs in World War II, see Lee Kennett, *G.I.: The American Soldier in World War II* (New York: Warner Books, 1987); Peter Schrijvers, *The Crash of Ruin: American Combat Soldier in Europe during World War II* (New York: New York University Press, 1998); and Peter Schrijvers, *The GI War against Japan: American*

Soldiers in Asia and the Pacific during World War II (New York: New York University Press, 2002). In recent years, a small number of scholars have noted the interconnections between military service and travel. For an introduction to this scholarship, see Bertram M. Gordon, *War Tourism: Second World War France from Defeat and Occupation to the Creation of Heritage* (Ithaca, NY: Cornell University Press, 2018); Debbie Lisle, *Holidays in the Danger Zone: Entanglements of War and Tourism* (Minneapolis: University of Minnesota Press, 2016); and Vernadette Vicuña Gonzalez and Jana K. Lipman, "Tours of Duty and Tours of Leisure," *American Quarterly* 68, no. 3 (September 2016): 507–21. The latter work is the introduction to a special issue of *American Quarterly* on the emerging field of "militourism" that contains several essays exploring the intersection of military service and travel. On the specific issue of souvenir collecting, see Mark D. Van Ells, "An Amazing Collection: American GIs and Their Souvenirs of World War II," in *War and Memorials: The Second World War and Beyond*, eds. Frank Jacob and Kenneth Pearl (Paderborn: Ferdinand Schöningh, 2019), 105–48.

5. Mary Louise Roberts, *Sheer Misery: Soldiers in Battle in WWII* (Chicago: University of Chicago Press, 2021), 3.

Chapter 1

1. For an introduction to the origins and development of the US Army division, see John B. Wilson, *Maneuver and Firepower: The Evolution of Divisions and Separate Brigades* (Washington, DC: Center of Military History, 1998).

2. Wisconsin Legislative Reference Bureau, *Wisconsin Blue Book, 1927* (Madison: State of Wisconsin, 1927), 404; Michigan Adjutant General's Office, *Report of the Adjutant General, 1860* (Lansing: State of Michigan, 1860), 9; *Historical and Pictorial Review, National Guard of the State of Michigan, 1940* (Baton Rouge: Army and Navy Publishing, 1940). For an introduction to American militia and National Guard history, see Jerry M. Cooper, *Rise of the National Guard: The Evolution of the American Militia, 1865–1920* (Lincoln: University of Nebraska Press, 1997); Ricardo A. Herrera, *For Liberty and the Republic: The American Citizen and Soldier, 1776–1861* (New York: New York University Press, 2015); and John K. Mahon, *History of the Militia and the National Guard* (New York: Macmillan, 1983). Jim Dan Hill, the author of *The Minute Man in Peace and War: A History of the National Guard* (Harrisburg, PA: Stackpole, 1964) served as an officer in the Wisconsin National Guard in the years before World War II.

3. For an introduction to the Iron Brigade, see Alan T. Nolan and Sharon Eggleston Vipond, *Giants in Their Tall Black Hats: Essays on the Iron Brigade* (Bloomington: Indiana University Press, 1998).

4. Wisconsin Legislative Reference Bureau, *Wisconsin Blue Book 1962*, 208–12, 217. For more on the 1886 Bay View Massacre, see Jerry M. Cooper, "The Wisconsin National Guard in the Milwaukee Riots of 1886," *Wisconsin Magazine of History* 55, no. 1 (Autumn 1971): 31–48.

5. J. Tracy Hale Jr., "Fire and Fall Back: Memories of a Saturday Soldier," Edward T. Lauer Papers, WVM, I:16.

6. Hale, "Fire and Fall Back," I:21.

7. Joint War History Commissions of Michigan and Wisconsin, *The 32nd Division in the World War, 1917–1919* (Madison: Wisconsin War History Commission, 1920).

8. For an introduction to US participation in World War I, see Edward M. Coffman, *The War to End All Wars: The American Military Experience in World War I* (Madison: University of Wisconsin Press, 1986); Jennifer D. Keene, *World War I: The American Soldier Experience* (Lincoln: University of Nebraska Press, 2011); and Edward G. Lengel, *Thunder and Flames: Americans in the Crucible of Combat, 1917–1918* (Lawrence: University Press of Kansas, 2015). The Thirty-Second Division's official World War I history is the Joint War History Commissions' *The 32nd Division in the World War*. For more on the division's World War I experience, see John W. Barry, *The Midwest Goes to War: The 32nd Division in the Great War* (Lanham, MD: Scarecrow Press, 2007).

9. Robert C. McCoy interview with Thomas Doherty, 1979, Wisconsin Veterans Oral History Program (hereafter cited as WVOHP), WVM.

10. Joint War History Commissions, *The 32nd Division in the World War*, 62.

11. Hale, "Fire and Fall Back," I:173–74.

12. Hale, I:195.

13. Leonard P. Ayers, *The War with Germany: A Statistical Summary* (Washington, DC: Government Printing Office, 1919), 117.

14. Joint War History Commissions, *The 32nd Division in the World War*, 127.

15. Robert Dalessandro, *Organization and Insignia of the American Expeditionary Force, 1917–1923* (Atglen, PA: Schiffer, 2008), 164; Wilson, *Maneuver and Firepower*, 111.

16. Hale, "Fire and Fall Back," II:8.

17. Wilson, *Maneuver and Firepower*, 87.

18. Hale, "Fire and Fall Back," II:8–9.

19. "Cavalry Unit for This City Seems Assured," *Alma* (MI) *Record*, 26 May 1921.

20. Herbert M. Smith, *Four Score and Ten: Happenings in the Life of Herbert M. Smith* (Eau Claire, WI: Heins Publications, 1994), 169.

21. Herbert A. Smith interview with Tom Doherty, 2008, WVOHP, WVM.

22. "Bill to Abolish Guard Passed by House," *Eau Claire Leader-Telegram*, 21 February 1923.

23. "Senator Is Opposed to Action Taken by Assembly," *Capital Times* (Madison), 23 February 1923.

24. Wisconsin Adjutant General, *Biennial Report of the Adjutant General of the State of Wisconsin for the Two Fiscal Years Ending June 30, 1924* (Madison: State of Wisconsin, 1924), 34.

25. "State Guard Lacks Funds for Training," *News-Palladium* (Benton Harbor, MI), 22 June 1925.

26. Hale, "Fire and Fall Back," II:46

27. Smith, *Four Score and Ten*, 188–89.

28. *National Guard of the State of Michigan*, xii.

29. Wisconsin Adjutant General, *Biennial Report of the Adjutant General of the State of Wisconsin for the Two Fiscal Years Ending June 30, 1928* (Madison: State of Wisconsin, 1928), 14.

30. Wisconsin Adjutant General, *Biennial Report of the Adjutant General of the State of Wisconsin for the Two Fiscal Years Ending June 30, 1930* (Madison: State of Wisconsin, 1930), 82.

31. Smith, *Four Score and Ten*, 188.

32. Smith, *Four Score and Ten*, 188.

33. Herbert A. Smith interview.

34. Hale, "Fire and Fall Back," II:16–17.

35. Wisconsin Adjutant General, *Biennial Report of the Adjutant General of the State of Wisconsin for the Two Fiscal Years Ending June 30, 1932* (Madison: State of Wisconsin, 1932), 13.

36. Hale, "Fire and Fall Back," II:31.

37. Herbert A. Smith interview. The US Army has since rechristened numerous facilities like Fort Benning that were named for Confederate leaders. This work will refer to installations as they were known during World War II. Fort Benning is now Fort Moore. Other renamed installations that appear in this work are Fort Bragg (now Fort Liberty) and Fort Polk, then Camp Polk (now Fort Johnson).

38. Smith, *Four Score and Ten*, 182.

39. Smith, *Four Score and Ten*, 184.

40. Oral History Interview with Brigadier General Robert B. Hughes by John J. Cooney, April 1976, WHS.

41. Donald Knox, *Death March: Survivors of Bataan* (New York: Harcourt Brace Jovanovich, 1981), 9.

42. Herbert A. Smith interview.

43. "Gen. Wilson Sends Greetings to Wisconsin," *Wisconsin National Guard Review*, July 1936, 1; "Maneuvers a Wonderful Success," *Wisconsin National Guard Review*, September 1936, 1.

44. Hale, "Fire and Fall Back," II:35.

45. "Forces of Two States Function as One," *Wisconsin National Guard Review*, September 1936, 5.

46. Wisconsin Adjutant General, *Biennial Report of the Adjutant General of the State of Wisconsin for the Two Fiscal Years Ending June 30, 1924*, 30.

47. "Guards Patrol Tornado Ruins at Eau Claire," *Capital Times*, 15 June 1930; Wisconsin Adjutant General, *Biennial Report for the Two Fiscal Years Ending June 30, 1930*, 5.

48. Herbert Jacobs, "The Wisconsin Milk Strikes," *Wisconsin Magazine of History* 35, no. 1 (Autumn 1951): 34.

49. "Striker Called Out for Duty with His Company of Troops," *Chicago Tribune*, 14 January 1937.

50. For more on the Flint strike, see Sidney Fine, *Sit-Down: The General Motors Strike of 1936–1937* (Ann Arbor: University of Michigan Press, 1969).

51. Wisconsin Adjutant General, *Biennial Report of the Adjutant General of the State of Wisconsin for the Two Fiscal Years Ending June 30, 1934* (Madison: State of Wisconsin, 1934), 15–17, 41–42.

52. Smith, *Four Score and Ten*, 189.

53. Wisconsin Adjutant General, *Biennial Report for the Two Fiscal Years Ending June 30, 1932*, 14.

54. Richard A. Stoelb, *Time in Hell: The Battle for Buna on the Island of New Guinea* (Sheboygan: Sheboygan Historical Society, 2012), 11.

55. Clarence Jungwirth, *Diary of a National Guardsman in World War II, 1940–1945* (self-published, 1991), 3.

56. Steve Janicki interview with Frank Boring, 20 August 2007, GVSU.

57. John Maino, *Frontlines, World War II: Personal Accounts of Wisconsin Veterans* (Appleton, WI: JP Graphics, 2006), 87.

58. Ervin Sartell interview with Mik Derks, Janesville, Wisconsin, 8 October 2002, WVOHP, WVM.

59. Erwin A. Pichotte survey, World War II Veterans Surveys, 32d Infantry Division, USAHEC.

60. Jungwirth, *Diary of a National Guardsman*, 3–4.

61. Stoelb, *Time in Hell*, 11.

62. Maino, *Frontlines*, 87.

63. Jungwirth, Diary of a National Guardsman, 4.

64. Maino, *Frontlines*, 86.

65. Erwin T. Veneklase interview with John Mingerink and Rick Mingerink, 4 November 2005, GVSU.

66. For studies of the US Army during World War II, a good starting point is the army's own official history series, *The US Army in World War II*, published by the Center of Military History and commonly referred to as the "Green Books." For the works in the series on the initial wartime mobilization, see Kent Roberts Greenfield, Robert R. Palmer, and Bell I. Wiley, *The Organization of Ground Combat Troops* (Washington, DC: Center of Military History, 1987) and Robert R. Palmer, Bell I. Wiley, and William R. Keast, *The Procurement and Training of Ground Combat Troops* (Washington, DC: Center of Military History, 1991). See also J. Garry Clifford and Samuel R. Spencer Jr., *The First Peacetime Draft* (Lawrence: University Press of Kansas, 1986) and Paul Dickson, *The Rise of the G.I. Army, 1940–1941* (New York: Atlantic Monthly Press, 2020). For specific focus on the National Guard, see Robert Bruce Sligh, *The National Guard and National Defense: The Mobilization of the Guard in World War II* (Westport, CT: Praeger, 1992) and Michael E. Weaver, *Guard Wars: The 28th Infantry Division in World War II* (Bloomington: Indiana University Press, 2010).

67. Clifford and Spencer, *First Peacetime Draft*, 6.

68. Christopher R. Gabel, *The U.S. Army GHQ Maneuvers of 1941* (Washington, DC: Center of Military History, 1992), 13.

69. "B Company in Its First Big Maneuver," *Eau Claire Leader-Telegram*, 17 August 1940.

70. Thomas Doherty, "Blitzkrieg for Beginners: The Maneuvers of 1940 in Central Wisconsin," *Wisconsin Magazine of History* 68, no. 2 (Winter 1984–1985): 101.

71. McCoy interview.

72. Diary of J. Tracy Hale Jr., 12 August 1940, 15 August 1940, J. Tracy Hale Jr. Papers, Milwaukee County Historical Society, Milwaukee, Wisconsin.

73. "B Company in Its First Big Maneuver."

74. "Butter Scare in 'War Zone,' Visitors Say," *Capital Times*, 28 August 1940.

75. Walter F. Choinski Jr., "The Military Connection," Walter F. Choinski Jr. Papers, WHS, 11.

76. Hale, "Fire and Fall Back," III:3; "Corps Exercise at Camp M'Coy Is Begun in Rain," *Chicago Tribune*, 25 August 1940; "2D Army Troops Halt Mimic War in Rain and Mist," *Chicago Tribune*, 27 August 1940.

77. "2D Army Troops."

78. Doherty, "Blitzkrieg for Beginners," 102.

79. "2D Army Troops."

80. Hale, "Fire and Fall Back," II:2.

81. Richard Van Hammen interview with Dan Bush and Chris Vredeveld, 11 November, 2005, GVSU.

82. Hale, "Fire and Fall Back," III:3.

83. "Finds Officers Inferior," *New York Times*, 29 August 1940.

84. "All of Army Found in Need of Training and Guns," *New York Times*, 9 September 1940.

85. Gabel, *GHQ Maneuvers*, 14.

86. "Guard May Be Called by October 16: Immell," *Capital Times*, 5 September 1940. The 135th Medical Regiment, later designated the 135th Medical Group, entered federal service in January 1941. Like the Thirty-Second Division, it went to the Southwest Pacific, and at times portions of the organization were attached to the Red Arrow and treated its casualties. For a history of the organization see James R. Moore and Anselm M. Keefe, *Official Outline of the History of the 135th Medical Group* (Wisconsin: 135th Medical Battalion, 1964).

87. Jungwirth, *Diary of a National Guardsman*, 6.

88. Robert J. Bable, *Beyond Pongani Mission* (Ann Arbor, MI: Bokmal Press, 2001), n.p.

89. Benjamin Winneshiek interview with Tom Doherty, 1989, WVOHP, WVM.

90. Roy M. Campbell, *Kindling for the Devil's Fires: Journals of an Infantryman* (Victoria, BC: Trafford, 2005), 32–38.

91. Campbell, *Kindling for the Devil's Fires*, 35.

Chapter 2

1. "150 Guardsmen Inducted into 32nd Division in Mobilization Here Today," *Capital Times* (Madison), 15 October 1940.

2. Herbert M. Smith, *O-241957: The Early Years of World War II* (Eau Claire, WI: Heins Publications, 1995), 6.

3. "Rapid Population Boom Causing Some Problems," *Town Talk* (Alexandria, LA), 22 November 1940.

4. Clarence Jungwirth, *Diary of a National Guardsman in World War II, 1940–1945* (self-published, 1991), 6.

5. John Maino, *Frontlines, World War II: Personal Accounts of Wisconsin Veterans* (Appleton, WI: JP Graphics, 2006), 87.

6. "Seven Officers and 565 Men Rejected," *Wisconsin National Guard Review*, December 1940.

7. "Guard Units Get Orders to Head for Camp," *Port Huron Times Herald*, 19 October 1940.

8. Benjamin Winneshiek interview with Tom Doherty, 1989, Wisconsin Veterans Oral History Program (hereafter cited as WVOHP), WVM.

9. Arthur J. Kessenich memoir, in Kessenich file, World War II Veterans Surveys, 32nd Infantry Division, USAHEC, 2.

10. Gordon Zuverink interview with Anita Van Til, 27 September 2011, GVSU.

11. Roy M. Campbell, *Kindling for the Devil's Fires: Journals of an Infantryman* (Victoria, BC: Trafford, 2005), 45–46.

12. "First of Guard from State Off," *Detroit Free Press*, 20 October 1940.

13. "The Trek South with the 121st F.A.," *Wisconsin National Guard Review*, December 1940.

14. "Two Wisconsin Deaths Come Early After Call," *Wisconsin National Guard Review*, December 1940.

15. "12 Planes in Detroit Squadron Are Coming," *Town Talk*, 25 October 1941; Tom Doherty, "Too Little, Too Late: Janesville's 'Lost Children' of the Armored Force," *Wisconsin Magazine of History* 75, no. 4 (Summer 1992): 242–83.

16. Campbell, *Kindling for the Devil's Fires*, 46.

17. Campbell, *Kindling for the Devil's Fires*, 47–48.

18. "First Regimental Retreat Held; 9,100 at Work on Four Camp Sites," *Town Talk*, 29 October 1940.

19. Jungwirth, *Diary of a National Guardsman*, 11.

20. Smith, *O-241957*, 2.

21. Orville Suckow to Minda Dockar, 30 October 1940, Minda Dockar Papers, WHS.

22. Kessenich memoir, 3; "First Regimental Retreat Held," *Town Talk*, 29 October 1940.

23. Campbell, *Kindling for the Devil's Fires*, 47.

24. Maino, *Frontlines*, 87.

25. "First Regimental Retreat Held," *Town Talk*, 29 October 1940.

26. William A. Sikkel interview with Anita Van Til, 14 June 2007, GVSU.

27. "Beauregard Notes," *Town Talk*, 21 November 1940.

28. Suckow to Dockar, 30 October 1940, Dockar Papers.

29. "Insulation Eating Goats Inspire Ode to 127th Infantry," *Town Talk*, 11 November 1940.

30. Smith, *O-241957*, 2.

31. Smith, *O-241957*, 2.

32. "Holiday Week in the 121st F.A.," *Wisconsin National Guard Review*, February 1941.

33. "First Regimental Retreat Held," *Town Talk*, 29 October 1940.

34. "Every Regiment Has at Least One Like This in the Mess," *Wisconsin National Guard Review*, January 1941.

35. "Wisconsin Boys Say 'Eats' Are Swell at Beauregard," *Town Talk*, 24 October 1940.

36. Gifford Coleman interview with Mark D. Van Ells, 10 November 1994, WVOHP, WVM.

37. Smith, *O-241957*, 7.

38. "Naturally the Q.M. Would Get the Sheets," *Wisconsin National Guard Review*, December 1940.

39. Kessenich memoir, 3.

40. Diary of J. Tracy Hale Jr., 18 November 1940, J. Tracy Hale Jr. Papers, Milwaukee County Historical Society, Milwaukee, Wisconsin.

41. Campbell, *Kindling for the Devil's Fires*, 50.

42. Kessenich memoir, 4.

43. "Guardsmen 'Different Men' After First Month," *Town Talk*, 26 November 1940.

44. "Gen. Immell's View of Camp Beauregard," *Wisconsin National Guard Review*, January 1941.

45. Ervin Sartell interview with Mik Derks, Janesville, Wisconsin, 8 October 2002, WVOHP, WVM.

46. Smith, *O-241957*, 6.

47. United States War Department, *Completion Report, 1942* (Alexandria, LA: Office of the Area Engineer, Camp Livingston and Vicinity, 1942), 1.

48. "Camp Livingston a Great Camp," *Wisconsin National Guard Review*, May 1941.

49. Jungwirth, *Diary of a National Guardsman*, 13.

50. "Camp Livingston a Great Camp."

51. "Camp Livingston Appears a Dream," *Wisconsin National Guard Review*, March 1941.

52. "32nd Division Answers 'Call to Arms,'" *Town Talk*, 25 March 1941.

53. "Two Regiments in Mock Battle Near Alexandria," *Town Talk*, 28 March 1941.

54. Monte L. Ball, *190 Letters: A Soldier's Story of World War II* (Mustang, OK: Tate Publishing, 2013), 17.

55. Lawrence Thayer, *My War* (Palmyra, WI: Palmyra Historical Society, 2003), 1.

56. Martin Bolt interview with Frank Boring, 20 July 2007, GVSU.

57. Paul A. Rettell, *A Soldier's True Story: The Life of an Infantry Soldier in World War II* (self-published, 1993), 2.

58. Thayer, *My War*, 1.

59. Steve Janicki interview with Frank Boring, 20 August 2007, GVSU.

60. Bolt interview.

61. Maino, *Frontlines*, 88.

62. "Army Personnel Within the Guard," *Wisconsin National Guard Review*, February 1941.

63. Diary of J. Tracy Hale Jr., 20 April 1941, J. Tracy Hale Jr. Papers, Milwaukee County Historical Society, Milwaukee, Wisconsin.

64. Wendell Trogdon, *Out Front: The Cladie Bailey Story* (Mooresville, IN: Backroads Press, 1994), 53.

65. Rettell, *Soldier's True Story*, 4.

66. "Schools and Still More School," *Wisconsin National Guard Review*, May 1941.

67. Bernd G. Baetcke to Dorothy and Colt, 28 December 1941, Baetcke Family Papers, USAHEC (hereafter cited as Baetcke Papers).

68. "Camp Livingston a Great Camp," *Wisconsin National Guard Review*, May 1941.

69. Winneshiek interview; "The Army Uses Indians to Work Out Code Enemy Probably Won't Crack," *Kerrville Times*, 4 September 1941. In 2013, the code talkers received a Congressional Gold Medal for their wartime work. Sadly, Benjamin Winneshiek and many others received their awards post-humously. For more, see William Meadows, "An Honor Long Overdue: The 2013 Congressional Gold and Silver Medal Ceremonies in Honor of Native American Code Talkers," *American Indian Culture and Research Journal* 40, no. 2 (2016): 91–121.

70. Ball, *190 Letters*, 35.

71. Ball, 32–33.

72. Erling M. Smestad interview with Kelli Brockschmidt and Jennifer Goven, November 2006, GVSU.

73. Byron Gibbs, "My Experiences and Observations," *Sebewa Recollector* (Portland, MI), October 2003.

74. Janicki interview.

75. Hans Sannes interview with James McIntosh, 1999, WVOHP, WVM.

76. Ernie Long to Edith Wiseman, 16 June 1941, Edith Wiseman Papers, Filson Historical Society, Louisville, Kentucky.

77. For an introduction to the Louisiana Maneuvers, see G. Patrick Murray, "The Louisiana Maneuvers: Practice for War," *Louisiana History* 13, no. 2 (1972): 117–138; and Christopher R. Gabel, *The U.S. Army GHQ Maneuvers of 1941* (Washington, DC: Center of Military History, 1992).

78. "Gale Holds Back War Game Start," *New York Times*, 15 September 1941.

79. Mark W. Clark, *Calculated Risk* (New York: Harper and Brothers, 1950), 15.

80. "The Gun That Wasn't There," *New York Times*, 19 September 1942.

81. Kevin C. Holzimmer, *General Walter Kruger: Unsung Hero of the Pacific War* (Lawrence: University Press of Kansas, 2007), 14.

82. J. Tracy Hale Jr., "Fire and Fall Back: Memories of a Saturday Soldier," Edward T. Lauer Papers, WVM, III:20.

83. Ball, *190 Letters*, 23–24.

84. Francis G. Smith, *History of the Third Army* (Historical Section, Army Ground Forces, 1946), 17.

85. Ball, *190 Letters*, 43.

86. Jungwirth, *Diary of a National Guardsman*, 16.

87. Ball, *190 Letters*, 43.

88. "Review of 32nd Maneuver Activities," *Wisconsin National Guard Review*, November 1941.

89. Ball, *190 Letters*, 48.

90. Ball, *190 Letters*, 45.

91. Clark, *Calculated Risk*, 15.

92. "Big Maneuvers Test U.S. Army," *LIFE*, 6 October 1941.

93. "Third Army Prepares to Meet Lear's Tanks in War's Major Test," *Town Talk*, 16 September 1941.

94. "Review of 32nd Maneuver Activities," *Wisconsin National Guard Review*, November 1941.

95. "Soldiers Enter City for Weekend 'Holiday,'" *Town Talk*, 20 September 1941.

96. "Review of 32nd Maneuver Activities," *Wisconsin National Guard Review*, November 1941.

97. Hale, "Fire and Fall Back," III:24.

98. "Review of 32nd Maneuver Activities," *Wisconsin National Guard Review*, November 1941.

99. Richard Correll to Elizabeth Harwood, 27 August 1941, Elizabeth Harwood Katz Papers, University of Alabama Library, Tuscaloosa, Alabama (hereafter cited as Katz Papers).

100. Gibbs, "Experiences and Observations," October 2003.

101. Jungwirth, *Diary of a National Guardsman*, 16.

102. Jungwirth, *Diary of a National Guardsman*, 16.

103. Sartell interview.

104. Sartell interview.

105. Rettell, *Soldier's True Story*, 4.

106. "War Games Show Army Still Lags," *New York Times*, 30 September 1941.

107. "Notes on trip—September 27—to V Corps CP at Lena," Walter Krueger Papers, United States Military Academy, West Point, New York (hereafter cited as Krueger Papers).

108. Jim Dan Hill, *The Minute Man in Peace and War: A History of the National Guard* (Harrisburg, PA: Stackpole, 1964), 431.

109. "Morale Is High during Maneuver Writes a Private," *Wisconsin National Guard Review*, November 1941.

110. "M'Nair Deplores 'Weak Discipline,'" *New York Times*, 1 October 1941.

111. "Review of 32nd Maneuver Activities," *Wisconsin National Guard Review*, November 1941.

112. Dwight D. Eisenhower, *At Ease: Stories I Tell My Friends* (Garden City, NY: Doubleday, 1967), 243.

113. Robert J. Bable, *Beyond Pongani Mission* (Ann Arbor, MI: Bokmal Press, 2001), 22.

114. Erwin T. Veneklase interview with John Mingerink and Rick Mingerink, 4 November 2005, GVSU.

115. Coleman interview.

116. Walter F. Choinski Jr., "The Military Connection," Walter F. Choinski Jr. Papers, WHS, 14, 37.

117. Geoffrey Perret, *There's a War to Be Won: The United States Army in World War II* (New York: Random House, 1991), 44.

118. Walter Krueger, *From Down Under to Nippon: The Story of the Sixth Army in World War II* (Nashville, TN: Battery Classics, 1989), 5.

119. Eisenhower, *At Ease*, 243.

120. Hale, "Fire and Fall Back," III:26.

121. Archie Van Gorden, "Red Arrow 'Red': Letters Home from World War II," Cyrena M. Van Gorden Dierauer Family Papers, 1941–1945, WHS, 5–6.

122. Herbert M. Smith, *Four Score and Ten: Happenings in the Life of Herbert M. Smith* (Eau Claire, WI: Heins Publications, 1994), 37.

123. Harold W. Blakeley, *32d Infantry Division in World War II* (Madison: Thirty-Second Infantry Division History Commission, 1957), 15, 24.

124. "32nd Division Officers, Men Have 'Big Time,'" *Town Talk*, 11 November 1940.

125. "Beauregard Notes," *Town Talk*, 26 October 1940.

126. Coleman interview.

127. "Louisiana Town Booms as the Army Moves In," *Milwaukee Journal*, 24 November 1940.

128. "Beauregard Notes," *Town Talk*, 11 November 1940.

129. "Service Units to Be Inducted First," *Wisconsin National Guard Review*, November 1940.

130. "Beauregard Notes," *Town Talk*, 29 October 1940.

131. "Beauregard Notes," *Town Talk*, 4 December 1940.

132. "Northern Boys Meet the Deep South, Find Much in Common, America First," *Milwaukee Journal*, 10 November 1940.

133. Campbell, *Kindling for the Devil's Fires*, 58.

134. Sikkel interview.

135. Anthony Harkins, *Hillbilly: A Cultural History of an American Icon* (New York: Oxford University Press, 2004), 4.

136. Baetcke to parents, n.d. [ca. Winter 1940–1941], Baetcke Papers.

137. Byron Gibbs, "My WWII Experiences and Observations," *Sebewa Recollector* (Portland, MI), December 2003.

138. Ball, *190 Letters*, 47.

139. Byron Gibbs, "My WWII Experiences and Observations," *Sebewa Recollector*, February 2004.

140. Ball, *190 Letters*, 30.

141. Kessenich memoir, 6.

142. "Claim Soldiers Are Doped and Robbed," *Wisconsin National Guard Review*, July 1941.

143. "Local Taxi Drivers Accused of Murder in Fatal Gangfight," *Town Talk*, 15 July 1941.

144. Hale, "Fire and Fall Back," III:22–23.

145. Kessenich memoir, 4–5.

146. "Protest Relative to Alleged Vice Near Beauregard," *Wisconsin National Guard Review*, March 1941.

147. Jungwirth, *Diary of a National Guardsman*, 12.

148. Jungwirth, 12.

149. Marilyn E. Hegarty, *Victory Girls, Khaki-Whackies, and Patriotutes: The Regulation of Female Sexuality during World War II* (New York: New York University Press, 2008), 2, 6. For more on the sexual politics of the United States during the war, see also Beth Bailey and David Farber, *The First Strange Place: Race and Sex in World War II Hawaii* (Baltimore: Johns Hopkins University Press, 1992); Mary Louise Roberts, *What Soldiers Do: Sex and the American GI in World War II France* (Chicago: University of Chicago Press, 2013); and Meghan K. Winchell, *Good Girls, Good Food, Good Fun: The Story of USO Hostesses during World War II* (Chapel Hill: University of North Carolina Press, 2008).

150. Ball, *190 Letters*, 42.

151. "Beauregard Notes," *Town Talk*, 3 December 1940.

152. Richard A. Stoelb, *Time in Hell: The Battle for Buna on the Island of New Guinea* (Sheboygan: Sheboygan Historical Society, 2012), 21.

153. Ball, *190 Letters*, 21.

154. Kessenich memoir, 4.

155. Jungwirth, *Diary of A National Guardsman*, 14.

156. "Beauregard Notes," *Town Talk*, 11 November 1940.

157. "Guardsmen 'Slick Up' for Dance Here Tonight," *Town Talk*, 25 January 1941.

158. For an introduction to GI morale and recreation during World War II, see James J. Cooke, *American Girls, Beer, and Glenn Miller: GI Morale in World War II* (Columbia: University of Missouri Press, 2012); James J. Cooke, *Chewing Gum, Candy Bars, and Beer: The Army PX in World War II* (Columbia: University of Missouri Press, 2006); and Winchell, *Good Girls, Good Food, Good Fun*.

159. Ball, *190 Letters*, 36.

160. "Chorus of 600 for Easter Service," *Wisconsin National Guard Review*, February 1941.

161. "Looks Like the 121st Ran Away with the 32nd Motor Show," *Wisconsin National Guard Review*, March 1941.

162. Hale, "Fire and Fall Back," III:18.

163. "Beauregard Notes," *Town Talk*, 28 November 1940.

164. "128th Infantry Wins Football Championship," *Wisconsin National Guard Review*, March 1941.

165. Hale, "Fire and Fall Back," III:16–17.

166. "Guardsmen Training Here to Visit Battlegrounds," *Town Talk*, 22 November 1940; "Beauregard Notes," *Town Talk*, 6 December 1940.

167. "Recreational Area on Coast to Be Invaded," *Town Talk*, 2 July 1941.

168. "Holiday Week in the 121st F.A.," *Wisconsin National Guard Review*, February 1941.

169. Ball, *190 Letters*, 28–32.

170. Stoelb, *Time in Hell*, 21.

171. Jungwirth, *Diary of a National Guardsman*, 12.

172. Hale, "Fire and Fall Back," III:12.

173. Campbell, *Kindling for the Devil's Fires*, 53–60.

174. "Beauregard Notes," *Town Talk*, 4 December 1940.

175. "Beauregard Notes," *Town Talk*, 26 October 1940.

176. Suckow to Dockar, 30 October 1940, Dockar Papers.

177. Kessenich memoir, 2.

178. Correll to Harwood, 14 November 1941, Katz Papers.

179. "Beauregard Notes," *Town Talk*, 21 November 1940.

180. Jungwirth, *Diary of a National Guardsman*, 14.

181. "G Company Coming Home for Christmas; Men Rejoice," *Capital Times*, 12 December 1940.

182. "Enthusiastic Welcome Given Members of Batteries Sunday," *Green Bay Press-Gazette*, 23 December 1940.

183. Edgar G. Connor, "My Most Memorable Christmases," in Connor file, World War II Veterans Surveys, Infantry Regiments, Separate, 125th Infantry Regiment, USAHEC, 1.

184. Kessenich memoir, 6.

185. Van Gorden, "Red Arrow Red," 1–3.

186. Baetcke to parents, n.d. [ca. Winter 1940–1941], Baetcke Papers.

187. "Soldiers' Wives, Here in Trailers, Like South," *Town Talk*, 11 November 1940.

188. William Lorenz Jr. to William Lorenz, 10 February 1941, William Lorenz Papers, WHS.

189. "Capt. Kobs Weds Wisconsin Girl in Alexandria, La.," *Wisconsin National Guard Review*, September 1941.

190. Kessenich memoir, 7–8.

191. Jungwirth, *Diary of a National Guardsman*, 16.

192. Ball, *190 Letters*, 55.

Chapter 3

1. Martin Bolt interview with Frank Boring, 20 July 2007, GVSU.

2. Roy M. Campbell, *Kindling for the Devil's Fires: Journals of an Infantryman* (Victoria, BC: Trafford, 2005), 63.

3. Historical studies of World War II in the Pacific are numerous. The best overview remains Ronald H. Spector, *Eagle Against the Sun: The American War with Japan* (New York: Vintage, 1985). For recent quality works on the early stages of the Pacific War, see Richard B. Frank, *Tower of Skulls: A History of the Asia-Pacific War, July 1937–May 1942* (New York: Norton, 2020) and John C. McManus, *Fire and Fortitude: The US Army in the Pacific War, 1941–1943* (New York: Caliber, 2019). General MacArthur, a figure who loomed large in the history of the Red Arrow Division, has been the subject of numerous biographies and historical studies. For an introduction to this important and controversial figure, see Richard B. Frank, *MacArthur* (New York: St. Martins Griffin, 2007); Geoffrey Perret, *Old Soldiers Never Die: The Life of Douglas MacArthur* (New York: Random House, 1996); and Michael Schaller, *Douglas MacArthur: The Far Eastern General* (New York: Oxford University Press, 1989). D. Clayton James, *The Years of MacArthur: Volume II, 1941–1945* (Boston: Houghton Mifflin, 1975) is the second work in his comprehensive three-volume history of MacArthur and focuses specifically on his activities during World War II.

4. Archie Van Gorden, "Red Arrow 'Red': Letters Home from World War II," Cyrena M. Van Gorden Dierauer Family Papers, 1941–1945, WHS, 6.

5. Steve Janicki interview with Frank Boring, 20 August 2007, GVSU.

6. Campbell, *Kindling for the Devil's Fires*, 69–70.

7. Arthur J. Kessenich memoir, in Kessenich file, World War II Veterans Surveys, 32nd Infantry Division, USAHEC, 8.

8. Campbell, *Kindling for the Devil's Fires*, 67–68.

9. Bolt interview.

10. Unit Journal, 7 December 1941, 126th Infantry Regiment, Unit Journal—Training (7 Dec 1941–30 May 1942), World War II Operations Reports, 32nd Infantry Division, Reports Relating to World War II and Korean War Combat Operations and to Activities in Occupied Areas, 1940–1954, Record Group 407: Records of the Adjutant General's Office, NARA (hereafter cited as RG 407).

11. Ball, *190 Letters*, 76.

12. Unit Journal, 12 December 1941, 126th Infantry Regiment, Unit Journal—Training (7 Dec 1941–30 May 1942), RG 407.

13. Unit Journal, 16 December 1941, 126th Infantry Regiment, Unit Journal—Training (7 Dec 1941–30 May 1942), RG 407.

14. Dr. Harry H. Heiden to Wanda and Harriet Heiden, 8 December 1941, Harry H. Heiden Papers, WVM.

15. J. Tracy Hale Jr., "Fire and Fall Back: Memories of a Saturday Soldier," Edward T. Lauer Papers, WVM, III:31.

16. Edgar G. Connor, "My Most Memorable Christmases," in Connor file, World War II Veterans Surveys, Infantry Regiments, Separate, 125th Infantry Regiment, USAHEC, 2.

17. William B. Cunningham and Thomas B. Colwell, *Let the Drum Beat: 125th Infantry: Its History during the First Year of World War II* (self-published, n.d.).

18. Truman K. Gibson, *Knocking Down Barriers: My Fight for Black America* (Evanston, IL: Northwestern University Press, 2005), 10. For an introduction to the climate of race relations in Louisiana in the early years of World War II, see Philip J. Johnson, "The Limits of Interracial Compromise: Louisiana, 1941, *Journal of Southern History* 69, no. 2 (2003): 319–348.

19. "Why Army Had Race Rioting," *PM*, 23 January 1942.

20. "Army Censors Facts on Riot," *PM*, 22 January 1942.

21. James B. LaFourche to Walter White, 19 January 1942, Racial Tension in Alexandria, La., 1942, General Office File, Records of the National Association for the Advancement of Colored People, Library of Congress, Washington, DC (hereafter cited as NAACP Records).

22. Joe Wilson Jr., *The 758th Tank Battalion in World War II: The U.S. Army's First All African American Tank Unit* (Jefferson, NC: McFarland, 2018), 32.

23. "M.P.'s Used Gas and Guns on Unarmed Soldiers," *Afro American (Baltimore, MD)*, 24 January 1942.

24. "Night of Horror Vividly Recalled by Brutalized Victims of White MP's, State and Civilian Police in Riot," *Louisiana Weekly*, 24 January 1942.

25. H-T. to Walter White, 13 January 1942, NAACP Records.

26. "10 Soldiers Killed, Report Charges," *Pittsburgh Courier*, 24 January 1942.

27. "Army Censors Facts on Riot," *PM*, 22 January 1942.

28. "No Deaths as a Result of Saturday Night Clash Here Corps Says," *Town Talk* (Alexandria, LA), 12 January 1942.

29. LaFourche to White, 19 January 1942, NAACP Records.

30. Ralph Robinson to Mr. and Mrs. Clem Jones, 11 January 1942, NAACP Records.

31. James B. LaFourche to Walter White, 31 January 1942, NAACP Records; Statement of Sgt. John Hines, NAACP Records.

32. William M. Simpson, "A Tale Untold?: The Alexandria, Louisiana Lee Street Riot (January 10, 1942)," *Louisiana History* 35, no. 2 (Spring 1994): 142–45. A few reports at the time also speculated that white MPs may have been killed. The *Louisiana Weekly* noted rumors that "at least two white M.P.'s were dead when they reached the army hospital." The *Afro American*, a Baltimore-based newspaper with a national readership, printed an account from a Black soldier who was in an automobile escaping the violence when another soldier produced a pistol and opened fire on police from the car window. "I am certain he plugged an MP in the right ear," the soldier wrote, "because I saw his hand fly up in pain." LaFourche, in a letter to Walter White, wrote that "one of these white M.P.'s was almost certainly stabbed to death" in the initial struggle in front of the Ritz Theater. "Night of Horror Vividly Recalled," *Louisiana Weekly*, 24 January 1942; "One Soldier Shot Back at La. M.P.'s," *Afro American*, 24 January 1942; James B. LaFourche to Walter White, 19 January 1942, NAACP Records.

33. "Night of Horror Vividly Recalled," *Louisiana Weekly*, 24 January 1942.

34. "M.P.'s Used Gas and Guns."

35. "Army Censors Facts on Riot."

36. "Army Censors Facts on Riot."

37. Walter Krueger to William Dryden, 17 January 1942, Military File 1941–1942, Walter Krueger Papers, United States Military Academy, West Point, New York.

38. J. D. Daniels to Walter White, 11 March 1942, NAACP Records.

39. War Department memorandum, 23 January 1942, NAACP Records; Simpson, "A Tale Untold," 133–149.

40. Matthew F. Delmont, *Half American: The Epic Story of African Americans Fighting World War II at Home and Abroad* (New York: Viking, 2022), 156.

41. Simpson, "A Tale Untold," 144.

42. Clarence Jungwirth, *Diary of a National Guardsman in World War II, 1940–1945* (self-published, 1991), 40.

43. Jungwirth, *Diary of a National Guardsman*, 40.

44. Van Gorden, "Red Arrow Red," 18.

45. Hans Sannes interview with James McIntosh, 1999, Wisconsin Veterans Oral History Program, WVM. The 101st Airborne originated as a reserve division in Wisconsin in the years after World War I. It adopted the emblem of a bald eagle head, an homage to "Old Abe the War Eagle," the mascot of the Eighth Wisconsin Infantry during the Civil War. Though its association with Wisconsin had been severed by 1942, the 101st Airborne Division retained Old Abe's image on its emblem and became known as the "Screaming Eagles." For more on Old Abe, see Richard H. Zeitlin, *Old Able the War Eagle: A True Story of the Civil War and Reconstruction* (Madison: Wisconsin Historical Society Press, 1986).

46. Van Gorden, "Red Arrow Red," 16, 20.

47. Joe H. Camp Jr., *32 Answered: A South Carolina Veterans' Story* (Charleston, SC: Joe H. Camp, Jr., 2015), 47–75.

48. Van Gorden, "Red Arrow Red," 20.

49. "Telling a Colonel the Tradition of His Regiment," *Wisconsin National Guard Review*, March 1942.

50. Walter F. Choinski Jr., "The Military Connection," Walter F. Choinski Jr. Papers, WHS, 44.

51. For examples of his poetry, see Edwin Forrest Harding, *Lays of the Mei-kuo ying-p'an* (Peking: publisher not identified, 1920s).

52. Leslie Anders, *Gentle Knight: The Life and Times of Major General Edwin Forrest Harding* (Kent, OH: Kent State University Press, 1985), 159.

53. George C. Marshall interview with Forrest Pogue, Transcript of Tape 12M and 19M, George C. Marshall Papers, Virginia Military Institute, Lexington, Virginia.

54. Hale, "Fire and Fall Back," III:33.

55. "Many Changes in the 32nd Division," *Wisconsin National Guard Review*, March 1942.

56. "Confidence in Major General Harding," *Wisconsin National Guard Review*, May 1942.

57. Hale, "Fire and Fall Back," III:33.

58. "Confidence in Major General Harding," *Wisconsin National Guard Review*, May 1942.

59. Hale, "Fire and Fall Back," III:30–31.

60. Frederick Stonehouse, *Combat Engineer!: The History of the 107th Engineering Battalion, 1881–1981* (107th Engineer Association, 1981), 62.

61. Robert C. McCoy to Alberta McCoy, n.d. [ca. 13 or 20 February 1942], McCoy Family Papers, WVM (hereafter cited as McCoy Papers).

62. Jungwirth, *Diary of a National Guardsman*, 40.

63. Charles C. McCoy to Alberta McCoy, n.d., ca. 13 or 20 February 1942, McCoy Papers.

64. Kessenich memoir, 9.

65. Campbell, *Kindling for the Devil's Fires*, 91–94.

66. Van Gorden, "Red Arrow Red," 27–28.

67. Janicki interview.

68. Paul A. Rettell, *A Soldier's True Story: The Life of an Infantry Soldier in World War II* (self-published, 1993), 12.

69. Kessenich memoir, 9.

70. Campbell, *Kindling for the Devil's Fires*, 95.

71. Ball, *190 Letters*, 104.

72. Van Gorden, "Red Arrow Red," 29.

73. Van Gorden, 29.

74. Campbell, *Kindling for the Devil's Fires*, 95–97.

75. Herbert M. Smith, *O-241957: The Early Years of World War II* (Eau Claire, WI: Heins Publications, 1995), 19.

76. Anders, *Gentle Knight*, 211–212.

77. Sheldon Ennis to E. J. Kahn Jr., 10 December 1941, E. J. Kahn Papers, New York Public Library, New York, New York (hereafter cited as Kahn Papers).

78. Jeanette Genetty to E.J. Kahn Jr., n.d. [December 1941], Kahn Papers.

79. E. J. Kahn Jr., *About the New Yorker and Me: A Sentimental Journey* (New York: Penguin, 1979), 63.

80. E. J. Kahn Jr., *The Army Life* (New York: Simon & Schuster, 1942), xii.

81. Spector, *Eagle Against the Sun*, 151.

82. Campbell, *Kindling for the Devil's Fires*, 97.

83. Jungwirth, *Diary of a National Guardsman*, 41.

84. Address by Colonel Lawrence A. Quinn, Commanding Officer of the 126th Infantry, on Eve of Departure of Regiment to Meet the Enemy, 7 April 1942, 126th Infantry Regiment, Journal and File—Buna (Papuan) Campaign (1–31 October 1942), RG 407.

85. Adrian Stransky, *Dear Dorothy: Letters from the Pacific Theater, 1941–1944* (Madison, WI: Marie T. Trest and Dennis Trest, 2014), n.p.

86. Ball, *190 Letters*, 107–8.

87. Hale, "Fire and Fall Back," III:40.

88. Kahn, *Army Life*, 150.

89. Ball, *190 Letters*, 107.

90. Hale, "Fire and Fall Back," III:41.

91. Jungwirth, *Diary of a National Guardsman*, 41.

92. Ball, *190 Letters*, 108.

93. Ball, 107.

94. McCoy to family, 16 April 1942, McCoy Papers.

95. Ball, *190 Letters*, 107.

96. Campbell, *Kindling for the Devil's Fires*, 100.

97. Stransky, *Dear Dorothy*, n.p.

98. Diary of J. Tracy Hale Jr., 15 April 1942, J. Tracy Hale Jr. Papers, Milwaukee County Historical Society, Milwaukee, Wisconsin.

99. Kessenich memoir, 10.

100. Smith, *O-241957*, 21.

101. McCoy to family, 16 April 1942; McCoy to Alberta McCoy, n.d. [April 1942], McCoy Papers.

102. Campbell, *Kindling for the Devil's Fires*, 101–102.

103. Correll to Harwood, 14 April 1942, Elizabeth Harwood Katz Papers, University of Alabama Library, Tuscaloosa, Alabama.

104. Ball, *190 Letters*, 109.

105. Rettell, *Soldier's True Story*, 14.

106. Raymond F. Dasmann, *Called by the Wild: The Autobiography of a Conservationist* (Berkeley: University of California Press, 2002), 23–24.

107. Howard E. Kelley, *Born in the U.S.A.: A World War II Memoir* (Eau Claire, WI: Heins Publications, 1999), 2.

108. Thomas R. St. George, *C/O Postmaster* (New York: Thomas Y. Crowell, 1943), 1.

109. St. George, *C/O Postmaster*, 2, 4.

110. Kelley, *Born in the USA*, 13–14.

111. Campbell, *Kindling for the Devil's Fires*, 101.

112. McCoy to family, n.d. [April 1942], McCoy Papers.

113. St. George. *C/O Postmaster*, 1–8.

114. "Robert Thompson, U.S. Communist Leader, Dies," *New York Times*, 17 October 1965; Saul

Wellman to Sylvia Hall Thompson, 10 May 1966, Sylvia Hall Thompson Papers, Tamiment Library and Robert F. Wagner Labor Archives, New York University, New York, New York. For an introduction to Spanish Civil War veterans in the US armed forces during World War II and the travails they faced, see Peter N. Carroll, Michael Nash, and Melvin Small, eds., *The Good Fight Continues: World War II Letters from the Abraham Lincoln Brigade* (New York: New York University Press, 2006).

115. "Captain Herman Bottcher: A Brief Account of His Service to America," Herman Bottcher File, Abraham Lincoln Brigade Archive, Tamiment Library and Robert F. Wagner Labor Archives, New York University, New York, New York.

116. McCoy to family, 16 April 42, McCoy Papers.

Chapter 4

1. Donald Knox, *Death March: Survivors of Bataan* (New York: Harcourt Brace Jovanovich, 1981), 134. For more on the experiences of American prisoners in Japanese captivity, see E. Bartlett Kerr, *Surrender and Survival: The Experience of American POWs in the Pacific, 1941–1945* (New York: Morrow, 1985).

2. Roy M. Campbell, *Kindling for the Devil's Fires: Journals of an Infantryman* (Victoria, BC: Trafford, 2005), 103.

3. Thomas R. St. George, *C/O Postmaster* (New York: Thomas Y. Crowell, 1943), 18–19.

4. Campbell, *Kindling for the Devil's Fires*, 104.

5. Diary of J. Tracy Hale Jr., 22 April 1942, J. Tracy Hale Jr. Papers, Milwaukee County Historical Society, Milwaukee, Wisconsin.

6. Howard E. Kelley, *Born in the U.S.A.: A World War II Memoir* (Eau Claire, WI: Heins Publications, 1999), 17. For more on transoceanic troop transport during World War II, see Mark D. Van Ells, "War Crossings: The American GI as Transatlantic Traveler," in *Off Shore: Perspectives on Atlantic Pleasure Travel since the 19th Century*, ed. Brigit Braasch and Claudia Müller (Zürich: Lit, 2020), 129–60.

7. Arthur J. Kessenich memoir, in Kessenich file, World War II Veterans Surveys, 32nd Infantry Division, USAHEC, 10.

8. Kelley, *Born in the USA*, 17.

9. Claire O. Ehle interview with Mik Derks, Stoughton, Wisconsin, 25 November 2002, Wisconsin Veterans Oral History Program, WVM.

10. St. George, *C/O Postmaster*, 23.

11. Richard A. Stoelb, *Time in Hell: The Battle for Buna on the Island of New Guinea* (Sheboygan: Sheboygan Historical Society, 2012), 27.

12. Compilation of letters from Dr. Harry Heiden, n.d., Heiden Papers, WVM.

13. Clarence Jungwirth, *Diary of a National Guardsman in World War II, 1940–1945* (self-published, 1991), 28.

14. Ehle interview.

15. Kenneth G. Springer, "Australia and New Guinea: World War II Memoirs," in Springer file, World War II Veterans Surveys, 32d Infantry Division, USAHEC, 5.

16. "Sight a Sub and Save Our Ship," *The Stalker*, 9 May 1942.

17. Kessenich memoir, 11.

18. E. J. Kahn, *G.I. Jungle: An American Soldier in Australia and New Guinea* (New York: Simon & Schuster, 1943), 2.

19. Raymond F. Dasmann, *Called by the Wild: The Autobiography of a Conservationist* (Berkeley: University of California Press, 2002), 26.

20. St. George, *C/O Postmaster*, 33–34.

21. Dasmann, *Called by the Wild*, 25.

22. Lenord Sill, *Buna and Beyond: 32nd Infantry Division World War II* (self-published, 2002), 27.

23. Campbell, *Kindling for the Devil's Fires*, 109.

24. Herbert M. Smith, *O-241957: The Early Years of World War II* (Eau Claire, WI: Heins Publications, 1995), 22–23.

25. Jungwirth, *Diary of a National Guardsman*, 42–43.

26. Campbell, *Kindling for the Devil's Fires*, 109.

27. Joe H. Camp Jr., *32 Answered: A South Carolina Veterans' Story* (Charleston, SC: Joe H. Camp, Jr., 2015), 90.

28. Kahn, *G.I. Jungle*, 7.

29. "Pvt. Wasserman Wins Essay Contest," *The Stalker*, 4 May 1942.

30. Archie Van Gorden, "Red Arrow 'Red': Letters Home from World War II," Cyrena M. Van Gorden Dierauer Family Papers, 1941–1945, WHS, 44.

31. St. George, *C/O Postmaster*, 29.

32. Kessenich memoir, 11.

33. Campbell, *Kindling for the Devil's Fires*, 110.

34. St. George, *C/O Postmaster*, 25.

35. Jungwirth, *Diary of a National Guardsman*, 43.

36. Kahn, *G.I. Jungle*, 8.

37. Camp, *32 Answered*, 89.

38. Campbell, *Kindling for the Devil's Fires*, 114.

39. Smith, *O-241957*, 25.

40. Smith, *O-241957*, 25.

41. St. George, *C/O Postmaster*, 38.

42. Kahn, *G.I. Jungle*, 15.

43. Sill, *Buna and Beyond*, 31.

44. E. Daniel Potts and Annette Potts, *Yanks Down Under: The American Impact on Australia* (Melbourne: Oxford University Press, 1985), 82.

45. Campbell, *Kindling for the Devil's Fires*, 116.

46. Springer, "Australia and New Guinea," 6.

47. Jungwirth, *Diary of a National Guardsman*, 44.

48. Stoelb, *Time in Hell*, 31.

49. St. George, *C/O Postmaster*, 79.

50. 107th Medical Battalion—History (15 Oct 1940–1 Mar 1943), Record Group 407: Records of the Adjutant General's Office, NARA (hereafter cited as RG 407).

51. Kelley, *Born in the USA*, 21–22.

52. St. George, *C/O Postmaster*, 55.

53. Van Gorden, "Red Arrow Red," 65.

54. Campbell, *Kindling for the Devil's Fires*, 116.

55. Adrian Stransky, *Dear Dorothy: Letters from the Pacific Theater, 1941–1944* (Madison, WI: Marie T. Trest and Dennis Trest, 2014), n.p.

56. 128th Infantry Regiment—History (15 Oct 1940–28 Feb 1943), RG 407.

57. Advance Unit Journal, 19 July 1942, 126 Infantry Regiment—Unit Journal and File—Training—Australia (10 June–31 August 1942), RG 407.

58. Smith, *O-241957*, 35.

59. Kahn, *G.I. Jungle*, 41.

60. General Order No. 37, 126 Infantry Regiment—Unit Journal and File—Training—Australia (10 June–31 August 1942), RG 407.

61. "2 High Army Awards Given to Soldier," *Battle Creek Enquirer*, 20 September 1942.

62. Memorial address, 30 August 1942, 126 Infantry Regiment—Unit Journal and File—Training—Australia (10 June–31 August 1942), RG 407.

63. Unit Journal, 30 August 1942, 126 Infantry Regiment—Unit Journal and File—Training—Australia (10 June–31 August 1942), RG 407.

64. United States War Department, *FM 31-20: Jungle Warfare* (Washington, DC: Government Printing Office, 1941), 1, 3, 15.

65. Jungwirth, *Diary of a National Guardsman*, 46–47.

66. Campbell, *Kindling for the Devil's Fires*, 121.

67. Dasmann, *Called by the Wild*, 32.

68. Dasmann, *Called by the Wild*, 32–33.

69. Kelley, *Born in the USA*, 28.

70. 128th Infantry Regiment—History (15 Oct 1940–28 Feb 1943), RG 407.

71. Smith, *O-241957*, 41.

72. General Harding's marginal comments, Background Files to the Study of "Victory in Papua," Department of Defense, Department of the Army, Office of the Chief of Military History, Record Group 319: Records of the Army Staff, 1903–2009, NARA.

73. Robert L. Eichelberger, *Our Jungle Road to Tokyo* (New York: Viking, 1950), 11.

74. Campbell, *Kindling for the Devil's Fires*, 120.

75. St. George, *C/O Postmaster*, 181.

76. Jungwirth, *Diary of a National Guardsman*, 46.

77. Potts and Potts, *Yanks Down Under*, 83.

78. Kahn, *G.I. Jungle*, 42.

79. Dasmann, *Called by the Wild*, 29.

80. Springer, "Australia and New Guinea," 8.

81. Ball, *190 Letters*, 118.

82. Kelley, *Born in the USA*, 28.

83. Kahn, *G.I. Jungle*, 42–43.

84. Kahn, *G.I. Jungle*, 14.

85. Campbell, *Kindling for the Devil's Fires*, 114.

86. Kahn, *G.I. Jungle*, 18. For an introduction to the cultural interactions between Americans and Australians during World War II, see John Hammond Moore, *Over-Sexed, Over-Paid, and Over Here: Americans in Australia, 1941–1945* (St. Lucia: University of Queensland Press, 1981); and Potts and Potts, *Yanks Down Under*. For a wider perspective on the Australia the Red Arrow entered, see Peter J. Dean, ed., *Australia 1942: In the Shadow of War* (Melbourne: Cambridge University Press, 2013).

87. Dasmann, *Called by the Wild*, 27.

88. Dasmann, *Called by the Wild*, 30.

89. Byron Gibbs, "My Experiences and Observations," *Sebewa Recollector* (Portland, MI), April 2004.

90. St. George, *C/O Postmaster*, 106.

91. St. George, *C/O Postmaster*, 58.

92. Paul M. Kinder to mother, 9 June 1942, Paul M. Kinder Letters, World War II Letters Collection, State Historical Society of Missouri, Columbia, Missouri (hereafter cited as Kinder Letters).

93. Kahn, *G.I. Jungle*, 17.

94. Van Gorden, "Red Arrow Red," 52.

95. Kelley, *Born in the USA*, 23–24.

96. Kahn, *G.I. Jungle*, 19.

97. Paul Kinder to Ruth and Sam, 21 April 1942, Kinder Letters.

98. Kessenich memoir, 13.

99. Kahn, *G.I. Jungle*, 19.

100. St. George, *C/O Postmaster*, 137.

101. Kahn, *G.I. Jungle*, 19.

102. St. George, *C/O Postmaster*, 138–39.

103. St. George, *C/O Postmaster*, 59, 95.

104. Lawrence Thayer, *My War* (Palmyra, WI: Palmyra Historical Society, 2003), 6.

105. St. George, *C/O Postmaster*, 60.

106. Jungwirth, *Diary of a National Guardsman*, 45.

107. John Maino, *Frontlines, World War II: Personal Accounts of Wisconsin Veterans* (Appleton, WI: JP Graphics, 2006), 90.

108. Thayer, *My War*, 6.

109. St. George, *C/O Postmaster*, 149.

110. Jungwirth, *Diary of a National Guardsman*, 45.

111. Jungwirth, *Diary of a National Guardsman*, 44.

112. Ehle interview.

113. Camp, *32 Answered*, 114.

114. Moore, *Over-Sexed*, 91.

115. Kinder to Ruth and Sam, 9 June 1942, Kinder Letters.

116. St. George, *C/O Postmaster*, 61.

117. Hughes interview, WHS.

118. Richard Correll to Elizabeth Harwood Correll, 31 July 1942, Elizabeth Harwood Katz Papers, University of Alabama Library, Tuscaloosa, Alabama.

119. Van Gorden, "Red Arrow Red," 46.

120. Moore, *Over-Sexed*, 91.

121. Robert J. Bable, *Beyond Pongani Mission* (Ann Arbor, MI: Bokmal Press, 2001), 5–6.

122. Thayer, *My War*, 5.

123. St. George, *C/O Postmaster*, 102–3.

124. Stoelb, *Time in Hell*, 32.

125. Jungwirth, *Diary of a National Guardsman*, 44–45.

126. "A.W.A.S. Marries U.S.A. Soldier," *Mail* (Adelaide, South Australia), 11 July 1942; "Saturday Weddings," *Advertiser* (Adelaide, South Australia), 13 July 1943.

127. "Adelaide Horsewoman to Marry U.S. Soldier," *News* (Adelaide, South Australia), 2 July 1942.

128. Thayer, *My War*, 5.

129. Jungwirth, *Diary of a National Guardsman*, 47.

Chapter 5

1. The official US Army history of the Papuan campaign is Samuel Milner, *Victory in Papua* (Washington, DC: Center of Military History, 1989). For a quality summary of the Red Arrow Division in Papua, see Jay Luvaas, "Buna: 19 November 1942–2 January 1943: A 'Leavenworth Nightmare,'" in *America's First Battles, 1776–1965*, ed. Charles E. Heller and William A. Stofft (Lawrence: University Press of Kansas, 1986). Works for general readers about the campaign include James Campbell, *The Ghost Mountain Boys: Their Epic March and the Terrifying Battle for New Guinea—The Forgotten War of the South Pacific* (New York: Crown, 2007); Harry A. Gailey, *MacArthur Strikes Back: Decision at Buna, New Guinea, 1942–1943* (Novato, CA: Presidio, 2000); and Lida Mayo, *Bloody Buna* (New York: Doubleday, 1974). The official Australian history of the Papuan campaign is Dudley McCarthy, *South-West Pacific Area—The First Year: Kokoda to Wau* (Canberra: Australian War Memorial, 1959). See also Peter J. Dean, *MacArthur's Coalition: US and Australian Operations in the Southwest Pacific Area* (Lawrence: University Press of Kansas, 2018) and Peter Williams, *The Kokoda Campaign: Myth and Reality* (Melbourne: Cambridge University Press, 2012).

2. E. J. Kahn, "Terrible Days of Company E," *Saturday Evening Post*, 8 January 1944.

3. For an introduction to New Guinea history, see John Waiko, *A Short History of Papua New Guinea*, 2nd ed. (South Melbourne: Oxford University Press, 2007).

4. Noah Riseman, "Australian [Mis]treatment of Indigenous Labor in World War II Papua and New Guinea," *Labour History* 98 (May 2010): 166.

5. Waiko, *Short History of Papua New Guinea*, 83, 86.

6. Jonathan Ritchie, "Papua New Guineans Reconstructing Their Histories: The Pacific War Revisited," *Oceania* 87, no. 2 (July 2017): 125. For an introduction to World War II from the perspective of Papua New Guineans and other Melanesians, see Neville K. Robinson, *Villagers at War: Some*

Papua New Guinean Experiences in World War II (Canberra: Australian National University, 1981) and Geoffrey M. White and Lamont Lindstrom, *The Pacific Theater: Island Representations of World War II* (Honolulu: University of Hawaii Press, 1989). In the years immediately after the war the experiences and perspectives of the peoples of New Guinea largely went unrecorded, though in recent decades anthropologists and historians have worked diligently to collect and preserve them. For more on these preservation efforts, see Ritchie, "Papua New Guineans Reconstructing Their Histories" and *Voices from the War: Papua New Guinean Stories of the Kokoda Campaign, World War II* (Canberra: Kokoda Initiative, 2015).

7. Riseman, "Australian [Mis]treatment," 172–73.

8. For an introduction to ANGAU, see Alan Powell, *The Third Force: ANGAU's New Guinea War, 1942–1945* (Melbourne: Oxford University Press, 2003).

9. For an introduction to the battle at Guadalcanal, see Richard B. Frank, *Guadalcanal* (New York: Random House, 1990); Stanley Coleman Jersey and Edward W. Snedeker, *Hell's Islands: The Untold Story of Guadalcanal* (College Station: Texas A&M University Press, 2008); and John Miller Jr., *Guadalcanal: The First Offensive* (Washington, DC: Center of Military History, 1949).

10. Kenneth G. Springer, "Australia and New Guinea: World War II Memoirs," in Springer file, World War II Veterans Surveys, 32d Infantry Division, USAHEC, 8.

11. Robert Eichelberger to Richard Sutherland, 6 September 1942, Record Group 30: Papers of Lieutenant General Richard K. Sutherland, MMA.

12. Clovis E. Byers diary, 5 September 1942, Clovis E. Byers Papers, Hoover Institution Archives, Stanford University, Palo Alto, California (hereafter cited as Byers Papers).

13. Robert L. Eichelberger, *Our Jungle Road to Tokyo* (New York: Viking, 1950), 11–12.

14. Clovis E. Byers interview with D. Clayton James, Washington, DC, 24 June 1971, Record Group 49: D. Clayton James Collection, MMA.

15. Harold W. Blakeley, *32d Infantry Division in World War II* (Madison: Thirty-Second Infantry Division History Commission, 1957), 27–31.

16. General Harding's marginal comments on Samuel Milner manuscript draft, Record Group 319: Records of the Army Staff, 1903–2009, NARA (hereafter cited as RG 319).

17. Hanford MacNider to Margaret MacNider, 14 May 1942, 18 June 1942, 19 September 1942, 29 September 1942, 9 October 1942, Hanford MacNider Papers, Herbert Hoover Presidential Library, West Branch, Iowa. For a biography of MacNider, see Dorothy H. Rankin, "Hanford MacNider," *Annals of Iowa* 33, no. 4 (April 1956): 233–67.

18. 128th Infantry Regiment—History (15 Oct 1940–28 Feb 1943), Record Group 407: Records of the Adjutant General's Office, NARA (hereafter cited as RG 407).

19. George C. Kenney, *General Kenney Reports: A Personal History of the Pacific War* (New York: Duell, Sloan and Pearce, 1949), 97–98.

20. Samuel Milner, *Victory in Papua* (Washington, DC: Center of Military History, 1989), 94.

21. Kahn, "Terrible Days of Company E."

22. Kenney, *General Kenney Reports*, 99–100.

23. Joe H. Camp Jr., *32 Answered: A South Carolina Veterans' Story* (Charleston, SC: Joe H. Camp, Jr., 2015), 147.

24. Lawrence Thayer, *My War* (Palmyra, WI: Palmyra Historical Society, 2003), 8.

25. Kessenich memoir, 14.

26. Herman A. Owen interview with Mark D. Van Ells, 13 September 1994, Wisconsin Veterans Oral History Program, WVM.

27. Roy M. Campbell, *Kindling for the Devil's Fires: Journals of an Infantryman* (Victoria, BC: Trafford, 2005), 125–26.

28. Herbert M. Smith, *O-241957: The Early Years of World War II* (Eau Claire, WI: Heins Publications, 1995), 44.

29. Monte L. Ball, *190 Letters: A Soldier's Story of World War II* (Mustang, OK: Tate Publishing, 2013), 128.

30. Paul A. Rettell, *A Soldier's True Story: The Life of an Infantry Soldier in World War II* (self-published, 1993), 23.

31. Byron Gibbs, "My Experiences and Observations," *Sebewa Recollector* (Portland, MI), April 2004.

32. E. J. Kahn, *G.I. Jungle: An American Soldier in Australia and New Guinea* (New York: Simon & Schuster, 1943), 59–60.

33. Campbell, *Kindling for the Devil's Fires*, 126.

34. Herman Owen interview.

35. Springer, "Australia and New Guinea," 11.

36. Eric Bergerud, *Touched with Fire: The Land War in the South Pacific* (New York: Viking, 1996), 60.

37. Robert J. Bable, *Beyond Pongani Mission* (Ann Arbor, MI: Bokmal Press, 2001), 19–20.

38. Bable, *Beyond Pongani Mission*, 26.

39. Kahn, *G.I. Jungle*, 60.

40. Kahn, *G.I. Jungle*, 61.

41. Ball, *190 Letters*, 124.

42. Kahn, *G.I. Jungle*, 60.

43. White and Lindstrom, *Pacific Theater*, 7.

44. Alfred Medendorp, "Trek Over the Owen Stanley Mountains," Edward T. Lauer Papers, WVM, 5.

45. Allied Forces, Southwest Pacific Area, Allied Geographical Section, *You and the Native: Notes for the Guidance of Members of the Forces in Their Relations with New Guinea Natives*, General Headquarters, SWPA, 1943, 3–4.

46. Campbell, *Kindling for the Devil's Fires*, 127.

47. Ball, *190 Letters*, 124.

48. Report of Reconnaissance Coberageri—Jaure Track, 126th Infantry Regiment—Patrol Reports along Kalamazoo—Laruni—Jaure Trail—Buna, Papuan Campaign (17 Oct–8 Nov 1942), RG 407; Patrol Report—Laruni to Jaure, 126th Infantry Regiment—Patrol Reports along Kalamazoo—Laruni—Jaure Trail—Buna, Papuan Campaign (17 Oct–8 Nov 1942), RG 407.

49. Campbell, *Ghost Mountain Boys*, 104.

50. Alfred Medendorp "Our Friends the Natives," addendum to "Trek Over the Owen Stanley Mountains," Lauer Papers, 8.

51. Medendorp, "Our Friends the Natives," 9–10.

52. Medendorp, "Our Friends the Natives," 12.

53. History of the Medical Activities of the 19th Portable Surgical Hospital, 126th Infantry Regiment—S-2 & S-3—Reports on Trail Operations—Buna, Papuan Campaign (17 Oct–8 Nov 1942), RG 407.

54. Herbert M. Smith, *Hannibal Had Elephants II: Papua, New Guinea, 1942* (Eau Claire, WI: Heins Publications, 1995), 18.

55. Kahn, "Terrible Days of Company E."

56. George L. Moorad, "Fire and Blood in the Jungle," *Liberty Magazine*, 3 July 1943, 38.

57. Medendorp, "Our Friends the Natives," 16–18.

58. Springer, "Australia and New Guinea," 13.

59. Alfred Medendorp, *March and Operations of the Antitank and Cannon Companies, 126th Infantry (32d Infantry Division) in the attack on Wairopi, 4 October–28 November 1942 (Papuan Campaign)* (Fort Benning, GA: The Infantry School, ca. 1948–1949), 8.

60. Kahn, "Terrible Days of Company E."

61. Wendell Trogdon, *Out Front: The Cladie Bailey Story* (Mooresville, IN: Backroads Press, 1994), 74.

62. Kahn, "Terrible Days of Company E."

63. Trogdon, *Cladie Bailey*, 76.

64. Kahn, "Terrible Days of Company E."

65. Moorad, "Fire and Blood," 38.

66. Medendorp, *March and Operations*, 7.

67. Moorad, "Fire and Blood," 33.

68. Medendorp, *March and Operations*, 10; Medendorp, "Our Friends the Natives," 8–15.

69. Campbell, *Ghost Mountain Boys*, 128.

70. Harry E. Maule, *A Book of War Letters* (New York: Random House, 1943), 218.

71. Medendorp, "Our Friends the Natives," 12.

72. Campbell, *Ghost Mountain Boys*, 128.

73. Medendorp, "Trek Over the Owen Stanley," 8.

74. Kahn, "Terrible Days of Company E."

75. Moorad, "Fire and Blood," 33.

76. 126th Infantry Regiment—History—Buna (Papuan) Campaign, Sep 1942–Jan 43), RG 407.

77. Kahn, "Terrible Days of Company E."

78. Smith, *O-241957*, 56; Smith, *Hannibal Had Elephants*, 15.

79. Medendorp, "Trek Over the Owen Stanley," H.

80. Medendorp, "Our Friends the Natives," 15–16.

81. Trogdon, *Cladie Bailey*, 76.

82. Kahn, "Terrible Days of Company E."

83. Smith, *Hannibal Had Elephants*, 19; Smith, *O-241957*, 60.

84. Smith, *Hannibal Had Elephants*, 20.

85. Medendorp, "Our Friends the Natives," 16.

86. Kahn, "Terrible Days of Company E."

87. Kahn, "Terrible Days of Company E."

88. Smith, *0241957*, 60; Smith, *Hannibal Had Elephants*, 20.

89. Medendorp, *March and Operations*, 12.

90. Medendorp, "Our Friends the Natives," 16.

91. Smith, *O-241957*, 61.

92. Medendorp, "Our Friends the Natives," 16–18.

93. Kahn, "Terrible Days of Company E."

94. Smith, *Hannibal Had Elephants*, 22.

95. Moorad, "Fire and Blood," 38.

96. Smith, *O-241957*, 63.

97. "Doughboys' March High Point in War," *New York Times*, 7 May 1944.

98. Mayo, *Bloody Buna*, 75.

99. Medendorp, *March and Operations*, 14.

100. Kahn, "Terrible Days of Company E."

101. Kristen Gilpatrick, *The Hero Next Door Returns: Stories from Wisconsin's World War II Veterans* (Oregon, WI: Badger Books, 2001), 166.

102. Campbell, *Kindling for the Devil's Fires*, 128.

103. James F. Kincaid, Reminiscence, James F. Kincaid Papers, WVM, n.p.

104. Gilpatrick, *Hero Next Door*, 168.

105. Bruce Fahnestock and Sheridan Fahnestock, *Stars to Windward* (New York: Harcourt Brace, 1938). Their mother, Mary Sheridan Fahnestock, accompanied her sons on a portion of the expedition and published her own account, *I Ran Away to Sea at Fifty* (New York: Harcourt Brace, 1939). For more on later voyages, see James McKee, "South Sea Collection Comes to Folk Archive," *Folklife Center News* 10, no. 2 (Spring 1988): 4–6. For more on the Small Ships Section, see Kenneth J. Babcock, "MacArthur's Small Ships: Improvising Water Transport in the South Pacific," *Army History* 90 (Winter 2014); and Bill Lunney and Ruth Lunney, *Forgotten Fleet 2: An Updated and Expanded History of the Part Played by Australian Men and Ships in the U.S. Army Small Ships Section in New Guinea, 1942–1945* (Medowie, Australia: Forfleet Publishing, 2004).

106. Ladislaw Reday, *The Raggle Taggle Fleet* (Coomba Park, Australia: U.S. Small Ships Association, 2004), 27.

107. Kincaid reminiscence, n.p.; 114th Engineer Combat Battalion—History (4 Apr 1942–28 Feb 1943), RG 407; Kelsie E. Miller to Samuel Milner, 2 January 1952, RG 319.

108. During this airlift, a plane carrying twenty soldiers and three crewmembers crashed into the jungle about thirty minutes out of Port Moresby. Survivors desperately wandered through the jungles in search of aid. Only six of them eventually "made their way overland to Abau," according to one report, "where they arrived a month later." 126th Infantry Regiment—History (15 Oct 1940–28 Feb 1940), RG 407.

109. Rettell, *Soldier's True Story*, 23–25.

110. Camp, *32 Answered*, 175.

111. Philip La Follette was one of the most successful governors in Wisconsin history and aspired to the presidency, but an April 28, 1938, campaign event in Madison severely damaged his public image—and it had a Wisconsin National Guard connection. La Follette held the rally to announce the creation of a new political party, the National Progressives of America. Wisconsin adjutant general Ralph Immell, a political ally, organized the event. A military band played while University of Wisconsin football players lined the stage. Also featured was the new party's emblem, a blue X inside a white circle. La Follette intended for it to symbolize a marked ballot, but critics noted its similarity to the Nazi swastika; critics even dubbed it a "circumcised swastika." The martial tunes, burly football players, and unfortunate party emblem smacked of fascism to some at a time when Nazi aggression in Europe intensified, and many supporters subsequently abandoned La Follette. He lost the 1938 Wisconsin gubernatorial race to Republican Julius Heil. For more on La Follette's political career, including the 1938 campaign debacle, see Jonathan Kasparek, *Fighting Son: A Biography of Philip F. La Follette* (Madison: Wisconsin Historical Society Press, 2006).

112. Philip F. La Follette to Senator Robert M. La Follette Jr., 11 November 1942, Personal Papers, Correspondence file, Philip F. La Follette Papers, WHS.

113. E. J. Kahn Jr., *About the New Yorker and Me: A Sentimental Journey* (New York: Penguin, 1979), 235.

114. La Follette spent the rest of the war as a public affairs officer at MacArthur's headquarters. For more on his World War II experiences, see Edward M. Coffman and Paul H. Hass, eds., "With MacArthur in the Pacific: A Memoir by Philip F. La Follette," *Wisconsin Magazine of History* 64, no. 2 (Winter 1980–1981): 83–106.

115. Kenney, *General Kenney Reports*, 127, 138.

Chapter 6

1. Eric Bergerud, *Touched with Fire: The Land War in the South Pacific* (New York: Viking, 1996), 217.

2. Robert L. Eichelberger, *History of the Buna Campaign: December 1, 1942–January 25, 1943* (Allied Forces, South West Pacific Area, 1943), 10.

3. J. Tracy Hale, "Papuan Campaign to 3 December 1942," WWII Files, Hanson W. Baldwin Papers, Virginia Military Institute, Lexington, Virginia (hereafter cited as Baldwin Papers); J. Tracy Hale Jr., "Fire and Fall Back: Memories of a Saturday Soldier," Edward T. Lauer Papers, WVM (hereafter cited as Lauer Papers), III:72.

4. Diary of Robert J. Doyle, 16 November 1942, Robert J. Doyle Papers, WHS (hereafter cited as Doyle Papers).

5. Benjamin Winneshiek with Tom Doherty, 1989, Wisconsin Veterans Oral History Program (hereafter cited as WVOHP), WVM.

6. Doyle diary, 16 November 1942, Doyle Papers.

7. Roy M. Campbell, *Kindling for the Devil's Fires: Journals of an Infantryman* (Victoria, BC: Trafford, 2005), 135.

8. Major David B. Parker, "Notes on Operations Near Buna, New Guinea, Nov. 14–23, 1942," Record Group 319: Records of the Army Staff, 1903–2009, NARA (hereafter cited as RG 319).

9. Richard David Wissolik and Barbara J. Wissolik, eds., *An Honor to Serve* (Latrobe, PA: Publications of the Saint Vincent College Center for Northern Appalachian Studies, 2007), 127–28.

10. Kincaid reminiscence, James F. Kincaid Papers, WVM, n.p.; 114th Engineer Combat Battalion—History (4 Apr 1942–28 Feb 1943), Record Group 407: Records of the Adjutant General's Office, NARA (hereafter cited as RG 407); Kelsie E. Miller to Samuel Milner, 2 January 1952, RG 319.

11. James Bement, *Baseball, Battle, and a Bride: An Okie in World War II* (Victoria, BC: Trafford, 2009), 57.

12. Parker, "Notes on Operations Near Buna," RG 319.

13. Alexander MacNab to Samuel Milner, 15 August 1950, RG 319.

14. Wissolik and Wissolik, *An Honor to Serve*, 131.

15. Campbell, *Kindling for the Devil's Fires*, 140.

16. Wissolik and Wissolik, *An Honor to Serve*, 128.

17. Unit Journal, 22 November 1942, 126th Infantry Regiment—Company K—Journal—Buna (Papuan) Campaign (10 Nov 1942–18 Jan 1943), RG 407.

18. Steve Janicki interview with Frank Boring, 20 August 2007, GVSU.

19. Bergerud, *Touched with Fire*, 369.

20. Bergerud, *Touched with Fire*, 369.

21. Kenneth G. Springer, "Australia and New Guinea: World War II Memoirs," in Springer file, World War II Veterans Surveys, 32d Infantry Division, USAHEC, 15–17.

22. Springer, "Australia and New Guinea," 17.

23. E. J. Kahn, "Terrible Days of Company E, Part II" *Saturday Evening Post*, 15 January 1944.

24. Bergerud, *Touched with Fire*, 218.

25. Herbert A. Smith to Samuel Milner, 20 January 1950, RG 319.

26. Smith to Milner, 20 January 1950, RG 319.

27. Herbert M. Smith, *Four Score and Ten: Happenings in the Life of Herbert M. Smith* (Eau Claire, WI: Heins Publications, 1994), 95.

28. Edwin Forrest Harding to Samuel Milner, 24 July 1951, RG 319.

29. Corrections in account of Buna campaign, n.d., Baldwin Papers.

30. Memorandum—Colonel John Mott, 10 December 1942, RG 319.

31. Smith, *Four Score and Ten*, 96.

32. George L. Moorad, "Fire and Blood in the Jungle," *Liberty Magazine*, 3 July 1943, 38.

33. Narrative of Robert Odell (Samuel Milner transcription), December 1942, RG 319.

34. Herbert M. Smith, *Hannibal Had Elephants II: Papua, New Guinea, 1942* (Eau Claire, WI: Heins Publications, 1995), 43.

35. Affidavit of Joseph M. Stehling, 1 February 1988, David Rubitsky Papers, WVM.

36. Herbert A. Smith to Congressman Les Aspin, 3 March 1988, Rubitsky Papers.

37. Affidavit of Herbert A. Smith, 11 January 1988, Rubitsky Papers.

38. Smith to Aspin, 11 January 1988, Rubitsky Papers.

39. "Army Cites Strong Evidence in Barring Medal," *New York Times*, 16 December 1989.

40. "Army Cites Strong Evidence," *New York Times*.

41. "Medal Eludes Jewish Veteran," *New York Times*, 15 December 1989.

42. MacNab to Milner, 15 November 1949, RG 319.

43. 32nd Quartermaster Company—Activities of the 107th Quartermaster Detachment at Oro Bay and Hariko—New Guinea (3 Oct 1942–Mar 1943), RG 407.

44. 32nd Quartermaster Company—Activities of the 107th Quartermaster Detachment at Dobodura (Papua)—New Guinea (27 Nov 1942–5 Jan 1943), RG 407.

45. Campbell, *Kindling for the Devil's Fires*, 142–43.

46. Robert J. Bable, *Beyond Pongani Mission* (Ann Arbor, MI: Bokmal Press, 2001), 69.

47. 32nd Quartermaster Company—Report on Activities—Buna (Papuan) Campaign (2 Oct 1942–1 March 1943), RG 407.

48. Vincent Riddle, "One GI's Enlistment," in Record Group 111: GHQ Honor Guard Papers, MMA, n.p.

49. James E. Myers, *Hell Is a Foxhole: An Autobiography—1942 to 1946* (New York: Vantage, 1966), 29.

50. Gifford Coleman interview with Mark D. Van Ells, 10 November 1994, WVOHP, WVM.

51. William G. De Mers survey, World War II Veterans Surveys, 32d Infantry Division, USAHEC.

52. MacNab to Milner, 15 November 1949, RG 319.

53. J. Tracy Hale to Edwin Forrest Harding, 7 November 1949, RG 319.

54. George C. Kenney, *General Kenney Reports: A Personal History of the Pacific War* (New York: Duell, Sloan and Pearce, 1949), 151.

55. Diary of Edwin Forrest Harding, 30 November 1942, RG 319.

56. Clovis E. Byers interview, RG 49, MMA.

57. Diary of Clovis E. Byers, 30 November 1942, Byers Papers; Robert L. Eichelberger, *Our Jungle Road to Tokyo* (New York: Viking, 1950) 21. In his diary, Byers recorded MacArthur's words as "If you don't take Buna I want to hear that you and Byers are buried there."

58. Eichelberger, *Our Jungle Road to Tokyo*, 22.

59. Byers interview.

60. Eichelberger, *Our Jungle Road to Tokyo*, 24.

61. Robert L. Eichelberger to Richard K. Sutherland, 1 December 1942, General Richard K. Sutherland Papers, NARA (hereafter cited as Sutherland Papers).

62. Jay Luvaas, *Dear Miss Em: General Eichelberger's War in the Pacific, 1942–1945* (Westport, CT: Greenwood Press, 1972), 39.

63. Harding diary, 2 December 1942, RG 319.

64. Luvaas, *Dear Miss Em*, 37.

65. Herbert M. Smith, *O-241957: The Early Years of World War II* (Eau Claire, WI: Heins Publications, 1995), 72.

66. Eichelberger to Sutherland, 3 December 1942, Sutherland Papers.

67. Harding diary, 2 December 1942, RG 319.

68. Hale to Harding, 7 November 1949, RG 319.

69. Eichelberger to Sutherland, 3 December 1942, Sutherland Papers.

70. Samuel Sloan Auchincloss Jr., *The Memoirs of Samuel Sloan Auchincloss, Jr, October 12, 1903–November 5, 1991* (self-published, ca. 1991), 183.

71. George DeGraaf to Robert L. Eichelberger, 5 March 1948, in Robert M. White Papers, Record Group 15: Contributions from the Public, MMA.

72. Susan R. Schad, "And MacArthur Declared No More Bunas," unpublished manuscript, McCoy Family Papers, WVM.

73. Lawrence Thayer, *My War* (Palmyra, WI: Palmyra Historical Society, 2003), 16–17.

74. Bable, *Beyond Pongani Mission*, 97.

75. Campbell, *Kindling for the Devil's Fires*, 160.

76. Eichelberger, *Our Jungle Road to Tokyo*, 28–29.

77. Smith, *O-241957*, 75.

78. John Edwin Grose diary, 5 December 1942, John Edwin Grose Papers, USAHEC.

79. Byers diary, 5 December 1942, Byers Papers.

80. Gordon B. Rogers to Orlando Ward, 5 July 1950, RG 319.

81. Moorad, "Fire and Blood," 39.

82. Rogers to Ward, 5 July 1950, RG 319.

83. Moorad, "Fire and Blood," 39.

84. Odell diary, RG 319.

85. Smith, *O-241957*, 79; Smith, *Four Score and Ten*, 101.

86. Kahn, "Terrible Days of Company E, Part II."

87. 127th Infantry Regiment—Tactical history during Papuan Campaign, Buna area (15 Nov 1942–1 Mar 1943), RG 407.

88. 32nd Quartermaster Company—Activities of the 107th Quartermaster Detachment at Dobodura (Papua)—New Guinea (27 Nov 1942–5 Jan 1943), RG 407.

89. 32nd Quartermaster Company—Report on Activities—Buna (Papuan) Campaign (2 Oct 1942–1 March 1943), RG 407.

90. Clarence Jungwirth, *Diary of a National Guardsman in World War II, 1940–1945* (self-published, 1991), 52.

91. Raymond F. Dasmann, *Called by the Wild: The Autobiography of a Conservationist* (Berkeley: University of California Press, 2002), 40.

92. Bergerud, *Touched with Fire*, 373. For more on the US Army's deployment of flamethrowers during World War II, see Leo P. Brophy, Wyndham D. Miles, and Rexmond C. Cochrane, *The Chemical Warfare Service: From Laboratory to Field* (Washington, DC: Government Printing Office, 1988), and Leonard L. McKinney, *Portable Flame Thrower Operations in World War II* (Washington, DC: Office of the Chief, Chemical Corps, 1949).

93. Dasmann, *Called by the Wild*, 40–41.

94. Howard E. Kelley, *Born in the U.S.A.: A World War II Memoir* (Eau Claire, WI: Heins Publications, 1999), 42.

95. Wissolik and Wissolik, *An Honor to Serve*, 130.

96. John Maino, *Frontlines, World War II: Personal Accounts of Wisconsin Veterans* (Appleton, WI: JP Graphics, 2006), 97.

97. Unit Journal, 10 November 1942, 27 November 1942, 126th Infantry Regiment—Company K—Journal—Buna (Papuan) Campaign (10 Nov 1942–18 Jan 1943), RG 407.

98. Gerald F. Linderman, *The World within War: America's Combat Experience in World War II* (New York: Free Press, 1997), 11–12.

99. For an introduction to the World War II combat experience, see John Ellis, *The Sharp End: The Fighting Man in World War II* (New York: Scribner's, 1980); Linderman, *The World within War*; and John C. McManus, *The Deadly Brotherhood: The American Combat Soldier in World War II* (New York: Ballantine, 1998).

100. Kelley, *Born in the USA*, 47.

101. Paul A. Rettell, *A Soldier's True Story: The Life of an Infantry Soldier in World War II* (self-published, 1993), 36.

102. Campbell, *Kindling for the Devil's Fires*, 140.

103. Alfred Medendorp, "Trek Over the Owen Stanley Mountains," Lauer Papers, 35.

104. Wissolik and Wissolik, *An Honor to Serve*, 128.

105. Wissolik and Wissolik, *An Honor to Serve*, 128.

106. Campbell, *Kindling for the Devil's Fires*, 161–62.

107. Letter, 1942, Hershel Horton Papers, World War II Letters Collection, State Historical Society of Missouri, Columbia, Missouri. For an introduction to the religious world of US military personnel during the war, see G. Kurt Piehler, *A Religious History of the American GI in World War II* (Lincoln: University of Nebraska Press, 2021).

108. Dasmann, *Called by the Wild*, 39.

109. Byron Gibbs, "My WWII Experiences and Observations," *Sebewa Recollector*, August 2004.

110. Bergerud, *Touched with Fire*, 219, 430.

111. Springer, "Australia and New Guinea," 16.

112. Dasmann, *Called by the Wild*, 41.

113. Unit Journal, 13 December 1942, 126th Infantry Regiment—Company K—Journal—Buna (Papuan) Campaign (10 Nov 1942–18 Jan 1943), RG 407.

114. Bergerud, *Touched with Fire*, 219–20, 452.

115. Thayer, *My War*, 17–18.

116. Coleman interview.

117. Oral History Interview with Brigadier General Robert B. Hughes, 1976, WHS.

118. Myers, *Hell Is a Foxhole*, 32–33.

119. Richard A. Stoelb, *Time in Hell: The Battle for Buna on the Island of New Guinea* (Sheboygan: Sheboygan Historical Society, 2012), 44–45.

120. Bergerud, *Touched with Fire*, 218.

121. John Dower, *War without Mercy: Race and Power in the Pacific War* (New York: Pantheon, 1986), 215. For an introduction to the rise of the modern Japanese military, see Edward J. Drea, *Japan's Imperial Army: Its Rise and Fall, 1853–1945* (Lawrence: University Press of Kansas, 2009).

122. Dower, *War without Mercy*, 11.
123. Rettell, *Soldier's True Story*, 36.
124. Odell diary, RG 319.
125. Stoelb, *Time in Hell*, 45.
126. 127th Infantry Regiment—Tactical history during Papuan Campaign, Buna area (15 Nov 1942–1 Mar 1943), RG 407.
127. Field message, Douglas MacArthur to Robert L. Eichelberger, 14 December 1942, Sutherland Papers.
128. Byers diary, 16 December 1942, Byers Papers.
129. MacNider to MacNider, 22 December 1942, Hanford MacNider Papers, Herbert Hoover Presidential Library, West Branch, Iowa.
130. Smith to Milner, 20 March 1951, RG 319.
131. Roy F. Zinzer to General Byers, 1 March 1951, RG 319.
132. Zinzer to Byers, 1 March 1951, RG 319.
133. Eichelberger to Sutherland, 16 December 1942, Sutherland Papers.
134. Bergerud, *Touched with Fire*, 222.
135. Eichelberger to Sutherland, 18 December 1942, Sutherland Papers.
136. Unit Journal, 21 December 1942, 128th Infantry Regiment—1st Battalion—Journal—Buna (Papuan) Campaign (17 Sep 1942–3 Jan 1943), RG 407.
137. Alan E. Kent, "Wisconsin and the Medal of Honor," *Wisconsin Magazine of History* 36, no. 2 (Winter 1952–1953): 107–8. For more on the Medal of Honor, see *The Congressional Medal of Honor* (Sharp and Dunnigan, 1984); George Lang, Raymond Collins, and Gerard White, *Medal of Honor Recipients, 1863–1994*, 2 vols. (New York: Facts of File, 1995); and James H. Willbanks, ed., *Medal of Honor Recipients from the Civil War to Afghanistan* (Westport, CT: Greenwood, 2013).
138. Stoelb, *Time in Hell*, 55–57.
139. 127th Infantry Regiment—Tactical history during Papuan Campaign, Buna area (15 Nov 1942–1 Mar 1943), RG 407.
140. Eichelberger to MacArthur, 29 December 1942, Sutherland Papers.
141. John E. Grose, "Comments on the Buna-Sanada [sic] Operation of the Papuan Campaign," RG 319.
142. Colonel Grose's comments on Ch. XIV, RG 319.
143. Jungwirth, *Diary of a National Guardsman*, 56.
144. Campbell, *Kindling for the Devil's Fires*, 174–75.
145. MacNab to Milner, 18 April 1950, RG 319.
146. Myers, *Hell Is a Foxhole*, 37–38.
147. Kelley, *Born in the USA*, 52.
148. Bergerud, *Touched with Fire*, 419.
149. 127th Infantry Regiment—Tactical history during Papuan Campaign, Buna area (15 Nov 1942–1 Mar 1943), RG 407.
150. 127th Infantry Regiment—Tactical history during Papuan Campaign, Buna area (15 Nov 1942–1 Mar 1943), RG 407.
151. Jungwirth, *Diary of a National Guardsman*, 57.
152. Bable, *Beyond Pongani Mission*, 128–29.
153. Interrogation of Matsuoka, Ryoju Captured Japanese Prisoner, 3 January 1943, 127th Infantry Regiment—Urbana Force—Journal—Buna (Papuan) Campaign (4 Dec 1942–1 Mar 1943), RG 407.
154. Interrogation of Ps'W (Koreans), 2 January 1943, 127th Infantry Regiment—Urbana Force—Journal—Buna (Papuan) Campaign (4 Dec 1942–1 Mar 1943), RG 407.
155. Campbell, *Kindling for the Devil's Fires*, 175–96.
156. Jungwirth, *Diary of a National Guardsman*, 58–59.
157. Springer, "Australia and New Guinea," 18.
158. Wellington F. Homminga interview with Frank Boring, 19 February 2009, GVSU.
159. Eichelberger to Sutherland, 7 January 1943, Sutherland Papers.

160. Douglas MacArthur, *Reports of General MacArthur, Vol. 1: The Campaigns of General MacArthur in the Pacific* (Washington, DC: Government Printing Office, 1966), 98.

161. "Certificate, Robert Thompson, S. Sgt, Co C, 127th Infantry, U.S. Army. For gallantry in action in the TARAKENA AREA, NEW GUINEA, on January 11, 1943," Sylvia Hall Thompson Papers, Tamiment Library and Robert F. Wagner Labor Archives, New York University, New York, New York.

162. "Lincoln Brigade Vets Charge Army Keeps Them from the Front," *PM*, 26 January 1943.

163. Unit Journal, 17 January 1943, 127th Infantry Regiment—Urbana Force—Journal—Buna (Papuan) Campaign (4 Dec 1942–1 Mar 1943), RG 407.

164. Hughes interview.

165. Maino, *Frontlines*, 99.

166. 127th Infantry Regiment—Tactical history during Papuan Campaign, Buna area (15 Nov 1942–1 Mar 1943), RG 407.

167. Unit Journal, 26 January 1943, Journal of the Headquarters, 1st Battalion, 127th Infantry Regiment—1st Battalion—Unit Journals—All Campaigns (14 Nov 1942–29 Aug 1945), RG 407.

168. Unit Journal, 1 February 1943, 127th Infantry Regiment—Urbana Force—Journal—Buna (Papuan) Campaign (4 Dec 1942–1 Mar 1943), RG 407.

169. Eichelberger, *History of the Buna Campaign*, 105.

170. Samuel Milner, *Victory in Papua* (Washington, DC: Center of Military History, 1989), 371–72.

171. Richard B. Frank, *MacArthur* (New York: St. Martins Griffin, 2007), 63.

172. Eichelberger, *Our Jungle Road to Tokyo*, 22.

173. Myers, *Hell Is a Foxhole*, 40.

Chapter 7

1. Lawrence Thayer, *My War* (Palmyra, WI: Palmyra Historical Society, 2003), 22.

2. Robert J. Bable, *Beyond Pongani Mission* (Ann Arbor, MI: Bokmal Press, 2001), 148.

3. Vincent Riddle, "One GI's Enlistment," in Record Group 111: GHQ Honor Guard Papers, MMA, n.p.

4. Raymond F. Dasmann, *Called by the Wild: The Autobiography of a Conservationist* (Berkeley: University of California Press, 2002), 43.

5. Monte L. Ball, *190 Letters: A Soldier's Story of World War II* (Mustang, OK: Tate Publishing, 2013), 141.

6. Kristen Gilpatrick, *The Hero Next Door Returns: Stories from Wisconsin's World War II Veterans* (Oregon, WI: Badger Books, 2001), 175.

7. Oral History Interview with Brigadier General Robert B. Hughes, 1976, WHS.

8. Ball, *190 Letters*, 140.

9. Thayer, *My War*, 23.

10. Clarence Jungwirth, *Diary of a National Guardsman in World War II, 1940–1945* (self-published, 1991), 73.

11. Richard David Wissolik and Barbara J. Wissolik, eds., *An Honor to Serve* (Latrobe, PA: Publications of the Saint Vincent College Center for Northern Appalachian Studies, 2007), 132.

12. Archie Van Gorden, "Red Arrow 'Red': Letters Home from World War II," Cyrena M. Van Gorden Dierauer Family Papers, 1941–1945, WHS, 109–10.

13. Alfred Medendorp, "Trek Over the Owen Stanley Mountains," Edward T. Lauer Papers, WVM, 43.

14. Herbert M. Smith, *O-241957: The Early Years of World War II* (Eau Claire, WI: Heins Publications, 1995), 82–89.

15. Smith, *O-241957*, 92. Medical problems continued to plague Smith while on duty in Melbourne. He returned to the United States in October 1943 and retired from the army.

16. "Wounded Men of Famed Red Arrow Division Return Here with Stories of the Pacific War," *Battle Creek Enquirer*, 12 March 1943.

17. "First Battle Casualty Here for Treatment," *Milwaukee Sentinel*, 23 September 1943.

18. Robert Thompson, "Miscellaneous Notes on Jungle Tactics," Sylvia Hall Thompson Papers, Tami-

ment Library and Robert F. Wagner Labor Archives, New York University, New York, New York; Robert Thompson, "Sniping and Antisniping," *Infantry Journal* 53, no. 6 (December 1943): 22. Upon his return to the United States, Thompson continued his communist activities. In Cold War America, that meant trouble. In 1949, he was sentenced to three years in prison on the grounds that his political activities advocated the violent overthrow of the government. Thompson jumped bail and when recaptured had four more years added to his sentence. After his release from prison, Thompson remained active in the communist movement until suffering a fatal heart attack in 1966. Despite the objections of the Department of Defense, Thompson's remains were interred at Arlington National Cemetery.

19. Kevin C. Holzimmer, *General Walter Krueger: Unsung Hero of the Pacific War* (Lawrence: University Press of Kansas, 2007), 103.

20. Stephen R. Taaffe, *Marshall and His Generals: U.S. Army Commanders in World War II* (Lawrence: University Press of Kansas, 2011), 33.

21. On paper, the US Sixth Army came under the authority of an Australian, General Blamey, head of SWPA ground forces, but Buna exposed considerable tensions between American and Australian commanders. MacArthur disliked the idea of placing American forces under a foreign commander. To get around Blamey, he designated the Sixth Army as a special task force, dubbed the Alamo Force, that came directly under MacArthur's authority, effectively removing Blamey from its chain of command.

22. William H. Gill and Edward Jaquelin Smith, *Always a Commander: The Reminiscences of Major-General William H. Gill as told to Edward Jaquelin Smith* (Colorado Springs: Colorado College, 1974), 43.

23. Gill and Smith, *Always a Commander*, 45, 52.

24. "Account of proceedings when Major General Gill made his first appearance before the officers and enlisted men of the 127th Infantry Regiment at Camp Fingal, Australia, in March 1943," Hanson W. Baldwin Papers, Virginia Military Institute, Lexington, Virginia.

25. Herbert A. Smith interview with Tom Doherty, 2008, Wisconsin Veterans Oral History Program (hereafter cited as WVOHP), WVM.

26. For an introduction to the replacement system, see Leonard L. Lerwill, *The Personnel Replacement System in the United States Army* (Washington, DC: Department of the Army, 1954).

27. Dean W. Andersen, *Praise the Lord and Pass the Penicillin: Memoir of a Combat Medic in the Pacific in World War II* (Jefferson, NC: McFarland, 2003), 30–31.

28. Jesse Coker, *My Unforgettable Memories of World War II* (self-published, 1994), 49.

29. Howard E. Kelley, *Born in the U.S.A.: A World War II Memoir* (Eau Claire, WI: Heins Publications, 1999), 68.

30. Andersen, *Praise the Lord*, 32.

31. Riddle, "One GI's Enlistment," n.p.

32. Jesse Coker survey, World War II Veterans Surveys, 32d Infantry Division, USAHEC.

33. Paul A. Rettell, *A Soldier's True Story: The Life of an Infantry Soldier in World War II* (self-published, 1993), 43.

34. Jungwirth, *Diary of a National Guardsman*, 76.

35. Kelley, *Born in the USA*, 69.

36. Arthur J. Kessenich memoir, in Kessenich file, World War II Veterans Surveys, 32nd Infantry Division, USAHEC, 15.

37. Charles A. Brennan survey, World War II Veterans Surveys, 32d Infantry Division, USAHEC.

38. Medendorp, "Over the Owen Stanley Mountains," 44–46.

39. Diary of Clovis E. Byers, 22 March 1943, Byers Papers.

40. History of the 126th Infantry Regiment (during the Period beginning 1 February 1943 and ending 30 June 1943), 126th Infantry Regiment—Unit Journal and File—New Guinea and Australia (1 May–31 July 1933), Record Group 407: Records of the Adjutant General's Office, NARA (hereafter cited as RG 407).

41. Claire O. Ehle interview with Mik Derks, Stoughton, Wisconsin, 25 November 2002, WVOHP, WVM.

42. Riddle, "One GI's Enlistment," n.p.

43. Coker, *Unforgettable Memories*, 65.

44. James E. Myers, *Hell Is a Foxhole: An Autobiography—1942 to 1946* (New York: Vantage, 1966), 49–50.

45. Coker, *Unforgettable Memories*, 69–72.

46. Coker, *Unforgettable Memories*, 68.

47. Coker, *Unforgettable Memories*, 68–69.

48. Riddle, "One GI's Enlistment," n.p.

49. Coker, *Unforgettable Memories*, 77.

50. History of the 126th Infantry Regiment (during the Period beginning 1 February 1943 and ending 30 June 1943), 126th Infantry Regiment—Unit Journal and File—New Guinea and Australia (1 May–31 July 1933), RG 407.

51. Byers diary, 26 April 1943.

52. Medical History of the Medical Detachment, 127th Infantry Regiment, From April 1, 1943, to June 30, 1943, 127th Infantry Regiment—Medical Detachment—Medical History—All Campaigns and Occupation of Japan (1 Oct 42–31 Dec 45), RG 407.

53. Jungwirth, *Diary of a National Guardsman*, 77.

54. Bable, *Beyond Pongani Mission*, 159.

55. Informal Monthly History, 6 October 1943, 128th Infantry Regiment—Medical Detachment—Medical History—All Campaigns and Occupation of Japan (1 Mar 1943–31 Dec 1945), RG 407.

56. Diary of Robert L. Eichelberger, 17 July 1943, Papers of Robert L. Eichelberger, Duke University Library Special Collections, Durham, North Carolina.

57. Informal Monthly History, 6 October 1943, 128th Infantry Regiment—Medical Detachment—Medical History—All Campaigns and Occupation of Japan (1 Mar 1943–31 Dec 1945), RG 407.

58. Jungwirth, *Diary of a National Guardsman*, 77–79.

59. Hughes interview.

60. G. G. Duncan, "Quinacrine Hydrochloride as a Malaria-Suppressive Agent for Combat Troops," *War Medicine* 8, no. 5 (November–December 1945): 305–18; Leonard D. Heaton, *Internal Medicine in World War II: Vol. II, Infectious Diseases* (Washington, DC: Office of the Surgeon General, United States Army, 1963). For an introduction to the army's struggle with malaria, see Mary Ellen Condon-Rall, "The Army's War Against Malaria: Collaboration in Drug Research during World War II," *Armed Forces and Society* 21, no. 1 (Fall 1994): 129–43; John T. Greenwood, "The Fight against Malaria in the Papua and New Guinea Campaigns," *Army History* 59 (Summer–Fall 2003): 16–28; and Leo B. Slater, *War and Disease: Biomedical Research on Malaria in the Twentieth Century* (New Brunswick, NJ: Rutgers University Press, 2009).

61. Medical History of the Medical Detachment, 127th Infantry Regiment, From April 1, 1943, to June 30, 1943, 127th Infantry Regiment—Medical Detachment—Medical History—All Campaigns and Occupation of Japan (1 Oct 42–31 Dec 45), RG 407; Medical History of the Medical Detachment, 127th Infantry Regiment, From July 1, 1943, to September 30, 1943, 127th Infantry Regiment—Medical Detachment—Medical History—All Campaigns and Occupation of Japan (1 Oct 42–31 Dec 45), RG 407.

62. Roy M. Campbell, *Kindling for the Devil's Fires: Journals of an Infantryman* (Victoria, BC: Trafford, 2005), 185.

63. Medical History of the Medical Detachment, 127th Infantry Regiment, From April 1, 1943, to June 30, 1943, 127th Infantry Regiment—Medical Detachment—Medical History—All Campaigns and Occupation of Japan (1 Oct 42–31 Dec 45), RG 407.

64. Dasmann, *Called by the Wild*, 43.

65. Kenneth G. Springer, "Australia and New Guinea: World War II Memoirs," in Springer file, World War II Veterans Surveys, 32d Infantry Division, USAHEC, 21.

66. James Campbell, *The Ghost Mountain Boys: Their Epic March and the Terrifying Battle for New Guinea—The Forgotten War of the South Pacific* (New York: Crown, 2007), 284–85.

67. Medendorp, "Over the Owen Stanley Mountains," 44–46. Medendorp eventually convinced the army to declare him fit for action. "It took the medics five minutes to mark me unfit for combat duty," he wrote, "but it took a week to declare me fit for general duty."

68. Van Gorden, "Red Arrow Red," 142.

69. Byers diary, 22 June 1943.

70. Byers diary, 30 June 1943.

71. Eichelberger to Krueger, 6 June 1943, 19 July 1943, Walter Krueger Papers, United States Military Academy, West Point, New York.

72. Coker, *Unforgettable Memories*, 62.

73. James R. Mayo to Mrs. Edgar Penticast, 13 September 1943, James R. Mayo Papers, Tennessee State Library and Archives, Nashville, Tennessee (hereafter cited as Mayo Papers).

74. Myers, *Hell Is a Foxhole*, 47.

75. Springer, "Australia and New Guinea," 21.

76. Joyce Perkins to General Douglas MacArthur, n.d. [ca. January 1943]; CINC Correspondence file, MMA; Joyce Perkins to Lieutenant Colonel Charles H. Morehouse, 15 February 1943, CINC Correspondence file, MMA.

77. Dasmann, *Called by the Wild*, 55–66.

78. Myers, *Hell Is a Foxhole*, 45–46.

79. Coker, *Unforgettable Memories*, 62.

80. Erwin A. Pichotte survey, World War II Veterans Surveys, 32d Infantry Division, USAHEC.

81. Myers, *Hell Is a Foxhole*, 51–52.

82. Coker, *Unforgettable Memories*, 62–63.

83. "Mrs. Roosevelt Speaks to 3,000 at Sydney Rally," *New York Herald Tribune*, 8 September 1943.

84. Bable, *Beyond Pongani Mission*, 180.

85. Rettell, *Soldier's True Story*, 48

86. Bable, *Beyond Pongani Mission*, 181–82.

87. "My Day," *Milwaukee Sentinel*, 14 September 1943.

88. Orville Prescott, "Books of the Times," *New York Times*, 16 September 1943.

89. "Best Selling Books, Here and Elsewhere," *New York Times*, 5 December 1943.

90. Stanley Hyman, "When Yank Meets Dinkum Cobber," *New York Times*, 19 September 1943.

91. Harriet Fryer Reid to E. J. Kahn Jr., 27 October 1943, E. J. Kahn Papers, New York Public Library, New York, New York.

92. E. J. Kahn, "The Men Behind the By-Lines," *Saturday Evening Post*, September 11, 1943. The articles on Company E are cited above.

93. "The Battle of Buna," *LIFE*, 15 February 1943; "Booty and Buna," *LIFE*, 22 February 1943.

94. "How the Heroic Boys of Buna Drove the Japs into the Sea," *LIFE*, 22 February 1943.

95. Peter Maslowski, *Armed with Cameras: The American Military Photographers of World War II* (New York: Free Press, 1993), 78, 80.

96. "First Pictures of Sicily Invasion," *LIFE*, August 2, 1943. For an introduction to US government censorship during World War II, see George H. Roeder Jr., *The Censored War: American Visual Experience during World War II* (New Haven, CT: Yale University Press, 1993); and Michael S. Sweeney, *Secrets of Victory: The Office of Censorship and the American Press and Radio in World War II* (Chapel Hill: University of North Carolina Press, 2001). On images of American dead specifically, see Mary A. Dudziak, " 'You didn't see him lying . . . beside the gravel road in France': Death, Distance, and American War Politics," *Diplomatic History* 42, no. 1 (2018): 1–16; and James J. Kimble, "Spectral Soldiers: Domestic Propaganda, Visual Culture, and Images of Death on the World War II Home Front," *Rhetoric and Public Affairs* 19, no. 4 (2016): 535–70.

97. "Three Americans," *LIFE*, September 20, 1943.

98. "Letters to the Editors," *LIFE*, October 11, 1943.

99. "Think of Them," *Atlanta Constitution*, 24 September 1943.
100. The official US Army account of the operation is John Miller Jr., *Cartwheel: The Reduction of Rabaul* (Washington, DC: Center of Military History, 1959). The Red Arrow Division fought alongside the 112th Cavalry Regiment in New Guinea and the Philippines. For an introduction to the regiment's history, see James S. Powell, *Learning Under Fire: The 112th Cavalry Regiment in World War II* (College Station: Texas A&M University Press, 2010).
101. Rettell, *Soldier's True Story*, 50.
102. Andersen, *Praise the Lord*, 56.
103. Andersen, *Praise the Lord*, 58.
104. Coker, *Unforgettable Memories*, 79.
105. Herman Bottcher to Harold Hantleman, 29 January 1944, Tamiment Library and Robert F. Wagner Labor Archives, New York University, New York, New York.
106. 114th Engineer Combat Battalion—Historical Report—Goodenough Island and Saidor—New Guinea (1 Oct 1943–10 Feb 1944), RG 407.
107. Bable, *Beyond Pongani Mission*, 189–91.
108. Dasmann, *Called by the Wild*, 59–60.
109. Coker, *Unforgettable Memories*, 82.
110. Andersen, *Praise the Lord*, 62.
111. Bable, *Beyond Pongani Mission*, 196.
112. Andersen, *Praise the Lord*, 61–62.
113. Rettell, *Soldier's True Story*, 50.
114. Coker, *Unforgettable Memories*, 88.
115. Douglas MacArthur, *Reminiscences* (New York: Fawcett, 1964), 199.
116. D. Clayton James, *The Years of MacArthur: Volume II, 1941–1945* (Boston: Houghton Mifflin, 1975), 372–73.

Chapter 8

1. Douglas MacArthur, *Reminiscences* (New York: Fawcett, 1964), 182.
2. Daniel E. Barbey, *MacArthur's Amphibious Navy: Seventh Amphibious Force Operations, 1943–1945* (Annapolis, MD: United States Naval Institute, 1969), 128.
3. Dean W. Andersen, *Praise the Lord and Pass the Penicillin: Memoir of a Combat Medic in the Pacific in World War II* (Jefferson, NC: McFarland, 2003), 60.
4. Monte L. Ball, *190 Letters: A Soldier's Story of World War II* (Mustang, OK: Tate Publishing, 2013), 178.
5. Barbey, *MacArthur's Amphibious Navy*, 130.
6. Andersen, *Praise the Lord*, 62–63.
7. "Heavy Fire Covered New Guinea Landing," *Wisconsin National Guard Review*, July 1944, 6.
8. Eric Bergerud, *Touched with Fire: The Land War in the South Pacific* (New York: Viking, 1996), 508.
9. Diary, Operations of the Michaelmas Task Force, Phase II, 126th Infantry Regiment—Unit Journal and File—Saidor—New Guinea (1 Feb–30 Apr 44), Record Group 407: Records of the Adjutant General's Office, NARA (hereafter cited as RG 407).
10. Barbey, *MacArthur's Amphibious Navy*, 131.
11. Bergerud, *Touched with Fire*, 508.
12. Barbey, *MacArthur's Amphibious Navy*, 131–32.
13. Diary, Operations of the Michaelmas Task Force, Phase II, 126th Infantry Regiment—Unit Journal and File—Saidor—New Guinea (1 Feb–30 Apr 44), RG 407.
14. Diary, Operations of the Michaelmas Task Force, Phase II, 126th Infantry Regiment—Unit Journal and File—Saidor—New Guinea (1 Feb–30 Apr 44), RG 407.
15. Walter Krueger, *From Down Under to Nippon: The Story of the Sixth Army in World War II* (Nashville, TN: Battery Classics, 1989), 38.
16. John L. Mohl, *Operations of a Special Patrol from Units of the 2d Battalion, 126th Infantry*

(*32d Infantry Division*) *at Saidor, New Guinea, 22–26 January 1944 (Personal Experience of a Patrol Leader)* (Fort Benning, GA: General Subjects Section, Academic Department, The Infantry School, ca. 1948–1949).

17. John Miller Jr., *Cartwheel: The Reduction of Rabaul* (Washington, DC: Center of Military History, 1959), 303.

18. Daily S-3 Report, 29 January 1944, 128th Infantry Regiment—Unit Journal and File—Michaelmas Operations (27 Jan—2 Feb 1944), RG 407; "Japs Nearly Overcame Yank Patrol at Saidor," *Milwaukee Journal*, 5 February 1944; "Leaders Killed in Rescue Try," *Milwaukee Journal*, 8 February 1944.

19. Krueger, *From Down Under to Nippon*, 38.

20. James E. Myers, *Hell Is a Foxhole: An Autobiography—1942 to 1946* (New York: Vantage, 1966), 57.

21. Jesse Coker, *My Unforgettable Memories of World War II* (self-published, 1994), 109–111.

22. Ball, *190 Letters*, 181.

23. Robert J. Bable, *Beyond Pongani Mission* (Ann Arbor, MI: Bokmal Press, 2001), 213–14.

24. Ball, *190 Letters*, 183.

25. Andersen, *Praise the Lord*, 66.

26. Exhibit A: Patrol Report, 15 March 1944, 32nd Cavalry Reconnaissance Troop—Operations Report—Aitape (10 Feb–15 Aug 1944), RG 407.

27. Exhibit C: Patrol Report, 15 March 1944, 32nd Cavalry Reconnaissance Troop—Operations Report—Aitape (10 Feb–15 Aug 1944), RG 407.

28. Bable, *Beyond Pongani Mission*, 218.

29. Andersen, *Praise the Lord*, 66–67.

30. Richard David Wissolik and Barbara J. Wissolik, eds., *An Honor to Serve* (Latrobe, PA: Publications of the Saint Vincent College Center for Northern Appalachian Studies, 2007), 134.

31. G-2 Report, 29 January 1944, 128th Infantry Regiment—Unit Journal and File—Michaelmas Operations (27 Jan–2 Feb 1944), RG 407.

32. Myers, *Hell Is a Foxhole*, 54.

33. "Heavy Fire Covered New Guinea Landing," *Wisconsin National Guard Review*, July 1944, 6.

34. Andersen, *Praise the Lord*, 88.

35. Joe H. Camp Jr., *32 Answered: A South Carolina Veterans' Story* (Charleston, SC: Joe H. Camp, Jr., 2015), 327.

36. Peter J. Dean, *MacArthur's Coalition: US and Australian Operations in the Southwest Pacific Area* (Lawrence: University Press of Kansas, 2018), 322–23.

37. Krueger, *From Down Under to Nippon*, 33.

38. William H. Gill and Edward Jaquelin Smith, *Always a Commander: The Reminiscences of Major General William H. Gill as told to Edward Jaquelin Smith* (Colorado Springs: Colorado College, 1974), 56.

39. Stephen R. Taaffe, *MacArthur's Jungle War: The 1944 New Guinea Campaign* (Lawrence: University Press of Kansas, 1998), 28. The official US Army history of MacArthur's campaign through northern New Guinea is Robert Ross Smith, *The Approach to the Philippines* (Washington, DC: Center of Military History, 1996). For an introduction to the last two years of fighting in the Pacific War, see also Max Hastings, *Retribution: The Battle for Japan* (New York: Knopf, 2008); Waldo Heinrichs and Marc Gallicchio, *Implacable Foes: The War in the Pacific, 1944–1945* (New York: Oxford University Press, 2017); John C. McManus, *Island Infernos: The US Army's Pacific War Odyssey, 1944* (New York: Dutton, 2021); and John C. McManus, *To the End of the Earth: The US Army and the Downfall of Japan, 1945* (New York: Dutton, 2023).

40. Howard E. Kelley, *Born in the U.S.A.: A World War II Memoir* (Eau Claire, WI: Heins Publications, 1999), 71.

41. 127th Infantry Regiment—Unit Journal—New Guinea (23 Mar–4 May 1944), RG 407.

42. Andersen, *Praise the Lord*, 91.

43. Daily Bulletin, 31 May 1944, 128th Infantry Regiment—Journal and File—Aitape Campaign (4 May–27 June 1944), RG 407.

44. Heinrichs and Gallicchio, *Implacable Foes*, 67–68.
45. 121st Field Artillery Battalion—Historical Report—Biak Operation (27 May–20 August 1944), RG 407.
46. Edward J. Drea, *MacArthur's Ultra: Codebreaking and the War against Japan, 1942–1945* (Lawrence: University Press of Kansas, 1992), 144.
47. Heinrichs and Gallicchio, *Implacable Foes*, 72.
48. Taaffe, *MacArthur's Jungle War*, 188.
49. Andersen, *Praise the Lord*, 96.
50. Unit Report No. 27, 19 May 1944, 127th Infantry Regiment—Unit Journal—Aitape Campaign (4 May–6 Jun 1944), RG 407.
51. Unit Report No. 29, 21 May 1944, 127th Infantry Regiment—Unit Journal—Aitape Campaign (4 May–6 Jun 1944), RG 407.
52. Andersen, *Praise the Lord*, 96–97.
53. Andersen, *Praise the Lord*, 95.
54. Telephone message, Capt. Wiley to S-3 127, 2 June 1944, 127th Infantry Regiment—Unit Journal—Aitape Campaign (4 May–6 Jun 1944), RG 407.
55. Kelley, *Born in the USA*, 77.
56. Unit Report No. 40, 1 June 1944, 127th Infantry Regiment—Unit Journal—Aitape Campaign (4 May–6 Jun 1944), RG 407.
57. Heinrichs and Gallicchio, *Implacable Foes*, 72.
58. Henry C. Zabierek, *Beyond Pearl Harbor: I Company in the Pacific of WWII* (Shippensburg, PA: Burd Street Press, 2010), 5.
59. Kelley, *Born in the USA*, 74–75.
60. Wissolik and Wissolik, *An Honor to Serve*, 134.
61. Drea, *MacArthur's Ultra*, 145–46.
62. Gerhard L. Weinberg, *A World at Arms: A Global History of World War II*, 2nd ed. (New York: Cambridge University Press, 2005), xx.
63. Heinrichs and Gallicchio, *Implaccable Foes*, 75.
64. Krueger, *From Down Under to Nippon*, 72.
65. Coker, *Unforgettable Memories*, 131.
66. Wissolik and Wissolik, *An Honor to Serve*, 134.
67. Zabierek, *Beyond Pearl Harbor*, 5.
68. Coker, *Unforgettable Memories*, 134–37.
69. Zabierek, *Beyond Pearl Harbor*, 6.
70. 128th Infantry Regiment—Operations Report—Aitape Campaign (4 May–25 August 1945), RG 407.
71. Coker, *Unforgettable Memories*, 142.
72. Smith, *Approach to the Philippines*, 182.
73. Roy M. Campbell, *Kindling for the Devil's Fires: Journals of an Infantryman* (Victoria, BC: Trafford, 2005), 207.
74. James R. Mayo to Lorene Abernathy, 20 August 44, Mayo Papers.
75. John H. Walters interview with Mark D. Van Ells, Madison, Wisconsin, 27 October 1997, Wisconsin Veterans Oral History Program (hereafter cited as WVOHP), WVM; John Walters to family, 28 April 1944; 11 June 1944, John H. Walters Papers, WVM (hereafter cited as Walters Papers).
76. Robert S. Hiatt, *The Red Arrow: An Infantryman's War Account* (Georgetown, TX: Armadillo, 2004), 39.
77. Edward R. Guhl survey, World War II Veterans Surveys, 32d Infantry Division, USAHEC.
78. Campbell, *Kindling for the Devil's Fires*, 191, 208–9.
79. Newman Phillips survey, World War II Veterans Surveys, 32d Infantry Division, USAHEC.
80. Whayland H. Greene survey, World War II Veterans Surveys, 32d Infantry Division, USAHEC.
81. Walters interview.

82. Kristen Gilpatrick, *The Hero Next Door Returns: Stories from Wisconsin's World War II Veterans* (Oregon, WI: Badger Books, 2001), 176.

83. Zabierek, *Beyond Pearl Harbor*, 8–9.

84. Phillips survey.

85. Campbell, *Kindling for the Devil's Fires*, 197–98, 207.

86. Walters interview.

87. Walters to family, 15 August 1944, Walters Papers.

88. Paul A. Rettell, *A Soldier's True Story: The Life of an Infantry Soldier in World War II* (self-published, 1993), 59.

89. Coker, *Unforgettable Memories*, 149.

90. Mary Ellen Condon-Rall and Albert E. Cowdrey, *Medical Service in the War Against Japan* (Washington: Center for Military History, 1998), 208.

91. The Medical History of the 107th Medical Battalion from 1 April 1944 to 30 June 1944, 107th Medical Battalion—Medical History—All Campaigns and Occupation of Japan (1 Jan 1943–10 Jan 1946), RG 407.

92. Campbell, *Kindling for the Devil's Fires*, 198.

93. Medical History of the Medical Detachment, 128th Infantry Regiment—Medical Detachment—Medical History—All Campaigns and Occupation of Japan (1 Mar 43–31 Dec 45), RG 407.

94. Condon-Rall and Cowdrey, *Medical Service in the War against Japan*, 206.

95. The Medical History of the 107th Medical Battalion from 1 July 1944 to 30 September 1944, 107th Medical Battalion—Medical History—All Campaigns and Occupation of Japan (1 Jan 1943–10 Jan 1946), RG 407.

96. Andersen, *Praise the Lord*, 95, 105.

97. For more on the development of the U.S. Army's rotation policies, see Leonard L. Lerwill, *The Personnel Replacement System in the United States Army* (Washington, DC: Department of the Army, 1954), 328–38.

98. "Men of 32nd Division Scheduled to Start Journeys Home in March," *Milwaukee Journal*, 28 January 1944.

99. Kelley, *Born in the USA*, 83.

100. "Back from Hell and New Guinea Come Michigan's Jungle-Toughened Red Arrow Men," *Detroit Free Press*, 16 April 1944.

101. "First of 32nd Reaching City," *Milwaukee Journal*, 14 April 1944.

102. The Medical History of the 107th Medical Battalion from 1 April 1944 to 30 June 1944, 107th Medical Battalion—Medical History—All Campaigns and Occupation of Japan (1 Jan 1943–10 Jan 1946), RG 407.

103. Bable, *Beyond Pongani Mission*, 265–66.

104. Ball, *190 Letters*, 210–211, 218.

105. Walters to family, 16 August 1944, Walters Papers.

106. Coker, *Unforgettable Memories*, 158–59.

107. Campbell, *Kindling for the Devil's Fires*, 210–11.

108. Benjamin Winnesheik interview with Tom Doherty, 1989, WVOHP, WVM.

109. Walters to family, 15 August 1944, Walters Papers.

110. Myers, *Hell Is a Foxhole*, 69.

111. Rettell, *Soldier's True Story*, 62.

Chapter 9

1. Douglas MacArthur, *Reminiscences* (New York: Fawcett, 1964), 214–17.

2. MacArthur, *Reminiscences*, 215, 245.

3. The US Army campaigns in the Philippines during 1944–1945 have received relatively little scholarly attention. Many of the general works on the Pacific War cited earlier discuss the conduct of the 1944–1945 campaigns, but few quality monographs have been dedicated specifically to them.

The official US Army study of the Leyte campaign is M. Hamlin Cannon, *Leyte: The Return to the Philippines* (Washington, DC: Center of Military History, 1993). See also Stanley L. Falk, *Decision at Leyte* (New York: Norton, 1966).

4. Walter Krueger, *From Down Under to Nippon: The Story of the Sixth Army in World War II* (Nashville, TN: Battery Classics, 1989), 129.

5. Whayland H. Greene, *Why Are You So Yellow?: 38520190: 32nd Division*, rev. 1992, in Greene file, World War II Veterans Surveys, 32d Infantry Division, USAHEC, n.p.

6. Dean W. Andersen, *Praise the Lord and Pass the Penicillin: Memoir of a Combat Medic in the Pacific in World War II* (Jefferson, NC: McFarland, 2003), 114.

7. After Action Report, Morotai Operation, 126th Infantry Regiment—After Action Reports with Attached Papers—All Campaigns (12 Sep 1942–30 Nov 1945), Record Group 407: Records of the Adjutant General's Office, NARA (hereafter cited as RG 407).

8. After Action Report, Morotai Operation, 126th Infantry Regiment—After Action Reports with Attached Papers—All Campaigns (12 Sep 1942–30 Nov 1945), RG 407.

9. Richard Van Hammen interview with Dan Bush and Chris Vredeveld, 11 November, 2005, GVSU.

10. Jesse Coker, *My Unforgettable Memories of World War II* (self-published, 1994), 159.

11. Training Memorandum No. 4., 1 October 1944, 128th Infantry Regiment—Unit Journal and File—Camp Walker and Hollandia—New Guinea (2–28 October 1944), RG 407.

12. 128th Infantry Regiment, Historical Operations Report—Hollandia—New Guinea (2–28 Oct 1944), RG 407.

13. James E. Myers, *Hell Is a Foxhole: An Autobiography—1942 to 1946* (New York: Vantage, 1966), 72.

14. Maggie Rivas-Rodriguez, Juliana A. Torres, Melissa DiPiero-D'Sa, and Lindsay Fitzpatrick, *A Legacy Greater than Words: Stories of U.S. Latinos and Latinas of the WWII Generation* (Austin: University of Texas Press, 2007), 120.

15. Monte Howell, *The Young Draftee* (San Jose, CA: Writer's Showcase, 2002), 23.

16. Howard E. Kelley, *Born in the U.S.A.: A World War II Memoir* (Eau Claire, WI: Heins Publications, 1999), 84.

17. History, 127th Infantry, Leyte Campaign, RG 407.

18. Howell, *Young Draftee*, 21.

19. Coker, *Unforgettable Memories*, 162.

20. Howell, *Young Draftee*, 23.

21. Walters to family, 14 October 1944, John H. Walters Papers, WVM (hereafter cited as Walters Papers).

22. For an introduction to the Battle of Leyte Gulf, see John Prados, *Storm over Leyte: The Philippine Invasion and the Destruction of the Japanese Navy* (New York: NAL Caliber, 2016).

23. Falk, *Decision at Leyte*, 245.

24. Krueger, *From Down Under to Nippon*, 169.

25. Roy M. Campbell, *Kindling for the Devil's Fires: Journals of an Infantryman* (Victoria, BC: Trafford, 2005), 212.

26. Robert S. Hiatt, *The Red Arrow: An Infantryman's War Account* (Georgetown, TX: Armadillo, 2004), 52–55.

27. Hiatt, *Red Arrow*, 54.

28. Campbell, *Kindling for the Devil's Fires*, 215.

29. Hiatt, *Red Arrow*, 57–58.

30. Whayland H. Greene, *Grateful Soldiers . . . Not Great Soldiers* (Vivian, LA: Whitecotton Printing, 1996), 8.

31. Andersen, *Praise the Lord*, 125–26.

32. Paul A. Rettell, *A Soldier's True Story: The Life of an Infantry Soldier in World War II* (self-published, 1993), 72.

33. For an introduction to the Japanese occupation of the Philippines, see Alfred W. McCoy, "'Politics by Other Means': World War II in the Western Visayas," in Alfred W. McCoy, ed., *Southeast Asia*

under Japanese Occupation (New Haven: Yale University Southeast Asia Studies, 1980): 191–245; Ikehata Setsuho and Ricardo Trota Jose, *The Philippines under Japan: Occupation Policy and Reaction* (Manila: Ateneo de Manila University, 1999); and Lydia Yu-Jose, *Japan Views the Philippines, 1900–1944* (Manila: Ateneo de Manila University, 1992).

34. For an introduction to guerrilla operations in the Philippines, see James Kelley Morningstar, *War and Resistance in the Philippines, 1942–1944* (Annapolis: Naval Institute Press, 2021); and James A. Villanueva, *Awaiting MacArthur's Return: World War II Guerrilla Resistance against the Japanese in the Philippines* (Manhattan: University Press of Kansas, 2022).

35. Villanueva, *Awaiting MacArthur's Return*, 124.

36. Andersen, *Praise the Lord*, 129.

37. Hiatt, *Red Arrow*, 60–63.

38. Greene, *Why Are You So Yellow?*, n.p.

39. Campbell, *Kindling for the Devil's Fires*, 216.

40. Hiatt, *Red Arrow*, 62.

41. Rettell, *Soldier's True Story*, 67.

42. Andersen, *Praise the Lord*, 128.

43. Greene, *Grateful Soldiers*, 8.

44. Hiatt, *Red Arrow*, 64.

45. Howell, *Young Draftee*, 37.

46. Andersen, *Praise the Lord*, 127.

47. Rettell, *Soldier's True Story*, 72.

48. Greene, *Grateful Soldiers*, 9.

49. Hiatt, *Red Arrow*, 65.

50. 128th Infantry Regiment—Historical Record—Leyte (14 Nov–25 Dec 1944), RG 407.

51. 128th Infantry Regiment—1st Battalion—Operations Report—Leyte (14 Nov–25 Dec 1944), RG 407.

52. Campbell, *Kindling for the Devil's Fires*, 218–22.

53. 128th Infantry Regiment—3rd Battalion—Unit History (14 November–25 December 1944), RG 407.

54. Myers, *Hell Is a Foxhole*, 79.

55. Coker, *Unforgettable Memories*, 170–72.

56. Myers, *Hell Is a Foxhole*, 80.

57. Coker, *Unforgettable Memories*, 172–74.

58. Coker, 173–77; Myers, *Hell Is a Foxhole*, 80–82.

59. Coker, 178.

60. Myers, *Hell Is a Foxhole*, 83.

61. Zabierek, *Beyond Pearl Harbor*, 13–26.

62. Mayo to Abernathy, 14 April 1944, Mayo Papers.

63. Falk, *Decision at Leyte*, 261.

64. Coker, *Unforgettable Memories*, 186.

65. Report After Action Leyte Operation, 126th Infantry Regiment—After Action Reports with Attached Papers—All Campaigns (12 Sep 1942–30 Nov 1945), RG 407.

66. Hiatt, *Red Arrow*, 107–8.

67. Richard David Wissolik and Barbara J. Wissolik, eds., *An Honor to Serve* (Latrobe, PA: Publications of the Saint Vincent College Center for Northern Appalachian Studies, 2007), 138.

68. Andersen, *Praise the Lord*, 132.

69. Hiatt, *Red Arrow*, 109.

70. Campbell, *Kindling for the Devil's Fires*, 236.

71. Wendell Trogdon, *Out Front: The Cladie Bailey Story* (Mooresville, IN: Backroads Press, 1994), 101.

72. Hiatt, *Red Arrow*, 112.

73. Greene, *Why Are You So Yellow?*, n.p.

74. Andersen, *Praise the Lord*, 133.

75. Wissolik and Wissolik, *An Honor to Serve*, 137.

76. Andersen, *Praise the Lord*, 134.

77. Martin Bolt interview interview with Frank Boring, 20 July 2007, GVSU.

78. Greene, *Why Are You So Yellow?*, n.p.

79. Howell, *Young Draftee*, 38.

80. Whayland H. Greene interview with Richard Misenheimer, 2 March 2017, National Museum of the Pacific War, Fredericksburg, Texas.

81. Hiatt, *Red Arrow*, 90–91.

82. 127th Infantry Regiment—History—Leyte (6 Nov 1944–3 Jan 1945), RG 407.

83. Report After Action Leyte Operation, 126th Infantry Regiment—After Action Reports with Attached Papers—All Campaigns (12 Sep 1942–30 Nov 1945), RG 407.

84. Campbell, *Kindling for the Devil's Fires*, 226–27.

85. Coker, *Unforgettable Memories*, 198.

86. Joe H. Camp Jr., *32 Answered: A South Carolina Veterans' Story* (Charleston, SC: Joe H. Camp, Jr., 2015), 353.

87. 32nd Cavalry Reconnaissance Troop—Unit Historical Report—Leyte (17 Nov 1944–2 Jan 1945), RG 407.

88. Harold W. Blakeley, *32d Infantry Division in World War II* (Madison: Thirty-Second Infantry Division History Commission, 1957), 187–92.

89. Blakeley, *32d Infantry Division*, 192–93; Trogdon, *Cladie Bailey*, 104–5.

90. Jay Luvaas, *Dear Miss Em: General Eichelberger's War in the Pacific, 1942–1945* (Westport, CT: Greenwood Press, 1972), 176.

91. Coker, *Unforgettable Memories*, 197.

92. Greene, *Grateful Soldiers*, 11.

93. Greene, *Why Are You So Yellow?*, n.p.

94. Hiatt, *Red Arrow*, 81.

95. Hiatt, 87–88.

96. Greene, *Why Are You So Yellow?*, n.p.

97. John Rawls, "On My Religion," in *A Brief Inquiry into the Meaning of Sin and Faith: With "On My Religion,"* ed. Thomas Nagel (Cambridge, MA: Harvard University Press, 2009), 262.

98. Campbell, *Kindling for the Devil's Fires*, 229, 233.

99. Campbell, *Kindling for the Devil's Fires*, 220.

100. Rettell, *Soldier's True Story*, 74.

101. Kristen Gilpatrick, *The Hero Next Door Returns: Stories from Wisconsin's World War II Veterans* (Oregon, WI: Badger Books, 2001), 179.

102. Wissolik and Wissolik, *An Honor to Serve*, 138.

103. 127th Infantry Regiment—History—Leyte (6 Nov 1944–3 Jan 1945), RG 407.

104. Cannon, *Leyte*, 342.

105. 127th Infantry Regiment—History—Leyte (6 Nov 1944–3 Jan 1945), RG 407.

106. Hiatt, *Red Arrow*, 124.

107. Hiatt, *Red Arrow*, 125.

108. 127th Infantry Regiment—History—Leyte (6 Nov 1944–3 Jan 1945), RG 407.

109. Hiatt, *Red Arrow*, 125.

110. Campbell, *Kindling for the Devil's Fires*, 242.

111. 127th Infantry Regiment—History—Leyte (6 Nov 1944–3 Jan 1945), RG 407.

112. Hiatt, *Red Arrow*, 126.

113. Coker, *Unforgettable Memories*, 200–203.

114. Campbell, *Kindling for the Devil's Fires*, 245.

115. 127th Infantry Regiment—History—Leyte (6 Nov 1944–3 Jan 1945), RG 407.

116. Hiatt, *Red Arrow*, 127.

117. Coker, *Unforgettable Memories*, 206–9.

118. 32nd Cavalry Reconnaissance Troop—Unit Historical Report—Leyte (17 Nov 1944–2 Jan 1945), RG 407; Supplementary After Action Report, Leyte, 32nd Cavalry Reconnaissance Troop, 26 December 1944–21 January 1945, RG 407.

119. "Our Captain Bottcher," *New Masses*, 26 March 1946, 11; 32nd Cavalry Reconnaissance Troop—Unit Historical Report—Leyte (17 Nov 1944–2 Jan 1945), RG 407; Supplementary After Action Report, Leyte, 32nd Cavalry Reconnaissance Troop, 26 December 1944–21 January 1945, RG 407.

120. "German to American," *Yank*, 3 March 1945.

121. Raymond F. Dasmann, *Called by the Wild: The Autobiography of a Conservationist* (Berkeley: University of California Press, 2002), 66.

122. Tribute to Captain Herman Bottcher, Manhattan Center, Thursday, May 17, 1945, Tamiment Library and Robert F. Wagner Labor Archives, New York University, New York, New York (hereafter cited as ALBA).

123. Speech delivered by Gustav Faber, Editor of the German American, Secretary of the German-American Trade Union Committee, at Manhattan Center, May 17, 1945, ALBA.

124. Press release, Veterans of the Abraham Lincoln Brigade, May 14, 1945, ALBA.

125. Cannon, *Leyte*, 238.

126. Howell, *Young Draftee*, 59.

127. Coker, *Unforgettable Memories*, 213–16.

128. Myers, *Hell Is a Foxhole*, 86.

129. John Walters to Jewell Walters, 14 January 1945, Walters Papers.

Chapter 10

1. Annie Norder to General Douglas MacArthur, 2 February 1945, CINC Correspondence file, MMA.

2. The official US Army history of the Luzon campaign is Robert Ross Smith, *Triumph in the Philippines* (Washington, DC: Center of Military History, 1993). See also Robert M. Young, *Pacific Hurtgen: The American Army in Northern Luzon, 1945* (Washington, DC: Westphalia Press, 2017).

3. Walter Krueger, *From Down Under to Nippon: The Story of the Sixth Army in World War II* (Nashville, TN: Battery Classics, 1989), 227–28.

4. Waldo Heinrichs and Marc Gallicchio, *Implacable Foes: The War in the Pacific, 1944–1945* (New York: Oxford University Press, 2017), 240.

5. Dean W. Andersen, *Praise the Lord and Pass the Penicillin: Memoir of a Combat Medic in the Pacific in World War II* (Jefferson, NC: McFarland, 2003), 155.

6. Roy M. Campbell, *Kindling for the Devil's Fires: Journals of an Infantryman* (Victoria, BC: Trafford, 2005), 147–48.

7. 128th Infantry Regiment—Historical Report—Luzon (27 Jan–30 Jun 1945), Record Group 407: Records of the Adjutant General's Office, NARA (hereafter cited as RG 407).

8. 128th Infantry Regiment—Historical Report—Luzon (27 Jan–30 Jun 1945), RG 407.

9. Jesse Coker, *My Unforgettable Memories of World War II* (self-published, 1994), 219.

10. Campbell, *Kindling for the Devil's Fires*, 249.

11. The Villa Verde Trail was just one of many roadbuilding projects Father Villaverde undertook. For more on his work and legacy, see Guillermo Tejon, *Juan Villaverde, O.P.: Missionary and Road Builder* (Manila: University of Santo Tomas, 1982).

12. 127th Infantry Regiment—History—Luzon (27 Jan–30 Jun 1945), RG 407.

13. 127th Infantry Regiment—History—Luzon (27 Jan–30 Jun 1945), RG 407.

14. Robert L. Eichelberger, *Our Jungle Road to Tokyo* (New York: Viking, 1950), 200.

15. Among the liberated American prisoners of war were members of Company A of the 192nd Tank Battalion, the former Thirty-Second Tank Company out of Janesville, Wisconsin. Other Janesville tankers had been transported out of the Philippines and remained captive in China, Japan, Korea, and Taiwan. These prisoners did not see liberation until the end of the war, if they survived that long. Of the ninety-nine members of the Janesville company when it was mobilized in 1940, only

thirty-five lived to the end of the war. For more on the company, see "Tom Doherty, "Too Little, Too Late: Janesville's 'Lost Children' of the Armored Force," *Wisconsin Magazine of History 75*, no. 4 (Summer 1992): 242–83; and Dale Dopkins, *The Janesville 99* (self-published, 1981).

16. 127th Infantry Regiment—History—Luzon (27 Jan–30 Jun 1945), RG 407.

17. Harold W. Blakeley, *32d Infantry Division in World War II* (Madison: Thirty-Second Infantry Division History Commission, 1957), 215–16.

18. John H. Walters interview with Mark D. Van Ells, Madison, Wisconsin, 27 October 1997, Wisconsin Veterans Oral History Program (hereafter cited as WVOHP), WVM.

19. James E. Myers, *Hell Is a Foxhole: An Autobiography—1942 to 1946* (New York: Vantage, 1966), 89.

20. Campbell *Kindling for the Devil's Fires*, 250.

21. Coker, *Unforgettable Memories*, 226.

22. Joe H. Camp Jr., *32 Answered: A South Carolina Veterans' Story* (Charleston, SC: Joe H. Camp, Jr., 2015), 360.

23. 127th Infantry Regiment—History—Luzon (27 Jan–30 Jun 1945), RG 407.

24. Coker, *Unforgettable Memories*, 225–31.

25. Smith, *Triumph in the Philippines*, 499.

26. Walters to family, 25 March 1945, John H. Walters Papers, WVM (hereafter cited as Walters Papers).

27. 128th Infantry Regiment—Historical Report—Luzon (27 Jan–30 Jun 1945), RG 407.

28. Campbell, *Kindling for the Devil's Fires*, 250.

29. Myers, *Hell Is a Foxhole*, 92.

30. 128th Infantry Regiment—Historical Report—Luzon (27 Jan–30 Jun 1945), RG 407.

31. Luzon Campaign, M-2 Operation, 126th Infantry Regiment—After Action Reports with Attached Papers—All Campaigns (12 Sep 1942–30 Nov 1945), RG 407.

32. William H. Gill and Edward Jaquelin Smith, *Always a Commander: The Reminiscences of Major General William H. Gill as told to Edward Jaquelin Smith* (Colorado Springs: Colorado College, 1974), 87.

33. Charles P. Murdock, "The Red Arrow Pierced Every Line," *Saturday Evening Post*, November 10, 1945.

34. 128th Infantry Regiment—Historical Report—Luzon (27 Jan–30 Jun 1945), RG 407.

35. "Battle of Caves Fought in Clouds," *Pittsburgh Post-Gazette*, 1 June 1945.

36. William E. Painter interview with Ronald E. Marcello, Denton, Texas, 21 December 1998, University of North Texas Library Special Collections, Denton, Texas.

37. Whayland H. Greene, *Why Are You So Yellow?: 38520190: 32nd Division*, rev. 1992, in Greene file, World War II Veterans Surveys, 32d Infantry Division, USAHEC, n.p.

38. Jerry R. Angel survey, World War II Veterans Surveys, 32d Infantry Division, USAHEC.

39. Henry C. Zabierek, *Beyond Pearl Harbor: I Company in the Pacific of WWII* (Shippensburg, PA: Burd Street Press, 2010), 32.

40. Greene, Why Are You So Yellow?, n.p.

41. Zabierek, *Beyond Pearl Harbor*, 36.

42. For an introduction to the Igorots, see Gerard A. Finin, *The Making of the Igorot: Ramut ti Pangkaykayse dagiti taga Cordillera (Contours of Cordillera Consciousness)* (Manila: Ateneo de Manila University Press, 2005); Rebecca Tinio McKenna, *American Imperial Pastoral: The Architecture of US Colonialism in the Philippines* (Chicago: University of Chicago Press, 2017); and William Henry Scott, *On the Cordillera: A Look at the Peoples and Cultures of the Mountain Province* (Manila: MCS Enterprises, 1966).

43. 114th Engineer Combat Battalion—Historical Report—M-1 Operation—Luzon (27 Jan–30 June 1945), RG 417.

44. Zabierek, *Beyond Pearl Harbor*, 34.

45. Ray C. Hunt and Bernard Norling, *Behind Japanese Lines: An American Guerrilla in the Philippines* (Lexington: University Press of Kentucky, 1986), 206.

46. 114th Engineer Combat Battalion—Historical Report—M-1 Operation—Luzon (27 Jan–30 June 1945), RG 417.

47. Action on Hill 505, 22 June 1945, 128th Infantry Regiment—Historical Report—Luzon (27 Jan–30 Jun 1945), RG 407.

48. Zabierek, *Beyond Pearl Harbor*, 37.

49. Coker, *Unforgettable Memories*, 243–44.

50. Zabierek, *Beyond Pearl Harbor*, 30.

51. John M. Carlisle, *Red Arrow Men: Stories About the 32nd Division on the Villa Verde Front* (Detroit: Arnold-Powers, 1945), 65.

52. Monte Howell, *The Young Draftee* (San Jose, CA: Writer's Showcase, 2002), 79.

53. 128th Infantry Regiment—Historical Report—Luzon (27 Jan–30 Jun 1945), RG 407.

54. Hunt and Norling, *Behind Japanese Lines*, 209.

55. 128th Infantry Regiment—Historical Report—Luzon (27 Jan–30 Jun 1945), RG 407.

56. Coker, *Unforgettable Memories*, 241–43.

57. Myers, *Hell Is a Foxhole*, 91–92.

58. 127th Infantry Regiment—History—Luzon (27 Jan–30 Jun 1945), RG 407.

59. Raul Morin, *Among the Valiant: Mexican-Americans in WWII and Korea* (Alhambra, CA: Borden Publishing Company, 1966), 218–23.

60. Carlisle, *Red Arrow Men*, 85.

61. Coker, *Unforgettable Memories*, 263–65.

62. Carlisle, *Red Arrow Men*, 86.

63. 107th Medical Battalion—After Action Report—M-1 Operation—Luzon (1 Jan–30 Nov 1945), RG 407.

64. Andersen, *Praise the Lord*, 167.

65. 107th Medical Battalion—Historical Report (27 Jan–4 Jun 1945), RG 407.

66. "Midget Planes Evacuate Wounded," *Pittsburgh Post-Gazette*, 30 May 1945.

67. Coker, *Unforgettable Memories*, 266.

68. 127th Infantry Regiment—History—Luzon (27 Jan–30 Jun 1945), RG 407.

69. Myers, *Hell Is a Foxhole*, 94.

70. 127th Infantry Regiment—History—Luzon (27 Jan–30 Jun 1945), RG 407.

71. Edward R. Guhl survey, World War II Veterans Surveys, 32d Infantry Division, USAHEC.

72. Walters to family, 3 May 1945, 12 May 1945, Walters Papers.

73. John Rawls, "On My Religion," in *A Brief Inquiry into the Meaning of Sin and Faith: With "On My Religion,"* ed. Thomas Nagel (Cambridge, MA: Harvard University Press, 2009), 262.

74. Guhl survey.

75. Robert L. Foist survey, World War II Veterans Surveys, 32d Infantry Division, USAHEC.

76. Painter interview.

77. Walters to family, 21 April 1945, Walters Papers.

78. 127th Infantry Regiment—History—Luzon (27 Jan–30 Jun 1945), RG 407.

79. Andersen, *Praise the Lord*, 169.

80. Robert Eichelberger to Emmaline Eichelberger, 18 February 1945, 23 February 1945, Papers of Robert L. Eichelberger, Duke University Library Special Collections, Durham, North Carolina.

81. 127th Infantry Regiment—History—Luzon (27 Jan–30 Jun 1945), RG 407.

82. Andersen, *Praise the Lord*, 169.

83. Albert E. Cowdrey, *Fighting for Life: American Military Medicine in World War II* (New York: Free Press, 1994), 151. See also Rebecca Schwartz Greene, *Breaking Point: The Ironic Evolution of Psychiatry in World War II* (New York: Fordham University Press, 2023).

84. Smith, *Triumph in the Philippines*, 504.

85. Gifford Coleman interview with Mark D. Van Ells, 10 November 1994, WVOHP, WVM.

86. Walters to family, 27 April 1945, Walters Papers.

87. Hunt, *Behind Japanese Lines*, 208–9.

88. Murdock, "The Red Arrow Pierced Every Line."

89. Walters to family, 19 April 1945, Walters Papers.

90. "Baby Burma Road Built on Luzon," *Pittsburgh Post-Gazette*, 24 May 1945.

91. Walters to family, 30 March 1945, 1 April 1945, Walters Papers.

92. Painter interview.

93. Andersen, *Praise the Lord*, 170.

94. Walters to family, 17 June 1945, Walters Papers.

95. Myers, *Hell Is a Foxhole*, 95–96.

96. Coker, *Unforgettable Memories*, 219–21.

97. Walters to family, 16 July 1945, Walters Papers.

98. Andersen, *Praise the Lord*, 158.

99. Donald R. Dill survey, World War II Veterans Surveys, 32d Infantry Division, USAHEC.

100. Walters to family, 31 May 1945, Walters Papers.

101. Howell, *Young Draftee*, 84.

102. Howell, *Young Draftee*, 88.

103. Coker, *Unforgettable Memories*, 223–24.

104. Andersen, *Praise the Lord*, 178–79.

105. Dill survey.

106. Howell, *Young Draftee*, 89.

107. Memorandum No. 7, 10 February 1945, 128th Infantry Regiment—Unit Journal and File—Luzon (10–19 Feb 1945), RG 407.

108. Andersen, *Praise the Lord*, 178.

109. 107th Medical Battalion—After Action Report—M-1 Operation—Luzon (1 Jan–30 Nov 1945), RG 407.

110. Andersen, *Praise the Lord*, 178.

111. Carlisle, *Red Arrow Men*, 68.

112. Myers, *Hell Is a Foxhole*, 97.

113. Andersen, *Praise the Lord*, 181.

114. Andersen, *Praise the Lord*, 181.

115. United Service Organizations, *USO, Five Years of Service: Report of the President* (Washington, DC: United Service Organizations, 1946), 11–12.

116. Andersen, *Praise the Lord*, 181.

117. Carlisle, *Red Arrow Men*, 57–60; "Pass, Beer Spur Capture of Japs," *Pittsburgh Post-Gazette*, 31 May 1945, 11.

118. Luzon Campaign, M-2 Operation, 126th Infantry Regiment—After Action Reports with Attached Papers—All Campaigns (12 Sep 1942–30 Nov 1945), RG 407.

119. The codename for the invasion of Japan was Operation Downfall. It would have been the largest amphibious operation in history—dwarfing the 1944 invasion of Normandy—and MacArthur was to command it. In the first phase of the operation, scheduled for November 1945 and codenamed Operation Olympic, Krueger's Sixth Army was to invade Kyushu, the southernmost of the Japanese home islands. Then in March 1946 Operation Coronet was to seize Tokyo and its environs. The Coronet force was to consist of two armies: Eichelberger's Eighth and the First Army under General Courtney H. Hodges, made up of divisions transferred from Europe. According to the plan, Eichelberger's Eighth Army (including the Red Arrow Division) was to land southwest of Tokyo on the shores of Sagami Bay, then secure the west shore of Tokyo Bay. A few days later, Hodges' First Army was to strike east of Tokyo. For an introduction to Operation Downfall, see Richard B. Frank, *Downfall: The End of the Imperial Japanese Empire* (New York: Penguin, 1999) and D. M. Giangreco, *Hell to Pay: Operation Downfall and the Invasion of Japan, 1945–1947* (Annapolis, MD: Naval Institute Press, 2009).

120. Dill survey.

121. 127th Infantry Regiment—History—Northern Luzon Highway 11 (1 Jul–30 Sep 1945), RG 407.

122. Campbell, *Kindling for the Devil's Fires*, 253–58.
123. 127th Infantry Regiment—History—Northern Luzon Highway 11 (1 Jul–30 Sep 1945), RG 407.
124. Greene, *Why Are You So Yellow?*, n.p.
125. Campbell, *Kindling for the Devil's Fires*, 255.
126. Charles A. Dunnam interview with Richard Misenheimer, 17 October 2014, National Museum of the Pacific War, Fredericksburg, Texas.
127. 127th Infantry Regiment—History—Northern Luzon Highway 11 (1 Jul–30 Sep 1945), RG 407.
128. Zabierek, *Beyond Pearl Harbor*, 47.
129. Angel survey.
130. Walters to family, 9 August 1945, Walters Papers.
131. Andersen, *Praise the Lord*, 185.
132. Dill survey.
133. James W. Casteel to Mrs. J. W. Casteel, n.d. [ca. August 1945], World War II letters, State Historical Society of Missouri, Columbia, Missouri.
134. Zabierek, *Beyond Pearl Harbor*, 49.
135. Andersen, *Praise the Lord*, 187.
136. Painter interview.
137. Walters to family, 15 August 1945, Walters Papers.
138. Greene, Why Are You So Yellow?, n.p.
139. Myers, *Hell Is a Foxhole*, 99.
140. Zabierek, *Beyond Pearl Harbor*, 50–51.
141. 127th Infantry Regiment—History—Northern Luzon Highway 11 (1 Jul–30 Sep 1945), RG 407.
142. G-2 Period Report, 19 August 1945, 128th Infantry Regiment—Journal and File—Luzon (23–31 Aug 1945), RG 407.
143. 127th Infantry Regiment—History—Northern Luzon Highway 11 (1 Jul–30 Sep 1945), RG 407.
144. Zabierek, *Beyond Pearl Harbor*, 49.
145. Zabierek, *Beyond Pearl Harbor*, 49–50.
146. 127th Infantry Regiment—History—Northern Luzon Highway 11 (1 Jul–30 Sep 1945), RG 407.
147. G-2 Period Report, 20 August 1945, 128th Infantry Regiment—Journal and File—Luzon (23–31 Aug 1945), RG 407.
148. Greene, Why Are You So Yellow?, n.p.
149. Eichelberger, *Our Jungle Road to Tokyo*, 257.
150. Blakeley, *32d Infantry Division*, 271.
151. Gill and Smith, *Always a Commander*, 100.
152. Eichelberger, *Our Jungle Road to Tokyo*, 258.
153. Eichelberger, *Our Jungle Road to Tokyo*, 258.
154. Carlisle, *Red Arrow Men*, 214.
155. Gill and Smith, *Always a Commander*, 97.
156. Whayland H. Greene, *Grateful Soldiers . . . Not Great Soldiers* (Vivian, LA: Whitecotton Printing, 1996), 17.
157. Zabierek, *Beyond Pearl Harbor*, 51.
158. Dunnam interview.
159. Dill survey.
160. Greene, *Why Are You So Yellow?*, n.p.
161. Dill survey.
162. 127th Infantry Regiment—History—Northern Luzon Highway 11 (1 Jul–30 Sep 1945), RG 407.
163. Dill survey.
164. Andersen, *Praise the Lord*, 188–89.
165. 127th Infantry Regiment—History—Northern Luzon Highway 11 (1 Jul–30 Sep 1945), RG 407.
166. Krueger, *From Down Under to Nippon*, 328.

Chapter 11

1. Walters to family, 15 August 1945, John H. Walters Papers, WVM (hereafter cited as Walters Papers).

2. Monte Howell, *The Young Draftee* (San Jose, CA: Writer's Showcase, 2002), 103. For an introduction to the demobilization process see John C. Sparrow, *History of Personnel Demobilization in the United States Army* (Washington, DC: Department of the Army, 1952) and Jack Stokes Ballard, *The Shock of Peace: Military and Economic Demobilization after World War II* (Washington: University Press of America, 1983).

3. Henry C. Zabierek, *Beyond Pearl Harbor: I Company in the Pacific of WWII* (Shippensburg, PA: Burd Street Press, 2010), 55–56.

4. Dean W. Andersen, *Praise the Lord and Pass the Penicillin: Memoir of a Combat Medic in the Pacific in World War II* (Jefferson, NC: McFarland, 2003), 197.

5. Roy M. Campbell, *Kindling for the Devil's Fires: Journals of an Infantryman* (Victoria, BC: Trafford, 2005), 263, 265.

6. Andersen, *Praise the Lord*, 198.

7. Campbell, *Kindling for the Devil's Fires*, 266.

8. Andersen, *Praise the Lord*, 198.

9. Andersen, *Praise the Lord*, 199.

10. Campbell, *Kindling for the Devil's Fires*, 268.

11. Campbell, *Kindling for the Devil's Fires*, 274–75.

12. Sparrow, *History of Personnel Demobilization*, 211.

13. Andersen, *Praise the Lord*, 200.

14. Campbell, *Kindling for the Devil's Fires*, 277–78.

15. For an introduction to the US occupation and to postwar Japan, see John Dower, *Embracing Defeat: Japan in the Wake of World War II* (New York: Norton, 1999); Douglas MacArthur, *Reports of General MacArthur*, vol. 1 supplement, *MacArthur in Japan: The Occupation; The Military Phase* (Washington, DC: Government Printing Office, 1966); and Michael Schaller, *The American Occupation of Japan: The Origins of the Cold War in Asia* (New York: Oxford University Press, 1985).

16. 127th Infantry Regiment—History—Blacklist Operation—Occupation of Japan (7 Sep–30 Nov 1945), Record Group 407: Records of the Adjutant General's Office, NARA (hereafter cited as RG 407); William E. Painter interview, University of North Texas Library Special Collections, Denton, Texas; 127th Infantry Regiment—1st Battalion—S-3 Operations Report (7 Sep–30 Nov 1945), RG 407.

17. Howell, *Young Draftee*, 105.

18. 127th Infantry Regiment—History—Blacklist Operation—Occupation of Japan (7 Sep–30 Nov 1945), RG 407.

19. James E. Myers, *Hell Is a Foxhole: An Autobiography—1942 to 1946* (New York: Vantage, 1966), 105.

20. Walters to family, 15 October 1945, Walters Papers.

21. Zabierek, *Beyond Pearl Harbor*, 61.

22. 127th Infantry Regiment—History—Blacklist Operation—Occupation of Japan (7 Sep–30 Nov 1945), RG 407.

23. Unit History, 1st Battalion, 128th Infantry Regiment—Battalions—Operations Report—Occupation of Japan (1 Dec 1945–28 Feb 1946), RG 407.

24. Quarterly History, 10 January 1946, 107th Medical Battalion—Unit Journal—Luzon and Occupation of Japan (23 Jul 1945–23 Feb 1946), RG 407.

25. Zabierek, *Beyond Pearl Harbor*, 62.

26. Walters to family, 19 October 1945, Walters Papers.

27. Howell, *Young Draftee*, 106.

28. 126th Infantry Regiment—Operations Report—Occupation of Japan (1 Dec 1945–28 Feb 1945), RG 407.

29. Myers, *Hell Is a Foxhole*, 105.

30. Field Order 14, 28 September 1945, 126th Infantry Regiment—Unit Journal and File—Occupation of Japan (7 Sep–30 Nov 1945), RG 407.

31. 127th Infantry Regiment—2nd Battalion—Occupation Report—Blacklist Operation—Occupation of Japan (19 Oct–5 Nov 1945), RG 407.

32. Field Order 14, 28 September 1945, 126th Infantry Regiment—Unit Journal and File—Occupation of Japan (7 Sep–30 Nov 1945), RG 407.

33. 127th Infantry Regiment—History—Blacklist Operation—Occupation of Japan (7 Sep–30 Nov 1945), RG 407.

34. Walters to family, 19 October 1945, Walters Papers.

35. Zabierek, *Beyond Pearl Harbor*, 68.

36. Walters to family, 6 November 1945, Walters Papers.

37. 127th Infantry Regiment—3rd Battalion—S-3 Report—Occupation of Japan (23 Sep–10 Dec 1945), RG 407.

38. Howell, *Young Draftee*, 112.

39. Walters to family, 19 October 1945, Walters Papers.

40. Painter interview.

41. 128th Infantry Regiment—1st Battalion—Unit History—Occupation of Japan (1 Dec 1945–28 Feb 1946), RG 407.

42. 127th Infantry Regiment—History—Blacklist Operation—Occupation of Japan (1 Dec–28 Feb 1946), RG 407.

43. 128th Infantry Regiment—1st Battalion—Unit History—Occupation of Japan (1 Dec 1945–28 Feb 1946), RG 407.

44. Unit Report No. 38, 30 November 1945, 126th Infantry Regiment—Unit Journal and File—Occupation of Japan (7 Sep–30 Nov 1945), RG 407.

45. Unit Report No. 22, 14 November 1945, 126th Infantry Regiment—Unit Journal and File—Occupation of Japan (7 Sep–30 Nov 1945), RG 407.

46. Unit Journal, 7 December 1945, 128th Infantry Regiment—Journal and File—Occupation of Japan (1 Dec 1945–15 Feb 1946), RG 407.

47. Painter interview.

48. 127th Infantry Regiment—History—Blacklist Operation—Occupation of Japan (1 Dec–28 Feb 1946), RG 407.

49. MacArthur, *Reports: Supplement*, 1:154.

50. 128th Infantry Regiment—1st Battalion—Unit History—Occupation of Japan (1 Dec 1945–28 Feb 1946), RG 407.

51. Occupation Operations Report, 14 February 1946, 128th Infantry Regiment—Battalions—Operations Report—Occupation of Japan (1 Dec 1945–28 Feb 1946), RG 407.

52. 128th Infantry Regiment—1st Battalion—Unit History—Occupation of Japan (1 Dec 1945–28 Feb 1946), RG 407.

53. 126th Infantry Regiment—Operations Report—Occupation of Japan (1 Dec 1945–28 Feb 1945), RG 407.

54. 128th Infantry Regiment—1st Battalion—Unit History—Occupation of Japan (1 Dec 1945–28 Feb 1946), RG 407; Occupation Operations Report, 17 February 1946, 128th Infantry Regiment—Battalions—Operations Report—Occupation of Japan (1 Dec 1945–28 Feb 1946), RG 407.

55. MacArthur, *Reports: Supplement*, 1:152–55.

56. 126th Infantry Regiment—Operations Report—Occupation of Japan (1 Dec 1945–28 Feb 1945), RG 407.

57. MacArthur, *Reports: Supplement*, 1:136.

58. 127th Infantry Regiment—History—Blacklist Operation—Occupation of Japan (1 Dec–28 Feb 1946), RG 407.

59. 128th Infantry Regiment—1st Battalion—Unit History—Occupation of Japan (1 Dec 1945–28 Feb 1946), RG 407.

60. Occupations Operations Report, 17 February 1946, 128th Infantry Regiment—Battalions—Operation Report—Occupation of Japan (1 Dec 1945–28 Feb 1946), RG 407.

61. 127th Infantry Regiment—3rd Battalion—S-3 Report—Occupation of Japan (23 Sep–10 Dec 1945), RG 407.

62. Occupation Operations Report, 14 February 1946, 128th Infantry Regiment—Battalions—Operation Report—Occupation of Japan (1 Dec 1945–28 Feb 1946), RG 407.

63. 126th Infantry Regiment—Operations Report—Occupation of Japan (1 Dec 1945–28 Feb 1945), RG 407.

64. Occupation Operations Report, 17 February 1946, 128th Infantry Regiment—Battalions—Operation Report—Occupation of Japan (1 Dec 1945–28 Feb 1946), RG 407.

65. 128th Infantry Regiment—1st Battalion—Unit History—Occupation of Japan (1 Dec 1945–28 Feb 1946), RG 07.

66. Zabierek, *Beyond Pearl Harbor*, 63–66.

67. 127th Infantry Regiment—History—Blacklist Operation—Occupation of Japan (7 Sep–30 Nov 1945), RG 407; 126th Infantry Regiment—After Action Report—Blacklist Operation—Occupation of Japan (7 Sep–30 Nov 1945), RG 407.

68. 127th Infantry Regiment—History—Blacklist Operation—Occupation of Japan (1 Dec–28 Feb 1946), RG 407.

69. Unit Report No. 22, 14 November 1945, 126th Infantry Regiment—Unit Journal and File—Occupation of Japan (7 Sep–30 Nov 1945), RG 407; Unit Report No. 23, 15 November 1945, 126th Infantry Regiment—Unit Journal and File—Occupation of Japan (7 Sep–30 Nov 1945), RG 407.

70. 126th Infantry Regiment—Operations Report—Occupation of Japan (1 Dec 1945–28 Feb 1945), RG 407.

71. Occupation Operations Report, 14 February 1946, 128th Infantry Regiment—Journal and File—Occupation of Japan (1 Dec 1945–15 Feb 1946), RG 407.

72. Walters to family, 19 October 1945, 21 October 1945, Walters Papers.

73. Eloy Duran to Maria Acosta Duran and Margarita Acosta Duran, 8 December 1945, James and Margarita Mendez Papers, Chicano Studies Research Center, University of California at Los Angeles, Los Angeles, California.

74. Walters to family, 19 October 1945, 21 October 1945, Walters Papers.

75. Myers, *Hell Is a Foxhole*, 105.

76. Howell, *Young Draftee*, 114.

77. Myers, *Hell Is a Foxhole*, 112.

78. Anthony Chavez interview with George Banda, Cudahy, Wisconsin, 27 October 2016, Wisconsin Veterans Oral History Program, WVM.

79. Zabierek, *Beyond Pearl Harbor*, 68.

80. Daily Bulletin No. 1, 2 January 1946, 128th Infantry Regiment—Daily Bulletins—Occupation of Japan (1 Dec 1945–15 Feb 1946), RG 407.

81. Zabierek, *Beyond Pearl Harbor*, 68.

82. Howell, *Young Draftee*, 114.

83. Myers, *Hell Is a Foxhole*, 108–9.

84. Military Police Platoon—Operations Report—Occupation of Japan (1 Dec 1945–28 Feb 1946), RG 407.

85. For an introduction to the history of intimacy between American soldiers and Japanese women and its impact on US-Japanese relations, see Sarah Kovner, *Occupying Power: Sex Workers and Servicemen in Postwar Japan* (Stanford: Stanford University Press, 2012); Robert Kramm, *Sanitized Sex: Regulating Prostitution, Venereal Disease, and Intimacy in Occupied Japan, 1945–1952* (Berkeley: University of California Press, 2017); and Naoko Shibusawa, *America's Geisha Ally: Reimagining the Japanese Enemy* (Cambridge, MA: Harvard University Press, 2006).

86. Howell, *Young Draftee*, 114–15.

87. Holly Sanders, "*Panpan*: Streetwalking in Occupied Japan," *Pacific Historical Review* 81, no. 3 (August 1944): 408.

88. Kramm, *Sanitized Sex*, 207.

89. Painter interview.

90. Dower, *Embracing Defeat*, 138.

91. Occupation Operations Report, 17 February 1946, 128th Infantry Regiment—Battalions—Operation Report—Occupation of Japan (1 Dec 1945–28 Feb 1946), RG 407.

92. Medical History of the 127th Regimental Combat Team, 1 December 1945–15 February 1946, 127th Infantry Regiment—Medical Detachment—Medical Histories—All Campaigns and Occupation of Japan (1 Oct 1942–31 Dec 1945), RG 407.

93. 127th Infantry Regiment—History—Blacklist Operation—Occupation of Japan (1 Dec 1945–28 Feb 1946), RG 407.

94. Howell, *Young Draftee*, 115.

95. Military Police Platoon—Operations Report—Occupation of Japan (1 Dec 1945–28 Feb 1946), RG 407.

96. Dower, *Embracing Defeat*, 139.

97. S-2 Periodic Report No. 76, 26 January 1946, 127th Infantry Regiment—3rd Battalion—S-2 Periodic Reports—Occupation of Japan (30 Nov 1945–28 Feb 1946), RG 407.

98. 128th Infantry Regiment—1st Battalion—Unit History—Occupation of Japan (1 Dec 1945–28 Feb 1946), RG 407.

99. Owen Griffiths, "Need, Greed, and Protest in Japan's Black Market, 1938–1949," *Journal of Social History* 39, no. 4 (Summer 2002): 848.

100. Military Police Platoon—Operations Report—Occupation of Japan (1 Dec 1945–28 Feb 1946), RG 407.

101. 126th Infantry Regiment—Operations Report—Occupation of Japan (1 Dec 1945–28 Feb 1945), RG 407.

102. John Rawls reminiscence, John Rawls Papers, Harvard University, Cambridge, Massachusetts.

103. Special Court Martial Order No. 4, 13 January 1946, 128th Infantry Regiment—Special Court Martial Orders—Occupation of Japan (1 Dec 1945–15 Feb 1946), RG 407.

104. Myers, *Hell Is a Foxhole*, 106–10.

105. 126th Infantry Regiment—Operations Report—Occupation of Japan (1 Dec 1945–28 Feb 1945), RG 407.

106. 127th Infantry Regiment—Operation Report—Occupation of Japan (1 Dec 1945–28 Feb 1946), RG 407. The United States Armed Forces Institute, based in Madison, Wisconsin, offered correspondence courses for military personnel on a wide range of topics, from trigonometry to farming, in association with US colleges and universities. For more on the USAFI, see Spence Benbow, "University of the Armed Forces," *Journal of Educational Sociology* 16, no. 9 (May 1943): 577–90; and Miles R. Palmer, "The United States Armed Forces Institute," *Public Administration Review* 15, no. 4 (Autumn 1955): 272–74.

107. 127th Infantry Regiment—Operation Report—Occupation of Japan (1 Dec 1945–28 Feb 1946), RG 407.

108. Occupation Operations Report, 14 February 1946, 128th Infantry Regiment—Journal and File—Occupation of Japan (1 Dec 1945–15 Feb 1946), RG 407.

109. Occupation Operations Report, 17 February 1946, 128th Infantry Regiment—Battalions—Operation Report—Occupation of Japan (1 Dec 1945–28 Feb 1946), RG 407.

110. Walters to family, 21 October 1945, Walters Papers.

111. MacArthur, *Reports: Supplement*, 1:58.

112. Quarterly History, 10 January 1946, 107th Medical Battalion—Unit Journal—Luzon and Occupation of Japan (23 Jul 1945–23 Feb 1946), RG 407.

113. Myers, *Hell Is a Foxhole*, 111.

114. Howell, *Young Draftee*, 118.

115. Walters to family, 30 October 1945, 2 Nov 1945, 3 November 1945, 11 November 1945, Walters Papers.
116. "GI's in the Pacific Aim Fire at Congress," *New York Times*, 11 December 1945.
117. "4000 GIs Parade in Manila Protest," *New York Times*, 26 December 1945.
118. "GI Protest on Slow Demobilization," *New York Times*, 13 January 1946.
119. R. Alton Lee, "The Army 'Mutiny' of 1946," *Journal of American History* 53, no. 3 (December 1966): 570.
120. Susan L. Carruthers, *The Good Occupation: American Soldiers and the Hazards of Peace* (Cambridge, MA: Harvard University Press, 2016), 191.
121. "'Bring Back Daddy' Appeal to Goodland," *Capital Times*, 17 December 1945.
122. Walters to family, 15 November 1945, 21 November 1945, 26 November 1945, Walters Papers.
123. Howell, *Young Draftee*, 121–22.
124. Myers, *Hell Is a Foxhole*, 112.
125. 127th Infantry Regiment—Operations Report—Occupation of Japan (1 Dec 1945–28 Feb 1946), RG 407.
126. Painter interview.
127. Chavez interview.
128. Occupation Operations Report, 14 February 1946, 128th Infantry Regiment—Journal and File—Occupation of Japan (1 Dec 1945–15 Feb 1946), RG 407.
129. 127th Infantry Regiment—Operations Report—Occupation of Japan (1 Dec 1945–28 Feb 1946), RG 407.
130. 126th Infantry Regiment—Operations Report—Occupation of Japan (1 Dec 1945–28 Feb 1945), RG 407.
131. "Last Ceremony Slated," *Red Arrow News*, 13 February 1946; General Order No. 1, 1 February 1946, 128th Infantry Regiment—Daily Bulletins—Occupation of Japan (1 Dec 1945–15 Feb 1946), RG 407.
132. Occupation Operations Report, 1 December 1945–28 February 1946, RG 407.
133. Unit Journal, 21–28 February 1946, 732nd Ordnance Company (LM)—Unit Journal—Record of Events—All Campaigns and Occupation of Japan (20 Oct 1943–28 Feb 1946), RG 407.
134. 127th Infantry Regiment—Operation Report—Occupation of Japan (1 Dec 1945–28 Feb 1946), RG 407.

Epilogue

1. John M. Carlisle, *Red Arrow Men: Stories About the 32nd Division on the Villa Verde Front* (Detroit: Arnold-Powers, 1945), 214–15.
2. United States Department of the Army, *Army Battle Casualties and Nonbattle Deaths in World War II: Final Report, 7 December 1941–31 December 1946* (Washington, DC: Department of the Army, 1953), 90. It should be noted that while the Thirty-Second Division suffered more casualties in World War I than in World War II, the infantry division in the latter conflict was also considerably smaller. At full strength, the World War I "square" division had roughly twenty-eight thousand soldiers, whereas in World War II the "triangular" division had fifteen thousand.
3. Harold W. Blakeley, *32d Infantry Division in World War II* (Madison: Thirty-Second Infantry Division History Commission, 1957), 279–80.
4. Paul A. Rettell, *A Soldier's True Story: The Life of an Infantry Soldier in World War II* (self-published, 1993), 79.
5. Benjamin Winneshiek interview with Tom Doherty, 1989, Wisconsin Veterans Oral History Program, WVM.
6. Arthur J. Kessenich memoir, in Kessenich file, World War II Veterans Surveys, 32nd Infantry Division, USAHEC, 21.
7. Monte Howell, *The Young Draftee* (San Jose, CA: Writer's Showcase, 2002), 124.

8. Donald R. Dill survey, World War II Veterans Surveys, 32d Infantry Division, USAHEC.

9. Erwin A. Pichotte survey, World War II Veterans Surveys, 32d Infantry Division, USAHEC. It should be noted that women and people of color often benefitted less from the GI Bill due to discriminatory policies in banking and education. For an introduction to the history of the GI Bill and its impact on American society, see Glenn C. Altschuler and Stuart M. Blumin, *The GI Bill: A New Deal for Veterans* (New York: Oxford University Press, 2009); Suzanne Mettler, *Soldiers to Citizens: The GI Bill and the Making of the Greatest Generation* (New York: Oxford University Press, 2005); and Keith W. Olson, *The GI Bill, the Veterans, and the Colleges* (Lexington: University Press of Kentucky, 1974).

10. Raymond F. Dasmann, *Called by the Wild: The Autobiography of a Conservationist* (Berkeley: University of California Press, 2002), 72.

11. Richard A. Stoelb, *Time in Hell: The Battle for Buna on the Island of New Guinea* (Sheboygan: Sheboygan Historical Society, 2012), 84.

12. Whayland H. Greene, *Why Are You So Yellow?: 38520190: 32nd Division*, rev. 1992, in Greene file, World War II Veterans Surveys, 32d Infantry Division, USAHEC, n.p.

13. Jesse Coker, *My Unforgettable Memories of World War II* (self-published, 1994), 300. For an introduction to veteran readjustment after World War II, see Michael D. Gambone, *The Greatest Generation Comes Home: The Veteran in American Society* (College Station: Texas A&M University Press, 2005); Robert Saxe, *Settling Down: World War II Veterans' Challenge to the Postwar Consensus* (New York: Palgrave Macmillan, 2007); and Mark D. Van Ells, *To Hear Only Thunder Again: America's World War II Veterans Come Home* (Lanham, MD: Lexington Books, 2001). The latter work focuses specifically on Wisconsin.

14. "James Myers," *The Times* (London), 16 May 2001.

15. "Songwriter's Big Hit Is His Final Tribute," *Philadelphia Inquirer*, 17 May 2001.

16. For an introduction to war brides, see Elfrieda Berthiaume Shukert and Barbara Smith Scibetta, *War Brides of World War II* (New York: Penguin, 1989) and Susan Zeiger, *Entangling Alliances: Foreign War Brides and American Society in the Twentieth Century* (New York: New York University Press, 2010).

17. Dasmann, *Called by the Wild*, 72.

18. "Raymond Dasmann, a Founding Father of Environmentalism," *Los Angeles Times*, 9 November 2002.

19. John Rawls, "On My Religion," in *A Brief Inquiry into the Meaning of Sin and Faith: With "On My Religion,"* ed. Thomas Nagel (Cambridge, MA: Harvard University Press, 2009), 261–63.

20. John Rawls, "50 Years After Hiroshima," *Dissent* 44, no. 3 (Summer 1995): 323–27. For an introduction to Rawls and his work, see Thomas Pogge, *John Rawls: His Life and Theory of Justice* (New York: Oxford University Press, 2007).

21. Ralph J. Olson, "The Wisconsin National Guard," *Wisconsin Magazine of History* 39, no. 4 (Summer 1956): 270.

22. Wisconsin Legislative Reference Bureau, *Wisconsin Blue Book* (Madison: State of Wisconsin, 1962), 204.

23. David Maraniss, *When Pride Still Mattered: A Life of Vince Lombardi* (New York: Simon & Schuster, 1999), 285.

24. "Guardsman from Loyal Dies in Iraq," *Wisconsin State Journal*, 28 December 2004.

25. Charles P. Murdock, "The Red Arrow Pierced Every Line," *Saturday Evening Post*, November 10, 1945.

26. Dean W. Andersen, *Praise the Lord and Pass the Penicillin: Memoir of a Combat Medic in the Pacific in World War II* (Jefferson, NC: McFarland, 2003), 196.

27. Edward R. Guhl survey, World War II Veterans Surveys, 32d Infantry Division, USAHEC.

28. E. J. Kahn, "You Get Imbued," *New Yorker*, 5 January 1962, 34.

29. Newman Phillips survey, World War II Veterans Surveys, 32d Infantry Division, USAHEC.

30. Elizabeth D. Samet, *Looking for the Good War: American Amnesia and the Violent Pursuit of Happiness* (New York: Farrar, Straus, Giroux, 2021), 337. For a further introduction to Good War mythology, see John Bodnar, *The "Good War" in American Memory* (Baltimore: Johns Hopkins University Press, 2010) and Studs Terkel, *"The Good War": An Oral History of World War II* (New York: New Press, 1984).

31. Clarence Jungwirth, *Diary of a National Guardsman in World War II, 1940–1945* (self-published, 1991), front matter.

Name Index

Subject Index

Page numbers in *italic* refer to images.
*PNG = Papua New Guinea
*DEI= Dutch East Indies

About the Author

Mark D. Van Ells is a professor of history at Queensborough Community College of the City University of New York. He received his PhD in history from the University of Wisconsin–Madison and is a native of the Badger State. He is the author of *To Hear Only Thunder Again: America's World War II Veterans Come Home* and *America and World War I: A Traveler's Guide*. His website is markdvanells.com.